# THE NEW FOOD PROCESSOR BIBLE

## 30TH ANNIVERSARY EDITION

# norene gilletz

whitecap

Copyright © 1979, 1994, 2002, 2011
by Norene Gilletz
FIRST EDITION published 1980
SECOND EDITION 1994
THIRD EDITION 2002
FOURTH EDITION 2011

Whitecap Books

Portions of this book have previously been published under the titles *The Pleasures of Your Food Processor* and *The Pleasures of Your Processor*.

Whitecap Books is known for its expertise in the cookbook market, and has produced some of the most innovative and familiar titles found in kitchens across North America. Visit our website at www.whitecap.ca.

EDITED BY Cameron Johnson
PREVIOUS EDITION EDITED BY Alison Maclean
COVER DESIGN BY Michelle Furbacher. Front cover photograph courtesy of Cuisinart
INTERIOR DESIGN BY Mauve Pagé, Tanya Lloyd Kyi and Jacqui Thomas

PRINTED IN Canada at Webcom Inc.

LIBRARY AND ARCHIVES CANADA CATALOGUING IN PUBLICATION

Gilletz, Norene
　The new food processor bible / Norene Gilletz. — 30th anniversary ed.

Includes index.
First ed. published under title : The pleasures of your processor.
ISBN 978-1-77050-028-0

　1. Food processor cooking.　2. Jewish cooking.
I. Title.

TX840.F6G58 2010　　　641.5'892
C2010-905825-9

The publisher acknowledges the financial support of the Government of Canada through the Canada Book Fund (CBF) and the Province of British Columbia through the Book Publishing Tax Credit.

11 12 13 14 15　5 4 3 2 1

# CONTENTS

v   Introduction

1   Using Your Food Processor

47   Nutritional Analysis

49   Appetizers

80   Soups, Sauces and Marinades

114   Fish and Dairy Dishes

170   Meat and Poultry

222   Vegetables and Side Dishes

265   Super Salads and Dressings

295   Yeast Doughs, Quick Breads and Muffins

342   Cakes and Frostings

389   Desserts and Tortes

420   Chocolates, Cookies and Squares

465   Pies and Pastries

490   Passover

528   Acknowledgments

530   Index

*This book is dedicated to my mom, Belle Rykiss, who was my culinary inspiration and my very first cooking teacher. She used a food processor almost every day for 35 years until her midnineties, creating magical food memories in her miracle machine with the simplest of ingredients. Sadly, my mother passed away as this revised edition neared the final stages of production. Mom inspired my love of cooking and I know she will continue to watch over me, cooking over my shoulder.*

# INTRODUCTION

The food processor has revolutionized the way we cook and eat.

When I bought my first food processor in 1975, I spent the first month making purée of dinner! My son Doug, who is now a chef and food photographer, hated vegetables when he was a young child. He was thrilled because I could put them in the processor and "make them disappear!"

My machine and I were in constant motion—chopping, grating and puréeing everything. Through trial and error, I became a processor whiz, quickly transforming simple ingredients into mouthwatering meals for family and friends. I compiled my recipes, tips and techniques into a bestselling cookbook, *The Pleasures of Your Processor*.

The original edition, bound in a bright yellow cover, has often been referred to as "the processor bible." (It's now out of print and is considered a collectible, so if you own a copy, treasure it!) Over the past 3 decades, I have received letters, phone calls and e-mails from people all over the world expressing how much pleasure my recipes have brought to them and their families.

With the new millennium came a new generation of food processors and a new generation of cooks. In 2002, I completely revised and updated my original processor cookbook, adding more than 100 new recipes reflecting changing food trends and using ingredients that were not readily available when the first edition was published. The result was the creation of a new book with a new look: *The Food Processor Bible*.

In this updated edition, *The New Food Processor Bible: 30th Anniversary Edition*, I've added many new features that my readers have requested.

I've incorporated up-to-date information on the newest generation of food processors, which are more powerful and include many innovative features—but of course the recipes still work well with older, basic models. In response to my readers' requests, there are many dairy-free, gluten-free and vegetarian alternatives, plus an additional 65 delicious new recipes that reflect the way we cook and eat today. I've also added a new section to help busy moms prepare homemade baby food easily. Since everyone (including me) loves sweets, there are lots of luscious desserts that are perfect for special celebrations.

I've added a nutritional analysis for each recipe (including the phosphorus content for those with kidney disease) to help you make healthier food choices. I've also trimmed the fat, calories and sodium from many (but not all) of my original recipes and added lighter, healthier variations that still taste terrific. Keeping in mind that portion control is important, I've reduced the serving size where appropriate.

I've incorporated contemporary cooking techniques, including grilling, roasting, slow cooking and microwave methods. You'll find freezing and reheating recommendations and guidelines on how long you can keep food, plus information on food safety.

Most recipes use ingredients that you probably have on hand in your refrigerator or pantry. Many can be prepared in advance and completed later, or can be prepared in several stages, so today's time-starved families can enjoy great meals in minutes! This revised edition has been completely reorganized, with hundreds of helpful tips and techniques to take the guesswork out of processing.

Because of my background, I've included many traditional Jewish dishes for today's kosher (or not) cook. However, you don't have to be Jewish to enjoy them! You'll also find a variety of ethnic recipes from the cuisines of the world that provide international flavor.

The **Smart Chart** (pages 24–41) (formerly called the Daily Use Food Guide) is the heart of this book. It has been alphabetized, reorganized and expanded to make it more user-friendly. Make sure that you read this section—you will find it an invaluable tool that will help you process almost any food like a pro!

I am the first to admit that there are times when it is faster or more practical to use a knife, garlic press or immersion blender. But the food processor has stood the test of time and become an indispensable kitchen appliance. I've worked with many different brands, models and sizes of food processors over the years, both at home and in my cooking demonstrations throughout North America. Although I could probably manage without a food processor, I certainly wouldn't want to!

When buying a food processor, choose the best and most powerful one you can afford—it is a worthwhile investment that will last you for many years. Make sure it is made by a reliable manufacturer and comes with a good warranty.

The latest models include many improvements and come in a variety of sizes, colors and prices. Features, accessories and warranties vary. The most versatile processors are also the most expensive. Top-quality machines have the power, capacity, versatility and accessories to handle almost any task.

My personal recommendation is to choose a machine with a capacity of 11 to 14 cups and a strong motor that can handle heavy loads without a problem. Smaller machines are fine for small tasks and small quantities. Choose a machine with features that best suit your needs. Some of the new models are taller and may not fit under your upper kitchen cabinet, so keep this in mind.

Processors with electronic touchpad controls are easier to clean than those with levers. The pulse feature is very helpful to control texture. Some models come with a dough cycle feature that works by spinning the blade at a slower speed when kneading yeast dough.

Nested work bowls offer more options for prepping ingredients. A wide-mouth feed tube accommodates larger ingredients, saving on pre-cutting time. A small oval and/or round pusher nested inside the large pusher offers more feed tube choices, from a single carrot to a whole tomato.

The Cuisinart Elite Collection 14-Cup Food Processor has many cutting-edge features. The adjustable **Slicing Disc** (1 to 6 mm) and a reversible **Shredding Disc** (fine or medium) offer 8 different options. More versatility from just 2 blades! The **Steel Blade** locks into place so it won't fall out when you empty the bowl. This feature also prevents leaks from the bottom. The seal-tight gasket around the inside of the lid prevents leaks from the top. This model comes with 3 nested bowls (14, 11 and 4½ cups) which have measurement markings and pouring spouts. It has a retractable cord and a storage case with a safety lock for the discs, blades and accessories. The **Steel Blade** and **Slicing** and **Shredding Discs** can be used in the medium or large bowl. The **Dough Blade** can only be used in the large bowl. To use the mini-bowl, all 3 bowls must be nested together.

The KitchenAid Architect 12-cup processor comes with 2 **Slicing Discs** (2 and 4 mm) and a 4 mm **Shredding Disc**. It also includes a **French Fry Disc**, egg whip attachment, citrus press and storage case. The innovative 3-piece food pusher offers various feed tube choices. This model comes with 3 nested bowls (12, 10 and 4 cups). The **Slicing** and **Shredding Discs** can be used in the medium or large bowl. The **Steel Blade** and **Dough Blade** can only be used in the large bowl. To use the mini-bowl, either nest all 3 bowls together or nest the mini-bowl inside the large bowl.

No matter which brand or model of food processor you own, this book will help you make the most of it. Be sure to keep your food processor on the counter, where you can count on it to be an extra pair of hands. It will help you have food fast—instead of "fast food"—right in your own kitchen!

Even if you are technically challenged, *The New Food Processor Bible* will help you become a more confident cook. Whether you are a novice or a well-seasoned cook, you'll learn how to adapt your favorite recipes with ease. You might even create new culinary delights of your own.

I hope that this book will help the next generation of cooks discover the joy—and not the "oy"—of processing!

# USING YOUR FOOD PROCESSOR

1   Basic Processor Parts

6   Safety Tips

7   Quick Cleanups

8   Dos and Don'ts

9   Blades and How to Use Them

12   Optional Blades and Discs

12   Nested Work Bowls

13   How Much Food Can I Process at a Time?

14   Tips, Tricks and Techniques

16   Organic or Not?

16   Baby Food

19   Baby Food Chart

22   Kids' Cuisine

24   Smart Chart

42   Freezing Tips

42   Microwave Oven Tips

44   Metric Equivalent Charts

Your food processor does the hard work so you don't have to! No matter which brand or model of food processor you own, this cookbook will help you make the most of this indispensable kitchen appliance and give you the power to be a processor pro.

Food processors come in a variety of sizes, shapes and colors. Your little "kitchen magician" takes up less than a square foot of counter space, but it can replace many appliances and utensils: an electric mixer, blender, bread machine, meat grinder, grater, garlic press, parsley chopper, chef's knife, cheese mill, pastry blender, whisk, food mill, peanut butter maker and nut chopper. The food processor requires almost no maintenance. Blades can be changed in a snap, and they stay sharp indefinitely.

The speed at which different foods are chopped, minced, puréed, blended or kneaded can vary from model to model because of differences in horsepower and blades.

It's easy to adjust most of your favorite recipes for the processor, but the method and sequence of adding ingredients is often quite different. Use the recipes in this book as a guide to adapt your favorite recipes. If your processor comes with nested bowls, refer to the Nested Bowl Method found at the end of many recipes throughout this book.

Read your manual thoroughly to become familiar with your machine and its basic and optional parts, as well as its particular strengths and weaknesses. The information in this book is not intended to replace your manual.

## BASIC PROCESSOR PARTS

The following components are found on most brands of food processors. I've also included features found on the newest generation of processors. (See illustrations on pages 2 and 13.)

BASE (1): The motor is housed inside the base. Some models have stronger motors than others. Better-quality machines have a direct drive motor and an automatic temperature-controlled circuit breaker in their motor to protect against burnout when processing heavy batters or doughs. Some models feature built-in cord storage. The controls to turn your processor on and off are usually located on the base.

ON/OFF CONTROLS (2): The first food processors were turned on by twisting the cover in one direction, then turned off by twisting in the oppo-

# PARTS OF A FOOD PROCESSOR

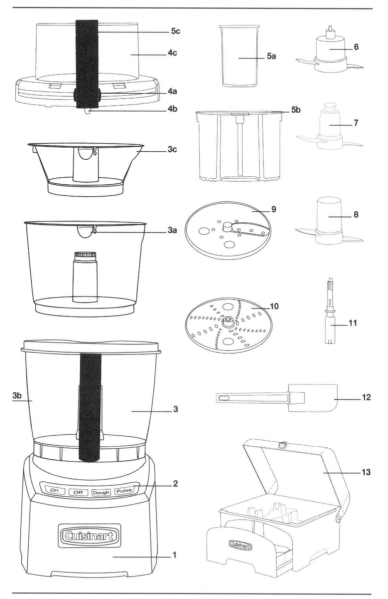

Image courtesy of Cuisinart

site direction. Subsequent models from different manufacturers came with levers, buttons or dials to operate the machine. The pulse control was added to help prevent overprocessing. Some models have multiple speeds. The newest generation of food processors features an easy-to-clean electronic touchpad with On, Off, Pulse and Dough options.

**WORK BOWL(S) (3):** The most popular models have a capacity of 7, 11, 12 or 14 cups. There are smaller and larger models available, ranging from 22 ounces up to 20 cups. The majority of recipes in this book can be made in a standard (7 cup) food processor, but a larger bowl is definitely an advantage. The work bowl on better-quality models is shatter- and heat-resistant. It should not be used in the microwave oven.

Some models feature 2 or 3 nested work bowls that fit into each other. Many come with finger recesses (3a), measurement markings (3b) and pouring spouts (3c). On models with 3 bowls, you can use all 3 bowls nested together or you can nest the medium bowl inside the large bowl. Choose the appropriate-sized bowl, blade and disc for the task and amount of food being processed.

**TO INSERT A BOWL:** Place your thumbs in the 2 finger recesses (3a) at the top, then turn the bowl until it slides into place. Push down firmly to lock into place. For Cuisinart Elite models, align the bowl with the pouring spout (3c) facing opposite the work bowl handle. To remove a bowl, place your thumbs in the finger recesses and lift up.

To use the mini-bowl on the 14-cup Cuisinart Elite, nest all 3 bowls together, place the mini-blade (6) on the stem adapter (11) and press down to lock the blade into place.

To use the mini-bowl on the 12-cup KitchenAid, either nest all 3 bowls together, or nest the mini-bowl inside the large bowl and insert the mini-blade—you don't need to use the disc stem.

**WORK BOWL COVER/FEED TUBE (4A, 4B, 4C):** The cover has a vertical feed tube that is located in either the front or the back. Food is put through the feed tube when slicing or grating, or when adding ingredients while the machine is running.

The original food processors were made with a standard oval feed tube. This type of feed tube is still available on many models and is very simple to use. However, food must be cut or trimmed to fit the feed tube, which has a capacity of about 1 cup.

The wide-mouth feed tube (4c) is about 2½ times the size of the standard feed tube. It eliminates much of the trimming needed when slicing or shredding whole fruits and vegetables. You can process batch after batch of food quickly, shortening preparation time. Don't fill the feed tube above the maximum fill line or the machine won't start.

The pusher assembly (5b) of the wide-mouth feed tube (4c) houses 1 or 2 smaller feed tubes, with capacities ranging from ½ cup to 1 cup.

The Cuisinart Elite processor features a seal-tight gasket around the inside of the work bowl cover. This allows for maximum bowl capacity when processing liquids, and it prevents leaks from the top. To place the cover onto the work bowl, position it directly over the bowl(s) then push down on the front and back to lock it into place. To remove the cover, push in the release buttons (4a) located on either side of the handle interlock (4b) and lift up. The cover will fit, lock and seal on the large bowl with any nested bowl combination (see illustration on page 13).

An optional flat cover is available on some models. It is used with the **Steel Blade** for chopping and mixing, but cannot be used when slicing or grating. The flat cover simplifies cleanup.

PUSHER ASSEMBLY (5A, 5B, 5C): The pusher guides food through the feed tube. It also prevents splashing when working with liquids. The standard feed tube comes with a 1-piece pusher. The wide-mouth feed tube (4c) has a 2-piece pusher assembly (5a and 5b). (The KitchenAid 12-Cup Architect has a 3-piece pusher assembly.)

The small pusher (5a) fits inside the large pusher (5b), allowing you to accommodate ingredients of various sizes. The small pusher is used for narrow fruits and vegetables and for adding ingredients while the machine is running. Some pushers have a tiny hole in the bottom to drizzle oil in slowly when making mayonnaise. Some models have measurement markings on the pusher.

The large pusher lock (5c), located on the handle, can be used when processing heavy loads. Pull it out to lock and push in to unlock.

SMALL CHOPPING/MIXING BLADE (6): This stainless steel mini-blade will chop or mix anything in your mini-bowl.

STEEL BLADE (7): This is the most useful blade of all. It is often referred to as the multipurpose blade and performs about 95% of the tasks (see page 9). On the Cuisinart Elite 14-cup model, the stainless **Steel Blade** can be used with the medium or large work bowl. The blade locks into place so it doesn't fall out when you empty the bowl. This locking feature also prevents leaks from the bottom of the bowl. On the KitchenAid Architect, the **Steel Blade** can be used only with the large bowl.

Some models come with a **Plastic Mixing Blade**, which is used for light mixing tasks and to avoid over-processing delicate ingredients (e.g., flaked tuna).

DOUGH BLADE (8): This blade works with the slower **Dough Cycle** to knead all types of dough without overheating. However, machines without a **Dough Cycle** or **Dough Blade** can still produce great yeast dough. On models with nested bowls, the **Dough Blade** can be used only in the large bowl.

SLICING DISC (9): Also referred to as the **Slicer** throughout this book. The medium (4 mm) **Slicing Disc** produces approximately ⅛-inch slices and the thin (2 mm) **Slicing Disc** produces 1/16-inch slices. Cuisinart's Elite processor comes with a versatile 6-in-1 **Slicing Disc** that can produce thin, medium or thick slices (1 to 6 mm) with a quick twist of a dial. One disc, 6 choices! Use the finger holes when handling the **Slicing Disc**. On models with nested bowls, the **Slicing Disc** can be used with the large or medium bowl. See page 10 for tips.

SHREDDING DISC (10): Also referred to as the **Grater** throughout this book. The medium (4 mm) **Shredding Disc** produces approximately ⅛-inch shreds. The Cuisinart Elite's reversible **Shredding Disc** provides the option of either fine or medium shreds. Just decide which side to use and grate away! Use the finger holes when handling the **Shredding Disc**. On models with nested bowls, the **Shredding Disc** can be used with the large or medium bowl. See pages 10–11 for tips.

STEM ADAPTER (11): Many models come with detachable disc stem(s) or a stem adapter for compact storage. The stem adapter is used to attach the discs/blades to the power shaft.

OTHER FEATURES: A spatula (12) is ideal for removing food from bowls, discs and blades. Some models come with a retractable cord. A storage case (13) helps organize and protect the discs, blades and accessories. (Cuisinart's storage case features a unique safety lock and a storage drawer for the discs.) Manufacturers offer various attachments (some optional, some included) and a wide array of colors and finishes (e.g., brushed metal, white, black).

MINI-PREPS: These mini-processors are small enough to keep on your counter and are handy for small tasks. They're also relatively inexpensive. Popular models have a capacity of 3 to 4 cups. Put the desired food into the work bowl, lock the cover in place and press either the chop or grind control button. The double-sided blade is sharp on one side and dull on the other, moving in one direction to chop and the other to grind.

Use the chop function for herbs, garlic, onion, crumbs, nuts, cheese, dips, sauces, salad dressings and baby food. Use the grind function for hard items such as chocolate, peppercorns, nutmeg and other whole spices. For more even chopping or grinding, use quick on/off pulses by pressing the desired button quickly. When making salad dressings and marinades, first chop harder ingredients (e.g., garlic, ginger) using quick pulses, then add softer ingredients and liquids and pulse to combine.

However, mini-processors don't slice or shred foods and can only process small quantities at a time. The mini-bowl on most models can process about 1 cup of liquid or ½ to ¾ cup solids. Refer to your manual for capacity guidelines.

Most models come with dishwasher-safe parts, making cleanup easy. Because the parts are small, place them securely on the top rack of the dishwasher to prevent them from falling through.

The powerful Ninja Master Prep does the work of two appliances: a mini food processor and a blender. The interchangeable motor head (Master Pod) switches easily to fit on top of the 2-cup prep bowl or the 6-cup pitcher. The Ninja's quad-blade assembly (4 blades, not 2) is composed of an upper and lower set of blades. You can quickly chop an onion, mince garlic, make salsa or purée baby food in the 2-cup prep bowl. The 6-cup pitcher is perfect for ice-based drinks, smoothies and shakes.

Always insert the blade assembly first, then add ingredients to the prep bowl or pitcher. Note: When chopping or mincing in the prep bowl, cut harder foods (e.g., onions, chicken) into 1-inch chunks. Next, place the splash guard on top of the prep bowl or pitcher. Then place the powerhead on top, making sure it is securely in place.

The manufacturer recommends using short pulses for chopping/mincing in the prep bowl and long pulses in the pitcher. To prevent overprocessing when chopping ingredients in the prep bowl, let the blades stop completely between pulses. You can only process small amounts at a time in the prep bowl, so don't overfill it.

NOTE: Do not operate the Ninja continuously for more than 20 seconds. Don't add more than 2 cups of dry or 1 cup of liquid ingredients to the prep bowl as this will strain the motor and may cause it to overflow. Never run the Ninja empty. Always make sure the blades have stopped completely before removing the splash guard.

The prep bowl, pitcher, blades and splash guards are dishwasher-safe. The prep bowl and pitcher are microwavable. Always follow assembly and operating directions in your manual.

MAXI-MACHINES: These come with a heavy-duty motor and a work bowl with a capacity of 16 to 20 cups. They are very powerful and are ideal for catering and restaurant use, or for the serious home chef with a large family. Although they're expensive, they are a worthwhile investment and will give you many years of service.

OTHER OPTIONS TO CONSIDER: Features, sizes and prices of food processors vary, depending on the manufacturer and model. Instructional DVDs and online videos on manufacturers' websites are helpful how-to guides. Models with a chute attachment allow you to continually slice and grate large quantities directly into a separate bowl. Some machines come with multiple speeds, and others include a blender/immersion blender option. There are many chopper/mixer combos available, offering varying degrees of quality and performance.

Which brand and model of food processor should you choose? There's no simple answer. Use the Web to research various models, compare brands and read reviews about features and prices.

Ask friends and family for their recommendations. If you frequently cook for a crowd or make a lot of yeast dough, choose a machine with a large capacity (14 cups) and a direct drive motor that can handle heavy loads. Otherwise, a smaller machine (7 to 11 cups) will do the job. Models with nested work bowls offer more options.

Top-quality models come with the power, capacity, versatility and accessories to handle almost any task, with many cutting-edge innovations. Choose a food processor made by a reliable manufacturer with features that suit your needs. A top-quality food processor may be expensive, but it is a worthwhile investment that will bring you many years of cooking and eating pleasure.

### SAFETY TIPS

Read your manual thoroughly and follow the manufacturer's safety recommendations.

The blades and discs are very sharp, so store them in a safe place, preferably in a blade holder or storage container. Keep them out of the reach of children. Don't store blades in a drawer where you may reach in blindly and cut yourself. Handle blades with care, especially if you are rushed or distracted.

To avoid injury, hold the **Steel Blade** by the hub, not by the blades. When handling the **Slicing** or **Shredding Disc**, use the finger holes on discs that come with this feature. Otherwise, hold it by its outer edges.

If the **Slicing** or **Shredding Disc** has a detachable disc stem, place the disc upside down on a flat surface before connecting the stem and locking it in place. If your machine comes with a stem adapter, place it on the motor shaft before assembling the discs. (Refer to your manual for assembly instructions.)

Never put the blades or discs on the motor shaft until the work bowl is locked in place. Then push the blade or disc all the way down as far as it will go.

Always insert the **Steel Blade** into the bowl before adding ingredients. Press down to lock the **Steel Blade** in place in models with this feature.

Use the pusher to guide food through the feed tube when slicing or grating. Never put your fingers or any kitchen utensil in the feed tube, especially while the machine is running.

On wide-mouth feed tube models, the pusher assembly has been designed so you can't take it apart—this is a safety feature. With the **Slicing** or **Shredding Disc** in place and the feed tube area exposed without the pusher covering it, someone could reach the rotating disc with their hand and be seriously injured. The safety design prevents this from happening.

Always wait until the blade or discs stop spinning completely before removing the pusher assembly or cover from the work bowl. Never use your fingers, a spatula or any other kitchen utensil to try and stop the blades.

If a piece of food becomes wedged between the bowl and blade, turn off the machine immediately, unplug it, and carefully remove the blade and trapped food.

On models without a **Blade Lock** system, be careful that the **Steel Blade** does not fall out of the bowl when emptying it. Remove the bowl from the base, then either remove the blade or hold it in place with your finger or a spatula when you tip the bowl to empty it.

On models with a **Blade Lock** system, the innovative blade has been designed to stay locked in place when you empty the bowl. To remove the blade on models with this feature, first remove the bowl from the base and place on a flat surface. Place the heel of your hand on the outside rim of the bowl, then firmly pull straight up on the plastic hub of the blade to remove it. Place your other hand on the outside of the bowl, away from the top. If it is difficult to remove the blade, use a little extra force.

Be careful—the blade is very sharp. Otherwise, just place the bowl and blade back on the base; the blade will release.

If the motor begins to labor (e.g., when mixing heavy, sticky doughs) turn off the machine immediately to protect the motor. If the motor stops because of overheating, wait for it to cool down before continuing. It usually takes 10 to 15 minutes.

Always make sure the machine has been turned off when you are finished using the processor. Models with electronic touchpad controls have an indicator light that will glow until you touch the OFF button.

Always store the processor with the work bowl and cover in the unlocked position when it is not in use to prevent damage to the spring mechanism.

Don't let the cord touch hot surfaces or hang over the edge of a counter or table where it can be pulled down accidentally.

Manufacturers recommend unplugging the machine before putting on or taking off parts, before removing food, and before cleaning. Keep machine unplugged when not in use.

## QUICK CLEANUPS

Plan ahead to keep cleanups to a minimum. Process dry or hard foods first (e.g., nuts, cheese, chocolate, crumbs), then process wet foods. Use paper towels to wipe out the bowl between steps.

To clean batter from the **Steel Blade** quickly, empty the contents of the bowl. Return the bowl and blade to the base of the machine, replace the cover, then turn on the processor. The blade will spin itself clean in seconds!

SELF-CLEANING PROCESSOR: Pour 2 cups of hot water into a Pyrex measuring cup and add a drop or two of dish soap. Return the dirty bowl and **Steel Blade** to the base, replace the lid and start the machine. Gradually pour soapy water through the feed tube while the machine is running, adding just enough to come *almost* to the top of the bowl where it meets the lid. (You may not need to add all the water—it depends on the capacity of the work bowl. If you add too much water, it will leak out where the lid and bowl meet.) Let the machine run for 30 to 60 seconds; a few quick on/off pulses will also help clean out the bowl and underside of the lid. Stop the machine and immediately remove the bowl and blade from the base to prevent leaking. Pour out the soapy liquid, rinse the bowl, blade and lid well, wipe dry and you're good to go again!

Cuisinart Elite models won't leak using this self-cleaning method because of their SealTight Advantage system. The high-powered motor will force the water to clean out the bowl as well as any bits and pieces trapped in the rubber gasket on the underside of the lid. Clean Cuisine-Art!

To avoid "ring around the counter," turn the cover upside down before placing it on your counter. Place the blade on top of the inverted cover. (This isn't possible with all models.)

When using the **Steel Blade** or **Dough Blade**, stretch a piece of plastic wrap across the top of the work bowl before clicking on the lid. This will keep the underside of the processor lid clean. It also prevents tiny food particles from getting stuck in the rubber gasket on Cuisinart Elite models. No need to wash the lid in the dishwasher—a quick rinse does the trick. (Thanks to Sandy Glazier for sharing this terrific tip.)

Rinse the bowl, cover and blades immediately after use so food won't dry on them. A bottle brush or dish brush simplifies cleanup. Handle sharp blades and discs carefully, using the plastic hubs on the blades and the finger holes on the discs.

Place the pushers upside down for drainage. If food lodges in the pusher, remove it by running water through it, or use a bottle brush.

Make sure that the bowl, cover and blades for your model are dishwasher-safe—check your manual. Load them away from exposed heating elements in the dishwasher. On models with nested work bowls, the measurement markings may fade or disappear after repeated washings.

Be careful not to cut yourself on the sharp blades and discs when loading and unloading the dishwasher or when washing by hand. In the dishwasher, place them flat and in full view on the top rack.

*Never* let the blades soak in soapy water, as you can accidentally cut yourself by reaching in blindly. When washing by hand, don't use abrasive cleansers or scouring pads; they can scratch or cloud the bowl and cover. Use a dish brush to clean the bowl and blades. A spray attachment is also effective. A cotton swab will remove sticky dough or batter from the hole on the underside of the **Steel Blade**, or from the underside of the rim of the **Slicing** or **Shredding Disc**.

An easy way to wash the **Steel Blade** is to fill the work bowl with soapy water, then hold the blade by its plastic hub and move it rapidly up and down on the center shaft of the work bowl.

STICKY TIP: To remove tiny food particles that may get trapped in the rubber gasket on the underside of the lid of Cuisinart Elite models, use a small metal spatula (the thin, flexible kind used to frost cakes). Works perfectly!

Another trick is to turn the lid upside down and rinse it under running water, pushing up and down on the gasket rapidly to release any tiny bits. A toothbrush also does a good job. You can also use a spray attachment to run water through the small openings in the top of the lid.

Wipe up spills on the base or cord quickly with a clean, damp sponge or nonabrasive cloth, then wipe dry. Never immerse the base in liquid as there is a danger of electric shock. Unplug the processor before cleaning.

To prevent the bowl from developing an odor (especially from strong-smelling foods like onions or garlic), leave it uncovered and exposed to air after washing. Also, don't store the pusher in the feed tube when the machine is not in use.

To prevent food poisoning, any processor parts that come in contact with raw or cooked foods must be sanitized. Experts recommend washing all parts with hot soapy water for at least 20 seconds. You can sanitize the bowl, blades and pusher (even your sponge and dish brush) on the top rack in the dishwasher. Also clean all preparation areas and utensils thoroughly (e.g., cutting boards, counters, knives). And always wash your hands thoroughly with soap and water before handling food!

The 4 rubber feet on the underside of the base keep the machine from moving on most work surfaces when processing heavy loads. If the rubber feet leave spots on the counter, spray them with a spot remover or nonabrasive cleaner, then wipe with a damp sponge.

## DOS AND DON'TS

Although your food processor can process almost anything, the following tasks are best done using other appliances, gadgets or a sharp knife.

Most manufacturers don't recommend grinding hard spices, grains or coffee beans in a food processor. Although you can use a mini-prep for hard spices, the bowl will quickly get scuffed and cloudy, and hard spices such as cinnamon sticks will turn into coarse crumbs rather than powder. A coffee grinder does a good job of grinding hard spices and is also better for coffee beans.

Mary M. Rodgers, director of marketing communications for Cuisinart & Waring, recommends using a burr grinder for coffee beans to preserve their quality. With a grinder, the coffee beans get crushed, not chopped. She also advises that ice cubes should never be chopped in a food processor, as they will ricochet around the bowl and scratch it. A blender is better for chopping ice and liquefying solid foods.

Potatoes are better when mashed with a potato masher, electric mixer or food mill. Cooked potatoes develop a sticky, gluey texture when processed with the **Steel Blade**. However, this actually makes a delicious topping for Shepherd's Pie!

A sharp knife does a better job of chopping or dicing foods when size, shape and appearance are important. A mini-prep is handy for small quantities and quick tasks.

An immersion blender is often easier to use when puréeing soups and sauces. However, some new models of food processors are able to process larger quantities of liquids and purées as a result of design improvements.

Use a heavy-duty electric mixer for sponge and chiffon cakes, whipping egg whites and kneading big batches of yeast dough.

For light, fluffy whipped cream with maximum volume, use an electric mixer. Processor whipped cream is lower in volume, but is great for garnishing as it holds its shape. Some models of food processors include an egg whip or whisk attachment that can whip heavy cream and egg whites for meringues, mousses and desserts. For best results, whip at least 1 cup of heavy cream or 3 egg whites at a time. Whipping smaller quantities may not result in maximum volume.

Don't use the processor bowl in a microwave oven. Instead, empty the contents into a microwavable container.

## BLADES AND HOW TO USE THEM

### STEEL BLADE

This is the "do-almost-everything" blade. If you are not slicing or grating, then you are probably using the **Steel Blade**. See the **Smart Chart** (pages 24–41) for techniques for processing specific foods. Always follow the guidelines in your manual.

Use the **Steel Blade** to chop foods, using quick on/off pulses. You can also mince, grind, purée, emulsify, mix, blend, knead and whip by letting the machine run until the desired results are achieved. You can control the exact consistency you want, from coarse to fine, even to a purée.

This multipurpose blade is used for cake batters, frostings, pastries, crumb crusts, cookies, yeast doughs, muffins and quick breads. It will mix up crêpe batters, salad dressings, dips, mayonnaise, sauces and baby foods. It can grind raw or cooked meat, fish and poultry; make peanut butter; mince garlic, parsley and herbs; grate Parmesan cheese; make bread crumbs; and chop, mince or purée raw or cooked fruits and vegetables. What a versatile blade! It rarely needs replacing, unless you use it frequently to chop very hard foods such as chocolate. (I've never had to replace my **Steel Blade** and I cook a lot.)

Food may be added directly to the work bowl or through the feed tube. Food placed directly in the bowl should be evenly distributed around the blade. Small or very hard foods (e.g., garlic) should be dropped in through the feed tube while the machine is running. It will be drawn into the centrifuge produced by the whirling blades. The food is then flung outward once it has been processed. Very hard foods (e.g., chocolate, nuts) make a loud noise at first, so don't be alarmed.

Quick on/off pulses will help you control texture and prevent overprocessing. Practice this basic technique a few times without any food in the bowl—it won't take very long to master this essential technique.

Let your eyes be your guide. Times given for processing are only estimates. Each person counts differently, or turns the machine on and off at a different rate. Times also vary according to texture, temperature and size of food being processed. Check often to prevent overprocessing.

For uniform chopping, cut the foods being processed into chunks that are the same size, 1 to 1½ inches. Instead of using a ruler, a quick way to measure is to make a circle with your thumb and index finger. The food should not be larger in diameter than the circle.

When chopping, process in batches for best results (see pages 13–14 for recommended capacity of work bowl). If you overfill the bowl, you may end up with mush! When chopping or mincing, make sure the bowl, blade and food are dry.

For a finer chop, use quick on/off pulses until the desired texture is reached. Onions, zucchini, bell peppers and other foods that have a high water content will quickly become puréed if overprocessed. A quick pat with paper towels after processing helps to absorb excess moisture from veggies.

Mincing takes 6 to 8 seconds, mixing cake batters takes 1½ to 2 minutes and kneading yeast doughs takes less than a minute. You may have to stop the processor once or twice to scrape down the sides of the bowl with a rubber spatula. When mincing, either hold the PULSE button down or press the ON button to run the machine continuously.

For smoother purées, process the solids first, then slowly add liquid through the feed tube while the machine is running. Scrape down the sides of the bowl as needed. This technique is excellent for preparing baby food.

You can grate foods using the **Steel Blade** when appearance is not important (e.g., cheese for sauces, vegetables for soups). Parmesan cheese can also be grated on the **Steel Blade**.

To keep liquids from leaking from the center opening of the work bowl, be sure to push the **Steel Blade** all the way down before adding ingredients. (On models with a **Blade Lock** feature, twist into position and push down firmly to lock.) Remove the mixture from the bowl as soon as you are finished processing. Do not remove the blade first. (On models without a **Blade Lock** feature, remove the bowl, blade and contents together and press down firmly on the hub of the blade to keep it secure.)

Don't remove the blade if liquids in the bowl are above the hub or they will leak out. Some machines have the maximum liquid level indicated on the bowls.

NOTE: The **Blade Lock** feature on Cuisinart Elite models is designed to keep the **Steel Blade** in place during processing, pouring, lifting and handling tasks, and also prevents leaking. The blade is not permanently attached, so handle with care. The **Steel Blade** can be used in the medium and the large work bowls. The blades and discs from earlier models won't fit Cuisinart Elite models with a **Blade Lock** feature.

### MINI-BLADE

On models with nested bowls, use the mini-blade in the mini-bowl for small tasks. Chop a handful of fresh herbs, mince a few cloves of garlic or a single onion, blend salad dressings and marinades, make guacamole or salsa, grind cracker crumbs or make baby food purées. To prevent leakage, don't fill the mini-bowl with liquid above the hub.

### SHREDDING DISC/GRATER AND SLICING DISC/SLICER

See the **Smart Chart** (pages 24–41) for techniques for shredding/grating and slicing specific foods.

Use the **Shredding Disc** (also called the **Grater**) for grating/shredding firm cheeses, raw vegetables (e.g., potatoes, carrots, zucchini), chocolate or nuts. Use the **Slicing Disc** (also called the **Slicer**) for slicing vegetables, fruits, chilled meats or firm cheeses. Assembly instructions vary, so refer to your manual.

Some models come with a detachable stem that locks onto the discs. To assemble, place the desired disc upside down on a flat surface, connect the stem and lock into place. Next, place the bowl on the base. Fit the stem of the disc onto the center post (power shaft) of the base, pushing it all the way down. Place the cover on the bowl.

Other models come with a stem adapter. First, place the bowl on the base. Next, position the stem adapter on the center post (power shaft) of the base, twist into position and push down to lock into place. Align and insert the disc onto the stem adapter. Place the cover on the bowl.

Cuisinart Elite models feature a reversible **Shredding Disc**, an adjustable **Slicing Disc** and 2 or 3 nested work bowls. Decide which side of the **Shredding Disc** to use (fine or medium) or select the desired slicing thickness (1 to 6 mm) before assembling. Use the finger holes when handling discs. You can use the **Shredding** and **Slicing Discs** with either the medium or large bowl on models with nested bowls.

Cut food to fit the feed tube. Cut the bottom ends flat so that food lies stable on the disc. Remove any large hard pits and seeds from fruits before processing; peel if desired. When shredding cheese, be sure that it is well chilled. Freeze softer cheeses such as mozzarella for 15 to 20 minutes before processing. Apply very little pressure on the pusher.

Food should be as large as possible before placing it in the feed tube. Measure the food against the length and width of the pusher as a convenient guide to size. Cut large foods, such as eggplant or cabbage, into wedges. Some recipes will tell you to cut the food in 1-inch pieces, chunks or halves. Place food in the feed tube (either horizontally or vertically). Don't fill the wide-mouth feed tube above the maximum fill line or the machine won't start. Food should fit the feed tube snugly, but not so snugly that the pusher can't move.

Use the pusher to guide food through the feed tube. Adjust the pressure according to the texture of the food being processed. Use light pressure for soft foods (e.g., bananas and mushrooms). Use medium pressure for most foods (e.g., apples, potatoes, zucchini). Use firm pressure for harder foods (e.g., turnips, sweet potatoes, partially frozen meats or poultry). Never process any food that is so hard or firmly frozen that it can't be pierced with the point of a sharp knife.

For maximum control, keep the palm of your hand flat on the top of the pusher. Empty the work bowl as often as needed.

For small round slices or short shreds (e.g., carrots, zucchini), cut food to fit feed tube vertically.

For long slices or shreds (e.g., potatoes), cut food to fit the feed tube horizontally.

For very thin slices or fine shreds, let foods "self-feed" (i.e., use almost no pressure on the pusher). When slicing or grating hard foods, use either light, medium or firm pressure, depending on the texture desired. Be careful when slicing soft or delicate foods (e.g., kiwis, tomatoes) to avoid crushing them.

For diagonal slices, use the standard or small feed tube. Place 1 or 2 pieces of food on an angle in the feed tube. Slice, using medium pressure. This is ideal for stir-fries (e.g., celery, zucchini).

Combine foods if you don't have enough of one, making a tighter fit (e.g., pack green onions in the indentation of celery stalks). The small feed tube is handy for small quantities.

If foods are narrow at 1 end (e.g., carrots), pack them in pairs, alternating 1 narrow end up, 1 wide end up.

Small quantities of long, narrow foods (e.g., 2 carrots) can be packed into a standard feed tube more securely if you cut them in half to make 4 shorter pieces.

To slice leafy vegetables (e.g., lettuce, spinach), pile the leaves in a stack, then roll them up into a cylinder. Insert the cylinder upright in the feed tube and slice, using light pressure.

The wide-mouth feed tube on the new generation of food processors has been redesigned for greater ease when slicing or grating. It's very easy to process consecutive batches of food in minutes. Reload the feed tube with 1 hand and press down on the pusher with your other hand. When processing several batches, select the ON button. If you want more control, use the PULSE button; the machine will stop instantly when you lift your finger off the button. Refer to your manual for further information.

## OPTIONAL BLADES AND DISCS

Some machines come with additional blades and discs, other pieces are optional. Not all parts are available for all makes and models. Only you can determine whether you need additional blades and discs.

The **Thin Slicing Disc** (2 mm) is ideal for slicing cabbage for coleslaw. (If you don't have this disc, use the **Medium Slicing Disc** (4 mm) and let food "self-feed" for thinner slices.) The **Thick Slicing Disc** (6 mm) makes ¼-inch-thick slices. An **Extra-Thin Slicing Disc** (1 mm), **Extra-Thick Slicing Disc** (8 mm), **Fine Shredding Disc** (2 mm) and **Thick Shredding Disc** (6 mm) are available for some models.

The **Julienne Disc** produces thin, matchstick strips that are ideal for hash browns, wraps, sushi and garnishes. Use it for beets, carrots, jicama and zucchini when making salads.

The **French Fry Disc** makes curved sticks about 2 inches long and ¼ inch wide (5 cm × 6 mm) that look like short, shoestring strips rather than traditional fries. Use firm pressure to process potatoes and sweet potatoes into skinny fries. You can also use it for eggplant, zucchini, cucumber and beets.

**Plastic Blade:** Some earlier models came with a plastic **Mixing Blade**. It can be used for light mixing and blending of foods, usually where a change of texture is not desired (e.g., dips, spreads). Use it to coarsely chop mushrooms, nuts or cookie crumbs. When processing thin liquids, there is more chance of leakage.

Some models come with a special **Dough Blade**, which is used to mix and knead yeast doughs. It creates less friction than the **Steel Blade**, reducing any chances of overheating. Follow the manufacturer's guidelines for use.

## NESTED WORK BOWLS

New-generation food processors often come with 2 or 3 nested work bowls. For optimal efficiency, use the work bowls in a way that saves on cleanup. For example, if your recipe calls for using multiple bowls, begin with the smallest bowl. This way, it will serve as a prep bowl to reserve the processed ingredients for a recipe.

Choose the appropriate-sized bowl and blade or disc for the task and amount of food being processed. For example, when making a carrot cake in the Cuisinart Elite 14-cup processor which comes with 3 nested bowls:

- Chop nuts in the mini-bowl, using the mini-blade.
- Process dry ingredients in the medium bowl, using the **Steel Blade**.
- Shred carrots in the large bowl, using the **Shredding Disc**. Transfer carrots to a 2-cup glass measure. (Note: If using a KitchenAid processor with 3 nested bowls, shred carrots in the medium/chef bowl and process dry ingredients in the large bowl. Transfer dry ingredients to a mixing bowl.)
- Process batter ingredients (e.g., oil, sugar, eggs, etc.) in the large bowl, using the **Steel Blade**.
- Add prepped ingredients to the large bowl as directed in the recipe, using the **Steel Blade**.

The Cuisinart Elite's nested work bowls are slightly tapered and lock into place so you can pour or remove food while they are still nested together. You can also use the finger recesses to remove the small and medium bowls along with their contents.

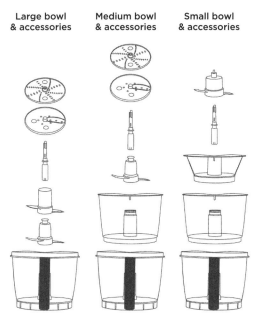

Large bowl & accessories    Medium bowl & accessories    Small bowl & accessories

Image courtesy of Cuisinart

On models with nested bowls, the **Slicing** and **Shredding Discs** can be used in the medium or large bowl. The **Steel Blade** and **Dough Blade** can only be used in the large bowl. (Note: The **Steel Blade** can be also used in the medium bowl of the Cuisinart 14-Cup Elite.)

To use the mini-bowl in the Cuisinart Elite, all 3 bowls must be nested together. To use the mini-bowl in the KitchenAid processor, either nest all 3 bowls together or nest the mini-bowl inside the large bowl.

## HOW MUCH FOOD CAN I PROCESS AT A TIME?

Quantities vary according to the food being processed and the task you are performing. The bowl holds more when slicing or shredding foods than when chopping or mincing.

Food processors are classified according to their dry ingredient capacity, ranging from 3 to 20 cups. As a general guideline, the liquid capacity is about half the dry ingredient capacity. Follow the guidelines in your manual for recommended capacities.

When chopping and puréeing fruits or vegetables, don't fill the bowl more than one-third to one-half full. For larger quantities, process food in batches.

The thicker the liquid, the more you can process in one batch. If liquid leaks out between the bowl and cover when the machine is running, you've added too much liquid. Some models have a maximum liquid fill line on the bowl, which indicates the maximum amount of liquid that can be processed at a time.

To prevent liquids from leaking from the bottom of the bowl, remove the bowl and **Steel Blade** together as soon as you've finished processing. Do not remove the blade first, especially if liquids in the bowl are above the hub of the blade. Otherwise, liquids will leak out from the center opening in the bowl when you remove the blade.

The following guide outlines the recommended maximum capacity for a standard (7-cup) processor. A medium (11-cup) or large (14-cup) processor can process 1½ to 2 times the amounts listed.

NOTE: Cuisinart Elite models can process larger quantities of liquids because of their improved design. The higher center post in the work bowl and the special rubber seal around the inside of the lid prevent leaking when processing liquids. The maximum liquid fill line is marked on the bowls. You can process up to 10 cups of liquid (e.g., soups, batters, salad dressings) in the large (14-cup) bowl, 8 cups in the medium bowl and 3 cups in the mini-bowl. When processing thin liquids (e.g., quiche, frittatas), reduce maximum capacity by 2 cups.

MAXIMUM CAPACITY GUIDE

- Sliced or grated vegetables or cheese: 7 cups.
- Chopped fruits, vegetables or nuts: 1½ cups.
- Chopped meat, poultry or fish: 1 lb/500 g (2 cups).

- Thin mixtures: 1½ cups (e.g., 1 milkshake).
- Thick mixtures: 3 cups. (For thick soups, strain vegetables from liquid and purée the solids in batches.)
- White bread dough: 1 loaf (3 to 3¼ cups of flour).
- Whole wheat bread dough:1 loaf (2½ to 3 cups of flour).
- Pastry: one 2-crust pie (2 cups of flour).
- Cakes: Recipes generally not exceeding 2 to 2½ cups flour or 1 box (18.5 oz) cake mix. See Cakes and Frostings (page 344) for more information.
- Cookie dough: 4 to 5 dozen (based on an average chocolate chip cookie recipe).

## TIPS, TRICKS AND TECHNIQUES

- Most of your favorite recipes can be adapted easily to the food processor. Use the appropriate disc or blade to slice, grate, chop, mince or mix. On models with nested bowls, choose the appropriate-sized bowl for the task. Read the recipe completely, then organize the processing tasks for maximum efficiency and minimal cleanup.
- Assemble and measure the ingredients. Cut food to fit the feed tube if slicing or grating. Cut food into chunks if chopping or mincing.
- For uniform results when chopping, all the pieces should be about the same size. When mincing, it's not as important. Do not process larger quantities than recommended in 1 batch.
- Process hard or dry ingredients first, then soft or wet ingredients (e.g., chop onions, then add eggs and mayonnaise for egg salad).
- Combine ingredients of the same texture. If foods have different textures, process them separately.
- Never process foods that are too hard to cut with a knife. You could damage the blade or the machine.

- Check often to avoid overprocessing.
- Wait for the blades to stop spinning before removing the cover. If the cover does not move or fit easily, rub a little cooking oil around the rim of the cover and bowl.
- When slicing or grating, if food doesn't fit through the top of the feed tube, try inserting it through the bottom, which is slightly larger.
- If appearance is important, pack the feed tube carefully. Otherwise, don't fuss.
- To slice small items such as mushrooms, strawberries or radishes, trim the bottom ends flat so food sits upright in the feed tube. Place a few pieces cut side down directly on the **Slicer**. (If your processor comes with a wide-mouth feed tube, place food directly in the feed tube. Be careful—the **Slicer** is very sharp. Use the smaller feed tube when processing small quantities.) Stack the remaining pieces in the feed tube. The bottom layer will produce perfect slices for garnishing.
- When slicing small items (e.g., strawberries, mushrooms) in the wide-mouth feed tube, keep the small pusher inside the small feed tube. Otherwise, the food will ride up inside the small feed tube and won't slice properly.
- To avoid slanted slices when slicing small amounts, place the food to be sliced in an upright position on the right side of the feed tube if disc spins counter-clockwise, and on the left side if disc spins clockwise.
- For round fruits or vegetables, remove a thick slice on the bottom of the food so that it sits upright in the feed tube. If food doesn't fit in the feed tube, cut it in halves or quarters to fit; trim if necessary. Process using steady pressure.
- For julienne strips or matchsticks, you need to slice twice! Cut food to fit the feed tube horizontally. Place food horizontally in the feed tube and slice, using steady pressure on

the pusher. You will get long, plank-like slices. Restack the slices and position them vertically in the feed tube, wedging them in snugly. Slice once again using steady pressure, making long julienne strips. Ideal for carrots, potatoes, turnips and zucchini.

- If you have a **Julienne Disc**, you only need to slice once! Cut food to fit the feed tube horizontally. Place food horizontally in the feed tube and cut into julienne strips using medium pressure. With harder foods such as carrots, use firmer pressure on the pusher.

- CHEATER CHOP: This time-saving technique eliminates emptying the bowl when chopping a large quantity of vegetables (e.g., onions, bell peppers). Place 1-inch chunks of food in the feed tube. Process on the **Slicer** or **French Fry Disc** using almost no pressure. Perfect for salsa!

- It is normal for sliced or grated food to pile up on 1 side of the bowl. Empty bowl as necessary. Don't let food press up against the bottom of the **Slicing** or **Shredding Disc**.

- Sometimes a small amount of food will not pass through the **Slicing** or **Shredding Disc**. Usually, the next item being sliced or shredded will force it through. Otherwise, this tidbit is a snack for the cook. (But no raw chicken, please!)

- The processor can process hot or cold foods. The bowl goes in the refrigerator or freezer (but not in the microwave oven), unless otherwise directed in your manual.

- Butter and cream cheese can be processed directly from the refrigerator—no need to soften them first.

- When adding flour to cake batter, etc., blend in with on/off pulses, just until it disappears. Overprocessing results in poor volume or heavy cakes. Refer to Cakes and Frostings (page 344) for more information.

- Remove the bowl and **Steel Blade** from the base as soon as you are finished processing. When they are removed together, the blade drops down around the central opening, forming a seal.

- On Cuisinart Elite models, make sure to lock the **Steel Blade** into place before adding food so that the blade won't fall out when you empty the bowl.

- If your model doesn't come with this feature, here's how to hold the **Steel Blade** in place when emptying the work bowl. Make sure your hands are dry. Insert your index or middle finger through the hole in the bottom of the bowl, securing the **Steel Blade** so it doesn't slip. Grip the outside edge of the bowl with your thumb. Tip the bowl to empty it, scraping out the contents with a spatula.

- Another method is to hold the blade in place with a rubber spatula while emptying the bowl. Be careful not to drop the blade into the food!

- Put a potholder, towel or small mat underneath the base of your processor. It will be easier to move the machine around on the counter.

- If your processor moves around when processing heavy loads, place a rubber waffled refrigerator liner under the base. This will allow air to circulate under the base and it rinses clean quickly.

- Be prepared! To save time and cleanup, process more food than you need (e.g., grated chocolate, cheese, nuts, crumbs, parsley, onions). Refrigerate or freeze extras for future use.

- First things first! Process nuts, chocolate and streusel mixtures for coffee cakes first, while the processor bowl is dry, to avoid extra washing of the bowl and blade.

- Paper towels are handy to wipe out the processor bowl for easy cleanups between steps.

- Leftover cooked vegetables will thicken gravies, sauces and soups with minimal calories. Purée on the **Steel Blade** until smooth.

- Puréed meals are ideal as "senior food" for people on a soft diet, or those with chewing, swallowing, digestive or dental difficulties.
- INSTANT FRUIT SAUCE: Defrost a 10 oz package of frozen unsweetened raspberries or strawberries (or use 2 cups cut-up fresh berries, peaches or mangoes). Purée on the **Steel Blade** until smooth. For each cup of fruit, add 1 to 2 Tbsp sugar (to taste), 1 tsp orange liqueur and a squeeze of lemon juice. Perfect over ice cream or fruit!

## ORGANIC OR NOT?

To avoid pesticides, use organic produce. The following guidelines will help you choose which conventionally grown fruits and vegetables to choose if organic produce isn't available. (For more information, visit www.foodnews.org.) Remember to always wash all produce thoroughly before eating or cooking to avoid chemical residue. Remove the peel, pits and any seeds or cores.

### THE DIRTY DOZEN

These fruits and vegetables have been found to be the most contaminated with pesticide residues. Most have either thin skin or no skin, which makes them more susceptible to pesticide residues. The following are listed from most to least contaminated:

1. celery
2. peaches
3. strawberries
4. apples
5. blueberries (domestic)
6. nectarines
7. bell peppers
8. spinach
9. cherries
10. kale/collard greens
11. potatoes
12. grapes (imported)

### THE CLEAN FIFTEEN

The following fruits and vegetables are listed from least to most contaminated. Most have thick skins which protect them from sprayed pesticides:

1. onions
2. avocados
3. sweet corn (frozen)
4. pineapple
5. mango (subtropical and tropical)
6. sweet peas (frozen)
7. asparagus
8. kiwi (subtropical and tropical)
9. cabbage
10. eggplant
11. cantaloupe (domestic)
12. watermelon
13. grapefruit
14. sweet potato
15. honeydew melon

## BABY FOOD

- It's easy and economical to make your own baby food. Commercially prepared baby foods often contain additives such as sugar, salt and modified starch. Check labels for ingredients.
- To avoid pesticides, use organic fruits and vegetables. Refer to Organic or Not? (above) for guidelines. It is very important to reduce the exposure of pesticides to babies and young children in order to minimize risks to their vital organ systems which continue to grow and mature.
- Wash fruits and vegetables thoroughly before eating or cooking. Remove the peel, pits, seeds and cores. Cut into 1-inch chunks before cooking or puréeing.
- Steaming is an excellent way to preserve nutrients. Place cut-up fruits or veggies in a vegetable steamer over 2 inches of water in a tightly covered saucepan. Steam until very soft, following times listed on the **Baby Food Chart** (pages 19–21). Drain, reserving liquid from bottom of steamer. Purée food to desired consistency, adding 1 to 2 Tbsp of reserved cooking liquid.
- To microwave, place cut-up fruits or vegetables in a microwavable bowl; sprinkle with 2 Tbsp water. Cover bowl with a damp paper towel or

parchment paper. (Don't use plastic wrap—plasticizers can leach into food when heated.) Calculate 2 to 3 minutes' cooking time on High per cup.

- Boiling, roasting and baking are other cooking methods. Some foods require no cooking at all (e.g., avocado, bananas).

- A mini-prep food processor is very convenient, takes up little space on the counter and is easy to clean. It can only process small amounts but is ideal when baby first starts eating solid foods.

- Food processors are perfect for puréeing larger batches of baby food. Cook in bulk, then purée and freeze. Many processors now include a mini-bowl and mini-blade, which are ideal for smaller quantities. (A blender requires adding extra water to process baby food to the right consistency, which means the food won't be as packed with nutrients.)

- Prior to preparing baby food, wash your hands thoroughly with soap and warm water. Make sure that all equipment, utensils and cooking areas have been sanitized before you start. Always use the freshest ingredients.

- Purée solids until very smooth for infants and to a coarser texture for older babies. For a smoother texture, process solids first, then add liquids. To start, purées should be quite runny, resembling the texture of a thick soup.

- If the purée is too thick, add a little of the reserved cooking liquid from the bottom of the steamer, or some of your baby's usual milk (e.g., breast milk or formula). Start by adding 1 Tbsp of liquid at a time, then add more as needed. Thicken purées by stirring in 1 or 2 spoonfuls of baby rice cereal.

- Follow your doctor's guidelines on when to introduce your baby to new foods. First foods should be easy to digest and unlikely to provoke an allergic reaction.

- When you first start your baby on food, it's not a good idea to introduce mixtures of food other than rice cereal (rice cereal is gluten-free) mixed with a single-fruit or single-vegetable purée. When foods are mixed together, it is difficult to tell which one is causing a problem. Once you've established that a food is tolerated, usually after a 3-day trial, you can create your own combinations.

- FIRST VEGETABLES: Carrots, potatoes, parsnips, butternut squash, potatoes and sweet potatoes. Root vegetables are the most popular ones with young babies (e.g., carrots, sweet potatoes, squash) because they make sweet, smooth purées. After first tastes, you can introduce stronger-flavored vegetables (e.g., broccoli, cauliflower, green/yellow beans, green peas, zucchini).

- If you introduce vegetables before fruit, starting with stronger-tasting veggies first, babies will become accustomed to bitter flavors. Stefanie Goldschmied, one of the moms in my focus group, did this and never experienced any rejection of foods from her babies, unlike a lot of her friends who started their babies on root vegetables and apples.

- Potatoes become gluey if puréed on their own in a food processor—use a food mill instead. However, when combined with other veggies, they can be puréed successfully in a processor or mini-prep. (Note: Instead of boiling potatoes, bake them to retain nutrients, then mash with a fork.)

- FIRST FRUITS: Apples, pears, bananas, peaches and ripe avocados (yes, it's a fruit!).

- POULTRY AND MEAT: Puréed chicken, turkey, beef and veal can be combined with root vegetables to produce a smoother texture, making them easier for young babies to swallow.

- For toddlers, process foods with quick on/off pulses to achieve a chunky texture. For variety, combine 2 or more fruits or vegetables.
- FISH/DAIRY/EGGS/WHEAT/NUTS/SOY/ CITRUS FRUITS: Check with your physician as to when to introduce these foods, especially if there is a family history of food allergies.
- Iron-rich foods should be introduced at 6 months.
- Honey should only be given to children who are over 1 year of age.
- Dietician Ilana Kobric recommends introducing textures to babies as early as you think they are able to handle them. Some signs that they are ready for this include rotary chewing motion and a lack of interest in purées. Teeth are not necessarily an indication of readiness for texture.
- CUBE FOOD: Baby food keeps 24 to 48 hours in the coldest part of the refrigerator. Prepare extra baby food and freeze in ice cube trays; wrap or seal well. Label foods, indicating the date and contents. Cubes will keep 4 to 6 weeks in the freezer. One cube equals about 2 Tbsp.
- CUBE CUISINE: Combine cubes to make interesting combinations (e.g., apple/pear, apple/ carrot, carrot/parsnip, carrot/potato, carrot/ sweet potato).
- Defrost baby food in the refrigerator (never at room temperature). It takes about 30 seconds to defrost 1 cube in the microwave. Stir well to eliminate any hot spots.
- Always test the temperature of food before feeding it to your baby. Food should be at room temperature or lukewarm.
- Discard leftovers, as bacteria from the baby's mouth can contaminate foods.
- QUANTITIES: It's difficult to predict how much a baby will eat since appetites differ. At the beginning, your baby will probably only take 1 or 2 Tbsp of purée (1 cube). As your baby grows, offer 5 to 6 Tbsp (3 cubes) and increase as needed.
- If you wish to prepare a food that is not on this list, follow directions for a food that is similar in shape and/or texture.
- Yields are approximate and are only provided as guidelines. Final yields may vary, depending on size, trimming and method of preparation.

| FRUIT | |
|---|---|
| **Apple Purée** | Choose sweet, ripe fruit. Wash, peel and core 4 medium apples; cut into small chunks. Place in saucepan with ¼ cup water or unsweetened apple juice. Cook on low heat 6 to 8 minutes, until very soft. Purée to desired consistency, adding a little cooking liquid. (Cinnamon may cause an allergic reaction, so check first with your doctor before adding.) Makes 8 cubes. |
| **Apple Pear Purée** | Prepare as for Apple Purée, using 2 apples and 2 pears. Makes 8 cubes. |
| **Apple or Pear Purée with Blueberries** | Prepare as for Apple Purée, using 3 apples or pears and ¾ cup blueberries. Add a little rice cereal to thicken. (Blueberries may cause an allergic reaction, so check first with your doctor.) Makes 8 cubes. |
| **Avocado Purée** | Avocado is actually a fruit. Cut ripe avocado in half and remove pit. Scoop out flesh. Purée to desired consistency. Add some of baby's usual milk if too thick. Serve immediately. (Tip: Wrap leftover avocado purée tightly. Refrigerate or freeze—or make guacamole.) Makes 3 to 4 cubes. |
| **Banana Purée** | Peel half of a small ripe banana; cut into small chunks. Purée to desired consistency. If desired, add some of baby's usual milk to thin it down. Serve immediately. Bananas blend well with other fruits. (Tip: Make extra purée and freeze to use in muffins or smoothies.) Makes 1 serving. |
| **Peach Purée** | Choose sweet, ripe fruit. Cut an X on base of fruit. Plunge 4 peaches into boiling water for 1 to 2 minutes. Drain, cool and peel. Cut into small chunks and discard pit. Steam until very soft, 5 to 6 minutes. Purée to desired consistency, adding a little water from bottom of steamer. (Combines well with Apple Purée.) Makes 8 cubes. |
| **Pear Purée** | Prepare as for Apple Purée, but cook pears for 5 to 6 minutes. Makes 8 cubes. |
| **Plum, Nectarine or Apricot Purée** | Prepare as for Peach Purée. Makes 4 to 6 cubes. |

*Continued*

USING YOUR FOOD PROCESSOR

## VEGETABLES

| | |
|---|---|
| **Bean Purée (Green/Yellow)** | Wash, trim and chop 2 cups of green or yellow beans. Steam until very soft, 12 to 15 minutes. Purée to desired consistency, adding a little water from bottom of steamer or baby's usual milk. If necessary, strain through a fine sieve to remove tough skins. Makes 8 cubes. |
| **Broccoli or Cauliflower Purée** | Wash broccoli or cauliflower florets well. Steam 3 cups of florets until very soft, 10 to 12 minutes. Purée to desired consistency, adding a little water from bottom of steamer or baby's usual milk. (Broccoli has a strong taste on its own but combines nicely with potato, sweet potato or carrots.) Makes 8 cubes. |
| **Butternut Squash Purée** | Wash, peel and seed squash. Cut into small chunks. (Tip: Microwave first on High for a few minutes to make squash easier to cut, or buy cut-up squash at your supermarket.) Steam until very soft, 15 to 20 minutes. (**Baked Squash**: Cut in half, place cut side down on parchment-lined baking sheet and bake at 375°F about 1 hour. Scoop out and discard seeds.) Purée squash to desired consistency, adding a little water from bottom of steamer, boiled water or baby's usual milk. (Tip: Squash also combines very well with Apple or Pear Purée.) Makes 10 cubes. |
| **Carrot Purée** | Wash, peel and cut 4 medium carrots into small chunks. Steam until very soft, 15 to 20 minutes. Purée to desired consistency, adding a little water from bottom of steamer or baby's usual milk. Amount of liquid needed will depend on your baby. Makes 8 cubes. |
| **Carrot Apple Purée** | Wash, peel and cut 2 carrots into small chunks. Steam for 15 minutes. Wash, peel and core 1 apple, then cut into small chunks. Add to carrots and steam 6 to 8 minutes longer, until very soft. Purée to desired consistency, adding a little water from bottom of steamer or baby's usual milk. Makes 8 cubes. |
| **Green Pea Purée** | Frozen peas are convenient to use and can be frozen again after cooking. Steam 2 cups of frozen peas until very soft, 12 to 15 minutes. Purée to desired consistency, adding a little water from bottom of steamer or baby's usual milk. If necessary, strain through a fine sieve to remove tough skins. (Tip: Peas combine well with sweet potato or squash.) Makes 8 cubes. |
| **Mixed Root Vegetable Purée** | Mix and match 3 root vegetables (carrot, potato, sweet potato, squash, parsnip). Wash, peel and cut 1 cup of each vegetable into small chunks. (Tip: Use only ½ cup of parsnip—it has a strong taste.) Steam until very soft, 15 to 20 minutes. Purée to desired consistency, adding a little water from bottom of steamer or baby's usual milk. Makes 8 to 10 cubes. |

| | |
|---|---|
| **Spinach Purée** | Wash 4 cups of spinach leaves well, then remove stems. Steam spinach 5 to 6 minutes, until very soft. Drain well. Purée to desired consistency, adding a little of baby's usual milk. Makes 5 to 6 cubes. (Tip: Spinach has a strong taste on its own, so mix with potato, sweet potato or squash.) |
| **Sweet Potato Purée** | Wash 2 medium sweet potatoes and pierce all over with a fork. Bake at 375°F for 1 hour, until tender. (Can also microwave on High about 10 minutes; turn over halfway through cooking time. Let stand 5 minutes.) Cut in half and scoop out flesh. Purée to desired consistency, adding a little boiled water or baby's usual milk. (Tip: Sweet potato chunks take 15 to 20 minutes to steam.) Makes 10 to 12 cubes. |
| **Sweet Potato Broccoli Purée** | Wash and peel 1 medium sweet potato; cut into small chunks. Steam 10 to 12 minutes. Add 1 cup of small broccoli florets and steam 8 to 10 minutes longer, until very soft. Purée to desired consistency, adding a little water from bottom of steamer or baby's usual milk. Makes 8 cubes. |
| **Triple Veggie Purée** | Wash, peel and cut 1 potato and 2 carrots into chunks (about 1 cup of each). Steam 10 to 12 minutes. Add 1 cup of cut-up broccoli florets and steam 8 to 10 minutes longer, until very soft. Purée to desired consistency, adding a little water from bottom of steamer or baby's usual milk. Makes 8 to 10 cubes. (Variations: Replace potato with sweet potato or squash. Replace broccoli with cauliflower or unpeeled zucchini chunks.) |

| **MEAT/POULTRY** | |
|---|---|
| **Baby Meat Purée** | Cut 1 cup of cooked meat (e.g., beef, veal, chicken) into small pieces. Process 20 to 30 seconds, until minced. Add 2 to 4 Tbsp cooking liquid and process 1 to 2 minutes, to desired consistency. (Tip: For a smoother texture, combine with root vegetables.) Makes 8 cubes. |
| **Baby Chicken Purée** | Rinse 1 single boneless, skinless chicken breast or 2 boneless thighs. Place in saucepan and add enough water to barely cover chicken. Bring to a boil. Reduce heat, cover and simmer 15 minutes. Remove from heat and let chicken cool in cooking liquid. Chicken should be firm with no traces of pink. Reserve liquid. Cut chicken into small pieces. Process 20 to 30 seconds, until minced. Add 2 to 4 Tbsp cooking liquid and process 1 to 2 minutes, to desired consistency. Makes 8 to 10 cubes. |
| **Chicken Combos** | Wash, peel and cut 1 cup of vegetables into 1-inch chunks (e.g., carrots, potatoes, parsnips, sweet potatoes, butternut squash, broccoli/cauliflower florets). Cook veggies together with chicken as for Chicken Purée and process as directed. Makes 12 cubes. |

## KIDS' CUISINE

- You'll find many family-friendly recipes throughout this book, from old favorites to delectable new dishes that will appeal to today's generation of time-starved cooks.
- Transform part of your family's meal into infant or toddler food. This works very well with macaroni and cheese, tuna noodle casserole, lasagna, chili, pasta with tomato sauce and veggies (e.g., broccoli, carrots, peas), boiled chicken with carrots, noodles or rice, meatballs (add mixed veggies to the sauce), shepherd's pie, any kind of vegetable-based soup—the possibilities are endless.
- Remember to ease up on the salt shaker. What tastes bland to you may not taste bland to your baby or toddler.
- Penne, rotini or elbows are ideal as finger food for toddlers, and vegetable purées make a tasty sauce for pasta. Cook desired pasta 1 minute longer than recommended on the package. Mix 1 cup pasta with ½ cup vegetable purée (e.g., squash) and sprinkle with Parmesan cheese.
- Broccoli florets are fun to dip into a cheese sauce, some grated Parmesan or your favorite dip. Rinse 1 cup florets and place in a 2-cup glass measure. There's no need to add extra water. Cover with a damp microwavable paper towel (not plastic wrap) and microwave for 2 minutes on High. Cool to lukewarm, then dip away.
- Couscous is quick to make and has a neutral taste. Combine ½ cup couscous with ¾ cup boiling water, cover and let stand 5 to 10 minutes. You can substitute cooked quinoa or orzo for cooked couscous. Fluff with a fork, add desired steamed veggies (e.g., minced broccoli, carrots, bell peppers, peas, zucchini) or finely chopped cooked chicken and mix together.

## FUSSY EATERS

- Many children are extremely fussy and go through phases. Noodles are the mainstay of my grandson Sam's diet. (It must be genetic—his dad would only eat white food when he was young!) However, his younger brother, Zak, will try almost anything and so will my sister's grandsons, Jesse, Ari and Jack. When my grandson Max was little, he loved to eat pasta with Pesto (page 105–6) that I made using half basil and half spinach. Meatballs, shepherd's pie, salmon patties and tuna casserole have always been favorites with the children in our family.
- Kids love finger foods, so look for ways to create fun foods for little hands to hold. If you're frustrated because your child refuses to eat anything that resembles a vegetable, your food processor can be a huge help. Instead of letting mealtime become a power struggle, hide healthy foods inside the ones that your child already likes and will eat. Combine foods that have similar colors or textures. If they can't see, smell or taste anything too different, you might be able to sneak some extra nutrition into them by adding puréed veggies to their favorite foods. Camouflage works wonders on the food battleground!
- SNEAKY SOUPS: Puréed vegetable-based soups (e.g., carrot, sweet potato) are a super way to get children to eat more veggies. Use a slotted spoon to remove some of the vegetables and purée to the desired consistency for babies and fussy eaters.
- SNEAKY BEAN CUISINE: Rinse and drain red lentils, then add to vegetable soups and spaghetti sauces—the lentils will "disappear" when cooked. Add ½ cup puréed canned or cooked lentils, chickpeas or vegetables to your favorite meatball mixture, pasta sauce, chili, burgers and meatloaf.

- **SNEAKY VEGGIE CUISINE:** Add ½ cup puréed squash or sweet potato to salmon patties. Add ½ cup puréed cauliflower or squash to macaroni and cheese—camouflage the taste with a little extra grated cheese.

- **SNEAKY SAUCE CUISINE:** Add puréed carrots to tomato sauce—it's perfect in lasagna, over pasta or on mini pizzas. Decorate mini pizzas with cut-up veggies to make faces!

- **WHITE'S ALL RIGHT:** Blend a couple of spoonfuls of puréed cottage cheese or silken tofu into pancake batter. Blend ½ cup tofu into the cheese filling when making lasagna. Add puréed white beans to mashed potatoes.

- **SNEAKY FRUIT CUISINE:** Combine yogurt with frozen chunks of banana and strawberries in the food processor to make an extra-thick smoothie and call it "ice cream for breakfast"!

- **SNEAKY FROZEN CUISINE:** Add different-colored fruit purées to yogurt (e.g., strawberries, mangoes, blueberries). Layer alternating colors in molds and freeze to make rainbow pops.

- **SNEAKY FUN CUISINE:** Cut fruits and vegetables into novelty shapes with mini cutters. Make dried Apple Chips as a healthy snack (see page 415 for recipe).

- **SNEAKY BAKING:** Replace part of the flour in muffins and quick breads with finely ground rolled oats. Add Prune Purée (page 346) to brownie batter and unsweetened applesauce to cake and muffin batters. Make zucchini bread, carrot cake or banana muffins, baking them in mini muffin pans.

OTHER FOOD IDEAS FOR KIDS

- **BETTER BREADING:** Most kids love fish or chicken fingers (or make tofu fingers using extra-firm tofu). For the crumb mixture, process whole-grain bread, crispy cereal or crackers until fine. You can also add 1 or 2 spoonfuls of wheat germ. Sesame seeds will add some crunch. This delicious coating is excellent on chicken drumettes and chicken schnitzel.

- **CRUMMY NEWS:** Instead of regular bread crumbs, add rolled oats, oat bran and/or a spoonful of wheat germ to meatballs and mini burgers.

- **TOASTY IDEAS:** Cut each slice of whole wheat bread into 4 strips. Dip in beaten egg, then in crushed cereal crumbs to make crunchy French toast sticks. Instead of cutting bread into strips, cut into different shapes with cookie cutters—use trimmings to make bread crumbs.

- **CHEESY FRENCH TOAST TRIANGLES:** Try a different "angle" on the grilled cheese sandwich. Place sliced cheese between 2 slices of whole grain bread (trim off crusts for fussy kids). Cut sandwich into 4 triangles. Dip in beaten egg (add a splash of milk), then in crushed cereal crumbs and cook as for French toast. Calci-yummy!

- **NICE BROWN RICE:** Disguise the color of brown rice by turning it into fried rice. Add a splash of soy sauce or any Asian-style sauce, some colorful veggies (e.g., peas, finely chopped carrots, red peppers), bits of cooked chicken or tofu, and a scrambled egg. Soy good!

- **USE YOUR NOODLE:** Many brands of whole wheat pasta have evolved to become taste-bud friendly, and turn lighter in color after cooking. Choose fun shapes of multigrain pasta and give the dish a fun name (e.g., noodle-doodles, whirly-curlies). Marketing, marketing!

- **MINIATURE KUGELS:** Instead of baking vegetable or noodle kugel mixtures in a large casserole, make mini kugels. Bake in sprayed muffin pans until golden brown, 35 to 45 minutes. Baking times will vary, depending on the mixture.

- ON THE BALL: Make tiny meatballs using ground chicken and finely minced vegetables. Add them to your chicken soup for the last 30 minutes of cooking. See Chicken Meatball Soup (page 88). Easy one-pot cooking!

- When children help prepare a dish, they're more likely to eat it. My granddaughters Lauren and Camille love to help their mom cook. Lauren now makes dinner for the family (stir-fry is one of her specialties) and Camille chose a cooking party for her 10th birthday. My sister's 4-year-old granddaughter, Mikaela, loves to help cook and is allowed to push the button to start the processor—with supervision, of course! Mikaela asks her mom, "Do I press PULSE or ON?"

## SMART CHART

IMPORTANT!

- To avoid pesticides, you may prefer to buy organic products. (See "The Dirty Dozen" and "The Clean Fifteen" on page 16.)

- Wash produce thoroughly. Peel, core and remove any pits or seeds if necessary.

- To use the **Slicer** or **Grater**, cut food in the largest possible size to fit the feed tube. Pack food in the feed tube evenly when slicing. For smaller amounts of food, use the smaller feed tube if your processor has one. Adjust the pressure according to the texture of the food being processed. Use light pressure for soft foods, medium pressure for medium foods and firm pressure for harder foods.

- To use the **Steel Blade**, cut food in even-sized chunks (1 to 1½ inches). Fill the bowl no more than one-third to one-half full. Process in batches if necessary. Use quick on/off pulses to chop; let the machine run to mince, grind or purée.

- Equivalents given for each food are approximate and are only provided as a guideline. Final yields may vary, depending on trimming, method of preparation and processing techniques.

- If a food you wish to process is not on this list, follow directions for a food that is similar in shape or texture.

| FRUITS | |
|---|---|
| **Apples** | (1 lb/500 g yields 3 cups; 1 medium yields ¾ cup sliced or chopped.) |
| Slicer or Grater | Medium pressure. |
| Steel Blade | Cut in chunks. On/off pulses to chop, let machine run to mince. Sprinkle with lemon juice to prevent discoloration. |
| **Applesauce** | (6 medium apples yield about 3 cups.) |
| Steel Blade | Peel and core apples; cook until tender. Process in batches with quick on/offs for chunky texture, let machine run for puréed texture. (A food mill does a better job on unpeeled apples.) |
| **Apricots** | *See* Fruits, Dried. *See also* Peaches. |
| **Avocados** | (1 medium avocado yields 1 cup purée.) |
| Steel Blade | Peel, remove pit and cut in chunks. Quick on/off pulses to chop; let machine run to mince or purée. Sprinkle with lemon juice to prevent discoloration. |

| **Bananas** | (2 medium bananas yield 1½ cups sliced, 1 cup purée.) |
|---|---|
| Slicer | Use firm bananas. Light pressure. Use small feed tube for 1 or 2 bananas. Sprinkle with lemon juice to prevent discoloration. |
| Steel Blade | The riper the better! Cut in chunks. Let machine run until puréed. Extras can be frozen for future use. |
| **Berries** | *See* Strawberries. |
| **Coconut** | (1 medium coconut yields 4 cups grated.) |
| Steel Blade | Pierce the eyes with a nail; drain out liquid from coconut. Place in a 400°F oven for about 20 minutes. Remove from oven and crack shell with a hammer. Peel off inner brown skin with a potato peeler. Rinse, pat dry and cut in 1-inch chunks. Process 1 cup at a time. On/off pulses, then let machine run until minced. Refrigerate for 3 days or freeze. |
| **Fruits, Dried** | Dried Apricots, Cherries, Cranberries, Dates, Mangoes, Prunes, Raisins <br> (1 lb/500 g yields 2½ cups.) |
| Steel Blade | Freeze sticky fruit for 10 minutes. Check pitted prunes carefully to make sure all pits have been removed. (Tip: If dates or other dried fruits are very dry, soak in hot water first, then pat dry.) To prevent sticking, add about ¼ cup flour if called for in recipe. Quick on/off pulses to chop candied or dried fruits. To grind or purée dried fruits, let machine run until fine. |
| **Kiwis** | (2 kiwis yield ¾ cup.) |
| Slicer | Use firm fruit. Chill before slicing, then peel. Fill feed tube snugly or use small feed tube. Use light pressure to prevent crushing. |
| **Lemons** | Also Limes, Oranges <br> (1 medium lemon yields 2 tsp zest and 3 Tbsp juice. <br> 1 medium lime yields 1 tsp zest and 1 to 2 Tbsp juice. <br> 1 medium orange yields 2 Tbsp zest and ⅓ to ½ cup juice.) |
| Slicer | Do not peel; scrub well. Cut ends flat. Medium pressure. Use wide-mouth feed tube for whole oranges, or cut to fit feed tube. |
| Steel Blade | Cut in quarters; remove any seeds. Process until fine—just a few seconds for peeled fruits, 20 to 30 seconds for unpeeled fruits. Use thin-skinned fruits as there is less bitter white pith. <br><br> ZEST (RIND): Use peeler to remove colored rind from fruit. Add part of sugar called for in recipe to rind. Start with on/off pulses, then let machine run until finely minced, 30 to 60 seconds. Refrigerate or freeze extra zest. (When recipe calls for zest and juice, remove rind first, then squeeze out juice.) |

| | |
|---|---|
| **Mangoes** | (1 medium yields ¾ to 1 cup.) |
| Steel Blade | Peel and pit; cut flesh into 1-inch pieces. On/off pulses to chop, let machine run to purée. Sprinkle with a few drops of lemon or lime juice. |
| **Nectarines** | *See* Peaches. |
| **Oranges** | *See* Lemons. |
| **Peaches** | Also Apricots, Nectarines, Pears, Plums <br> (1 lb/500 g yields 2 to 2½ cups.) |
| Slicer | Remove pits or core. Peel if desired. Light pressure. |
| Steel Blade | On/off pulses to chop, let machine run to mince or purée. Sprinkle with lemon juice to prevent discoloration. |
| **Pineapple** | (1 medium yields 4 cups.) |
| Slicer | Peel, then remove eyes with point of sharp knife. Cut in wedges to fit feed tube; remove core. Cut flat ends. Medium to firm pressure. Makes thin slices. |
| Steel Blade | Cut in chunks; process in batches. Fill bowl one-quarter to one-third full. Use on/off pulses to chop. (If recipe calls for canned crushed pineapple but you only have slices or chunks, drain well and process 6 to 8 seconds, until crushed.) |
| **Prunes** | *See* Fruits, Dried. *Also see* Prune Purée (page 346). |
| **Purées (Fruit)** | (1 cup fruit or berries [fresh or frozen] yields about ½ cup purée.) |
| Steel Blade | Choose ripe fruit. Frozen fruit should be thawed first. *See individual listings.* |
| | Peel; remove pits or core. Cut fruit in chunks. For cooked purées, cook or steam until tender. Drain, reserving cooking liquid (1 to 2 Tbsp per cup of fruit). Fill bowl one-third full. Process in batches until smooth; scrape down sides of bowl and add liquid as needed to achieve desired consistency. *Also see* **Baby Food Chart** (pages 19–21). |
| **Rhubarb** | (1 lb/500 g yields 2 cups chopped and cooked.) |
| Slicer | Trim; peel with vegetable peeler. Discard leaves (they are poisonous). Place stalks upright in feed tube. Medium pressure. Makes thin slices. |
| Steel Blade | Quick on/off pulses to chop; let machine run to purée. |
| **Strawberries** | (1 pint fresh berries yields about 2 cups; a 10 oz/300 g package frozen yields 1½ cups.) |
| Slicer | Strawberries should be firm; remove stems. Stack on their sides in feed tube. Light pressure. (Partially thaw frozen strawberries and use medium pressure.) |
| Steel Blade | Use fresh or frozen berries, thawed and drained. Let machine run until puréed. Strain to remove seeds, if desired. |

## VEGETABLES

**Beans, Green/Wax** — (1 lb/500 g yields 3 cups; 1 cup yields ½ cup purée.)

| | |
|---|---|
| Slicer | **FRENCH STYLE:** Trim and cut beans to fit feed tube crosswise. Cook in boiling salted water for 1 minute, then plunge into ice water. Drain, dry and slice. Medium pressure. |
| Steel Blade | Process cooked beans with quick on/offs to chop, let machine run to mince or purée. Use in soups, spreads or latkes (pancakes). |

**Beets** — (1 medium beet yields ½ to ¾ cup.)

| | |
|---|---|
| Slicer or Grater | **RAW:** Peel and trim. Firm pressure, with bouncing motion on pusher. (Shredded raw beets will cook in just 3 minutes.)<br>**COOKED:** Parboil with skins on to retain color. Peel and trim. Light pressure. |
| Steel Blade | Cut raw or cooked beets in chunks. Process in batches if necessary. Fill bowl one-quarter to one-third full. On/off pulses to chop, let machine run to mince or purée. |

**Broccoli** — (1 lb/500 g yields 2 cups chopped [raw] or 1 cup purée [cooked].)

| | |
|---|---|
| Slicer or Grater | Peel and trim raw broccoli stems. Medium pressure. (Reserve florets for stir-fries; they will crumble if sliced.) Substitute grated/shredded broccoli stems for cabbage in coleslaw. |
| Steel Blade | Cut raw or cooked broccoli in chunks. Process in batches if necessary. Fill bowl one-quarter to one-third full. On/off pulses to chop; let machine run to mince or purée. |

**Cabbage** — (1 medium cabbage [about 2 lb/1 kg] yields 8 cups.)

| | |
|---|---|
| Slicer | Use **Slicer** to "grate." Young cabbages are best. Cut in wedges to fit feed tube; remove core. Light to no pressure.<br><br>For coleslaw, let cabbage self-feed, with almost no pressure.<br><br>Roll soft, outer leaves into a cylinder. Light pressure. |
| Grater | Medium pressure. Ideal for egg rolls, extra-fine coleslaw. |
| Steel Blade | Cut in 1-inch chunks. Fill bowl one-quarter to one-third full. On/off pulses to chop; let machine run to mince. |

**Carrots** — Also Parsnips
(1 lb/500 g [6 medium carrots] yields 3 cups; 2 medium carrots yield ½ cup purée. Substitute 3 or 4 baby carrots for 1 medium carrot.)

| | |
|---|---|
| Slicer or Grater | Medium to firm pressure. If grating, use bouncing motion with pusher. For small round slices or short shreds, pack upright in feed tube. For long slices or shreds, pack horizontally in feed tube. To slice 1 or 2 carrots, use small feed tube. |
| Steel Blade | Cut raw or cooked carrots in chunks. Process in batches if necessary. Fill bowl one-quarter to one-third full. Quick on/off pulses to chop, let machine run to mince or purée. |

| **Cauliflower** | (1 lb/500 g yields 2 cups chopped [raw] or 1 cup purée [cooked].) |
|---|---|
| Grater | Cut raw cauliflower into large chunks. Medium pressure produces rice-like texture which is ideal for Low-Carb "Fried Rice" (page 250). |
| Steel Blade | Cut raw or cooked cauliflower in chunks. Process in batches if necessary. Fill bowl one-quarter to one-third full. On/off pulses to chop; let machine run to mince or purée. (Crumbles if sliced.) |
| **Celery** | (2 medium stalks yield ½ to ¾ cup.) |
| Slicer | Peel and trim; pat dry. Medium pressure. For diagonal slices, place on an angle in feed tube. |
| Steel Blade | Cut in chunks. On/off pulses to chop; let machine run to mince. *See* "Cheater Chop" (page 15). |
| **Celery Root** | (1½ lb/750 g yields 4 cups grated.) |
| Grater or Julienne Disc | Peel and trim, using a sharp knife. Cut to fit feed tube. Medium pressure. |
| **Cucumbers** | (1 medium English cucumber yields 1½ cups.) |
| Slicer | Long, slim, firm cucumbers are best and have fewer seeds. Trim and cut to fit feed tube. Place upright in feed tube for round slices. Place horizontally in feed tube for long slices. Medium pressure. Pat dry before using. Use small feed tube for small quantities.<br><br>CRESCENTS: Cut in half lengthwise; scoop out seeds with a spoon. Cut to fit feed tube. Slice, using medium pressure. Pretty for salads! |
| Grater | Trim and cut to fit feed tube. Place upright in feed tube for short shreds. Place horizontally in feed tube for long shreds. Medium pressure. Pat dry. |
| Steel Blade | Remove seeds. Cut in chunks. On/off pulses to chop. Do not overprocess because of high water content. Drain or pat dry. |
| **Eggplant** | (1 lb/500 g yields 3½ cups chopped [raw] or 1½ cups purée [cooked].) |
| Slicer | Trim; peel if desired. Cut in wedges to fit feed tube. Medium pressure. Makes thin slices. Use wide-mouth feed tube for large slices. *See* "Cheater Chop" (page 15). |
| Steel Blade | Trim; peel if desired. Cut in chunks; process in batches if necessary. Quick on/off pulses to chop raw eggplant. Do not overprocess cooked eggplant. |
| **Fennel** | (1 lb/500 g equals 2 medium bulbs. 1 medium bulb yields 1 to 1½ cups.) |
| Slicer | Trim off fronds and stalks (reserve feathery fronds as a garnish). Peel and trim bulb. Cut in half (or quarters) lengthwise to fit feed tube. Medium pressure.<br><br>STALKS: Cut to fit feed tube upright; pack tightly. Medium pressure. (Tip: Use stalks instead of celery in soups and stews, or add to poaching liquid for fish. Fennel has a pronounced licorice flavor.) |

| | |
|---|---|
| Steel Blade | FRONDS: Process as for Parsley. Add to salads or use as a garnish. |
| | BULB: Cut bulb in chunks. Quick on/off pulses to chop or mince. |
| **Garlic** | (1 head contains 12 to 15 cloves; 1 medium clove yields ½ tsp.) |
| Steel Blade | Not necessary to peel if bowl and blade are dry. Drop through feed tube while machine is running; process until minced, 8 to 10 seconds. Discard peel. (Pieces are easy to pick out if bowl is dry.) Don't bother if garlic is to be cooked; peel disintegrates during cooking. |
| **Ginger** | (1-inch piece yields 1 Tbsp; 4 oz/125 g yields ½ cup.) |
| Steel Blade | Peel; cut in pieces. Drop through feed tube while machine is running; process until minced. Process extra ginger, then place in a glass jar, adding sherry to cover. Refrigerate up to 3 months. (Sherry can be used in cooking.) |
| **Green Onions** | *See* Leeks. |
| **Herbs, Fresh** | (1 Tbsp fresh chopped herbs equals 1 tsp dried.) |
| Steel Blade | Herbs, bowl and blade must be clean and dry. Quick on/off pulses to chop; let machine run to mince. *Also see* Parsley. |
| **Jicama** | (1 medium root yields 1 cup.) |
| Slicer or Grater | Peel just before using; cut to fit feed tube. Firm pressure. (Tip: Taste is similar to a pear or apple. Use raw in salads or cook briefly in stir-fries.) |
| Steel Blade | Cut in chunks. Quick on/off pulses to chop or mince. |
| **Leeks** | Also Green Onions/Scallions<br>(1 lb/500 g leeks yields 2 cups; 1 or 2 green onions yields ¼ cup. For 1 leek, substitute 6 green onions.) |
| Slicer | Trim off most of green portion from leeks and green onions; cut to fit feed tube. Wash very well, especially leeks. Pack upright in feed tube or use small feed tube. If slicing small quantities, combine with other foods (e.g., pack green onions in the hollow of celery stalks). Medium pressure. Some slivering will occur. |
| Steel Blade | Cut in 1-inch chunks. On/off pulses to chop; let machine run to mince. Some slivering will occur. |
| **Lemon Grass** | (1 stalk yields 3 to 4 Tbsp minced.) |
| Steel Blade | Cut off bulb, remove and discard tough outer leaves. Cut stalk in 1-inch pieces. Drop through feed tube while machine is running; process until minced. (Tip: Substitute zest of a lemon for 1 stalk lemon grass.) |
| **Lettuce** | (1 lb/500 g yields 6 cups.) |
| Slicer | To shred, roll leaves together and place upright in feed tube. Medium pressure. Good for layered salads, sandwiches, tacos. For tossed salads, tear by hand into pieces. |

## VEGETABLES *(CONTINUED)*

| | |
|---|---|
| **Mushrooms** | (½ lb/250 g yields 2 to 2½ cups.) |
| Slicer | The firmer the better. If appearance is not important, stack feed tube at random. Use small feed tube for small amounts. Remove and discard stems from portobello mushrooms.<br><br>HAMMERHEAD SLICES: Trim ends. Stack mushrooms on their sides, alternating direction of caps (one facing right, the next facing left). Light to medium pressure.<br><br>ROUND SLICES: Remove stems; place mushrooms rounded side down. Light to medium pressure. |
| Grater | Medium pressure. |
| Steel Blade | Quick on/off pulses to chop; let machine run to mince. If overprocessed, make Mushroom Duxelles (page 235) or quiche. |
| **Olives** | *See* Pickles. |
| **Onions** | (1 lb/500 g equals 4 medium; 1 medium yields ½ to ¾ cup.) |
| Slicer | For round rings, onions must be small or processor must have wide-mouth feed tube. Light to medium pressure. For "diced" onions, cut onions in 1-inch chunks. Slice, using light pressure. For "grated" onions, **Steel Blade** is better as some catching may take place with **Grater**. (For milder flavor, soak onions in ice-cold water for 15 minutes after slicing.) |
| Steel Blade | Cut small onions in half, larger onions in quarters or chunks. On/off pulses to chop (1 onion takes 2 to 3 quick on/off pulses, 2 onions take 3 to 4 pulses). To mince or grate, let machine run 8 to 10 seconds. Overprocessing onions produces a purée. *Also see* "Cheater Chop" (page 15). |
| **Parsley, Fresh** | Also Fresh Herbs: Basil, Coriander/Cilantro, Dill, etc.<br>(1 cup loosely packed sprigs yields ⅓ cup minced.) |
| Steel Blade | Discard tough stems. Herbs, bowl and blade should be clean and dry. For best results, chop or mince at least ½ cup (or up to a whole bowlful) at a time. On/off pulses, then let machine run until minced. For small quantities, drop through feed tube while machine is running; process until minced. Wrap in paper towels and store in an airtight bag in refrigerator for up to a week. (Tip: Instead of mincing herbs first, add to cooked soups or sauces and process them together.)<br><br>HERB CUBES: Process 3 cups fresh herbs with 2 cups water for 30 to 45 seconds. Mixture will look like thick slush. Freeze in ice cube trays. Transfer to freezer bags. One cube equals 2 Tbsp fresh or 2 tsp dried herbs. Best used in cooked dishes. |

| **Parsnips** | (4 medium parsnips is about 1 lb/500 g and yields 2 to 2½ cups.) |
| | Process as for Carrots. |
| **Peppers, Bell** | (1 medium yields ¾ to 1 cup.) |
| Slicer | Remove stems and seeds. |
| | PEPPER RINGS: Cut stem end flat. Use wide-mouth feed tube for large peppers. For standard feed tube, use small peppers that will fit through bottom of feed tube. If too big, cut down 1 side; roll up to fit snugly in feed tube. Medium to firm pressure. |
| | LONG SLICES: Cut in half or quarters. Place horizontally in feed tube. |
| | NARROW SLICES: Cut in half or quarters. Place upright in feed tube or use small feed tube. Medium pressure. |
| Steel Blade | Cut in 1-inch chunks. Quick on/off pulses to chop; do not overprocess. Pat dry with paper towels. Let machine run to mince. *Also see* "Cheater Chop" (page 15). (Tip: Peppers chop more evenly when combined with onions.) |
| | ROASTED PEPPERS: 2 or 3 quick on/off pulses to chop, let machine run to mince or purée. |
| **Peppers, Hot** | (1 medium yields 3 to 4 Tbsp.) |
| Slicer | Remove stem, rib and seeds (use rubber gloves). Place upright in feed tube or use small feed tube. Medium pressure. |
| Steel Blade | Remove stem, ribs and seeds (use rubber gloves). Cut in 1-inch chunks. Quick on/off pulses to chop; do not overprocess. Let machine run to mince. Caution—don't rub your eyes (or any sensitive body parts) after handling hot peppers! |
| **Pickles** | Also Olives, Water Chestnuts |
| Slicer | PICKLES: Choose firm pickles. Arrange either upright or horizontally in feed tube. Medium pressure. |
| | OLIVES: Arrange pitted olives with flat ends down in feed tube. Medium pressure. (Hand-slicing may be easier.) |
| | WATER CHESTNUTS: Peel fresh water chestnuts just before using. Firm pressure. |
| Steel Blade | Quick on/off pulses to chop; let machine run to mince. |
| **Potatoes** | Also Sweet Potatoes, Yams |
| | (1 lb/500 g yields 3½ to 4 cups.) |
| Slicer | Cut in largest size possible to fit feed tube. Medium pressure for raw potatoes, firm pressure for raw sweet potatoes or yams. (Cooked potatoes crumble somewhat when sliced.) |

*Continued*

**Potatoes** *(continued)*

| | |
|---|---|
| Grater | Light to medium pressure, depending on texture desired. Makes long shreds. (Store grated or sliced raw potatoes in cold water to prevent discoloration. Dry well before using.) |
| Steel Blade | Cut in chunks; process in batches. Fill bowl one-quarter to one-third full. On/off pulses to chop, let machine run to mince or "grate." Processor-mashed potatoes will be glue-like and sticky. (*See* Rescued Mashed Potatoes on page 225.) |
| French Fry Disc | Place horizontally in feed tube. Medium pressure. (For best results, use wide-mouth feed tube.) Makes short shoestring strips rather than traditional fries. *See* Skinny No-Fries (page 237). |
| Julienne Disc | Place horizontally in feed tube. Medium pressure. Use for hash browns. |
| **Purées (Vegetable)** | (1 cup cooked vegetables yields about ½ cup purée.) Excellent for most cooked or leftover vegetables except starchy ones like potatoes. |
| Steel Blade | Cook or steam vegetables until tender. Drain, reserving cooking liquid (1 to 2 Tbsp per cup of vegetables). Fill bowl one-third full. Process in batches until smooth; scrape down sides of bowl and add liquid as needed to achieve desired consistency. Broth or cream can replace cooking liquid. Season with salt, freshly ground black pepper and a little butter or margarine, if desired. *Also see* **Baby Food Chart**, pages 19–21. |
| | PURÉED SOUPS: Strain out solids. Process in batches until smooth; scrape down sides of bowl as needed. Add up to ¼ cup liquid for each cup of vegetables. |
| **Radishes** | (½ lb/250 g yields 1½ cups sliced.) |
| Slicer | Trim ends; place cut side down in feed tube. Firm pressure. |
| Grater | Large varieties (e.g., black radish, daikon) should be cut to fit feed tube; grate to use in salads. Medium pressure. |
| Steel Blade | Quick on/off pulses to chop; let machine run to mince. |
| **Scallions** | (Also called green onions.) *See* Leeks. |
| **Shallots** | (These are a cross between garlic and onions. Don't confuse with green onions. 1 yields 1 to 2 Tbsp.) |
| Steel Blade | For small quantities, drop through feed tube while machine is running. On/off pulses to chop; let machine run to mince. |
| **Spinach** | (1 lb/500 g fresh yields about 10 cups raw or 1½ cups cooked and drained. A 10 oz/300 g package frozen yields 1 cup cooked and drained.) |
| Slicer | To shred, stack leaves. Roll up into a cylinder and stand upright in feed tube. Medium pressure. Use in stir-fries, salads and wraps. |

| Steel Blade | Discard tough stalks. Process in batches if necessary. Fill bowl one-quarter to one-third full. On/off pulses to chop; let machine run to mince or purée. (Tip: Squeeze cooked spinach dry before processing.) |
|---|---|
| **Squash, Winter** | Also Acorn, Butternut, Hubbard, etc. <br> (1 lb/500 g yields 2 to 2½ cups chopped [raw] or 1 cup purée [cooked].) |
| Slicer or Grater | Cut in half. Scoop out and discard seeds. Peel and trim; cut to fit feed tube. Firm pressure. (Tip: Squash is easier to cut if you microwave it first on High for 4 to 5 minutes. You can also buy cut-up squash at your supermarket.) |
| Steel Blade | Process in batches if necessary. Fill bowl one-quarter to one-third full. On/off pulses to chop. For raw or cooked squash, let machine run to mince or purée. |
| **Swiss Chard** | Process as for Spinach. |
| **Tomatoes** | (1 lb/500 g [3 medium tomatoes] yields 1½ to 2 cups.) |
| Slicer | For standard feed tube, cut firm tomatoes in half and cut ends flat. Medium pressure. Whole firm tomatoes can be sliced in wide-mouth feed tube. Cherry tomatoes can be sliced in small feed tube. Drain well after slicing. |
| Steel Blade | Cut in quarters. Peeling is not necessary if cooking tomatoes as blade does an excellent job on skins. On/off pulses to chop or mince. If desired, squeeze out seeds and juice before processing. In season, freeze ripe chopped tomatoes to use in sauces. <br><br> CANNED TOMATOES: Drain liquid. On/off pulses to chop, let machine run to mince or purée. |
| **Turnips** | (1 lb/500 g yields 2 to 2½ cups chopped [raw] or 1 cup purée [cooked].) |
| Slicer or Grater | Peel and trim. Cut to fit feed tube. Firm pressure, with bouncing motion on pusher. |
| Steel Blade | Process in batches if necessary. Fill bowl one-quarter to one-third full. On/off pulses to chop. For raw or cooked turnips, let machine run to mince or purée. |
| **Watercress** | Process as for Parsley; use as garnish. |
| **Zucchini** | Also Summer Squash <br> (1 lb/500 g yields 3 cups.) |
| Slicer | Trim; peel if desired. Cut to fit feed tube. Place upright in feed tube for round slices. Place horizontally in feed tube for long slices. Use small feed tube for small quantities. Medium pressure. |
| Grater | Trim; peel if desired. Cut to fit feed tube. Place upright in feed tube for short shreds. Place horizontally in feed tube for long shreds. Medium pressure. |

*Continued*

**Zucchini** *(continued)*

| | |
|---|---|
| Steel Blade | Cut in chunks. Process in batches if necessary. On/off pulses to chop; let run to mince or purée. |

## CHEESE, EGGS, FISH, MEAT, POULTRY, TOFU

| | |
|---|---|
| **Cheeses, Hard** | Parmesan<br>(¼ lb/125 g yields 1 cup grated.) |
| Steel Blade | Parmesan cheese should be at room temperature. Break into small chunks with a blunt knife or chisel. Process no more than 1 cup at a time. Drop pieces through feed tube while machine is running; let machine run until finely grated, 20 to 30 seconds. Refrigerate or freeze extras. Never process cheeses that cannot be pierced with the tip of a sharp knife. |
| **Cheeses, Semihard or Soft** | Cheddar, Swiss or Mozzarella<br>(¼ lb/125 g yields 1 cup grated.) |
| Grater | Chill thoroughly for best results (especially mozzarella). If not cold enough, freeze for 15 to 20 minutes before grating. Light pressure produces fine shreds, medium pressure produces coarser shreds. Grate extra to use in salads, casseroles or pizzas, and refrigerate or freeze. |
| Slicer | Don't slice soft cheese (e.g., mozzarella) or hard cheese (e.g., Parmesan). You may damage the blade! Cut cheese to fit feed tube. Place in freezer until partially frozen; you should be able to pierce it with the tip of a sharp knife. Light to medium pressure. |
| Steel Blade | Cut in chunks. On/off pulses to chop. Use when appearance is not important (e.g., sauces, casseroles). |
| **Cheeses, Soft** | Cream Cheese, Cottage Cheese, Ricotta<br>(½ lb/250 g yields 1 cup.) |
| Steel Blade | May be used directly from refrigerator.<br><br>CREAM CHEESE: Cut in chunks; process until smooth. Scrape down bowl as necessary.<br><br>COTTAGE CHEESE: Process until very smooth and lump-free, scraping down bowl as necessary. For dry cottage cheese, you may need to add a little milk.<br><br>CRÊPE OR BLINTZ FILLING: Use fewer eggs in cheese mixture; processor makes cheese very creamy. |
| **Eggs** | (1 large egg yields ¼ cup.) |
| Grater | HARD-COOKED: Light pressure. **Steel Blade** "grates" better. For slices, slice by hand for best results. |

| | |
|---|---|
| Steel Blade | **HARD-COOKED:** Cut in half. On/off pulses. For egg salad, chop or mince vegetables first, then add eggs, mayonnaise and seasonings. (Up to 1 dozen eggs at a time.) |
| | **RAW:** Process for 2 or 3 seconds, until blended. For omelets or frittatas, the processor is faster than a fork! |
| **Egg Whites** | (1 egg white yields 2 Tbsp; 8 egg whites equal 1 cup.) |
| Steel Blade | To process, use at least 3 egg whites, or up to 8. Egg whites should be at room temperature. For each egg white, add 1 tsp lemon juice or vinegar. Bowl and blade must be absolutely clean and grease-free. Process until firm, 1½ to 2 minutes. Do not use for meringues. (Tip: An electric mixer or whisk produces firmer whites and greater volume.) |
| **Fish, Raw** | (1 lb/500 g fillets yields 2 cups.) |
| Steel Blade | Remove skin and bones; cut in chunks. Grind in batches (2 to 3 cups at a time). On/off pulses to chop coarsely, or let machine run until smooth, about 15 to 20 seconds. |
| **Fish, Cooked/Canned** | (6 to 7 oz can [170 to 213 g] yields ½ to ⅔ cup drained.) |
| Steel Blade | 2 or 3 quick on/off pulses. Maximum 2 to 3 cups at a time. Chop or mince vegetables first, then add fish, mayonnaise and seasonings. On/off pulses to combine. If overprocessed, flaked tuna will have a gritty texture. |
| **Meat and Poultry, Cooked** | Beef, Lamb, Veal, Chicken, Turkey<br>(1 lb/500 g yields 2 cups.) |
| Slicer | Chill first. The firmer the meat, the better it will slice. Trim fat, gristle and bones. Cut to fit feed tube. Cut ends flat. Firm pressure. |
| | **ROASTS/BRISKET:** Slices will be narrow. You may prefer to slice by hand. |
| | **BONELESS CHICKEN BREASTS:** Chilled breasts slice well for sandwiches or salads. Firm pressure. |
| | **SALAMI OR PEPPERONI:** Cut to fit feed tube or use small feed tube. If soft, freeze until partially frozen, following directions for raw meat. You should be able to insert the point of a knife. Firm pressure. |
| | **JULIENNE STRIPS:** Roll up sliced deli meat into a cylinder. Fill feed tube snugly. Ideal for salads. Medium pressure. |
| Steel Blade | Trim fat, gristle and bones from meat. Remove and discard skin from poultry. Cut in chunks. Process in batches. Fill bowl one-quarter to one-third full. On/off pulses to chop coarsely, or let machine run 8 to 10 seconds, until finely chopped. Blend in additional ingredients with quick on/off pulses. |

## CHEESE, EGGS, FISH, MEAT, POULTRY, TOFU *(CONTINUED)*

| | |
|---|---|
| **Meat and Poultry, Raw** | Beef, Lamb, Veal, Chicken, Turkey<br>(1 lb/500 g boneless yields 2 cups.) |
| Slicer | (**Slicer** must be *serrated* to slice raw meat or poultry. Refer to your manual.) Remove skin, bones and excess fat. Cut pieces as large as possible to fit feed tube. Freeze 30 to 60 minutes, or until semifrozen. (Time will vary, depending on thickness.) Food is ready to slice when easily pierced with the tip of a sharp knife. For maximum tenderness, slice across the grain. Firm pressure. (If not firm enough, food won't slice well. If too firm, partially thaw until you can do the knife test.) Ideal for stir-fries. |
| Steel Blade | GRIND YOUR OWN: Remove bones, excess fat and gristle from meat. Remove skin and bones from poultry. Cut in 1-inch chunks. Should be very cold but not frozen. Process in batches. Fill work bowl one-quarter to one-third full. On/off pulses to chop coarsely. To grind, use on/off pulses, until desired texture is reached. Scrape down sides of bowl as needed. Check texture often to prevent overprocessing. |
| **Tofu, Blended** | (10 oz/300 g package yields about ¾ cup.) |
| Steel Blade | Drain liquid. Process silken, firm or extra-firm tofu until well blended, about 2 minutes. Scrape down sides of bowl as necessary. Use as a substitute for mayonnaise or to replace eggs in baking. It can also replace uncooked eggs in desserts. Use ¼ cup silken tofu for each egg. Refrigerate for up to 1 week. |

## CRUMBS

| | |
|---|---|
| **Bread Crumbs, Dried/Toasted** | (1 slice yields ¼ cup crumbs.) |
| Steel Blade | Store scraps of bread or rolls in freezer. To dry, place on a baking sheet; dry at 300°F for 1 hour. Process chunks until fine. Store at room temperature.<br><br>ITALIAN SEASONED CRUMBS: To each cup of crumbs, add ½ tsp salt, dash pepper, oregano, basil and ¼ cup grated Parmesan cheese (optional). Process a few seconds to combine. |
| **Bread Crumbs, Soft** | (1 slice yields ½ cup crumbs.) |
| Steel Blade | Tear fresh bread or rolls in chunks. Process up to 4 slices at a time. For larger quantities, add additional chunks through feed tube while machine is running. Process to make fine crumbs. Store in freezer or crumbs will get moldy.<br><br>BUTTERED CRUMBS: Blend 1 to 2 Tbsp butter or oil into crumbs with on/off pulses.<br><br>CRUMB TOPPING: Blend 1 to 2 Tbsp oil, salt, pepper and your favorite herbs into crumbs. |

| | |
|---|---|
| **Crumbs, Homemade Panko** | (6 slices yield 1 cup crumbs.) |
| Steel Blade | Remove and discard crusts from slightly stale white bread. Tear in chunks; add through feed tube while machine is running. Process to make crumbs, 20 to 30 seconds. Spread on a rimmed baking sheet. Bake at 300°F for 15 to 20 minutes, until dried out; do not brown. (You can also microwave on High for 2 minutes; stir, breaking up crumbs with your fingers. Microwave 1 to 2 minutes longer, until dry.) Store in an airtight container or freeze. (Tip: Panko crumbs are more elongated than regular bread crumbs and paler in color.) |
| **Crumbs (Cookies, Crackers, Corn Flakes)** | For 1 cup crumbs use:<br>• 18 chocolate wafers<br>• 22 to 26 vanilla wafers<br>• 12 to 14 single graham wafers<br>• 15 ginger snaps<br>• 28 soda crackers<br>• 4 cups corn flakes |
| Steel Blade | Break cookies or crackers in chunks. Place in work bowl or drop through feed tube while machine is running. Process until fine. |
| **Matzo Meal** | (3 matzos or 2 cups matzo farfel yield 1 cup.) |
| Steel Blade | Break matzos into chunks. Process matzos or farfel until fine, 45 to 60 seconds. |

USING YOUR FOOD PROCESSOR

## DOUGHS (BATTERS, PASTRY DOUGHS, YEAST DOUGHS)

| | |
|---|---|
| **Batters** | Quick Breads, Cakes, Cookies |
| Steel Blade | Sift dry ingredients together by processing 10 seconds; remove and reserve. Process fats and sugars together 1 to 2 minutes, then blend in remaining liquid ingredients (e.g., eggs, flavoring). Pulse in reserved dry ingredients. Any ingredients that need to be coarsely chopped can be added with dry ingredients. For finely chopped ingredients, chop separately (use small bowl on models with nested bowls); add to batter at the end using quick on/off pulses.<br>CAKE MIXES: Place dry mixture in work bowl. Add eggs and liquid while machine is running; process for 1 minute, scraping down sides of bowl as needed. |

| **DOUGHS (BATTERS, PASTRY DOUGHS, YEAST DOUGHS) (*CONTINUED*)** | |
|---|---|
| **Pastry Doughs** | Refer to Pies and Pastries chapter (pages 466–469) for full information. |
| Steel Blade | STANDARD (7-CUP) PROCESSOR: One 2-crust pie (1½ to 2 cups flour). |
| | LARGE (14-CUP) PROCESSOR: Two 2-crust pies (3 cups flour). Cut chilled butter or margarine in 1-inch chunks. Combine with dry ingredients in processor. Use quick on/off pulses, *just* until mixture resembles coarse oatmeal. Slowly drizzle cold water through feed tube while machine is running. Process *just* until dough begins to gather around blades, 12 to 15 seconds. Do not overprocess or dough will be tough. If too dry, add extra liquid a few drops at a time. If too sticky, remove dough from processor and gently knead in a little more flour. |
| **Yeast Doughs** | Refer to Yeast Doughs chapter (pages 295–300) for full information. Some models are not strong enough to process yeast doughs. Check manual for guidelines. |
| | STANDARD (7-CUP) PROCESSOR: Recommended capacity is 3 to 3¼ cups flour for white bread dough, 2½ to 3 cups for whole wheat bread dough. |
| | LARGE (14-CUP) PROCESSOR: Recommended capacity is 6 cups flour for white bread dough, 4 cups for whole wheat bread dough. If recipe calls for more flour than recommended, mix and knead dough in equal batches. |
| Dough Blade or Steel Blade | Use **Dough Blade** if your model has one; otherwise use **Steel Blade**. Models with a **Dough Cycle** work at reduced speed so dough won't get too warm during kneading. |
| | Proof yeast in warm liquid. Process dry ingredients in work bowl until combined. Use **Dough Cycle** if available. Start machine; add yeast mixture and liquids gradually through feed tube while machine is running. Process until dough cleans sides of bowl; continue processing 45 seconds longer. Dough should be soft and pliable, yet slightly sticky. If dough is too wet, add flour (1 to 2 Tbsp at a time) through feed tube. If dough is too dry, drizzle liquid (1 to 2 Tbsp at a time) through feed tube. |
| | (Tip: Sweet doughs are rich and sticky and may not clean sides of bowl; you may need to scrape out bowl with a spatula.) |

| MISCELLANEOUS | |
|---|---|
| **Baby Food** | *See* **Baby Food Chart**, pages 19–21. |
| **Butter/Margarine** | (¼ lb/125 g [1 stick] yields ½ cup.) |
|   Slicer | Butter must be cold, but not frozen. Medium to firm pressure. |
|   Steel Blade | **PIES:** Use frozen butter or margarine. Cut in chunks with a sharp knife. |
| | **BAKING:** Use butter or margarine directly from refrigerator or at room temperature. Cut in chunks. |
| | **FLAVORED BUTTERS/MARGARINE:** Chop garlic or herbs first. |
| | **HOMEMADE BUTTER:** *See* Whipping Cream. |
| | **LIGHTER BUTTER/MARGARINE:** Process 1 cup soft butter or margarine until smooth. Gradually add ½ cup cold water through feed tube while machine is running. Process 2 to 3 minutes, scraping down bowl as needed. Contains half the calories of regular butter or margarine. (Tip: Excellent as a spread; don't use for baking.) |
| **Candy, Hard** | Peppermint sticks, cinnamon candy |
|   Steel Blade | Drop chunks through feed tube while machine is running, keeping your hand on top to prevent pieces from flying out. Process until fine. |
| **Chocolate** | (1 oz/30 g square yields ¼ cup grated; 6 oz/175 g chocolate chips yields 1 cup.) |
|   Grater | Chill chocolate. Medium to firm pressure. (Processor will be extremely noisy!) Grate extras and refrigerate or freeze. Ideal for garnishing. (Tip: If recipe calls for melted chocolate, use the equivalent grated volume. It will melt in moments!) |
|   Steel Blade | Use chocolate chips or cut chocolate squares in half. On/off pulses to start, then let machine run until desired degree of fineness is reached (10 to 15 seconds for coarsely chopped, 20 to 30 seconds for finely chopped). Texture will be more pebbly than grated, but is fine where appearance is not important (e.g., cake batters). |
| **Coffee** | Most manufacturers do not recommend grinding coffee beans. A burr coffee grinder is preferable. Refer to your manual. |
|   Steel Blade | **CAFFÈ LATTE:** Heat milk until steaming. Process for 20 to 30 seconds, until foamy. Fill cups half full with hot espresso, then top with foamy milk. Sprinkle with ground cinnamon and/or grated chocolate. |
| **Flax Seed** | |
|   Steel Blade | Process until finely ground, 2 to 3 minutes. A coffee grinder does a better job. Store in freezer to prevent rancidity. (Some manufacturers do not recommend grinding seeds, spices or grains. Check your manual.) |

## MISCELLANEOUS (*CONTINUED*)

| | |
|---|---|
| **Ice** | Not recommended by most manufacturers as ice can dull or damage blades or bowl. A blender does a better job of chopping ice because rotation speed of blades is much faster and action of blades is more effective. |
| **Milkshakes/ Smoothies** | |
| Steel Blade | **MILKSHAKES:** Not more than one at a time to prevent leakage. Add ice cream first; then add milk through feed tube while machine is running. Process until blended. |
| | **SMOOTHIES:** Process cut-up fruit (e.g., bananas, mangoes) or berries first, then add cold milk (skim or soy) or orange juice through feed tube while machine is running. Most manufacturers do not recommend processing ice cubes. |
| **Nuts** | (¼ lb/125 g yields 1 cup.) |
| Grater or Slicer | Medium pressure. **Grater** produces fine texture. **Slicer** produces coarser texture. |
| Steel Blade | Timing depends on hardness of nuts used and degree of fineness desired. Do not overprocess or you will get nut butter! Process in batches (up to 1½ cups in a standard processor, 3 cups in a large processor). (Tip: If recipe calls for flour or sugar, add some to nuts before chopping so you can chop them as fine as you want without making nut butter.) |
| | **COARSELY CHOPPED:** 6 to 8 on/off pulses, or let machine run 6 to 8 seconds. |
| | **FINELY GROUND:** On/off pulses to start, then process 20 to 30 seconds, until desired texture is reached. Freeze or refrigerate extras. |
| **Nut Butter/Peanut Butter** | (2 cups nuts yield 1 cup of nut butter.) |
| Steel Blade | **PEANUT BUTTER:** Process 2 cups salted or dry-roasted peanuts. Use on/off pulses to start, then process for 2½ to 4 minutes, until drops of oil are visible and mixture is very smooth. Stop machine several times to scrape down sides of bowl. For a smoother texture, add 2 to 3 Tbsp oil. |
| | **CHOCOLATE PEANUT BUTTER:** Process 1½ cups peanuts and ½ cup chocolate chips for 2½ minutes, scraping down sides of bowl as needed. |
| | **NUT BUTTER:** Prepare as for Peanut Butter, using toasted almonds or cashews. Try a ratio of 1 cup almonds and ½ cup each of cashews and walnuts or pecans. |

| | |
|---|---|
| **Almond Flour** | (¼ lb/125 g/1 cup whole blanched almonds yields 1 cup almond flour.) |
| Steel Blade | On/off pulses to start, then process 25 to 30 seconds, until finely ground. Don't overprocess or you will get almond butter! (Tip: Use Almond Flour to replace up to 50% of flour in baked goods.) |
| **Oat Flour** | (1 cup rolled oats yields ⅞ cup [1 cup less 2 Tbsp] oat flour.) |
| Steel Blade | Quick on/offs to start, then let machine run 25 to 30 seconds, until finely ground. (Tip: Use oat flour to replace up to 25% of flour in baked goods.) |
| **Sugar (Fruit/Caster Sugar, Brown Sugar, Icing Sugar)** | (1 lb/500 g granulated yields 2 cups. <br> 1 lb/500 g brown sugar yields 2¼ cups packed. <br> 1 lb/500 g icing sugar yields 4 cups.) |
| Steel Blade | FRUIT (CASTER) SUGAR: Process granulated sugar for 1 minute, or until fine. Measure after processing. <br><br> BROWN SUGAR: To remove lumps, process 15 to 20 seconds. (Tips: If very hard, soften by placing ½ apple, cut side up, in bag or jar and seal tightly. Discard apple the next day. Chunks of very hard sugar can be used in cooking [e.g., sweet and sour meatballs].) <br><br> ICING SUGAR: See recipe (page 493). |
| **Toffee/Skor Bits** | (4 bars [1.4 oz/39 g each] yield 1 cup chopped.) |
| Steel Blade | Chill before processing. Break into chunks. On/off pulses until desired texture is reached. Use for cookies, coffee cake toppings, desserts. |
| **Whipping Cream** | Also Dessert Topping <br> (1 cup or package yields 1½ cups when whipped.) |
| Steel Blade | Will be firmer, but less volume than with an electric mixer. Good for garnishing. Use well-chilled whipping cream. If it is too warm or is overprocessed, it will turn into butter! <br><br> METHOD: Chill bowl and blade for 15 minutes. Do not insert pusher in feed tube. Whip chilled cream until texture of sour cream, 35 to 40 seconds. Add sugar and process 5 to 10 seconds longer, just until firm. Dessert topping takes about 2 minutes. <br><br> HOMEMADE BUTTER: Process up to 2 cups whipping cream at a time. Let machine run about 2 minutes, until cream separates and forms butter. Add a little salt if desired. Drain liquid; rinse butter well and pat dry. Refrigerate or freeze. An excellent way to use up leftover whipping cream or to rescue overwhipped cream! Drained liquid can be used in baked goods. |

## FREEZING TIPS

- Cooked foods, such as meats, roasts, stews (without potatoes), poultry (without stuffing), fish, pasta, grains, soups, sauces and most baked goods, freeze well. Potatoes may become slightly grainy. Rice may get hard if frozen, unless there is an adequate amount of sauce. Don't freeze cream fillings, puddings, salad greens, mayonnaise or hard-cooked eggs. Refer to specific recipes in this book as to whether a dish freezes well.

- Cool foods quickly to room temperature before freezing by placing the dish in a larger pan of ice water; stir occasionally. Then wrap well to prevent freezer burn and loss of flavor.

- Pack it right! Use freezer-safe containers or heavy-duty freezer bags, or double-wrap with heavy-duty foil. Remove as much air as possible and seal tightly. More food can be packaged in square or oblong containers than in round or cylindrical shapes. To save on cleanup, use ovenproof or microwavable dishes to freeze cooked casseroles. Avoid surprises—mark packages with contents, quantity and date frozen.

- HERE'S A GREAT TRICK: Freeze food in a casserole dish that has been lined with heavy-duty foil. When it is completely frozen, remove the foil-wrapped food from the dish. Now your casserole dish is free for everyday use! To thaw or reheat, unwrap the food and place it back in the original casserole.

- Make double or triple batches of recipes for future meals. Freeze in portions suitable for your family. Pack some single portions for unexpected company or for quick, kid-sized meals. Smaller packages freeze and thaw faster than larger ones.

- Foods can be stored longer in an upright or chest freezer than in the freezer compartment of your refrigerator. Although foods may be safe to eat if frozen beyond the recommended time, taste or texture may be affected.

- If there is a power failure, don't panic. Be sure to keep the freezer door closed to prevent cold air from escaping. If your freezer is fully stocked, the contents will remain frozen for at least 2 days. If it is half-full, the contents will stay frozen at least 1 full day. If the power remains off longer, place dry ice on top of the food.

- Once food has thawed, use it as soon as possible. If there are still some ice crystals, it can be refrozen, but texture may be affected. You can refreeze cookies, cakes and breads even if they have thawed completely. Raw fish, chicken or meat that has thawed must be cooked before you can freeze it again.

- Thaw foods before reheating unless otherwise indicated. Your microwave oven is ideal for thawing. Foods can also be thawed overnight in the refrigerator. Do not thaw meat, poultry or fish at room temperature.

- When reheating foods, cover them to prevent them from drying out. Crispy foods should be reheated uncovered to prevent them from becoming soggy. Most casseroles, roasts and poultry should be reheated in a covered casserole at 350°F for about 20 minutes. When reheating in the microwave, allow 1 to 2 minutes on High per cup of food. Two pieces of chicken or a serving of soup will take about 2 minutes to reheat.

- To test if a food is fully heated, insert the blade of a knife into the center. When you remove the knife, it should feel hot when you touch it!

## MICROWAVE OVEN TIPS

- Glass baking dishes are ovenproof and microwavable.

- Parchment paper makes an excellent cover. Wet it first so you can mold it easily around the dish.

- Do not microwave foods in disposable plastic containers from the supermarket, plastic bags or plastic wrap. When subjected to heat, chemicals can leach and migrate into foods, especially fatty foods.
- Cooking times are based on a 650- to 700-watt microwave oven. (One cup of water boils in 2½ minutes on High.) If you have a 1000-watt microwave oven, reduce cooking times by approximately 25%.
- Always check food shortly before estimated cooking time is completed. Always allow for standing time.
- To double the recipe, allow half to two-thirds more cooking time. To make half the recipe, allow one-third less cooking time.

# METRIC EQUIVALENT CHARTS

## METRIC PAN EQUIVALENTS

- To prevent sticking, use a nonstick spray made of canola oil and spray pans lightly.
- When baking in glass or dark baking pans, reduce temperatures by 25°F (10°C).

| Pan | Metric Measure | Capacity |
|---|---|---|
| 8- × 8- × 2-inch (square) pan | 20 × 20 × 5 cm | 2 litres (8 cups) |
| 9- × 9- × 2-inch (square) pan | 23 × 23 × 5 cm | 2.5 litres (10 cups) |
| 9- × 5- × 3-inch loaf pan | 23 × 13 × 6 cm | 2 litres (8 cups) |
| 10- × 3½-inch fluted tube pan (Bundt) | 25 × 9 cm | 3 litres (12 cups) |
| 10- × 4-inch tube pan | 25 × 10 cm | 4 litres (16 cups) |
| 8- × 2-inch round layer pan | 20 × 5 cm | 1.5 litres (6 cups) |
| 9- × 2-inch round layer pan | 23 × 5 cm | 2 litres (8 cups) |
| 7- × 11- × 2-inch glass baking dish | 18 × 28 × 5 cm | 2 litres (8 cups) |
| 9- × 13- × 2-inch glass baking dish | 22 × 33 × 5 cm | 3.5 litres (15 cups) |
| 9-inch pie plate | 23 cm | 1 litre (4 cups) |
| 10- × 15- × 1-inch cookie sheet | 25 × 38 × 3 cm | 2.5 litres (10 cups) |
| 9-inch springform pan | 23 cm | 2.5 litres (10 cups) |
| 10-inch springform pan | 25 cm | 3 litres (12 cups) |
| 5-quart casserole dish | 47 × 32 cm | 5.7 litres (23 cups) |

## METRIC MEASUREMENT EQUIVALENTS

One inch equals 2.5 cm, and 5 cm is 2 inches.

| ⅛ inch | 0.3 cm |
|---|---|
| ¼ inch | 0.6 cm |
| ½ inch | 1.2 cm |
| 1 inch | 2.5 cm |
| 4 inches | 10 cm |
| 6 inches | 15 cm |
| 12 inches | 30 cm |

## METRIC TEMPERATURE CONVERSIONS

To convert from °F to °C:
(__°F − 32) divided by 1.8 = __°C.
To convert from °C to °F:
(__°C × 1.8) plus 32 = __°F.

| 0°F | − 18°C | Freezer temperature |
|---|---|---|
| 32°F | 0°C | Water freezes |
| 40°F | 4°C | Refrigerator temperature |
| 68°F | 20°C | Room temperature |
| 105°F–115°F | 41°C–46°C | Water temperature to proof yeast |
| 212°F | 100°C | Water boils |

## OVEN TEMPERATURES

| | |
|---|---|
| 250°F | 120°C |
| 275°F | 135°C |
| 300°F | 150°C |
| 325°F | 160°C |
| 350°F | 180°C |
| 375°F | 190°C |
| 400°F | 200°C |
| 425°F | 220°C |
| 450°F | 230°C |
| 475°F | 240°C |
| 500°F | 260°C |

## METRIC MEASUREMENTS FOR VOLUME AND WEIGHT

Quick Conversions (Approximate)

TO OUNCES: Drop the last digit from the number of millilitres (mL) or grams (g) and divide by 3. For example, 156 mL is about 5 oz (15 divided by 3 equals 5).

TO MILLILITRES OR GRAMS: Multiply the number of ounces by 30. For example, 1 ounce is about 30 mL or grams.

## APPROXIMATE METRIC EQUIVALENTS (VOLUME)

| | |
|---|---|
| ¼ tsp | 1 mL |
| ½ tsp | 2 mL |
| 1 tsp | 5 mL |
| 1 Tbsp | 15 mL |
| 2 Tbsp | 25 mL |
| ¼ cup | 50 mL |
| ⅓ cup | 75 mL |
| ½ cup | 125 mL |
| ¾ cup | 175 mL |
| 1 cup | 250 mL |
| 4 cups | 1 L |

## APPROXIMATE METRIC EQUIVALENTS (WEIGHT)

| | |
|---|---|
| 1 oz | 30 g (actual is 28.4 g) |
| 2 oz | 60 g |
| 3 oz | 85 g |
| 3½ oz | 100 g |
| ½ lb | 250 g (actual is 227 g) |
| ¾ lb | 375 g |
| 1 lb | 500 g (actual is 454 g) |
| 2 generous lb | 1 kg |

## METRIC PACKAGING

| Common can/bottle sizes | |
|---|---|
| 3 oz | 85 mL |
| 5½ oz | 156 mL |
| 7½ oz | 213 mL |
| 8 oz | 227 mL |
| 8.8 oz | 250 mL |
| 10 oz | 284 mL |
| 12 oz | 340 mL |
| 14 oz | 398 mL |
| 16 oz | 454 mL |
| 17.6 oz | 500 mL |
| 19 oz | 540 mL |
| 28 oz | 796 mL |
| 35.2 oz | 1 L |
| 48 oz | 1.36 L |

## METRIC EQUIVALENTS FOR INGREDIENTS

### Butter, Margarine

| | | |
|---|---|---|
| 115 g | ½ cup | ¼ lb |
| 250 g | 1 generous cup | ½ lb |

### Cheeses, Hard

| | | |
|---|---|---|
| 125 g | 1 cup grated | ¼ lb/4 oz |
| 227 to 250 g | 2 cups grated | ½ lb/8 oz |

### Cheeses, Soft (Cottage/Ricotta/Cream Cheese)

| | | |
|---|---|---|
| 125 g | ½ cup | ¼ lb/4 oz |
| 227 to 250 g | 1 cup | ½ lb/8 oz |
| 454 to 500 g | 2 cups | 1 lb/16 oz |

### Chocolate, Chocolate Chips, Cocoa

| | | |
|---|---|---|
| 30 g | ¼ cup grated chocolate | 1 oz (1 square) |
| 175 g | 1 cup chocolate chips | 6 oz |
| 110 g | 1 cup cocoa | 3¾ oz |

### Cream, Milk, Sour Cream, Yogurt, Ice Cream

| | | |
|---|---|---|
| 227 to 250 mL/g | 1 cup | 8 oz |
| 454 to 500 mL/g | 2 cups | 16 oz |
| 1 L | about 4 cups | 35.2 oz |

### Dried Fruits, Nuts

| | | |
|---|---|---|
| 150 g | 1 cup dates, raisins | 5¼ oz |
| 115 g | 1 cup chopped walnuts | 4 oz |
| 110 g | 1 cup ground almonds | 3¾ oz |

### Fish/Meat/Poultry, Fruits/Vegetables (Fresh)

| | |
|---|---|
| 227 to 250 g | ½ lb |
| 454 to 500 g | 1 lb |
| 1 kg | 2.2 lb |
| 1.5 kg | 3½ lb (an average chicken) |
| 5 kg | 11 lb (an average turkey) |

### Fruits and Vegetables (Frozen)

| | |
|---|---|
| 300 g | 10 oz pkg |
| 454 to 500 g | 16 oz pkg (1 lb) |
| 1 kg | 2.2 lb |

### Flour, Cornstarch, Crumbs, Cereal

| | | |
|---|---|---|
| 145 g | 1 cup all-purpose flour | 5 oz |
| 125 g | 1 cup cornstarch | 4½ oz |
| 110 g | 1 cup cookie crumbs | 3¾ oz |
| 125 g | 1 cup dried bread crumbs | 4½ oz |
| 90 g | 1 cup oats | 3¼ oz |

### Pasta, Grains, Dried Beans

| | |
|---|---|
| 200 g | 1 cup split peas, lentils, rice |
| 250 g | 8 oz pkg |
| 375 g | 12 oz pkg |
| 454 to 500 g | 16 oz pkg (1 lb) |
| 1 kg | 2.2 lb |

### Sugar, Honey

| | | |
|---|---|---|
| 200 g | 1 cup sugar | 7¾ oz |
| 170 g | 1 cup packed brown sugar | 6 oz |
| 150 g | 1 cup icing sugar | 5 oz |
| 340 g | 1 cup honey | 12 oz |

- The nutritional analysis was calculated using data from ESHA (The Food Processor SQL Edition 10.4) and, when necessary, manufacturers' food labels.
- If a recipe indicated a range of servings (4 to 6 servings), it was analyzed for 4 servings.
- If there was a choice of ingredients, the first ingredient was analyzed (e.g., skim milk was analyzed when a recipe called for 1 cup skim milk or orange juice). The analysis does not include optional ingredients or those with no specified amounts.
- The smaller measure of an ingredient was analyzed when a range was given (e.g., ¼ cup was analyzed when a recipe called for ¼ to ⅓ cup).
- The nutrient values were not rounded off for carbohydrates, fiber and fat, but they were rounded off for calories, protein, cholesterol, sodium, potassium, iron, calcium and phosphorus.
- The phosphorus content included in the analysis is helpful for people with medical problems, including kidney disease.
- A serving of at least 2 grams of fiber is considered a moderate source, 4 grams is a high source, and 6 grams of fiber is considered a very high source of fiber.
- Olive and canola oils were the oils of choice. In recipes calling for margarine, soft tub margarine was used, unless otherwise indicated.
- When eggs were called for, the recipe was analyzed using large eggs.
- Recipes that gave an option of using sugar or granular Splenda were analyzed for sugar. An analysis with Splenda was also provided when there was a significant difference in carbohydrates and/or calories.
- Specific measurements of salt were included in the analysis (e.g., 1 tsp salt). When a recipe didn't give a specific measurement (e.g., salt to taste), then salt wasn't included in the analysis. If the sodium content of my original recipe was very high, lower-sodium products were used for the analysis unless otherwise indicated. To reduce sodium content, choose low-sodium or salt-free products (e.g., tomato sauce, tomato paste, canned tomatoes, tomato juice, barbecue sauce, canned beans, canned tuna/salmon, soy sauce, cheeses, nuts, crackers, butter).
- When cheese was called for, the recipe was analyzed using low-fat or reduced-fat cheese (e.g., cheddar, mozzarella, Swiss), light cream cheese or ricotta cheese, or 1% cottage cheese, unless otherwise indicated. Many cheeses are high in salt, so check labels if this is important for your health.
- When mayonnaise was called for, the recipe was analyzed using light mayonnaise, unless otherwise indicated.
- When sour cream or yogurt were called for, the recipe was analyzed using light sour cream or fat-free yogurt, unless otherwise indicated.
- When milk was called for, the recipe was analyzed using 1% milk unless otherwise indicated. For very young children or the elderly, you may prefer to use 2% or whole milk (3.5%).
- Nutrient values were not given for recipe variations if there were no significant differences between the main recipe and the variations.
- Garnishes weren't calculated unless a specific quantity was indicated.

# APPETIZERS
## recipe list

52 Best Vegetable Dip

52 Curry Dip

53 Roasted Red Pepper Dip

53 Sun-Dried Tomato Spread

54 Olive Tapenade

54 Guacamole

55 Egg and Avocado Spread

55 Simply Salsa

56 Hummus

57 Eggplant Spread

57 Vegetarian Chopped Liver

58 Chopped Liver

59 Chicken or Turkey Salad Spread

60 Chopped Egg Spread

60 Tuna Spread

61 Antipasto Spread

61 Chopped Herring

62 Sardine Spread

62 Salmon Spread

63 Salmon or Tuna Mousse

63 Lox and Cheese Spread

64 Herbed Cheese Log

65 Garlic Butter

66 Salmon Tortilla Pinwheels

67 Mango Quesadillas

67 Asparagus Cheese Rolls

68 Bruschetta

69 Make-and-Bake Pizza

70 Pizza Tarts

71 Sesame Cheese Straws

72 Gougères (French Cheese Puffs)

73 Roasted Red Pepper Crescents

73 Spanakopita (Phyllo Triangles)

74 Mushroom Turnovers

75 Stuffed Italian Mushrooms

76 Vegetarian Egg Rolls

77 Egg Roll Filling

78 Falafel

78 Party Meatballs

- You can make delicious dips, spreads and hors d'oeuvres in minutes using your processor, making anytime party time!
- Refer to the **Smart Chart** (pages 24–41) for basic techniques.
- WORK BOWLS, BLADES AND DISCS: If your food processor comes with nested bowls, choose the appropriate-sized bowl and blade or disc for the task and the amount of food being processed. Use the small or medium bowl to prep ingredients that will be added later (e.g., chop/mince herbs or nuts in the small bowl, grate/slice cheese or veggies in the medium bowl). Use the large bowl for most tasks (chop, mince, purée, slice or grate ingredients). Use the large bowl for mixing and kneading dough (use **Dough Blade** and **Dough Cycle** for yeast doughs if your processor has these features). Models differ, so always follow manufacturer's recommendations.
- Use the thick (6 mm) or regular (4 mm) **Slicer** for vegetables to serve with dips. Long vegetables (such as carrots, zucchini, celery) can be cut to fit crosswise in the feed tube rather than upright. Use fairly firm pressure or slices may be too thin. For a decorative effect, pull fork tines down the length of zucchini or cucumber. Cut into pieces slightly shorter than the feed tube; trim both ends flat. Stand the pieces upright in the feed tube. Slice, using medium pressure.
- Some vegetables require hand slicing (e.g., cauliflower or broccoli florets, tomato wedges).
- Add color, flavor and nutrients to dips and spreads with finely chopped carrots, celery, bell peppers, onions and herbs.
- DOUBLE DIP: If you have a larger processor (e.g., 11, 12 or 14 cup), you can double the recipe for your favorite dips or spreads. If you have a smaller processor (7 cup), it takes moments to whip up another batch. Don't exceed the maximum amount recommended in your user's manual.
- Tofu Mayonnaise (page 112) is excellent in dips and spreads.
- Leftover dips can be thinned with a little milk and used as salad dressings. Chop leftover veggies on the **Steel Blade** and use in soups, sauces, etc.
- Creative containers for dips and spreads can be made from hollowed-out bell peppers, tomatoes, grapefruit, melon or avocado shells. Cut

bottoms flat so they won't tip. Pumpernickel bread also makes a great container. Cut 1 inch off the top. Hollow out, leaving ½-inch-thick sides. Fill with dip and serve with crudités and the hollowed-out bread, cut into cubes.

- PITAS, WRAPS AND ROLL-UPS: Fill mini pitas with your favorite spread (e.g., tuna, chicken salad, hummus). Or spread plain or flavored tortillas with your favorite filling. Fold up the bottom of the tortilla about 1 inch, then roll it around the filling. Wrap well and refrigerate. For pinwheels, trim off the ends and cut into 1-inch slices.

- Many appetizers may be served as a main dish, or vice versa. A main dish for 4 people will serve 6 to 8 as an appetizer. Assorted latkes, such as Easy Potato Latkes (page 245), are great as miniatures. Other bite-sized delights are Zucchini Puffs (page 242) and Broccoli Cheese Squares (page 153).

- Make quick pastry canapés with leftover pastry. Roll it out and cut out 2-inch rounds. Bake on an ungreased cookie sheet in a preheated 400°F oven for a few minutes, until golden. Top with grated cheese and veggies, such as mushrooms or bell peppers. Broil for 3 or 4 minutes, until the cheese is melted.

- EASY NACHOS: Leftover salsa (page 55)? Make nachos! Spread a layer of tortilla chips on a microwavable plate. Sprinkle with 1 to 2 cups grated cheddar and/or Monterey Jack cheese, then top with a few dollops of salsa. Microwave on High about 2 minutes, until cheese is melted. Easy, cheesy!

## BEST VEGETABLE DIP

I used this recipe
in my catering
business for years,
with rave reviews!

Yield: About 2½ cups.
Keeps 3 or 4 days
in the refrigerator.
Do not freeze.

1 clove garlic, peeled

2 green onions or ½ small onion

2 baby carrots

½ red bell pepper

1 cup sour cream (light or regular)

1 cup mayonnaise (light or regular)

1 tsp Worcestershire sauce

dash each salt and freshly ground
black pepper

¼ tsp each dried basil and oregano

STEEL BLADE: Drop garlic through feed tube while machine is running; process until minced. Add onions, carrots and red pepper; process until minced. Add remaining ingredients and process until blended, for 8 to 10 seconds. Chill.

29 calories per Tbsp, 1.2 g carbohydrates, 0.1 g fiber, 0 g protein, 2.6 g fat (0.7 g saturated fat), 4 mg cholesterol, 50 mg sodium, 23 mg potassium, 0 mg iron, 10 mg calcium, 8 mg phosphorus

### variations

- Eliminate Worcestershire sauce, basil and oregano. Add any of the following: 2 or 3 Tbsp cucumber; 1 Tbsp horseradish; 2 or 3 Tbsp anchovy paste; 2 or 3 Tbsp chili or barbecue sauce. Add 2 Tbsp each parsley, basil and/or dill.

### lighter variation

Substitute fat-free plain yogurt and 1% creamed cottage cheese for the sour cream and mayonnaise. Increase processing time to 45 seconds, until smooth and creamy. One Tbsp contains 10 calories and 0.3 g fat.

## CURRY DIP

Yield: About 1 cup.
Doubles easily. Keeps
3 or 4 days in the
refrigerator.
Do not freeze.

1 or 2 cloves garlic

2 Tbsp fresh coriander or parsley

2 baby carrots

½ cup mayonnaise (light or regular)

½ cup sour cream or yogurt
(light or regular)

1 tsp curry powder

1 Tbsp chili sauce or ketchup

3 or 4 drops hot sauce

salt and freshly ground black
pepper to taste

dash ground cumin

STEEL BLADE: Process garlic, coriander or parsley and carrots until minced, about 10 seconds. Add remaining ingredients and process until smooth, for 8 to 10 seconds. Chill. Serve with assorted raw vegetables, or as a chip dip.

31 calories per Tbsp, 1.4 g carbohydrates, 0.1 g fiber, 0 g protein, 2.8 g fat (0.8 g saturated fat), 4 mg cholesterol, 60 mg sodium, 21 mg potassium, 0 mg iron, 11 mg calcium, 8 mg phosphorus

# ROASTED RED PEPPER DIP

Roasted peppers
from a jar should
be rinsed well
and patted dry to
remove the vinegary
taste. When
peppers are in
season, it's cheaper
to roast your own.

Yield: About 1 cup.
Doubles easily. Keeps
3 or 4 days in the
refrigerator.
Do not freeze.

1 clove garlic

2 green onions, cut in chunks

2 Tbsp fresh basil (or 1 tsp
    dried basil)

1 large roasted red pepper (below)
    (or ½ cup roasted red peppers
    from a jar)

½ cup firm tofu or light cream cheese

2 tsp extra-virgin olive oil

1 tsp fresh lemon juice

salt and freshly ground black pepper
    to taste

pinch sugar

dash cayenne pepper or hot sauce

STEEL BLADE: Drop garlic and green onions through feed tube while machine is running; process until minced. Add basil, red pepper and tofu or cream cheese. Process until very smooth, about 45 seconds, scraping down sides of bowl as needed. Add remaining ingredients and process briefly to blend. Chill well before serving.

19 calories per Tbsp, 0.8 g carbohydrates, 0.3 g fiber, 1 g protein, 1.3 g fat (0.2 g saturated fat), 0 mg cholesterol, 1 mg sodium, 32 mg potassium, 0 mg iron, 56 mg calcium, 17 mg phosphorus

## roasted red peppers

Preheat broiler or barbecue. Cut bell peppers in half and discard stem, core and seeds. Broil or grill peppers until skin is blackened and blistered. Transfer peppers to a bowl, cover and let cool. Rub with paper towels to remove blackened skin. Freezes well. One roasted pepper contains 20 calories, 5 g carbohydrates and 0.1 g fat.

# SUN-DRIED TOMATO SPREAD

Great for Salmon
Tortilla Pinwheels
(page 66) and
delicious with
bagels, rolls or
crackers.

Yield: About 1½ cups.
Doubles easily. Keeps
3 or 4 days in the
refrigerator.
Do not freeze.

¼ cup oil-packed sun-dried
    tomatoes, well drained

⅓ cup pitted black olives

2 green onions, cut in chunks

2 Tbsp fresh basil (or 1 tsp dried basil)

1 cup cream cheese, cut in chunks
    (light or regular)

2 Tbsp yogurt or sour cream (low-fat
    or regular)

STEEL BLADE: Process sun-dried tomatoes, olives, green onions and basil until finely chopped, about 10 seconds. Add cream cheese and yogurt or sour cream. Process with quick on/off pulses to combine. Do not overprocess. Chill before serving.

24 calories per Tbsp, 1.1 g carbohydrates, 0.2 g fiber, 1 g protein, 1.7 g fat (0.9 g saturated fat), 5 mg cholesterol, 65 mg sodium, 24 mg potassium, 0 mg iron, 35 mg calcium, 4 mg phosphorus

## chef's tip

To use this as a dip, thin it with a little milk.

APPETIZERS

# OLIVE TAPENADE

If you like olives, you'll love tapenade.

Yield: About 2 cups. Keeps about a month in the refrigerator. Do not freeze.

1 lb (500 g) pitted kalamata or other brine-cured black olives, drained
5 to 6 oil-packed anchovy fillets (half of a 2 oz/56 g can), drained
3 cloves garlic
2 Tbsp capers, drained and rinsed
1 Tbsp lemon juice
⅓ cup extra-virgin olive oil
½ tsp dried thyme

STEEL BLADE: Process olives, anchovies, garlic and capers until coarsely chopped, about 10 to 12 seconds. Scrape down sides of bowl. Add lemon juice, olive oil and thyme. Process with quick on/off pulses, just until combined. Do not overprocess. Transfer to a container, cover and refrigerate until ready to use.

51 calories per Tbsp, 1.2 g carbohydrates, 0.1 g fiber, 0 g protein, 4.9 g fat (0.6 g saturated fat), 1 mg cholesterol, 224 mg sodium, 6 mg potassium, 0 mg iron, 7 mg calcium, 2 mg phosphorus

## chef's tips

Tapenade is a delicious dip for raw veggies and it makes a great spread for a toasted baguette or sourdough bread. Add a dollop or 2 to pasta to boost the flavor, or spread a thin layer over fish fillets before grilling or broiling. Spread tapenade on tortilla wraps instead of using mayonnaise.

# GUACAMOLE

Yield: 2 cups. Keeps 1 to 2 days in the refrigerator. Do not freeze.

1 small onion, halved
½ green bell pepper or chili pepper, cored and seeded
1 ripe tomato, quartered
1 ripe avocado, peeled, pitted and cut in chunks (preferably Hass)
¼ cup mayonnaise (light or regular)
1 Tbsp lemon or lime juice
salt and freshly ground black pepper to taste
2 or 3 drops hot sauce

STEEL BLADE: Process onion and pepper until minced, about 6 seconds. Add tomato and process a few seconds longer. Add remaining ingredients and process until smooth, 20 to 30 seconds, scraping down bowl as necessary. (Or for a chunkier version, process with several quick on/offs, until desired texture is reached.)

Transfer to a serving bowl, cover tightly with plastic wrap, pressing wrap directly against surface of guacamole to prevent discoloration. Serve chilled as a dip with tortilla chips or crackers.

17 calories per Tbsp, 1.1 g carbohydrates, 0.5 g fiber, 0 g protein, 1.4 g fat (0.2 g saturated fat), 1 mg cholesterol, 13 mg sodium, 43 mg potassium, 0 mg iron, 2 mg calcium, 5 mg phosphorus

## EGG AND AVOCADO SPREAD

My mother's favorite!

Yield: 1¼ cups. Doubles easily. Keeps 2 days in the refrigerator. Do not freeze.

½ small onion (or 2 green onions, cut in chunks)

1 ripe avocado, cut in half (preferably Hass)

3 hard-cooked eggs, halved (discard 2 yolks)

1 Tbsp mayonnaise (light or regular)

½ tsp salt (or to taste)

freshly ground black pepper to taste

STEEL BLADE: Process onion until minced, about 6 seconds. Scoop out avocado pulp and add in chunks to processor bowl. Add egg, egg whites, mayonnaise, salt and pepper. Process with 3 or 4 quick on/offs, until coarsely chopped. Don't overprocess.

Transfer to a serving bowl and cover tightly with plastic wrap, pressing wrap directly against surface of mixture to prevent discoloration. Serve chilled.

20 calories per Tbsp, 0.9 g carbohydrates, 0.6 g fiber, 1 g protein, 1.6 g fat (0.3 g saturated fat), 9 mg cholesterol, 59 mg sodium, 48 mg potassium, 0 mg iron, 3 mg calcium, 9 mg phosphorus

## SIMPLY SALSA

Excellent served with crudités or tortilla chips, or as a topping for fish or chicken. Delicious as an omelet filling or as a topping for nachos (page 51).

2 cloves garlic

4 Roma (Italian plum) tomatoes, cored and halved

½ small onion (or 2 green onions)

¼ cup fresh basil (or 1 tsp dried basil)

¼ cup fresh parsley or coriander

1 Tbsp lemon juice

1 tsp extra-virgin olive oil

salt and freshly ground black pepper to taste

dash of sugar and cayenne pepper to taste

APPETIZERS

STEEL BLADE: Drop garlic through feed tube while machine is running; process until minced. Add remaining ingredients and process with quick on/off pulses until coarsely chopped. Don't overprocess. Adjust seasonings to taste.

5 calories per Tbsp, 0.8 g carbohydrates, 0.2 g fiber, 0 g protein, 0.2 g fat (0 g saturated fat), 0 mg cholesterol, 1 mg sodium, 36 mg potassium, 0 mg iron, 4 mg calcium, 4 mg phosphorus

## HUMMUS

Serve this Middle Eastern spread with pita bread or assorted vegetables.

¼ cup fresh parsley
2 or 3 cloves garlic
1 can (19 oz/540 mL) chickpeas, drained and rinsed
⅔ cup extra-virgin olive oil
½ cup tahini (sesame seed paste)
6 Tbsp fresh lemon juice

1 tsp salt (or to taste)
freshly ground black pepper to taste
½ tsp ground cumin (or to taste)
additional olive oil, for garnish
paprika and olives, for garnish (optional)

STEEL BLADE: Make sure parsley and processor bowl are dry. Process parsley until minced. Set aside. Drop garlic through feed tube while machine is running; process until minced. Add chickpeas, olive oil, tahini, lemon juice, salt, pepper and cumin. Process until very smooth, about 2 minutes, scraping down the sides of the bowl as needed.

Spread mixture on large flat serving plate. Drizzle with additional oil and sprinkle with reserved parsley. Garnish with paprika and olives (if desired). Serve chilled.

46 calories per Tbsp, 2.5 g carbohydrates, 0.5 g fiber, 1 g protein, 3.8 g fat (0.5 g saturated fat), 0 mg cholesterol, 66 mg sodium, 28 mg potassium, 0 mg iron, 6 mg calcium, 24 mg phosphorus

### variations

- "GOURD FOR YOU" HUMMUS: Add 1 cup baked butternut squash or pumpkin to desired hummus mixture; process 30 seconds longer, until smooth. Garnish with toasted pumpkin seeds. (For insructions on baking squash, see Butternut Squash Purée in the **Baby Food Chart** on page 20 or Pumpkin Purée on page 101.)

- ROASTED RED PEPPER HUMMUS: Process ½ cup roasted red peppers (from a jar or homemade—see page 53) along with chickpeas and remaining ingredients.

### lighter variation

- Reduce olive oil to 2 Tbsp and tahini to 3 Tbsp. Reserve liquid from canned chickpeas; blend ⅓ to ½ cup chickpea liquid into hummus mixture. One Tbsp contains 23 calories and 1.2 g fat.s

# EGGPLANT SPREAD

Yield: About 4 cups.

Keeps 3 or 4 days in the

refrigerator. Freezes well.

**2 eggplants (about 1¼ lb)**

**1 medium onion or 6 green onions (scallions)**

**2 cloves garlic**

**1 green bell pepper, seeded and cut in chunks**

**½ stalk celery, cut in chunks**

**1 tomato, quartered**

**salt and freshly ground black pepper to taste**

**1 Tbsp extra-virgin olive oil**

**1 Tbsp vinegar or lemon juice**

**½ tsp sugar**

Cut eggplants in half lengthwise and place cut side down on broiling rack. Preheat broiler. Broil eggplant about 4 inches from heat for 15 minutes. Do not turn. (This gives eggplant a charred flavor.) Let cool.

STEEL BLADE: Process onion with garlic until minced, 6 to 8 seconds. Add green pepper and celery and process with 2 or 3 quick on/off pulses, until coarsely chopped. Remove any long strands of seeds from eggplant and discard (they're often bitter). Scoop out eggplant pulp with a spoon and add to processor bowl with remaining ingredients. Process with 3 or 4 quick on/offs, just until mixed. Adjust seasonings to taste. Chill before serving.

6 calories per Tbsp, 1.2 g carbohydrates, 0.3 g fiber, 0 g protein, 0.2 g fat (0 g saturated fat), 0 mg cholesterol, 0 mg sodium, 21 mg potassium, 0 mg iron, 1 mg calcium, 3 mg phosphorus

### to microwave eggplants

Pierce eggplants in several places with a fork. Place on microwavable rack and microwave on High for 5 to 6 minutes. Turn eggplants over and microwave 5 to 6 minutes longer, until tender. For a smoky taste, add 3 drops liquid smoke.

# VEGETARIAN CHOPPED LIVER

Yield: 4 servings.

Doubles easily. Keeps

3 or 4 days in the

refrigerator.

Do not freeze.

**½ lb green or yellow beans**

**4 green onions, cut in 3-inch lengths**

**3 hard-cooked eggs, halved**

**2 tsp mayonnaise (light or regular)**

**salt and freshly ground black pepper to taste**

Trim ends off beans and cook in boiling salted water until tender, 10 to 15 minutes. Drain well.

STEEL BLADE: Drop onions through feed tube while machine is running. Process until minced. Add remaining ingredients and process 6 to 8 seconds longer. Chill.

*Continued*

APPETIZERS

89 calories per serving, 5.7 g carbohydrates, 2.4 g fiber, 6 g protein, 5 g fat (1.4 g saturated fat), 160 mg cholesterol, 64 mg sodium, 161 mg potassium, 1 mg iron, 51 mg calcium, 85 mg phosphorus

### variations

#### lighter variation

Instead of 3 eggs, use 1 hard-cooked egg plus 3 whites. One serving contains 62 calories, 2.3 g fat and 54 mg cholesterol.

#### traditional variation

One can (14 oz/398 mL) green or wax beans, well drained, may be substituted for fresh. Two chopped onions sautéed in 1 Tbsp canola oil can replace green onions. Add ¼ cup walnuts or almonds for a protein boost. Process with quick on/off pulses to combine. One serving contains 186 calories, 13.3 g fat and 160 mg cholesterol.

APPETIZERS

## CHOPPED LIVER

Mayonnaise gives this a "schmaltzy" flavor. It's wonderful topped with lots of fried onions.

Yield: 6 to 8 servings. Keeps 2 days in the refrigerator. May be frozen for up to 1 month.

| | |
|---|---|
| 1 lb (500 g) beef or calf liver | 1 Tbsp light or regular mayonnaise |
| 3 or 4 medium onions, quartered | (optional) |
| 2 to 3 Tbsp oil | salt and freshly ground black pepper |
| 3 hard-cooked eggs, halved | to taste |
| 2 or 3 Tbsp chicken broth (preferably | |
| low-sodium) | |

Broil liver on both sides. Do not overcook. Cool completely. (May be prepared in advance and refrigerated until needed.) Cut in 1½-inch chunks.

STEEL BLADE: If necessary, process onions in 2 batches, depending on the capacity of your processor bowl. Process with several quick on/off pulses, until coarsely chopped. Heat oil in large skillet on medium heat. Sauté onions slowly in oil until browned, about 10 minutes. Cool slightly.

Process liver until minced, 15 to 20 seconds. Add onions along with remaining ingredients and process until combined, 10 to 15 seconds longer, scraping down sides of bowl as necessary. Mixture should be moist rather than dry, as it will firm up when refrigerated.

210 calories per serving, 8.3 g carbohydrates, 0.9 g fiber, 20 g protein, 10.3 g fat (2.1 g saturated fat), 328 mg cholesterol, 79 mg sodium, 313 mg potassium, 4 mg iron, 29 mg calcium, 339 mg phosphorus

### chef's tip

If liver is hot when processed, texture will be more like a pâté. Chicken livers may be substituted for beef or calf liver, but processing time will only be 10 to 12 seconds.

# CHICKEN OR TURKEY SALAD SPREAD

If you don't have enough chicken, add 2 or 3 hard-cooked eggs.

Yield: 4 to 6 servings. Keeps 2 days in the refrigerator. Do not freeze.

4 radishes, trimmed
1 stalk celery, cut in chunks
½ medium onion
½ carrot
2 Tbsp fresh dill or basil

2 cups cooked chicken or turkey, cut in chunks (discard skin and bones)
¼ to ⅓ cup mayonnaise or salad dressing (light or regular)
salt and freshly ground black pepper to taste

STEEL BLADE: Process radishes, celery, onion, carrot and dill until minced, 8 to 10 seconds. Add remaining ingredients and process with several quick on/offs, scraping down bowl once or twice. Do not overprocess. Refrigerate.

193 calories per serving, 3.7 g carbohydrates, 0.7 g fiber, 21 g protein, 10.2 g fat (2.2 g saturated fat), 69 mg cholesterol, 177 mg sodium, 259 mg potassium, 1 mg iron, 23 mg calcium, 152 mg phosphorus

APPETIZERS

## CHOPPED EGG SPREAD

Yield: Filling for
6 sandwiches. Keeps
2 days in the refrigerator.
Do not freeze.

½ small onion, cut in chunks (or
    2 green onions)
6 hard-cooked eggs, halved
3 Tbsp light or regular mayonnaise
    (approximately)

salt and freshly ground black pepper
    to taste
dash Dijon mustard (optional)

STEEL BLADE: Drop onion through feed tube while machine is running. Process until minced. Add remaining ingredients and process with 3 or 4 quick on/off pulses, until desired texture is reached. Scrape down bowl once or twice; do not overprocess.

104 calories per serving, 1.7 g carbohydrates, 0.1 g fiber, 6 g protein, 7.8 g fat (2 g saturated fat), 215 mg cholesterol, 113 mg sodium, 75 mg potassium, 1 mg iron, 27 mg calcium, 90 mg phosphorus

### note

Up to 1 dozen eggs may be processed in 1 batch in a 7-cup processor, 1½ dozen eggs can be processed in an 11- to 14-cup processor and 2 dozen eggs can be processed in a 16-cup processor. Use ½ Tbsp mayonnaise for each egg.

### lighter variation

Replace up to half of the eggs with egg whites, using 2 whites for each egg. Use light mayonnaise. One serving contains 81 calories, 5.2 g fat and 109 mg cholesterol.

## TUNA SPREAD

Yield: Filling for
3 sandwiches. Recipe
may be doubled. Keeps
2 days in the refrigerator.
Do not freeze.

½ stalk celery, cut in chunks
2 green onions, cut in chunks
3 baby carrots
2 or 3 sprigs fresh dill
1 can (6 oz/170 g) white tuna, drained

2 to 3 Tbsp mayonnaise (light or
    regular)
dash salt and freshly ground black
    pepper

STEEL BLADE: Process celery, onions, carrots and dill until minced, 6 to 8 seconds. Add remaining ingredients. Process with quick on/off pulses, just until mixed. (Use 3 or 4 pulses for solid tuna, 2 or 3 quick pulses for flaked or chunk tuna.) If necessary, scrape down sides of bowl once or twice. Do not overprocess or tuna will have a very gritty texture.

105 calories per serving, 2.3 g carbohydrates, 0.7 g fiber, 15 g protein, 3.8 g fat (0.7 g saturated fat), 21 mg cholesterol, 109 mg sodium, 201 mg potassium, 1 mg iron, 18 mg calcium, 103 mg phosphorus

## ANTIPASTO SPREAD

*Serve on lettuce leaves as an appetizer or as a spread with assorted crackers.*

*Yield: About 8 cups. Keeps about a month in the refrigerator. Freezes well.*

2 cans (6 oz/170 g each) tuna, drained

2 cups sweet mixed pickles, drained

1 jar (12 oz/375 mL) cocktail onions, drained (optional)

1 jar (12 oz/375 mL) stuffed olives, drained

1 can (10 oz/284 mL) mushrooms, drained

1 medium onion, cut in chunks

2 medium carrots, cut in chunks

1½ cups ketchup

1¼ cups chili sauce

1 Tbsp Worcestershire sauce

2 Tbsp lemon juice

STEEL BLADE: If using solid tuna, process with 2 or 3 quick on/off pulses, just until flaked. Do not overprocess. Empty flaked tuna into large bowl. Process sweet mixed pickles with 3 or 4 quick on/offs. Add to tuna. Repeat with cocktail onions (if using), stuffed olives, mushrooms, onion and carrots, emptying bowl each time. Ingredients must be processed separately with quick on/offs to avoid overprocessing.

Combine all ingredients in bowl and mix well. Store in tightly closed jars in refrigerator.

15 calories per Tbsp, 2.6 g carbohydrates, 0.1 g fiber, 1 g protein, 0.2 g fat (0 g saturated fat), 1 mg cholesterol, 106 mg sodium, 21 mg potassium, 0 mg iron, 1 mg calcium, 6 mg phosphorus

chef's tip

To reduce sodium, rinse pickles, cocktail onions, olives and mushrooms under cold running water for at least 1 minute, then pat dry.

## CHOPPED HERRING

*Yield: About 2 cups. Keeps about 10 days to 2 weeks in the refrigerator. Do not freeze.*

1 jar (7 oz/200 g) marinated herring fillets

1 apple, cored and cut in chunks (peel if desired)

1 slice challah or rye bread

2 hard-cooked eggs, halved (or 3 hard-cooked whites)

1 tsp sugar

Empty contents of herring jar (herring pieces, onions, pickling spices and liquid) into colander. Discard any pickling spices. Rinse herring and onions under cold running water. *Continued*

STEEL BLADE: Process apple until minced, about 10 seconds. Scrape down sides of bowl. Moisten bread with a little water and squeeze out excess. Add bread, herring and onions to processor bowl. Process until coarsely chopped, about 8 seconds. Add eggs and sugar and process 6 to 8 seconds longer, until finely chopped. Refrigerate.

28 calories per Tbsp, 1.9 g carbohydrates, 0.1 g fiber, 1 g protein, 1.6 g fat (0.3 g saturated fat), 12 mg cholesterol, 70 mg sodium, 14 mg potassium, 0 mg iron, 8 mg calcium, 12 mg phosphorus

## SARDINE SPREAD

This tastes almost like chopped herring! Sardines are a great source of calcium.

Yield: About 6 servings or 2½ cups. Keeps 2 or 3 days in the refrigerator. Do not freeze.

1 medium onion, halved

1 apple, peeled, cored and quartered

2 cans (3¼ oz/106 g each) sardines, well drained

1 slice bread

3 hard-cooked eggs, halved (or 1 hard-cooked egg plus 3 whites)

3 to 4 Tbsp white vinegar (or to taste)

1 tsp sugar

dash salt

STEEL BLADE: Process onion and apple until finely minced, 6 to 8 seconds. Scrape down sides of bowl. Add sardines. Process about 6 seconds longer. Moisten bread with cold water and squeeze out excess moisture. Add chunks of bread along with remaining ingredients. Process 8 to 10 seconds longer, until blended. Refrigerate.

18 calories per Tbsp, 1.1 g carbohydrates, 0.1 g fiber, 2 g protein, 0.8 g fat (0.2 g saturated fat), 20 mg cholesterol, 32 mg sodium, 28 mg potassium, 0 mg iron, 19 mg calcium, 27 mg phosphorus

## SALMON SPREAD

Yield: Filling for 3 sandwiches (about 1 cup). Recipe may be doubled. Keeps 2 days in the refrigerator. Do not freeze.

½ stalk celery, cut in chunks

2 green onions, cut in chunks

2 or 3 sprigs fresh dill

1 can (7¾ oz/213 g) salmon (or ¾ cup cooked salmon)

1 or 2 Tbsp mayonnaise or Caesar dressing (light or regular)

dash freshly ground black pepper

dash lemon juice

STEEL BLADE: Process celery, green onions and dill until minced, 6 to 8 seconds. Add remaining ingredients and process with 3 or 4 quick on/offs, just until mixed. If necessary, scrape down sides of bowl once or twice. Do not overprocess or you will have mush! Serve chilled.

130 calories per serving, 1.1 g carbohydrates, 0.4 g fiber, 13 g protein, 8.7 g fat (1.8 g saturated fat), 42 mg cholesterol, 309 mg sodium, 42 mg potassium, 1 mg iron, 158 mg calcium, 6 mg phosphorus

## SALMON OR TUNA MOUSSE

This delicious
mousse is perfect
for any festive
occasion. Make it in
a fish-shaped mold,
using a grape for
the eye and a red
pepper strip for
the mouth. Insert a
hook, line and sinker
into the mouth as
the ultimate garnish!

Yield: Serves 16 to 20.
Keeps 2 to 3 days
in the refrigerator. Do
not freeze.

1 envelope (1 Tbsp) unflavored
  gelatin
¼ cup cold water
½ cup boiling water
4 green onions, cut in chunks
¼ cup fresh dill (or 1 Tbsp
  dried dill)
½ cup mayonnaise (light or
  regular)

1 cup cream cheese (light or regular)
2 cans salmon (7¾ oz/213 g each) or
  tuna (6 oz/170 g each), drained and
  flaked
1 Tbsp lemon juice
6 drops hot sauce
¾ tsp salt
dash freshly ground black pepper

In a measuring cup, sprinkle gelatin over ¼ cup cold water. Let stand for 5 minutes to soften. Add ½ cup boiling water and stir to dissolve. Cool slightly.

STEEL BLADE: Process green onions and dill until minced. Add mayonnaise and cream cheese; process until smooth. Blend in dissolved gelatin. Add remaining ingredients and blend with on/off pulses, scraping down sides of bowl as needed.

Pour mixture into sprayed 4-cup (1 L) fish mold. Cover and refrigerate overnight. (Can be made a day or 2 in advance.)

To unmold, loosen edges with a knife, dip mold three-quarters of the way into hot water, count to 3 and invert onto a lettuce-lined platter. Garnish with sliced lemon, dill, cucumbers and olives. Serve with crackers or black bread.

23 calories per Tbsp, 0.4 g carbohydrates, 0 g fiber, 2 g protein, 1.7 g fat (0.6 g saturated fat), 6 mg cholesterol, 81 mg sodium, 3 mg potassium, 0 mg iron, 26 mg calcium, 1 mg phosphorus

### variations

- Substitute 1½ to 2 cups (375 to 500 mL) fresh cooked salmon.
- Instead of pouring mixture into a mold, pour into a large fish-shaped glass platter. Garnish as directed above once it has set. Serve directly from platter. There's no need to unmold.

## LOX AND CHEESE SPREAD

Yield: About 1¼ cups.
Doubles easily. Keeps
3 or 4 days in the
refrigerator. Freezes well.

3 or 4 green onions, cut in 2-inch
  lengths
1 cup light cream cheese or pressed
  cottage cheese, cut in chunks

1 to 2 Tbsp milk (if mixture is
  too thick)
¼ lb (250 g) lox/smoked salmon

STEEL BLADE: Drop green onions through feed tube while machine is running; process until minced. Add cheese and process until smooth. If necessary, add milk to soften. Add lox and process with 3 or 4 quick on/offs, just until mixed (or let machine run to blend thoroughly, making the mixture a pale salmon color). Chill and serve with bagels, pumpernickel bread, pita or assorted crackers.

23 calories per Tbsp, 0.6 g carbohydrates, 0.1 g fiber, 2 g protein, 1.5 g fat (0.9 g saturated fat), 5 mg cholesterol, 133 mg sodium, 12 mg potassium, 0 mg iron, 30 mg calcium, 8 mg phosphorus

### variations

- LOX AND CHEESE RING: Completely line bottom and sides of a sprayed 4-cup ring mold with strips of lox (you'll need about 12 oz/375 g). Make triple the amount of Lox and Cheese Spread. Fill mold, smoothing top with a spatula. Cover with plastic wrap and refrigerate several hours or overnight. Unwrap and carefully unmold onto a serving platter. Perfect for a party.

- Spread strips of lox with lox/cheese spread. Roll up jelly-roll style. Stand on end and insert a sprig of parsley in the center of each roll. Great as a garnish.

### dairy-free variation
Use Tofutti imitation cream cheese instead of cream cheese. Omit milk.

---

# HERBED CHEESE LOG

An easy and elegant centerpiece for your holiday buffet table. Serve with assorted crackers and/or pumpernickel bread. The variations are also excellent.

Yield: 12 to 15 servings. Keeps 3 or 4 days in the refrigerator. Do not freeze.

1 cup pecans, walnuts or shelled pistachios

2 bunches fresh parsley, washed and well dried

2 or 3 cloves garlic

4 green onions, cut in chunks

3 cups (1½ lb/750 g) chilled cream cheese (light or regular), cut in chunks

2 Tbsp sour cream (light or regular)

2 tsp Worcestershire sauce

½ tsp each dried basil and oregano

roasted red pepper strips (from a jar or homemade, page 53), for garnish

For machines with nested bowls, see method on page 65.

STEEL BLADE: Process nuts with 5 or 6 quick on/off pulses, until finely chopped. Empty bowl. Process parsley until fine, for 12 to 15 seconds. Reserve 1 Tbsp parsley and spread remainder in a 10-inch square on a piece of aluminum foil.

Drop garlic and onions through feed tube while machine is running; process until minced. Add cheese, sour cream, Worcestershire sauce, basil, oregano and reserved parsley. Process until smooth, about 30 seconds, scraping down sides of bowl once or twice.

Spread cheese mixture over parsley to within ½ inch of edges. Sprinkle nuts over cheese. Roll up parsley-cheese mixture like a jelly roll. (Use foil as a guide, but don't roll it up with the cheese!) Wrap log loosely with foil, sealing edges well. Refrigerate until firm. (Can be made up to 2 days in advance.) Unwrap and carefully transfer to a long platter. Garnish with strips of red pepper.

29 calories per Tbsp, 1.1 g carbohydrates, 0.3 g fiber, 1 g protein, 2.3 g fat (1 g saturated fat), 5 mg cholesterol, 47 mg sodium, 27 mg potassium, 0 mg iron, 36 mg calcium, 6 mg phosphorus

### nested bowl method

Use mini-bowl and mini-blade to chop nuts. Use large bowl and STEEL BLADE to mince parsley and prepare cheese mixture.

### variations

- Cheese mixture may be piped through a pastry tube onto crackers or celery stalks, or used as a filling for tiny cream puffs. It's also delicious as a spread for bagels.

- Replace oregano and basil with 2 Tbsp (30 mL) fresh dill, if desired.

- Add ½ cup drained sun-dried tomatoes or roasted red peppers (from a jar or homemade, page 53) to cheese mixture; process with quick on/off pulses to combine. Don't overprocess.

- Have a ball! Prepare cheese mixture as directed above; shape into 1-inch balls. (Use a melon baller to scoop mixture.) Roll in chopped pistachios and/or parsley. Serve chilled.

## GARLIC BUTTER

Yield: About ½ cup.
Recipe may be doubled.
Keeps about a month in the refrigerator.
Freezes well.

**2 cloves garlic**
**3 sprigs fresh parsley**

**½ cup soft butter or margarine (or Lighter Butter, page 39)**
**1 Tbsp chopped chives (optional)**

STEEL BLADE: Process garlic and parsley until finely minced, about 10 seconds. Add chunks of butter or margarine and process until well blended, scraping down sides of bowl as necessary. Blend in chives (if using). *Continued*

101 calories per Tbsp, 0.3 g carbohydrates, 0 g fiber, 0 g protein, 11.3 g fat (7.1 g saturated fat), 30 mg cholesterol, 80 mg sodium, 8 mg potassium, 0 mg iron, 5 mg calcium, 5 mg phosphorus

### variations

- DILL BUTTER: Omit garlic and parsley. Use 2 Tbsp (30 mL) fresh dill. Terrific with fish or potatoes.
- Add 2 Tbsp (30 mL) of your favorite fresh herbs (e.g., basil, thyme).

## SALMON TORTILLA PINWHEELS

Tortilla pinwheels are today's version of party sandwiches. Blend salmon with cream cheese to make this creamy filling. For a dairy-free version, use tofu "cream cheese" (Tofutti) and mayonnaise.

Yield: About 32. Keeps 1 day in the refrigerator. These can be frozen if you omit spinach when filling the tortillas.

2 green onions, cut in chunks
2 Tbsp fresh dill
1 cup cream cheese (light or regular)
2 Tbsp honey mustard
1 can (7¾ oz/213 g) salmon, drained
2 Tbsp sour cream or mayonnaise (light or regular)
four 10-inch flour tortillas
half of a 10 oz (300 g) pkg baby spinach leaves
grape tomatoes, for garnish

STEEL BLADE: Process green onions and dill until minced, about 10 seconds. Add cream cheese, mustard, salmon and sour cream or mayonnaise. Process until blended, 15 to 20 seconds longer, scraping down sides of bowl as needed.

Spread mixture evenly on tortillas. Cover with a layer of spinach leaves, leaving ½-inch border around the outside edge of each tortilla so that it will stick together when rolled up. Use any remaining spinach leaves to line serving platter.

Roll tortillas up tightly and wrap in plastic wrap. Refrigerate for at least an hour or overnight.

At serving time, slice each roll on the diagonal into 8 slices. (The ends are for nibbling!) Arrange on a large platter lined with spinach; garnish with grape tomatoes.

56 calories per pinwheel, 5.7 g carbohydrates, 0.6 g fiber, 3 g protein, 2.5 g fat (1 g saturated fat), 7 mg cholesterol, 128 mg sodium, 18 mg potassium, 1 mg iron, 53 mg calcium, 12 mg phosphorus

### variations

- Replace spinach with red leaf lettuce. Place a narrow band of roasted red bell peppers (store-bought or homemade, page 53) along one edge of tortillas before rolling them up. Roasted asparagus spears also make a pretty presentation.
- Try other fillings: Lox and Cheese Spread (page 63), Chopped Egg Spread (page 60), Salmon Spread (page 62), Tuna Spread (page 60), Sun-Dried Tomato Spread (page 53). Do not freeze fillings containing mayonnaise.

# MANGO QUESADILLAS

This recipe comes from a great little cookbook called *Simply Irresistible: Easy, Elegant, Fearless, Fussless Cooking* by Sheilah Kaufman of Potomac, Maryland. Ideal as appetizers or a main course. Assemble these a few hours in advance and pop them into the oven just before serving.

Yield: 12 wedges. Do not freeze.

8 oz (250 g) chilled Monterey Jack cheese (2 cups grated)
1 cup roasted red peppers (from a jar or homemade, page 53), drained
dash hot sauce
1 large mango, peeled and cut into chunks

four 10-inch flour tortillas
4 Tbsp Pesto (page 105), or use store-bought
2 Tbsp butter or margarine
salsa and sour cream, for serving

Preheat oven to 375°F. For machines with nested bowls, see method below.

GRATER: Grate cheese, using medium pressure. Remove from bowl and set aside.

STEEL BLADE: Process red peppers and hot sauce until smooth. Place mixture in small bowl. (Prepare ahead of time if desired, then cover and refrigerate.) Chop mango using quick on/off pulses.

Place tortillas on work surface and brush 1 Tbsp pesto over half of each tortilla. Sprinkle one-quarter of cheese and mango over pesto. Fold in half. Melt 1 Tbsp butter or margarine in a large skillet over medium heat. Cook quesadillas until golden brown on each side, adding more butter as needed.

Transfer to large baking sheet and brush tops with red pepper mixture. Bake at 375°F until cheese melts and tortillas are crisp, 5 to 10 minutes. Cut each quesadilla into 3 wedges. Serve with salsa and sour cream.

200 calories per wedge, 16.1 g carbohydrates, 1.3 g fiber, 8 g protein, 11.9 g fat (5.9 g saturated fat), 24 mg cholesterol, 305 mg sodium, 113 mg potassium, 1 mg iron, 211 mg calcium, 136 mg phosphorus

### nested bowl method

Use mini-bowl and mini-blade to process red peppers and hot sauce. Use medium bowl and GRATER/SHREDDING DISC to grate cheese. Use large bowl and STEEL BLADE to chop mango.

# ASPARAGUS CHEESE ROLLS

Prepare these in advance and pop them under the broiler when your company arrives.

18 slices thinly sliced white or whole wheat bread, crusts removed
8 oz (250 g) chilled low-fat cheddar cheese (2 cups grated)
½ cup soft butter or light margarine, cut in chunks

1 tsp Dijon mustard
1 tsp Worcestershire sauce
18 steamed asparagus spears

Leftover cheese mixture can be used as a spread.

Yield: 3 dozen.
Freezes well.

Flatten bread slices lightly with a rolling pin.

GRATER: Grate cheese, using medium pressure. Leave cheese in processor bowl.

STEEL BLADE: Insert blade, pushing it all the way down. Add butter or margarine, mustard and Worcestershire sauce. Process until mixed, scraping down bowl as needed. Spread on bread slices.

Place an asparagus spear on each slice of bread, trimming asparagus to fit. Roll up and cut in half. Place seam side down in a single layer on a cookie sheet. Wrap well; refrigerate or freeze until needed. Broil until golden. Serve hot.

69 calories each, 6.8 g carbohydrates, 0.4 g fiber, 3 g protein, 3.4 g fat (2 g saturated fat), 8 mg cholesterol, 148 mg sodium, 36 mg potassium, 1 mg iron, 48 mg calcium, 48 mg phosphorus

# BRUSCHETTA

This easy and healthy appetizer tastes best when fresh tomatoes are in season. The tomato mixture also makes a terrific topping for grilled fish or chicken.

Yield: 8 bruschetta.
Tomato mixture keeps 1 to 2 days in the refrigerator. Do not freeze.

1 clove garlic
¼ cup fresh basil leaves
4 firm, ripe tomatoes, cored and quartered
salt and freshly ground black pepper to taste

2 to 3 Tbsp extra-virgin olive oil
eight 1-inch slices French or Italian crusty bread
2 additional cloves garlic, cut in half

STEEL BLADE: Process 1 clove garlic with basil until minced. Add tomatoes and process with several quick on/off pulses, until coarsely chopped. Do not overprocess. Season with salt, pepper and 1 Tbsp of the olive oil. (Can be prepared in advance and refrigerated.)

Toast or grill bread slices on both sides until crisp and golden. Rub 1 side of bread slices with cut garlic. Brush lightly with remaining olive oil. Top with tomato mixture and serve immediately.

230 calories each, 38.9 g carbohydrates, 2.3 g fiber, 8 g protein, 4.8 g fat (0.8 g saturated fat), 0 mg cholesterol, 419 mg sodium, 236 mg potassium, 3 mg iron, 39 mg calcium, 90 mg phosphorus

## variation

Top with grated low-fat mozzarella or crumbled feta cheese. You will need ¾ to 1 cup cheese. Broil just until melted. One serving contains 262 calories, 6.9 g fat and 6 mg cholesterol.

# MAKE-AND-BAKE PIZZA

Warning: Once you
try this recipe, you
may never order
from the local
pizzeria again!
Pizzas may be
frozen unbaked;
when ready to bake,
pop the frozen
pizza into the oven
and increase baking
time by 5 minutes.
Pizzas may also be
frozen after baking.

Yield: 2 large or
12 miniature pizzas.
Keeps 2 days in the
refrigerator. Reheats
and/or freezes well.

## DOUGH

1 pkg dry yeast (2¼ tsp)

¼ cup warm water (105°F to 115°F)

2¾ cups flour (half whole wheat flour
   may be used)

1 Tbsp sugar

1 tsp salt

1 Tbsp extra-virgin olive oil

1 cup lukewarm water

## TOPPING

2 tsp extra-virgin olive oil

1 cup tomato or pizza sauce (unsalted
   or regular, bottled or homemade)

dash dried oregano and dried basil

1 cup mushrooms

1 green, red and/or yellow bell pepper,
   halved and seeded

8 oz (250 g) chilled low-fat mozzarella
   cheese (2 cups grated)

For dough: Sprinkle yeast over ¼ cup warm water and let stand for 8 to 10 minutes. Stir to dissolve.

STEEL BLADE (or DOUGH BLADE and DOUGH CYCLE): Process flour, sugar and salt for 6 seconds. Add yeast mixture and process 10 seconds longer. Combine 1 tbsp oil and lukewarm water in a glass measuring cup. Turn on machine and slowly drizzle liquid through feed tube while machine is running. Process until dough gathers together, cleans sides of processor bowl and forms a mass around the blades. (Have an additional ¼ cup flour ready in case the machine begins to slow down; dump in through feed tube, if necessary.) Process dough 30 to 40 seconds longer. Dough should be somewhat sticky. (See Chef's Tips, page 70.)

Divide dough in half. Knead on a floured surface into 2 smooth balls. Flatten and roll into two 12-inch circles (or make 12 smaller circles). Place on sprayed pizza pans or baking sheets. Turn edges to raise slightly. Let rise 10 to 15 minutes in pans. (You can let dough rise for up to 2 hours.)

For topping: Preheat oven to 425°F. Brush dough with remaining 2 tsp oil. Spread with sauce and sprinkle with seasonings.

SLICER: Slice mushrooms and peppers, using light pressure. Spread over sauce.

GRATER: Grate cheese, using medium pressure. Top pizzas.

Bake on lowest rack for 20 minutes for large pizzas and 12 to 15 minutes for mini pizzas. Cut each large pizza into 6 wedges and serve.

201 calories per slice or mini pizza, 27.5 g carbohydrates, 1.6 g fiber, 9 g protein, 6.1 g fat
(2.7 g saturated fat), 10 mg cholesterol, 298 mg sodium, 191 mg potassium,
2 mg iron, 149 mg calcium, 152 mg phosphorus

*Continued*

APPETIZERS

### variations

Top pizzas with any of the following toppings: Pesto (page 105), chopped sun-dried tomatoes, roasted red bell pepper strips, thinly sliced zucchini, tomatoes, onions, potatoes, olives, marinated artichoke hearts, basil leaves, chopped spinach, thinly sliced smoked salmon, drained and flaked tuna, grated Parmesan cheese, crumbled feta cheese . . . Design your own personal pizza!

### chef's tips

- DO-AHEAD DOUGH: Store in a large resealable plastic bag in the refrigerator for 4 or 5 days. Punch down, divide in half, roll out and continue as directed.

- For more information about yeast doughs, see pages 296–300.

- For a crispier crust when reheating pizza, reheat on a parchment-lined baking sheet at 400°F for 5 to 7 minutes. The parchment paper absorbs extra moisture. Saves on cleanup, too!

## PIZZA TARTS

*Kids love these tasty tarts. They also make a terrific appetizer for adults.*

*Yield: 24 tarts. Doubles easily. Keeps 2 days in the refrigerator. Reheats and/or freezes well.*

Flaky Ginger Ale Pastry (page 471) or
    Cream Cheese Pastry (page 472)
1 clove garlic
1 medium onion, quartered
1 red bell pepper, quartered and
    seeded
1½ cups mushrooms

1 Tbsp olive or canola oil
1 cup tomato or pizza sauce
salt and pepper to taste
dried oregano and basil to taste
8 oz (250 g) chilled low-fat mozzarella
    cheese (2 cups grated)

Prepare pastry as directed. Roll out on a lightly floured surface into a large rectangle. Cut into 3½-inch circles. Lightly spray 24 muffin cups with nonstick spray. Line muffin cups with dough.

STEEL BLADE: Drop garlic through feed tube while machine is running. Process until minced. Add onion and process with 2 or 3 quick on/offs, until coarsely chopped. (No need to empty processor bowl.)

SLICER: Slice red pepper and mushrooms, using light pressure. Heat oil in a skillet on medium heat. Add garlic, onion, pepper and mushrooms and sauté 5 minutes. Stir in sauce and seasonings. Simmer, uncovered, 2 or 3 minutes longer. Let cool.

GRATER: Grate cheese, using medium pressure.

Place about 1 Tbsp vegetable mixture in each tart shell. Top with grated cheese. Bake in preheated 400°F oven for 20 minutes, until golden.

95 calories each, 6.4 g carbohydrates, 0.5 g fiber, 3 g protein, 6.4 g fat (2 g saturated fat), 5 mg cholesterol, 148 mg sodium, 78 mg potassium, 1 mg iron, 73 mg calcium, 64 mg phosphorus

## SESAME CHEESE STRAWS

Yield: 7 to 8 dozen. Store in an airtight container for about a week. May be frozen either baked or unbaked. It is not necessary to thaw them before baking.

**4 oz (125 g) chilled low-fat cheddar cheese (about 1 cup grated)**
**1 cup flour**
**½ tsp salt**
**¼ tsp paprika**

**⅓ cup chilled butter or margarine, cut in 1-inch chunks**
**½ tsp Worcestershire sauce**
**2 to 3 Tbsp cold water**
**¼ cup sesame seeds**

Preheat oven to 400°F. For machines with nested work bowls, see method below.

GRATER: Grate cheese, using light pressure. Set aside.

STEEL BLADE: For dough, process flour, salt, paprika and butter or margarine for 8 to 10 seconds, until particles are size of small peas. Add cheese, Worcestershire sauce, 2 Tbsp water and sesame seeds. Process just until dough begins to gather in a ball around the blades, 12 to 15 seconds. Add an extra Tbsp of water if dough seems too dry. Do not overprocess.

Divide mixture in half. Roll out each part on a floured surface into 8- × 12-inch rectangle about ⅛ inch thick. Using a sharp knife or fluted pastry wheel, cut in strips about ½ inch × 3 inches.

Place on ungreased parchment- or foil-lined cookie sheets. Bake for 10 to 12 minutes, until golden. Serve at room temperature.

17 calories each, 1.3 g carbohydrates, 0.1 g fiber, 1 g protein, 1.1 g fat (0.6 g saturated fat), 2 mg cholesterol, 28 mg sodium, 5 mg potassium, 0 mg iron, 10 mg calcium, 11 mg phosphorus

### nested bowl method

Use medium bowl and GRATER/SHREDDING DISC to grate cheese. Use large bowl and STEEL BLADE to prepare dough.

# GOUGÈRES (FRENCH CHEESE PUFFS)

You can use any kind of hard, sharp cheese in this savory version of cream puffs.

Yield: 5 dozen bite-sized puffs. Reheats and/or freezes well.

handful chives or green onions (to yield 3 to 4 Tbsp)
8 oz (250 g) chilled sharp Gruyère or cheddar cheese (2 cups grated)
6 Tbsp butter or margarine
1 cup water
½ tsp salt
1 cup flour
4 eggs
1 tsp dry mustard
¼ tsp cayenne

Preheat oven to 375°F. Line 2 baking sheets with parchment paper. For machines with nested bowls, see method below.

STEEL BLADE: Mince chives or green onions. Set aside.

GRATER: Grate cheese, using medium pressure. Reserve 1½ cups for mixture and ½ cup to sprinkle on top.

Combine butter or margarine, water and salt in a medium, heavy saucepan. Bring to a boil, stirring occasionally. As soon as butter is melted, remove from heat and dump in flour all at once. Stir vigorously with a wooden spoon until mixture pulls away from sides of pan and forms a ball. Cool 5 minutes.

STEEL BLADE: Transfer mixture from saucepan to processor bowl. Process for 5 seconds. Drop eggs through feed tube 1 at a time while machine is running. Process 20 to 25 seconds after you've added the eggs. Mixture should be smooth and shiny. Add 1½ cups grated cheese, chives, mustard and cayenne and process briefly to combine.

Drop mixture by rounded teaspoonfuls onto prepared baking sheets, forming mounds about the size of small cherry tomatoes. Leave about an inch between each mound. Sprinkle tops with reserved cheese. (Can be prepared up to this point and baked just before guests arrive.)

Bake for 25 minutes, until puffy and nicely browned. For extra-crispy puffs, 5 minutes before they're done, poke the side of each puff with a sharp knife so steam can escape. Then return them to the oven to finish baking. Best served warm.

38 calories each, 1.7 g carbohydrates, 0.1 g fiber, 2 g protein, 2.7 g fat (1.5 g saturated fat), 21 g cholesterol, 44 mg sodium, 10 mg potassium, 0 mg iron, 39 mg calcium, 30 mg phosphorus

### nested bowl method

Use mini-bowl and mini-blade to mince chives. Use medium bowl and GRATER/SHREDDING DISC for cheese. Use large bowl and STEEL BLADE to process mixture.

# ROASTED RED PEPPER CRESCENTS

Quick and easy for entertaining! If desired, mix some chopped black olives into the goat cheese.

Cream Cheese Pastry (page 472)

½ cup grated Parmesan cheese, divided

2 large roasted red bell peppers (page 53), or 1 cup roasted red bell peppers from a jar

½ cup soft goat cheese (herb or plain)

dried basil, dried thyme and paprika, to taste

2 Tbsp additional Parmesan cheese

Yield: 2 dozen. Doubles easily. Keeps 2 days in the refrigerator. Reheats and/or freezes well.

Preheat oven to 375°F.

Prepare pastry as directed; divide into 2 balls. Flour dough lightly. Roll out 1 portion of dough on floured surface into 9-inch circle. Sprinkle with half the Parmesan cheese. Cut circle into quarters, then cut each quarter into 3 triangles, making 12 triangles in total. (Use a pizza cutter or sharp knife.)

Pat red peppers dry with paper towels. Cut into 24 pieces. Place 1 tsp goat cheese at outside edge of each triangle. Top with piece of red pepper. Sprinkle dough with basil, thyme and paprika. Roll up tightly from the outside edge towards the center and shape into a crescent. Place on ungreased parchment- or foil-lined baking sheet. Repeat with remaining dough and filling. Sprinkle crescents with additional Parmesan cheese.

Bake for 18 to 20 minutes, until lightly browned.

93 calories each, 5.1 g carbohydrates, 0.2 g fiber, 3 g protein, 6.8 g fat (4.3 g saturated fat), 19 mg cholesterol, 120 mg sodium, 24 mg potassium, 0 mg iron, 64 mg calcium, 35 mg phosphorus

# SPANAKOPITA (PHYLLO TRIANGLES)

Although this Greek specialty is usually filled with spinach and cheese, try the variations on page 74—they are also delicious.

FILLING

2 pkgs (10 oz/300 g each) frozen spinach

1 onion, quartered

2 Tbsp olive oil

¼ cup grated Parmesan cheese

1 cup light ricotta or pressed cottage cheese (or ½ cup feta and ½ cup cottage cheese)

1 or 2 eggs

salt and freshly ground black pepper to taste

¼ tsp nutmeg

DOUGH

1 lb (500 g) phyllo dough (see About Phyllo Dough, page 74)

½ cup melted butter, margarine or oil

Yield: About 100 hors d'oeuvres. Keeps 2 to 3 days in the refrigerator. Freezes well. To reheat, bake uncovered at 300°F about 10 minutes.

Cook spinach according to package directions. Let cool, then squeeze out excess moisture.

STEEL BLADE: Process onion with 2 or 3 quick on/offs, until coarsely chopped.

*Continued*

Sauté in olive oil on medium heat for 5 minutes, until golden. Process spinach until finely chopped, about 10 seconds. Add onion, Parmesan, ricotta, 1 egg and seasonings; process just until mixed. (Add second egg only if mixture seems dry.)

Preheat oven to 350°F about 20 minutes before baking. Place 1 sheet of phyllo dough on dry surface. (Cover remaining dough with plastic wrap to prevent it from drying out.) Brush dough with melted butter. Top with second sheet of dough; brush again with butter. Cut each sheet into 8 strips about 2 inches wide. Place about 1 tsp filling 1 inch from bottom of each strip. Fold upward to cover filling.

Bring right-bottom corner of dough upwards to meet left edge, making a triangle. Continue folding upwards and from side to side until strip is completely folded into a triangle. Repeat with remaining dough and filling. Place triangles seam side down on lightly sprayed baking pan. Brush with additional melted butter. (May be frozen at this point. No need to thaw before baking; just add 2 or 3 minutes to baking time.)

Bake for 20 minutes, until golden.

31 calories each, 2.8 g carbohydrates, 0.3 g fiber, 1 g protein, 1.8 g fat (0.9 g saturated fat), 6 mg cholesterol, 40 mg sodium, 23 mg potassium, 0 mg iron, 17 mg calcium, 13 mg phosphorus

### variations

Add ¼ cup (60 mL) fresh dill and/or parsley; process with spinach. You can replace spinach with broccoli or use Cheese Filling (page 166). For Chicken or Meat Filling (page 257), use oil to brush dough.

### about phyllo dough

A 1 lb (500 g) package of frozen or fresh phyllo dough contains 20 to 28 sheets. To thaw, place package in refrigerator overnight. Dough will keep for 2 or 3 weeks in the refrigerator. When working with phyllo, keep it well covered with plastic wrap to prevent it from drying out. If dough tears, don't worry. Just patch it together with melted butter or margarine!

## MUSHROOM TURNOVERS

You can freeze these baked or unbaked. No need to thaw them first; just increase the baking time by 3 or 4 minutes.

Flaky Ginger Ale Pastry (page 471) or
  Cream Cheese Pastry (page 472)

FILLING
2 medium onions, quartered
2 Tbsp olive or canola oil

½ lb (250 g) button or cremini
  mushrooms (or try a medley of wild
  mushrooms)
¼ cup sour cream (light or regular) or
  2 Tbsp red wine
salt and pepper to taste
½ tsp dried thyme

Prepare desired dough as directed, divide in half, wrap well and chill for 1 hour.

STEEL BLADE: For filling, process onions with 3 or 4 quick on/offs, until coarsely chopped. Heat oil in a large skillet. Add onions and sauté on medium-high heat for 3 minutes. Process mushrooms with 4 or 5 quick on/offs, until finely chopped. Add to onions and sauté until golden, 7 or 8 minutes. Remove from heat and stir in sour cream and seasonings; let cool.

Assembly: Thinly roll out 1 portion of dough on a pastry cloth or floured surface into a 9- × 12-inch rectangle. Cut dough into 12 squares or circles. Place a scant teaspoon (5 mL) of filling in center of each square. Brush edges of dough lightly with water, then fold over to form a triangle or crescent. Seal edges of dough well; prick tops of turnover 2 or 3 times with a fork so steam can escape during baking. Repeat with remaining dough and filling. (Can be baked immediately or frozen in a single layer on baking sheet until solid, then transferred to freezer containers and frozen until needed.)

Preheat oven to 375°F. Bake on parchment-lined baking sheet for 18 to 20 minutes, until lightly browned.

74 calories each, 5.8 g carbohydrates, 0.4 g fiber, 1 g protein, 5.3 g fat (1.1 g saturated fat), 1 mg cholesterol, 47 mg sodium, 56 mg potassium, 0 mg iron, 8 mg calcium, 19 mg phosphorus

### variations

- SPINACH CHEESE TURNOVERS: Make 4 batches of desired pastry. Use Spanakopita filling (page 73).

- CHICKEN OR MEAT TURNOVERS: Use Flaky Ginger Ale Pastry (page 471). Fill with Chicken or Meat Filling (page 257).

## STUFFED ITALIAN MUSHROOMS

*Ideal as an appetizer or a side dish.*

*Yield: 4 servings.*

*Doubles easily. Keeps 1 to 2 days in the refrigerator. To freeze, bake for only 10 minutes at 350°F. When cool, wrap well and freeze until needed.*

1 dozen very large mushrooms (or 2 dozen medium)
1 clove garlic
1 Tbsp olive oil
1 small onion
1 stalk celery, cut in chunks
½ red bell pepper

⅓ cup dried bread crumbs
salt and freshly ground black pepper to taste
pinch each of dried oregano and dried basil (or 1 Tbsp each fresh oregano and basil)
2 oz (60 g) chilled low-fat mozzarella cheese (½ cup grated)

Preheat oven to 350°F.

Wash mushrooms quickly and pat dry with paper towels. Remove stems and set aside.
*Continued*

STEEL BLADE: Drop garlic through feed tube while machine is running; process until minced. Add mushroom stems and process until finely chopped, 6 to 8 seconds. Heat oil in large skillet; add garlic and chopped mushrooms. Process onion, celery and red pepper until minced, 6 to 8 seconds. Add to skillet and sauté about 5 minutes on medium heat. Stir in bread crumbs and seasonings.

Stuff mushroom caps with mixture and arrange in single layer in sprayed baking dish.

GRATER: Grate cheese, using medium pressure. Sprinkle stuffed mushrooms with cheese. (Can be made in advance and refrigerated.)

Bake, uncovered, for 15 to 20 minutes.

*Bake frozen mushrooms, covered, at 350°F for 15 minutes. Uncover and broil until golden.*

47 calories each, 4.1 g carbohydrates, 0.6 g fiber, 3 g protein, 2.4 g fat (0.8 g saturated fat), 3 mg cholesterol, 51 mg sodium, 113 mg potassium, 0 mg iron, 44 mg calcium, 54 mg phosphorus

### variation

Omit celery, red bell pepper and mozzarella cheese. Process ¼ cup almonds on STEEL BLADE for 15 seconds, until coarsely chopped. Add ¼ cup each of sun-dried tomatoes and roasted red bell peppers to almonds. Process with 3 or 4 quick on/offs. Add almond mixture, bread crumbs and seasonings to sautéed mushrooms stems. Stuff mushrooms; sprinkle lightly with 2 Tbsp grated Parmesan cheese or melted margarine. Bake as directed. One mushroom contains 55 calories and 3.2 g fat.

## VEGETARIAN EGG ROLLS

*To save time, you can buy frozen egg roll wrappers, available in most supermarkets, instead of making your own.*

| | |
|---|---|
| 2¼ cups flour | Egg Roll Filling (page 77) |
| ½ tsp salt | 1 egg, lightly beaten |
| 2 eggs | oil for deep-frying (about 2 cups) |
| ¼ cup warm water (approximately) | plum sauce or duck sauce, for dipping |

STEEL BLADE: Process flour, salt, 2 eggs and water until dough forms a ball on the blade and is well kneaded, 25 to 30 seconds. Remove from bowl, cover and let stand for 15 minutes. Prepare filling as directed and let cool.

Divide dough in half. Roll 1 piece out into a large, thin rectangle. Cut in 4-inch squares for large egg rolls, or into 2- × 4-inch rectangles for miniatures. Brush edges of dough with beaten egg. Place spoonful of filling along lower edge of dough. Roll up and press edges to seal. Repeat with remaining dough and filling.

Yield: About 24 to
30 large or 50 to
60 small egg rolls.
Keeps 3 to 4 days in the
refrigerator. Reheats
and/or freezes well.

Heat oil to 375°F in deep-fryer or deep saucepan. Fry egg rolls until golden, about 5 minutes. Drain well on paper towels. (May be frozen at this point. Thaw before reheating.)

To reheat: Place in single layer on foil-lined cookie sheet and heat, uncovered, at 350°F until piping hot and crisp, 10 to 15 minutes.

118 calories each (large size), 11.6 g carbohydrates, 1 g fiber, 3 g protein, 6.8 g fat (0.7 g saturated fat), 26 mg cholesterol, 146 mg sodium, 98 mg potassium, 1 mg iron, 13 mg calcium, 45 mg phosphorus

## EGG ROLL FILLING

Yield: Filling for 24 to
30 egg rolls or 16 to
20 crêpes.

1 or 2 cloves garlic

1 slice fresh ginger, peeled (1 Tbsp)

2 medium onions, quartered

2 stalks celery, cut in chunks

1 green or red bell pepper, cut in chunks

1 cup mushrooms

2 Tbsp canola oil

1 lb (500 g) fresh bean sprouts

2 Tbsp soy sauce (low-sodium or regular)

1 tsp toasted sesame oil

dash freshly ground black pepper

STEEL BLADE: Drop garlic and ginger through feed tube while machine is running; process until minced. Process onions with 3 or 4 quick on/off pulses, until coarsely chopped. Empty bowl. Repeat with celery, bell pepper and mushrooms. In large skillet or wok, quickly brown chopped vegetables in hot oil on high heat. Add bean sprouts and stir-fry until mixture is fairly dry, about 2 minutes. Stir in soy sauce, sesame oil and pepper.

25 calories per serving (1/24 of recipe), 2.6 g carbohydrates, 0.7 g fiber, 1 g protein, 1.4 g fat (0.1 g saturated fat), 0 mg cholesterol, 88 mg sodium, 77 mg potassium, 0 mg iron, 8 mg calcium, 21 mg phosphorus

### variations

- About half a medium cabbage or bok choy may be substituted for bean sprouts. Process on SLICER, using light pressure. Measure approximately 3 cups.

- Add some thinly sliced water chestnuts, bamboo shoots, green onions, grated zucchini and/or carrots, if desired. The choice is yours!

# FALAFEL

Serve this Middle
Eastern specialty
in warmed pita
pockets with
garnishes such as
chopped onion,
cucumber, hot
pepper, pickles,
tomatoes, peppers
and lettuce. Drizzle
with Tahini Dressing
(page 108).

Yield: About 100 balls.
Keeps 2 days in the
refrigerator. Reheats
and/or freezes well.

2 cups dried chickpeas

4 to 6 cloves garlic

2 large onions, quartered

½ cup fresh parsley

6 Tbsp dried bread crumbs

2 eggs

1½ tsp salt (or to taste)

1 tsp ground cumin (or to taste)

½ tsp baking powder

freshly ground black pepper to taste

dash cayenne pepper or ground
    coriander

oil for deep-frying (about 4 cups)

Pick over chickpeas, discarding any stones or debris. Soak overnight in cold water. Drain thoroughly. Divide ingredients in half and process in 2 batches. (If you have a larger processor—11 cups or more—process ingredients in 1 batch.)

STEEL BLADE: Drop garlic through feed tube while machine is running; process until minced. Add onions and parsley; process until minced. Add remaining ingredients, except oil, and process until finely ground, 20 to 30 seconds, scraping down bowl as necessary. Transfer to mixing bowl and repeat with second batch of ingredients. Form into 1-inch balls.

Heat oil to 375°F in deep-fryer or deep saucepan. Fry falafel in hot oil until crisp and golden, about 5 minutes. They will float to the surface when done. Drain on paper towels.

60 calories each, 3 g carbohydrates, 0.4 g fiber, 1 g protein, 5 g fat (0.4 g saturated fat), 4 mg cholesterol, 42 mg sodium, 9 mg potassium, 0 mg iron, 8 mg calcium, 4 mg phosphorus

### notes

- If desired, substitute 4 cups drained canned chickpeas for the dried chickpeas. Soaking is not necessary.
- To reheat, place falafel in single layer on foil-lined rimmed baking sheet. Heat, uncovered, at 350°F until piping hot and crisp, 10 to 15 minutes.

# PARTY MEATBALLS

These meatballs
can also be made
with ground veal,
chicken, turkey or
vegetarian meat
substitute.

1 clove garlic

1 small onion, halved

2 lb (1 kg) lean ground beef
    (or see Grind Your Own, page 36)

1 egg (or 2 egg whites)

2 Tbsp dried bread crumbs or
    matzo meal

1 tsp salt (or to taste)

dash freshly ground black pepper

1⅓ cups chili or barbecue sauce

1 cup grape jelly

2 Tbsp lemon juice

2 lb (1 kg) hot dogs (optional)

Yield: About
50 meatballs and 50 hot
dog slices. Keeps 2 days
in the refrigerator.
Freezes well. Reheat
in oven at 300°F
until piping hot, 20 to
25 minutes.

STEEL BLADE: Process garlic and onion until minced. Combine with ground meat in a large mixing bowl. Add egg, crumbs or matzo meal, salt and pepper; mix lightly.

STEEL BLADE: Process chili or barbecue sauce, grape jelly and lemon juice until mixed, 6 to 8 seconds. Transfer to a large saucepan and bring to a simmer. (If desired, mix 2 or 3 Tbsp sauce into meat mixture.)

Form meat mixture into walnut-sized meatballs and drop into simmering sauce. Cover partially and simmer for about 1 hour. If desired, add hot dogs, sliced diagonally into ½-inch pieces. Simmer for 5 minutes to heat through.

60 calories per meatball, 6.7 g carbohydrates, 0 g fiber, 4 g protein, 2.1 g fat (0.8 g saturated fat), 13 mg cholesterol, 158 mg sodium, 47 mg potassium, 0 mg iron, 3 mg calcium, 25 mg phosphorus

### variations

Try forming the following recipes into tiny balls and serving them at the buffet table: Hawaiian Meatballs (page 191), Mmm-Good Meatballs (page 192), Cranberry Chicken Meatballs (page 193), Pineapple Chicken Meatballs (page 195), Passover Cranberry Sweet and Sour Meatballs (page 497).

# SOUPS, SAUCES AND MARINADES
recipe list

84  Quick Vegetable Broth
84  Flanken (Short Ribs) and
    Barley Soup
85  Gazpacho
85  Dairy Beet Borscht
86  Vegetarian Cabbage Soup
87  As-You-Like-It Vegetable
    Soup
87  Mom's Vegetable Soup
    with Matzo Balls
88  Matzo Balls
88  Chicken Meatball Soup
90  Slow Cooker Chicken
    Soup
90  Easy Lentil Vegetable
    Soup
91  Vegetarian Minestrone
92  Quick Potato Soup
92  Phony Minestrone
93  Penny's Tomato Bisque
94  Potato Mushroom Soup
94  Parmentier Soup
95  Carrot and Sweet Potato
    Soup

96  Zucchini and Two Potato
    Soup
97  Zucchini Noodle Soup
97  Broccoli Lentil Soup
98  Herbed Cauliflower or
    Broccoli Soup
99  Roasted Squash Soup
99  Sweet Potato Squash
    Soup
100 Cream of Pumpkin Soup
101 Vegetable Cheese
    Chowder
102 Manhattan Fish Chowder
103 Onion Soup au Gratin
103 Béchamel (White) Sauce
104 Mushroom Sauce
105 Easy Barbecue Sauce
105 Quick Tomato Sauce
105 Pesto
106 Vegetarian Spaghetti
    Sauce
107 Rina's Red Pepper Sauce
107 Mango Salsa
108 Tahini Dressing

108 Chinese Sweet and Sour Sauce

108 Teriyaki Marinade

109 Cantonese Marinade

109 Chinese Marinade

110 Honey Garlic Sparerib Sauce

110 Peanut Butter Sauce

110 Horseradish

111 Mayonnaise

112 Tofu Mayonnaise

- I usually have chicken soup in my freezer. How-ever, if you don't have homemade broth on hand, use canned soup, instant powdered soup mix or bouillon cubes dissolved in water. Look for low-sodium or salt-free brands. You can also use the cooking water from vegetables.

- Quick Vegetable Broth (page 84) is very simple to make. Or cut 1 onion, 2 stalks celery and 2 carrots in chunks. Place in a saucepan with a few parsley stems, green onion tops and 1 or 2 garlic cloves. Add water to cover, bring to a boil and simmer for 20 minutes, then strain. Use immediately, refrigerate or freeze.

- BROTH IN A BOX: Good-quality brands of vegetable broth are available in most supermarkets and are handy in a pinch. You can use Imagine Organic No-Chicken Broth, which is kosher, vegetarian and fat-free. One box contains about 4 cups and it doesn't require refrigeration until it has been opened. One cup contains 10 calories, 2 g carbohydrates and 470 mg sodium, so it's lower in sodium than canned broth but higher than homemade.

- To add extra flavor to broths or soups, save the soaking water from dried mushrooms or sun-dried tomatoes. Freeze in ice cube trays until needed. One cube equals 2 Tbsp.

- To prepare vegetables, peel and/or trim them, and rinse well. Cut into chunks if chopping or mincing with the **Steel Blade**. Cut to fit the feed tube if slicing or shredding/grating.

- Use leftover cooked vegetables to thicken soups. Strain vegetables, then purée on the **Steel Blade** until smooth, about 10 seconds. For thick purées (vegetables only), process 3 to 3½ cups at a time in a standard (7-cup) processor. For thin purées (vegetables and liquid), process 2½ cups at a time. The food processor produces a slightly more rustic texture than a blender. Approximately 1 cup of puréed vegetables or legumes will thicken 3 to 4 cups of broth.

- Larger and newer models of food processors can process bigger batches at a time. Processors are classified according to their dry ingredient capacity, ranging from 3 to 20 cups. As a general guideline, the liquid capacity is about half the dry ingredient capacity. Work in batches if necessary. Always check your manual for capacity guidelines.

- The Cuisinart Elite food processor is excellent because it can process up to 10 cups of soup in 1 batch in the 14-cup bowl and 8 cups in the 11-cup bowl. Also, the **Steel Blade** locks into place and doesn't fall out when you pour liquid out of the bowl after processing. The higher center post in the work bowl and the special rubber seal around the inside of the lid (SealTight Advantage) prevent leaking when processing liquids.

- Note: The chopping/mixing blades should not be removed if liquid contents in the bowl are above the hub of the blade or it will leak.

- NESTED WORK BOWLS: Choose the appropriate bowl and blade or disc for the task. Use the mini-bowl and mini-blade to mince garlic, chop herbs and make marinades. Use the medium or large bowl and appropriate disc to slice or shred/grate veggies, cheese, etc. Use the large bowl and **Steel Blade** to chop/mince veggies and to purée soups and sauces. (You can also use the **Steel Blade** in the medium bowl on Cuisinart Elite models.)

- Add meat or chicken bones to soups for a heartier flavor.

- Barley, beans, lentils and split peas add vitamins and fiber to soups.

- Add chopped fresh herbs (e.g., basil, dill) to soups in the last few minutes of cooking. A squeeze of fresh lemon juice also improves the taste.

- Don't throw out those celery tops. Chop with the **Steel Blade** and add them to soups for a fresh flavor.

- When freezing soups, leave 2 inches at the top of the container to allow for expansion. To defrost, place the container in hot water for a few seconds, then transfer the soup to a microwavable bowl. One cup of frozen soup takes 4 minutes on High to defrost, plus 2 to 3 minutes to reheat. Stir often.

- SLOW COOKERS: Soups are a cinch to make in the slow cooker, especially those made with lentils, beans, split peas, barley or root vegetables. Puréed vegetable soups and long-simmered meat soups also work well. There is less evaporation, so start with less liquid than when cooking on the stovetop—the liquid should barely cover the solid ingredients. Additional liquid will release from the vegetables during the long, slow cooking time.

- SLOW COOKER CONVERSION TIMES: If your regular recipe calls for 15 to 30 minutes of cooking, cook it for 4 to 8 hours on Low or 1½ to 2 hours on High. If it calls for 30 to 60 minutes, cook it for 6 to 8 hours on Low or 3 to 4 hours on High. If it calls for 2 to 3 hours, cook it for 8 to 12 hours on Low or 4 to 6 hours on High. No peeking! Every time you lift the lid, it prolongs the cooking time by an additional 20 minutes. Late for dinner? Timing isn't crucial. An extra hour of cooking in the slow cooker usually won't affect soup recipes.

- Refrigerate soups and gravies overnight. Discard congealed fat and say goodbye to unwanted calories and cholesterol!

- Thicken sauces and gravies with leftover cooked vegetables (e.g., potatoes, carrots, cauliflower, squash). Purée the vegetables, then add hot broth or pan juices through the feed tube until the desired texture is reached. Season to taste.

- Dump those lumps! Make sauces smooth by processing them for a few seconds on the **Steel Blade**.

- Marinades enhance flavor and increase tenderness; they also prevent harmful carcinogens from forming during grilling. Raw meats and poultry can be marinated for 24 to 48 hours in the refrigerator. Fish only needs to be marinated for 1 hour. Even 10 or 15 minutes of marinating will add flavor. Never marinate foods at room temperature for longer than an hour—transfer them to the refrigerator.

- Marinades used for meat, poultry or fish can be brushed on cooked food or used as a sauce, but they must first be boiled for 5 minutes to kill any harmful bacteria.

- To prevent cross-contamination, don't serve cooked food on the same plate that was used to carry raw marinated meat, poultry or fish from the kitchen to the grill. Use separate plates and utensils for raw foods and cooked foods.

## QUICK VEGETABLE BROTH

All or part of the cooked vegetables can be processed on the **Steel Blade** and then stirred back into the broth. A dash of soy sauce boosts the flavor.

Yield: About 6 cups. Keeps 3 days in the refrigerator. Reheats and/or freezes well.

2 onions (no need to peel)

2 or 3 stalks celery

3 or 4 carrots

1 red bell pepper

3 cloves garlic

½ cup parsley stems

¼ cup fresh dill

8 cups water (approximately)

pinch salt and pepper

Cut onions, celery, carrots and red pepper in chunks. Combine in a large soup pot with garlic, parsley stems, dill, water, salt and pepper. Water should cover vegetables by about an inch. Bring to a boil. Reduce heat and simmer, partially covered, for 35 to 45 minutes. Strain. Refrigerate or freeze broth.

About 20 calories per cup of clear broth, 2 g carbohydrates, 0 g fiber, 0 g protein, 0 g fat, 0 mg cholesterol, 140 mg sodium

## FLANKEN (SHORT RIBS) AND BARLEY SOUP

Yield: 10 to 12 hearty servings. Keeps 2 to 3 days in the refrigerator. Reheats and/or freezes well. Thin with a little water if necessary when reheating.

6 or 8 strips lean flanken (short ribs) (about 4½ lb/2 kg, or 2 lb/1 kg boneless lean stewing beef)

12 cups cold water

2 to 3 tsp salt (or to taste)

2 medium onions, quartered

3 stalks celery, cut in chunks

3 carrots, cut in chunks

½ turnip, cut in chunks

1 cup pearl barley, rinsed and drained

¼ tsp freshly ground black pepper

Place meat in large soup pot. Add cold water and salt. Bring to a boil and skim well.

STEEL BLADE: Process onions and celery until finely minced, 6 to 8 seconds. Add to soup. Repeat with carrots and turnip. Add barley and pepper to soup. Cover and simmer slowly for 3 hours. Taste to correct seasonings. Chill overnight to remove excess fat.

265 calories per serving, 20.1 g carbohydrates, 4.3 g fiber, 22 g protein, 10.5 g fat (4.4 g saturated fat), 48 mg cholesterol, 542 mg sodium, 375 mg potassium, 2 mg iron, 50 mg calcium, 171 mg phosphorus

### passover variations

- Omit barley. Cut 2 potatoes or sweet potatoes into chunks and process until minced. Add with remaining ingredients to soup.

- Replace barley with 1 cup quinoa, well rinsed and drained. Add to soup for the last half hour of cooking.

# GAZPACHO

A cold uncooked
soup, sometimes
known as
salad soup.

Yield: 6 servings. Keeps
about 1 week in the
refrigerator.
Do not freeze.

1 English cucumber (do not peel)

1 green bell pepper, seeded

1 medium onion

6 ripe, firm tomatoes

4 cloves garlic

juice of ½ lemon (2 Tbsp lemon juice)

2 Tbsp extra-virgin olive or canola oil

½ tsp each chili powder and dried
basil

2 tsp salt (or to taste)

1 can (19 oz/540 mL) tomato juice
(salt-free or regular)

Cut cucumber, green pepper, onion and tomatoes into 1-inch chunks.

STEEL BLADE: Process cucumber with 4 or 5 on/off pulses, until finely chopped. Transfer to large bowl. Repeat with green pepper, onion and tomatoes, adding each in turn to mixing bowl. Drop garlic through feed tube while machine is running; process until minced. Add lemon juice, oil, chili powder, basil, salt and half the tomato juice. Process until smooth. Add to chopped vegetables along with remaining tomato juice. Adjust seasonings to taste. Chill for several hours to blend flavors. Serve with croutons and additional chopped vegetables if desired.

104 calories per serving, 14.5 g carbohydrates, 2.9 g fiber, 3 g protein, 5.1 g fat (0.7 g saturated fat), 0 mg cholesterol, 796 mg sodium, 666 mg potassium, 1 mg iron, 42 mg calcium, 72 mg phosphorus

### note

For a coarser texture, vegetables can be processed on the FRENCH FRY DISC or SLICER. Cut into 1-inch chunks and process, using very light pressure.

# DAIRY BEET BORSCHT

Serve this refreshing
soup ice cold with
sour cream or
yogurt. Perfect
summer fare!

Yield: 8 servings. Keeps
2 to 3 weeks in the
refrigerator. Freezes well.

2½ lb (1.2 kg) beets (about
8 medium), peeled

1 medium onion

8 cups cold water

1 can (19 oz/540 mL) tomato juice
(salt-free or regular)

2 Tbsp lemon juice

1 cup sugar

2 tsp salt

few sprigs fresh dill

sour cream or plain yogurt, for garnish

GRATER: Cut beets to fit feed tube. Grate, using fairly firm pressure. (A slight bouncing motion with the pusher is best.) Grate onion. Combine in large saucepan with water. Bring to a boil, reduce heat to simmer and add remaining ingredients, except sour cream or yogurt.

Simmer for 1 hour, partially covered. Taste to adjust seasonings. Refrigerate. Garnish with a dollop of sour cream or yogurt. *Continued*

SOUPS, SAUCES
AND MARINADES

176 calories per serving, 43.3 g carbohydrates, 3.2 g fiber, 3 g protein, 0.3 g fat (0 g saturated fat), 0 mg cholesterol, 703 mg sodium, 606 mg potassium, 1 mg iron, 40 mg calcium, 69 mg phosphorus

### sugar-free variation

Substitute 1 cup granular Splenda for sugar (or use Passover sugar substitute to equal 1 cup). One serving contains 88 calories and 20.8 g carbohydrates.

## VEGETARIAN CABBAGE SOUP

Yield: 12 hearty servings. Keeps 3 to 4 days in the refrigerator. Reheats and/or freezes well.

**10 cups boiling water**
**1 can (28 oz/796 mL) tomatoes**
**1 can (5½ oz/156 mL) tomato paste**
**1 can (8 oz/227 mL) tomato sauce**
**1 medium onion, quartered lengthwise**
**½ head cabbage**

**½ to ¾ cup brown or granulated sugar (or to taste)**
**2 Tbsp lemon juice**
**salt and freshly ground black pepper to taste**

Combine water, tomatoes, tomato paste and tomato sauce in large soup pot and bring to a boil.

SLICER: Slice onion using light pressure. Cut cabbage in wedges to fit feed tube. Discard core. Slice using very light pressure. Add to soup along with remaining ingredients. Cover and simmer for 1½ to 2 hours. Adjust seasonings to taste.

75 calories per serving, 18.4 g carbohydrates, 2.6 g fiber, 2 g protein, 0.2 g fat (0 g saturated fat), 0 mg cholesterol, 224 mg sodium, 411 mg potassium, 2 mg iron, 58 mg calcium, 41 mg phosphorus

### meatball soup

Make your favorite meatball mixture. (Process 1 lb/500 g lean ground beef, 1 egg, 2 Tbsp matzo meal, 1 clove minced garlic, salt and pepper with quick on/offs, just until combined.) Shape into tiny balls and add to soup. Cover and simmer for 2 hours. If desired, stir in ½ cup uncooked rice and simmer 20 to 25 minutes longer.

175 calories per serving, 19.6 g carbohydrates, 2.6 g fiber, 10 g protein, 5.9 g fat (2.2 g saturated fat), 40 mg cholesterol, 253 mg sodium, 520 mg potassium, 2 mg iron, 65 mg calcium, 110 mg phosphorus

# AS-YOU-LIKE-IT VEGETABLE SOUP

Yield: 6 servings. Keeps 3 to 4 days in the refrigerator. Reheats and/or freezes well.

3 tomatoes, quartered

2 medium onions, halved

2 medium carrots, cut in chunks

2 or 3 parsnips, cut in chunks (optional)

3 stalks celery, cut in chunks

1 cup green beans, broccoli and/or cauliflower, cut in chunks

salt and freshly ground black pepper to taste

3 cups water

1 Tbsp instant pareve chicken soup mix (optional)

½ tsp dried dill (or 1 Tbsp fresh dill)

STEEL BLADE: Process tomatoes until puréed. Add to saucepan along with remaining ingredients. Cover and simmer until vegetables are tender, about 40 minutes.

Remove vegetables from liquid with slotted spoon and place in processor bowl. Process until puréed, 30 to 45 seconds. Return mixture to saucepan and adjust seasonings to taste.

44 calories per serving, 9.9 g carbohydrates, 2.9 g fiber, 2 g protein, 0.3 g fat (0.1 g saturated fat), 0 mg cholesterol, 40 mg sodium, 351 mg potassium, 1 mg iron, 43 mg calcium, 49 mg phosphorus

### variation

Any combination of raw or leftover cooked vegetables may be added. Two cups of skim milk plus 1 tsp margarine may be added for a creamier soup, making 8 servings of 58 calories each with 0.8 g fat.

# MOM'S VEGETABLE SOUP WITH MATZO BALLS

Yield: 8 hearty servings. Keeps 3 days in the refrigerator. Reheats and/or freezes well.

3 stalks celery

1 large potato

2 to 3 carrots

1 large onion

8 cups water or vegetable broth

½ cup pearl barley, rinsed and drained

salt and freshly ground black pepper to taste

1½ cups frozen green peas

1 Tbsp tub margarine

Matzo Balls (page 88)

GRATER: Cut celery, potato, carrots and onion to fit feed tube. Grate using medium pressure. Place in a large saucepan with water or broth, barley, salt and pepper. Bring to a boil, reduce heat and simmer, partially covered, for 1½ hours. Add peas and simmer 10 to 15 minutes longer. Adjust seasonings to taste. Add margarine and cooked Matzo Balls. *Continued*

310 calories per serving, 31.2 g carbohydrates, 3.9 g fiber, 8 g protein, 18.3 g fat (2.1 g saturated fat), 106 mg cholesterol, 275 mg sodium, 364 mg potassium, 2 mg iron, 63 mg calcium, 118 mg phosphorus

### variation

Omit Matzo Balls and add 1 cup macaroni or tiny pasta to soup during last 15 minutes of cooking. One serving contains 179 calories, 27.5 g carbohydrates and 4.4 g fat.

## MATZO BALLS

Baking powder makes the matzo balls light as a cloud. Omit during Passover (or use Passover baking powder)!

Yield: About 16. Keeps 3 days in the refrigerator. Freezes well. Place on cookie sheet to freeze, then transfer to freezer bags. You can also freeze cooked matzo balls in soup.

| | |
|---|---|
| 4 eggs | ½ tsp salt |
| ½ cup oil | ½ tsp baking powder |
| 1 cup matzo meal | |

STEEL BLADE: Process all ingredients just until smooth, about 10 seconds. Place in refrigerator for 1 hour, or in freezer for 20 minutes, until thickened.

Shape into small balls, wetting your hands for easier handling. Drop matzo balls into boiling salted water in a large pot and cook, partially covered, for about 40 minutes.

109 calories each, 6.9 g carbohydrates, 0.3 g fiber, 2 g protein, 8.3 g fat (0.9 g saturated fat), 53 mg cholesterol, 106 mg sodium, 17 mg potassium, 0 mg iron, 15 mg calcium, 27 mg phosphorus

### chef's tip

Freeze uncooked matzo ball mixture in ice cube trays. When needed, drop frozen matzo balls in boiling water and cook, partially covered, for 35 to 40 minutes, then add to soup. Kids love them in different shapes!

### lighter variation

Use 2 eggs plus 4 egg whites. Reduce oil to ¼ cup. One matzo ball contains 73 calories and 4.2 g fat.

## CHICKEN MEATBALL SOUP

SOUP

Chicken soup is the ultimate comfort food. The whole family will love this nourishing soup!

| | |
|---|---|
| 3 lb (1.4 kg) chicken pieces | 3 or 4 stalks celery |
| 10 cups water (approximately) | 2 tsp salt (or to taste) |
| 1 large or 2 medium onions | ½ tsp pepper |
| 4 to 6 carrots | ½ cup fresh dill |

Yield: About 10 cups
soup. Keeps 3 days in
the refrigerator. Reheats
and/or freezes well.

CHICKEN MEATBALLS

| | |
|---|---|
| **1 small onion** | **1 egg** |
| **1 stalk celery** | **2 Tbsp water** |
| **1 medium carrot** | **3 Tbsp matzo meal** |
| **1 lb (500 g) lean minced chicken (or see Grind Your Own, page 36)** | **salt and pepper to taste** |
| | **¼ tsp dried basil** |

For soup: Trim and discard excess fat from chicken. Place in a large pot and add enough water to completely cover chicken by at least 1 inch. Bring to a boil over high heat. Use a slotted spoon to skim off the scum that rises to the surface of the soup. Add onion, carrots, celery, salt and pepper. Reduce heat and simmer, partially covered, for 1 hour. If desired, remove cooked chicken and vegetables. (See Chef's Tips below.) Meanwhile, prepare meatball mixture.

For meatballs: Process onion, celery and carrot on the STEEL BLADE until minced, about 10 seconds. Add remaining meatball ingredients. Process with several quick on/off pulses, just until mixed. Shape into small meatballs (approximately 30), wetting your hands for easier handling.

Drop meatballs into simmering soup. Add dill and simmer 30 minutes longer. Serve soup with fine noodles or Matzo Balls (page 88).

20 calories per cup of clear broth (without chicken or vegetables), 2 g carbohydrates, 0 g fiber, 1 g protein, 0.5 g fat (0 g saturated fat), 5 mg cholesterol, 570 mg sodium, 20 mg calcium

38 calories per meatball, 1.1 g carbohydrates, 0.1 g fiber, 4 g protein, 2.1 g fat (0.1 g saturated fat), 19 mg cholesterol, 15 mg sodium, 58 mg potassium, 0 mg iron, 6 mg calcium, 5 mg phosphorus

### chef's tips

- A stockpot with a pasta insert is excellent for cooking chicken soup as there's no need to strain out the chicken, bones and vegetables after cooking. Cook soup for 1 hour, then lift out pasta insert with its contents; transfer to a large container. Add meatballs to simmering soup and cook 30 minutes longer. Meanwhile, remove skin and bones from chicken pieces and discard. Cut chicken and vegetables into bite-sized pieces and add to soup.
- Use leftover cooked chicken in stir-fries, casseroles, salads, wraps, etc.

## SLOW COOKER CHICKEN SOUP

Yield: About 8 cups broth. Keeps 3 days in the refrigerator. Reheats and/or freezes well.

4 lb (1.8 kg) chicken bones (wings, carcasses, etc.)

1 large onion, halved

4 carrots, halved

3 stalks celery, halved

water (approximately 8 to 10 cups)

salt and pepper to taste

½ cup dill sprigs

Place chicken bones in a slow cooker insert. Add onion, carrots and celery. Cover with water just to the top of the bones and vegetables. (If you add too much water, it will dilute the flavor.) Add salt and pepper, cover and cook on Low for 8 hours. Add dill in the last half hour of cooking. Let cool.

Strain into a container and discard bones, vegetables and dill. Refrigerate overnight. Remove and discard hardened fat from soup.

20 calories per cup, 2 g carbohydrates, 1 g fiber, 1 g protein, 0.5 g fat (0 g saturated fat), 5 mg cholesterol, 570 mg sodium, 0 mg iron, 20 mg calcium, 30 mg phosphorus

## EASY LENTIL VEGETABLE SOUP

This soup is versatile and quick. Use whatever frozen vegetables you have on hand. Leftover cooked vegetables can be substituted for some or all of the frozen veggies.

Yield: 12 servings. Keeps 3 to 4 days in the refrigerator. Reheats and/or freezes well.

2 or 3 cloves garlic

2 medium onions, cut in chunks

2 stalks celery, cut in chunks

2 Tbsp olive oil

10 cups boiling water

1 Tbsp instant pareve chicken soup mix

2 cups bottled tomato sauce

1½ cups red lentils, rinsed and drained

5 to 6 cups frozen mixed vegetables (e.g., broccoli, cauliflower, peas, carrots)

salt and freshly ground black pepper to taste

1 tsp dried basil

1 to 2 Tbsp lemon juice

STEEL BLADE: Drop garlic through feed tube while machine is running; process until minced. Add onions and celery. Process with several quick on/off pulses, until coarsely chopped.

Heat oil in large soup pot. Sauté garlic, onions and celery on medium heat for 7 to 8 minutes, until golden. Add water, soup mix, tomato sauce and lentils. Bring to a boil. Simmer, partially covered, for 35 to 40 minutes. Add frozen vegetables and simmer 10 to 15 minutes longer, stirring occasionally. Add salt, pepper, basil and lemon juice. If too thick, thin with a little water.

Optional: Place a strainer over a large bowl or saucepan. Strain soup. Purée half the solids on the STEEL BLADE until smooth. Stir vegetables back into soup.

138 calories per serving, 20.7 g carbohydrates, 3.3 g fiber, 8 g protein, 2.5 g fat (0.4 g saturated fat), 0 mg cholesterol, 340 mg sodium, 186 mg potassium, 1 mg iron, 42 mg calcium, 20 mg phosphorus

# VEGETARIAN MINESTRONE

Yield: 12 servings. Keeps
3 to 4 days in the
refrigerator. Reheats
and/or freezes well.

3 medium onions

2 carrots

2 stalks celery

4 medium potatoes, peeled

¼ head cabbage (2 cups sliced)

2 medium zucchini (do not peel)

2 Tbsp olive or vegetable oil

2 cloves garlic

½ lb (250 g) fresh green beans,
trimmed and halved

1 can (28 oz/796 mL) tomatoes (or
2 lb/500 g ripe tomatoes)

8 cups water

3 Tbsp pareve instant beef or chicken
soup mix

salt and freshly ground black pepper
to taste

1 tsp dried oregano

½ tsp dried basil

2 cups dried pasta (e.g., shells,
macaroni)

grated Parmesan cheese, for garnish

Cut onions, carrots, celery and potatoes into chunks. Cut cabbage and zucchini
to fit feed tube.

STEEL BLADE: Process onions with 3 or 4 quick on/offs, until coarsely chopped.
Heat oil in large soup pot. Add onions and sauté on medium-high heat until
golden, about 5 minutes.

Process garlic until minced. Add carrots and process with on/off pulses until
coarsely chopped. Add to pot. Repeat with celery and potatoes.

SLICER: Slice cabbage and zucchini, using medium pressure. Add to soup pot
with green beans, tomatoes, water, soup mix, salt, pepper, oregano and basil. (Fresh
tomatoes should be puréed on STEEL BLADE before adding them to soup.)

Cover and simmer slowly for 2 to 2½ hours. Add pasta and cook about 10 minutes longer. Serve with a bowl of grated Parmesan cheese.

138 calories per serving, 20.7 g carbohydrates, 3.3 g fiber, 8 g protein, 2.5 g fat (0.4 g saturated fat), 0 mg
cholesterol, 340 mg sodium, 186 mg potassium, 1 mg iron, 42 mg calcium, 20 mg phosphorus

## variations

- If desired, add a 19 oz (540 mL) can of drained and rinsed lima or kidney
  beans 15 minutes before soup is completed.

### passover variation
Omit green beans, canned beans and pasta.

## QUICK POTATO SOUP

An excellent lunch
for the kids.

Yield: 4 to 6 servings.
Keeps 2 to 3 days in
the refrigerator. Reheat
gently; do not boil. If
freezing soup, add milk
after thawing it.

3 medium potatoes or 2 sweet
   potatoes, peeled
2 Tbsp fresh dill
1 medium onion
1 large or 2 medium carrots

1 stalk celery
3 cups boiling water
1 to 2 tsp salt (or to taste)
¼ tsp freshly ground black pepper
1½ cups milk (1% or 2%)

STEEL BLADE: Cut potatoes in chunks. Process with dill until minced, 8 to 10 seconds. Transfer to a 3-quart saucepan. Cut onion, carrot and celery in chunks. Process until minced. Add to potatoes along with boiling water, salt and pepper. Cover and simmer for 15 to 20 minutes, until vegetables are tender. Add milk and heat just to boiling.

167 calories per serving, 34.3 g carbohydrates, 3.4 g fiber, 6 g protein, 1.1 g fat (0.6 g saturated fat), 5 mg cholesterol, 658 mg sodium, 671 mg potassium, 1 mg iron, 141 mg calcium, 155 mg phosphorus

### variation

Prepare Quick Potato Soup as directed. Grate 4 oz (125 g) chilled low-fat Swiss or cheddar cheese, using medium pressure (about 1 cup grated). Stir into soup. Adjust seasonings to taste. If too thick, add more water or milk. Serve with crusty fresh rolls. May be frozen, but add cheese when reheating. One serving contains 217 calories, 14 g protein, 2.6 g fat and 414 mg calcium.

## PHONY MINESTRONE

When my kids were
young, they called
this "spaghetti
soup"! For a
vegetarian version,
omit chicken and
substitute vegetable
broth for water. To
reduce the sodium,
use salt-free tomato
paste and canned
tomatoes.

2 whole chicken breasts, bone in
   (remove and discard skin)
6 cups cold water
2 to 3 tsp salt
3 or 4 cloves garlic
1 large onion, cut in chunks
2 carrots, cut in chunks
2 stalks celery, cut in chunks
½ cup green split peas, rinsed
   and drained
¼ cup barley, rinsed and drained
1 can (5½ oz/156 mL) tomato paste
1 can (28 oz/796 mL) tomatoes,
   drained (reserve juice)

2 bay leaves
freshly ground black pepper to taste
½ tsp each dried basil and dried
   oregano
¼ tsp each dried rosemary and dried
   thyme
1 cup fresh green beans (optional)
2 additional carrots
1 cup canned baked beans
1 can (14 oz/398 mL) green peas,
   drained
1½ to 2 cups spaghetti, broken
   into 2-inch pieces

SOUPS, SAUCES
AND MARINADES

Yield: 12 hearty servings.
Keeps 3 days in the
refrigerator. Reheats
and/or freezes well.

Place chicken, cold water and salt in large soup pot. Bring to a boil. Skim.

STEEL BLADE: Drop garlic through feed tube while machine is running; process until minced. Add onion, 2 carrots and celery and process until fine. Add to soup. Add split peas, barley, tomato paste and reserved juice from canned tomatoes to soup.

Process drained tomatoes on STEEL BLADE until puréed, about 6 seconds. Add to soup. Add bay leaves, pepper, basil, oregano, rosemary and thyme. Cover and simmer for 2 hours, stirring occasionally.

SLICER: Cut green beans (if using) to fit crosswise in feed tube. Slice, using firm pressure. Slice additional 2 carrots, using firm pressure. Add all remaining ingredients to soup. Simmer about 25 minutes longer, stirring occasionally. Adjust seasonings.

Remove chicken from bones, cut into bite-sized pieces and return to soup to heat through. Discard chicken bones and bay leaves.

232 calories per serving, 33.7 g carbohydrates, 7.4 g fiber, 20 g protein, 2.3 g fat (0.6 g saturated fat), 34 mg cholesterol, 714 mg sodium, 615 mg potassium, 3 mg iron, 69 mg calcium, 212 mg phosphorus

## PENNY'S TOMATO BISQUE

I first ate this
wonderful soup at
a family gathering
in Vancouver.
Penny Sprackman
has lightened up
her recipe over
the years by using
skim milk instead
of heavy cream but
still adds ¼ lb butter.
I've reduced the fat
even further but the
final choice is yours!

| | |
|---|---|
| 2 medium onions (1 cup chopped) | 1 tsp dried marjoram or oregano |
| 2 stalks celery (1 cup chopped) | 1 bay leaf |
| 1 medium carrot (½ cup chopped) | 4 cups vegetable broth (low-sodium |
| 3 to 4 Tbsp butter or margarine | or regular) |
| ⅓ cup flour | 2 cups milk (skim or 1%) |
| 2 cans (28 oz/796 mL each) whole | ½ tsp sweet paprika |
| tomatoes (salt-free or regular) | ½ tsp curry powder |
| 2 tsp sugar | ¼ tsp pepper |
| 1 tsp dried basil | salt to taste |

Yield: 8 servings. Keeps
3 days in the refrigerator.
Reheat gently; do not
boil. If freezing, add milk
after defrosting.

Cut onions, celery and carrot in chunks.

STEEL BLADE: Process onions, celery and carrot with several quick on/offs, until coarsely chopped. Melt butter in a large saucepan on medium heat. Add chopped vegetables and sauté until tender, 6 to 8 minutes. Stir in flour and cook 2 minutes longer, stirring constantly.

Drain tomatoes. Chop on STEEL BLADE, using quick on/off pulses. Add tomatoes to saucepan along with sugar, basil, marjoram, bay leaf and vegetable broth. Bring to a boil. Reduce heat, cover and simmer for 30 minutes, stirring occasionally. Discard bay leaf. Purée soup in batches on STEEL BLADE. Add milk, paprika, curry powder and pepper; stir well. Add salt to taste. Serve hot or cold.

147 calories per serving, 22.4 g carbohydrates, 3.4 g fiber, 5 g protein, 4.8 g fat (2.8 g saturated fat), 13 mg cholesterol, 161 mg sodium, 600 mg potassium, 3 mg iron, 171 mg calcium, 126 mg phosphorus

SOUPS, SAUCES
AND MARINADES

# POTATO MUSHROOM SOUP

An old European recipe that was in the original edition of this cookbook.

2 onions, quartered

2 Tbsp butter or margarine

4 or 5 medium potatoes, peeled

2½ cups mushrooms

5 cups boiling water

1 tsp salt

freshly ground pepper to taste

Yield: 4 to 6 servings. Keeps 2 to 3 days in the refrigerator. Reheats and/or freezes well.

STEEL BLADE: Process onions with 3 or 4 quick on/offs, until coarsely chopped.

Melt butter or margarine in a heavy 3-quart sauce-pan. Sauté onions for 5 minutes on medium heat.

SLICER: Cut potatoes to fit feed tube. Slice, using medium pressure. (If you have a FRENCH FRY DISC, process with light pressure.) Use either blade for the mushrooms, applying medium pressure.

Add all ingredients to saucepan, cover and simmer for 20 to 25 minutes, until tender.

131 calories per serving, 18.4 g carbohydrates, 2.2 g fiber, 2 g protein, 6.0 g fat (3.7 g saturated fat), 15 mg cholesterol, 639 mg sodium, 389 mg potassium, 1 mg iron, 20 mg calcium, 63 mg phosphorus

# PARMENTIER SOUP

Yield: 6 servings. Keeps 3 days in the refrigerator. Reheats and/or freezes well.

¼ cup fresh parsley

2 large leeks (or a combination of leeks and onions, about 3 cups sliced)

2 Tbsp margarine or butter

3 Tbsp flour

6 cups water

4 medium potatoes, peeled and cut in chunks

salt and freshly ground black pepper to taste

2 cups milk (1% or 2%)

1 Tbsp additional butter (optional)

STEEL BLADE: Process parsley until minced. (Use mini-bowl and mini-blade if available.) Set aside.

SLICER: Wash leeks well. Cut to fit feed tube, discarding most of green part. Slice, using firm pressure.

Melt margarine or butter in heavy saucepan. Add leeks and/or onions, cover pan and cook for 5 minutes over low heat without browning. Blend in flour and cook for 1 minute more without browning. Add water gradually, blending with a whisk.

STEEL BLADE: Chop potatoes in 2 batches with on/off pulses, until coarsely chopped. Add potatoes, salt and pepper to saucepan; bring to a boil, cover and simmer for 30 to 35 minutes. Add milk and additional butter (if desired) and garnish with parsley. Adjust seasonings, if necessary.

192 calories per serving, 32.7 g carbohydrates, 2.6 g fiber, 6 g protein, 4.8 g fat (1.2 g saturated fat), 4 mg cholesterol, 88 mg sodium, 542 mg potassium, 1 mg iron, 129 mg calcium, 135 mg phosphorus

## variations

- **VICHYSSOISE:** Prepare as for Parmentier Soup, but strain vegetables through a sieve over another saucepan. Purée vegetables (in batches if necessary) on the STEEL BLADE. Return to cooking liquid. Stir in milk plus ½ cup heavy or light cream. Omit additional butter. Cover and refrigerate. Garnish with parsley to serve. One serving made with heavy cream contains 261 calories and 12.2 g fat.

### lighter variation
Substitute a 10 oz (300 g) package of frozen chopped broccoli or cauliflower (or 3 cups florets) for the potatoes. One serving contains 109 calories, 12.9 g carbohydrates and 2 g fiber.

# CARROT AND SWEET POTATO SOUP

This easy, nutritious soup is packed with beta-carotene. You can use a combination of carrots and squash for a tasty variation.

Yield: 10 servings. Delicious hot or cold. Keeps 3 days in the refrigerator. Reheats and/or freezes well.

2 cloves garlic
1 slice fresh ginger, peeled (about 1 Tbsp)
1 large onion, cut in chunks
1 or 2 stalks celery, cut in chunks
1 Tbsp olive oil
1½ lb (750 g) carrots, cut in chunks (4 cups)
2 medium sweet potatoes

1 medium potato
8 cups water or vegetable broth
2 tsp salt (or to taste)
freshly ground black pepper to taste
2 Tbsp fresh basil
2 Tbsp fresh dill
1 to 2 Tbsp lemon juice (or to taste)
1 to 2 Tbsp honey (or to taste)

STEEL BLADE: Drop garlic and ginger through feed tube while machine is running; process until minced. (Use mini-bowl and mini-blade if available.) Set aside. Process onion and celery with quick on/off pulses, until coarsely chopped.

Heat oil in large soup pot. Sauté onion and celery for 6 or 7 minutes, until tender, stirring occasionally. Add a little water if vegetables begin to stick.

Process carrots with quick on/off pulses, until coarsely chopped. Add to soup pot along with reserved garlic and ginger; cook 2 minutes longer. Coarsely chop potato and sweet potatoes. Add to soup pot along with water or broth, salt and pepper.

Bring to a boil, reduce heat and simmer, partially covered, about 30 minutes, until vegetables are tender. Process basil and dill until minced, about 10 seconds.

Because of the quantity, it may be easier to use an immersion blender and purée soup directly in the pot. (To purée soup in the processor, place a strainer over

*Continued*

a large bowl or saucepan. Strain soup. Purée solids on the STEEL BLADE until smooth, working in batches if necessary. Stir puréed vegetables into cooking liquid.) Add basil, dill, lemon juice and honey; season with salt and pepper to taste. Add additional water or broth if soup is too thick.

102 calories per serving, 20.9 g carbohydrates, 3.7 g fiber, 2 g protein, 1.7 g fat (0.2 g saturated fat), 0 mg cholesterol, 538 mg sodium, 483 mg potassium, 1 mg iron, 50 mg calcium, 57 mg phosphorus

### carrot soup

Eliminate sweet potatoes and use 2 lb (1 kg) carrots. If desired, eliminate dill and add 1 tsp ground cumin. For a calcium boost, add 1 cup of 1% milk or soy milk to puréed soup when reheating. Garnish with chopped chives, green onions or a drizzle of Pesto (page 105), if desired. One serving contains 89 calories, 16.9 g carbohydrates and 3.1 g fiber.

## ZUCCHINI AND TWO POTATO SOUP

This quick and easy soup is sure to become a family favorite!

Yield: 10 to 12 servings. Keeps 3 days in the refrigerator. Reheats and/or freezes well.

3 cloves garlic
2 medium onions, cut in chunks
1 stalk celery, cut in chunks
2 Tbsp oil or margarine
2 medium zucchini (about 3 cups grated)
2 medium sweet potatoes (about 4 cups grated)

2 potatoes (about 2 cups grated)
8 cups vegetable broth (low-sodium or regular)
1 to 2 tsp salt (or to taste)
freshly ground black pepper to taste
1 tsp dried basil
2 Tbsp minced fresh dill (or 1 tsp dried dill)

STEEL BLADE: Drop garlic through feed tube while machine is running; process until minced. Process onions and celery with several on/off pulses, until coarsely chopped. Heat oil or melt margarine in large soup pot. Add garlic, onions and celery. Sauté on medium-high heat until lightly browned, 7 or 8 minutes.

GRATER: Cut zucchini, sweet potatoes and potatoes to fit feed tube. Grate, using medium pressure. Add to soup pot along with remaining ingredients. Bring to a boil, reduce heat and simmer, partially covered, for 30 minutes. Adjust seasonings to taste.

117 calories per serving, 20 g carbohydrates, 2.9 g fiber, 2 g protein, 3 g fat (0.2 g saturated fat), 0 mg cholesterol, 364 mg sodium, 394 mg potassium, 1 mg iron, 45 mg calcium, 52 mg phosphorus

# ZUCCHINI NOODLE SOUP

This is one of my favorite soups.

Yield: 8 servings. Keeps 3 days in the refrigerator. Freezes well, but texture is better if you add milk after thawing soup.

¼ cup fresh parsley

2 medium onions, quartered

2 Tbsp butter or margarine

2 Tbsp flour

4 zucchini, unpeeled (about 1½ lb/750 g)

3 carrots

6 cups boiling water

6 tsp instant pareve chicken soup mix

salt and freshly ground black pepper to taste

½ tsp dried tarragon (optional)

1 cup fine egg noodles

2 cups milk, soy milk or water

STEEL BLADE: Process parsley until minced. Empty bowl. Process onions with 3 or 4 quick on/off pulses, until coarsely chopped. Melt butter or margarine in a heavy saucepan. Add onions and sauté for 7 or 8 minutes, until golden. Stir in flour and cook 1 to 2 minutes longer, stirring. Do not brown. Remove from heat.

GRATER: Cut zucchini and carrots to fit feed tube. Grate zucchini, using medium pressure. Grate carrots, using firm pressure. Add zucchini, carrots, water, soup mix, salt, pepper and tarragon (if using) to saucepan along with parsley. Cover and simmer for half an hour. Add noodles and cook 15 minutes longer, stirring occasionally.

Thin soup with milk or water. Adjust seasonings to taste.

109 calories per serving, 14.9 g carbohydrates, 2.1 g fiber, 4 g protein, 4 g fat (2.3 g saturated fat), 15 mg cholesterol, 348 mg sodium, 383 mg potassium, 1 mg iron, 106 mg calcium, 117 mg phosphorus

# BROCCOLI LENTIL SOUP

This nutritious, low-fat soup is a terrific way to sneak some fiber into your day!

Yield: 6 to 8 servings. Keeps 3 days in the refrigerator. Reheats and/or freezes well.

2 Tbsp fresh dill (or 1 tsp dried dill)

1 large or 2 medium onions, cut in chunks

1 Tbsp olive or canola oil

2 or 3 carrots, cut in chunks

2 medium potatoes, cut in chunks

1 large bunch broccoli (3 to 4 cups, cut up)

6 cups vegetable or chicken broth

1 tsp soy sauce

½ cup red lentils, rinsed and drained

salt and freshly ground black pepper to taste

1 Tbsp fresh lemon juice (or to taste)

STEEL BLADE: If using fresh dill, process until minced, about 10 seconds. Remove from bowl and set aside.

Process onion with quick on/off pulses, until coarsely chopped. Heat oil in large saucepan and sauté onion on medium-high heat for 5 to 7 minutes, until golden.

Chop carrots and potatoes with quick on/off pulses; add to pan. Chop broccoli with quick on/off pulses. Add to pan along with broth, soy sauce and lentils. Bring

*Continued*

to a boil and reduce heat. Simmer, partially covered, for 25 to 30 minutes, stirring occasionally, until lentils soften. Season with salt and pepper.

Purée soup in batches until fairly smooth. If soup is too thick, thin with a little water or broth. Add dill and lemon juice; adjust seasonings to taste.

168 calories per serving, 28.9 g carbohydrates, 3.6 g fiber, 6 g protein, 3 g fat (0.4 g saturated fat), 0 mg cholesterol, 524 mg sodium, 261 mg potassium, 1 mg iron, 41 mg calcium, 36 mg phosphorus

## HERBED CAULIFLOWER OR BROCCOLI SOUP

My friend Shelly Glass modified my recipe from *MicroWays*, making it dairy-free. He microwaves it on High in a 5-quart microwavable casserole; cooking time is the same. Try it with cauliflower—it tastes a lot like potato soup, but has fewer calories and carbs.

Yield: 6 servings (about 9 cups). Keeps 3 days in the refrigerator. Reheats and/or freezes well.

2 cloves garlic
2 medium onions, cut in chunks
1 to 2 Tbsp olive oil
2 medium carrots, cut in chunks (about 1 cup)
2 medium potatoes, peeled and cut in chunks (about 2 cups)
1 head cauliflower or 1 bunch broccoli, cut into florets (about 8 cups)

6 cups vegetable broth (or 6 cups water plus 2 Tbsp instant pareve chicken soup mix)
salt and pepper to taste
2 Tbsp fresh parsley
2 Tbsp fresh dill
2 Tbsp fresh basil

STEEL BLADE: Drop garlic through feed tube while machine is running; process until minced. Add onions and process with 3 or 4 quick on/offs, until coarsely chopped.

Heat oil in a large pot on medium-high heat. Add garlic and onions and sauté for 5 minutes, until golden. Add carrots, potatoes and cauliflower or broccoli to pot. Add broth; it should barely cover the vegetables. Season with salt and pepper.

Bring to a boil, reduce heat, cover partially and simmer 25 to 30 minutes, stirring occasionally.

Remove solids with a slotted spoon and process in batches on the STEEL BLADE together with parsley, dill and basil.

154 calories per serving, 28.1 g carbohydrates, 6.3 g fiber, 5 g protein, 3.1 g fat (0.4 g saturated fat), 0 mg cholesterol, 514 mg sodium, 688 mg potassium, 1 mg iron, 70 mg calcium, 99 mg phosphorus

# ROASTED SQUASH SOUP

All the cooking for this flavorful, fat-free soup takes place in your oven! It can also be made with a combination of butternut, hubbard and/or acorn squash.

Yield: 6 servings. Keeps 3 days in the refrigerator. Reheats and/or freezes well.

2½ to 3 lb (1.2 to 1.4 kg) butternut squash

4 or 5 cloves garlic

1 large onion (unpeeled)

2 large, firm apples, unpeeled (e.g., Cortland)

3 cups vegetable broth (low-sodium or regular)

1 cup skim milk or soy milk

1 tsp curry powder or ground cumin

½ tsp dried basil

¼ tsp chili powder

salt and freshly ground black pepper to taste

Preheat oven to 400°F.

Cut squash in half lengthwise and scoop out seeds. (It will be easier to cut if you microwave it first for 5 minutes on High.) Place cut side down on a sprayed foil-lined baking sheet. Wrap garlic cloves in foil. Rinse unpeeled onion and apples, pierce skin in several places with sharp knife and place on baking sheet along with garlic and squash. Roast for 45 minutes, until tender. Don't worry if apples burst open during cooking. Remove pan from oven. When cool enough to handle, discard skins from squash, onion and apples. Discard apple cores.

STEEL BLADE: Place squash, garlic, onion and apples in processor bowl. Process until smooth, about 25 to 30 seconds, scraping down sides of bowl as needed. You will have about 4 cups of purée. Transfer mixture to large saucepan or microwavable bowl; stir in broth and milk. Add remaining ingredients and heat until piping hot.

137 calories per serving, 32.7 g carbohydrates, 6.5 g fiber, 4 g protein, 0.4 g fat (0.1 g saturated fat), 1 mg cholesterol, 96 mg sodium, 637 mg potassium, 1 mg iron, 142 mg calcium, 105 mg phosphorus

# SWEET POTATO SQUASH SOUP

So delicious. Perfect for the whole family!

Yield: 8 servings. Keeps 3 days in the refrigerator. Reheats and/or freezes well.

2 cloves garlic

1 slice ginger (about 1 Tbsp)

1 large or 2 medium onions, cut in chunks

4 tsp olive or canola oil

4 large sweet potatoes, peeled and cut in chunks (about 8 cups)

2 medium carrots, cut in chunks (or 1 cup baby carrots)

4 cups butternut squash or frozen squash cubes (see Chef's Tip, page 100)

6 cups water

2 tsp salt

¼ tsp pepper

2 Tbsp fresh dill

2 Tbsp fresh basil

2 Tbsp brown sugar (or to taste)

STEEL BLADE: Drop garlic and ginger through feed tube while machine is running. Process until minced. Add onion to processor bowl and process with 3 or 4 quick on/offs, until coarsely chopped. Heat oil in a large pot on medium heat. Add garlic, ginger and onion and sauté 5 to 7 minutes, until tender.

Add sweet potatoes, carrots, squash, water, salt and pepper. Bring to a boil. Reduce heat, cover partially and simmer for 30 to 35 minutes, stirring occasionally.

Remove solids with a slotted spoon and process in batches on the STEEL BLADE together with dill, basil and brown sugar until smooth, 30 to 45 seconds. If soup is too thick, thin it by adding a little water.

182 calories per serving, 38.5 g carbohydrates, 6.4 g fiber, 3 g protein, 2.5 g fat (0.4 g saturated fat), 0 mg cholesterol, 672 mg sodium, 687 mg potassium, 1 mg iron, 83 mg calcium, 91 mg phosphorus

### baby's dinner

Omit salt and sugar from soup (you can add it to the remaining soup later). Purée 1 cup of vegetables from soup with 1 to 2 Tbsp cooking liquid. Freeze in ice cube trays.

### chef's tip

To cut up butternut squash: Pierce in several places with a sharp knife. Microwave for 5 minutes on High; let cool slightly. Cut squash in 2 pieces at its neck, using a chef's knife or cleaver. Cut round bottom part in half and use a large spoon to scoop out stringy fiber and seeds. Peel squash with a vegetable peeler. Cut in chunks.

## CREAM OF PUMPKIN SOUP

A delicious way to use up leftover pumpkin purée from Pumpkin Pie (page 480). Try it with cooked squash.

Yield: 4 servings. Keeps 2 or 3 days in the refrigerator. May be frozen. Reheat on low heat; do not boil.

| | |
|---|---|
| 1 medium onion, halved | ¾ tsp salt |
| 1 to 2 Tbsp margarine or butter | freshly ground black pepper to taste |
| 2¼ cups boiling water | 1 Tbsp minced fresh dill (or ½ tsp dried |
| 2 cups canned or fresh pumpkin | dill) |
| purée (see facing page) | 1¼ cups milk or soy milk |
| 2 tsp instant pareve chicken soup mix | 2 tsp additional margarine or butter |

STEEL BLADE: Process onion with 3 or 4 quick on/off pulses, until coarsely chopped. Melt margarine or butter in a saucepan and sauté onion for 3 or 4 minutes on medium heat, until golden. Add water, pumpkin, soup mix, salt, pepper and dill. Cover partially and simmer for 15 to 20 minutes.

Process soup on STEEL BLADE about 30 seconds, until smooth. Return mixture to saucepan. Pour milk into processor and process for a few seconds to remove any purée clinging to bowl. Add milk to saucepan along with 2 tsp additional margarine or butter. Season to taste. Serve hot or cold.

129 calories per serving, 16.3 g carbohydrates, 3.9 g fiber, 4 g protein, 6 g fat (1.5 g saturated fat), 4 mg cholesterol, 707 mg sodium, 411 mg potassium, 2 mg iron, 134 mg calcium, 126 mg phosphorus

## pumpkin purée

Cut pumpkin in half with a sharp knife. Scoop out seeds and fibers. Save seeds for roasting (below). Place pumpkin halves, cut side down, on a sprayed foil-lined baking sheet. Cover with additional foil.

Bake in a preheated 350°F oven for 1 hour, until tender. Let cool. Scrape out the pulp and process on the STEEL BLADE about 30 to 45 seconds, until smooth. Makes 2 to 3 cups. May be frozen, but drain off any excess liquid when thawed. A 4 lb (2 kg) pumpkin yields about 2 cups purée.

25 calories per ½ cup, 6 g carbohydrates, 1.3 g fiber, 1 g protein, 0 g fat (0 g saturated fat), 0 mg cholesterol, 1 mg sodium, 282 mg potassium, 1 mg iron, 18 mg calcium, 37 mg phosphorus

## roasted pumpkin seeds

For a tasty snack, roast the pumpkin seeds in a preheated 200°F oven until dry and crisp, about 1 hour. If desired, sprinkle lightly with oil during roasting. Sprinkle with salt and cool on paper towels.

# VEGETABLE CHEESE CHOWDER

Yield: 6 generous servings. Keeps 2 to 3 days in the refrigerator. Reheat on low heat. May be frozen but texture may be affected.

| | |
|---|---|
| 2 large potatoes, peeled and cut in chunks | 2 Tbsp butter or margarine |
| 1 large onion, quartered | ¼ cup flour |
| 2 stalks celery, cut in chunks | dash salt |
| 6 medium tomatoes, quartered | ½ tsp dry mustard |
| 2½ cups boiling water | 1 tsp Worcestershire sauce |
| 1 to 2 tsp salt (or to taste) | 6 oz (180 g) chilled low-fat cheddar cheese (1½ cups grated) |
| ½ tsp freshly ground black pepper | 1 Tbsp chopped fresh parsley |
| ¼ tsp dried oregano | |
| 2 cups milk (skim or soy milk are fine) | |

STEEL BLADE: Process each vegetable separately, using 4 or 5 quick on/off pulses. Process tomatoes in 2 batches. Empty bowl each time. (Instead of the STEEL BLADE, the FRENCH FRY DISC or SLICER can be used to dice vegetables; see

*Continued*

"Cheater Chop" technique on page 15. Use very light pressure with the pusher. The smaller you wish to dice the vegetables, the smaller the chunks should be.)

Place all vegetables in large saucepan with boiling water, salt, ¼ tsp of pepper and oregano. Bring to a boil, cover and simmer for 15 to 20 minutes, until vegetables are tender.

In a 4-cup glass measuring cup, microwave milk on High for 3½ to 4 minutes, until steaming hot.

Process butter or margarine with flour, salt, mustard and ¼ tsp pepper on the STEEL BLADE for 5 or 6 seconds. Pour hot milk and Worcestershire sauce through feed tube while machine is running. Process until blended. Pour sauce mixture back into measuring cup and microwave 1 to 2 minutes on High, stirring once or twice, until thickened and bubbling.

GRATER: Grate cheese, using medium pressure. Add to sauce and stir until melted. Add to vegetables along with parsley. Bring to a boil, then serve.

252 calories per serving, 36.5 g carbohydrates, 3.4 g fiber, 14 g protein, 6.3 g fat (3.8 g saturated fat), 18 mg cholesterol, 715 mg sodium, 833 mg potassium, 2 mg iron, 260 mg calcium, 312 mg phosphorus

## MANHATTAN FISH CHOWDER

Serve this with crusty rolls as a light "meal-in-one."

Yield: 8 hearty servings. Reheat on low but do not boil. Keeps 2 to 3 days in the refrigerator. Do not freeze.

| | |
|---|---|
| 1 clove garlic | ¼ cup ketchup |
| 2 medium onions, cut in chunks | 1½ lb (750 g) sole fillets, cut in large |
| 1 green bell pepper, cut in chunks | chunks |
| 2 stalks celery, cut in chunks | 6 cups water |
| 1 cup mushrooms | salt to taste |
| 2 Tbsp olive or canola oil | ¼ tsp freshly ground black pepper |
| 3 carrots | 1 bay leaf, crumbled |
| 3 medium potatoes | ½ tsp dried thyme |
| 1 can (19 oz/540 mL) tomatoes | |

STEEL BLADE: Drop garlic through feed tube while machine is running; process until minced. Process onions, green pepper and celery with quick on/offs, until coarsely chopped.

SLICER: Slice mushrooms, using medium pressure.

Heat oil in a large soup pot over medium heat and sauté onions, pepper, celery and mushrooms for about 10 minutes, stirring occasionally. Cut carrots and potatoes to fit feed tube. Slice, using fairly firm pressure. Add with remaining ingredients to soup pot and bring to a boil. Reduce heat to simmer and cook, covered, about 30 minutes, or until vegetables are tender.

204 calories per serving, 24.1 g carbohydrates, 3.5 g fiber, 17 g protein, 4.8 g fat (0.8 g saturated fat), 40 mg cholesterol, 275 mg sodium, 862 mg potassium, 2 mg iron, 66 mg calcium, 255 mg phosphorus

# ONION SOUP AU GRATIN

Place soup bowls on a baking sheet lined with foil to catch any drips.

Yield: 8 servings. Soup keeps 3 days in the refrigerator. Reheats and/or freezes well. Shortly before serving, top soup with bread slices, sprinkle with cheese and bake.

6 medium onions, halved

3 Tbsp oil or margarine

½ tsp sugar

2 Tbsp flour

8 cups hot broth (e.g., low-sodium vegetable broth or onion soup mix)

½ cup red wine or sherry

1 bay leaf

¼ tsp dried basil

¼ tsp nutmeg

salt and freshly ground black pepper to taste

eight 1-inch slices French bread

6 oz (180 g) chilled low-fat mozzarella cheese

6 oz (180 g) chilled low-fat Swiss cheese

¼ cup grated Parmesan cheese

SLICER: Slice onions, using medium pressure. Heat oil in heavy 4-quart saucepan. Stir in onions. Cook, uncovered, on low heat for 25 to 30 minutes, until deep golden brown, stirring often.

Stir in sugar and flour and cook for 2 minutes. Add broth, wine, bay leaf, basil, nutmeg, salt and pepper. Cover and simmer 20 to 25 minutes. (Soup may be prepared to this point and refrigerated or frozen. Discard bay leaf.)

Place bread slices in preheated 325°F oven for about half an hour to dry. Remove bread. Increase oven temperature to 350°F.

GRATER: Grate mozzarella and Swiss cheeses, using medium pressure. You should have about 3 cups. Mix lightly.

Ladle soup into individual ovenproof bowls. Top each bowl with a bread slice. Sprinkle with combined mozzarella and Swiss cheeses. Top with a little Parmesan cheese. Bake at 350°F about 20 minutes, then broil lightly to brown cheeses. (If soup is already hot when you ladle it into bowls, eliminate baking and just broil for 4 to 5 minutes, until bubbly and golden.)

417 calories per serving, 50.1 g carbohydrates, 3.1 g fiber, 21 g protein, 12.7 g fat (4.6 g saturated fat), 21 mg cholesterol, 765 mg sodium, 268 mg potassium, 3 mg iron, 453 mg calcium, 362 mg phosphorus

# BÉCHAMEL (WHITE) SAUCE

This technique makes a creamy, lump-free sauce.

2 Tbsp butter or margarine

2 Tbsp flour

¼ tsp salt

dash white pepper

1 cup milk (2%, 1% or skim)

STEEL BLADE: Process butter or margarine with flour, salt and pepper until blended, about 5 seconds.

Microwave milk in a 2-cup glass measuring cup on High for 1½ to 2 minutes, until steaming hot. Pour hot milk through feed tube while machine is running.

*Continued*

Yield: 1 cup (4 servings).
Reheat on low heat.
Keeps 2 days in the
refrigerator.
May be frozen.

Process until smooth. Pour sauce back into measuring cup and microwave on High for 30 to 60 seconds, until bubbly and thickened. Stir once or twice.

91 calories per serving, 6.1 g carbohydrates, 0.1 g fiber, 3 g protein, 6.4 g fat (4 g saturated fat), 18 mg cholesterol, 213 mg sodium, 98 mg potassium, 0 mg iron, 75 mg calcium, 64 mg phosphorus

## note

Recipe may be doubled. For a thinner sauce, use 1 Tbsp butter and 1 Tbsp flour for each cup of milk. For a thicker sauce, use 3 Tbsp butter and 3 Tbsp flour for each cup of milk.

## variations

- Substitute chicken stock for milk and use nondairy (pareve) margarine instead of butter.

- CHEESE SAUCE: Stir 1 cup grated cheddar or Swiss cheese (low-fat or regular), ¼ tsp dry mustard and ½ tsp Worcestershire sauce into hot Béchamel Sauce. Stir until cheese melts. One serving (¼ cup) contains 141 calories, 6.8 g carbohydrates and 8.4 g fat.

## gluten-free/passover variation

- Substitute ½ Tbsp potato starch for each Tbsp of flour.

# MUSHROOM SAUCE

Yield: About 1¾ cups
(6 servings). Reheat on
low heat. Keeps 2 days in
the refrigerator.
May be frozen.

| | |
|---|---|
| 1 cup mushrooms | ¾ tsp salt |
| 3 Tbsp butter or margarine | ¼ tsp white pepper |
| 3 Tbsp flour | dash nutmeg (optional) |
| 1½ cups hot milk (2%, 1% or skim), or soy milk or broth | |

SLICER: Slice mushrooms, using light pressure. Melt 1 Tbsp of the butter or margarine in a nonstick skillet. Sauté mushrooms until golden. Set aside.

STEEL BLADE: Process remaining 2 Tbsp butter with flour until blended, about 5 seconds. Pour hot liquid through feed tube while machine is running. Add seasonings. Process until smooth.

Transfer sauce to 4-cup glass measuring cup. Microwave on High for 1 to 2 minutes, until bubbly and thick, stirring once or twice. Stir in mushrooms.

93 calories per serving, 6.5 g carbohydrates, 0.3 g fiber, 3 g protein, 6.4 g fat (4 g saturated fat), 18 mg cholesterol, 359 mg sodium, 128 mg potassium, 0 mg iron, 76 mg calcium, 72 mg phosphorus

# EASY BARBECUE SAUCE

Use for spare ribs, London broil, chicken or tofu.

1 clove garlic
½ cup brown sugar, packed

½ cup bottled barbecue sauce or ketchup
½ cup applesauce

Yield: About 1½ cups. Keeps up to 10 days in the refrigerator. Freezes well.

STEEL BLADE: Drop garlic through feed tube while machine is running; process until minced, about 8 seconds. Scrape down sides of bowl. Add remaining ingredients and process just until blended.

27 calories per Tbsp, 6.9 g carbohydrates, 0.1 g fiber, 0 g protein, 0 g fat (0 g saturated fat), 0 mg cholesterol, 64 mg sodium, 22 mg potassium, 0 mg iron, 5 mg calcium, 2 mg phosphorus

# QUICK TOMATO SAUCE

A delicious substitute for bottled spaghetti sauce.

3 or 4 cloves garlic
1 large onion, cut in chunks
1 can (28 oz/796 mL) tomatoes (with juice)
1 can (5½ oz/156 mL) tomato paste
¼ tsp each salt, dried basil, dried oregano and sugar

freshly ground black pepper to taste
¼ tsp cayenne pepper or red pepper flakes
3 to 4 Tbsp red wine or water
1 Tbsp olive oil

Yield: About 4 cups. Keeps about a week in the refrigerator. Reheats and/or freezes well.

STEEL BLADE: Add garlic through feed tube while machine is running; process until minced. Add onion and process until minced, 6 to 8 seconds.

Combine all ingredients in covered microwave casserole or large saucepan. To microwave, cook, covered, on High for 12 to 15 minutes, stirring once or twice. To cook conventionally, bring to a boil, reduce heat and simmer, covered, for 25 to 30 minutes, stirring occasionally. Adjust seasonings to taste.

50 calories per ½ cup, 7.9 g carbohydrates, 1.7 g fiber, 2 g protein, 1.6 g fat (0.2 g saturated fat), 0 mg cholesterol, 185 mg sodium, 337 mg potassium, 1 mg iron, 36 mg calcium, 35 mg phosphorus

# PESTO

When basil is expensive, use a combination of basil and fresh spinach leaves. Pesto is

4 cloves garlic
1 cup fresh basil, tightly packed
¼ cup fresh parsley
¼ cup pine nuts or almonds
½ tsp salt (or to taste)

freshly ground black pepper to taste
½ cup olive oil (preferably extra-virgin)
⅓ to ½ cup grated Parmesan cheese

perfect with pasta,
fish or in salad
dressings, soups
and casseroles.

STEEL BLADE: Drop garlic through feed tube while machine is running; process until minced. Add basil, parsley, nuts, salt and pepper. Process until finely minced, about 20 seconds. Drizzle oil through feed tube while machine is running and process until blended. Blend in Parmesan cheese.

Transfer pesto to a bowl, cover and refrigerate. If you cover it with a thin layer of olive oil, it will keep about a week to 10 days in the refrigerator.

Yield: About 1 cup.
Keeps 4 or 5 days in
the refrigerator or
freezes well.

85 calories per Tbsp, 0.7 g carbohydrates, 0.2 g fiber, 1 g protein, 8.8 g fat (1.3 g saturated fat), 1 mg cholesterol, 97 mg sodium, 30 mg potassium, 0 mg iron, 26 mg calcium, 27 mg phosphorus

### lighter variation

Use ¼ cup olive oil and ¼ cup tomato juice or vegetable broth. Reduce cheese to 3 Tbsp and nuts to 2 Tbsp. One Tbsp contains 49 calories and 4.9 g fat.

## VEGETARIAN SPAGHETTI SAUCE

This nutritious sauce
is great on pasta or
spaghetti squash.

Yield: 6 to 8 servings.
Keeps 3 or 4 days in the
refrigerator. Freezes well.

2 or 3 cloves garlic

2 medium onions, quartered

1 green or red bell pepper,
    cut in chunks

2 Tbsp olive oil

1 eggplant, peeled
    (about 1¼ lb/625 g)

1 medium zucchini, peeled ¼ tsp
    each dried oregano, dried basil
    and chili powder

1 cup mushrooms

1 can (19 oz/540 mL) tomatoes

2 cans (5½ oz/156 mL each)
    tomato paste

¼ cup dry red wine (optional)

1 bay leaf (optional)

salt and freshly ground black
    pepper to taste

STEEL BLADE: Drop garlic through feed tube while machine is running; process until minced. Add onions and bell pepper. Process with 3 or 4 quick on/off pulses, until coarsely chopped. Heat oil in a large pot. Sauté garlic, onions and pepper for 5 minutes on medium heat, until tender.

SLICER: Slice mushrooms, using light pressure. Add to pan and cook 2 minutes longer.

GRATER: Cut eggplant to fit feed tube. Grate, using medium pressure. Repeat with zucchini. Add to pan and cook 5 minutes longer. Stir in remaining ingredients, cover and simmer about 45 minutes, stirring occasionally. Taste and adjust seasonings.

159 calories per serving, 27.6 g carbohydrates, 6.7 g fiber, 5 g protein, 5.4 g fat (0.8 g saturated fat), 0 mg cholesterol, 184 mg sodium, 987 mg potassium, 3 mg iron, 68 mg calcium, 107 mg phosphorus

# RINA'S RED PEPPER SAUCE

This delicious sauce comes from the personal recipe collection of Rina Perry of Israel. Rina can't imagine life without her food processor! Serve with pasta, meat patties or your favorite fish.

Yield: About 3 cups. Keeps 2 weeks in the refrigerator. Freezes well.

**8 large red bell peppers**

**3 cloves garlic**

**½ cup extra-virgin olive oil**

**¼ cup white vinegar**

**1 tsp salt**

**2 tsp sugar**

Broil or grill peppers on all sides until skin is blackened and blistered. Transfer them to a bowl, cover and let cool. Remove the blackened skin. Cut peppers in half; discard the core and seeds.

STEEL BLADE: Drop garlic through feed tube while machine is running; process until minced. Add remaining ingredients and process until you get a smooth sauce, scraping down sides of bowl as necessary. Adjust seasonings to taste. Pour sauce into a glass container, seal the top with additional olive oil and store tightly covered in the refrigerator.

Sauce will keep 2 weeks in the refrigerator. If you have extra sauce left and want to keep it longer, bring it to a boil for a few minutes, let cool, then transfer to a clean glass container. Seal again with olive oil. The oil will harden and form a seal on top of the sauce.

16 calories per Tbsp, 1 g carbohydrates, 0.2 g fiber, 0 g protein, 1.3 g fat (0.2 g saturated fat), 0 mg cholesterol, 26 mg sodium, 22 mg potassium, 0 mg iron, 1 mg calcium, 3 mg phosphorus

# MANGO SALSA

This is wonderful with grilled sea bass or boneless chicken breasts. Try fresh pineapple or papaya instead of mango. Ginger adds a wonderful kick!

Yield: About 1½ cups. Keeps 1 or 2 days in the refrigerator. Do not freeze.

**1 large ripe mango, peeled (about 1 cup)**

**1 slice fresh ginger, peeled (about 1 Tbsp)**

**¼ cup fresh coriander or parsley**

**½ small red onion (or 2 green onions)**

**½ red bell pepper, cut in chunks**

**1 jalapeño pepper, cored and seeded**

**2 Tbsp fresh basil**

**¼ cup fresh lime juice (juice of 2 limes)**

**2 tsp extra-virgin olive oil**

**1 tsp honey**

**salt and freshly ground black pepper to taste**

Using a sharp knife, cut down 1 side of the flesh of the mango, feeling for the pit with your knife. Repeat on the other side. You will have 2 large pieces. Cut in chunks.

STEEL BLADE: Process ginger with coriander or parsley until minced. Add mango, onion and peppers. Process with quick on/off pulses, until coarsely chopped. Add remaining ingredients and process with 2 or 3 quick on/offs to combine. May be prepared up to a day in advance and refrigerated. Bring to room temperature before serving.

11 calories per Tbsp, 2 g carbohydrates, 0.2 g fiber, 0 g protein, 0.4 g fat (0.1 g saturated fat), 0 mg cholesterol, 1 mg sodium, 25 mg potassium, 0 mg iron, 2 mg calcium, 3 mg phosphorus

# TAHINI DRESSING

Yield: About ¾ cup.
Keeps about 2 weeks in
the refrigerator.
Do not freeze.

1 clove garlic

½ cup tahini (sesame paste)

⅓ cup water

2 Tbsp lemon juice

½ tsp salt (or to taste)

freshly ground black pepper to taste

dash ground cumin (optional)

STEEL BLADE: Drop garlic through feed tube while machine is running; process until minced. Add remaining ingredients and process until smooth and creamy, 10 to 15 seconds.

46 calories per Tbsp, 1.9 g carbohydrates, 0.4 g fiber, 1 g protein, 4.1 g fat (0.6 g saturated fat), 0 mg cholesterol, 77 mg sodium, 38 mg potassium, 0 mg iron, 12 mg calcium, 61 mg phosphorus

# CHINESE SWEET AND SOUR SAUCE

Fabulous with fish
or chicken.

Yield: 3 cups. Keeps
about 1 month in the
refrigerator.
Freezes well.

½ cup ketchup

½ cup vinegar

¾ cup cold water

2 Tbsp lemon juice

1¼ cups granulated sugar

½ cup brown sugar, lightly packed

3 Tbsp cornstarch dissolved in ¼ cup cold water

Combine all ingredients except cornstarch mixture in an 8-cup microwavable bowl and stir well. Microwave uncovered on High for 6 to 7 minutes, until boiling, stirring at half time. Stir cornstarch mixture into sauce. Microwave on High for 2 minutes longer, until bubbling and thickened.

27 calories per Tbsp, 7 g carbohydrates, 0 g fiber, 0 g protein, 0 g fat (0 g saturated fat), 0 mg cholesterol, 23 mg sodium, 11 mg potassium, 0 mg iron, 2 mg calcium, 1 mg phosphorus

# TERIYAKI MARINADE

This is a marvelous marinade for beef, chicken, turkey, tofu or fish. It also makes an excellent sauce (see page 109).

Yield: About ¾ cup.
Keeps 7 to 10 days in the
refrigerator. Freezes well.

1 or 2 slices fresh ginger, peeled (about 1 to 2 Tbsp)

3 cloves garlic

¼ cup soy sauce (low-sodium or regular)

¼ cup honey, maple syrup or brown sugar

¼ cup white wine or water

2 tsp toasted sesame oil (optional)

STEEL BLADE: Drop ginger and garlic through feed tube while machine is running; process until minced. Add remaining ingredients and process for 8 to 10 seconds to blend.

Marinate meat, poultry or tofu for 1 to 2 hours or up to 24 hours in the refrigerator. Fish only needs to be marinated for 1 to 2 hours.

24 calories per Tbsp, 5.4 g carbohydrates, 0.1 g fiber, 0 g protein, 0 g fat (0 g saturated fat), 0 mg cholesterol, 144 mg sodium, 15 mg potassium, 0 mg iron, 2 mg calcium, 6 mg phosphorus

### teriyaki sauce

Prepare marinade as directed; heat until boiling. Dissolve 1 Tbsp cornstarch in 2 Tbsp cold water or orange juice. Stir into boiling marinade and cook, stirring constantly, until smooth and thickened, about 2 minutes. Serve as a sauce over fish, poultry, meat or tofu. One Tbsp contains 22 calories and 5 g carbohydrates.

## CANTONESE MARINADE

Delicious for spare ribs, chicken, London Broil or tofu.

2 cloves garlic
1 slice fresh ginger, peeled (or 1 tsp ground ginger)
¼ cup soy sauce

¼ cup honey
¼ cup apricot jam
¾ cup pineapple or orange juice

Yield: 1½ cups. Keeps 7 to 10 days in the refrigerator.

STEEL BLADE: Drop garlic and fresh ginger through feed tube while machine is running; process until minced. Add remaining ingredients and process a few seconds longer to blend.

21 calories per Tbsp, 5.3 g carbohydrates, 0 g fiber, 0 g protein, 0 g fat (0 g saturated fat), 0 mg cholesterol, 129 mg sodium, 19 mg potassium, 0 mg iron, 2 mg calcium, 3 mg phosphorus

## CHINESE MARINADE

Excellent on chicken, London broil, spare ribs or tofu.

2 cloves garlic
4 green onions
2 Tbsp soy sauce
2 Tbsp dry sherry or wine
2 Tbsp honey or corn syrup

1 Tbsp ketchup
1 Tbsp chili sauce
dash salt and freshly ground black pepper

Yield: Enough marinade for 3 lb meat or chicken. Keeps 7 to 10 days in the refrigerator.

STEEL BLADE: Drop garlic and green onions through feed tube while machine is running; process until minced. Scrape down sides of bowl. Add remaining ingredients and process for a few seconds to blend.

22 calories per Tbsp, 5.4 g carbohydrates, 0.2 g fiber, 0 g protein, 0 g fat (0 g saturated fat), 0 mg cholesterol, 202 mg sodium, 26 mg potassium, 0 mg iron, 5 mg calcium, 6 mg phosphorus

## HONEY GARLIC SPARERIB SAUCE

This is delicious as a sauce or marinade for spare ribs, chicken, tofu or brisket.

1 or 2 cloves garlic
½ small onion
¾ cup honey
2 Tbsp soy sauce
1 Tbsp ketchup or chili sauce

1 Tbsp lemon juice or vinegar
½ tsp salt
¼ tsp each dry mustard, ground ginger, chili powder and freshly ground black pepper

Yield: 1 cup. Recipe may be doubled. Keeps in the refrigerator for about 1 month. Freezes well.

STEEL BLADE: Drop garlic through feed tube while machine is running; process until minced. Add onion and process until minced. Scrape down sides of bowl. Add remaining ingredients and process for 3 or 4 seconds to blend.

Transfer to 2-cup glass measuring cup and microwave on High for 2 minutes, or until bubbling. Stir well. Microwave 1 minute longer.

35 calories per Tbsp, 9.1 g carbohydrates, 0.1 g fiber, 0 g protein, 0 g fat (0 g saturated fat), 0 mg cholesterol, 132 mg sodium, 15 mg potassium, 0 mg iron, 2 mg calcium, 3 mg phosphorus

## PEANUT BUTTER SAUCE

Wonderful with chicken, tofu, pasta or in a stir-fry.

3 or 4 cloves garlic
2 slices fresh ginger, peeled (about 2 Tbsp)
¼ cup soy sauce (low-sodium or regular)
¼ cup peanut butter

2 Tbsp honey
2 Tbsp apricot jam
1 Tbsp lemon juice or rice vinegar
1 to 2 tsp toasted sesame oil
dash cayenne pepper or several drops hot sauce

Yield: About ¾ cup. Keeps in the refrigerator for up to 1 month. If too thick, thin with a little water. Reheat gently; do not boil, as sauce may separate. Do not freeze.

STEEL BLADE: Drop garlic and ginger through feed tube while machine is running; process until minced. Add remaining ingredients and process until blended, about 12 to 15 seconds. Scrape down sides of bowl as needed.

42 calories per Tbsp, 5.2 g carbohydrates, 0.3 g fiber, 1 g protein, 2.2 g fat (0.4 g saturated fat), 0 mg cholesterol, 147 mg sodium, 39 mg potassium, 0 mg iron, 5 mg calcium, 18 mg phosphorus

## HORSERADISH

The fumes from fresh horseradish are very intense, so be careful. Serve with Gefilte Fish (page 118),

½ lb (250 g) fresh horseradish root, peeled and cut in chunks
1 can (14 oz/398 mL) whole beets, drained
2 to 3 Tbsp beet juice

1 Tbsp sugar (or to taste)
¼ tsp salt
dash freshly ground black pepper
½ cup white vinegar (approximately)

boiled short ribs
or roast beef.

Yield: About 3 cups.
Keeps in the refrigerator
for several months.
Freezes well but it may
lose some of its strength.

STEEL BLADE: Process horseradish until finely minced, about 30 seconds. Add beets through feed tube and process until fine. (Don't remove processor cover just yet; the fumes will be very strong.) Add remaining ingredients and process until well blended, about 30 seconds.

Store in refrigerator in tightly closed jars. This will keep for months, but will lose strength gradually.

9 calories per Tbsp, 1.9 g carbohydrates, 0.6 g fiber, 0 g protein, 0.1 g fat (0 g saturated fat), 0 mg cholesterol, 27 mg sodium, 36 mg potassium, 0 mg iron, 7 mg calcium, 5 mg phosphorus

### variation

For white horseradish, omit beets and beet juice.

# MAYONNAISE

My method of
making mayonnaise
follows food safety
recommendations
of heating the yolks.
If you are using
pasteurized eggs
or are not worried
about getting
food poisoning
from raw eggs,
make Traditional
Mayonnaise (below).

Yield: About 1 cup.
Keeps about 1 week.
Do not freeze.

**2 egg yolks (or 1 egg)**
**2 Tbsp fresh or bottled lemon juice**
**2 Tbsp water**
**½ tsp sugar**
**2 tsp Dijon mustard or 1 tsp dry mustard**

**¼ tsp salt (or to taste)**
**dash white pepper**
**1 cup canola oil**

Combine egg yolks, lemon juice, water and sugar in a small saucepan. Heat on very low heat, constantly stirring and scraping bottom of pan with rubber spatula. When mixture begins to thicken, *immediately* remove pan from heat, stirring constantly. Place pan in cold water to stop the cooking. Transfer mixture to processor and cool for 5 minutes.

STEEL BLADE: Add mustard, salt and pepper to egg yolk mixture. Process for 5 seconds. While machine is running, add oil in a very slow, steady stream through feed tube; process until thickened. Total time is approximately 45 seconds. Transfer to a clean container and refrigerate immediately.

107 calories per Tbsp, 0.3 g carbohydrates, 0 g fiber, 0 g protein, 11.8 g fat (1 g saturated fat), 22 mg cholesterol, 36 mg sodium, 4 mg potassium, 0 mg iron, 3 mg calcium, 8 mg phosphorus

### variations

• TRADITIONAL MAYONNAISE: Combine egg yolks, lemon juice, mustard, salt and pepper in processor bowl. (Omit water and sugar.) Process for 5 seconds. While machine is running, add oil in a very slow, steady stream through the feed tube; process until thickened. (There's a tiny hole specifically for this purpose in the feed tube on many processors.) *Continued*

- ROASTED RED PEPPER MAYONNAISE: Process 1 roasted red pepper (see page 53) until minced. Add 1 cup mayonnaise (homemade or store-bought) and process a few seconds longer, until blended.

- TARTAR SAUCE: Process 2 small pickles, 2 green onions and a few sprigs of parsley until minced. Add 1 cup mayonnaise (homemade or store-bought) and process a few seconds longer, until blended. Delicious with fish.

## TOFU MAYONNAISE

This is a wonderful substitute for mayonnaise in salad dressings, dips and spreads. Tofu contains no cholesterol and is dairy-free.

1 or 2 cloves garlic
1 pkg (10 oz/300 g) silken tofu, drained (1% tofu is ideal)
1 tsp Dijon mustard

2 tsp lemon juice or cider vinegar
½ tsp salt
2 to 3 Tbsp olive or canola oil

STEEL BLADE: Drop garlic through feed tube while machine is running; process until minced. Add tofu and process for 2 to 3 minutes, until very smooth, scraping down sides of bowl as necessary.

Blend in mustard, lemon juice or vinegar and salt. Slowly drizzle oil through feed tube while machine is running; process until blended. Adjust seasonings to taste.

Yield: About ¾ cup. Store in a tightly covered container in the refrigerator for about 1 week. Do not freeze.

18 calories per Tbsp, 0.3 g carbohydrates, 0 g fiber, 1 g protein, 1.5 g fat (0.2 g saturated fat), 0 mg cholesterol, 58 mg sodium, 1 mg potassium, 0 mg iron, 9 mg calcium, 0 mg phosphorus

### variation

Add ¼ cup parsley, 2 Tbsp fresh basil and ¼ cup green onions. Process until blended. If desired, add a spoonful or 2 of mayonnaise. This makes a terrific topping for baked potatoes.

# FISH AND DAIRY DISHES
recite list

118 Gefilte Fish
119 Tricolor Gefilte Fish Mold
120 Pickled Salmon
120 Dishwasher Salmon
121 Baked Salmon with Mushroom Stuffing
122 Mushroom Stuffing
122 Baked Salmon with Mango Salsa
123 Balsamic Baked Fish with Onions and Mushrooms
123 Orange Teriyaki Grilled Salmon
124 Baked Halibut and Potato Casserole
125 Salsa Just for the Halibut!
125 Poached Fish
126 Easy Fish Bake
127 Oven-Fried Fish
128 Deep-Fry Beer Batter
128 Fish Fillets Amandine
129 Broiled Cheesy Fillets
129 Stuffed Fish Fillets au Gratin

130 Broccoli-Stuffed Fillets with Mushroom Sauce
131 Fish Italian Style
132 Sole Mornay
132 Fish Patties
133 Sweet and Sour Fish Patties
134 Salmon Patties
134 Salmon Burgers
135 Tuna Patties
135 Tuna Patties in Spanish Sauce
136 Tuna Strudel
137 Swiss Tuna Bake
137 Favorite Tuna Casserole
138 Tuna and Mushroom Lasagna
139 Luscious Vegetarian Lasagna
140 Tortilla Lasagna Florentine
141 Pasta Vegetable Medley
142 Penne with Roasted Tomatoes and Garlic au Gratin

| | |
|---|---|
| 143 | Buttermilk Noodle Kugel |
| 144 | Cookie's Hot Milk Cheese Kugel |
| 144 | Florentine Noodle Kugel |
| 145 | Pineapple Noodle Kugel |
| 145 | Almost Sour Cream! |
| 146 | Three-Cheese Sweet Kugel |
| 147 | Hot Cheese Cake |
| 148 | Cheddar Cheese Puff |
| 148 | Italian Cheese Puff |
| 149 | Bagel, Salmon and Broccoli Casserole |
| 149 | Spinach Cheese Phyllo Puff |
| 150 | Spinach Soufflé |
| 151 | Baked Frittata |
| 152 | Cheesy Broccoli Casserole |
| 153 | Broccoli Cheese Squares |
| 154 | Spinach Cheese Bake |
| 154 | Spinach Borekas |
| 155 | No-Dough Cheese Knishes |
| 156 | Cheese Knishes |
| 156 | Onion Cheese Quiche |
| 158 | Sour Cream Tuna Quiche |
| 158 | Pareve Vegetable Quiche |
| 159 | No-Crust Cheese and Spinach Pie |
| 159 | No-Crust Zucchini Quiche |
| 160 | Luncheon Puff |
| 161 | Easy Cottage Cheese Pancakes |
| 161 | Buttermilk Pancakes |
| 162 | Basic Crêpe Batter |
| 163 | Florentine Crêpes |
| 164 | Salmon Crêpes |
| 164 | Cheese Cannelloni (Crêpes Italiano) |
| 165 | Cheese Blintzes |
| 166 | Cheese Filling |
| 166 | Blintz Soufflé |
| 167 | Crazy Blintz Soufflé |
| 168 | Cheese Fondue |

- Calculate 1 lb (500 g) per serving when buying a whole fish. One pound of fillets serves 2 to 3.
- Cook fish within 24 hours of purchase for maximum flavor. Store in the coldest part of your refrigerator.
- Fish can be stored for about 1 month in the freezer section of your refrigerator, or up to 3 months in a deep freezer.
- Thaw fish in the refrigerator, not at room temperature. Calculate 6 hours per pound in the refrigerator. In the microwave, allow 4 to 6 minutes per pound on Defrost; a few ice crystals should remain. Place in cold water for a few minutes, until ice melts. Cook and serve within a day.
- COOKING TIMES: For fresh fish, allow 10 minutes per inch of thickness at 450°F; for frozen fish, allow 20 minutes per inch of thickness. Measure fish at the thickest point. If baked in sauce, increase cooking time by about 5 minutes per inch of thickness. Cook fish just until it flakes. When done, fish should be opaque and juices on surface will be white.
- Microwave fish (e.g., salmon, halibut) between wet lettuce leaves to stop it from popping during cooking. Calculate 4 minutes per pound on High as your microwave cooking time.
- Baking, steaming, poaching, broiling, grilling and microwaving are excellent low-fat cooking methods for fish.
- Thin fish fillets don't need to be turned when broiled. Cook about 3 inches from heat on 1 side only, just until cooked.
- Infants, young children, the elderly and those with weakened immune systems should avoid raw or undercooked eggs. Pasteurized liquid egg product can be substituted—¼ cup equals 1 egg. For more information on egg safety, proper storage, etc., check out www.aeb.org or www.fightbac.org.
- After boiling hard-cooked eggs, drain the hot water and place them under cold running water to stop the cooking process. Drain again, then vigorously shake the pot back and forth to crack the shells. Cover eggs with cold water and let stand for 2 or 3 minutes. Shells will slip off easily! If desired, discard some of the yolks.
- In the Jewish kitchen, cheese and dairy dishes such as blintzes and noodle kugels (puddings) are considered main dishes and not desserts!

Team them up with a big bowl of soup and fruit or vegetable salad.

- Dishes that contain dairy ingredients (e.g., cottage or cream cheese, sour cream, yogurt, butter, milk) are traditionally served in Jewish homes as part of a dairy meal. Although they can be served as either side or main dishes, they are in this chapter because of their dairy content (e.g., Cookie's Hot Milk Cheese Kugel, page 144). For side dishes that can be served with either meat or dairy meals, see the Vegetables and Side Dishes chapter (pages 222–263).
- See "Cheese" in the **Smart Chart** (page 34) for tips on processing.
- Be sure that cheeses are well chilled before shredding or slicing. Freeze softer cheeses such as mozzarella for at least 15 to 20 minutes before processing. Apply very little pressure on the pusher. Process more than you need and store in resealable bags in the freezer.

- Harder cheeses can be grated on the **Steel Blade** when appearance is not important (e.g., when adding them to soups and sauces).
- **FLAVORED CHEESE SPREADS:** Mince any of the following, using the **Steel Blade**: green onions, carrots, sun-dried tomatoes, roasted peppers, spinach. Add your favorite herbs (e.g., dill, basil), plus cream cheese or cottage cheese. Process until combined.
- **NESTED WORK BOWLS:** Choose the appropriate bowl and blade or disc for the task. Use the medium or large bowl and appropriate disc to slice or shred/grate veggies, cheese, etc. Use the large bowl and **Steel Blade** to chop/mince veggies or grind fish and to combine ingredients. (You can also use the **Steel Blade** in the medium bowl on Cuisinart Elite models.)

# GEFILTE FISH

Use whatever fish is available locally. I use whitefish and doré (pickerel), and have even used fresh salmon. Serve this hot or cold with Horseradish (page 110) or Simply Salsa (page 55).

Yield: 12 to 14 servings. Keeps 3 or 4 days in the refrigerator. If frozen, fish may become watery. Simmer thawed fish balls for about 15 minutes in water to cover. Drain well. Fish will taste freshly cooked!

## FISH STOCK

head, skin and bones from fish (optional)

4 cups cold water (approximately)

2 medium onions

2 medium carrots

1 tsp salt

1 tsp sugar

## FISH MIXTURE

2 medium onions, cut in chunks

2 medium carrots, cut in chunks

2 lb (1 kg) fish fillets (or ground fish)

4 eggs (or 2 eggs plus 4 egg whites)

3 to 4 Tbsp matzo meal (or substitute potato starch or finely ground almonds for gluten-free)

¼ cup cold water

1½ tsp salt

½ tsp freshly ground black pepper

1 tsp sugar (or to taste)

For fish stock: Place head, skin and bones from fish (if using) in large wide pot or fish poacher. Add enough water to barely cover fish trimmings.

SLICER: Slice onions and carrots, using firm pressure. Add with salt and sugar to pot. Cover and simmer for half an hour. (If you are not using fish trimmings, just bring water, vegetables and seasonings to a boil before adding gefilte fish balls.)

For fish mixture: Process ingredients in 2 batches if you have a small (7-cup) processor. Otherwise, process in 1 batch.

STEEL BLADE: Process onions and carrots until finely minced, about 10 seconds. Add fish and process until very smooth, about 45 seconds. (If fish is already minced, reduce processing time to 20 seconds.) Add remaining ingredients and process 15 seconds longer, until well mixed, scraping down sides of bowl as necessary. (If using a small processor, transfer mixture to large mixing bowl. Repeat with remaining ingredients. Combine both batches and mix well.)

Assembly: Moisten your hands with cold water. Shape fish into balls and add to simmering liquid. Cover and simmer for 2 hours. Remove cover the last half hour of cooking to reduce liquid. Cool. Carefully remove fish from broth and transfer to a large platter. Garnish with cooked carrots.

151 calories per serving, 5.1 g carbohydrates, 0.8 g fiber, 17 g protein, 6.4 g fat (1.3 g saturated fat), 117 mg cholesterol, 360 mg sodium, 329 mg potassium, 1 mg iron, 37 mg calcium, 248 mg phosphorus

## notes

- Gefilte fish leftovers are a great way to entice children to eat fish. Slice fish into ½-inch slices. Coat with beaten egg and seasoned bread crumbs or matzo meal. Heat 1 to 2 Tbsp oil in a nonstick skillet. Brown fish slices quickly on both sides, until golden and crisp. Serve immediately.

- For those who prefer sweet gefilte fish, use 2 Tbsp sugar in the fish mixture and 1 Tbsp sugar in the fish stock. (I've met people who add as much as ½ cup sugar to both the fish mixture and water!)

## TRICOLOR GEFILTE FISH MOLD

Brenda Shenken of New Zealand e-mailed me, "This is a lovely, colorful dish to serve guests at a summer buffet. The original recipe called for a loaf of frozen gefilte fish, which isn't available in New Zealand, so I prepare my own fish mixture."

Yield: 20 to 24 slices. Keeps in the refrigerator for 3 or 4 days. Do not freeze.

**5 carrots, cut up (or 20 mini carrots)**

**1 pkg (10 oz/300 g) frozen chopped spinach**

**Gefilte Fish Mixture (page 118)**

Cook carrots in boiling water until tender, 15 to 20 minutes. Drain well. Microwave spinach on High for 3 to 4 minutes, until defrosted. Let cool; squeeze dry. Prepare fish mixture as directed. Divide fish mixture in 3. Spray a 12-cup fluted tube pan with nonstick spray.

STEEL BLADE: Process spinach until finely ground, about 15 seconds. Add one-third of fish mixture and blend well. Spread evenly in pan. Spread with a second layer of fish mixture. Process cooked carrots about 15 seconds; add remaining fish mixture and blend well. Spread evenly in pan to make the third layer.

Place a piece of parchment paper or sprayed waxed paper on top of fish, then cover pan with foil. Bake in preheated 350°F oven for 1½ hours. (See Note.) Remove from oven and cool for 20 to 30 minutes. Remove foil and parchment. Carefully unmold onto a large platter. Wipe up any juices that collect on the plate. Cool completely, cover and refrigerate overnight. (Can be made up to 2 days in advance.)

97 calories per slice, 4.2 g carbohydrates, 1.1 g fiber, 11 g protein, 3.9 g fat (0.8 g saturated fat), 70 mg cholesterol, 231 mg sodium, 247 mg potassium, 1 mg iron, 41 mg calcium, 156 mg phosphorus

### note

This can also be made in 2 loaf pans, but reduce baking time to 1 hour. When done, top should be firm to the touch and edges should pull away from sides of pan. A skewer inserted into fish halfway between center and outside edge should come out clean. Cool for 20 to 30 minutes. Loosen fish with a long, narrow spatula. Cover pan with a serving plate, invert and shake gently to unmold. Serve with horseradish, lettuce, tomatoes and cucumber slices.

## PICKLED SALMON

An excellent summer meal or perfect for a brunch! You can substitute halibut or pike, with equally delicious results.

Yield: 10 to 12 servings as a main course. Allow 1 steak per person as a main course, or half as an appetizer. Keeps about 1 week in the refrigerator. Do not freeze.

**2 large cooking onions**
**2 cups water**
**½ tsp salt**
**¼ tsp freshly ground black pepper**
**3 to 4 lb (1.4 to 1.8 kg) fresh salmon, sliced in 1-inch-thick steaks or fillets**
**1½ cups white vinegar**
**2 tsp pickling spices**
**½ cup sugar**
**1 large sweet onion (e.g., Spanish or Vidalia)**

SLICER: Cut cooking onions to fit feed tube. Slice, using medium pressure. Place in large pot or fish poacher with water, salt and pepper. Bring to a boil. Cook for 20 minutes. Add salmon, cover and simmer for 10 minutes. Remove fish from stock and place in 9- × 13-inch glass baking dish. Add vinegar, pickling spices and sugar to fish stock. Boil 5 minutes longer. Pour stock through a sieve over fish.

SLICER: Cut sweet onion to fit feed tube. Slice, using light pressure. Add to fish. When cool, refrigerate 2 to 3 days before serving.

244 calories per serving, 6.7 g carbohydrates, 0.3 g fiber, 36 g protein, 6.5 g fat (1.6 g saturated fat), 113 mg cholesterol, 225 mg sodium, 721 mg potassium, 1 mg iron, 42 mg calcium, 10 mg phosphorus

## DISHWASHER SALMON

No dishes, no soap, please! Be sure to use heavy-duty aluminum foil. Regular foil could tear from the water pressure and you might end up with fish in your filter—"gefiltered fish!"

Yield: 6 servings. Recipe can be doubled easily. Salmon keeps 2 or 3 days in the refrigerator. Freezes well.

**Simply Salsa (page 55)**
**¼ cup fresh basil or dill**
**6 salmon fillets (6 to 8 oz/180 to 250 g each)**
**1 to 2 Tbsp olive oil**
**salt and freshly ground black pepper to taste**
**juice of 1 lemon or lime**
**fresh chopped basil or dill (for garnish)**

STEEL BLADE: Prepare salsa as directed; refrigerate. Process basil or dill until minced.

Cut 3 squares of heavy-duty aluminum foil. Spray each piece of foil with non-stick spray. Place 2 salmon fillets in a single layer on each piece of foil. Brush salmon lightly with oil. Sprinkle with salt, pepper and juice. Top with basil or dill.

Wrap tightly, pressing out air and sealing edges of foil securely so water won't get in. Place foil packets seam side up on top rack of dishwasher. Run dishwasher through the normal cycle, including the full drying cycle—approximately 50 minutes. Carefully unwrap fish and serve with salsa. Delicious hot or cold.

359 calories per serving, 3.6 g carbohydrates, 0.8 g fiber, 35 g protein, 22.1 g fat (4.3 g saturated fat), 96 mg cholesterol, 97 mg sodium, 730 mg potassium, 1 mg iron, 38 mg calcium, 402 mg phosphorus

### variation

Serve with Rina's Red Pepper Sauce (page 107) or Mango Salsa (page 107).

# BAKED SALMON WITH MUSHROOM STUFFING

This works well with Arctic char, bass or any whole fish. The baked salmon is also excellent without the stuffing, but stuffing turns it into an elegant company dish. Garnish with lemon slices that have been dipped in chopped parsley and serve with Mango Salsa (page 107).

Yield: 8 to 10 servings. Keeps 2 or 3 days in the refrigerator. Remove stuffing and store separately. Salmon freezes well.

| | |
|---|---|
| 4 to 5 lb (1.8 to 2.3 kg) whole salmon, scaled with head removed (see Note) | 2 tsp paprika |
| | ½ tsp each dried thyme and dried oregano |
| 3 cloves garlic | juice of ½ lemon |
| ¼ cup fresh dill | 2 Tbsp olive oil |
| 2 Tbsp fresh basil | 2 large onions, halved |
| 1 Tbsp salt (or to taste) | Mushroom Stuffing (optional) |
| freshly ground black pepper to taste | (page 122) |

Preheat oven to 450°F. Wash salmon and pat dry. Place in well-sprayed, large glass baking dish.

STEEL BLADE: Drop garlic through feed tube while machine is running; process until minced. Add dill and basil; process until minced. Rub fish with the minced mixture, salt, pepper, thyme, paprika, oregano, lemon juice and oil.

SLICER: Slice onions, using light pressure. Arrange onions around fish. If desired, stuff with Mushroom Stuffing just before baking. Cut slits in skin of fish on top side in 3 or 4 places.

Bake, uncovered, for approximately 30 minutes (allow 10 minutes cooking time for each inch of thickness). When done, fish should flake easily at the thickest point and the flesh should be opaque.

366 calories per serving (without stuffing), 4.3 g carbohydrates, 0.7 g fiber, 35 g protein, 22.6 g fat (4.3 g saturated fat), 96 mg cholesterol, 967 mg sodium, 667 mg potassium, 1 mg iron, 38 mg calcium, 402 mg phosphorus

### note

Instead of using a whole salmon, you can use 2 salmon fillets, weighing 1½ to 2 lb (750 g to 1 kg) each.

## MUSHROOM STUFFING

Yield: 8 servings.
Do not freeze.

½ **cup fresh parsley**

**3 or 4 green onions**

**1 to 2 Tbsp olive oil**

**3 cups mushrooms**

¾ **cup dried bread crumbs or matzo**
   **meal**

**2 to 3 Tbsp dry white wine**

**salt and freshly ground black pepper**
   **to taste**

STEEL BLADE: Process parsley and green onions until minced. Sauté in olive oil in a nonstick skillet for about 2 minutes over medium heat. Coarsely chop mushrooms with several quick on/offs. Add to skillet and cook 2 to 3 minutes longer. Add remaining ingredients, using just enough wine to moisten stuffing. Mix well. Cool before using. (Can be made up to a day in advance and refrigerated.)

Stuff fish and fasten with skewers. Bake as directed (see page 121). Stuffing must be cooked until it reaches 165°F on an instant-read thermometer.

67 calories per serving, 8.9 g carbohydrates, 1.2 g fiber, 2 g protein, 2.4 g fat (0.4 g saturated fat), 0 mg cholesterol, 77 mg sodium, 121 mg potassium, 1 mg iron, 28 mg calcium, 37 mg phosphorus

### variation

Substitute 2 cups cooked rice, couscous or quinoa for the bread crumbs. Omit wine and add 1 lightly beaten egg to bind the stuffing together. If desired, add other vegetables to boost the color and flavor (e.g., grated zucchini, chopped red pepper, spinach). One serving contains 78 calories, 12.8 g carbohydrates and 0.9 g fiber.

## BAKED SALMON WITH MANGO SALSA

You'll be hooked on salmon once you try this dish. It tastes fabulous either hot or cold. A fillet of salmon in 1 piece makes a beautiful presentation.

**1 lime, ends trimmed**

**1 slice fresh ginger, peeled (1 Tbsp)**

¼ **cup fresh basil**

**2½ to 3 lb (1.2 to 1.4 kg) salmon**
   **fillets (or 6 to 8 fillets)**

**salt, freshly ground black pepper and**
   **paprika to taste**

**juice of 1 lime (2 Tbsp)**

**1 to 2 Tbsp honey**

**Mango Salsa (page 107)**

SLICER: Slice lime, using medium pressure. (If you don't have a wide-mouth feed tube, cut lime in half to fit feed tube.) Reserve to use as a garnish.

STEEL BLADE: Process ginger and basil until minced, about 10 seconds.

Line baking sheet with foil; spray with nonstick spray. Place salmon on baking sheet and sprinkle with salt, pepper and paprika. Rub with lime juice and honey; sprinkle with ginger and basil. (Can be prepared up to 2 hours in advance and refrigerated.)

Prepare salsa as directed and refrigerate up to a day in advance. Bring to room temperature before serving.

Bake salmon, uncovered, in preheated 450°F oven about 15 minutes, or until fish flakes with a fork. Calculate cooking time as 10 minutes per inch of thickness of fish at its thickest point. Transfer to large platter. Garnish with lime slices and serve with salsa.

Yield: 6 to 8 servings. Salmon keeps 2 or 3 days in the refrigerator and freezes well. Salsa can be prepared a day in advance. Do not freeze.

414 calories per serving, 12.8 g carbohydrates, 1.2 g fiber, 38 g protein, 22.8 g fat (4.5 g saturated fat), 107 mg cholesterol, 106 mg sodium, 784 mg potassium, 1 mg iron, 39 mg calcium, 443 mg phosphorus

## BALSAMIC BAKED FISH WITH ONIONS AND MUSHROOMS

This is also excellent with halibut or sea bass. Cooking the fish and vegetables together in 1 pan saves time and cleanup!

2 large onions, cut in quarters

2 cups mushrooms

2 Tbsp olive oil

4 salmon fillets (about 2 lb/1 kg)

¼ cup balsamic vinegar

2 Tbsp honey

salt, freshly ground black pepper and dried basil to taste

SLICER: Slice onions and mushrooms, using medium pressure. Place on sprayed, foil-lined baking sheet and drizzle with olive oil.

Place salmon on baking sheet. Drizzle salmon, onions and mushrooms with balsamic vinegar and honey. Season with salt, pepper and basil. Marinate for 15 to 20 minutes.

Yield: 4 servings. Keeps 2 days in the refrigerator. Veggies become soggy if frozen.

Bake, uncovered, in preheated 425°F oven for 15 minutes. Salmon will be nicely browned on the outside, but still juicy inside. Onions and mushrooms should be tender and golden. Serve immediately.

565 calories per serving, 19.1 g carbohydrates, 1.5 g fiber, 47 g protein, 32.5 g fat (6.1 g saturated fat), 129 mg cholesterol, 131 mg sodium, 1004 mg potassium, 1 mg iron, 51 mg calcium, 563 mg phosphorus

## ORANGE TERIYAKI GRILLED SALMON

Halibut or sea bass may be substituted for salmon. The marinade is also excellent with chicken, tofu or vegetables.

1 slice fresh ginger, peeled (1 Tbsp)

1 clove garlic

2 Tbsp soy sauce

2 Tbsp orange juice

2 Tbsp orange marmalade

2 tsp sugar

1 tsp toasted sesame oil

¼ tsp dried basil

4 salmon fillets or steaks (6 to 8 oz/180 to 250 g each)

1 tsp cornstarch dissolved in 3 Tbsp orange juice

Grill over heat, not flame, to prevent flare-ups. You can also use an indoor grill, following manufacturer's directions for cooking times.

Yield: 4 servings. Keeps 2 to 3 days in the refrigerator. Freezes well.

STEEL BLADE: Drop ginger and garlic through feed tube while machine is running; process until minced. Add soy sauce, 2 Tbsp orange juice, marmalade, sugar, sesame oil and basil. Process until combined, 8 to 10 seconds.

Arrange salmon in single layer in glass baking dish. Pour marinade over salmon and marinate at room temperature for 30 minutes (or refrigerate up to 2 hours).

Preheat barbecue or grill. Remove fish from marinade, reserving any leftover marinade. Grill for 3 to 4 minutes per side, basting occasionally. Do not overcook or fish will be dry.

Meanwhile, bring leftover marinade to a boil. Stir cornstarch mixture into boiling marinade and simmer for 3 to 4 minutes, until thickened, stirring often. Drizzle sauce over fish and serve immediately. Delicious over rice.

376 calories per serving, 12.5 g carbohydrates, 0.2 g fiber, 35 g protein, 20.1 g fat (4 g saturated fat), 96 mg cholesterol, 551 mg sodium, 659 mg potassium, 1 mg iron, 33 mg calcium, 401 mg phosphorus

## chef's tips

- If you don't have a grill, place marinated salmon on a sprayed foil-lined baking sheet. Bake, uncovered, in preheated 425°F oven for 15 minutes, until fish flakes with a fork.

- WOOD CHIPS TIPS!: Soak 3 or 4 handfuls of wood chips (mesquite, applewood, hickory) in water while food is marinating. Toss the soaked chips on top of the hot coals just before placing food on the barbecue.

# BAKED HALIBUT AND POTATO CASSEROLE

Yield: 4 servings. Best eaten the same day. Do not freeze.

3 or 4 large potatoes, peeled
salt, freshly ground black pepper
    and paprika to taste
4 halibut steaks (6 oz/180 g each,
    about ¾ inch thick)

2 medium onions, halved
1 Tbsp butter or oil
1½ cups milk (1%) or tomato juice
    (approximately)

Preheat oven to 350°F.

SLICER: Cut potatoes to fit feed tube. Slice potatoes, using firm pressure. Arrange half of potatoes in sprayed 9- × 13-inch glass baking dish. Sprinkle with salt, pepper and paprika. Season fish and arrange over potatoes.

Cut onions to fit feed tube. Slice, using light pressure. Top fish with onions and remaining potatoes. Season again and dot with butter or drizzle with oil. Cover with milk or tomato juice. Bake, uncovered, for about 1 hour, until tender.

479 calories per serving, 56.8 g carbohydrates, 5.6 g fiber, 45 g protein, 8 g fat (3 g saturated fat), 67 mg cholesterol, 176 mg sodium, 2180 mg potassium, 4 mg iron, 233 mg calcium, 639 mg phosphorus

# SALSA JUST FOR THE HALIBUT!

So quick, so easy, so good! To make this pizza-style, top with grated mozzarella cheese. It's equally good with red snapper or sea bass.

Yield: 4 to 6 servings. Delicious hot or at room temperature. Keeps 2 days in the refrigerator. Do not freeze.

¼ cup fresh parsley

Simply Salsa (page 55)

4 to 6 halibut steaks or fillets (about 2 lb/1 kg)

salt and lemon pepper to taste

¼ cup grated Parmesan cheese (optional)

STEEL BLADE: Process parsley until minced, about 10 seconds. Empty bowl and set aside. Prepare salsa as directed. (Salsa can be prepared up to a day in advance and refrigerated.)

Spoon some salsa into bottom of sprayed 9- × 13-inch glass baking dish. Arrange halibut in single layer on top of salsa. Sprinkle fish lightly with salt and lemon pepper. Top with remaining salsa and sprinkle with cheese (if desired).

Bake in preheated 400°F oven for 10 to 12 minutes, just until fish flakes. (Cooking time depends on thickness of fish; allow 10 minutes per inch, measured at the thickest point.) Sprinkle with parsley.

279 calories per serving, 4.6 g carbohydrates, 1.2 g fiber, 48 g protein, 6.6 g fat (0.9 g saturated fat), 73 mg cholesterol, 130 mg sodium, 1239 mg potassium, 3 mg iron, 133 mg calcium, 530 mg phosphorus

# POACHED FISH

This is delicious with Mango Salsa (page 107), Dill Butter (page 66), Chinese Sweet and Sour Sauce (page 108) or Teriyaki Sauce (page 109).

Yield: About 8 servings. Keeps 2 or 3 days in the refrigerator. Leftovers freeze well or can be used to make Quick Fish Salad (page 126).

4 lb (1.8 kg) whole fish, fish steaks or fillets (e.g., salmon, halibut, sole, haddock)

salt to taste

8 cups boiling water

1 cup dry white wine

¼ cup lemon juice

1 Tbsp salt

8 peppercorns

½ tsp dried thyme

1 bay leaf

few sprigs fresh parsley

1 Tbsp butter or margarine (optional)

2 stalks celery, with tops

1 lemon

1 or 2 medium onions, halved

If fish is whole, remove head and tail. Salt inside of fish. Wrap carefully in several layers of cheesecloth.

Place boiling water, wine, lemon juice, salt, peppercorns, thyme, bay leaf, parsley and butter or margarine (if using) in fish poacher or large roasting pan and bring to a boil.

STEEL BLADE: Cut celery into chunks. Process with quick on/off pulses, until coarsely chopped.

SLICER: Slice lemon and onion, using medium pressure. Add celery, lemon and onion to poacher and simmer, covered, for 20 minutes. Carefully place fish in poacher. *Continued*

125

Once water returns to a simmer, begin timing fish. Allow 10 minutes for each inch of thickness measured at its thickest point. If frozen, allow 20 minutes per inch. Cook covered.

Whole fish takes about 30 to 40 minutes. If fish is large, it may have to be turned over during cooking. The cheesecloth makes it easier. (Small fillets take 3 to 4 minutes; fish steaks take 10 to 15 minutes.)

When done, remove fish from liquid and drain well. It should flake easily with a fork. Remove from cheesecloth. If desired, strip off skin from whole fish, being careful not to tear the flesh. Transfer carefully to large serving platter. Garnish with additional lemon slices, chopped parsley and strips of pimento. Serve hot or chilled.

256 calories per serving (based on 8 oz/250 g raw salmon fillet), 1 g carbohydrates, 0 g fiber, 51 g protein, 5.9 g fat (1.6 g saturated fat), 65 mg cholesterol, 180 mg sodium, 846 mg potassium, 2 mg iron, 114 mg calcium, 1682 mg phosphorus

### quick fish salad

Mince 1 small onion, 1 stalk celery and 1 carrot on STEEL BLADE. Add 1 cup leftover cooked fish, 2 Tbsp light mayonnaise, salt and freshly ground black pepper. Process with quick on/off pulses until mixed. Serve chilled. Yield: 2 to 3 servings. Multiplies easily. Do not freeze.

153 calories per serving, 8 g carbohydrates, 1.7 g fiber, 16 g protein, 6.8 g fat (1.3 g saturated fat), 24 mg cholesterol, 192 mg sodium, 453 mg potassium, 1 mg iron, 61 mg calcium, 521 mg phosphorus

## EASY FISH BAKE

Yield: 6 servings.
Leftovers keep 2 days in the refrigerator.
Crumb coating becomes soggy if frozen.

2 lb (1 kg) fish fillets (e.g., sole, tilapia, haddock)
½ cup Italian Salad Dressing (page 286) or bottled dressing (low-fat is fine)
½ cup dried bread, cracker or cereal crumbs (see "Bread Crumbs" in the Smart Chart, pages 36–37)
¼ cup grated Parmesan cheese
dash each of salt and freshly ground black pepper

Dip fish on both sides in salad dressing. Arrange in single layer on sprayed foil-lined baking sheet.

STEEL BLADE: Process crumbs with cheese, salt and pepper for a few seconds to mix. Sprinkle over fish. Bake, uncovered, in preheated 425°F oven for 10 to 12 minutes, until fish flakes with a fork. Best served immediately.

296 calories per serving, 6.9 g carbohydrates, 0.4 g fiber, 28 g protein, 16.6 g fat (3 g saturated fat), 74 mg cholesterol, 428 mg sodium, 385 mg potassium, 1 mg iron, 74 mg calcium, 341 mg phosphorus

### note

Four slices of dried bread, 25 to 30 crackers or 4 cups corn flakes or similar crispy cereal will yield 1 cup crumbs. Make a big batch and store in an airtight container in the refrigerator. Also try this with Panko crumbs (page 37).

### variation

Omit crumbs and Parmesan. Process about 3 cups of potato chips or tortilla chips on the STEEL BLADE until crushed. Dip fish in salad dressing, then in crushed chips. Grate 4 oz (125 g) chilled cheddar cheese (1 cup grated), using medium pressure. Sprinkle over fish and bake as directed. One serving contains 666 calories, 35.9 g carbohydrates, 3.1 g fiber and 43 g fat.

---

## OVEN-FRIED FISH

Yield: 4 servings.
Leftovers keep 2 days in the refrigerator.
Crumb coating becomes soggy if frozen.

| | |
|---|---|
| 1 cup bread, Panko or cracker crumbs (see "Bread Crumbs" in the Smart Chart, pages 36–37) | dash each of garlic powder and paprika |
| ½ to 1 tsp salt (to taste) | 1 egg plus 2 Tbsp water |
| dash freshly ground black pepper | 1½ lb (750 g) fish fillets (e.g., sole, tilapia) |
| | 1 to 2 Tbsp melted butter or olive oil |

STEEL BLADE: Process crumbs with seasonings for 2 or 3 seconds to blend. Transfer to flat dish. Process egg with water for a few seconds to blend. Transfer to another flat dish. Dip fish fillets in egg, then in crumbs. Place in single layer on sprayed cookie sheet. Drizzle with butter or oil.

Bake in preheated 450°F oven for 10 to 12 minutes, until crispy. Serve immediately.

289 calories per serving, 19.7 g carbohydrates, 1.3 g fiber, 34 g protein, 7.4 g fat (3 g saturated fat), 140 mg cholesterol, 648 mg sodium, 476 mg potassium, 2 mg iron, 78 mg calcium, 407 mg phosphorus

### variations

- Add ⅓ cup grated Parmesan cheese and/or sesame seeds to crumb mixture.
- Instead of bread or cracker crumbs, substitute croutons. Caesar croutons are especially delicious, but omit the salt.

# DEEP-FRY BEER BATTER

This batter recipe is
ideal for fish, onion
rings, boneless
chicken breasts, etc.

1½ **cups flour**
1½ **cups beer**

**dash each of salt, cayenne and**
**paprika**

Process all ingredients on the STEEL BLADE until smooth, about 10 seconds. Let
stand at least 4 hours, either at room temperature or in the refrigerator. Dip food
in the batter and deep-fry in hot oil (375°F) until crisp and golden brown. Drain
well. Foods fried in this batter can be kept in a warm oven and will remain crisp.
Freezes well.

# FISH FILLETS AMANDINE

Everyone goes nuts
when they try this
classic fish dish.
Panko crumbs add a
crunchy texture.

1½ **to 2 lb (750 g to 1 kg) fish**
 **fillets (sole, doré/pickerel**
 **or tilapia)**
**salt and freshly ground black pepper**
1¼ **cups dried bread crumbs or Panko**
 **crumbs (pages 36–37)**
¼ **tsp each salt, freshly ground black**
 **pepper, dried thyme and paprika**

2 **eggs plus 2 Tbsp water**
⅓ **to ½ cup flour**
1 **Tbsp butter or margarine**
1 **Tbsp oil**
½ **cup toasted slivered almonds (for**
 **garnish)**

Yield: 4 to 6 servings.
May be reheated.
Leftovers keep 2 days in
the refrigerator. Coating
may become soggy if
frozen.

Sprinkle fish lightly with salt and pepper.

STEEL BLADE: Process crumbs with salt, pepper, thyme and paprika until
blended, about 5 seconds. Spread on large piece of waxed paper. Process eggs with
water until blended, about 2 seconds. Transfer to pie plate. Spread another piece
of waxed paper with flour. Dip fish in flour, then in egg, then in crumbs. (May be
prepared in advance up to this point and refrigerated.)

Heat butter or margarine with oil in large nonstick skillet. Pan-fry fish on
medium-high heat 2 to 3 minutes per side, until golden brown and crispy. Drain
on paper towels. Garnish with almonds. Serve immediately.

395 calories per serving, 30.7 g carbohydrates, 1.8 g fiber, 37 g protein, 12.7 g fat (3.7 g saturated fat),
193 mg cholesterol, 568 mg sodium, 514 mg potassium, 3 mg iron, 100 mg calcium, 448 mg phosphorus

## note

To toast almonds, bake at 350°F for 5 to 10 minutes, or microwave,
uncovered, on High for 2 to 3 minutes, stirring once. Nuts will darken
during standing time.

## BROILED CHEESY FILLETS

This is a new twist on an old favorite. Excellent for company!

Yield: 6 servings. Leftovers keep 2 days in the refrigerator. Freezing isn't recommended.

2 lb (1 kg) fish fillets (e.g., sole, tilapia, orange roughy)
1 to 2 Tbsp oil or melted butter
salt, freshly ground black pepper and dried thyme to taste

4 or 5 sprigs fresh parsley
1 cup mushrooms
⅓ cup oil-packed sun-dried tomatoes, well drained
4 oz (125 g) chilled low-fat Swiss cheese (1 cup grated)

Place fish on well-sprayed broiler pan and brush both sides with oil or butter. Sprinkle with salt, pepper and thyme.

STEEL BLADE: Coarsely chop parsley, mushrooms and sun-dried tomatoes with 3 or 4 quick on/off pulses.

GRATER: Grate cheese, using medium pressure. Mix cheese with mushroom mixture.

Broil fish about 3 inches from heat for 4 to 5 minutes, until fish flakes with a fork. Spread mushroom/cheese mixture on fillets and broil 2 to 3 minutes longer, until cheese melts (see Note below).

192 calories per serving, 2.6 g carbohydrates, 0.6 g fiber, 31 g protein, 5.8 g fat (1.3 g saturated fat), 78 mg cholesterol, 176 mg sodium, 510 mg potassium, 1 mg iron, 205 mg calcium, 432 mg phosphorus

### note

To save a step, combine cheese with mushroom mixture and spread on fillets. Instead of broiling, bake in preheated 400°F oven for 10 to 12 minutes, until golden.

## STUFFED FISH FILLETS AU GRATIN

An easy do-ahead company dish.

Yield: 4 servings. Keeps 2 days in the refrigerator. Reheats well. Leftovers can be frozen.

8 sole, tilapia or whitefish fillets (about 2 lb/1 kg)
salt, freshly ground black pepper, paprika and dried thyme to taste
1 large onion, quartered
2 stalks celery, cut in chunks
2 Tbsp butter or margarine, divided

½ green or red bell pepper, cut in chunks
1 cup mushrooms
8 slices whole wheat or rye bread
⅓ cup grated Parmesan cheese

Sprinkle fish lightly on both sides with salt, pepper, paprika and thyme. Arrange half of fillets in single layer in sprayed 7- × 11-inch glass baking dish.

STEEL BLADE: Process onion and celery with quick on/off pulses, until coarsely chopped. Melt 1 Tbsp butter or margarine in large nonstick skillet; add onion

*Continued*

and celery. Repeat with bell pepper and mushrooms. Add to skillet and sauté on medium heat for about 10 minutes, until fairly dry.

Tear bread into chunks and drop through feed tube while machine is running. Process to make fine crumbs. Add to sautéed vegetables and mix well. Season to taste. Let cool.

To assemble: Top each fillet in baking dish with stuffing. Place remaining fillets on top. Dot with reserved butter and sprinkle with Parmesan cheese. (May be assembled up to this point and refrigerated overnight.) Bake, uncovered, in pre-heated 375°F oven for 30 to 35 minutes, until fish flakes with a fork.

541 calories per serving, 29.2 g carbohydrates, 5 g fiber, 72 g protein, 13.6 g fat (6.2 g saturated fat), 194 mg cholesterol, 693 mg sodium, 1203 mg potassium, 3 mg iron, 199 mg calcium, 928 mg phosphorus

### variations

- Instead of topping fish with butter and Parmesan cheese, sprinkle with 1 cup grated low-fat cheddar cheese.

#### passover variation
Substitute 4 cups crumbled matzo or matzo farfel for bread.

## BROCCOLI-STUFFED FILLETS WITH MUSHROOM SAUCE

*Any firm-fleshed fish fillets will work in this recipe. Try it with sole, tilapia or snapper.*

1 pkg (10 oz/300 g) frozen chopped broccoli (or 2 cups fresh broccoli)
4 tsp margarine
1 medium onion, halved

salt, freshly ground black pepper and dried thyme to taste
1 slice bread, quartered
6 fish fillets (about 2 lb/1 kg)
Mushroom Sauce (page 104)

*Yield: 6 servings. Keeps 1 to 2 days in the refrigerator. Reheats well. Do not freeze.*

Cook frozen broccoli according to package directions. Fresh broccoli can be micro-waved, covered, on High for 4 to 5 minutes, until tender. Microwave margarine on High for 30 seconds, until melted. Remove 2 tsp margarine and set aside for crumb topping.

STEEL BLADE: Process onion with quick on/off pulses, until coarsely chopped. Microwave, uncovered, with 2 tsp margarine on High for 3 minutes, until tender. Process broccoli with 3 or 4 quick on/off pulses, until finely chopped. Add to onion. Season to taste.

For crumb topping: Process bread with reserved margarine until fine crumbs are formed. Set aside.

Season fillets on dark side. Spread each fillet with about 3 Tbsp of broccoli mixture and roll up. Place seam side down in a sprayed oven-to-table casserole dish.

Prepare sauce as directed and let cool. Pour over fish. Sprinkle with reserved crumb topping. (May be assembled in advance up until this point and refrigerated overnight.) Bake, uncovered, in preheated 375°F oven for 30 to 35 minutes.

294 calories per serving, 12.5 g carbohydrates, 1.9 g fiber, 35 g protein, 11.1 g fat (5 g saturated fat), 105 mg cholesterol, 552 mg sodium, 670 mg potassium, 1 mg iron, 130 mg calcium, 471 mg phosphorus

### variation

Substitute spinach for broccoli. Add ½ cup grated cheese to the sauce. Add ¼ tsp dry mustard if using cheddar cheese or ⅛ tsp nutmeg if using Swiss cheese.

## FISH ITALIAN STYLE

Yield: 6 servings. Leftovers keep 2 days in the refrigerator. Reheats and/or freezes well.

| | |
|---|---|
| 2 lb (1 kg) fish fillets or 6 halibut steaks | 1 or 2 cloves garlic |
| salt and freshly ground black pepper to taste | 1 cup tomato sauce |
| | ¼ cup chili sauce or ketchup |
| 6 oz (180 g) chilled low-fat mozzarella cheese (1½ cups grated) | ¼ tsp each dried oregano and dried basil |
| 1 cup mushrooms | few drops hot sauce (optional) |
| 1 green or red bell pepper, halved | |

For machines with nested bowls, see method on page 132.

Wash fish and pat dry. Sprinkle both sides with a little salt and pepper. Place in sprayed 9- × 13-inch glass baking dish.

GRATER: Grate cheese, using medium pressure. Set aside.

SLICER: Slice mushrooms and bell pepper, using medium pressure. Set aside.

For sauce: Insert STEEL BLADE. Drop garlic through feed tube while machine is running; process until minced. Add tomato sauce, chili sauce or ketchup, seasonings and hot sauce (if using). Process for a few seconds to blend.

To assemble: Pour sauce over fish. Sprinkle with vegetables; top with cheese.

Bake, uncovered, in preheated 375°F oven for 25 to 30 minutes, or until fish flakes with a fork. Halibut takes 35 to 40 minutes, depending on thickness.

240 calories per serving, 8.8 g carbohydrates, 1.1 g fiber, 34 g protein, 7.4 g fat (4 g saturated fat), 86 mg cholesterol, 627 mg sodium, 592 mg potassium, 1 mg iron, 235 mg calcium, 473 mg phosphorus

*Continued*

131

## SOLE MORNAY

A terrific company dish—easy and elegant. Also delicious with halibut—just increase the baking time to 35 or 40 minutes, depending on the thickness of the fish.

Yield: 6 servings. Leftovers keep 2 days in the refrigerator. Reheats well. Crumb topping won't be crispy if frozen.

2 lb (1 kg) sole fillets (or any fish fillets)

salt, freshly ground black pepper and paprika to taste

Mushroom Duxelles (page 235)

3 Tbsp butter or margarine, cut in chunks

3 Tbsp flour

4 oz chilled low-fat Swiss cheese, cut in chunks (1 cup grated)

¼ tsp dry mustard

1½ cups hot milk (2% or 1%)

½ cup dried bread crumbs

1 Tbsp melted butter or margarine

Sprinkle fish lightly with salt, pepper and paprika. Stuff fish with Mushroom Duxelles. Roll up (or fold in half) and fasten with a toothpick. Arrange seam side down in sprayed 7- × 11-inch glass baking dish.

STEEL BLADE: Process butter or margarine, flour and cheese until cheese is fine, 15 to 20 seconds. Add mustard and a little salt and pepper. Pour hot milk through feed tube while machine is running. Transfer sauce to 4-cup glass measure and microwave on High for 1 to 2 minutes, until thick and bubbling, stirring once or twice. Cool slightly. Pour sauce over fish. Top with crumbs and drizzle with melted butter or margarine. (Can be prepared up to this point and refrigerated up to 24 hours.)

Bake, uncovered, in preheated 375°F oven about 30 minutes.

346 calories per serving, 16 g carbohydrates, 1.1 g fiber, 35 g protein, 15.3 g fat (7.1 g saturated fat), 101 mg cholesterol, 629 mg sodium, 586 mg potassium, 1 mg iron, 298 mg calcium, 516 mg phosphorus

## FISH PATTIES

Yield: 4 servings (8 to 12 patties, depending on size). Keeps 2 days in the refrigerator. Reheats and/or freezes well.

1 medium onion, cut in chunks

1 small carrot, cut in chunks

½ stalk celery, cut in chunks

2 eggs (or 1 egg plus 2 whites)

1 lb (500 g) fish fillets (sole, haddock or perch), cut in chunks

½ cup dried bread crumbs or matzo meal

½ to 1 tsp salt (to taste)

freshly ground black pepper to taste

2 Tbsp oil for frying (approximately)

STEEL BLADE: Process onion, carrot and celery until minced, about 10 seconds. Add eggs and fish. Process 20 to 25 seconds, until fish is minced. Add crumbs or matzo meal, salt and pepper; process a few seconds longer to mix.

Heat oil in large nonstick skillet. Drop fish mixture from large spoon into hot oil. Flatten slightly with back of spoon. Fry both sides on medium-high heat until golden brown, 3 to 4 minutes per side. Add additional oil if needed. Drain on paper towels.

261 calories per serving, 13.7 g carbohydrates, 1.5 g fiber, 24 g protein, 11.6 g fat (1.8 g saturated fat), 159 mg cholesterol, 515 mg sodium, 408 mg potassium, 1 mg iron, 63 mg calcium, 304 mg phosphorus

### note

To double the recipe in a small processor (7 cups), process in 2 batches. You can double the recipe in 1 batch if the capacity of your processor is 11 cups or larger.

## SWEET AND SOUR FISH PATTIES

This is also delicious using Tuna Patties (page 135).

Yield: 8 servings. Keeps 2 days in the refrigerator. Reheats and/or freezes well. May be prepared in advance and baked at mealtime.

Fish Patties (page 132), double recipe
1 medium onion, halved
1 stalk celery
2 cups mushrooms

1 to 2 Tbsp oil
Chinese Sweet and Sour Sauce (page 108) (see Note)
2 cups tomato sauce (low-sodium or regular)

Cook patties as directed. Place in sprayed 9- × 13-inch glass baking dish.

SLICER: Slice onion, celery and mushrooms, using medium pressure. Heat oil in large nonstick skillet. Sauté vegetables in oil for about 5 minutes, until tender. Stir in sauces. Pour over patties.

Bake, uncovered, in preheated 325°F oven for 25 to 30 minutes. Serve over rice.

510 calories per serving, 72.1 g carbohydrates, 2.6 g fiber, 26 g protein, 13.5 g fat (1.9 g saturated fat), 159 mg cholesterol, 702 mg sodium, 567 mg potassium, 2 mg iron, 95 mg calcium, 327 mg phosphorus

### note

A 14 oz (398 mL) can of jellied cranberry sauce plus 2 Tbsp lemon juice may be used instead of Chinese Sweet and Sour Sauce. One serving made this way contains 395 calories, 43.3 g carbohydrates and 3.4 g fiber.

## SALMON PATTIES

For Passover, replace corn flakes with ⅓ cup matzo meal or ground crumbs from Passover crackers.

Yield: 6 servings (12 to 14 patties). Keeps 2 to 3 days in the refrigerator. Freezes well.

| | |
|---|---|
| 1 medium onion, cut in chunks | 2½ cups corn flakes or Special K cereal |
| 1 carrot, cut in chunks | 4 eggs (or 2 eggs plus 4 egg whites) |
| ¼ cup fresh dill | dash freshly ground black pepper |
| 2 cans (7¾ oz/213 g each) salmon | 2 Tbsp oil for frying |

STEEL BLADE: Process onion, carrot and dill until minced, about 8 seconds. Add salmon (including the skin, bones and juice), corn flakes, eggs and pepper. Process just until blended, 6 to 8 seconds. Mixture will be soft.

Heat oil in a large nonstick skillet. Drop salmon mixture from a large spoon into hot oil. Flatten slightly with the back of the spoon. Brown on medium heat on both sides, until golden. Drain well on paper towels.

123 calories per patty, 6.4 g carbohydrates, 0.5 g fiber, 10 g protein, 6.3 g fat (1.3 g saturated fat), 91 mg cholesterol, 282 mg sodium, 171 mg potassium, 2 mg iron, 90 mg calcium, 156 mg phosphorus

## SALMON BURGERS

Grill someone happy! You can pan-fry these if you don't have a grill. Serve these either as a main dish or in a bun topped with lettuce, tomatoes and mayonnaise. I usually don't need to add bread crumbs to the mixture.

Yield: 4 burgers. Recipe multiplies easily. Keeps 1 to 2 days in the refrigerator. Freezes well.

| | |
|---|---|
| 2 cloves garlic | 2 to 3 Tbsp light mayonnaise |
| 2 Tbsp fresh parsley (or 2 tsp dried) | 1 tsp Dijon mustard (optional) |
| ½ medium onion (or 2 green onions), cut in chunks | salt and pepper to taste |
| 1 lb (500 g) boneless, skinless salmon fillets, cut in chunks (remove any pin bones) | bread crumbs (optional) |

STEEL BLADE: Drop garlic, parsley and onion through feed tube while machine is running; process until minced. Add salmon chunks and process just until minced and slightly pasty, 18 to 20 seconds, scraping down sides of bowl as needed. Add mayonnaise, mustard (if using), salt and pepper; process briefly to combine. If necessary, add bread crumbs to bind mixture.

Shape mixture into burgers, oiling your hands slightly for easier handling. Cover and refrigerate for 20 to 30 minutes. (Can be prepared up to 24 hours in advance.)

Preheat grill. Cook burgers about 4 minutes on the first side, until firm, then 3 to 4 minutes on the second side. (Alternatively, heat 2 Tbsp olive oil in a large skillet on medium-high heat. Cook 3 to 4 minutes per side, until golden brown. Drain on paper towels.)

242 calories per burger, 2.4 g carbohydrates, 0.2 g fiber, 23 g protein, 15.1 g fat (3 g saturated fat), 67 mg cholesterol, 114 mg sodium, 426 mg potassium, 1 mg iron, 23 mg calcium, 267 mg phosphorus

## TUNA PATTIES

*Cans of tuna are smaller than they used to be, so I now use 3 cans to make this recipe.*

*Yield: 6 servings (12 patties). Keeps 2 to 3 days in the refrigerator. Freezes well.*

1 medium onion, cut in chunks

1 carrot, cut in chunks

3 cans (6 oz/170 g each) tuna, drained

4 eggs (or 2 eggs plus 4 egg whites)

½ cup dried bread crumbs or matzo meal

½ tsp salt

¼ tsp freshly ground black pepper

2 Tbsp oil for frying

STEEL BLADE: Process onion and carrot until minced, about 8 seconds. Add tuna, eggs, bread crumbs or matzo meal, salt and pepper. Process until mixed, about 10 seconds. Shape into patties or 1-inch balls.

Heat oil in a large nonstick skillet. Brown on medium heat on both sides, until golden. Drain well on paper towels.

117 calories per patty, 4.6 g carbohydrates, 0.4 g fiber, 13 g protein, 4.7 g fat (0.9 g saturated fat), 83 mg cholesterol, 174 mg sodium, 150 mg potassium, 1 mg iron, 24 mg calcium, 107 mg phosphorus

### variation

Mixture can also be shaped into a loaf and baked at 350°F for 45 to 50 minutes or fill muffin tins two-thirds full and bake for 25 minutes, until golden. Makes 10 to 12. May be sliced and used for sandwiches.

## TUNA PATTIES IN SPANISH SAUCE

*Yield: 6 servings. Keeps 2 days in the refrigerator. Reheats and/or freezes well.*

Tuna Patties (see above)

2 stalks celery

1 green and/or red bell pepper, halved

1 medium onion, halved

1 cup mushrooms

1 to 2 Tbsp oil

2 cups tomato sauce (unsalted or regular)

1 cup frozen peas and carrots

salt and freshly ground black pepper to taste

½ tsp dried basil

Prepare and fry patties as directed, and place in sprayed 9- × 13-inch glass baking dish.

*Continued*

SLICER: Cut celery, bell pepper and onion to fit feed tube. Slice, using medium pressure. Slice mushrooms, using light pressure. Sauté vegetables in oil in nonstick skillet for 5 minutes. Add tomato sauce, peas and carrots and seasonings; mix well. Pour over patties. Can be prepared in advance and refrigerated until serving time. You can also freeze it at this point; thaw overnight in refrigerator.

Bake, uncovered, in preheated 350°F oven for 20 to 25 minutes. Serve over rice.

268 calories per serving, 22.6 g carbohydrates, 3.8 g fiber, 25 g protein, 8.6 g fat (0.9 g saturated fat), 25 mg cholesterol, 345 mg sodium, 732 mg potassium, 3 mg iron, 62 mg calcium, 217 mg phosphorus

## TUNA STRUDEL

*Perfect for the buffet table.*

*Yield: 6 to 8 servings. Keeps 2 days in the refrigerator. Reheats and/or freezes well.*

Flaky Ginger Ale Pastry (page 471)
1 medium onion, cut in chunks
1 green and 1 red bell pepper, cut in chunks
1 Tbsp butter or margarine
½ cup grated Parmesan cheese
½ cup bread or cracker crumbs

3 cans (6 oz/170 g each) tuna, drained and flaked
1 cup sour cream (light or regular)
1 tsp dry mustard
dash salt and freshly ground black pepper
1 egg yolk blended with 2 tsp cold water

Prepare pastry as directed and chill.

STEEL BLADE: Process onion and bell peppers with quick on/off pulses, until coarsely chopped. Sauté in butter or margarine until golden, about 5 minutes.

Process Parmesan cheese with crumbs for 3 or 4 seconds. Remove about ¼ cup of crumb mixture and set aside. Combine tuna, sour cream, mustard, salt, pepper and sautéed vegetables with crumb mixture in processor bowl. Process with several quick on/offs, just until mixed.

Roll out half the dough on a lightly floured surface into an 8- × 10-inch rectangle. Sprinkle with half the reserved crumb mixture. Spoon half the tuna mixture onto pastry along 1 long edge. Leave a 1-inch border on remaining 3 sides; brush with egg yolk to help seal roll. Roll up, turning in ends. Transfer roll to sprayed baking sheet. Brush with egg yolk and cut several slits on the top. Repeat with remaining dough and filling. (Can be frozen unbaked up to 1 month. Thaw before baking.)

Bake in preheated 375°F oven for 35 to 45 minutes, until golden.

483 calories per serving, 32.4 g carbohydrates, 1.8 g fiber, 30 g protein, 25.8 g fat (8.6 g saturated fat), 86 mg cholesterol, 458 mg sodium, 440 mg potassium, 3 mg iron, 175 mg calcium, 280 mg phosphorus

### variation

Replace tuna with canned or leftover cooked salmon (1½ to 2 cups).

## SWISS TUNA BAKE

Easy and delicious!
Assemble this the
night before and
place it in the oven
an hour before your
guests arrive.

Yield: 6 servings.
Keeps 2 days in the
refrigerator. Reheats
and/or freezes well.

3 green onions, cut in chunks

¼ cup fresh dill

1 cup mushrooms

3 cans (6 oz/170 g each) tuna,
   drained and flaked

salt to taste

1 cup grated Parmesan cheese

8 oz (250 g) chilled Swiss cheese
   (low-fat or regular) (2 cups grated)

6 slices white or whole wheat bread

4 eggs (or 2 eggs plus 4 egg whites)

½ tsp dry mustard

1 tsp Worcestershire sauce

3 or 4 drops hot sauce

2 cups milk (1% or 2%)

STEEL BLADE: Process onions, dill and mushrooms with several on/off pulses, until finely chopped. Combine with tuna in a large mixing bowl. Add salt and half the Parmesan cheese.

GRATER: Grate Swiss cheese, using medium pressure. Add half to tuna. Add the rest to remaining Parmesan cheese and reserve.

Place bread slices in bottom of sprayed 7- × 11-inch glass baking dish, trimming slices to fit. Spread tuna mixture over bread.

STEEL BLADE: Process eggs with mustard, Worcestershire and hot sauce for 2 or 3 seconds. Add milk through feed tube while machine is running. Immediately pour over tuna mixture. Top with reserved cheeses. Cover and refrigerate at least 2 hours or overnight.

Bake, covered, in preheated 350°F oven for 30 minutes. Uncover and bake 30 minutes longer.

379 calories per serving, 20 g carbohydrates, 1 g fiber, 46 g protein, 11.7 g fat (5.5 g saturated fat), 195 mg cholesterol, 603 mg sodium, 500 mg potassium, 3 mg iron, 678 mg calcium, 630 mg phosphorus

## FAVORITE TUNA CASSEROLE

Sure to become a
family favorite.

Yield: 8 servings.
Keeps 2 days in the
refrigerator. Reheats
and/or freezes well.

1 pkg (7¼ oz/225 g) macaroni and
   cheese dinner

1½ cups broad noodles

1½ cups macaroni shells or spirals

12 cups boiling salted water

1 medium onion, halved

2 Tbsp butter or margarine

4 oz (125 g) chilled cheddar cheese
   (low-fat or regular), cut in chunks
   (1 cup grated)

¾ cup milk (1% or 2%)

1 can (10 oz/284 mL) condensed
   mushroom soup

2 cans (6 oz/170 g each) tuna, drained

salt and freshly ground black pepper
   to taste

Cook pasta in boiling salted water in large pot for 8 to 10 minutes. Drain and rinse well. Return pasta to pot.

STEEL BLADE: Process onion with 2 or 3 quick on/off pulses, until coarsely chopped. Sauté in butter or margarine on medium heat for 5 minutes. Process cheese on the STEEL BLADE until finely chopped, about 20 seconds. Add to pasta along with remaining ingredients, including the cheese packet that came with the box. Mix well. Place in sprayed 9- × 13-inch glass baking dish. (May be prepared in advance up to this point and refrigerated or frozen. Do not thaw frozen casserole. Drizzle an additional ½ cup milk over the top and bake, uncovered, at 350°F for 45 to 50 minutes.)

Bake, uncovered, in preheated 350°F oven for 35 minutes.

369 calories per serving, 48.6 g carbohydrates, 2.6 g fiber, 24 g protein, 8.2 g fat (3.5 g saturated fat), 34 mg cholesterol, 386 mg sodium, 245 mg potassium, 3 mg iron, 110 mg calcium, 261 mg phosphorus

## TUNA AND MUSHROOM LASAGNA

To reduce the sodium, make Béchamel (White) Sauce instead of using canned mushroom soup. See low-sodium variation on page 139.

Yield: 8 servings. Keeps 2 to 3 days in the refrigerator. Reheats and/or freezes well.

9 lasagna noodles (packaged or Homemade Pasta, page 259)
2 cloves garlic
2 medium onions, quartered
1 green or red bell pepper, cut in chunks
2 Tbsp margarine or oil
3 cans (6 oz/170 g each) tuna, drained and flaked

2 cans (10 oz/284 g each) condensed mushroom soup (or double recipe of Béchamel Sauce, page 103)
salt and freshly ground black pepper to taste
8 oz (250 g) chilled mozzarella cheese (low-fat or regular) (2 cups grated)
¼ cup grated Parmesan cheese
2 cups ricotta or cottage cheese (light or regular)
1 or 2 eggs

For machines with nested bowls, see method on page 139.

Cook noodles according to package directions. Drain well. Fresh pasta does not require cooking.

STEEL BLADE: Drop garlic through feed tube while machine is running; process until minced. Add onions and bell pepper. Process with quick on/off pulses, until coarsely chopped. Sauté garlic, onions and pepper in margarine or oil in a large nonstick skillet on medium heat for 5 minutes, until golden. Add tuna, soup, salt and pepper. Mix well.

GRATER: Grate mozzarella cheese, using medium pressure. Empty bowl and set aside.

STEEL BLADE: Process Parmesan cheese, ricotta cheese and 1 egg until mixed, 8 to 10 seconds. Add second egg if mixture seems dry.

Assembly: Spray 9- × 13-inch glass baking dish with nonstick spray. Place 3 lasagna noodles in bottom of dish. Spread with half the tuna mixture. Add another layer of noodles; spread with ricotta cheese mixture. Add remaining noodles; top with remaining tuna mixture. Sprinkle with mozzarella cheese. (Can be assembled up to this point and refrigerated.) Bake in preheated 350°F oven for 35 to 45 minutes.

448 calories per serving, 29.1 g carbohydrates, 1.3 g fiber, 36 g protein, 20.2 g fat (9 g saturated fat), 82 mg cholesterol, 817 mg sodium, 380 mg potassium, 3 mg iron, 430 mg calcium, 424 mg phosphorus

## nested bowl method

Use medium bowl and GRATER/SHREDDING DISC to grate mozzarella cheese. Use large bowl and STEEL BLADE for remaining processing tasks.

## variations

### low-sodium variation

Omit canned mushroom soup. Add 1 cup sliced mushrooms to vegetable mixture. Make a double recipe of Béchamel Sauce (page 103). One serving contains 390 calories, 24.6 g carbohydrates, 16.1 g fat and 342 mg sodium.

### passover variation

Follow assembly instructions above, but replace lasagna noodles with 7 matzos. Briefly moisten each matzo with hot water first; cut as needed to fit baking dish.

# LUSCIOUS VEGETARIAN LASAGNA

The name says it all!

Yield: 10 servings. Keeps 2 to 3 days in the refrigerator. Reheats and/or freezes well.

**Vegetarian Spaghetti Sauce (page 106)**

**9 lasagna noodles (packaged or Homemade Pasta, page 259)**

**12 oz (375 g) chilled mozzarella cheese (low-fat or regular) (3 cups grated)**

**1 green and/or red bell pepper, halved**

**1 cup mushrooms**

**3 cups ricotta or creamed cottage cheese (light or regular)**

**1 egg**

**¾ cup grated Parmesan cheese**

For machines with nested bowls, see method on page 140.

Prepare sauce as directed. Cook lasagna noodles according to package directions. Drain well; lay flat on clean towel. Fresh pasta does not require cooking.

GRATER: Cut mozzarella cheese to fit feed tube. Grate, using medium pressure. Empty bowl. *Continued*

SLICER: Slice pepper and mushrooms, using light pressure. Empty bowl.

STEEL BLADE: Process ricotta or cottage cheese with egg until blended, about 10 seconds.

Place about 1½ cups sauce in the bottom of sprayed 9- × 13-inch glass baking dish. Arrange 3 lasagna noodles over sauce. Spread with half the ricotta cheese; sprinkle with half the Parmesan and one-third of the mozzarella cheese. Repeat with sauce, noodles and cheeses. Top with noodles, sauce and mozzarella cheese. Garnish with pepper and mushrooms. (Can be refrigerated or frozen at this point. Thaw before baking.)

Bake in preheated 375°F oven about 45 minutes, until bubbling and golden.

404 calories per serving, 36.3 g carbohydrates, 4.9 g fiber, 26 g protein, 18.5 g fat (9.6 g saturated fat), 68 mg cholesterol, 719 mg sodium, 801 mg potassium, 3 mg iron, 562 mg calcium, 440 mg phosphorus

### nested bowl method

Use medium bowl and GRATER/SHREDDING DISC to grate mozzarella cheese; empty bowl. Use medium bowl and SLICER for pepper and mushrooms; leave them in bowl. Use large bowl and STEEL BLADE for ricotta mixture. Assemble as directed.

### variations

Add a 10 oz (300 g) package of chopped spinach, drained and squeezed dry, to ricotta cheese mixture. Tofu can replace part or all of the ricotta cheese.

# TORTILLA LASAGNA FLORENTINE

There's no need to cook pasta for this quick lasagna. I like to make it in 2 pie plates and freeze 1 for a future meal.

Yield: 8 servings. Keeps 2 days in the refrigerator. Reheats and/or freezes well.

12 oz (375 g) chilled mozzarella cheese (low-fat or regular) (3 cups grated)

2 cloves garlic

1 medium carrot, cut in chunks

3 cups (1½ lb/750 g) 1% dry cottage cheese

1 pkg (10 oz/300 g) frozen spinach, defrosted and squeezed dry

½ cup grated Parmesan cheese

salt and freshly ground black pepper to taste

½ tsp each dried basil and dried oregano

4 cups vegetarian tomato sauce (store-bought or homemade, preferably low-sodium)

6 large soft flour tortillas (10-inch round)

For machines with nested bowls, see method on page 141.

GRATER: Grate mozzarella cheese, using medium pressure. You should have 3 cups. Empty bowl.

STEEL BLADE: Process garlic and carrot until finely minced, about 10 seconds. Add cottage cheese, spinach, Parmesan cheese, salt, pepper, basil and oregano; process until blended. Scrape down sides of bowl as needed.

Spray two 9-inch glass pie plates with nonstick spray. In each pie plate, layer ½ cup sauce, 1 tortilla, one-quarter of the spinach mixture and ½ cup grated cheese. Repeat layering, ending with a tortilla. You will have 3 layers of tortillas and 2 layers of spinach mixture in each pie plate. Top with remaining sauce and grated cheese. (Can be prepared in advance up to this point and refrigerated.)

Bake, uncovered, in preheated 350°F oven for 30 minutes, until golden brown. Let stand for 5 minutes for easier slicing. Cut in wedges to serve.

427 calories per serving, 42.2 g carbohydrates, 3.9 g fiber, 31 g protein, 15.1 g fat (7.8 g saturated fat), 31 mg cholesterol, 695 mg sodium, 303 mg potassium, 4 mg iron, 552 mg calcium, 454 mg phosphorus

### nested bowl method

Use medium bowl and GRATER/SHREDDING DISC to grate mozzarella cheese. Use large bowl and STEEL BLADE for remaining processing tasks.

### variations

Use a combination of grated mozzarella and Swiss cheeses. Replace part or all of the cottage cheese with ricotta cheese or tofu.

## PASTA VEGETABLE MEDLEY

Yield: 6 servings. Keeps 2 days in the refrigerator. Reheats well. If frozen, vegetables may lose some of their texture.

1 pkg (1 lb/500 g) rotini or bow-tie pasta
3 cups broccoli florets
3 cloves garlic
1 medium onion, cut in chunks
1 red bell pepper, cut in chunks
1 cup mushrooms
1 Tbsp olive oil

2 Tbsp fresh chopped basil (or 1 tsp dried basil)
2 cups tomato sauce
¼ cup grated Parmesan cheese, plus extra for garnish
salt and freshly ground black pepper to taste

Bring large pot of salted water to a boil. Cook pasta for 8 minutes, until nearly tender. Add broccoli and cook 2 minutes longer, until broccoli is tender-crisp and pasta is al dente. Reserve about ½ cup of cooking liquid. Drain pasta but do not rinse. Return pasta and broccoli to pot.

STEEL BLADE: Drop garlic through feed tube while machine is running; process until minced. Add onion, red pepper and mushrooms; process with quick on/off pulses, until coarsely chopped. *Continued*

In large nonstick skillet or wok, heat oil. Sauté garlic, onion, red pepper and mushrooms on medium-high heat until tender, 5 to 7 minutes. Combine with pasta, broccoli, basil, tomato sauce and ¼ cup Parmesan cheese. Add reserved cooking liquid; mix well. Season with salt and pepper. Garnish with additional Parmesan cheese.

360 calories per serving, 67.5 g carbohydrates, 5.4 g fiber, 14 g protein, 4.8 g fat (1.3 g saturated fat), 3 mg cholesterol, 499 mg sodium, 590 mg potassium, 4 mg iron, 86 mg calcium, 196 mg phosphorus

### pasta tips

- Save on cleanup by adding firm vegetables (e.g., broccoli, baby carrots, snow peas, sun-dried tomatoes) to the pasta pot for the last 2 to 3 minutes of cooking, until tender-crisp.

- Don't add oil to the water when cooking pasta and don't rinse it once it's cooked.

- Reserve about ½ cup of the starchy cooking liquid when cooking pasta. It will help thicken the sauce.

## PENNE WITH ROASTED TOMATOES AND GARLIC AU GRATIN

This could be called "penne from heaven!" Make it when tomatoes and basil are in season. When basil is expensive, chop fresh parsley together with dried basil for a fresh taste.

Yield: 6 servings. Keeps 2 days in the refrigerator. Reheats and/or freezes well.

| | |
|---|---|
| 2 dozen Italian plum tomatoes | ¼ cup extra-virgin olive oil |
| 10 to 12 cloves garlic | 1 pkg (1 lb/500 g) penne (spirals can |
| ½ cup fresh basil, packed | be substituted) |
| (or ½ cup fresh parsley plus | 8 oz (250 g) chilled low-fat mozzarella |
| 2 tsp dried basil) | cheese (2 cups grated) |

For machines with nested bowls, see method on page 143.

Core tomatoes and cut in half lengthwise. Arrange cut side up in a single layer on nonstick baking pan.

STEEL BLADE: Process garlic and basil until minced, 10 to 12 seconds. Add olive oil and process briefly to mix. Spread mixture with a rubber spatula over tomatoes. Roast, uncovered, in preheated 350°F oven for 1½ hours, or until tomatoes are very tender and brown around the edges.

In large pot, cook pasta according to package directions. Reserve about ½ cup of cooking water. Drain pasta well and return to pot.

GRATER: Grate cheese, using medium pressure. Empty bowl.

STEEL BLADE: Coarsely chop tomatoes and pan juices, using several quick on/off pulses. Add to pasta along with reserved cooking water. Mix well. Transfer to sprayed 2-quart casserole and top with grated cheese. (Can be prepared in advance up to this point.)

Bake, uncovered, in preheated 350°F oven for 20 minutes, until cheese is melted and golden.

510 calories per serving, 67.2 g carbohydrates, 4.5 g fiber, 23 g protein, 16.6 g fat (4.8 g saturated fat), 20 mg cholesterol, 284 mg sodium, 618 mg potassium, 2 mg iron, 580 mg calcium, 69 mg phosphorus

### nested bowl method

Use mini-bowl and blade to process garlic/basil mixture. Use medium bowl and GRATER/SHREDDING DISC to grate cheese (there's no need to empty the bowl). Use large bowl and STEEL BLADE to chop tomatoes.

### variations

- Cut 2 medium onions and 1 red bell pepper in half. Roast with the tomatoes.

- Omit mozzarella cheese. Mix pasta with roasted chopped tomatoes and ½ cup cooking water. Place on individual dinner plates. Top with a little crumbled feta or grated Parmesan cheese. Serve immediately.

# BUTTERMILK NOODLE KUGEL

This kugel makes a great main dish and is suitable for diabetics. Serve it with Almost Sour Cream! (page 145) or yogurt and berries.

Yield: 12 servings. Keeps 2 to 3 days in the refrigerator. Reheats and/or freezes well.

| | |
|---|---|
| 1 pkg (12 oz/375 g) medium or broad noodles (yolk-free are fine) | 3 Tbsp sugar (or granular Splenda) |
| 4 eggs (or 2 eggs plus 4 egg whites) | salt to taste |
| 1 cup cottage cheese | dash ground cinnamon (optional) |
| | 4 cups buttermilk |

Cook noodles according to package directions. Drain and rinse well. Return noodles to saucepan.

STEEL BLADE: Process eggs with cottage cheese until blended, 12 to 15 seconds. Add to noodles along with remaining ingredients and mix well. Pour into sprayed 9- × 13-inch glass baking dish.

Bake in preheated 375°F oven for 50 to 60 minutes, until golden brown. Serve hot.

122 calories per serving, 14.8 g carbohydrates, 0.3 g fiber, 9 g protein, 3.1 g fat (1.2 g saturated fat), 84 mg cholesterol, 185 mg sodium, 169 mg potassium, 1 mg iron, 118 mg calcium, 146 mg phosphorus

# COOKIE'S HOT MILK CHEESE KUGEL

This scrumptious recipe from my sister Rhonda Matias is a winner. The lighter version is an excellent runner-up.

Yield: 12 servings. Keeps 2 to 3 days in the refrigerator. Reheats and/or freezes well.

1 pkg (12 oz/375 g) medium noodles or Homemade Pasta (page 259)

½ cup soft butter or margarine, cut in chunks

1½ cups creamed cottage cheese

4 eggs

3 Tbsp sugar (or to taste)

½ cup sour cream (light or regular)

2 cups hot milk (1%) (heat in microwave 3 to 4 minutes)

2 Tbsp melted butter or margarine

¼ cup corn flake crumbs

½ tsp ground cinnamon (optional)

sour cream or yogurt and berries for serving

Prepare noodles according to package or recipe directions. Drain and rinse well. Return noodles to saucepan.

STEEL BLADE: Process butter or margarine with cottage cheese, eggs, sugar and sour cream until well mixed, stopping machine once or twice to scrape down sides of bowl. Add to noodles. Add hot milk and mix well.

Grease 9- × 13-inch glass baking dish with melted butter or margarine. Add noodle mixture and top with crumbs and cinnamon (if desired). Bake in preheated 350°F oven for 1 hour, until golden. Serve hot with sour cream and berries.

225 calories per serving, 15.7 g carbohydrates, 0.4 g fiber, 8 g protein, 14.4 g fat (8.1 g saturated fat), 116 mg cholesterol, 226 mg sodium, 144 mg potassium, 1 mg iron, 99 mg calcium, 140 mg phosphorus

### lighter variation

Reduce butter or margarine to ¼ cup. Use 1% cottage cheese and skim milk. Instead of 4 eggs, use 2 eggs and 4 egg whites. Use light or fat-free sour cream. Use only 1 Tbsp melted butter or margarine to grease the pan. One serving contains 167 calories and 7.5 g fat.

# FLORENTINE NOODLE KUGEL

When I served this scrumptious dish for a buffet brunch, everyone kept going back for more!

Yield: 12 servings. Keeps 2 to 3 days in the refrigerator. Reheats and/or freezes well.

1 pkg (12 oz/375 g) medium noodles or Homemade Pasta (page 259)

1 pkg (10 oz/300 g) frozen spinach, thawed and squeezed dry

¼ cup fresh dill

2 Tbsp melted butter or margarine

2 cups (500 g) light ricotta cheese

½ cup light sour cream

4 eggs

2 tsp salt

½ tsp pepper

1½ cups milk (skim or 1% is fine)

Prepare noodles according to package or recipe directions. Drain and rinse well. Return noodles to saucepan.

STEEL BLADE: Process spinach with dill until minced, about 10 seconds. Add butter, ricotta cheese, sour cream, eggs, salt and pepper. Process until well mixed, about 30 seconds, stopping machine once or twice to scrape down sides of bowl. Add mixture to noodles. Add milk and mix well.

Spray a 9- × 13-inch glass baking dish with nonstick spray. Add noodle mixture and spread evenly.

Bake in preheated 350°F oven for 1 hour, until golden. Serve hot.

169 calories per serving, 12.6 g carbohydrates, 1 g fiber, 10 g protein, 8.7 g fat (4.6 g saturated fat), 102 mg cholesterol, 514 mg sodium, 208 mg potassium, 1 mg iron, 207 mg calcium, 172 mg phosphorus

## PINEAPPLE NOODLE KUGEL

*Yield: 8 servings. Keeps 2 to 3 days in the refrigerator. Reheats and/or freezes well.*

1 pkg (12 oz/375 g) medium noodles or Homemade Pasta (page 259)
1 cup cottage cheese (1% or regular)
½ cup sour cream (light or regular)
4 eggs (or 2 eggs plus 4 egg whites)
¼ cup sugar (or to taste)
½ cup raisins
1 can (14 oz/398 mL) crushed pineapple, well-drained

Prepare noodles according to package or recipe directions. Drain and rinse well. Return noodles to saucepan. Combine with remaining ingredients and mix well. Place in sprayed 7- × 11-inch glass baking dish.

Bake in preheated 375°F oven for 45 minutes, until golden. Serve hot with sour cream or Almost Sour Cream! (below).

206 calories per serving, 30.9 g carbohydrates, 1.5 g fiber, 10 g protein, 5.3 g fat (2.2 g saturated fat), 127 mg cholesterol, 163 mg sodium, 213 mg potassium, 1 mg iron, 64 mg calcium, 130 mg phosphorus

### chef's tip

If you only have pineapple slices or chunks on hand, it's easy to transform them into crushed pineapple. Drain well, then process pineapple with quick on/off pulses, until crushed.

## ALMOST SOUR CREAM!

*A terrific substitute for sour cream! If the mixture is too thick after processing, add a little water.*

2 cups small-curd cottage cheese (1%)

Process cottage cheese using the STEEL BLADE for 2 to 3 minutes, until smooth and creamy. Scrape down the sides of the bowl as needed. Transfer to a container, cover and refrigerate. *Continued*

Yield: 2 cups. Keeps
up to 1 week in
the refrigerator.
Do not freeze.

10 calories per Tbsp, 0.4 g carbohydrates, 0 g fiber, 2 g protein, 0.1 g fat (0.1 g saturated fat), 1 mg cholesterol, 57 mg sodium, 12 mg potassium, 0 mg iron, 9 mg calcium, 19 mg phosphorus

### variation

Blend in 1 to 2 Tbsp granular Splenda or sugar and a dash of pure vanilla extract. Use instead of sour cream over pancakes, blintzes or dairy kugels. To serve with potatoes, omit sweetener and vanilla extract.

## THREE-CHEESE SWEET KUGEL

Serve this hot
with sour cream.

Yield: 12 servings as a
side dish, 8 servings as
a main course. Keeps
2 to 3 days in the
refrigerator. Reheats
and/or freezes well.

1 pkg (12 oz/375 g) broad noodles or Homemade Pasta (page 259)

4 oz (125 g) chilled cheddar cheese (low-fat or regular) (1 cup grated)

½ cup cream cheese (light or regular)

3 eggs (or 2 eggs plus 2 egg whites)

1½ cups milk (skim or 1% is fine)

1 cup sour cream (light or regular)

½ cup sugar

½ cup cottage cheese (1% or regular)

¼ cup margarine

½ tsp salt

½ cup corn flake crumbs (see Note)

ground cinnamon

For machines with nested bowls, see method below.

Prepare noodles according to package or recipe directions. Drain and rinse well. Return noodles to saucepan.

GRATER: Grate cheddar cheese, using medium pressure. Empty bowl.

STEEL BLADE: Process cream cheese with eggs until smooth, about 20 seconds, scraping down sides of bowl once or twice.

Add all ingredients except corn flake crumbs and cinnamon to noodles; mix well. Place in sprayed 9- × 13-inch glass baking dish. Sprinkle with corn flake crumbs and cinnamon. Bake in preheated 350°F oven for 1 hour, until golden.

218 calories per serving (as a side dish), 23 g carbohydrates, 0.4 g fiber, 9 g protein, 9.9 g fat (3.9 g saturated fat), 77 mg cholesterol, 342 mg sodium, 135 mg potassium, 1 mg iron, 152 mg calcium, 147 mg phosphorus

### nested bowl method

Use mini-bowl and mini-blade to process corn flake crumbs. Use medium bowl and GRATER/SHREDDING DISC to grate cheddar cheese. Use large bowl and STEEL BLADE for cream cheese mixture.

### note

To make your own crumbs, process 2 cups corn flakes on the STEEL BLADE for 25 to 30 seconds. To save unnecessary washing of the processor bowl, prepare crumbs first.

# HOT CHEESE CAKE

A longtime favorite from my friend Roz Brown. This makes a fabulous main dish for a buffet or brunch. Serve it with sour cream and fresh fruit salad or berries.

Yield: 8 servings. Keeps 2 to 3 days in the refrigerator. Reheats and/or freezes well. Recipe may be doubled and baked in sprayed 9- × 13-inch glass baking dish. Baking time will be about the same.

## TOPPING

**1 cup corn flakes (or ¼ cup crumbs)**
**1 Tbsp brown sugar**
**½ tsp ground cinnamon**

## BASE

**¼ cup butter or margarine**
**2 Tbsp granulated sugar**
**1 egg**
**1 cup flour**
**½ tsp baking powder**
**½ tsp ground cinnamon**

## FILLING

**2 cups dry cottage cheese (fat-free or regular) (see Note)**
**2 eggs**
**½ cup granulated sugar**
**dash salt**
**2 Tbsp cornstarch**
**½ cup milk (1% or 2%)**

Use the STEEL BLADE to process all ingredients. For machines with nested bowls, see method below.

For topping: Process corn flakes with brown sugar and cinnamon until fine. Transfer to small bowl.

For base: Process butter or margarine with sugar and egg for about 1 minute, scraping down sides of bowl as necessary. Add flour, baking powder and cinnamon. Process just until dough begins to form a ball around the blades, about 10 seconds. Pat into sprayed 8-inch square glass baking dish or 9-inch pie plate.

For filling: Process cheese for 15 seconds. Add eggs, sugar and salt. Process 15 seconds longer. Dissolve cornstarch in milk and pour in through feed tube while machine is running. Process 10 seconds longer, until well mixed. Pour over base and sprinkle with reserved topping.

Bake in preheated 350°F oven for 1 hour. Serve hot.

258 calories per serving, 38 g carbohydrates, 0.8 g fiber, 9 g protein, 8.2 g fat (4.4. g saturated fat), 98 mg cholesterol, 275 mg sodium, 123 mg potassium, 2 mg iron, 85 mg calcium, 143 mg phosphorus

### nested bowl method

Use mini-bowl and blade for crumb mixture. Use large bowl and STEEL BLADE for remaining processing tasks.

### note

If you can't find dry or pressed cottage cheese in your supermarket, substitute small curd cottage cheese (low-fat or fat-free). Place in a strainer and press out excess liquid. You'll probably have to add extra cottage cheese to make up for the drained liquid; processing time will be slightly longer.

# CHEDDAR CHEESE PUFF

Great for brunch—
and so easy!

Yield: 6 to 8 servings.

Keeps 2 to 3 days in the refrigerator. Reheats well.

Do not freeze.

8 oz (250 g) chilled cheddar cheese (low-fat or regular) (2 cups grated)

6 slices bread (white, whole wheat or challah)

2 Tbsp melted butter (optional)

3 eggs (or 2 eggs plus 2 egg whites)

½ to 1 tsp salt (to taste)

¼ tsp freshly ground black pepper

¾ tsp dry mustard

2 cups milk (1% or 2%)

GRATER: Grate cheese, using light pressure. Empty into sprayed 7- × 11-inch glass baking dish.

STEEL BLADE: Tear bread into chunks and drop through feed tube while machine is running. Process to make soft bread crumbs. Add to cheese and mix well. Spread evenly in baking dish. Drizzle with melted butter (if using). Process remaining ingredients for 5 seconds. Immediately pour over bread/cheese mixture. Cover with foil and refrigerate for half an hour or up to 24 hours.

Bake, covered, in preheated 350°F oven for 30 minutes. Uncover and bake 30 minutes longer, until nicely browned.

207 calories per serving, 17.8 g carbohydrates, 0.6 g fiber, 17 g protein, 7 g fat (3.1 g saturated fat), 118 mg cholesterol, 661 mg sodium, 203 mg potassium, 2 mg iron, 305 mg calcium, 327 mg phosphorus

### note

If desired, cut bread into 1-inch squares instead of making soft bread crumbs.

# ITALIAN CHEESE PUFF

Yield: 2 servings.

Do not freeze.

2 slices whole wheat bread, quartered

½ cup grated low-fat mozzarella cheese

1 tomato, quartered

½ green bell pepper, cut in chunks

2 eggs (or ½ cup egg substitute)

1 cup skim or soy milk

¼ tsp each dried basil and dried oregano

salt and freshly ground black pepper to taste

STEEL BLADE: Process bread with cheese for 5 to 6 seconds. Empty bowl. Process tomato and bell pepper with quick on/off pulses. Return bread and cheese to processor along with remaining ingredients. Process with 2 or 3 quick on/offs to mix. Pour into 2 lightly greased onion soup bowls. Fill to within 1 inch from the top.

Bake in preheated 375°F oven for 25 to 30 minutes, until puffed and golden. Serve immediately.

279 calories per serving, 24.1 g carbohydrates, 2.8 g fiber, 23 g protein, 10.5 g fat (4.4 g saturated fat), 229 mg cholesterol, 453 mg sodium, 519 mg potassium, 2 mg iron, 622 mg calcium, 290 mg phosphorus

## BAGEL, SALMON AND BROCCOLI CASSEROLE

I usually have bagels in my freezer, canned salmon in my pantry and broccoli in my refrigerator. This calcium-packed dish makes a wonderful brunch dish for a crowd. To make half the recipe, bake it for 45 to 50 minutes.

Yield: 12 servings. Keeps 2 to 3 days in the refrigerator. Reheats and/or freezes well.

6 bagels, cut in bite-sized pieces (about 8 cups)
2 cans (7¾ oz/213 g each) salmon, drained and flaked
4 cups broccoli florets
8 oz (250 g) chilled cheddar cheese (low-fat or regular) (2 cups grated)
¼ cup fresh dill
1 medium onion, cut in chunks
6 eggs (or 4 eggs plus 4 egg whites)
1 cup cream cheese (light or regular)
2 cups milk (1% or skim)
salt to taste
½ tsp pepper

Spray a 3-quart oblong or oval casserole with nonstick spray. Spread bagel pieces evenly in casserole. Spread salmon over bagels.

Rinse broccoli, leaving some water clinging to the florets. Microwave, covered, on High for 5 minutes. Cool slightly, then spoon over salmon layer.

GRATER: Grate cheese, using medium pressure. Sprinkle evenly over broccoli layer.

STEEL BLADE: Process dill and onion until fine. Add eggs and cream cheese; process until smooth, 25 to 30 seconds. (If you have a small processor, you may have to do this in 2 batches.) Add milk, salt and pepper; process briefly to combine. Pour evenly over bagel mixture. Cover and refrigerate for at least 1 hour or up to 24 hours.

Bake, uncovered, in a preheated 375°F oven for 1 hour, or until puffed and golden. Remove from oven and let stand 10 minutes for easier cutting.

351 calories per serving, 35.8 g carbohydrates, 2.2 g fiber, 25 g protein, 12.1 g fat (4.7 g saturated fat), 144 mg cholesterol, 714 mg sodium, 244 mg potassium, 3 mg iron, 309 mg calcium, 245 mg phosphorus

### variation

Instead of canned salmon, substitute 8 oz (250 g) chopped lox. Instead of cream cheese, substitute light sour cream or yogurt.

## SPINACH CHEESE PHYLLO PUFF

Yield: 8 servings. Keeps 2 days in the refrigerator. Can be frozen before or after baking.

1 medium onion, halved
1 Tbsp butter
1 pkg (10 oz/300 g) frozen spinach, thawed and squeezed dry
¼ cup fresh dill
½ cup grated Parmesan cheese
1½ cups cottage or ricotta cheese (light or regular)
3 eggs (or 2 eggs plus 2 egg whites)
salt and freshly ground black pepper to taste
8 sheets phyllo dough
¼ cup additional butter, melted

STEEL BLADE: Coarsely chop onion using quick on/off pulses. Heat butter in nonstick skillet and sauté onion over medium heat for 5 minutes. Add spinach and cook until moisture has evaporated. Process dill with Parmesan cheese until fine. Add cottage or ricotta cheese and eggs; process until well mixed. Add spinach mixture and process with several on/offs, just until mixed. Season to taste.

Keep phyllo dough covered with plastic wrap as it dries out quickly. Line sprayed 7- × 11-inch glass baking dish with 4 sheets of phyllo dough, brushing each sheet lightly with melted butter. Let edges of dough hang over pan.

Spread filling evenly over dough. Cover with remaining dough, brushing each sheet lightly with butter. Fold overhanging edges over the top; brush with butter. (May be prepared in advance and refrigerated or frozen until needed. Thaw before baking.)

Bake in preheated 350°F oven for 30 minutes, until puffed and golden. Serve immediately. If reheated, it will not puff up.

216 calories per serving, 14.1 g carbohydrates, 1.5 g fiber, 12 g protein, 12.5 g fat (6.6 g saturated fat), 105 mg cholesterol, 442 mg sodium, 187 mg potassium, 2 mg iron, 140 mg calcium, 160 mg phosphorus

### variations

- Margarine or oil can be used instead of butter. If using fresh spinach, wash and drain well. Chop in batches on STEEL BLADE. Sauté as directed.

- CHEESE FILLING: For the filling, use 3 cups pressed cottage cheese or light ricotta cheese, 2 eggs, ¼ cup sugar and 2 Tbsp lemon juice. Process on the STEEL BLADE until smooth, about 20 seconds. Serve with sour cream and fresh berries. One serving contains 220 calories, 20.6 g carbohydrates, 0.4 g fiber and 10.4 g fat.

## SPINACH SOUFFLÉ

Yield: 4 servings.
Serve immediately.
Do not freeze. (See
Roulade, page 151,
which can be frozen.)

3 Tbsp butter or margarine
¼ cup flour
½ tsp salt
dash freshly ground black pepper
  and nutmeg
1 cup hot milk (1% or 2%)
5 egg yolks

1 pkg (10 oz/300 g) fresh or frozen
  spinach, cooked, drained and
  squeezed dry
2 Tbsp grated Parmesan cheese
7 egg whites
¼ tsp cream of tartar

Preheat oven to 375°F.

STEEL BLADE: Process butter or margarine, flour and seasonings for 5 or 6 seconds. Add hot milk through feed tube while machine is running. Add egg yolks and blend 5 seconds longer. Place mixture in a saucepan and cook over medium heat, stirring constantly, until thick. Remove from heat. Do not boil.

Process spinach until minced, 10 to 12 seconds. Add spinach and Parmesan cheese to saucepan. (May be prepared in advance to this point. Beaten egg whites can be folded in just before baking.)

Beat egg whites and cream of tartar with electric mixer until stiff peaks form. Quickly stir about one-quarter of egg whites into soufflé mixture. Then carefully fold in remaining whites.

Turn into lightly buttered 8-cup soufflé dish. Bake at 375°F for 25 to 30 minutes, until puffed and golden. Serve immediately.

264 calories per serving, 12.9 g carbohydrates, 2.3 g fiber, 16 g protein, 16.9 g fat (8.4 g saturated fat), 294 mg cholesterol, 576 mg sodium, 406 mg potassium, 2 mg iron, 221 mg calcium, 224 mg phosphorus

## variations

- Substitute 1½ cups cooked broccoli for spinach. Process on STEEL BLADE until minced, 12 to 15 seconds. Or substitute Mushroom Duxelles (page 235) for spinach.

- ROULADE: To make a rolled soufflé (roulade), line large jelly roll pan with parchment paper; spray with nonstick spray. Prepare desired soufflé mixture and spread evenly in pan. Bake in preheated 400°F oven for about 15 minutes. Invert carefully onto a towel; carefully peel off parchment paper. Sprinkle with ¼ cup grated Parmesan cheese or Mushroom Duxelles (page 235). Roll up from the short side to form a jelly roll. Serve with Mushroom Sauce (page 104) or Cheese Sauce (page 104). May be frozen. Serves 6.

## BAKED FRITTATA

Yield: 4 servings.
Serve hot or at
room temperature.
Do not freeze.

¼ cup fresh dill
¼ cup fresh basil
¼ cup cut-up onion
¼ cup roasted red peppers (from a jar or homemade, page 53)
8 eggs (or 2 cups liquid egg substitute)

salt and freshly ground black pepper to taste
2 to 3 oz (60 to 90 g) chilled low-fat mozzarella cheese (½ to ¾ cup grated)

STEEL BLADE: Process dill, basil, onion and roasted peppers for 10 seconds. Add eggs or egg substitute, salt and pepper. Process 5 seconds longer. Pour into a sprayed 9-inch glass pie plate.

GRATER: Grate cheese, using medium pressure. Sprinkle evenly over egg mixture.

Bake in preheated 375°F oven for 25 to 30 minutes, until firm. Cut in wedges to serve.

203 calories per serving, 2.9 g carbohydrates, 0.2 g fiber, 17 g protein, 13.5 g fat (5.1 g saturated fat), 432 mg cholesterol, 199 mg sodium, 174 mg potassium, 1 mg iron, 161 mg calcium, 251 mg phosphorus

### lighter variation

If made with liquid egg substitute, 1 serving contains 156 calories and 7.1 g fat.

## CHEESY BROCCOLI CASSEROLE

This is a terrific do-ahead brunch dish! Assemble it the night before and bake it just before your guests arrive.

Yield: 6 to 8 servings. Keeps 1 to 2 days in the refrigerator. Reheats and/or freezes well.

1 pkg (10 oz/300 g) frozen broccoli, defrosted (or 4 cups fresh broccoli, cut in chunks)

4 oz (125 g) chilled cheddar cheese (low-fat or regular) (1 cup grated)

2 cups creamed cottage cheese (low-fat is fine)

3 eggs (or 2 eggs plus 2 egg whites)

2 Tbsp margarine (regular or light)

3 Tbsp flour

dash salt and freshly ground black pepper

STEEL BLADE: Chop broccoli with several quick on/off pulses, until coarsely chopped. (If using fresh broccoli, rinse in cold water; drain well. Microwave, covered, on High for 4 minutes. Chop with quick on/off pulses.) Place in sprayed 9- × 13-inch glass baking dish.

GRATER: Grate cheese, using medium pressure.

STEEL BLADE: Add remaining ingredients to grated cheese. Process just until mixed, 8 to 10 seconds. Pour over broccoli and mix well. (Can be assembled up to this point and refrigerated overnight.) Bake in preheated 325°F oven about 1 hour.

187 calories per serving, 8.2 g carbohydrates, 1.5 g fiber, 19 g protein, 8.6 g fat (2.8 g saturated fat), 113 mg cholesterol, 495 mg sodium, 199 mg potassium, 1 mg iron, 162 mg calcium, 266 mg phosphorus

# BROCCOLI CHEESE SQUARES

Easy and versatile! These make a great vegetarian brunch dish or side dish and can be adapted easily for Passover. For an easy hors d'oeuvre, cut into bite-sized squares.

**8 oz (250 g) chilled low-fat Swiss and/or cheddar cheese (2 cups grated)**
**1 Tbsp grated Parmesan cheese**
**2 cloves garlic**
**1 medium onion, cut in chunks**
**1 carrot, cut in chunks**
**1 Tbsp olive oil**
**4 cups cut-up broccoli**

**2 Tbsp fresh parsley**
**3 eggs (or 2 eggs plus 2 egg whites)**
**¼ cup dried bread crumbs or matzo meal**
**½ tsp salt**
**¼ tsp each dried basil and dried oregano**
**dash chili powder (optional)**

Yield: 6 servings as a main dish or 8 to 10 servings as a side dish. Keeps 2 days in the refrigerator. Reheats and/or freezes well.

For machines with nested bowls, see method below.

GRATER: Grate Swiss or cheddar cheese, using medium pressure. Transfer to bowl. Remove 2 Tbsp grated cheese, combine with Parmesan cheese and reserve as a topping.

STEEL BLADE: Drop garlic through feed tube while machine is running; process until minced. Add onion and carrot; process with several quick on/off pulses, until coarsely chopped. Heat oil in nonstick skillet. Sauté garlic, onion and carrot on medium heat until softened, about 5 minutes.

Meanwhile, rinse broccoli in cold water; drain well. Microwave, covered, on High for 4 minutes. Cool slightly.

Process broccoli and parsley with several on/off pulses, until coarsely chopped. Add sautéed vegetables and grated cheese (excluding reserved cheese topping), along with all remaining ingredients. Process 8 to 10 seconds longer, until combined. Spread mixture evenly in sprayed 7- × 11-inch glass baking dish. Sprinkle with reserved cheese topping.

Bake in preheated 325°F oven for 30 to 35 minutes, until golden. Cool slightly; cut into squares.

174 calories per serving (main dish), 10.9 g carbohydrates, 2.3 g fiber, 16 g protein, 7.6 g fat (2.6 g saturated fat), 119 mg cholesterol, 389 mg sodium, 277 mg potassium, 1 mg iron, 406 mg calcium, 316 mg phosphorus

## nested bowl method

Use medium bowl and GRATER/SHREDDING DISC for Swiss or cheddar cheese. Use large bowl and STEEL BLADE for remaining processing tasks.

## variation

Replace cooked broccoli with a 14 oz (398 mL) can of drained artichoke hearts. Substitute a red bell pepper for the carrot.

## SPINACH CHEESE BAKE

Serve this easy, versatile dish for brunch, lunch or as a side dish. To use as an appetizer, cut it into bite-sized squares. This also comes out delicious when made with gluten-free flour.

Yield: 6 servings as a main dish or 8 to 10 servings as a side dish. Keeps 2 days in the refrigerator. Reheats and/or freezes well.

2 Tbsp margarine or butter

1 pkg (10 oz/300 g) frozen spinach

8 oz (250 g) chilled cheddar, Muenster or Monterey Jack cheese (low-fat or regular) (2 cups grated)

2 eggs

½ cup milk (1% or skim)

½ cup flour (or Bob's Red Mill gluten-free flour)

½ tsp baking powder

½ tsp salt (to taste)

2 tsp fresh basil or dill (or ½ tsp dried)

Preheat oven to 350°F. For machines with nested bowls, see method below.

Place margarine in a 7- × 11-inch baking dish or 10-inch ceramic quiche dish. Place in oven for 5 minutes to melt butter. Microwave spinach on High for 3 minutes to thaw. Cool slightly; squeeze out excess moisture.

GRATER: Grate cheese, using medium pressure. Set aside.

STEEL BLADE: Process eggs, milk, flour, baking powder, salt and basil until blended, about 10 seconds. Add melted butter, spinach and cheese; process 10 to 15 seconds longer to combine. Spread mixture evenly in baking dish.

Bake for 30 to 35 minutes, until golden brown. Let stand a few minutes for easier cutting.

165 calories per serving (main dish), 7.8 g carbohydrates, 1.5 g fiber, 14 g protein, 8.7 g fat (3 g saturated fat), 80 mg cholesterol, 562 mg sodium, 196 mg potassium, 1 mg iron, 271 mg calcium, 264 mg phosphorus

### nested bowl method

Use medium bowl and GRATER/SHREDDING DISC to grate cheese. Use large bowl and STEEL BLADE to process all ingredients.

## SPINACH BOREKAS

These little pies or turnovers are a Middle Eastern delight! Popular fillings are spinach, cheese or meat.

double recipe of Cream Cheese Pastry (page 472) or Flaky Ginger Ale Pastry (page 471)

1 pkg (10 oz/300 g) frozen spinach, thawed and squeezed dry

4 green onions

2 Tbsp fresh dill

½ cup feta cheese

½ cup cottage cheese (1% or regular)

3 Tbsp grated Parmesan cheese

2 eggs (reserve 1 yolk to glaze dough)

salt and freshly ground black pepper to taste

sesame seeds for sprinkling

Prepare dough as directed and divide in 3 or 4 pieces. Wrap well and refrigerate for half an hour.

Yield: About 3 dozen.
Can be frozen before
or after baking.
Keeps 2 days in the
refrigerator. Reheats
and/or freezes well.

STEEL BLADE: Process spinach with green onions and dill until minced, about 10 seconds. Scrape down sides of bowl. Add cheeses, 1 egg, 1 egg white and salt and pepper. Mix well. (Dough and filling can be prepared up to a day in advance and refrigerated.)

Roll out 1 piece of dough as thin as possible into a large square on a floured surface. Cut in 3-inch circles. Place about 1 Tbsp filling on lower half of each circle. Fold over into a half-moon shape and press edges with fork to seal. Repeat with remaining dough and filling. (Dough scraps can be gathered into a ball and rolled again.)

Place borekas on ungreased foil-lined baking sheet. Brush lightly with egg yolk mixed with a few drops of water. Sprinkle with sesame seeds. Bake in preheated 375°F oven for 20 minutes, until golden. Serve hot or at room temperature.

99 calories each, 6.3 g carbohydrates, 0.5 g fiber, 3 g protein, 7 g fat (4.3 g saturated fat), 31 mg cholesterol, 118 mg sodium, 39 mg potassium, 1 mg iron, 51 mg calcium, 32 mg phosphorus

### note

For hors d'oeuvres, cut dough in 2-inch circles and use just a dab of filling. To freeze, place in freezer containers with waxed paper between layers to prevent sticking.

### variation

Spinach Borekas can also be made with commercial puff pastry or Sour Cream Pastry (page 473).

## NO-DOUGH CHEESE KNISHES

Quick and easy.
Serve these hot
with sour cream
and berries.

| | |
|---|---|
| 2 cups (1 lb/500 g) dry cottage cheese | ½ tsp salt |
| | ¼ cup sugar |
| 3 eggs (or 2 eggs plus 2 egg whites) | 1½ cups flour |
| ½ cup butter or margarine, melted | 2 tsp baking powder |

Yield: 18 to 20 knishes.
Keeps 2 days in the
refrigerator. Reheats
and/or freezes well.

STEEL BLADE: Process all ingredients together until well mixed, about 20 seconds. Drop by heaping spoonfuls onto generously sprayed foil-lined baking sheets.

Bake on middle rack in preheated 350°F oven for 25 to 30 minutes, until golden brown.

118 calories each, 12.1 g carbohydrates, 0.3 g fiber, 4 g protein, 6.2 g fat (3.6 g saturated fat), 50 mg cholesterol, 219 mg sodium, 45 mg potassium, 1 mg iron, 51 mg calcium, 69 mg phosphorus

# CHEESE KNISHES

Serve these cheese-filled crispy baked dumplings with sour cream or yogurt and berries.

Yield: 24 to 30 knishes. Keeps 2 days in the refrigerator. Reheats well. May be frozen before or after baking.

DOUGH

½ cup butter or margarine, cut in chunks

2 Tbsp sugar

2 eggs

2⅔ cups flour

2 tsp baking powder

½ cup milk (1% or 2%)

FILLING

4 cups (2 lb/1 kg) dry cottage cheese

1 egg

2 Tbsp lemon juice

¼ cup sugar

½ cup well-drained crushed pineapple (optional)

For dough: Use the STEEL BLADE. Process butter or margarine, sugar and eggs for 2 minutes, scraping down sides of bowl once or twice. Add flour, baking powder and milk and process 8 to 10 seconds longer, just until mixed. Do not overprocess. Remove from bowl and wrap well to prevent dough from drying out.

For filling: Process cheese, egg, lemon juice and sugar for 10 to 15 seconds, until blended. If using pineapple, mix in with 2 or 3 quick on/off pulses.

Divide dough into 4 equal parts. Coat lightly with flour. Roll 1 portion of dough into a rectangle on a floured surface.

Place about one-quarter of filling in a row along 1 edge, leaving 1-inch border on 3 sides. Roll up. Using the edge of your hand, gently press down on roll. Use a sawing motion to cut 2-inch pieces. Turn knishes on end, pressing ends in slightly. Repeat with remaining dough and filling. Place on sprayed baking sheet.

Bake in preheated 350°F oven for 35 minutes, until golden.

126 calories each, 15.9 g carbohydrates, 0.4 g fiber, 5 g protein, 4.8 g fat (2.7 g saturated fat), 39 mg cholesterol, 158 mg sodium, 66 mg potassium, 1 mg iron, 56 mg calcium, 86 mg phosphorus

# ONION CHEESE QUICHE

My son Steven used to wrap quiche in foil, bring it to school and heat it on the radiator for lunch!

Standard Butter Pastry, ½ recipe (page 470)

3 large onions, quartered

2 Tbsp butter or margarine

1 Tbsp flour

4 oz (125 g) chilled Swiss cheese (low-fat or regular) (1 cup grated)

2 eggs

⅔ cup milk (1% or 2%)

1 tsp salt

dash freshly ground black pepper and nutmeg

For machines with nested bowls, see method on page 157.

Yield: 6 to 8 servings. Keeps 2 days in the refrigerator. Reheats and/or freezes well.

Prepare pastry as directed. Roll out chilled pastry to fit 11-inch quiche pan with removable bottom or 9-inch pie pan. To minimize shrinkage, refrigerate for half an hour. Line crust with aluminum foil and weigh down with uncooked rice or dried beans.

Bake in preheated 400°F oven for 10 minutes; remove foil and beans or rice, and bake 5 minutes longer. Cool slightly. Reduce oven temperature to 375°F.

STEEL BLADE: Process onions with quick on/off pulses, until coarsely chopped. Sauté onions in melted butter or margarine over medium heat for about 10 minutes. Do not brown. Sprinkle in flour and mix well.

GRATER: Grate cheese, using medium pressure. Remove from bowl and set aside.

STEEL BLADE: Process eggs, milk, salt, pepper and nutmeg for a few seconds. Add onions and *half* of cheese. Process with 2 or 3 quick on/off turns to blend. Place in partially baked pastry shell. (Fill no higher than ¼ inch from top as quiche will puff during baking and may run over.) Sprinkle with remaining cheese. Bake immediately at 375°F for 30 to 35 minutes, until golden. A knife inserted in the center should come out clean.

318 calories per serving, 25.3 g carbohydrates, 1.5 g fiber, 11 g protein, 19.5 g fat (10 g saturated fat), 107 mg cholesterol, 718 mg sodium, 208 mg potassium, 2 mg iron, 141 mg calcium, 196 mg phosphorus

### nested bowl method

Use medium bowl and GRATER/SHREDDING DISC to grate cheese. Use large bowl and STEEL BLADE for remaining processing tasks.

### chef's tip

For that just-baked taste, prebake pastry shell, cool and freeze. Prepare filling up to 2 days in advance and refrigerate. About half an hour before serving, pour filling into frozen shell and bake for 30 to 35 minutes.

### variations

Use 2 cups raw or 1 cup cooked vegetables (e.g., onions, roasted red peppers, spinach, broccoli). Chop with quick on/off pulses. Sauté in butter or margarine until golden. Any gratable cheese may be used.

# SOUR CREAM TUNA QUICHE

Back due to popular demand! This recipe was in my original yellow processor book but wasn't included in *The Food Processor Bible* due to space constraints, so here it is once more. This quiche does not require prebaking of the crust.

Yield: 6 to 8 servings. Keeps 2 to 3 days in the refrigerator. Reheats and/or freezes well.

**Standard Butter Pastry, ½ recipe (page 470)**
**2 oz (60 g) chilled cheddar cheese (low-fat or regular) (½ cup grated)**
**3 eggs**

**1 cup sour cream (light or regular)**
**¾ tsp salt**
**dash pepper**
**¼ tsp Worcestershire sauce**
**1 can (6 oz/170 g) tuna, drained**
**1 can (3 oz/85 g) French's French Fried Onions**

For machines with nested bowls, see method below.

Preheat oven to 350°F. Prepare pastry as directed and place in a 9-inch glass pie plate. Flute edges, but do not prick pastry.

GRATER: Grate cheese, using medium pressure. Empty bowl and set aside.

STEEL BLADE. Process eggs, sour cream, salt, pepper and Worcestershire sauce for a few seconds to blend. Add tuna and cheese. Process with 3 or 4 very quick on/off pulses, just until mixed.

Place half the onions in a single layer in the pie shell. Add tuna mixture and top with remaining onions. Bake immediately for about 45 minutes, until set and golden.

268 calories per serving, 12.9 g carbohydrates, 0.3 g fiber, 14 g protein, 17.7 g fat (7.2 g saturated fat), 134 mg cholesterol, 615 mg sodium, 182 mg potassium, 1 mg iron, 139 mg calcium, 182 mg phosphorus

### nested bowl method

Use medium bowl and GRATER/SHREDDING DISC to grate cheese. Use large bowl and STEEL BLADE for remaining processing tasks.

# PAREVE VEGETABLE QUICHE

Use any combination of vegetables you like. This quiche is dairy-free.

Yield: 6 to 8 servings. Keeps 2 days in the refrigerator. Reheats and/or freezes well.

**Pareve Pie Crust (page 470)**
**2 medium onions or 1 bunch green onions, cut in chunks**
**2 stalks celery, cut in chunks**
**1 cup mushrooms**
**1 to 2 Tbsp oil**
**3 Tbsp flour**
**2 eggs**

**1 tsp pareve instant chicken soup mix**
**⅔ cup cold water or soy milk**
**¼ tsp each salt and freshly ground black pepper**
**⅛ tsp each garlic powder and dried basil**
**paprika, for garnish**

Prepare pastry as directed. Freeze half for another time. Roll out chilled pastry to fit 11-inch quiche pan or 9-inch pie pan. To minimize shrinkage, refrigerate for half an hour. Line crust with aluminum foil and fill with uncooked rice or dried beans.

Bake in preheated 400°F oven about 12 minutes. Remove foil and rice or beans; bake 6 to 8 minutes longer. Cool slightly. Reduce oven temperature to 375°F.

STEEL BLADE: Process onions with quick on/off pulses, until coarsely chopped. Empty bowl. Repeat with celery, then mushrooms, emptying bowl each time. Heat oil in large nonstick skillet. Add onions and celery and brown quickly over medium-high heat. Add mushrooms and cook a few minutes longer, until mixture is fairly dry. Remove from heat and stir in flour.

Process eggs with soup mix, water or soy milk, salt, pepper, garlic and basil for 3 or 4 seconds. Stir into vegetables. Pour vegetable mixture into baked crust and sprinkle with paprika. Bake immediately in preheated 375°F oven for 25 to 30 minutes, until golden.

257 calories per serving, 23.4 g carbohydrates, 1.5 g fiber, 5 g protein, 15.9 g fat (3.6 g saturated fat), 71 mg cholesterol, 291 mg sodium, 168 mg potassium, 2 mg iron, 27 mg calcium, 78 mg phosphorus

## NO-CRUST CHEESE AND SPINACH PIE

This easy, crustless pie can also be used for Passover.

Yield: 4 servings. Keeps 2 days in the refrigerator. Freezes and/or reheats well.

½ medium onion

1 pkg (10 oz/300 g) frozen spinach, cooked and squeezed dry

2 eggs

⅔ cup 1% cottage cheese

¾ tsp salt (or to taste)

dash freshly ground black pepper

¼ tsp dried dill

2 Tbsp grated Parmesan cheese

STEEL BLADE: Process onion and spinach until minced. Add remaining ingredients except Parmesan cheese and process until blended, 10 to 15 seconds. Place in sprayed 9-inch glass pie plate. Sprinkle with Parmesan cheese. Bake in preheated 350°F oven about 30 minutes.

101 calories per serving, 5.3 g carbohydrates, 2.2 g fiber, 11 g protein, 4.3 g fat (1.6 g saturated fat), 110 mg cholesterol, 712 mg sodium, 255 mg potassium, 2 mg iron, 151 mg calcium, 144 mg phosphorus

## NO-CRUST ZUCCHINI QUICHE

Yield: 6 servings. Keeps 2 days in the refrigerator. Reheats and/or freezes well.

3 medium zucchini, unpeeled

salt and freshly ground black pepper to taste

8 oz (250 g) chilled low-fat Swiss, mozzarella or cheddar cheese (2 cups grated)

½ medium onion

3 eggs (or 2 eggs plus 2 egg whites)

½ tsp each dried oregano and dried basil

3 Tbsp grated Parmesan cheese

GRATER: Cut zucchini to fit feed tube. Grate, using firm pressure. Transfer to strainer and sprinkle with salt. Let stand 10 minutes. Press out all liquid. Grate cheese and onion, using medium pressure. Do not empty bowl.

STEEL BLADE: Add zucchini, eggs, oregano and basil to processor bowl. Process with 3 or 4 quick on/off pulses, just until mixed. Place in sprayed 9-inch pie plate or 10-inch ceramic quiche dish. Sprinkle with Parmesan cheese.

Bake in preheated 350°F oven for 35 to 40 minutes, until set and golden.

128 calories per serving, 5 g carbohydrates, 1.1 g fiber, 15 g protein, 5.3 g fat (2.4 g saturated fat), 121 mg cholesterol, 165 mg sodium, 254 mg potassium, 1 mg iron, 399 mg calcium, 308 mg phosphorus

### variation

Replace zucchini with 2 cups chopped mushrooms. Omit basil and oregano. Add a dash of nutmeg.

## LUNCHEON PUFF

This baked pancake is quick and easy. Serve it with sour cream and berries or fresh fruit.

½ cup flour
½ cup milk (1%)
2 eggs
dash salt
½ tsp ground cinnamon

dash nutmeg
2 Tbsp butter or margarine
1 Tbsp lemon juice
2 Tbsp icing sugar

Yield: 2 servings.
Do not freeze.

Preheat oven to 425°F.

STEEL BLADE: Process flour with milk, eggs, salt, cinnamon and nutmeg for 8 to 10 seconds. Melt butter or margarine in shallow 1-quart casserole or 2 individual casseroles. Pour in batter, but do not stir. Sprinkle lightly with additional nutmeg and cinnamon.

Place immediately into oven and bake for 20 to 25 minutes, until browned on top. Sprinkle with lemon juice and icing sugar. Serve immediately.

346 calories per serving, 36 g carbohydrates, 1.2 g fiber, 12 g protein, 17.5 g fat (9.3 g saturated fat), 245 mg cholesterol, 257 mg sodium, 208 mg potassium, 2 mg iron, 115 mg calcium, 192 mg phosphorus

# EASY COTTAGE CHEESE PANCAKES

Serve these with yogurt, sour cream or Almost Sour Cream! (page 145).

Yield: About 15 pancakes. Keeps 2 days in the refrigerator. Reheats well in the microwave. Freezes well.

1 cup 1% cottage cheese
¼ cup sour cream or yogurt (light or regular)
2 eggs (or 1 egg plus 2 egg whites)
1 Tbsp melted butter or margarine
½ cup flour
¼ tsp salt
½ tsp baking powder
½ tsp ground cinnamon
combination of oil and butter, for frying

STEEL BLADE: Combine all ingredients, except oil and butter for frying, in processor and process until fairly smooth, 20 to 25 seconds.

Melt about 1 Tbsp oil and 1 Tbsp butter in large skillet. When bubbling, drop cheese mixture from large spoon into skillet. Brown on medium heat until golden, 2 to 3 minutes. Flip pancakes and brown other side. Repeat with remaining cheese mixture, adding more oil and butter as necessary. Serve hot.

64 calories each, 4.1 g carbohydrates, 0.2 g fiber, 3 g protein, 3.8 g fat (1.6 g saturated fat), 34 mg cholesterol, 138 mg sodium, 35 mg potassium, 0 mg iron, mg 29 calcium, 43 mg phosphorus

# BUTTERMILK PANCAKES

Children love it when you "write" their initials with pancake batter! Pour batter into the hot skillet to form the desired letters of the alphabet.

Yield: About fourteen 4-inch pancakes. Serve with maple syrup or honey. Keeps 2 days in the refrigerator. Reheats well in the microwave. Freezes well.

1¼ cups flour
1 Tbsp sugar
1 tsp baking powder
½ tsp salt
½ tsp baking soda
1¼ cups buttermilk
2 Tbsp oil or melted butter
1 egg

STEEL BLADE: Combine dry ingredients in processor and process for 3 or 4 seconds. Add remaining ingredients and process 6 to 8 seconds, until smooth, scraping down sides of bowl if necessary. Do not overprocess.

Pour onto hot, lightly greased griddle or skillet, using a scant ¼ cup batter for each pancake. Cook until bubbles appear on top side. Turn over and brown on other side.

76 calories each, 10.6 g carbohydrates, 0.3 g fiber, 2 g protein, 2.7 g fat (0.4 g saturated fat), 16 mg cholesterol, 190 mg sodium, 50 mg potassium, 1 mg iron, 48 mg calcium, 45 mg phosphorus

## variations

- Replace part of the all-purpose flour with whole wheat flour. Add 1 to 2 Tbsp wheat germ. If desired, add 1 cup grated carrots.

- No buttermilk? Use half yogurt and half milk.

- Stir ½ cup drained fresh or frozen blueberries into batter. *Continued*

- To make chocolate pancakes, prepare batter as directed, but add 3 Tbsp unsweetened cocoa powder with dry ingredients. Use 3 Tbsp sugar and 1⅓ cups of 1% or 2% milk. Serve pancakes with chocolate syrup if desired. One pancake contains 87 calories, 13.2 g carbohydrates and 0.7 g fiber.

## BASIC CRÊPE BATTER

Crêpes are a terrific way to use up leftovers and make a main course dish or dessert.

Yield: 12 to 14 crêpes or blintzes. Can be made in advance and refrigerated for 2 days or frozen for about a month.

¾ cup flour (you can use part whole wheat)

¼ tsp salt

3 eggs

1 cup milk (1%) or water

¼ cup canola oil

STEEL BLADE: Process all ingredients for 10 to 15 seconds, until blended. Refrigerate 30 minutes or overnight. Batter should be like heavy cream. If too thick, add a little milk or water.

Brush 8- or 9-inch nonstick skillet lightly with oil. Heat pan on medium-high heat for 2 minutes. Sprinkle with a few drops water. If it sizzles, pan is hot enough. Quickly pour 3 Tbsp batter into pan. Tilt in all directions to coat bottom evenly with batter. Immediately pour excess batter back into bowl.

Cook for 1 minute on first side. Flip with a spatula and cook 30 seconds on second side. (If making blintzes, cook only on 1 side.) Repeat with remaining batter. Place waxed paper between cooked crêpes to prevent sticking and stack them on a plate. Fill as desired.

98 calories each, 7.1 g carbohydrates, 0.2 g fiber, 3 g protein, 6.3 g fat (0.9 g saturated fat), 54 mg cholesterol, 73 mg sodium, 55 mg potassium, 1 mg iron, 32 mg calcium, 49 mg phosphorus

### note

In a standard-sized processor, process 1 batch of batter at a time to avoid leakage from bottom of bowl. Transfer to mixing bowl and repeat as many times as necessary. Recipe can be doubled if you have a large processor.

### crêpe shapes

To prevent tearing, crêpes should be at room temperature when filling.

- ROLL-UPS: Either spread filling in a thin layer over entire crêpe, or place 2 to 3 Tbsp filling on lower third of crêpe; roll up into a cylinder.
- ENVELOPES: Fold bottom edge up over filling, fold sides towards center and roll up (e.g., blintzes). Place seam side down.

- TORTES: Layers of crêpes, with filling in between, topped with sauce. (Great for people who have trouble rolling blintzes!)
- WEDGES/TRIANGLES: Fold in half, then in half once again. (Usually used for dessert crêpes.)

## FLORENTINE CRÊPES

Although there are several steps to this recipe, it is quite simple. Delicious!

Yield: 6 servings. Keeps 2 days in the refrigerator. Reheats and/or freezes well.

Basic Crêpe Batter (page 162)
Béchamel Sauce, double recipe (page 103)
¾ cup grated Parmesan cheese, divided
2 slices bread
1 Tbsp melted butter

2 pkgs (10 oz/300 g each) frozen or fresh spinach
1 egg
1 cup dry cottage cheese or light ricotta cheese
salt and freshly ground black pepper to taste

For machines with nested bowls, see method below.

Prepare crêpes as directed and refrigerate or freeze until needed. Prepare double recipe of sauce; stir in half the Parmesan cheese. Let cool.

STEEL BLADE: Tear bread in chunks. Process until fine crumbs are formed. Add melted butter and process a few seconds longer. Set aside.

Cook frozen spinach according to package directions. (Fresh spinach should be washed well and cooked in just the water clinging to the leaves for 4 to 5 minutes.) Drain well; squeeze dry. Process spinach on STEEL BLADE until fine, about 10 seconds. Add egg, cottage or ricotta cheese, salt and pepper and remaining Parmesan cheese. Process until mixed.

Place about 3 Tbsp filling on lower part of each crêpe and roll up. Place seam side down in sprayed 9- × 13-inch glass baking dish. Pour sauce over crêpes; top with crumbs. (May be prepared in advance and refrigerated.) Bake in preheated 350°F oven for 20 to 25 minutes.

454 calories per serving, 32.2 g carbohydrates, 3.5 g fiber, 21 g protein, 27.7 g fat (10.6 g saturated fat), 184 mg cholesterol, 815 mg sodium, 526 mg potassium, 3 mg iron, 425 mg calcium, 363 mg phosphorus

### nested bowl method

Use mini-bowl and blade to process bread. Use large bowl and STEEL BLADE for all other processing tasks.

## SALMON CRÊPES

Yield: 4 to 6 servings.
Keeps 2 days in the
refrigerator. May
be frozen, but best
prepared fresh.

**Béchamel Sauce, double recipe (page 103), or 1 can (10 oz/ 284 mL) condensed mushroom soup plus 5 oz milk (1%)**

**1 medium onion, halved**

**1 cup mushrooms**

**1 Tbsp butter or margarine**

**1½ cups cooked or canned salmon, drained**

**2 oz (60 g) chilled low-fat Swiss cheese (½ cup grated)**

**12 crêpes (page 162)**

Prepare sauce as directed, or whisk canned soup with milk, mixing well. Set aside.

STEEL BLADE: Process onion and mushrooms with quick on/off pulses, until coarsely chopped. Sauté in melted butter or margarine in large nonstick skillet over medium heat until golden. Process salmon with quick on/offs, until flaked; do not overprocess. Add to skillet along with half the sauce.

GRATER: Grate cheese, using medium pressure.

Place half the remaining sauce in sprayed 9- × 13-inch glass baking dish. Spread each crêpe with 3 Tbsp salmon mixture. Roll up and arrange in single layer in baking dish. Top with remaining sauce and sprinkle with grated cheese. (May be prepared in advance and refrigerated.)

Bake in preheated 400°F oven for 15 to 20 minutes, until bubbling hot.

477 calories per serving, 25.6 g carbohydrates, 1 g fiber, 28 g protein, 29.1 g fat (10.4 g saturated fat), 172 mg cholesterol, 559 mg sodium, 467 mg potassium, 2 mg iron, 519 mg calcium, 501 mg phosphorus

## CHEESE CANNELLONI (CRÊPES ITALIANO)

To reduce the
sodium, use salt-free
or reduced-sodium
cheeses and make
your own tomato
sauce.

Yield: 4 to 6 servings.
Keeps 2 days in the
refrigerator. Reheats
and/or freezes well.
(I have used the crêpes
directly from the freezer,

**Basic Crêpe Batter (page 162)**

**4 oz (125 g) chilled low-fat mozzarella cheese (1 cup grated)**

**½ cup grated Parmesan cheese**

**2 cups (1 lb/500 g) dry cottage or ricotta cheese**

**1 egg**

**salt and freshly ground black pepper to taste**

**2 cups tomato sauce (low-sodium or regular)**

**¼ tsp each garlic powder, dried basil and dried oregano**

Prepare crêpes as directed.

GRATER: Grate mozzarella cheese, using medium pressure. Set aside.

STEEL BLADE: Process Parmesan, cottage or ricotta cheese, egg, salt and pepper until mixed, about 15 seconds. Place 2 to 3 Tbsp cheese mixture on each crêpe. Roll up and place in sprayed 9- × 13-inch glass baking dish.

topped them with sauce and cheese, then baked them for 35 to 40 minutes.)

Combine tomato sauce with garlic, basil and oregano; pour over crêpes. Top with grated cheese. Bake in preheated 350°F oven for 25 to 30 minutes, until bubbly and golden.

519 calories per serving, 36.9 g carbohydrates, 1.7 g fiber, 32 g protein, 27.3 g fat (7.5 g saturated fat), 244 mg cholesterol, 849 mg sodium, 296 mg potassium, 3 mg iron, 702 mg calcium, 382 mg phosphorus

## CHEESE BLINTZES

Blintzes are paper-thin pancakes that are folded like an envelope, then fried or baked until golden. Serve them with sour cream, Almost Sour Cream! (page 145) or yogurt and berries.

**Basic Crêpe Batter (page 162)**        **2 to 3 Tbsp butter or margarine**
**Cheese Filling (page 166)**

Prepare crêpes as directed, browning them on 1 side only, just until no moisture remains on the top, 30 to 40 seconds.

Place about 3 Tbsp filling on lower third of browned side of each crêpe. Fold bottom edge up over filling, fold in sides and roll up. (Can be prepared in advance and refrigerated.)

To fry: Melt butter or margarine in a nonstick skillet. Place blintzes seam side down in pan. Brown on all sides on medium-low heat until golden.

To bake: Arrange blintzes in single layer in sprayed shallow casserole. Dot with butter or margarine; bake, uncovered, in preheated 400°F oven until golden, about 20 minutes. Serve hot.

Yield: 12 to 14 blintzes. Keeps 2 days in the refrigerator. To freeze, place filled blintzes on baking sheet in single layer. Freeze until firm, then store in plastic bags. Can be frozen for about 1 month.

159 calories each, 12.9 g carbohydrates, 0.2 g fiber, 7 g protein, 8.7 g fat (2.3 g saturated fat), 79 mg cholesterol, 207 mg sodium, 109 mg potassium, 1 mg iron, 66 mg calcium, 126 mg phosphorus

### variations

Use Potato Filling (half recipe, page 256). For fruit blintzes, fill with canned cherry, apple or blueberry pie filling or fruit jam. Delicious with Chicken or Meat Filling (page 257) and served with gravy. For Chinese Crêpes, place about 2 Tbsp Egg Roll Filling (page 77) on each crêpe and roll up. Serve hot with plum sauce. Do not freeze.

## CHEESE FILLING

Yield: 3 cups filling, enough for 12 to 16 blintzes or 30 kreplach.

3 cups (1½ lb/750 g) dry cottage cheese

1 egg yolk

3 Tbsp sugar or granular Splenda (or to taste)

2 Tbsp lemon or orange juice

STEEL BLADE: Process all ingredients until smooth, about 10 seconds.

44 calories per serving (¹⁄₁₂ of recipe), 5.8 g carbohydrates, 0 g fiber, 4 g protein, 0.5 g fat (0.2 g saturated fat), 20 mg cholesterol, 120 mg sodium, 54 mg potassium, 0 mg iron, 33 mg calcium, 76 mg phosphorus

## BLINTZ SOUFFLÉ

Serve these with yogurt or sour cream and berries.

Cheese Blintzes (page 165) or 1 dozen frozen blintzes (cheese, blueberry or cherry)

1½ cups sour cream or yogurt (light or regular)

1 tsp pure vanilla extract

½ cup sugar

4 eggs (or 1 cup egg substitute)

½ cup orange juice

Yield: 6 servings. Keeps 2 days in the refrigerator. Reheats and/or freezes well.

Place blintzes in single layer in sprayed 9- × 13-inch glass baking dish.

STEEL BLADE: Process sour cream or yogurt with vanilla extract and sugar for a few seconds. Add eggs and orange juice through feed tube while machine is running. Process until smooth. Immediately remove bowl from base of machine to prevent leakage. Pour topping over blintzes. (Can be prepared in advance and refrigerated.)

Bake in preheated 350°F oven for 1 hour, until puffed and golden.

529 calories per serving, 49.7 g carbohydrates, 0.5 g fiber, 21 g protein, 27.6 g fat (9.8 g saturated fat), 322 mg cholesterol, 500 mg sodium, 435 mg potassium, 2 mg iron, 238 mg calcium, 356 mg phosphorus

### lighter variation

If you make the topping with fat-free yogurt, granular Splenda and egg substitute, 1 serving contains 433 calories, 36 g carbohydrates and 21.9 g fat. To further reduce calories and fat, also use lighter ingredients in Cheese Blintzes.

# CRAZY BLINTZ SOUFFLÉ

Linda Warner of Farmington Hills, Michigan, sent me her recipe for this brunch dish. You can prepare the batter and filling a day in advance and assemble it just before baking. The original recipe called for 1 cup of butter. My version has a fraction of the fat! Serve this with sour cream or yogurt. Top with sliced almonds or jam.

Yield: 12 servings. Keeps 2 days in the refrigerator. Reheats and/or freezes well.

**BATTER**

1 cup flour
½ cup sugar
1 Tbsp baking powder
dash salt
½ cup margarine or butter, melted
   and cooled
2 eggs (or ½ cup egg substitute)
½ cup milk (skim or 1%)
1 tsp pure vanilla or ½ tsp almond
   extract

**FILLING**

3 cups (1½ lb/750 g) ricotta cheese
   (low-fat is fine)
2 cups (1 lb/500 g) light cream cheese
2 eggs (or ½ cup egg substitute)
¼ cup sugar
juice of a large lemon (3½ Tbsp)
1 tsp each lemon and orange zest
dash salt

Spray 9- × 13-inch glass baking dish with nonstick spray. (You can also use two 9-inch pie plates.) Use the STEEL BLADE to process all ingredients.

For batter: Combine all ingredients and blend until smooth, about 30 seconds, scraping down sides of bowl once or twice. Transfer batter to 4-cup measuring cup or bowl. (Don't bother washing processor bowl. Just scrape it out well with a spatula.)

For filling: Process ricotta cheese and cream cheese until smooth, about 30 seconds. Add remaining filling ingredients and process 30 seconds longer.

Assembly: Pour *half* the batter into prepared dish. Spoon filling overtop, gently spreading without mixing it into the batter. Pour remaining batter over filling. Bake in preheated 300°F oven about 1½ hours, until set and nicely browned. (If baked in 2 pie plates, baking time is about 1¼ hours.)

342 calories per serving, 27.6 g carbohydrates, 0.3 g fiber, 14 g protein, 19.6 g fat (8.5 g saturated fat), 108 mg cholesterol, 492 mg sodium, 135 mg potassium, 1 mg iron, 379 mg calcium, 191 mg phosphorus

### note

Cottage cheese can be used instead of ricotta. I've also made this using 4 cups ricotta and 1 cup cottage cheese, with excellent results.

# CHEESE FONDUE

Old is new—fondue parties are back in fashion! Make this company dish quickly using your processor and microwave. Fondue is delicious with boiled new potatoes, steamed cauliflower or broccoli.

Yield: 8 servings. Leftovers keep a day or 2 in the refrigerator. Add a little milk, reheat on Medium in the microwave and use as a sauce for steamed veggies or pasta. Do not freeze.

1½ lb (750 g) chilled Swiss cheese
(low-fat is fine)
1 Tbsp cornstarch
1 clove garlic, cut in half
3 cups dry white wine
¼ cup Kirsch

2 Tbsp fresh lemon juice
salt and freshly ground black pepper
to taste
French bread or baguettes, cut in bite-
sized chunks

GRATER: Grate cheese, using medium pressure. Combine cheese with cornstarch in plastic bag; shake well. Rub bottom and sides of ceramic cheese fondue pot or 2-quart microwavable casserole with garlic. Discard garlic.

Pour wine, Kirsch and lemon juice into casserole. Microwave, uncovered, on High for 6 to 7 minutes, just until bubbles start to appear; do not boil. Stir in cheese, salt and pepper. Reduce power to Medium (50%) and microwave 4 or 5 minutes longer, until smooth, whisking every 2 minutes. Transfer to fondue burner.

Spear the bread cubes on long-handled forks and dunk them in a figure-eight movement to keep the fondue well-stirred.

249 calories per serving, 10.2 g carbohydrates, 0 g fiber, 24 g protein, 4.3 g fat (2.8 g saturated fat), 30 mg cholesterol, 222 mg sodium, 102 mg potassium, 0 mg iron, 818 mg calcium, 516 mg phosphorus

# MEAT AND POULTRY
## recipe list

175  Herbed Rack of Lamb
175  Lamb Shanks with Classic Gremolata
176  Marinated Brisket
177  Super Roast Brisket
178  Savory Brisket or Top Rib
179  Overnight Roast
180  Oven-Roasted Pickled Brisket
180  Teriyaki Chuck Roast
181  Teriyaki Steak
182  Veal Brisket with Stuffing
182  Bread Stuffing
183  Minced Veal Stuffing
183  Italian Roasted Veal
184  Rozie's Osso Bucco with Gremolata
185  Gremolata
185  Baked Veal Chops
186  Cantonese Short Ribs
187  Honey Garlic Ribs
188  Spicy Short Ribs/Miami Ribs
189  Stew Italiano
190  Tasty Meatball Stew

191  Hawaiian Meatballs
192  Mmm-Good Meatballs
193  Cranberry Chicken Meatballs
194  Mandarin Chicken Meatballs
195  Pineapple Chicken Meatballs
196  Hamburgers à la Dutch
197  Chili
198  Chicken Chili
199  Super Spaghetti Sauce
200  Sneaky Spaghetti Sauce
201  Moist and Spicy Meat Loaf
201  Potato Kugel Meat Loaf
202  Turkey Popcorn Shepherd's Pie
203  Shipwreck
203  Stir-Fried Beef and Broccoli
204  Chinese Chicken Liver Stir-Fry
205  Teriyaki Turkey or Chicken Stir-Fry

206 Mushroom Almond
Chicken Stir-Fry

207 Moo Goo Guy Kew

208 Chicken Guy Kew

208 Chinese Chicken
Dinner-in-a-Dish

209 Chicken in Pineapple-
Orange Sauce

210 Tangy Orange Barbecue
Chicken

210 Marinated Barbecued
Chicken

211 Chicken and Vegetable
Bake

211 Heavenly Chicken

212 Italian Seasoned Chicken
with Potatoes

213 Crunchy Sesame Chicken

214 Potato-Crusted Chicken

214 Panko-Crusted Chicken
Fingers

215 Maple-Glazed Garlic
Chicken Breasts

215 Sticky Chicky

216 Roasted Turkey Breast
Balsamico

217 Turkey Cutlets with
Peppers and Mushrooms

218 Marinated Roast Turkey
with Cranberry Relish

220 Cranberry Relish

- Chop, purée or slice meats and poultry in moments in your processor (e.g., lean boneless beef, veal, chicken or turkey breasts). An added benefit is that you can also control the fat and cholesterol content. Refer to the **Smart Chart** (pages 35 and 36) for basic techniques.

- Grind your own meat or poultry (see page 36) using the **Steel Blade**. For best results, meat should be very cold. Use quick on/off pulses, checking texture often to avoid overprocessing.

- Depending on your food processor's capacity, you may have to combine ground meat or poultry with remaining ingredients in a large mixing bowl. Too large a quantity won't mix properly in smaller food processors. Meat at the bottom of the bowl will become overprocessed and meat at the top won't be mixed at all. Check guidelines in your user's manual for maximum quantities.

- SWITCH-A-GROUND: You can use lean ground turkey, chicken or veal in any recipe calling for ground beef (e.g., burgers, meatballs). Meat or poultry that you grind yourself will contain fewer calories and less fat and cholesterol than commercially ground meats. The choice is yours!

- Add grated vegetables such as zucchini, onions, carrots or mashed beans to replace a portion of the ground meat in recipes. Instead of grating

them, you can also grind them on the **Steel Blade**. (What a "grate" way to include more veggies in your meals, especially when dealing with fussy eaters!)

- Should you cook poultry with or without the skin? If roasting poultry without a sauce, leave the skin on during cooking to keep it moist; remove skin after cooking. If cooking poultry in a sauce, you can remove the skin either before or after cooking. I usually prefer to cook chicken with the skin on to keep it moist and flavorful, then I remove the skin after cooking to save on calories and fat.

- SKINNY SECRETS: When cooking chicken in a sauce, remove the skin before cooking if you plan to serve it immediately. Otherwise the fat from the skin melts and drains into the sauce. However, if you plan to serve the chicken the next day, you can cook it with the skin on, then refrigerate it overnight. Discard congealed fat before reheating. Remove the skin before eating.

- If you don't have a scale, remember that 2 cups meat cubes or 3 single, boneless, skinless chicken breasts weigh about 1 lb (500 g).

- BONE YOUR OWN: Pull the skin off the chicken breast; remove the breastbone and smaller bones with your fingers and a sharp knife. Pull out the white tendons from the breast meat. No need to be perfect—you will improve with practice!

- Slice your own uncooked boneless meat or poultry (see page 36). Be sure to chill it first. You will have perfect, paper-thin slices that are perfect for stir-fries!

- Cut pieces of boneless raw meat or poultry to fit feed tube. Wrap in plastic and freeze briefly, until very cold. It is ready to slice when it is hard to the touch but can be pierced easily with the tip of a sharp knife.

- Slice across the grain for maximum tenderness. To check which way the grain (muscle fiber) runs, slice off a thin piece from raw or cooked meat. Muscle fibers in chicken and turkey breasts run lengthwise, so cut across the width.

- Wash the bowl, blades and cover immediately after processing meat or poultry. Either wash by hand with hot, soapy water and a brush, use technique for "Self-Cleaning Processor" (page 7) or place on top rack of dishwasher. Blades and discs are very sharp, so handle with care!

- Use ground meat within 24 to 48 hours of purchase. Stewing meat, steaks, chicken and chops should be used within 2 days, and roasts within 3 days. Store in the coldest part of your refrigerator at 40°F or lower.

- You can freeze raw ground meat for 2 to 3 months. Roasts and steaks can be frozen for 8 to 12 months. Whole chicken and turkey can be frozen for 8 to 10 months, or 5 to 6 months if cut up. Freeze cooked meat and poultry dishes no longer than 2 months for maximum quality.

- Never stuff poultry or roasts in advance. Prepare stuffing and refrigerate; stuff just before cooking. Allow ½ cup stuffing for each pound of poultry. Stuff loosely, as stuffing expands during cooking. Stuffing must be cooked to 165°F; check the temperature with an instant-read thermometer.

- Stuffing may be baked separately in a covered casserole to prevent it from absorbing the fatty drippings. Bake at 350°F for about 45 minutes.

- Remove stuffing from poultry or roast before refrigerating or freezing leftovers.

- For maximum flavor, season poultry with desired marinade or spices, cover and marinate in the refrigerator for at least 1 hour or up to 48 hours.

- Brush up on food safety! Beware of cross-contamination from raw meat, poultry or the basting brush used during cooking. Boil marinade for 5 minutes; then you can use it as a sauce on cooked food. (Be sure to use a clean basting brush or spoon.)

- Clean all work surfaces, cutting boards, blades and processor bowl thoroughly; wash your hands with soap and hot water to help prevent cross-contamination.

- Do not leave raw or cooked meats and poultry at room temperature for more than 1 to 2 hours.

- Use your processor to slice, chop or shred foods quickly into uniform pieces; then stir-fry. Dinner will be ready in minutes! Use the recipe for Teriyaki Turkey or Chicken Stir-Fry (page 205) as a guideline on how to slice meat and vegetables for stir-fries using wide-mouth feed tube techniques.

- Leftover cooked meat or poultry is a blessing in disguise! Use it in fajitas, sandwiches, salads, stir-fries, pasta, stuffed bell peppers, crêpes, soufflés or omelets.

## SLOW COOKERS

- A slow cooker is excellent for cuts of meat that are usually cooked on top of the stove or braised in the oven. It's ideal for brisket, pot roast, stews, meatballs, chili and spaghetti sauce.

- Slow cookers come in a variety of sizes. I have an oval 6-quart model with a High and Low setting. A slow cooker cooks foods at a low heat ranging from 200°F to 300°F in a tightly sealed, moist environment. They work best when two-thirds to three-quarters full.

- Spray the insert with nonstick spray for easier cleanup or use a slow cooker bag/liner.

- It's not a good idea to cook frozen roasts or chicken in a slow cooker. It takes too long for the meat to thaw and reach a safe temperature.

- Cooking meats and poultry in a slow cooker is similar to braising them in your oven. However, slow cookers won't brown foods—and browning adds flavor. Heat oil in a large skillet on medium-high heat. Add beef, chicken pieces or ground meat to the skillet, working in batches if necessary. Brown on all sides and then transfer to the slow cooker. Scrape up any browned bits from the pan with a wooden spoon, adding a little water, wine or broth. Add liquid and browned bits to the slow cooker. Brown onions in the skillet until golden, then add them to the slow cooker.

- IN A STEW? Here's how to prevent the vegetables from becoming overcooked. Peel desired veggies (e.g., potatoes, parsnips, carrots) and cut into 1-inch chunks. Place in a bowl, drizzle with 1 Tbsp oil, then season with salt, pepper and desired herbs. Mix well and wrap tightly in foil. Place the foil packet on top of meat and liquid; cover and cook on low for 10 hours. Carefully unwrap veggies and stir into the stew just before serving.

- Reduce the amount of liquid by about 25% in your regular recipe to compensate for the fact that there will be little evaporation during cooking. If there's too much liquid left, uncover for the last hour of cooking and cook on High setting. Or you can strain the cooking liquid into

a saucepan and cook it uncovered on top of the stove over high heat until reduced.

- SLOW COOKER CONVERSION TIMES: If your regular recipe calls for 15 to 30 minutes of cooking, cook it for 4 to 8 hours on Low or 1½ to 2 hours on High setting. If it calls for 30 to 60 minutes, cook it for 6 to 8 hours on Low or 3 to 4 hours on High. If it calls for 2 to 3 hours, cook it for 8 to 12 hours on Low or 4 to 6 hours on High.

- No peeking! Every time you lift the lid it prolongs the cooking time by an additional 20 minutes.

- Boneless skinless chicken breasts get dry and tough if they are cooked too long in a slow cooker (thighs won't dry out as quickly). Boneless chicken pieces take 3 to 4 hours on Low. Cut-up chicken on the bone takes 4 to 6 hours on Low. Brown chicken in batches in a skillet first for maximum flavor.

- If a recipe calls for 4 hours of cooking and you work full-time, prepare and cook it in your slow cooker when you get home from work. It will be cooked by the time you're ready for bed. Transfer to shallow containers for quicker cooling and refrigerate overnight. The next day, remove and discard hardened fat. When you reheat the dish, the flavor will be enhanced.

- For recipes that require 8 to 12 hours of cooking, prepare and combine the ingredients in the removable insert and store in the refrigerator overnight. The next morning, put the insert into the heating unit and set the timer. When you get home, dinner will be done!

- Going out for a few hours? You can start the slow cooker on High while you're still home, then turn it down to Low just before you leave.

- Late for dinner? Timing isn't crucial. An extra hour of cooking in the slow cooker usually won't affect the recipe.

# HERBED RACK OF LAMB

This elegant, quick
recipe is excellent
for company. It
multiplies easily—
each rack serves
2 people.

Yield: 4 servings.

2 trimmed racks of lamb, about
  2 lb (1 kg) each (calculate 4 lamb
  chops per person)
salt and freshly ground black pepper
  to taste
4 cloves garlic
2 Tbsp fresh rosemary (or ½ tsp dried
  rosemary)

2 Tbsp fresh thyme (or ½ tsp dried
  thyme)
2 Tbsp olive oil
2 Tbsp lemon juice
2 Tbsp honey
2 Tbsp Dijon mustard
½ cup fresh parsley
2 slices bread, torn into pieces
¼ cup pecans

Rub lamb with salt and pepper.

STEEL BLADE: Drop garlic through feed tube while machine is running; process until minced. Add rosemary, thyme, oil, lemon juice, honey and mustard; process until blended, about 10 seconds. Rub mixture over lamb. Marinate at room temperature for 30 minutes or overnight in refrigerator.

Place lamb, meat side down, on rack in roasting pan. Roast in preheated 450°F oven for 10 minutes, until browned.

STEEL BLADE: Process parsley, bread and pecans until finely minced, 15 to 20 seconds. Turn lamb meat side up; pat crumb mixture evenly over meat. Return lamb to oven and roast about 10 minutes longer, or until meat thermometer registers 140°F for rare. Let stand for 10 minutes. Carve into chops and serve immediately.

732 calories per serving, 19.8 g carbohydrates, 1.6 g fiber, 42 g protein, 53.1 g fat (22.1 g saturated fat), 193 mg cholesterol, 355 mg sodium, 395 mg potassium, 5 mg iron, 88 mg calcium, 399 mg phosphorus

# LAMB SHANKS WITH CLASSIC GREMOLATA

I was never a big
fan of lamb until
I tried this recipe
from cookbook
author and culinary
expert Dana
McCauley. It's lick-
the-spoon good!

6 lamb shanks, about
  1 lb (500 g) each
¼ cup canola oil
1 large carrot
1 large onion
1 stalk celery
6 cloves garlic, peeled
2 Tbsp tomato paste
1 cup red wine

1 tsp salt (to taste)
2 tsp black peppercorns
2 cups chicken, lamb or veal stock
  (approximately)

GREMOLATA

1 lemon
1 cup lightly packed parsley leaves
3 garlic cloves
½ tsp coarsely ground pepper

Yield: 6 servings.
Keeps 2 days in the
refrigerator. Reheats
and/or freezes well.

Rinse lamb shanks under cold running water; drain and pat dry with paper towel. Preheat oven to 300°F.

Place a Dutch oven (or saucepan large enough to hold all of the lamb shanks) over high heat; add half the oil. Brown shanks, turning frequently, on all sides until well browned, about 5 minutes; work in batches if necessary. Remove shanks from pot and transfer to a platter. Tent with foil.

Meanwhile, cut carrot, onion, celery, and garlic in chunks and place in the bowl of a food processor fitted with the STEEL BLADE. Pulse to chop finely. Scrape into the hot pan and sauté for 2 minutes. Reduce heat to medium and stir in tomato paste. Using a flat, stiff spatula, cook for 2 minutes, scraping bottom of the pot as you stir to prevent scorching. At the first sign of scorching, deglaze pan with a splash of red wine. Continue to cook until tomato paste darkens and is almost brown.

Pour in remaining wine and mix well. Simmer for 10 minutes or until liquid is reduced by half. Return lamb shanks to the pot, stacking them like cord wood if necessary. Add salt and peppercorns and pour in enough stock to cover (add extra if necessary to cover meat). Bring to a boil over high heat. Cover tightly with a lid and transfer to the preheated oven. Braise for 1½ hours.

For gremolata: Use a vegetable peeler to remove skin from lemon, leaving as much of the white pith behind as possible. Use the blade of a knife to scrape away as much of the pith on the peel strips as possible. Discard pith. Place lemon strips, parsley and garlic in the mini-bowl of a food processor. Pulse until finely chopped. Cut lemon in half and squeeze out juice. Gently stir lemon juice and pepper into lemon/parsley mixture. Reserve.

Stir all but 2 Tbsp of the reserved gremolata into the braised lamb. (The lamb can be made and heated again when needed. In fact, the flavors develop wonderfully overnight.) Cool to room temperature; transfer to a storage container with a tight lid and refrigerate until needed. Reheat and serve the remaining gremolata on the side.

396 calories per serving, 9.8 g carbohydrates, 2.2 g fiber, 43 g protein, 17.7 g fat (3.6 g saturated fat), 140 mg cholesterol, 548 mg sodium, 566 mg potassium, 4 mg iron, 72 mg calcium, 254 mg phosphorus

## MARINATED BRISKET

Marinating, then
long, slow cooking
are the secrets to
this mouthwatering
brisket.

3 or 4 medium onions, cut in chunks

4 to 5 lb (1.8 to 2.3 kg) brisket, well-trimmed

salt and freshly ground black pepper to taste

1 Tbsp paprika

1 tsp dry mustard

4 cloves garlic

½ cup soy sauce (low-sodium or regular)

2 to 3 Tbsp honey or maple syrup

SLICER: Slice onions, using medium pressure. Place in large, sprayed roasting pan. Rub brisket on all sides with salt, pepper, paprika and mustard; place in pan.

STEEL BLADE: Drop garlic through feed tube while machine is running; process until minced. Add soy sauce and honey or maple syrup; process 2 or 3 seconds longer. Pour mixture over brisket and rub into meat on all sides. Cover pan with aluminum foil. Marinate in refrigerator for at least 1 hour or up to 24 hours.

Bake, covered, in preheated 325°F oven. Allow 45 minutes per lb, or until meat is fork-tender. Uncover for the last hour and baste occasionally. Let stand for 20 to 30 minutes before slicing. Reheat for a few minutes in pan gravy.

*328 calories per serving, 10.2 g carbohydrates, 1 g fiber, 40 g protein, 13.4 g fat (4.7 g saturated fat), 98 mg cholesterol, 626 mg sodium, 483 mg potassium, 4 mg iron, 23 mg calcium, 347 mg phosphorus*

### slow cooker method

Combine all ingredients in sprayed slow cooker insert and marinate up to 24 hours in the refrigerator. Place insert in slow cooker and cook, covered, on Low for 8 to 10 hours.

*Yield: 8 to 10 servings. Keeps 2 to 3 days in the refrigerator. Reheats and/or freezes well. Can be prepared in advance and refrigerated overnight. Discard congealed fat from gravy, slice and serve.*

# SUPER ROAST BRISKET

*A tried-and-true favorite and an excellent holiday dish.*

*Yield: 10 to 12 servings. Keeps 2 to 3 days in the refrigerator. Reheats and/or freezes well.*

| | |
|---|---|
| **5 to 6 lb (2.3 to 2.7 kg) brisket, well trimmed** | **¼ cup honey** |
| **2 or 3 cloves garlic** | **¼ cup cola** |
| **1 small onion, halved** | **3 Tbsp ketchup** |
| **2 Tbsp vinegar or lemon juice** | **2 to 3 tsp salt (to taste)** |
| **¼ cup red wine** | **1 tsp paprika** |
| **¼ cup oil** | **¼ tsp freshly ground black pepper** |

Place brisket in large, sprayed roasting pan.

STEEL BLADE: Process garlic and onion until minced. Add remaining ingredients and process a few seconds longer to blend. Pour over brisket, making sure to cover all surfaces. Cover pan with aluminum foil. Marinate in refrigerator for 1 to 2 hours, or up to 24 hours. Baste occasionally.

Bake, covered, in preheated 300°F oven for 5 hours, until very tender (about 1 hour per lb). When cool, refrigerate. Slices better the next day. Remove hardened fat and discard.

*374 calories per serving, 9.7 g carbohydrates, 0.2 g fiber, 39 g protein, 18.7 g fat (5.1 g saturated fat), 98 mg cholesterol, 607 mg sodium, 415 mg potassium, 4 mg iron, 131 mg calcium, 320 mg phosphorus*

*Continued*

## slow cooker method

Combine all ingredients in sprayed slow cooker insert and marinate up to 24 hours in the refrigerator. Place insert in slow cooker and cook, covered, on Low for 10 to 12 hours.

---

# SAVORY BRISKET OR TOP RIB

This easy, tasty recipe uses ingredients you always have on hand.

**3 large onions, cut in chunks**
**3 or 4 cloves garlic**
**1 tsp salt**
**¼ tsp freshly ground black pepper**
**¼ cup ketchup**

**¼ cup Dijon mustard**
**¼ cup brown sugar**
**4 to 5 lb (1.8 to 2.3 kg) brisket or top**
  **rib roast, well trimmed**

Yield: 8 to 10 servings. Keeps 2 to 3 days in the refrigerator. Reheats and/or freezes well.

SLICER: Slice onions, using medium pressure. Place in bottom of sprayed roasting pan.

STEEL BLADE: Drop garlic through feed tube while machine is running; process until minced. Scrape down sides of bowl. Add salt, pepper, ketchup, mustard and brown sugar. Process for a few seconds, just until blended. Spread mixture over meat on all sides. (Can be prepared up to this point and refrigerated overnight.)

Cook, covered, in preheated 325°F oven for 3½ hours, or until tender. Uncover the last half hour and baste with pan juices. It should not be necessary to add any liquid as the roast will produce its own gravy. Cool completely. Refrigerate several hours or overnight. Discard congealed fat from gravy. Slice and reheat in gravy in a covered casserole at 325°F for 20 to 25 minutes.

346 calories per serving, 15.4 g carbohydrates, 0.7 g fiber, 39 g protein, 13.2 g fat (4.7 g saturated fat), 98 mg cholesterol, 648 mg sodium, 491 mg potassium, 4 mg iron, 28 mg calcium, 333 mg phosphorus

## slow cooker method

Combine all ingredients in sprayed slow cooker insert and marinate up to 24 hours in the refrigerator. Place insert in slow cooker and cook, covered, on Low for 8 to 10 hours.

## savory turkey breast

Substitute a rolled boneless turkey breast (about 4 lb/1.8 kg) for the brisket. Calculate 30 minutes per lb in the oven as the cooking time. When done, a meat thermometer should register an internal temperature of 170°F. Let stand, covered, for 20 minutes. Slice and serve. Reheats well.

## OVERNIGHT ROAST

A great time-saver—set it and forget it!

Yield: 10 to 12 servings. Keeps 2 to 3 days in the refrigerator. Reheats and/or freezes well.

5 to 6 lb brisket or top rib roast (2.3 to 2.7 kg)

1 Tbsp paprika

2 tsp salt

½ tsp each freshly ground black pepper and dried basil

2 Tbsp soy sauce

4 cloves garlic

3 or 4 medium onions, cut in chunks

3 stalks celery

4 carrots

¾ cup red wine

¼ cup water (approximately)

Place meat in sprayed roasting pan; rub roast on all sides with paprika, salt, pepper, basil and soy sauce.

STEEL BLADE: Drop garlic through feed tube while machine is running; process until minced. Process half the onions with 3 or 4 quick on/off pulses, until coarsely chopped. Rub onion/garlic mixture over meat. Process remaining onions with quick on/offs and arrange around meat.

SLICER: Cut celery and carrots to fit feed tube. Slice, using medium pressure. Add to roasting pan. Add wine and water. Cover tightly and place in preheated 200°F oven. Cook overnight for 7 to 8 hours. (I put the roast into the oven just before going to sleep and remove it first thing in the morning.)

Uncover and cool; refrigerate until serving time. Discard congealed fat from gravy. Slice brisket and reheat in gravy.

323 calories per serving, 6.4 g carbohydrates, 1.5 g fiber, 40 g protein, 13.2 g fat (4.7 g saturated fat), 98 mg cholesterol, 759 mg sodium, 541 mg potassium, 4 mg iron, 31 mg calcium, 342 mg phosphorus

### slow cooker method

Combine all ingredients in sprayed slow cooker. Cook, covered, on Low for 10 to 12 hours.

### passover variation

Replace soy sauce with bottled barbecue sauce.

MEAT AND POULTRY

179

# OVEN-ROASTED PICKLED BRISKET

Pickled meats are extremely salty. To reduce sodium, boil the meat for 30 minutes, drain well, then roast. Another option is to soak the meat in cold water for several hours or overnight before roasting it, changing the water once or twice.

4 to 5 lb (1.8 to 2.3 kg) pickled brisket or top rib roast, well trimmed

2 tsp dry mustard (optional)

2 tsp paprika

⅓ cup brown sugar, packed

2 Tbsp honey

Wash spices off meat. Dry well. Line roasting pan with double thickness of aluminum foil large enough to wrap roast completely. Place meat on foil; sprinkle with seasonings and brown sugar on all sides. Drizzle honey over and rub into meat. Wrap tightly. Bake in preheated 325°F oven about 3 hours, or until tender. Let cool, then slice.

369 calories per serving, 12.7 g carbohydrates, 0.2 g fiber, 34 g protein, 19.3 g fat (6.4 g saturated fat), 178 mg cholesterol, 2118 mg sodium, 384 mg potassium, 4 mg iron, 22 mg calcium, 229 mg phosphorus

Yield: 10 servings. Keeps 2 to 3 days in the refrigerator. Reheats and/or freezes well.

### variations

- Roast brisket as directed. Process ½ cup orange marmalade, 2 Tbsp ketchup, 1 Tbsp lemon juice and 1 Tbsp horseradish with the STEEL BLADE, about 10 seconds. Brush mixture over roast. Bake, uncovered, at 350°F for a half hour longer, until glazed and crusty.

  Leftover meat may be used to make filling for knishes, blintzes, kreplach, etc. See Corned Beef Filling (page 257).

### passover variation

Omit mustard. If brown sugar is not available, substitute granulated sugar.

# TERIYAKI CHUCK ROAST

Yield: 8 servings. Keeps 2 to 3 days in the refrigerator. Reheats and/or freezes well.

4 lb (1.8 kg) boneless chuck roast, well trimmed

1 large onion, cut in chunks

2 to 3 cloves garlic

1 slice fresh ginger, peeled (1 Tbsp), or ½ tsp ground ginger

¼ cup oil

½ cup orange juice

¼ cup sherry or red wine

¼ cup soy sauce (low-sodium or regular)

1 to 2 Tbsp brown sugar or maple syrup

½ tsp red pepper flakes

Pierce roast deeply on both sides with a fork and place in sprayed 9- × 13-inch ovenproof dish.

SLICER: Slice onion, using medium pressure. Wrap well and refrigerate until needed.

STEEL BLADE: Drop garlic and ginger through feed tube while machine is running; process until minced. Add remaining ingredients except onion and process for a few seconds to blend. Pour marinade over meat. Cover and marinate in refrigerator for 2 to 3 hours, or overnight, turning meat once.

Drain most of marinade from meat. Refrigerate marinade until just before serving time. Add sliced onion to meat, cover tightly and bake in preheated 325°F oven about 3 hours, or until tender. Let stand about 20 minutes before slicing.

Place reserved marinade in a saucepan and bring to a boil. Cook for 5 minutes, stirring occasionally. Serve over sliced roast.

385 calories per serving, 7.3 g carbohydrates, 0.4 g fiber, 47 g protein, 17 g fat (4.3 g saturated fat), 95 mg cholesterol, 433 mg sodium, 461 mg potassium, 4 mg iron, 31 mg calcium, 305 mg phosphorus

## TERIYAKI STEAK

*The marinade is delicious on veal chops, chicken and tofu. Thinly sliced leftover meat is delicious cold in sandwiches or wrapped in tortillas.*

*Yield: 5 to 6 servings. Leftovers keep 2 days in the refrigerator. Freezes well.*

| | |
|---|---|
| 2 lb (1 kg) London broil (flank steak) | 1 Tbsp oil |
| 2 cloves garlic | 1 Tbsp ketchup (optional) |
| ¼ cup soy sauce (low-sodium or regular) | 2 to 3 Tbsp brown sugar |
| | ½ tsp ground ginger |
| ¼ cup pineapple juice | ¼ tsp paprika |
| 2 Tbsp lemon or lime juice | |

Place meat in nonreactive container.

STEEL BLADE: Drop garlic through feed tube while machine is running; process until minced. Add remaining ingredients and process 3 to 4 seconds longer. Pour over meat. Cover and marinate in refrigerator for 1 to 2 hours or up to 48 hours, turning meat over occasionally.

Preheat grill, barbecue or broiler. Remove meat from marinade. Cook until medium, 8 to 10 minutes per side, brushing meat with marinade during cooking. Slice meat across the grain. Discard leftover marinade.

401 calories per serving, 9.1 g carbohydrates, 0.2 g fiber, 51 g protein, 16.3 g fat (5.8 g saturated fat), 89 mg cholesterol, 532 mg sodium, 698 mg potassium, 4 mg iron, 42 mg calcium, 411 mg phosphorus

### variations

Use any of the following as a marinade: Chinese Marinade (page 109), Cantonese Marinade (page 109), Honey Garlic Sparerib Sauce (page 110) or your favorite bottled Asian sauce.

# VEAL BRISKET WITH STUFFING

This tender,
tasty brisket is
full of flavor!

Yield: 10 servings for a
boneless veal shoulder
or brisket, or 6 servings
for a veal brisket with
bones. Keeps 2 to 3 days
in the refrigerator.
Reheats and/or freezes
well, but remove stuffing
and reheat or freeze
it separately. Do not
freeze potatoes.

5 to 6 lb (2.3 to 2.7 kg) veal brisket
  or shoulder (have butcher make
  a pocket)
3 or 4 cloves garlic
2 tsp paprika
1 to 2 tsp salt (to taste)
1 tsp dry mustard
½ tsp dried thyme
¼ tsp freshly ground black pepper

Bread Stuffing (below) or Minced Veal
  Stuffing (page 183)
2 medium onions
3 stalks celery
24 baby carrots
½ cup chicken broth or water
¼ cup wine (red or white)
8 to 10 potatoes, cut up (optional)

Place roast in a large sprayed roasting pan.

STEEL BLADE: Drop garlic through feed tube while machine is running; process until minced. Remove from processor bowl with a rubber spatula and spread over meat. Rub roast inside and out with garlic and seasonings. Stuff loosely with desired stuffing and fasten with skewers. (If roast is very lean, rub with 1 Tbsp oil.)

SLICER: Cut onions and celery to fit feed tube. Slice, using medium pressure. Add to roasting pan along with carrots, broth and wine. Cover and bake in preheated 325°F oven for 3 hours, basting occasionally. Uncover and bake ¾ hour longer. If desired, add cut-up potatoes.

378 calories per serving, 12.9 g carbohydrates, 2.3 g fiber, 45 g protein, 14.6 g fat (5.4 g saturated fat), 227 mg cholesterol, 699 mg sodium, 665 mg potassium, 3 mg iron, 88 mg calcium, 390 mg phosphorus

### passover variation

Omit dry mustard; increase paprika to 1 Tbsp. Stuff brisket with Mostly Vegetable Stuffing (page 499) or Quick Matzo Meal Stuffing (page 500).

# BREAD STUFFING

Yield: For 5 lb (2.3 kg)
veal brisket, 2 roasting
chickens or a large
capon. Stuff loosely,
as stuffing expands
during cooking.

leftover bread or rolls (2¼ cups soft
  bread crumbs)
2 carrots, cut in chunks
2 stalks celery, cut in chunks
1 medium onion, halved

¼ cup fresh parsley
2 eggs (or 1 egg plus 2 egg whites)
1 tsp salt
freshly ground black pepper to taste
¼ tsp dried thyme

STEEL BLADE: Drop chunks of bread through feed tube while machine is running. Measure loosely packed; transfer to large mixing bowl. Process vegetables and parsley until minced, about 8 seconds. Add eggs and process 2 or 3 seconds longer. Add with remaining ingredients to bread crumbs and mix well.

Stuff meat or poultry just before cooking. Remove stuffing before refrigerating or freezing leftovers.

65 calories per serving (⅛ of recipe), 9.2 g carbohydrates, 1 g fiber, 3 g protein, 1.8 g fat (0.5 g saturated fat), 53 mg cholesterol, 409 mg sodium, 112 mg potassium, 1 mg iron, 39 mg calcium, 45 mg phosphorus

## MINCED VEAL STUFFING

Yield: For a 5 lb (2.3 kg) veal brisket, 2 roasting chickens or a large capon.

| | |
|---|---|
| 1 lb (500 g) lean ground veal (or see Grind Your Own, page 36) | 1 small onion |
| | 2 Tbsp ketchup |
| 1 or 2 cloves garlic | 1 egg (or 2 egg whites) |
| 1 medium potato | ¼ cup matzo meal |
| 1 large carrot | 1 Tbsp instant onion soup mix |
| 1 stalk celery | dash salt and freshly ground black pepper |
| ½ green or red bell pepper | |

Place meat in large mixing bowl.

STEEL BLADE: Drop garlic through feed tube while machine is running; process until minced. Process vegetables in batches until minced. Add to mixing bowl along with remaining ingredients; mix lightly to blend. Stuff meat or poultry just before cooking.

124 calories per serving (⅛ of recipe), 11.7 g carbohydrates, 1.1 g fiber, 11 g protein, 3.6 g fat (1.4 g saturated fat), 65 mg cholesterol, 186 mg sodium, 325 mg potassium, 1 mg iron, 22 mg calcium, 118 mg phosphorus

## ITALIAN ROASTED VEAL

The seasonings for this recipe may be used on any cut of veal (shoulder, breast, steaks, chops). Thinly sliced cold roast is delicious in sandwiches.

| | |
|---|---|
| 4 to 5 lb veal roast (1.8 to 2.3 kg) (or 8 veal steaks or chops) | 4 cloves garlic, cut in slivers |
| | 4 large carrots |
| 1 to 2 tsp seasoning salt | 2 large onions |
| freshly ground black pepper to taste | ½ cup tomato sauce and/or chicken broth |
| 2 tsp Italian seasoning (or 1 tsp each dried oregano and dried basil) | |
| | ½ cup dry red wine |
| 1 tsp dry mustard | 6 to 8 potatoes (optional) |

Rub meat with salt, pepper, Italian seasoning and mustard. Cut several slits in meat and insert garlic. Place in large sprayed roasting pan. *Continued*

SLICER: Cut carrots and onions to fit feed tube. Slice, using firm pressure. Add vegetables, tomato sauce and/or broth and wine to roasting pan. Cover and bake in preheated 300°F oven about 3 hours for a roast or 1½ hours for steaks or chops (see Note).

Uncover and roast 45 minutes longer, basting occasionally. If desired, sliced or quartered potatoes may be added when you uncover the meat.

Let roast stand for 20 minutes before slicing, or slice when cold and reheat in the pan gravy.

383 calories per serving, 8.5 g carbohydrates, 1.7 g fiber, 61 g protein, 9.2 g fat (2.5 g saturated fat), 258 mg cholesterol, 432 mg sodium, 821 mg potassium, 3 mg iron, 76 mg calcium, 492 mg phosphorus

Yield: 8 servings. Allow ½ lb per person for boneless roasts and ¾ to 1 lb per person if there is a large percentage of bone. Keeps 2 to 3 days in the refrigerator. Reheats and/or freezes well.

### note

The low cooking temperature is important. Allow 50 to 60 minutes cooking time per lb of meat and cook until fork-tender.

### passover variation

Omit mustard. Have butcher make a pocket in roast. Stuff with your favorite Passover stuffing. Allow an extra half hour cooking time.

## ROZIE'S OSSO BUCCO WITH GREMOLATA

Thanks to my friend Roz Brown of Montreal for this awesome Italian dish. It tastes even better the next day. Delicious over rice. *Buon appetito!*

Yield: 6 servings. Keeps 2 to 3 days in the refrigerator. Reheats and/or freezes well. Before reheating, skim off fat.

6 veal shanks, well trimmed (about 4 lb/1.8 kg)
⅓ cup flour
salt and freshly ground black pepper to taste
4 Tbsp olive oil
3 or 4 cloves garlic
3 medium carrots, cut in chunks
2 medium onions, cut in chunks
2 cups mushrooms
2 stalks celery

¾ to 1 cup dry white wine
1½ cups chicken broth (salt-free or regular)
1 can (28 oz/796 mL) tomatoes (salt-free or regular)
¼ cup fresh basil, minced (or 1 tsp dried basil)
1 tsp dried rosemary
½ tsp dried thyme (optional)
salt and pepper to taste
Gremolata (page 185)

Coat veal on all sides with flour, shaking off excess. Sprinkle with salt and pepper. Heat 3 Tbsp of the oil in a large skillet. Add veal (in batches) and brown slowly on all sides, about 10 minutes. Transfer to a platter. Discard fat from skillet.

STEEL BLADE: Drop garlic through feed tube while machine is running; process until minced. Add carrots and onions and process with quick on/off pulses, until coarsely chopped.

SLICER: Slice mushrooms and celery, using medium pressure. Heat remaining 1 Tbsp oil in skillet. Add vegetables and sauté on medium heat for 6 to 8 minutes, stirring occasionally. Add wine, reduce heat and cook 1 minute longer. Add broth, tomatoes and herbs. Season with salt and pepper. Add veal.

Cover and simmer for 2 hours, until tender. At serving time, sprinkle Gremolata over veal.

465 calories per serving, 19.9 g carbohydrates, 3.7 g fiber, 51 g protein, 17.4 g fat (3.5 g saturated fat), 209 mg cholesterol, 221 mg sodium, 947 mg potassium, 4 mg iron, 119 mg calcium, 427 mg phosphorus

### slow cooker method

Brown veal shanks as directed and transfer to sprayed slow cooker. Sauté vegetables. You'll need to add less liquid (use only ½ cup wine and 1 cup chicken broth). Add tomatoes, herbs, salt and pepper to vegetables.

Transfer mixture to slow cooker and stir to combine. Cook, covered, on Low for 8 hours.

## GREMOLATA

Yield: 4 to 6 servings.

**2 to 3 Tbsp lemon rind**
**¼ to ⅓ cup fresh parsley**

**2 to 3 cloves garlic**

STEEL BLADE: Process until finely minced, about 10 seconds. Delicious with veal, chicken or fish.

5 calories per serving, 1.2 g carbohydrates, 0.5 g fiber, 0 g protein, 0 g fat (0 g saturated fat), 0 mg cholesterol, 3 mg sodium, 32 mg potassium, 0 mg iron, 12 mg calcium, 5 mg phosphorus

## BAKED VEAL CHOPS

Yield: 4 to 6 servings.
Keeps 2 days in the
refrigerator. Reheats
and/or freezes well.

**30 crackers (or 1 cup dried bread crumbs)**
**1 tsp Italian seasoning**
**½ tsp salt (or to taste)**
**¼ tsp each freshly ground black pepper, paprika and garlic powder**
**1 egg plus 2 Tbsp water**

**4 to 6 veal chops (about 2 lb/1 kg)**
**2 Tbsp oil for frying**
**2 cloves garlic**
**2 cups tomato sauce**
**1 green or red bell pepper, cut in chunks**
**1 medium onion, cut in chunks**

STEEL BLADE: Process crackers with Italian seasoning, salt, pepper, paprika and garlic powder until fine crumbs are formed, about 30 seconds. Transfer to a flat plate or plastic bag. Process egg with water for 2 or 3 seconds. Transfer to a pie plate.

Dip chops in egg mixture, then in crumbs. Heat oil in large nonstick skillet over medium-high heat. Brown chops quickly on both sides, adding more oil if needed. Drain well on paper towels. Arrange in a single layer in large sprayed casserole.

STEEL BLADE: Drop garlic through feed tube while machine is running; process until minced. Add tomato sauce and dash of Italian seasoning. Process for a few seconds to blend. Pour over chops.

SLICER: Slice pepper and onion, using medium pressure. Add to casserole. Cover and bake in preheated 350°F oven for half an hour. Uncover and bake half an hour longer, or until tender.

432 calories per serving, 34 g carbohydrates, 3.1 g fiber, 35 g protein, 17.2 g fat (3.3 g saturated fat), 153 mg cholesterol, 593 mg sodium, 412 mg potassium, 4 mg iron, 113 mg calcium, 273 mg phosphorus

### passover variation

Replace cracker crumbs with matzo crackers or matzo meal. Replace Italian seasoning with mixture of fresh or dried basil, oregano and thyme.

## CANTONESE SHORT RIBS

Yield: 6 servings. Keeps 2 to 3 days in the refrigerator. Reheats well. If freezing, add pineapple and vegetables when reheating.

| | |
|---|---|
| 1 can (14 oz/398 mL) pineapple chunks | 2 medium onions, cut in chunks |
| Cantonese Marinade (page 109) | 1 green or red bell pepper, cut in chunks |
| 4 lb (1.8 kg) short ribs (flanken or Miami ribs), cut in serving-sized pieces | 2 cups mushrooms |
| | 2 cups bean sprouts |
| | 1 cup snow peas or sugar snap peas |

Drain pineapple. Reserve ¾ cup of the juice and use to prepare marinade as directed. Refrigerate pineapple until needed.

Place short ribs in sprayed 9- × 13-inch ovenproof dish. Pour marinade over ribs. Cover and marinate for 2 to 3 hours or up to 24 hours in the refrigerator, turning meat over several times.

Bake, covered, in preheated 300°F oven about 3 hours, or until tender, basting occasionally.

SLICER: Slice onions, bell pepper and mushrooms, using medium pressure. Add sliced vegetables, bean sprouts, peas and reserved pineapple to meat. Cook 10 minutes longer, until heated through. Serve over rice.

424 calories per serving, 39 g carbohydrates, 2.7 g fiber, 33 g protein, 15.8 g fat (6.6 g saturated fat), 73 mg cholesterol, 668 mg sodium, 631 mg potassium, 4 mg iron, 64 mg calcium, 244 mg phosphorus

## slow cooker method

Combine short ribs and marinade in sprayed slow cooker insert; marinate in refrigerator overnight. Place insert in slow cooker and cook, covered, on Low for 10 hours. Stir in vegetables and pineapple the last 15 minutes to heat through.

# HONEY GARLIC RIBS

Yield: 4 servings as a main course, 6 to 8 servings as an appetizer. Keeps 2 to 3 days in the refrigerator. Reheats and/or freezes well.

3 lb (1.4 kg) spareribs
salt and freshly ground black pepper to taste
1 slice fresh ginger, peeled (1 Tbsp) (or 1 tsp ground ginger)
2 or 3 cloves garlic

1 cup brown sugar or honey
¼ cup soy sauce (low-sodium or regular)
2 tsp white or rice vinegar
½ cup water

Place ribs in a single layer on broiling rack. Sprinkle with salt and pepper. Broil on both sides until brown. Drain on paper towels. Cut into individual ribs and place in sprayed 2-quart casserole.

STEEL BLADE: Drop ginger and garlic through feed tube while machine is running; process until minced. Add remaining ingredients and process a few seconds, until mixed. Pour over ribs.

Bake, uncovered, in preheated 300°F oven for 1½ hours, basting every 15 minutes.

518 calories per serving, 56.3 g carbohydrates, 0.2 g fiber, 34 g protein, 17.3 g fat (7.4 g saturated fat), 82 mg cholesterol, 613 mg sodium, 428 mg potassium, 4 mg iron, 81 mg calcium, 209 mg phosphorus

## variation

Cut spareribs into individual ribs. Place in saucepan, cover with water and simmer, covered, for half an hour. Drain well. Place in sprayed casserole; pour Honey Garlic Sparerib Sauce (page 110) over ribs. (No need to cook the sauce first!) Bake, uncovered, at 350°F about 1 hour, basting occasionally.

# SPICY SHORT RIBS/MIAMI RIBS

Yield: 4 to 6 servings. Keeps 2 to 3 days in the refrigerator. Reheats and/or freezes well.

8 strips short ribs (flanken or Miami ribs)

3 cloves garlic

1 can (14 oz/398 mL) peaches, drained (or 1 cup baby food peaches)

½ cup ketchup or chili sauce

¼ cup lemon juice or vinegar

3 Tbsp soy sauce (low-sodium or regular)

1 Tbsp Worcestershire or steak sauce

¼ cup brown sugar

½ tsp dry mustard

Arrange ribs in a single layer in sprayed 9- × 13-inch baking dish.

STEEL BLADE: Drop garlic through feed tube while machine is running; process until minced. Add remaining ingredients and process until smooth. Pour sauce over meat, cover and marinate 1 to 2 hours or up to 24 hours in refrigerator, basting occasionally.

Bake, covered, in preheated 325°F oven 2½ hours. Uncover and bake half an hour longer, or until very tender. Baste occasionally. Serve with rice or noodles.

540 calories per serving, 36.2 g carbohydrates, 0.8 g fiber, 46 g protein, 23.4 g fat (9.9 g saturated fat), 110 mg cholesterol, 869 mg sodium, 696 mg potassium, 5 mg iron, 70 mg calcium, 286 mg phosphorus

### slow cooker method

Place vegetables in bottom of sprayed slow cooker insert; add marinated meat and sauce. Place insert in slow cooker and cook, covered, on Low for 10 hours. One serving contains 684 calories, 78.1 g carbohydrates and 5.9 g fiber.

### oven stew

Replace short ribs with 2½ lb (1.2 kg) lean stewing beef or veal. Prepare sauce. Pour over meat, cover and marinate as directed above. Bake, covered, at 325°F for 2 hours. Slice 3 large carrots, 2 onions, 4 large potatoes and 3 stalks celery on the SLICER. Add vegetables to stew and cook, covered, 1 hour longer. (Omit potatoes if freezing.)

# STEW ITALIANO

Don't let the list of ingredients scare you—this is really quick and easy to make.

Yield: 4 to 6 servings. Keeps 2 to 3 days in the refrigerator. Reheats well. May be frozen, but omit potatoes and serve over broad noodles, bow ties or quinoa.

½ cup flour
½ tsp salt
¼ tsp paprika
dash freshly ground black pepper
2 to 2½ lb (about 1 kg) lean stewing beef or veal, cut in chunks
3 cloves garlic
2 medium onions, cut in chunks
oil for browning (about ¼ cup)
½ cup red wine
salt and freshly ground black pepper to taste

1 tsp each dried basil and dried oregano
1 bay leaf
1 Tbsp brown or granulated sugar
1 can (28 oz/796 mL) tomatoes (salt-free or regular), drained (reserve liquid)
4 carrots
2 cups mushrooms
4 potatoes, cut in chunks
1 pkg (10 oz/300 g) frozen green peas (1¼ cups)

Combine flour, salt, paprika and pepper in a plastic bag. Add meat a few pieces at a time and shake to coat well on all sides.

STEEL BLADE: Drop garlic through feed tube while machine is running; process until minced. Add onions and process with 3 or 4 very quick on/offs, until coarsely chopped.

Heat 1 to 2 Tbsp oil in large pot or Dutch oven. Add garlic and onions and brown over medium heat. Remove from pan. Add meat a few pieces at a time and brown on all sides. Remove from pan when ready. Add more oil as needed. Add wine to pan. Stir with a wooden spoon to scrape any browned bits from bottom of pan. Return browned meat, onions and garlic to the pan. Add salt, pepper, basil, oregano, bay leaf and sugar. Stir in reserved liquid from tomatoes.

Purée tomatoes on the STEEL BLADE until smooth; add to stew.

Cover and simmer about 2½ hours, until nearly tender. (If desired, stew may be baked in preheated 300°F oven.)

SLICER: Cut carrots to fit feed tube. Slice carrots and mushrooms, using medium pressure. Add with potatoes to stew. Cook 25 to 30 minutes longer. Add peas and cook 10 minutes more. Discard bay leaf.

691 calories per serving, 77.9 g carbohydrates, 11.5 g fiber, 43 g protein, 21.8 g fat (3.8 g saturated fat), 65 mg cholesterol, 442 mg sodium, 1974 mg potassium, 9 mg iron, 161 mg calcium, 468 mg phosphorus

## slow cooker method

Instead of cooking stew on the stovetop, transfer browned meat, onion/garlic mixture, pan juices and tomatoes to a sprayed slow cooker insert. Place sliced carrots, mushrooms and potatoes in a bowl. Add 1 Tbsp oil;

*Continued*

sprinkle with salt, pepper, basil and oregano. Mix well and wrap tightly in foil. Place foil packet on top of meat. Cover and cook on Low for 10 hours. Carefully unwrap vegetables and stir into stew along with peas. Cook 10 minutes longer.

### passover variation

Replace flour with potato starch. Replace peas with 1 zucchini, sliced.

---

# TASTY MEATBALL STEW

Yield: 6 to 8 servings. Keeps 2 days in the refrigerator. Reheats well. If freezing, omit potatoes.

## MEATBALLS

**2 cloves garlic**

**½ small onion**

**2 lb (1 kg) lean ground beef, veal, chicken or turkey (or see Grind Your Own, page 36)**

**¼ cup dried bread crumbs, oat bran or matzo meal**

**1 tsp salt (or to taste)**

**½ tsp freshly ground black pepper**

**1 Tbsp ketchup, barbecue or soy sauce**

**1 egg (or 2 egg whites)**

**¼ cup water**

## SAUCE

**2 cloves garlic**

**1 can (5½ oz/156 mL) tomato paste (unsalted or regular)**

**2 cups water (approximately)**

**salt and freshly ground black pepper to taste**

**¼ tsp dried oregano**

**1 bay leaf**

## VEGETABLES

**3 medium onions, cut in chunks**

**1 green and/or red bell pepper, cut in chunks**

**2 or 3 stalks celery**

**6 medium potatoes, peeled and quartered**

**2 dozen baby carrots**

For meatballs: Process garlic and onion on the STEEL BLADE until minced, 6 to 8 seconds. Transfer to a large mixing bowl, add remaining ingredients for meatballs and mix lightly to blend.

Shape into 1-inch balls, moistening your hands for easier handling. Place on sprayed baking sheet and bake in preheated 400°F oven for 20 to 25 minutes (or microwave on High for 10 to 12 minutes, stirring once or twice). Transfer meatballs to a large pot.

For sauce: Drop garlic through feed tube while machine is running; process until minced. Add tomato paste, water, salt, pepper and oregano and process for a few seconds, until mixed. Add with bay leaf to meatballs. Cover and simmer for 35 to 40 minutes.

For vegetables: Slice onions, bell pepper and celery on the SLICER, using medium pressure. Add to meatballs along with potatoes and carrots. Simmer half an hour longer, until vegetables are tender. Add more water if necessary. Remove bay leaf before serving.

519 calories per serving, 54.9 g carbohydrates, 7.1 g fiber, 36 g protein, 18 g fat (6.8 g saturated fat), 112 mg cholesterol, 597 mg sodium, 1415 mg potassium, 5 mg iron, 85 mg calcium, 299 mg phosphorus

### passover variation

For meatball mixture, use ketchup and matzo meal (or 1 medium potato, finely ground on the STEEL BLADE).

# HAWAIIAN MEATBALLS

Yield: 8 to 10 servings as an appetizer, 6 servings as a main course. Serve over rice. Keeps 2 days in the refrigerator. Reheats and/or freezes well, but omit pineapple and add when reheating.

MEATBALLS

1 clove garlic
1 small onion
1 egg (or 2 egg whites)
2 lb (1 kg) lean ground beef or veal
(or see Grind Your Own, page 36)
1 tsp salt (or to taste)
¼ tsp each freshly ground black
pepper and ground ginger
2 Tbsp dried bread crumbs
or rolled oats

SAUCE

1 can (19 oz/540 mL) pineapple
chunks
2 Tbsp cornstarch
½ cup orange juice
¼ cup honey
2 Tbsp lemon juice or vinegar
1 Tbsp soy sauce (low-sodium or
regular)
¼ tsp each ground ginger and garlic
powder

For meatballs: Process garlic and onion on the STEEL BLADE until minced, 6 to 8 seconds. Add egg and process 5 seconds longer. Transfer to a large mixing bowl. Add remaining ingredients for meatballs; mix lightly to blend.

Wet hands and form tiny meatballs as an appetizer or larger ones as a main course. Place on a sprayed baking sheet and bake in preheated 400°F oven for 25 minutes (or microwave, uncovered, on High for 10 to 12 minutes, stirring once or twice). Transfer to a 3-quart glass casserole.

For sauce: Drain pineapple, reserving ¾ cup juice. In a saucepan, dissolve cornstarch in pineapple and orange juices. Stir in remaining sauce ingredients, except pineapple chunks, and bring to a boil, stirring occasionally. Simmer 2 minutes longer, until thick and bubbling. (Or microwave on High for 5 to 6 minutes in a 4-cup glass measuring cup, stirring twice.) Carefully pour sauce over meatballs, add pineapple and mix gently. *Continued*

Cover and bake at 350°F for 45 minutes (or microwave, uncovered, on High for 6 to 8 minutes), stirring occasionally.

412 calories per serving, 32.9 g carbohydrates, 1.2 g fiber, 30 g protein, 17.4 g fat (6.7 g saturated fat),
112 mg cholesterol, 563 mg sodium, 467 mg potassium, 3 mg iron, 34 mg calcium, 178 mg phosphorus

# MMM-GOOD MEATBALLS

These are perfect as party fare or a main course.

Yield: About 100 meatballs (12 to 15 servings as a main dish). Keeps 2 days in the refrigerator. Freezes well. Tastes even better reheated. Recipe may be halved.

SAUCE

1 jar (9 oz/250 mL) grape jelly
2 cans (28 oz/796 mL each) tomatoes (salt-free or regular)
1 can (19 oz/540 mL) tomato juice (low-sodium or regular)
½ cup brown sugar or honey
2 Tbsp lemon juice
salt to taste

MEATBALLS

2 cloves garlic
4 slices bread, quartered
4 lb (1.8 kg) lean ground beef or veal (or see Grind Your Own, page 36)
2 eggs (or 1 egg plus 2 whites)
⅔ cup water
1 to 2 tsp salt (or to taste)
½ tsp freshly ground black pepper

For sauce: Spray large heavy pot with nonstick spray. Add ingredients for sauce. Heat slowly on low heat, stirring often to prevent jelly from scorching, until simmering.

For meatballs: Insert STEEL BLADE. Drop garlic through feed tube while machine is running; process until minced. Add bread and process to make fine crumbs. (You will have about 2 cups.) Combine with ground meat in a large mixing bowl. Process eggs, water, salt and pepper for 2 or 3 seconds. Add to meat and mix lightly to blend.

Wet your hands and form mixture into 1-inch meatballs. Drop into simmering sauce and cook, partially covered, for 2 hours, stirring occasionally. (Meatballs may also be baked in preheated 325°F oven for 2 hours.)

426 calories per serving, 35.4 g carbohydrates, 2 g fiber, 31 g protein, 17.6 g fat (6.7 g saturated fat),
112 mg cholesterol, 368 mg sodium, 649 mg potassium, 5 mg iron, 83 mg calcium, 201 mg phosphorus

### passover variation

Replace bread with ¾ cup matzo meal or grated potato.

### slow cooker method

Combine ingredients for sauce in sprayed slow cooker. Cook, covered, on High for 30 minutes, or until simmering. Meanwhile, prepare meat mixture. Form into meatballs and place on parchment-lined baking sheet.

Bake, uncovered, in preheated 400°F oven for 25 minutes. Uncover slow cooker and stir sauce. Add drained meatballs, cover and cook on Low for 6 to 8 hours.

# CRANBERRY CHICKEN MEATBALLS

These scrumptious meatballs can also be made with lean ground beef, veal or turkey.

Yield: 6 to 8 servings as a main course, 10 to 12 servings as an appetizer. Reheats and/or freezes well.

MEATBALLS

2 lb (1 kg) lean minced chicken (or see Grind Your Own, page 36)

1 medium onion, cut in chunks

1 carrot, cut in chunks

1 stalk celery, cut in chunks

1 egg (or 2 egg whites)

1 tsp salt (or to taste)

½ tsp garlic powder

¼ tsp freshly ground black pepper

⅓ cup dried bread crumbs or matzo meal

SAUCE

2 cans (14 oz/398 mL each) jellied cranberry sauce

½ tsp ground cinnamon

2 cups tomato sauce (salt-free or regular)

For meatballs: Place minced chicken in a large mixing bowl.

STEEL BLADE: Process onion, carrot and celery until minced, about 10 seconds. Add egg, salt, garlic powder and pepper and process a few seconds longer. Add with crumbs to chicken. Mix well.

Wet hands and form small meatballs for appetizers or larger ones for a main course. Place on sprayed, foil-lined baking sheet. Bake, uncovered, in preheated 350°F oven for 25 to 30 minutes. Transfer meatballs to large sprayed casserole.

For sauce: Place cranberry sauce and cinnamon in processor. Add tomato sauce through feed tube while machine is running. Process until blended. Pour over meatballs. Bake, covered, at 350°F for 1 hour, basting occasionally.

581 calories per serving, 63.5 g carbohydrates, 4.1 g fiber, 36 g protein, 20.2 g fat (0.4 g saturated fat), 153 mg cholesterol, 593 mg sodium, 816 mg potassium, 4 mg iron, 75 mg calcium, 61 mg phosphorus

### slow cooker method

Transfer baked meatballs to sprayed slow cooker. Prepare sauce and pour over meatballs. Cook, covered, on High for 1 hour. Then cook on Low for 4 hours for small meatballs and 5 to 6 hours for larger meatballs.

# MANDARIN CHICKEN MEATBALLS

I often double the meatball mixture of this recipe, but not the sauce. You can also use leftover cooked chicken or turkey.

Yield: 4 servings. Keeps 2 days in the refrigerator. Reheats well. If frozen, vegetables will not be as crisp.

**MEATBALLS**

½ small onion

1 lb (500 g) lean minced raw chicken (or 2 to 3 cups leftover cooked chicken or turkey)

2 eggs (or 1 egg plus 2 egg whites)

3 to 4 Tbsp dried bread crumbs or matzo meal

¼ tsp garlic powder

salt and freshly ground black pepper to taste

**SAUCE**

1½ cups Chinese Sweet and Sour Sauce (page 108) or bottled sauce

¾ cup duck sauce or plum sauce

1 cup mushrooms

1 green bell pepper, halved

1 medium onion, halved

1 stalk celery, cut in chunks

1 can (10 oz/300 mL) mandarin oranges, drained

For meatballs: Process onion on the STEEL BLADE until minced, about 8 seconds. Add remaining meatball ingredients. Process with several on/off pulses, just until mixed. Shape into small meatballs, wetting your hands for easier handling.

If using raw minced chicken, place meatballs on a sprayed foil-lined baking sheet and bake in preheated 400°F oven for 25 minutes. If using cooked chicken or turkey, brown meatballs on all sides in 1 to 2 Tbsp hot oil in a large nonstick skillet. Transfer to sprayed ovenproof casserole.

For sauce: Combine sauces and pour over meatballs.

SLICER: Slice vegetables, using medium pressure. Microwave, covered, on High for 3 to 4 minutes. Add vegetables and drained oranges to meatballs; mix gently. Cover and bake at 325°F for half an hour.

611 calories per serving, 84.2 g carbohydrates, 2.2 g fiber, 30 g protein, 17.3 g fat (0.9 g saturated fat), 195 mg cholesterol, 478 mg sodium, 689 mg potassium, 3 mg iron, 87 mg calcium, 94 mg phosphorus

### passover variation

Substitute potato starch for cornstarch in Chinese Sweet and Sour Sauce; use duck sauce instead of plum sauce. Pineapple chunks may be used instead of mandarin oranges. For meatballs, use matzo meal.

# PINEAPPLE CHICKEN MEATBALLS

Serve this over rice, couscous or quinoa as a main course. These can also be made with ground veal or turkey.

Yield: 6 to 8 servings as a main course or 12 servings as an appetizer. Keeps 2 days in the refrigerator. Reheats and/or freezes well.

## MEATBALLS

2 lb (1 kg) lean minced chicken (or see Grind Your Own, page 36)

2 or 3 cloves garlic

1 small onion, cut in chunks

1 small potato, cut in chunks

2 eggs (or 1 egg plus 2 egg whites)

1 tsp salt

¼ tsp freshly ground black pepper

⅓ cup dried bread crumbs or matzo meal

1 to 2 Tbsp oil for frying

## SAUCE

1 jar (8 oz/250 mL) Chinese cherry sauce (optional—see Note)

1½ cups Chinese Sweet and Sour Sauce (page 108)

1 cup tomato sauce (salt-free or regular)

1 green or red bell pepper, halved

1 medium onion, halved

1 can (14 oz/398 mL) pineapple chunks, drained (about 1 cup chunks)

For meatballs: Place minced chicken in large mixing bowl. Process garlic, onion and potato on the STEEL BLADE until minced, 8 to 10 seconds. Add eggs, salt and pepper and process a few seconds longer. Add to chicken along with crumbs. Mix well.

Wet hands and form small meatballs for appetizers or larger ones for a main course. Heat oil in large nonstick skillet. Brown meatballs on all sides. Drain well.

For sauce: In large pot, combine sauces and heat to boiling. Add meatballs, cover and simmer for 45 minutes.

SLICER: Slice green or red pepper and onion, using firm pressure. Add to meatballs along with pineapple chunks; simmer 5 to 10 minutes longer.

591 calories per serving, 56.7 g carbohydrates, 2.5 g fiber, 38 g protein, 23.4 g fat (0.8 g saturated fat), 189 mg cholesterol, 679 mg sodium, 909 mg potassium, 4 mg iron, 92 mg calcium, 89 mg phosphorus

### note

Bottled Chinese cherry sauce makes this dish higher in calories, carbohydrates and sodium, but you can add it if you like. The recipe is equally delicious without it.

# HAMBURGERS À LA DUTCH

This is one of my favorite meals, but I've lightened it considerably by using leaner cuts of meat and a nonstick skillet.

Yield: 6 servings. Keeps 2 days in the refrigerator. Reheats and/or freezes well.

## MEAT MIXTURE

**2 cloves garlic**

**1 small onion**

**2 egg whites (or 1 egg)**

**2 lb (1 kg) lean ground beef, veal, chicken or turkey (or see Grind Your Own, page 36)**

**6 Tbsp matzo meal**

**1 tsp salt (or to taste)**

**½ tsp each freshly ground black pepper and dried basil**

**¼ cup water**

**1 Tbsp olive oil**

## VEGETABLE MIXTURE

**3 or 4 medium onions, halved**

**2 green bell peppers, cut in chunks**

**2 red bell peppers, cut in chunks**

**2 cups mushrooms**

**2 stalks celery, cut to fit feed tube**

**salt and freshly ground black pepper to taste**

**2 tsp sweet paprika**

**½ cup dry red wine, water or chicken broth**

For meat mixture: Process garlic and onion on the STEEL BLADE until minced, 8 to 10 seconds. Add egg whites and process 2 to 3 seconds longer. Combine with remaining ingredients except oil in large mixing bowl; mix lightly to blend. Form into 10 burgers about ½ inch thick.

Heat oil in large nonstick skillet or electric skillet. Cook burgers about 5 minutes on each side, until browned. Transfer to a 2-quart ovenproof microwavable casserole.

For vegetable mixture: Slice onions, bell peppers, mushrooms and celery on the SLICER, using medium pressure. Add to skillet and brown in pan juices, stirring often, about 5 minutes. Add a little water if needed to prevent sticking. Sprinkle with salt, pepper and paprika, add wine and simmer 2 to 3 minutes longer. Add to hamburgers, cover and microwave on High for 6 to 8 minutes, stirring once or twice. (Alternatively, steam on the stove in a skillet on low heat, or bake in a 350°F oven, for 15 to 20 minutes.)

398 calories per serving, 21.1 g carbohydrates, 2.8 g fiber, 32 g protein, 19 g fat (6.8 g saturated fat), 77 mg cholesterol, 479 mg sodium, 645 mg potassium, 4 mg iron, 41 mg calcium, 204 mg phosphorus

### gluten-free variation

Replace matzo meal with 1 medium potato, finely ground on the STEEL BLADE.

# CHILI

Cocoa gives this chili a rich, dark color. If there's an excuse to include chocolate in a dish, I'll find it!

Yield: 8 servings. Keeps 2 days in the refrigerator. Reheats and/or freezes well. Delicious over pasta or rice.

1 or 2 cloves garlic
2 medium onions, cut in chunks
1 green bell pepper, cut in chunks
1 stalk celery, cut in chunks
2 lb (1 kg) lean ground beef or veal
   (or see Grind Your Own, page 36)
1 can (10 oz/284 mL) condensed
   tomato soup
½ soup can (5 oz) water

1 can (19 oz/540 mL) red kidney beans
   or chickpeas, with liquid
1 to 2 Tbsp chili powder
salt to taste
1 Tbsp unsweetened cocoa powder
½ tsp freshly ground black pepper
½ tsp ground cumin
6 to 8 drops hot sauce

STEEL BLADE: Drop garlic through feed tube while machine is running; process until minced. Process onions, green pepper and celery with quick on/offs, until coarsely chopped. Place vegetables and ground meat in a Dutch oven sprayed with nonstick spray (or a 3-quart microwavable casserole).

Brown meat and vegetables over medium-high heat, stirring often. (Or microwave, uncovered, on High for 10 minutes, until meat is cooked, stirring 2 or 3 times to break up meat.) Add remaining ingredients and mix well.

Simmer, uncovered, for about 1 hour, stirring often. (Or microwave, covered, on High for 20 to 25 minutes.) Taste and adjust seasonings. Flavor is even better the next day.

305 calories per serving, 21.1 g carbohydrates, 5.2 g fiber, 26 g protein, 12.8 g fat (4.9 g saturated fat), 58 mg cholesterol, 585 mg sodium, 477 mg potassium, 4 mg iron, 38 mg calcium, 189 mg phosphorus

## slow cooker method

(Tip: Drain off half the liquid from canned kidney beans or chickpeas.) Transfer sautéed vegetables and meat to sprayed slow cooker insert; stir in remaining ingredients. Cook, covered, on Low for 6 to 8 hours, or on High for 3 to 4 hours.

# CHICKEN CHILI

This chili comes together quickly and makes a big batch. You can make it either on the stovetop or in the slow cooker.

Yield: 10 to 12 servings. Reheats and/or freezes well.

3 cloves garlic

2 medium onions, cut in chunks

2 Tbsp olive oil

2 red bell peppers, quartered and seeded

2 cups mushrooms

1 can (28 oz/796 mL) whole tomatoes (salt-free or regular)

1 can (5½ oz/156 mL) tomato paste (salt-free or regular)

1 cup tomato sauce (salt-free or regular)

6 single boneless, skinless chicken breasts, cut in 1-inch chunks

1 can (19 oz/540 mL) black beans, drained and rinsed

1 can (19 oz/540 mL) white or red kidney beans, drained and rinsed

1 Tbsp chili powder (or to taste)

salt and pepper to taste

1 tsp dried basil

½ tsp dried oregano

1 tsp brown sugar

STEEL BLADE: Drop garlic through feed tube while machine is running; process until minced. Process onions with quick on/off pulses, until coarsely chopped. Heat oil in a Dutch oven or large pot on medium heat. Add onions and garlic and sauté for 3 or 4 minutes, until softened.

SLICER: Slice peppers and mushrooms, using medium pressure. Add to onions and sauté 3 or 4 minutes longer.

Drain liquid from tomatoes and add to vegetables. Purée drained tomatoes on the STEEL BLADE and add them to the pot. Add tomato paste, tomato sauce, chicken, drained beans, seasonings and sugar; stir well.

Cover and simmer for 30 minutes, stirring occasionally. Serve over spaghetti, rice, couscous or quinoa.

289 calories per serving, 36.9 g carbohydrates, 10.2 g fiber, 27 g protein, 5.2 g fat (1 g saturated fat), 44 mg cholesterol, 554 mg sodium, 820 mg potassium, 5 mg iron, 121 mg calcium, 179 mg phosphorus

## variations

- Replace chicken breasts with 4 cups shredded cooked chicken or turkey; add to chili 10 minutes before it finishes simmering.

- For a vegetarian version, use 2 packages (6 oz/170 g each) chicken-flavored vegetarian strips. Add to chili during the last 10 minutes of cooking. Add 1 cup well-drained canned corn, if desired.

## slow cooker method

Sauté the vegetables in a skillet as directed. Transfer to sprayed slow cooker insert and stir in remaining ingredients. Cook, covered, on Low for 3 to 4 hours.

# SUPER SPAGHETTI SAUCE

For a vegetarian version, omit salami and replace ground meat with vegetarian ground beef substitute.

Yield: 8 servings. Keeps 2 days in the refrigerator. Reheats and/or freezes well.

3 cloves garlic

2 medium onions, quartered

1 to 2 Tbsp oil

1 green or red bell pepper, cut in chunks

1 cup mushrooms

¼ lb salami or pepperoni, cut in chunks (optional)

2 lb (1 kg) lean ground beef or veal (or see Grind Your Own, page 36)

1 can (28 oz/796 mL) tomatoes (salt-free or regular)

2 cans (5½ oz/156 mL each) tomato paste (salt-free or regular)

¼ cup red wine

1 to 2 tsp salt (to taste)

½ tsp each freshly ground black pepper, dried basil, dried oregano and sugar

1 bay leaf

red pepper flakes or chili powder to taste

STEEL BLADE: Drop garlic through feed tube while machine is running; process until minced. Process onions with 3 or 4 quick on/off pulses, until coarsely chopped. Brown garlic and onions slowly in hot oil in a Dutch oven for 5 minutes. Process bell pepper and mushrooms with 3 or 4 quick on/offs, until coarsely chopped. Add to pot and cook 2 minutes longer. Remove vegetables from pot.

If using salami or pepperoni, process with several quick on/offs, until coarsely chopped. Add to pan along with ground meat. Brown slowly over medium heat for 10 minutes, stirring often.

Add remaining ingredients to pot, stirring well to break up tomatoes. Cover and simmer 1½ to 2 hours, stirring occasionally. Taste to adjust seasonings. Discard bay leaf.

297 calories per serving, 17.6 g carbohydrates, 3.7 g fiber, 25 g protein, 14.4 g fat (5 g saturated fat), 58 mg cholesterol, 389 mg sodium, 953 mg potassium, 5 mg iron, 67 mg calcium, 185 mg phosphorus

## slow cooker method

Sauté vegetables and meat as directed. Transfer to sprayed slow cooker insert and stir in remaining ingredients. Cook, covered, on Low for 6 to 8 hours or on High for 3 to 4 hours. If sauce is too thin, uncover and cook on High for 20 to 30 minutes longer.

# SNEAKY SPAGHETTI SAUCE

This vegetable-packed sauce comes together very quickly. Cutting the veggies into chunks and then slicing them one after the other speeds up prep time—no need to empty the bowl between batches. This is a wonderful way to get more veggies into your family!

Yield: 8 servings. Keeps 2 days in the refrigerator. Reheats and/or freezes well.

**1 lb (500 g) lean ground beef, veal or chicken (or see Grind Your Own, page 36)**

**3 medium zucchini (do not peel)**

**2 medium onions**

**2 red bell peppers**

**2 Japanese eggplants (1 lb/500 g) (do not peel)**

**1 to 2 Tbsp canola oil**

**1 can (28 oz/796 mL) tomatoes (salt-free or regular)**

**4 cloves garlic**

**1 can (5½ oz/156 mL) tomato paste (salt-free or regular)**

**1 tsp salt**

**½ tsp pepper**

**½ tsp red pepper flakes**

**1 tsp dried basil**

**1 tsp sugar**

Place ground meat in a large microwavable bowl and microwave on High for 5 to 6 minutes, stirring 2 or 3 times to break up meat. Drain off juices.

Cut zucchini, onions, peppers and eggplants in large chunks (about 2 inches is fine).

SLICER: Slice zucchini, onions and peppers, using light pressure. Spray a Dutch oven with nonstick spray. Add oil and heat on medium-high heat. Sauté zucchini, onions and peppers for 5 to 7 minutes, until softened.

Slice eggplants, using medium pressure. Add to skillet and cook 3 or 4 minutes longer, stirring occasionally. (Tip: If vegetable mixture begins to stick, add a little water or juice from canned tomatoes.)

Drain juices from tomatoes and add to vegetable mixture. Purée drained tomatoes with garlic on the STEEL BLADE. Add along with cooked meat, tomato paste and seasonings to the pot; stir well.

Cover and simmer 1½ to 2 hours, stirring occasionally. Taste to adjust seasonings.

203 calories per serving, 20.9 g carbohydrates, 4.8 g fiber, 14 g protein, 8.4 g fat (2.6 g saturated fat), 29 mg cholesterol, 348 mg sodium, 816 mg potassium, 3 mg iron, 67 mg calcium, 137 mg phosphorus

## slow cooker method

Cook meat and sauté vegetables as directed. Transfer to sprayed slow cooker and stir in remaining ingredients. Cook, covered, on Low for 6 to 8 hours, or on High for 3 to 4 hours. If sauce is too thin, uncover and cook on High for 20 to 30 minutes longer.

# MOIST AND SPICY MEAT LOAF

A delicious way
to stretch 1 lb of
meat to serve a
family. Chock-
full of vegetables
and vitamins.

Yield: 4 to 6 servings.
Keeps 2 days in the
refrigerator. Reheats
and/or freezes well.

### MEAT MIXTURE

1 lb (500 g) lean ground beef or veal
   (or see Grind Your Own, page 36)

1 or 2 cloves garlic

1 medium onion, cut in chunks

3 green onions, cut in chunks

1 small stalk celery, cut in chunks

½ green bell pepper, cut in chunks

4 slices whole wheat bread,
   in chunks

½ cup mushrooms

1 cup chicken or vegetable broth
   (salt-free or regular)

1 egg (or 2 egg whites)

½ tsp salt (or to taste)

¼ tsp freshly ground black pepper

½ tsp Italian seasoning

4 to 6 drops hot sauce

1 to 2 Tbsp dried bread crumbs, if
   needed

### TOPPING

2 to 3 Tbsp steak, duck or barbecue
   sauce

½ red bell pepper

1 cup mushrooms

For meat mixture: Place ground meat in large mixing bowl.

STEEL BLADE: Drop garlic through feed tube while machine is running; process until minced. Add onions, celery and green pepper and process until minced, about 10 seconds (work in batches if necessary). Add to ground meat. Process bread and mushrooms until coarsely ground, about 10 seconds. Add to meat mixture. Add remaining ingredients for meat mixture; mix well. Place mixture in sprayed 9- × 5-inch loaf pan, packing lightly.

For topping: Spread sauce over meat loaf. Slice red pepper and mushrooms on the SLICER, using light pressure. Top meat loaf with vegetables. Bake, uncovered, in preheated 350°F oven 1 hour and 10 minutes.

332 calories per serving, 19.4 g carbohydrates, 3.6 g fiber, 29 g protein, 15.1 g fat (5.6 g saturated fat), 117 mg cholesterol, 629 mg sodium, 502 mg potassium, 4 mg iron, 66 mg calcium, 224 mg phosphorus

# POTATO KUGEL MEAT LOAF

Finely grated raw
potatoes make an
unusual topping
for this version of
shepherd's pie. Tried
and true!

### MEAT MIXTURE

1 lb (500 g) lean ground beef or veal
   (or see Grind Your Own, page 36)

salt and freshly ground black pepper
   to taste

dash garlic powder

1 egg (or 2 egg whites)

2 Tbsp ketchup

### TOPPING

3 medium potatoes, cut in chunks

1 small onion, halved

2 eggs (or 1 egg plus 2 egg whites)

3 Tbsp flour or potato starch

¾ tsp salt (or to taste)

½ tsp baking powder

freshly ground black pepper to taste

Yield: 4 servings. Keeps
2 days in the refrigerator.
Reheats and/or
freezes well.

For meat mixture: In a large nonstick skillet, cook meat on medium heat about 4 to 5 minutes, until it loses its red color, mashing it to keep it crumbly. (Or microwave, uncovered, on High for 5 minutes, mashing meat once or twice during cooking.) Add remaining ingredients for meat mixture; mix well. Place in sprayed 1-quart shallow casserole.

For topping: Process potatoes, onion and eggs on the STEEL BLADE until fine, 12 to 15 seconds. Add remaining topping ingredients and process a few seconds longer, until combined. Spread over meat. Bake, uncovered, in preheated 375°F oven until browned and crisp, about 1 hour.

414 calories per serving, 35.9 g carbohydrates, 3.2 g fiber, 30 g protein, 16.4 g fat (6.1 g saturated fat), 217 mg cholesterol, 683 mg sodium, 993 mg potassium, 4 mg iron, 84 mg calcium, 289 mg phosphorus

## TURKEY POPCORN SHEPHERD'S PIE

Try this new twist on
turkey with stuffing!
Serve it with
Cranberry Relish
(page 220) and
steamed broccoli for
a delicious dinner.
Substitute chicken
if you prefer.

Yield: 6 servings.
Keeps 2 days in the
refrigerator. Reheats
and/or freezes well.

Popcorn Stuffing Mounds (page 261)
2 cloves garlic
1 medium onion, cut in chunks
1 stalk celery, cut in chunks
2 tsp olive oil
2 lb (1 kg) lean ground turkey (or
   see Grind Your Own, page 36)

⅓ cup matzo meal, dried bread
   crumbs or quick-cooking oats
2 eggs (or 1 egg plus 2 egg whites)
½ tsp each dried thyme and dried
   basil
salt and freshly ground black pepper
   to taste

Prepare stuffing mixture as directed; set aside.

STEEL BLADE: Drop garlic through feed tube while machine is running; process until minced. Add onion and celery and process until finely chopped, 6 to 8 seconds. Heat oil in nonstick skillet; sauté vegetables for 5 minutes, until golden.

In large mixing bowl, combine ground turkey with remaining ingredients. Add sautéed vegetables and mix well. Spread meat mixture evenly in sprayed 7- × 11-inch glass baking dish. Spread stuffing mixture over meat. Bake in preheated 350°F oven about 1 hour, or until lightly browned.

447 calories per serving, 25.2 g carbohydrates, 4 g fiber, 35 g protein, 23.2 g fat (5.2 g saturated fat), 261 mg cholesterol, 407 mg sodium, 727 mg potassium, 4 mg iron, 78 mg calcium, 385 mg phosphorus

### lighter variation

Instead of using store-bought ground turkey, you can Grind Your Own (page 36). Use air-popped popcorn in the stuffing. One serving contains 362 calories and 9.2 g fat.

## SHIPWRECK

My children loved this casserole when they were little, but they had trouble pronouncing the name—they thought the *p* was a *t*. If you have less time, make it in the microwave.

Yield: 4 to 6 servings. Keeps 2 days in the refrigerator. Reheats well. Do not freeze.

2 medium onions

2 potatoes

salt, freshly ground black pepper, garlic powder and paprika to taste

1½ lb (750 g) lean ground beef or veal (or see Grind Your Own, page 36)

½ cup uncooked rice

2 stalks celery

3 medium carrots

2 cups chicken broth (salt-free or regular)

SLICER: Cut onions and potatoes to fit feed tube. Slice, using medium pressure. Layer in sprayed, 2-quart round glass baking dish. Sprinkle lightly with salt, pepper, garlic and paprika. Spread ground meat evenly over potatoes; season lightly. Top with rice.

Slice celery and carrots, using medium pressure. Spread over rice; season once again. Pour broth over casserole.

Cover and bake at 250°F for 2½ to 3 hours. To microwave, cover and cook on High for 12 minutes. Reduce power to Medium (50%) and cook 45 minutes longer, rotating casserole twice during cooking. Let stand 5 minutes before serving.

499 calories per serving, 41 g carbohydrates, 4.4 g fiber, 39 g protein, 19.4 g fat (7.5 g saturated fat), 99 mg cholesterol, 176 mg sodium, 976 mg potassium, 5 mg iron, 51 mg calcium, 269 mg phosphorus

## STIR-FRIED BEEF AND BROCCOLI

I've simplified the preparation for this delicious family favorite. You can add snow peas, bean sprouts, bok choy or any vegetables you like. It's also scrumptious with chicken breasts.

Yield: 6 servings. Leftovers reheat well in the microwave. If frozen, vegetables will become soggy.

1½ lb (750 g) lean boneless steak

4 cloves garlic

¼ cup soy sauce (low-sodium or regular)

1 Tbsp lemon juice

1 Tbsp honey or maple syrup

1 Tbsp ketchup

1 pint mushrooms (about 2½ cups)

2 large onions, quartered

1 bunch fresh broccoli (about 1 lb/500 g)

oil for stir-frying (about 3 Tbsp)

2 Tbsp cornstarch dissolved in ¼ cup cold water or broth

1 tsp toasted sesame oil

cooked rice (optional)

For machines with nested bowls, see method on page 204.

Cut meat in pieces that will fit the feed tube snugly. Trim fat. Freeze meat until semifrozen, about 1 hour. It should be firm to the touch but easily pierced with the point of a sharp knife. If necessary, let meat stand for a few minutes until you can do the knife test. Meanwhile, prepare marinade.

STEEL BLADE: Drop garlic through feed tube; process until minced. Remove half of garlic and reserve. Add soy sauce, lemon juice, honey or maple syrup and ketchup to processor. Process a few seconds longer. Transfer to a large bowl.

*Continued*

SLICER: Slice meat, using firm pressure. Add to marinade and mix well. Cover and marinate for 1 hour or up to 24 hours in the refrigerator, stirring occasionally.

SLICER: Slice mushrooms and onions, using medium pressure. Transfer to a large mixing bowl. Cut florets from broccoli and add to vegetables. Slice broccoli stems, using medium pressure. Add sliced stems to vegetables.

Heat 1 Tbsp oil in a large wok or nonstick skillet. Stir-fry vegetables for 2 minutes on high heat. Add reserved garlic and stir-fry 30 seconds longer. Return to mixing bowl.

Remove meat from marinade with a slotted spoon and pat dry with paper towel. Reserve marinade. Stir-fry meat in 2 Tbsp hot oil about 2 to 3 minutes. If necessary, sprinkle with a little cornstarch to prevent splattering.

Return vegetables to wok and mix well. Add marinade and bring to a boil. Make a well in the center and stir in cornstarch mixture and sesame oil. Cook 1 to 2 minutes longer, until thickened, stirring constantly. Serve over rice (if desired).

361 calories per serving (without rice), 20.2 g carbohydrates, 4.4 g fiber, 28 g protein, 19.4 g fat (5.3 g saturated fat), 55 mg cholesterol, 461 mg sodium, 780 mg potassium, 5 mg iron, 55 mg calcium, 290 mg phosphorus

### nested bowl method

Use mini-bowl and mini-blade for marinade. Use medium bowl and SLICER for mushrooms, onions and broccoli stems. Use large bowl and SLICER for meat.

### stir-fried chicken and broccoli

Use boneless, skinless chicken breasts instead of steak. One serving contains 283 calories and 11.1 g fat.

# CHINESE CHICKEN LIVER STIR-FRY

Yield: 4 servings. If frozen, vegetables will become soggy.

1 lb (500 g) chicken livers, halved

2 cloves garlic

1 slice fresh ginger, peeled (1 Tbsp) or ½ tsp ground ginger

2 medium onions, quartered

2 green or red bell peppers, halved

1 pint fresh mushrooms (about 2½ cups)

1 cup snow peas or pea pods

1 to 2 Tbsp oil

2 Tbsp soy sauce (low-sodium or regular)

1 Tbsp brown sugar or honey

2 Tbsp cornstarch dissolved in ¼ cup cold water

freshly ground black pepper to taste

cooked rice (optional)

Broil chicken livers lightly on both sides. Set aside.

STEEL BLADE: Drop garlic and ginger through feed tube while machine is running; process until minced.

SLICER: Slice onions, bell peppers and mushrooms, using medium pressure.

Heat oil in large skillet or wok. Add sliced vegetables and snow peas. Stir-fry for 2 minutes on high heat. Add soy sauce, brown sugar or honey and chicken livers. Cook 2 minutes longer, stirring occasionally.

Stir in cornstarch mixture. Cook 1 to 2 minutes, until sauce is bubbly and thick, stirring constantly. Add pepper to taste. Serve over rice (if desired). Best served immediately.

263 calories per serving (without rice), 22.2 g carbohydrates, 3.3 g fiber, 23 g protein, 9.4 g fat (2.1 g saturated fat), 391 mg cholesterol, 354 mg sodium, 656 mg potassium, 12 mg iron, 53 mg calcium, 422 mg phosphorus

## variations

Add 1 tsp toasted sesame oil with soy sauce. Garnish with ½ cup toasted slivered almonds or sesame seeds.

## TERIYAKI TURKEY OR CHICKEN STIR-FRY

This colorful, versatile stir-fry is full of flavor! For a vegetarian version, substitute extra-firm tofu, cut in strips, for the meat.

Teriyaki Marinade (page 108)
1½ lb (750 g) turkey or chicken breasts
4 green onions
2 stalks celery
1 red and 1 yellow bell pepper
4 stalks bok choy

1 cup sugar snap peas, trimmed
2 cups bean sprouts
1 to 2 Tbsp oil
1 Tbsp cornstarch dissolved in 2 Tbsp cold water
cooked rice (optional)

Yield: 6 servings. Do not freeze or vegetables will lose their crispness. Leftovers can be reheated in the microwave.

For machines with nested bowls, see method on page 206.

Prepare marinade and set aside. Cut turkey or chicken breasts in half to fit feed tube snugly. Wrap and freeze for about 30 minutes, or until semifrozen. They are ready to slice when easily pierced with the tip of a sharp knife. If necessary, let them stand for a few minutes until you can do the knife test.

SLICER: Cut green onions, celery and peppers to fit feed tube. Slice, using medium pressure. (Use small feed tube if your machine has one.) Trim bok choy and cut to fit feed tube. Slice, using medium pressure. (Use wide-mouth feed tube if your machine has one.) Combine sliced vegetables with peas and bean sprouts in a large bowl. *Continued*

SLICER: Place turkey or chicken in feed tube cut side down. Slice, using firm pressure. Mix marinade and turkey or chicken in nonreactive dish, cover and marinate for 1 hour or up to 24 hours in the refrigerator, stirring occasionally.

Heat oil in wok or large nonstick skillet. Drain turkey or chicken, reserving marinade. Stir-fry on high heat for 2 minutes, or until chicken is white. Add vegetables and stir-fry 2 minutes longer. Add reserved marinade and bring to a boil. Stir in cornstarch mixture and cook 1 to 2 minutes longer, until sauce is bubbling and thickened. Serve over rice (if desired). Best served immediately.

245 calories per serving (without rice), 23.1 g carbohydrates, 2.3 g fiber, 30 g protein, 3.2 g fat (0.4 g saturated fat), 74 mg cholesterol, 424 mg sodium, 515 mg potassium, 3 mg iron, 56 mg calcium, 254 mg phosphorus

### nested bowl method

Use mini-bowl and mini-blade for marinade. Use medium bowl and SLICER for green onions, celery, peppers and bok choy. Use large bowl and SLICER for turkey or chicken.

## MUSHROOM ALMOND CHICKEN STIR-FRY

Yield: 4 servings. If frozen, vegetables will not be crispy.

4 single boneless, skinless chicken breasts
2 cups mushrooms
1 medium onion, halved
1 to 2 Tbsp oil
1 cup frozen peas (no need to thaw)
2 cloves garlic, crushed
¼ cup chicken broth (salt-free or regular)

1 to 2 Tbsp soy sauce (reduced-sodium or regular)
1 Tbsp cornstarch dissolved in 2 Tbsp cold water
freshly ground black pepper to taste
3 cups cooked rice
½ cup slivered almonds, toasted

Cut chicken breasts to fit feed tube snugly. Wrap and freeze for about 30 minutes, or until semifrozen. They will be ready to slice when easily pierced with the tip of a sharp knife. If necessary, let them stand for a few minutes until you can do the knife test.

SLICER: Slice chicken, using firm pressure. Empty bowl. Slice mushrooms and onion, using light pressure.

Heat oil in wok or large nonstick skillet. Add chicken and stir-fry over high heat for 2 minutes, until chicken is white. Add mushrooms, onion and peas; stir-fry 1 to 2 minutes longer.

Add garlic, broth and soy sauce and bring to a boil. Stir in cornstarch mixture;

cook 1 to 2 minutes longer, until sauce is bubbling and thickened, stirring constantly. Add pepper. Serve over rice; top with almonds. Best served immediately.

297 calories per serving (without rice), 13.7 g carbohydrates, 4.2 g fiber, 32 g protein, 12.6 g fat
(1.6 g saturated fat), 75 mg cholesterol, 231 mg sodium, 481 mg potassium, 2 mg iron,
62 mg calcium, 315 mg phosphorus

## MOO GOO GUY KEW

Yield: 6 servings. If frozen, vegetables will not be crispy.

Chicken Guy Kew (page 208)

1 large onion, cut in chunks

1 green or red bell pepper, cut in chunks

1 stalk celery, cut in chunks

1 cup mushrooms

2 cups broccoli florets

1 can (8 oz/250 mL) sliced water chestnuts, drained

2 or 3 cloves garlic, crushed

1 to 2 Tbsp oil

1 to 2 Tbsp reduced-sodium soy sauce (or to taste)

1 Tbsp cornstarch dissolved in ¼ cup chicken broth

cooked rice or noodles (optional)

Prepare chicken as directed; drain well. Keep warm. (May be prepared in advance and reheated.)

SLICER: Slice onion, bell pepper, celery and mushrooms, using medium pressure. Pat dry with paper towels. Combine with broccoli, water chestnuts and garlic in large bowl.

Heat oil in wok or large nonstick skillet. Stir-fry vegetables for 2 minutes on medium-high heat. Add soy sauce and cornstarch mixture and cook 1 to 2 minutes longer, stirring constantly. Add chicken and mix well. Serve over rice or noodles (if desired).

419 calories per serving (without rice), 27.5 g carbohydrates, 3.2 g fiber, 33 g protein, 19.5 g fat
(2.6 g saturated fat), 144 mg cholesterol, 716 mg sodium, 525 mg potassium,
3 mg iron, 73 mg calcium, 308 mg phosphorus

### variation

Replace water chestnuts with 1 cup snow peas. Omit soy sauce. Add 1½ cups Chinese Sweet and Sour Sauce (page 108) and 1 cup drained pineapple chunks to cooked chicken and vegetable mixture. Sprinkle with toasted sesame seeds. One serving contains 565 calories, 64.5 g carbohydrates, 3.3 g fiber and 679 g sodium.

## CHICKEN GUY KEW

Yield: 8 to 10 servings
as an hors d'oeuvre,
6 servings as a main
course. Allow for second
helpings! Freezes well.

Chinese Sweet and Sour Sauce
(page 108)

6 single boneless, skinless chicken
breasts

1 cup flour

1 Tbsp paprika

1 tsp salt

½ tsp baking powder

½ cup water or beer

2 Tbsp oil

2 eggs

additional oil for frying
(3 to 4 Tbsp)

Prepare sauce as directed. Cut chicken into 1-inch pieces with a sharp knife.

STEEL BLADE: Process flour, paprika, salt, baking powder, water or beer, 2 Tbsp oil and eggs until smooth, 10 to 15 seconds. Dip chicken pieces in batter. Fry in hot oil until brown on all sides, 2 to 3 minutes. Drain well on paper towels. Serve with sauce.

To reheat: Bake, uncovered, on foil-lined baking sheet in preheated 450°F oven until hot and crispy, 6 to 8 minutes.

350 calories per main-dish serving (without sauce), 16.8 g carbohydrates, 1 g fiber, 31 g protein, 16.8 g fat (2.3 g saturated fat), 144 mg cholesterol, 514 mg sodium, 288 mg potassium, 2 mg iron, 50 mg calcium, 259 mg phosphorus

## CHINESE CHICKEN DINNER-IN-A-DISH

My former student
Rivanna Stuhler
said, "This dish
will tempt even a
vegetarian like me!"

Yield: 4 to 6 servings.
Keeps 2 to 3 days in the
refrigerator. Reheats
well. Chicken freezes
well but rice may
get hard if frozen.

2 medium onions, cut in chunks

1 cup uncooked brown rice

1 red and/or green bell pepper, halved

1 cup mushrooms

3 lb (1.4 kg) chicken pieces

3 Tbsp soy sauce (low-sodium or
regular)

1 Tbsp rice vinegar

1 Tbsp honey

1 tsp toasted sesame oil

2 cups water

freshly ground black pepper and
paprika to taste

SLICER: Slice onions, using medium pressure. Place in sprayed 9- × 13-inch oven-proof casserole. Top with rice. Slice peppers and mushrooms, using light pressure. Add to casserole.

Remove skin and excess fat from chicken. Arrange chicken pieces in a single layer over rice and vegetables. Combine soy sauce, vinegar, honey and sesame oil. Drizzle over chicken pieces and marinate for 30 minutes.

Add water to casserole. Sprinkle chicken with pepper and paprika. Cover dish with foil. Bake in preheated 350°F oven for 1¾ hours, until chicken is tender. If necessary, add a little more water. Uncover and bake 15 minutes longer.

433 calories per serving (without skin), 48.7 g carbohydrates, 4.3 g fiber, 41 g protein, 7.8 g fat (1.8 g saturated fat), 114 mg cholesterol, 536 mg sodium, 648 mg potassium, 3 mg iron, 52 mg calcium, 459 mg phosphorus

## CHICKEN IN PINEAPPLE-ORANGE SAUCE

Yield: 8 servings. Keeps 2 to 3 days in the refrigerator. Freezes well, but do not garnish until serving time.

2 chickens, each cut in 8 pieces (3 lb/1.4 kg each)

salt and freshly ground black pepper to taste

1 Tbsp paprika

2 cloves garlic

1 cup tomato sauce (salt-free or regular)

¾ cup frozen concentrated orange juice (unthawed)

¼ cup brown sugar or maple syrup

½ tsp each dry mustard, ground cinnamon and ground ginger

1 can (14 oz/398 mL) pineapple chunks, drained (reserve juice)

1 medium orange, for garnish

cooked rice (optional)

Sprinkle chicken with salt, pepper and paprika on all sides. Place in a single layer in large sprayed roasting pan.

STEEL BLADE: Drop garlic through feed tube while machine is running; process until minced. Add tomato sauce, orange juice, brown sugar or maple syrup, mustard, cinnamon, ginger and ½ cup pineapple juice. Process for 2 or 3 seconds to blend. Pour over chicken.

Bake, uncovered, about 1½ hours in preheated 350°F oven, basting occasionally. If sauce cooks down too much, add a little more pineapple juice. Add pineapple chunks and bake 5 minutes longer.

SLICER: Cut orange in half lengthwise. Slice, using medium pressure. Serve chicken over rice (if desired), spoon sauce over and garnish with orange slices.

302 calories per serving (without skin), 26 g carbohydrates, 1.5 g fiber, 36 g protein, 5.4 g fat (1.3 g saturated fat), 114 mg cholesterol, 132 mg sodium, 757 mg potassium, 1 mg iron, 48 mg calcium, 315 mg phosphorus

### nutrition note

If you serve this with ½ cup rice, 1 serving contains 404 calories, 48 g carbohydrates and 1.7 g fiber.

# TANGY ORANGE BARBECUE CHICKEN

Yield: 8 servings.
Keeps 2 to 3 days in
the refrigerator. Tastes
even better reheated.
Freezes well.

2 chickens, each cut in 8 pieces
   (3 lb/1.4 kg each)
¾ cup frozen concentrated orange
   juice (unthawed)
¾ cup brown sugar, lightly packed
¾ cup barbecue sauce

1 green and 1 red bell pepper, halved
1 medium onion, halved
1 can (10 oz/300 mL) mandarin
   oranges, drained

Place chicken pieces in single layer in large sprayed roasting pan.

STEEL BLADE: Process orange juice, brown sugar and barbecue sauce until blended, 10 to 15 seconds. Pour over chicken. Cover and bake in preheated 350°F oven 1 hour. Uncover and bake about half an hour longer, basting occasionally.

SLICER: Slice bell peppers and onion, using medium pressure. Add with mandarin oranges to chicken. Cook 10 to 15 minutes longer.

378 calories per serving (without skin), 45.7 g carbohydrates, 1.2 g fiber, 36 g protein, 5.3 g fat
(1.3 g saturated fat), 114 mg cholesterol, 428 mg sodium, 743 mg potassium,
2 mg iron, 57 mg calcium, 316 mg phosphorus

# MARINATED BARBECUED CHICKEN

Barbecued chicken
will cook without
scorching and be
very juicy if you
precook it first in
the microwave.

5 to 6 lb chicken pieces
   (2.3 to 2.7 kg)
2 cloves garlic
¼ cup oil
3 Tbsp balsamic or wine vinegar

2 tsp paprika
1 tsp dry mustard
½ tsp chili powder
salt and freshly ground black pepper
   to taste

Yield: 8 servings.
Leftovers keep
2 to 3 days in the
refrigerator. Reheats
and/or freezes well.

Place chicken in nonreactive dish.

STEEL BLADE: Drop garlic through feed tube while machine is running; process until minced. Add remaining ingredients and process until blended, 2 or 3 seconds longer.

Pour marinade over chicken. Rub well to coat on all sides. Cover and marinate in refrigerator for at least 1 hour, or up to 24 hours, turning chicken over once or twice. Pat dry with paper towels. Discard marinade.

Preheat barbecue or grill. Place chicken as far away from hot coals as possible. (If using a gas grill, cook on medium heat.) Grill for 35 to 45 minutes, turning often to prevent scorching. (Chicken may also be baked on sprayed foil-lined baking sheet in preheated 400°F oven for 1 hour, until browned and crispy.)

To cut down on cooking time, microwave chicken pieces in large microwavable baking dish on High, allowing 4 minutes per lb. Immediately transfer chicken to preheated barbecue and cook for 15 minutes, until golden and crispy.

## CHICKEN AND VEGETABLE BAKE

Yield: 8 servings.
Keeps 2 to 3 days
in the refrigerator.
May be frozen, but
omit potatoes.

| | |
|---|---|
| **5 or 6 potatoes** | **1 tsp dried oregano** |
| **3 large onions** | **2 chickens, each cut in 8 pieces** |
| **3 or 4 carrots** | **⅔ cup barbecue sauce** |
| **2 medium zucchini, unpeeled** | **½ cup white wine** |
| **salt, freshly ground black pepper** | **1 Tbsp lemon juice** |
| **and garlic powder to taste** | **2 to 3 Tbsp maple syrup (optional)** |

SLICER: Cut vegetables to fit feed tube. Slice, using medium pressure. Arrange vegetables in layers in large sprayed casserole. Sprinkle with salt, pepper, garlic powder and oregano. Arrange chicken in a single layer over vegetables. Season again.

STEEL BLADE: Process barbecue sauce, wine, lemon juice and maple syrup (if using) for a few seconds to blend. Pour over chicken. Cover and bake in preheated 375°F oven for 1 hour. Uncover and bake half an hour longer, until browned and tender. Baste occasionally.

## HEAVENLY CHICKEN

You can use bottled
or homemade salad
dressing for any of
the variations (next
page) of this recipe.
Serve with rice or
couscous.

Yield: 8 servings. Keeps
2 to 3 days in the
refrigerator. Reheats
and/or freezes well.

| | |
|---|---|
| **2 broilers, each cut in 8 pieces** | **¾ to 1 cup apricot, peach or** |
| **¾ to 1 cup Italian Salad Dressing** | **pineapple jam** |
| **(page 286)** | **1 Tbsp lemon juice** |
| | **1 pkg (1.9 oz/54 g) dry onion soup mix** |

Place chicken pieces in large sprayed roasting pan.

STEEL BLADE: Combine remaining ingredients and process for a few seconds, until blended. Pour over chicken. (May be marinated for several hours or overnight in refrigerator; turn once.)

Bake, uncovered, in preheated 350°F oven about 2 hours, until golden brown. Baste occasionally.

*Continued*

431 calories per serving (without skin), 23 g carbohydrates, 0.4 g fiber, 36 g protein, 21.3 g fat
(3.6 g saturated fat), 115 mg cholesterol, 740 mg sodium, 443 mg potassium,
2 mg iron, 35 mg calcium, 297 mg phosphorus

## variations

Combine any of the following or use your imagination!

- Italian salad dressing or orange marmalade.
- Thousand Island salad dressing plus apricot jam.
- Sweet and Spicy French Dressing (page 288) plus peach or apricot jam.
- Best Vinaigrette Dressing (page 287) plus ½ cup orange marmalade and ½ cup peach jam.
- Any bottled low-calorie dressing plus sugar-free jam.

# ITALIAN SEASONED CHICKEN WITH POTATOES

Yield: 4 servings.
Keeps 2 to 3 days
in the refrigerator.
Reheats well. If freezing,
omit potatoes.

3½ lb (1.6 kg) chicken, cut in 8 pieces
1 tsp paprika
½ tsp each dry mustard, dried oregano and dried basil
¼ tsp dried thyme

salt and freshly ground black pepper to taste
2 cloves garlic
1 large onion, quartered
½ to ¾ cup chicken broth or water
4 medium potatoes

Place chicken pieces in large sprayed roasting pan and sprinkle with paprika, mustard, oregano, basil, thyme, salt and pepper.

STEEL BLADE: Drop garlic through feed tube while machine is running; process until minced. Add onion and process with 3 or 4 quick on/off pulses, until coarsely chopped. Rub onion and garlic over chicken. Let stand at least half an hour for maximum flavor.

Add broth or water. Roast, uncovered, in preheated 325°F oven for about 2 hours, or until tender and golden.

SLICER: About 45 minutes before chicken is done, cut potatoes to fit feed tube. Slice, using firm pressure. Add potatoes to chicken and sprinkle with additional seasonings. Baste occasionally, adding extra liquid if necessary.

413 calories per serving (without skin), 40.9 g carbohydrates, 4.6 g fiber, 46 g protein, 6.6 g fat
(1.6 g saturated fat), 133 mg cholesterol, 262 mg sodium, 1462 mg potassium,
4 mg iron, 67 mg calcium, 476 mg phosphorus

## variation

Add 2 cups baby carrots, 1 sliced red bell pepper and 2 cups sliced mushrooms along with potatoes (or substitute sweet potatoes). Replace broth

with a 19 oz (540 mL) can tomatoes (salt-free or regular), 2 Tbsp white wine and a bay leaf. Remove bay leaf before serving. One serving contains 484 calories, 56.4 g carbohydrates and 9.1 g fiber.

# CRUNCHY SESAME CHICKEN

Yield: 6 servings. Reheat in a preheated 400°F oven for 10 to 15 minutes; do not cover. Freezes well.

24 crackers (or ¾ cup dried bread crumbs)
½ tsp salt
freshly ground black pepper to taste
dash each of paprika and garlic powder

⅓ cup sesame seeds
1 egg plus 2 Tbsp water
6 single boneless, skinless chicken breasts
3 to 4 Tbsp oil for frying

STEEL BLADE: Process crackers with salt, pepper, paprika and garlic powder to make fine crumbs, about 30 seconds. Add sesame seeds and process 2 or 3 seconds longer to mix. Transfer to a flat plate or plastic bag.

Beat egg with water in a pie plate. Dip chicken pieces first in egg, then in crumb mixture. Heat 1 to 2 Tbsp oil in large nonstick skillet. Add chicken pieces and brown on medium heat about 5 minutes on each side, until golden and crispy. Add additional oil as needed. Drain well on paper towels.

316 calories per serving (with bread crumbs), 11.8 g carbohydrates, 1.6 g fiber, 31 g protein, 15.6 g fat (2.4 g saturated fat), 108 mg cholesterol, 368 mg sodium, 296 mg potassium, 3 mg iron, 120 mg calcium, 283 mg phosphorus

## variations

• BAKED CRUNCHY SESAME CHICKEN: Substitute 3 lb (1.4 kg) chicken pieces or breasts (including skin and bone). If using chicken wings, cut in half and discard wing tips. Bake, uncovered, on sprayed foil-lined baking sheet in preheated 400°F oven until browned. Chicken wings take 30 to 35 minutes. Chicken pieces or breasts take 45 to 60 minutes.

• PASSOVER CHICKEN OR TURKEY SCHNITZEL: Substitute 1 cup matzo meal or cake meal for crumbs; omit sesame seeds. Place chicken or turkey cutlets between 2 sheets of waxed paper and pound to ¼-inch thickness. Coat with egg, then seasoned matzo meal. Brown in hot oil on medium-high heat until golden, about 2 to 3 minutes per side. Keep warm in 275°F oven. Serve with lemon wedges.

# POTATO-CRUSTED CHICKEN

A delicious potato
pancake flavor.

Yield: 4 servings. Keeps
2 to 3 days in the
refrigerator. Reheats
and/or freezes well.

3 lb (1.4 kg) chicken pieces

salt, freshly ground black pepper,
    paprika, garlic powder and dried
    basil to taste

3 medium onions, halved

1 to 2 Tbsp oil

1 egg

2 Tbsp water

1 cup instant mashed potato flakes

seasoning salt to taste

¼ to ½ cup water (as needed)

Remove and discard skin and excess fat from chicken. Rub chicken with seasonings. Cover and refrigerate for at least 1 hour or overnight.

SLICER: Slice onions, using medium pressure. Heat oil in nonstick skillet on medium-high heat and sauté onions until golden. Place in large sprayed roasting pan.

Beat egg with water in a flat dish. Dip chicken pieces first in egg, then in potato flakes. Sprinkle lightly with seasoning salt. Arrange in a single layer over onions. Add water to bottom of pan. Bake, covered, in preheated 350°F oven for 1 hour. Uncover and bake 20 minutes longer, basting occasionally.

321 calories per serving, 17.3 g carbohydrates, 2 g fiber, 38.5 g protein, 10 g fat (2 g saturated fat), 167 mg
cholesterol, 159 mg sodium, 507 mg potassium, 2 mg iron, 42 mg calcium, 329 mg phosphorus

# PANKO-CRUSTED CHICKEN FINGERS

Panko crumbs are
Japanese-style
bread crumbs, and
they're so simple
to make yourself.
If there are nut
allergies in your
family, just omit the
nuts and increase
crumbs to 1¼ cups.

Yield: 4 servings.
Keeps 2 days in the
refrigerator. Reheats
and/or freezes well.

½ cup almonds or pecans

¾ cup Panko crumbs (page 37) or
    dried bread crumbs

2 Tbsp fresh parsley

salt, pepper and paprika to taste

4 single boneless skinless chicken
    breasts

⅓ cup light mayonnaise mixed with
    1 Tbsp honey mustard

Preheat oven to 375°F. Line a baking sheet with parchment paper.

STEEL BLADE: Process nuts, Panko crumbs and parsley with seasonings to form fine crumbs, 25 to 30 seconds. Transfer to a flat plate or plastic bag.

Cut chicken into long strips about 1-inch wide. Sprinkle lightly with seasonings. Dip strips in mayonnaise mixture, then in crumb mixture. Place in a single layer on baking sheet.

Bake, uncovered, for 10 minutes. Flip chicken strips over and bake 5 to 7 minutes longer, until crisp and golden. Serve with Dipping Sauce (page 215) or Easy Barbecue Sauce (page 105).

367 calories per serving, 24.2 g carbohydrates, 1.6 g fiber, 31 g protein, 16 g fat (2.4 g saturated fat),
80 mg cholesterol, 291 mg sodium, 322 mg potassium, 3 mg iron, 54 mg calcium, 261 mg phosphorus

### dipping sauce

Whisk together ½ cup apricot preserves, 1 Tbsp soy sauce, 1 Tbsp lemon juice and 1 Tbsp ketchup in a small bowl. One Tbsp contains 30 calories, 8 g carbohydrates and 0.1 g fiber.

## MAPLE-GLAZED GARLIC CHICKEN BREASTS

Ginger and garlic combine perfectly with maple syrup for an easy, tasty chicken dish. Great for company!

Yield: 8 servings. Keeps 2 to 3 days in the refrigerator. Leftovers are delicious cold. Reheats and/or freezes well.

8 single chicken breasts, with bone (or 2 chickens, cut up)
5 or 6 cloves garlic
2 slices fresh ginger, peeled (2 Tbsp)
½ cup maple syrup

¼ cup soy sauce (low-sodium or regular)
3 Tbsp orange juice
2 tsp toasted sesame oil
¼ tsp cayenne pepper
3 or 4 Tbsp sesame seeds

Remove skin from chicken. Arrange in a single layer in large, sprayed, nonreactive casserole or roasting pan.

STEEL BLADE: Drop garlic and ginger through feed tube while machine is running; process until minced. Add maple syrup, soy sauce, orange juice, sesame oil and cayenne. Process until blended, about 10 seconds. Pour mixture over chicken, cover and marinate for 1 hour or up to 24 hours in refrigerator. Turn chicken pieces over once or twice for even marinating.

Bake, covered, in preheated 350°F oven for 45 minutes. Uncover, baste chicken with sauce and sprinkle with sesame seeds. Bake, uncovered, 20 minutes longer. Chicken should be glazed and nicely browned. Baste occasionally.

239 calories per serving (without skin), 17 g carbohydrates, 0.6 g fiber, 28 g protein, 6 g fat (1.3 g saturated fat), 73 mg cholesterol, 784 mg sodium, 335 mg potassium, 2 mg iron, 64 mg calcium, 241 mg phosphorus

## STICKY CHICKY

Tried and true! Be sure to check out Sticky Tofu (page 249) for the vegetarians at your table.

4 lb (1.8 kg) chicken pieces
1 tsp paprika
1 tsp dry mustard
½ tsp garlic powder
salt and freshly ground black pepper to taste
2 cloves garlic

½ cup soy sauce (low-sodium or regular)
½ cup honey or corn syrup
2 Tbsp vinegar or lemon juice
½ tsp ground ginger
1 Tbsp cornstarch dissolved in 2 Tbsp cold water
2 to 3 Tbsp sesame seeds, for garnish

Rub chicken pieces with paprika, mustard, garlic powder, salt and pepper. Place skin side down in large sprayed casserole or roasting pan. Do not add any liquids. Roast, uncovered, in preheated 400°F oven for 20 minutes, then turn skin side up and roast 15 minutes longer.

STEEL BLADE: Drop garlic through feed tube while machine is running; process until minced. Add soy sauce, honey or syrup, vinegar or lemon juice and ginger. Process 2 or 3 seconds, until blended. Pour sauce over chicken pieces. Reduce heat to 350°F. Roast half an hour longer, basting occasionally.

Stir cornstarch mixture into bubbling sauce. Return chicken to oven and cook 2 or 3 minutes longer. Sprinkle with sesame seeds.

282 calories per serving (without skin), 26.6 g carbohydrates, 0.4 g fiber, 33 g protein, 4.7 g fat (1.2 g saturated fat), 102 mg cholesterol, 824 mg sodium, 402 mg potassium, 2 mg iron, 27 mg calcium, 280 mg phosphorus

*Yield: 6 servings. Keeps 2 to 3 days in the refrigerator. Reheats and/or freezes well.*

## ROASTED TURKEY BREAST BALSAMICO

*This is a wonderful alternative to roasting a whole turkey, no bones about it! Marinating keeps the turkey moist and flavorful. You can also use an unrolled boneless turkey breast.*

Balsamic Vinaigrette (page 287)

3 medium onions, cut in chunks

3 cloves garlic

1 boneless rolled turkey breast, about 4 lb (1.8 kg) (see Chef's Tip, page 217)

salt, freshly ground black pepper and paprika to taste

½ tsp each dried basil and dried thyme

Prepare Balsamic Vinaigrette as directed; measure ½ cup. Refrigerate remaining mixture to use another time.

STEEL BLADE: Process onions with several quick on/off pulses, until coarsely chopped. Place in the bottom of a sprayed casserole. Drop garlic through feed tube while machine is running; process until minced.

Place turkey in casserole; rub with garlic, salt, pepper, paprika, basil and thyme. Pour ½ cup vinaigrette overtop, turning turkey to coat on all sides. Cover and marinate in refrigerator for at least 1 hour or up to 24 hours, turning occasionally.

Cook, covered, in preheated 350°F oven. Calculate 30 minutes per lb as the cooking time. Uncover during the last half hour of cooking and baste occasionally. When done, a meat thermometer should register an internal temperature of 170°F to 175°F and juices will run clear when turkey is pierced. Let stand, covered, for 20 minutes for easier slicing. Slice turkey thinly. Serve with pan juices.

*Yield: 8 to 10 servings. Keeps 2 to 3 days in the refrigerator. Reheats and/or freezes well.*

300 calories per serving, 6 g carbohydrates, 0.6 g fiber, 54 g protein, 5.3 g fat (0.9 g saturated fat), 147 mg cholesterol, 238 mg sodium, 582 mg potassium, 3 mg iron, 33 mg calcium, 411 mg phosphorus

## chef's tip

Rolled turkey breast is not always available. If you use an unrolled turkey breast, cooking time will be 20 to 25 minutes per lb. If you can't find 1 large turkey breast, use 2 smaller ones. Since 2 smaller pieces require less cooking time than 1 large piece, use an instant-read thermometer to prevent overcooking.

## stuffed turkey breast

Ask your butcher to butterfly a boneless, skinless turkey breast. (To do it yourself, cut horizontally through the middle, leaving it hinged on 1 side, so that it opens flat like a book.) Place between 2 pieces of plastic wrap and pound lightly to flatten. Rub both sides with garlic and seasonings. Spread with your favorite stuffing mixture. Starting at the narrow end, roll up tightly. Tie with string in several places, about 3 inches apart. Place in casserole, pour vinaigrette over and roast as directed. Calculate 30 minutes per lb as the cooking time.

# TURKEY CUTLETS WITH PEPPERS AND MUSHROOMS

This makes a quick, healthy and delicious dinner! It is equally good using chicken breasts and is perfect over rice or pasta. Garnish with toasted slivered almonds for company.

Yield: 4 servings. Leftovers keep 2 days in the refrigerator and can be reheated in the microwave. Vegetables will become soggy if frozen.

| | |
|---|---|
| 1½ lb (750 g) thin turkey cutlets | 2 cups mushrooms |
| salt and freshly ground black pepper to taste | ½ cup chicken broth |
| ¼ cup flour (approximately) | ¼ cup dry white wine |
| 2 Tbsp olive oil | 2 Tbsp fresh lemon juice |
| ¼ cup fresh parsley | 2 tsp Dijon or honey mustard |
| 2 cloves garlic | ½ tsp each dried basil and dried thyme (or 1 Tbsp each fresh basil |
| 4 green onions (or 1 medium onion) | and fresh thyme) |
| 1 red and 1 yellow bell pepper, halved | |

For machines with nested bowls, see method on page 218.

Sprinkle cutlets with salt and pepper. Coat with flour, shaking off excess. Heat 1 Tbsp oil in large nonstick skillet. Brown turkey 1 to 2 minutes on each side. Transfer cutlets to a plate and cover with foil to keep warm.

STEEL BLADE: Process parsley until minced, about 10 seconds. Remove from bowl and reserve as a garnish. Drop garlic through feed tube and process until minced.

SLICER: Slice green onions, bell peppers and mushrooms, using medium pressure. Heat remaining oil in skillet. Sauté garlic, onions, peppers and mushrooms

*Continued*

for 3 to 4 minutes, until golden. Add broth, wine, lemon juice, mustard, basil and thyme. Return turkey to skillet. Simmer, uncovered, for 2 or 3 minutes, stirring occasionally, until sauce is slightly thickened. Adjust seasonings to taste. Sprinkle with reserved parsley.

331 calories per serving, 16.3 g carbohydrates, 2.3 g fiber, 45 g protein, 8.4 g fat (1.1 g saturated fat), 68 mg cholesterol, 314 mg sodium, 362 mg potassium, 4 mg iron, 36 mg calcium, 68 mg phosphorus

### nested bowl method

Use mini-bowl and blade to mince parsley. Use large bowl and STEEL BLADE for remaining tasks.

# MARINATED ROAST TURKEY WITH CRANBERRY RELISH

Yield: 12 to 14 servings. Leftovers keep 2 to 3 days in the refrigerator or may be frozen. Remove stuffing and wrap separately.

## MARINATED TURKEY

12 to 14 lb (5.5 to 6.4 kg) turkey

1 seedless orange

2 cloves garlic

2 Tbsp olive oil

2 Tbsp each lemon, orange and lime juice

2 Tbsp honey or maple syrup (or to taste)

1 tsp salt

1 tsp paprika

½ tsp dry mustard (optional)

¼ tsp each freshly ground black pepper, dried basil and dried thyme

## TURKEY STUFFING

12 slices bread (6 cups soft bread crumbs)

½ cup fresh parsley

2 medium onions, cut in chunks

2 stalks celery, cut in chunks

2 Tbsp oil

1 apple, peeled and cut in chunks

2 eggs (or 1 egg plus 2 egg whites)

1 tsp salt

1 tsp paprika

½ tsp each freshly ground black pepper, dried basil and dried thyme

¼ tsp each dried savory and dried sage (optional)

½ cup chicken broth or water (approximately)

For marinated turkey: Remove excess fat and giblets from turkey cavity. Place turkey in large sprayed roasting pan.

SLICER: If necessary, cut orange to fit feed tube; slice, using medium pressure. Place orange slices under turkey skin to keep turkey moist during cooking.

STEEL BLADE: Drop garlic through feed tube while machine is running; process until minced. Add oil, juices, honey or maple syrup and seasonings; process for 5 seconds to blend. Rub mixture over turkey. Cover and refrigerate overnight or up to 2 days. Remove from refrigerator about 1 hour before cooking.

For turkey stuffing: Drop chunks of bread through feed tube while the machine is running. Process on the STEEL BLADE until fine crumbs are formed; measure 6 cups. Place crumbs in large mixing bowl. Process parsley until minced, 8 to 10 seconds. Add to crumbs.

Process onions with quick on/off pulses, until coarsely chopped. Empty bowl; repeat with celery. Sauté onions and celery in oil on medium heat until golden, about 5 minutes. Add to crumbs.

Process apple until minced, about 10 seconds. Add eggs and process 2 or 3 seconds longer. Add to crumb mixture along with seasonings and enough broth to moisten; mix well. (May be made up to a day in advance and refrigerated.)

Assembly: Stuff cavity and neck of turkey loosely to allow for expansion during cooking. Close with skewers and string. Fasten legs close to the body with string. (Alternately, bake stuffing separately in large casserole in preheated 325°F oven for 50 to 60 minutes.)

Place turkey breast side down on sprayed roasting rack. Roast, uncovered, in preheated 325°F oven. Calculate 18 to 20 minutes per lb as your cooking time. (A 12 to 14 lb/5.4 to 6.4 kg stuffed turkey takes 3½ to 4 hours.) Turn breast side up halfway through cooking. Baste occasionally. If turkey gets too brown, cover loosely with a tent of foil. Let turkey stand for 20 minutes before carving. Serve with Cranberry Relish (page 220).

513 calories per serving, 20.4 g carbohydrates, 1.6 g fiber, 70 g protein, 15.2 g fat (3.9 g saturated fat), 233 mg cholesterol, 804 mg sodium, 105 mg potassium, 6 mg iron, 102 mg calcium, 648 mg phosphorus

### test for doneness

Turkey is done when a drumstick moves easily and juices run clear when turkey is pierced. An instant-read thermometer inserted into meaty portion of thigh should read 175°F. Stuffing temperature should be 165°F. Unstuffed turkey needs less cooking time; remove from oven when it reaches 165°F on an instant-read thermometer.

### turkey gravy

Pour pan juices from turkey into a container and freeze for about 15 minutes, or until fat rises to the top. Skim off fat. Measure ¼ cup fat and place it back in roasting pan. Add ¼ cup flour (or 2 Tbsp potato starch) and cook on low heat, stirring to loosen browned bits from bottom of pan. When golden brown, gradually blend in reserved pan juices from

*Continued*

turkey plus enough chicken or turkey broth to make 4 cups liquid. If desired, add 2 tsp soy sauce.

Simmer for 5 minutes, scraping any remaining browned bits from bottom of pan. Add salt and freshly ground black pepper to taste. This makes 4 cups thin gravy. For a thicker gravy, use ½ cup fat and ½ cup flour (or ¼ cup potato starch).

41 calories per ¼ cup serving, 1.4 g carbohydrates, 0 g fiber, 1 g protein, 3.3. g fat (1 g saturated fat), 9 mg cholesterol, 30 mg sodium, 2 mg potassium, 0 mg iron, 0 mg calcium, 2 mg phosphorus

## CRANBERRY RELISH

Yield: About 3½ cups. Keeps about 1 month in the refrigerator or may be frozen.

1 large seedless orange, cut in chunks
3 cups cranberries
1 cup sugar
½ cup apricot jam
1 tsp lemon juice

STEEL BLADE: Process orange until fine, about 15 seconds. Add cranberries and process until finely ground, 25 to 30 seconds. Scrape down sides of bowl as necessary. Add remaining ingredients and process until combined, about 10 seconds. Refrigerate for several hours to blend flavors.

26 calories per Tbsp, 6.7 g carbohydrates, 0.3 g fiber, 0 g protein, 0 g fat (0 g saturated fat), 0 mg cholesterol, 1 mg sodium, 12 mg potassium, 0 mg iron, 2 mg calcium, 1 mg phosphorus

# VEGETABLES AND SIDE DISHES
## recipe list

226 Roasted Asparagus with Portobello Mushrooms

226 French-Cut Green Beans

227 Asian Green Bean Bake

227 Easy Broccoli Bake

228 Apricot Candied Carrots

228 Pineapple Carrots

229 Carrot Ring

229 Carrot Soufflé

230 Eggplant Italiano

231 Sweet and Sour Eggplant

231 No-Fry Eggplant Parmesan

232 Mom's Caponata

233 Ratatouille

233 Sautéed Garlic Mushrooms

234 Chickpea Chili

235 Mushroom Duxelles

235 Honey-Glazed Roasted Roots

236 Barbecued Lyonnaise Potatoes

236 Best-Ever Scalloped Potatoes

237 Skinny No-Fries

238 Rösti Potatoes

238 Potato Kugel

239 Sweet Potato Kugel

239 Carrot Kugel

240 Lokshin Kugel (Noodle Pudding)

241 Onion Kugel

242 Mini Potato Zucchini Kugels

242 Zucchini Puffs

243 Breaded Zucchini

243 Carrot Latkes

244 Broccoli Latkes

245 Easy Potato Latkes

246 Noodle Latkes (Pancakes)

246 Veggie Latkes

247 Baked Veggie Patties

248 Hoisin Vegetable Stir-Fry

248 Pea Pod, Pepper and Mushroom Stir-Fry

249 Sticky Tofu

250 No-Fry Fried Rice

250 Low-Carb "Fried Rice"

251 Chinese Fried Rice

252 Rice Pilaf
253 Leek and Rice Skillet Casserole
253 Rapid Risotto
254 Rice, Spinach and Mushroom Bake
255 Vegetable Kishka
256 Potato Knishes
257 Corned Beef Filling
257 Chicken or Meat Filling
258 Kasha Knish
258 Kreplach
259 Homemade Pasta
261 Peanut Butter Pasta
261 Popcorn Stuffing Mounds
262 Stuffing Casserole

- Side dishes that do not contain any dairy products (e.g., Lokshin Kugel, page 240) can be served with either meat or dairy meals, so they are in this chapter. For side dishes containing dairy products, see the Fish and Dairy chapter.
- Refer to the **Smart Chart** (pages 27–34) for basic vegetable processing techniques.
- Choose vegetables that are firm and not too ripe. Remove the core, large pits and seeds before processing.
- The wide-mouth feed tube is excellent for slicing or grating whole round fruits and vegetables (e.g., lemons, tomatoes, onions).
- The small feed tube (mini-tube) is ideal for single or small items. If vegetables are wide at 1 end and narrow at the other (e.g., carrots), pack them in pairs, alternating 1 wide end up and 1 narrow end up.
- Before slicing or grating/shredding vegetables, cut the bottom ends flat; place them in the feed tube flat side down. Pack the feed tube snugly, but not so tightly that the pusher can't move.
- Cut vegetables in lengths to fit the feed tube. Some newer models of food processors have a marking on the feed tube to indicate the maximum height for filling. Don't overfill the feed tube or the machine won't start when you press down on the pusher!
- If the vegetables don't fit, try inserting them from the bottom of the feed tube where the opening is slightly larger.
- The mini-feed tube (if your machine has one) is ideal for slicing or shredding long vegetables or small items (e.g., 1 or 2 carrots, zucchini, green onions, celery).
- For short shreds, pack the vegetables (e.g., carrots, zucchini) in the feed tube upright. For long, narrow shreds, pack the feed tube horizontally.
- The pusher assembly for the wide-mouth feed tube has a small pusher that fits inside the small feed tube. The small pusher must be in place when using the wide-mouth feed tube; otherwise, food will bounce up and down in the small feed tube instead of being sliced or grated. (I speak from experience!)
- In general, use medium pressure for most vegetables (e.g., potatoes, celery, zucchini). Use firm pressure for hard vegetables (e.g., carrots, sweet potatoes). Use light pressure for tomatoes or cabbage.

- CHEATER CHOP: For an easy way to "chop" vegetables, cut them in 1-inch chunks, place them in the feed tube and process on the **Slicer**, using light pressure.

- For more control when slicing or grating vegetables, use the PULSE button. Press down on the pusher with 1 hand and press PULSE with the other; release pulse as soon as the food is sliced or shredded. The processor will stop instantly!

- For continuous feed, use either the ON or PULSE button. If you use the ON button, 1 hand will be free to refill the feed tube.

- Cooking time for vegetables varies depending on the type of vegetable and whether they are whole, sliced or chopped. Estimate 3 to 4 minutes for grated vegetables, 5 to 6 minutes for sliced vegetables, and 10 to 15 minutes for whole vegetables. Taste and check.

- To microwave vegetables, soak them in cold water and shake them dry. The water clinging to the vegetables provides enough steam to cook them. Allow 5 to 7 minutes per lb on High. Stir or turn vegetables over halfway through cooking. If they have a skin (e.g., potatoes, squash), pierce before microwaving.

- GRATINÉED VEGETABLES: Top cooked vegetables with Béchamel Sauce (page 103) or Cheese Sauce (page 104); sprinkle with buttered seasoned crumbs. Bake 15 to 20 minutes at 350°F, until bubbling and nicely browned.

- Store potatoes and onions separately in a cool, dark place to prevent spoiling. If refrigerated, potatoes will develop a sweet taste.

- RESCUED MASHED POTATOES: Here's a tried and true remedy to rescue overprocessed mashed potatoes, based on 3 to 4 potatoes. Add ¼ cup milk, 2 Tbsp margarine, 1 egg, ½ tsp baking powder, salt and freshly ground black pepper to mashed potatoes. Process on the **Steel Blade** 30 seconds, until smooth and sticky. Spread in a sprayed 9-inch pie plate, sprinkle with paprika and bake at 375°F about 30 minutes, until brown and crusty.

NOODLE KNOW-HOW

- To cook pasta, the general rule is 4 quarts of boiling water and 4 tsp salt for each lb of pasta. Do not cook pasta without salt or it will never taste right.

- Drain pasta as soon as it is cooked. Reheat quickly by placing in boiling water for a minute (or microwave on High, allowing 1 minute per cup). Undercook pasta slightly if you plan to reheat it later.

- Spaghetti and macaroni double when cooked. Other noodles swell slightly. One pound of spaghetti yields 5 to 6 servings. One cup uncooked noodles (2½ oz weight) yields 1¼ cups cooked (2 servings). You can freeze cooked pasta for 4 to 6 months.

- NESTED WORK BOWLS: Choose the appropriate bowl and blade or disc for the task. Use the small bowl to mince garlic or herbs, or for other small tasks. Use the medium or large bowl and appropriate disc to slice or shred/grate veggies, cheese, etc. Use the large bowl and **Steel Blade** to chop/mince vegetables and to combine ingredients. (You can also use the **Steel Blade** in the medium bowl on Cuisinart Elite models.)

- OTHER OPTIONS: The Cuisinart Elite food processor comes with an adjustable 6-in-1 slicing disc, which can produce thin, medium or thick slices (1 to 6 mm) with a quick twist of a dial. It also comes with a reversible shredding disc which can produce fine or medium shreds. Also refer to Optional Blades and Discs (page 12).

# ROASTED ASPARAGUS WITH PORTOBELLO MUSHROOMS

Deliciously easy! You can use shiitake or button mushrooms with equally good results.

Yield: 4 servings.

1 bunch asparagus (1 lb/500 g)

4 medium portobello mushrooms (½ to ¾ lb/250 to 375 g)

¼ cup Balsamic Vinaigrette (page 287)

salt and freshly ground black pepper to taste

Preheat oven to 425°F. Soak asparagus in cold water; drain well. Bend asparagus and snap off ends at the point where it breaks off naturally. (The ends can be peeled and used in soups.) Remove stems from mushrooms. Rinse mushrooms briefly and pat dry. If necessary, trim caps to fit feed tube. Insert SLICER. Slice mushrooms, using medium pressure.

Place asparagus and mushrooms in a single layer on a sprayed baking sheet. Drizzle with vinaigrette, and season with salt and pepper. Roast at 425°F for 10 to 12 minutes, or until tender and browned. Serve immediately. Also delicious at room temperature.

82 calories per serving, 9.1 g carbohydrates, 3 g fiber, 4 g protein, 4.2 g fat (0.5 g saturated fat), 0 mg cholesterol, 163 mg sodium, 511 mg potassium, 1 mg iron, 29 mg calcium, 131 mg phosphorus

# FRENCH-CUT GREEN BEANS

Yield: 4 servings. Can be reheated in the microwave.

1 lb (500 g) fresh green beans

2 Tbsp butter or margarine (or to taste)

salt and freshly ground black pepper

1 Tbsp fresh lemon or lime juice

SLICER: Wash and trim beans to fit width of feed tube. Stack horizontally in feed tube to within 1 inch of top. Slice, using medium pressure. Repeat with remaining beans in as many batches as necessary.

Place in saucepan with boiling salted water to cover. Cover and cook on medium heat for 6 to 8 minutes, until tender but still slightly crunchy. Drain well. Combine with remaining ingredients. Serve immediately.

91 calories per serving, 9.1 g carbohydrates, 3.6 g fiber, 2 g protein, 6.1 g fat (3.7 g saturated fat), 15 mg cholesterol, 42 mg sodium, 169 mg potassium, 1 mg iron, 51 mg calcium, 34 mg phosphorus

## variation

Cook and drain sliced green beans as directed. Sauté 1 chopped onion in 2 Tbsp Garlic Butter (page 65) until golden. Add green beans and ¼ cup slivered almonds; cook 2 to 3 minutes longer. Season to taste.

## ASIAN GREEN BEAN BAKE

An oldie, but a goodie! This is real comfort food. If you prefer fresh veggies, use 1 lb (500 g) green beans, 2 cups broccoli florets and 2 cups sliced mushrooms.

Yield: 8 servings. Keeps 2 days in the refrigerator. Reheats well. Do not freeze.

2 pkgs (10 oz/300 g each) French-style frozen green beans

1 pkg (10 oz/300 g) frozen broccoli spears

1 can (8 oz/250 mL) water chestnuts, drained

1 can (10 oz/300 mL) sliced mushrooms, drained

1 or 2 cloves garlic

2 cans (10 oz/284 mL each) condensed mushroom soup

2 Tbsp soy sauce (low-sodium or regular)

dash freshly ground black pepper

1 can (3 oz/85 g) French's French Fried Onions

Cook beans and broccoli according to package directions, undercooking slightly. Drain well. (If using fresh veggies, stir-fry them quickly in 1 Tbsp oil until tender-crisp.)

SLICER: Slice water chestnuts, using firm pressure. Combine with beans, broccoli and mushrooms in a lightly greased 9- × 13-inch glass baking dish. Mix well.

STEEL BLADE: Drop garlic through feed tube while machine is running; process until minced. Add soup, soy sauce and pepper and blend with several on/off pulses. Stir into vegetables. Top with French Fried Onions. (May be prepared in advance up to this point and refrigerated.)

Bake in preheated 350°F oven for 25 to 30 minutes, until bubbling and onions are nicely browned.

181 calories per serving, 20.5 g carbohydrates, 5.1 g fiber, 5 g protein, 9.9 g fat (2.4 g saturated fat), 0 mg cholesterol, 783 mg sodium, 250 mg potassium, 2 mg iron, 65 mg calcium, 75 mg phosphorus

## EASY BROCCOLI BAKE

Kosher condensed mushroom soup does not contain any dairy.

Yield: 4 to 6 servings. May be prepared up to a day in advance and baked just before needed.

2 pkgs (10 oz/300 g each) frozen broccoli spears (or 1 bunch fresh broccoli, cut up)

4 oz (125 g) chilled cheddar cheese (low-fat or regular), cut in chunks (1 cup)

1 can (10 oz/284 mL) condensed mushroom soup

½ cup corn flake or dried bread crumbs (or 3 oz/85 g can French's French Fried Onions)

1 Tbsp margarine or butter

Cook frozen broccoli according to package directions. (Or microwave fresh broccoli, covered, on High, allowing 5 to 6 minutes per lb.) Drain well. Spread evenly in a sprayed 9-inch pie plate.

STEEL BLADE: Process cheese until fine, 15 to 20 seconds. Add soup and blend in with quick on/off pulses. Spread over broccoli. Sprinkle with crumbs or onions. Dot with margarine or butter. Bake, uncovered, in preheated 350°F oven for about 20 minutes.

*Continued*

220 calories per serving, 22.6 g carbohydrates, 4.1 g fiber, 13 g protein, 9.5 g fat (2.8 g saturated fat), 6 mg cholesterol, 801 mg sodium, 304 mg potassium, 3 mg iron, 191 mg calcium, 231 mg phosphorus

### variation

Replace broccoli with 2 cups cooked cauliflower florets. Slice 1 medium onion and 1 cup mushrooms; sauté in 1 Tbsp oil for 5 minutes. Add to cauliflower and spread evenly in pie plate. Continue as directed.

## APRICOT CANDIED CARROTS

Gluten-free, easy and delicious!

Yield: 6 to 8 servings. Keeps 2 to 3 days in the refrigerator. Reheats and/or freezes well.

2 lb (1 kg) carrots, scraped and trimmed
½ cup boiling water
dash salt

½ cup apricot jam
8 marshmallows
1 Tbsp lemon juice

SLICER: Cut carrots to fit feed tube. Slice, using firm pressure.

Combine boiling water, salt and jam in a saucepan. Add carrots, cover tightly and simmer for 15 minutes or until tender. Remove cover and, if necessary, let liquid boil down to a depth of ½ inch. Add marshmallows and lemon juice and stir until dissolved.

144 calories per serving, 36.6 g carbohydrates, 4.3 g fiber, 1 g protein, 0.3 g fat (0 g saturated fat), 0 mg cholesterol, 148 mg sodium, 351 mg potassium, 1 mg iron, 48 mg calcium, 44 mg phosphorus

## PINEAPPLE CARROTS

Yield: 6 to 8 servings. Keeps 2 to 3 days in the refrigerator. Reheats and/or freezes well.

2 lb (1 kg) carrots
2 Tbsp cornstarch
1 cup unsweetened pineapple juice

½ tsp ground cinnamon (optional)
¼ cup sugar (or granular Splenda)

SLICER: Cut carrots 1 inch shorter than feed tube. Slice, using medium pressure. Cook in boiling salted water until tender, 12 to 15 minutes. Drain carrots well and return to saucepan.

Dissolve cornstarch in pineapple juice. Add with cinnamon (if using) and sugar to carrots and simmer until thickened, 2 to 3 minutes.

113 calories per serving, 27.6 g carbohydrates, 4.3 g fiber, 1 g protein, 0.3 g fat (0 g saturated fat), 0 mg cholesterol, 82 mg sodium, 381 mg potassium, 1 mg iron, 47 mg calcium, 45 mg phosphorus

### lighter variation

With Splenda, 1 serving contains 85 calories and 20.2 g carbohydrates.

## CARROT RING

Yield: 8 servings. Keeps
2 to 3 days in the
refrigerator. Reheats
and/or freezes well.

**5 or 6 medium carrots, cut in chunks**
  **(about 1½ cups)**
**2 eggs**
**½ cup canola oil**
**½ cup brown sugar, packed**
**¼ cup orange juice or water**
**1½ cups flour**

**2 tsp baking powder**
**1 tsp baking soda**
**1 tsp ground cinnamon**
**dash salt**
**1 cup green peas or broccoli (optional)**

STEEL BLADE: Process carrots until finely minced, 12 to 15 seconds. Add eggs, oil and brown sugar. Process until well mixed, about 45 seconds. Add remaining ingredients, except green peas or broccoli, and process with 4 or 5 quick on/offs, just until flour disappears.

Pour into sprayed 6-cup ring mold or small fluted tube pan. Bake in preheated 350°F oven for about 40 minutes, or until done. Invert onto serving plate. If desired, cook green peas or broccoli and fill center of ring. Serve warm.

294 calories per serving, 34.9 g carbohydrates, 1.4 g fiber, 4 g protein, 15.6 g fat (1.5 g saturated fat), 53 mg cholesterol, 333 mg sodium, 142 mg potassium, 2 mg iron, 100 mg calcium, 81 mg phosphorus

### variation

Replace oil with margarine and reduce baking powder to 1 tsp. Fill sprayed muffin tins three-quarters full. Bake at 350°F about 30 minutes. Serve hot. Makes 12 muffins. One muffin contains 196 calories, 23.3 g carbohydrates and 0.9 fiber.

## CARROT SOUFFLÉ

My niece Debbi-Jo
Matias gets rave
reviews when she
brings this moist,
light pudding to
dinner parties.

**2 lb (1 kg) carrots**
**½ cup margarine, cut in chunks**
**3 eggs**
**¾ cup brown sugar, firmly packed**

**¼ cup flour**
**1½ tsp baking powder**
**¾ tsp baking soda**

SLICER: Cut carrots 1 inch shorter than feed tube. Slice, using medium pressure. Cook in boiling salted water until tender, 10 to 15 minutes. Drain well.

STEEL BLADE: Process carrots with margarine until puréed, 20 to 30 seconds, stopping machine to scrape down sides as necessary. Add remaining ingredients and process until blended, about 15 seconds. *Continued*

Pour into sprayed 1½-quart soufflé or baking dish. Place dish in a pan filled with 1 inch of water. Bake, uncovered, in preheated 350°F oven about 1 hour. Serve immediately. It deflates slightly when it cools but still tastes terrific.

Yield: 8 servings.
Leftovers keep 2 to
3 days in the refrigerator.
Reheats well, but
do not freeze.

260 calories per serving, 32.4 g carbohydrates, 3.2 g fiber, 4 g protein, 13.6 g fat (2.7 g saturated fat), 80 mg cholesterol, 392 mg sodium, 303 mg potassium, 1 mg iron, 110 mg calcium, 88 mg phosphorus

### note

To avoid reheating, prepare batter earlier in the day, omitting baking powder and baking soda. Refrigerate until 1 hour before serving time. Stir in leavening and mix well. Bake as directed.

## EGGPLANT ITALIANO

If you don't tell them it's eggplant, I won't! It tastes like pizza without the crust. Serve as a side dish or main dish.

Yield: 4 to 6 servings. Keeps 2 to 3 days in the refrigerator. Reheats and/or freezes well.

2 cloves garlic
1 large onion, cut in chunks
1 stalk celery
1 green or red bell pepper
1 to 2 cups mushrooms
1 Tbsp oil
1 medium eggplant, peeled
salt and freshly ground black pepper
  to taste

½ tsp each dried basil and dried
  oregano
1 can (19 oz/540 mL) tomatoes (salt-
  free or regular)
4 to 8 oz (125 to 250 g) chilled low-
  fat mozzarella cheese (1 to 2 cups
  grated)

STEEL BLADE: Drop garlic through feed tube while machine is running; process until minced. Add onion and process with quick on/offs, until coarsely chopped.

SLICER: Cut celery and bell pepper 1 inch shorter than top of feed tube. (If your processor has a wide-mouth feed tube, cut veggies to fit small feed tube.) Slice celery, pepper and mushrooms, using light pressure. Heat oil in large nonstick skillet or wok. Sauté processed vegetables over medium heat, about 5 minutes, until tender.

Slice eggplant, using firm pressure. (If your processor has a standard feed tube, cut eggplant lengthwise in strips so slices won't be too large.) Add to skillet, stir well and cook 5 minutes longer. Add salt, pepper, basil, oregano and tomatoes. Cover and heat to simmering. Place in sprayed casserole. (May be prepared in advance and refrigerated or frozen.)

GRATER: Grate cheese, using medium pressure. Sprinkle over eggplant mixture. Bake in preheated 375°F oven 25 to 30 minutes, until bubbly and golden.

227 calories per serving, 27.6 g carbohydrates, 6.7 g fiber, 11 g protein, 9.9 g fat (4 g saturated fat), 15 mg cholesterol, 175 mg sodium, 669 mg potassium, 2 mg iron, 279 mg calcium, 231 mg phosphorus

# SWEET AND SOUR EGGPLANT

Geitie Kramer of Toronto makes this as an appetizer or side dish. It's delicious either hot or cold. I've even served it as a pasta sauce. Salting eggplant before cooking draws out its bitter juices.

Yield: 8 servings (about 6 cups). Keeps about 1 week in the refrigerator. Reheats and/or freezes well.

2 lb (1 kg) eggplant, peeled and cut in 1-inch chunks

salt for sprinkling

¼ cup fresh parsley

1 or 2 cloves garlic

1 large onion, cut in chunks

2 Tbsp olive oil

2 cans (19 oz/540 mL each) tomatoes (salt-free or regular)

¼ cup lemon juice

2 Tbsp balsamic vinegar

3 Tbsp sugar

¼ tsp freshly ground black pepper

SLICER: Slice eggplant, using medium pressure. Transfer to a colander and sprinkle with salt. Let drain for 1 hour. Rinse well; squeeze out excess moisture.

STEEL BLADE: Process parsley until minced. Remove from bowl and set aside. Drop garlic through feed tube while machine is running; process until minced. Add onion and process with quick on/off pulses, until coarsely chopped.

Heat oil in large nonstick skillet on medium heat. Sauté onion and garlic until soft and golden, about 5 minutes. Drain tomatoes, adding liquid to skillet.

Process tomatoes for a few seconds, until coarsely chopped. Add tomatoes, eggplant, parsley and remaining ingredients to skillet. Cook on low heat, partially covered, for 20 to 25 minutes, until eggplant is tender. Stir occasionally. Serve hot or cold.

125 calories per serving, 23 g carbohydrates, 4.4 g fiber, 2 g protein, 4 g fat (0.6 g saturated fat), 0 mg cholesterol, 309 mg sodium, 452 mg potassium, 2 mg iron, 60 mg calcium, 52 mg phosphorus

# NO-FRY EGGPLANT PARMESAN

This recipe may be halved for a small family, but I like to prepare the full recipe and freeze the leftovers.

Yield: 6 to 8 servings as a main dish, 12 servings as a side dish. Keeps 2 days in the refrigerator. Reheats well. If frozen, eggplant will be

2 eggplants (about 1½ lb/750 g each)

salt for sprinkling

½ cup grated Parmesan cheese

1 cup bread or cracker crumbs

dash salt and freshly ground black pepper

¼ tsp each garlic powder and dried basil

8 oz (250 g) chilled low-fat mozzarella cheese (2 cups grated)

2 eggs mixed with 2 Tbsp cold water

1½ cups tomato sauce (bottled or homemade, salt-free or regular)

¼ cup additional Parmesan cheese (optional)

1 pkg (1.9 oz/54 g) dry onion soup mix (optional)

Peel eggplants; slice crosswise into ½-inch slices. Sprinkle with salt and let stand for 20 minutes. Rinse well; pat dry with paper towels. *Continued*

somewhat softer but still tastes terrific.

STEEL BLADE: Process the ½ cup Parmesan cheese, crumbs, salt, pepper, garlic powder and basil for 3 or 4 seconds to mix. Transfer to a sheet of waxed paper.

GRATER: Grate mozzarella cheese, using medium pressure. Set aside.

Dip eggplant slices first in egg, then in crumb mixture. Arrange in a single layer on sprayed or parchment-lined baking sheets.

Bake, uncovered, in preheated 375°F oven for 15 to 20 minutes. Turn slices over. Top each slice with sauce. Add grated cheese and about 1 tsp dry onion soup mix (if desired). Bake 10 to 12 minutes longer, until golden.

340 calories per serving, 38.9 g carbohydrates, 7.1 g fiber, 19 g protein, 12.8 g fat (6.8 g saturated fat), 97 mg cholesterol, 488 mg sodium, 591 mg potassium, 2 mg iron, 413 mg calcium, 357 mg phosphorus

### passover eggplant parmesan

Replace crumbs with matzo meal, cake meal or crushed Passover crackers.

## MOM'S CAPONATA

My mother changed my recipe and boosted the flavor! Make this in minutes using your processor. Sprinkle with toasted pine nuts and chopped parsley. Serve chilled as an appetizer or hot over rice or pasta.

4 cloves garlic
2 medium onions, cut in chunks
2 stalks celery, cut in chunks
1 Tbsp olive oil
4 medium bell peppers (2 red, 1 green, 1 yellow)
1 jalapeño pepper
2 Japanese eggplants, unpeeled (1 lb/500 g)
1 Tbsp balsamic vinegar

1 can (28 oz/796 mL) tomatoes (salt-free or regular), drained (reserve liquid)
⅓ cup sultana raisins
1 Tbsp sugar
¼ tsp red pepper flakes
½ tsp each ground cumin and dried basil
salt and freshly ground black pepper to taste
¼ cup capers, rinsed and drained
1 cup pitted black and/or green olives

Yield: 8 to 10 servings (about 8 cups). This keeps about 10 days in the refrigerator or freezes well.

STEEL BLADE: Drop garlic through feed tube while machine is running; process until minced. Add onions and celery; process with quick on/off pulses, until coarsely chopped.

Heat oil in large pot. Sauté garlic, onions and celery on medium heat for 5 minutes, until soft.

SLICER: Cut bell and jalapeño peppers and eggplants in half; remove core and seeds from peppers. Slice peppers and eggplants, using medium pressure. Add to onion mixture and cook 10 minutes longer, stirring occasionally.

Add balsamic vinegar, drained tomatoes, raisins, sugar, pepper flakes, cumin, basil, salt and pepper. Cover partially and simmer 20 minutes longer, stirring occasionally. Add reserved tomato liquid as needed to prevent the mixture from becoming dry. Mixture should be thick, not watery. Stir in capers and olives at the end of cooking. Adjust seasonings to taste.

164 calories per serving, 28.1 g carbohydrates, 4.3 g fiber, 3 g protein, 5.5 g fat (0.3 g saturated fat), 0 mg cholesterol, 364 mg sodium, 546 mg potassium, 2 mg iron, 64 mg calcium, 66 mg phosphorus

## RATATOUILLE

Here is my mother's updated recipe— serve it chilled as an appetizer or hot as a sauce over pasta. The flavor is even better the next day!

Yield: 6 to 8 servings. Keeps in the refrigerator about a week, or freezes well.

3 cloves garlic

1 Spanish onion, cut in chunks

1 green and 1 red bell pepper, halved

1 cup mushrooms

3 stalks celery, cut in chunks

1 to 2 Tbsp olive oil

1 medium eggplant, cut in chunks

2 medium zucchini, cut in chunks

1 can (19 oz/540 mL) plum tomatoes
   (salt-free or regular)

1 Tbsp balsamic vinegar

1 tsp sugar

½ tsp each dried basil and dried
   oregano

¼ tsp red pepper flakes

salt and freshly ground black pepper
   to taste

dash Worcestershire sauce

STEEL BLADE: Drop garlic through feed tube while machine is running; process until minced.

SLICER: Slice onion, bell peppers, mushrooms and celery, using medium pressure. Spray a large pot with nonstick spray. Add oil and heat on medium heat. Sauté sliced vegetables 7 to 8 minutes, stirring occasionally.

Slice eggplant and zucchini, using medium pressure. Add to pot and cook 10 minutes more. Add remaining ingredients and simmer, uncovered, 10 minutes longer, stirring occasionally. Adjust seasonings to taste.

125 calories per serving, 25 g carbohydrates, 5.8 g fiber, 3 g protein, 3 g fat (0.4 g saturated fat), 0 mg cholesterol, 37 mg sodium, 657 mg potassium, 2 mg iron, 71 mg calcium, 90 mg phosphorus

## SAUTÉED GARLIC MUSHROOMS

If using a combination of wild and cultivated mushrooms, substitute olive oil and balsamic vinegar for

2 to 3 cloves garlic

2 Tbsp margarine or olive oil

1 lb (500 g) mushrooms, trimmed

1 Tbsp fresh lemon juice

salt and freshly ground black pepper
   to taste

STEEL BLADE: Drop garlic through feed tube while machine is running; process until minced. Heat margarine in a large nonstick skillet. Stir in garlic and cook for 1 to 2 minutes on medium heat. *Continued*

margarine and lemon juice.

SLICER: Stack mushrooms on their sides. Slice, using light pressure. Add to skillet and sauté on medium heat for 4 to 5 minutes, shaking pan to stir. Sprinkle with lemon juice, salt and pepper. Serve immediately.

Yield: 4 servings.
Do not freeze.

77 calories per serving, 5.3 g carbohydrates, 1.9 g fiber, 2 g protein, 6.1 g fat (1.1 g saturated fat), 0 mg cholesterol, 49 mg sodium, 307 mg potassium, 2 mg iron, 8 mg calcium, 75 mg phosphorus

## CHICKPEA CHILI

With the help of your processor, you can prepare this tasty, versatile chili in minutes. Serve as a side dish or vegetarian main dish over rice, polenta or pasta.

Yield: 8 servings. Keeps 4 or 5 days in the refrigerator. Reheats and/or freezes well

**3 cloves garlic**
**1 large onion, cut in chunks**
**2 Tbsp olive oil**
**1 red bell pepper, quartered**
**2 cups mushrooms**
**½ lb (250 g) eggplant, cut in long**
**    strips (e.g., Asian eggplant)**
**1 can (19 oz/540 mL) chickpeas,**
**    drained and rinsed**
**salt and freshly ground black pepper**
**    to taste**

**3 cups water**
**2 medium carrots**
**1 can (5½ oz/156 mL) tomato paste**
**    (salt-free or regular)**
**1 cup tomato sauce (salt-free or**
**    regular) (or 2 tomatoes, chopped)**
**½ cup bulgur or couscous**
**½ tsp each dried basil, dried oregano**
**    and chili powder**
**1 Tbsp honey or sugar**
**1 bay leaf**

STEEL BLADE: Drop garlic through feed tube while machine is running; process until minced. Add onion and chop coarsely, using quick on/off pulses. Heat oil in 5-quart saucepan. Add garlic and onion; sauté on medium heat until soft, about 5 minutes.

. SLICER: Slice bell pepper, mushrooms and eggplant, using medium pressure. Add to saucepan and sauté 6 or 7 minutes longer, until softened, stirring occasionally. Slice carrots. Add to saucepan along with remaining ingredients; mix well.

Bring to a boil, reduce heat and simmer, partially covered, for 25 to 30 minutes, until vegetables are tender, stirring occasionally. If mixture gets too thick, add a little water. Adjust seasonings to taste. Discard bay leaf before serving.

180 calories per serving, 31.4 g carbohydrates, 6.3 g fiber, 6 g protein, 4.6 g fat (0.6 g saturated fat), 0 mg cholesterol, 216 mg sodium, 593 mg potassium, 2 mg iron, 50 mg calcium, 114 mg phosphorus

### variation

Add 3 cups of cut-up cooked chicken the last 10 minutes of cooking. One serving contains 280 calories and 8.5 g fat.

### slow cooker method

Sauté the vegetables as directed. Combine all ingredients in sprayed slow cooker insert. Cook, covered, on Low for 4 hours.

# MUSHROOM DUXELLES

Yield: About 1 cup. Duxelles can be refrigerated for a week in a tightly covered container. To freeze, spoon mixture into ice cube trays. When frozen, transfer to a resealable plastic bag. For a "gourmet touch," add cubes to stews and soups!

1 medium onion or ½ cup shallots, cut in chunks

2 to 3 Tbsp margarine or butter

1 pint mushrooms (about ½ lb/250 g)

1 Tbsp lemon juice

¾ tsp salt

¼ tsp freshly ground black pepper

STEEL BLADE: Process onion or shallots until finely chopped, about 6 seconds. Melt margarine or butter in a nonstick skillet. Sauté onion on medium heat until transparent, about 5 minutes. Do not brown.

Process mushrooms until finely chopped, about 10 seconds. Wrap mushrooms in a tea towel and wring out excess moisture. Add mushrooms to skillet, sprinkle with lemon juice and cook, stirring, until dry, about 10 minutes. Add salt and pepper.

17 calories per Tbsp, 1 g carbohydrates, 0.2 g fiber, 0 g protein, 1.4 g fat (0.3 g saturated fat), 0 mg cholesterol, 119 mg sodium, 33 mg potassium, 0 mg iron, 2 mg calcium, 8 mg phosphorus

# HONEY-GLAZED ROASTED ROOTS

This is ideal for the Jewish high holidays, when honey and carrots are always on the menu at my house!

2 large onions

1 lb (500 g) parsnips

1 lb (500 g) carrots

1 lb (500 g) sweet potatoes

1 fennel bulb

1 slice ginger (about 1 Tbsp)

2 to 3 Tbsp extra-virgin olive oil

2 Tbsp lemon juice

¼ cup honey

salt and pepper to taste

1 tsp dried thyme

2 Tbsp chopped parsley

Yield: 8 servings. Keeps 2 days in the refrigerator. Reheats well. Do not freeze.

Preheat oven to 400°F. Line a large rimmed baking sheet with foil and spray with nonstick spray. Peel and trim vegetables; cut in large chunks or wedges to fit feed tube.

STEEL BLADE: Drop ginger through feed tube while machine is running; process until minced.

SLICER: (If you have an adjustable slicing disc, set it for 6 mm.) Slice onions, parsnips, carrots, sweet potatoes and fennel, using medium pressure.

Transfer ginger and sliced vegetables to baking sheet. Drizzle with olive oil, lemon juice and honey. Sprinkle with salt, pepper and thyme; mix well. Spread out in a single layer.

Bake, uncovered, for 45 to 50 minutes, until tender and nicely browned, stirring occasionally. Transfer to a serving platter and sprinkle with parsley.

182 calories per serving, 36.4 g carbohydrates, 6.7 g fiber, 3 g protein, 4 g fat (0.6 g saturated fat), 0 mg cholesterol, 209 mg sodium, 709 mg potassium, 1 mg iron, 78 mg calcium, 104 mg phosphorus

VEGETABLES AND SIDE DISHES

# BARBECUED LYONNAISE POTATOES

Yield: 4 to 6 servings. Leftovers can be reheated in the microwave or toaster oven. Do not freeze.

**4 to 6 medium potatoes, peeled**

**2 small onions**

**2 Tbsp margarine**

**salt and freshly ground black pepper to taste**

**paprika to taste**

**2 Tbsp each fresh parsley, dill and/or thyme**

Cut a large sheet of heavy-duty aluminum foil, or use a double-thickness of regular-strength foil.

SLICER: Cut potatoes and onions to fit feed tube. Slice, using medium pressure. Place on foil, making a layer ½ inch thick. Dot with margarine and sprinkle with salt, pepper and paprika.

STEEL BLADE: Chop parsley, dill and/or thyme until minced, about 5 seconds. Sprinkle over potatoes. Wrap loosely, sealing well.

Place on barbecue, about 4 inches from hot coals. Cook about 20 minutes, turning package over after 10 minutes. (Or bake in preheated 450°F oven about 20 minutes. Do not turn.)

225 calories per serving, 39.7 g carbohydrates, 4.3 g fiber, 5 g protein, 6 g fat (1.1 g saturated fat), 0 mg cholesterol, 66 mg sodium, 987 mg potassium, 2 mg iron, 36 mg calcium, 133 mg phosphorus

# BEST-EVER SCALLOPED POTATOES

This is a favorite with families all over the globe!

Yield: 4 to 6 servings. Keeps 2 days in the refrigerator. Reheats well. Do not freeze.

**4 to 6 medium potatoes, peeled**

**salt and freshly ground black pepper to taste**

**3 Tbsp margarine**

**3 Tbsp flour**

**2 tsp instant pareve chicken soup mix**

**1½ cups boiling water**

**paprika to taste**

SLICER: Cut potatoes to fit feed tube. Slice, using medium pressure. Arrange in layers in sprayed 2-quart casserole. Sprinkle each layer with salt and pepper.

STEEL BLADE: Process margarine with flour and soup mix until blended, about 5 seconds. Pour boiling water through feed tube while machine is running and process until smooth. Transfer sauce to 4-cup glass measure. Microwave on High for 30 to 60 seconds, until bubbly and thickened, stirring once or twice. Season with salt and pepper.

Pour hot sauce over potatoes. Sprinkle with paprika. Bake, uncovered, in pre-heated 350°F oven 1¼ hours, until tender and golden brown.

244 calories per serving, 38.1 g carbohydrates, 3.2 g fiber, 4 g protein, 8.9 g fat (1.6 g saturated fat), 0 mg cholesterol, 268 mg sodium, 559 mg potassium, 1 mg iron, 19 mg calcium, 75 mg phosphorus

### variation

Replace soup mix and boiling water with 1½ cups 1% milk or soy milk. Stir 1 cup grated low-fat Swiss or cheddar cheese into sauce; stir until melted.

334 calories per serving, 44 g carbohydrates, 3.2 g fiber, 15 g protein, 11.2 g fat (3.1 g saturated fat), 13 mg cholesterol, 202 mg sodium, 752 mg potassium, 1 mg iron, 405 mg calcium, 339 mg phosphorus

## SKINNY NO-FRIES

These come out best using a processor with a wide-mouth feed tube and using the french fry disc. No french fry disc? Use the match-stick method.

Yield: 4 servings.

Do not freeze.

4 medium Idaho (russet) potatoes

2 Tbsp olive oil

salt and pepper to taste

dried basil or rosemary to taste

paprika and garlic powder to taste

Preheat oven to 400°F. Line 1 or 2 large rimmed baking sheets with aluminum foil; spray with nonstick spray.

Peel potatoes (or scrub very well). Cut in largest size possible to fit feed tube horizontally.

FRENCH FRY DISC: Process potatoes, using medium pressure. You'll get skinny fries.

Matchstick method: Insert SLICER. Place potatoes horizontally in feed tube and process with even pressure to create long, plank-like slices. Replace stack of slices in feed tube vertically and process again using even pressure.

Spread potatoes out evenly in a single layer on prepared baking sheet(s). Drizzle with oil and sprinkle with seasonings; mix well. Bake, uncovered, for 30 to 35 minutes, or until brown and crispy, stirring 2 or 3 times. Spread out potatoes each time you stir them or they won't crisp up properly. Serve immediately.

223 calories per serving, 36.5 g carbohydrates, 3.8 g fiber, 4 g protein, 7.2 g fat (1 g saturated fat), 0 mg cholesterol, 17 mg sodium, 923 mg potassium, 2 mg iron, 26 mg calcium, 121 mg phosphorus

### sweet potato no-fries

Use 3 or 4 medium sweet potatoes, peeled and trimmed.

# RÖSTI POTATOES

This is the ultimate potato pancake! In Switzerland, *rösti* (pronounced "rooshti") means "crisp and golden." Grate the onion alternately with the potatoes to prevent them from turning black.

Yield: 3 to 4 servings. Leftovers (if any!) can be reheated in the toaster oven. Do not freeze.

**3 large or 4 medium Idaho (russet) potatoes, peeled (see Note)**

**1 medium onion, halved**

**1 Tbsp olive oil**

**salt and freshly ground black pepper to taste**

GRATER: Alternately grate potatoes and onion, using medium pressure.

Spray a heavy 10-inch nonstick skillet with nonstick spray. Add oil and heat on medium heat. Spread potato mixture evenly in skillet. Press down firmly on potatoes with a spatula to form a large pancake; sprinkle with salt and pepper. Cook on medium heat for 8 to 10 minutes, until bottom is browned and crusty.

Carefully invert onto a large round platter, then slide potatoes back into skillet, crusty side up. Press down once again with spatula. Cook until bottom is nicely browned and potatoes are cooked through, 6 to 8 minutes longer.

Cut in wedges and serve immediately.

224 calories per serving, 40.3 g carbohydrates, 4.4 g fiber, 5 g protein, 5 g fat (0.7 g saturated fat), 0 mg cholesterol, 25 mg sodium, 1004 mg potassium, 2 mg iron, 38 mg calcium, 134 mg phosphorus

### note

To shorten cooking time, parboil potatoes in boiling water for 2 to 3 minutes. Drain well and let stand, uncovered, for 10 minutes to dry before grating. (Potatoes can be precooked and refrigerated the night before.)

# POTATO KUGEL

My daughter Jodi and son-in-law Paul Sprackman love this crispy potato pudding. The processor makes it so easy!

Yield: 6 to 8 servings. Keeps 2 to 3 days in the refrigerator. Reheats well. Freezing is not recommended.

**3 to 4 Tbsp oil**

**4 large potatoes, peeled and cut in chunks**

**1 large onion, cut in chunks**

**3 eggs (or 2 eggs and 2 egg whites)**

**1½ tsp salt (or to taste)**

**¼ tsp freshly ground black pepper**

**¼ cup flour or potato starch**

Preheat oven to 375°F. Pour oil in 7- × 11-inch glass baking dish. Place casserole in oven and heat until oil is piping hot, about 5 minutes.

GRATER: Grate potatoes, using light pressure. (The harder you press, the coarser the texture.) Transfer potatoes to a colander. To wash out the starch and keep potatoes white, rinse under cold running water. Squeeze dry.

STEEL BLADE: Process onion until minced, about 8 seconds. Scrape down sides of bowl. Add eggs, salt and pepper. Process for 3 to 4 seconds. Combine with grated potatoes and flour or potato starch in a large mixing bowl. Add most of oil, leaving 1 Tbsp oil in casserole. Mix well.

Pour potato mixture into casserole. Sprinkle a little additional oil on top. Bake for about 1 hour, or until well browned and crispy.

302 calories per serving, 46.5 g carbohydrates, 4.1 g fiber, 7 g protein, 9.9 g fat (1.9 g saturated fat), 106 mg cholesterol, 623 mg sodium, 729 mg potassium, 1 mg iron, 35 mg calcium, 136 mg phosphorus

## SWEET POTATO KUGEL

This yummy pudding should be called "Puddin' on the Ritz!"

Yield: 8 to 10 servings. Keeps 2 to 3 days in the refrigerator. Reheats and/or freezes well. Recipe may be halved and baked in a 1½-quart casserole.

2 to 3 Tbsp oil
4 medium sweet potatoes, peeled (about 2 lb/1 kg)
1 medium onion, cut in chunks
6 eggs (or 4 eggs plus 4 egg whites)
¾ cup brown sugar, packed

2 tsp ground cinnamon (or to taste)
1 tsp salt
¼ tsp nutmeg
¼ tsp ground cloves
½ cup flour
½ tsp baking powder

Preheat oven to 400°F. Pour oil in 7- × 11-inch glass baking dish and heat until oil is piping hot, about 5 minutes.

GRATER: Cut sweet potatoes to fit feed tube. Grate, using medium pressure. Empty into large mixing bowl. You should have about 6 cups.

STEEL BLADE: Process onion until minced, about 8 seconds. Add eggs, brown sugar, cinnamon, salt, nutmeg and cloves. Process until blended, 8 to 10 seconds. Add to sweet potatoes. Add flour and baking powder and mix well.

Pour sweet potato mixture into baking dish. Sprinkle a little additional oil on top. Bake for about 1 hour, until nicely browned.

266 calories per serving, 42.8 g carbohydrates, 3 g fiber, 7 g protein, 7.7 g fat (1.5 g saturated fat), 159 mg cholesterol, 399 mg sodium, 434 mg potassium, 2 mg iron, 90 mg calcium, 122 mg phosphorus

## CARROT KUGEL

I enjoyed this gluten-free carrot kugel when I was a guest at Raisy Gittler's home in Fort Lauderdale, Florida. I eliminated almost half the fat in this scrumptious

2 lb (1 kg) carrots, cut in chunks
½ cup chopped nuts (e.g., walnuts or almonds)
¼ cup brown sugar, lightly packed
6 eggs (or 4 eggs plus 4 egg whites)
¼ cup potato starch

⅓ cup honey (or ½ cup sugar)
½ cup oil
2 tsp pure vanilla extract
2 tsp baking powder
½ tsp ground cinnamon
¼ tsp nutmeg (optional)

Cook carrots in boiling salted water until tender, about 20 minutes. Drain well and let cool.

*Continued*

pudding without
sacrificing flavor. It's
a winner!

STEEL BLADE: Process nuts and brown sugar until crumbly, 8 to 10 seconds. Remove from bowl and set aside. Wipe bowl clean with a damp paper towel. (If you have a machine with nested bowls, use mini-bowl and blade to process nuts and sugar.)

Purée carrots until smooth, 20 to 25 seconds. Add eggs and mix well. Add remaining ingredients (except for reserved nut mixture) and process until smooth, about 30 seconds longer. Scrape down sides of bowl as needed.

Pour mixture into sprayed 9- × 13-inch glass baking dish and sprinkle with reserved nut mixture. Bake in preheated 350°F oven about 1 hour, until nicely browned.

Yield: 12 servings.
Keeps 2 to 3 days in the
refrigerator. Reheats
and/or freezes well.
Delicious served hot or
at room temperature.

236 calories per serving, 21.8 g carbohydrates, 2.5 g fiber, 5 g protein, 15.3 g fat (1.8 g saturated fat), 106 mg cholesterol, 154 mg sodium, 229 mg potassium, 1 mg iron, 89 mg calcium, 98 mg phosphorus

### passover variation

Substitute Passover products. Passover baking powder is available and granulated sugar can be used if brown sugar is not available. Replace vanilla extract with Sabra liqueur or sweet wine.

## LOKSHIN KUGEL (NOODLE PUDDING)

Yield: 8 to 10 servings.
Freezes well.

Homemade Pasta (page 259) or
  1 pkg (12 oz/375 g) medium or
  broad noodles
2 to 3 Tbsp oil
1 large onion, quartered

4 or 5 eggs (or 3 eggs and 4 egg
  whites)
1 cup chicken soup (salt-free or
  regular)
salt and freshly ground black pepper
  to taste

Prepare noodles according to package or recipe directions. Drain well; return to saucepan. Preheat oven to 400°F. Place oil in 7- × 11-inch glass baking dish. Place dish in oven and heat until oil is piping hot, about 5 minutes.

STEEL BLADE: Process onion with quick on/offs, until coarsely chopped. Stir into hot oil. Place in oven about 5 minutes, until onion is lightly browned. Process eggs with chicken soup for 10 seconds. Combine with noodles, salt and pepper; mix well. Stir into oil/onion mixture.

Bake, uncovered, at 400°F for or 1 hour, until golden.

186 calories per serving, 19.9 g carbohydrates, 0.9 g fiber, 8 g protein, 7.9 g fat (1.6 g saturated fat), 162 mg cholesterol, 209 mg sodium, 99 mg potassium, 2 mg iron, 26 mg calcium, 95 mg phosphorus

# ONION KUGEL

If you love onions, you'll love this side dish that my friend Helene Medjuck shared with me. Its texture is similar to that of potato kugel. The processor makes quick work of slicing all those onions!

Yield: 8 servings. Keeps 2 to 3 days in the refrigerator. Reheats and/or freezes well.

| | |
|---|---|
| 5 or 6 onions, peeled, trimmed and cut in half | 2 tsp salt (or to taste) |
| 5 eggs | ½ tsp pepper |
| ½ cup canola oil | 1¼ cups flour |
| ½ cup water | 2 tsp baking powder |

Preheat oven to 350°F. Line a 7- × 11-inch baking pan with parchment paper.

SLICER: Slice onions, using light pressure. You should have about 6 cups. Transfer to a large mixing bowl and separate the onion slices with your fingers.

STEEL BLADE: Process eggs, oil, water, salt and pepper until combined, about 10 seconds. Add flour and baking powder. Process with quick on/off pulses to blend, scraping down sides of bowl as necessary. Pour batter over onions and mix well. It may look like you don't have enough batter, but you will—the batter will just coat the onions. Transfer to baking pan.

Bake, uncovered, for 45 to 55 minutes, until golden brown.

280 calories per serving, 23.8 g carbohydrates, 1.7 g fiber, 7 g protein, 17.7 g fat (2.1 g saturated fat), 133 mg cholesterol, 745 mg sodium, 193 mg potassium, 2 mg iron, 105 mg calcium, 128 mg phosphorus

## variation

Instead of onions, substitute 6 cups of thinly sliced leeks.

# MINI POTATO ZUCCHINI KUGELS

When my back was sore during Chanukah, I made these and told everyone they were kugel-latkes! They are also great for Passover. You can substitute a 10 oz (300 g) package of spinach, thawed and squeezed dry, for the zucchini.

Yield: 12 mini kugels. Keeps 2 to 3 days in the refrigerator. Reheats and/or freezes well.

3 large potatoes, scrubbed
1 medium zucchini
2 cloves garlic
1 medium onion
1 Tbsp fresh basil (or 1 tsp dried basil)
2 Tbsp fresh dill and/or parsley
3 eggs
¼ cup matzo meal
½ tsp salt (or to taste)
freshly ground black pepper to taste
1 to 2 Tbsp olive oil

Preheat oven to 375°F. Generously spray muffin pan with nonstick spray.

GRATER: Grate potatoes and zucchini, using medium pressure. Transfer to a strainer and rinse with cold water. Drain well; squeeze out excess moisture. You should have about 4 cups. Place in large mixing bowl.

STEEL BLADE: Process garlic, onion, basil, dill and parsley until minced, 10 to 15 seconds. Add eggs and process a few seconds longer to blend. Transfer to mixing bowl and add matzo meal, salt and pepper; mix well. Spoon mixture into muffin pan; brush tops with oil.

Bake for about 30 minutes, until golden brown and firm. Let stand about 5 minutes, then loosen carefully with a flexible spatula and remove from pan.

115 calories per serving, 19.6 g carbohydrates, 2 g fiber, 4 g protein, 2.6 g fat (0.6 g saturated fat), 53 mg cholesterol, 121 mg sodium, 459 mg potassium, 1 mg iron, 22 mg calcium, 82 mg phosphorus

# ZUCCHINI PUFFS

Yield: 10 puffs. Keeps 2 days in the refrigerator. Reheats and/or freezes well.

3 oz (85 g) chilled low-fat mozzarella cheese (¾ cup grated)
2 medium zucchini (2 cups grated)
½ small onion
2 eggs (or 1 egg plus 2 egg whites)
½ tsp salt
dash freshly ground black pepper
½ cup dried bread crumbs

For machines with nested bowls, see method on page 243.

GRATER: Grate cheese using medium pressure. Empty bowl. Cut zucchini to fit feed tube; grate, using firm pressure. Measure 2 cups, lightly packed.

STEEL BLADE: Process onion until minced, about 6 seconds. Add eggs, salt and pepper and process for 2 seconds. Add bread crumbs, zucchini and cheese to egg mixture. Process with 2 or 3 quick on/offs, just until mixed. Do not overprocess.

Divide mixture evenly among 10 sprayed muffin cups. Bake in preheated 375°F oven for 30 minutes. They will fall slightly upon standing, but taste and texture won't be affected. Serve hot.

67 calories each, 5.4 g carbohydrates, 0.6 g fiber, 4 g protein, 3.1 g fat (1.5 g saturated fat), 47 mg cholesterol, 214 mg sodium, 85 mg potassium, 1 mg iron, 80 mg calcium, 79 mg phosphorus

## BREADED ZUCCHINI

*The zucchini comes out crispy and scrumptious.*

*Yield: 3 to 4 servings. Do not freeze. May be made ahead and refrigerated until needed. Bake in preheated 425°F oven until hot and crispy.*

3 or 4 slender zucchini (about 1 lb/500 g)
salt for sprinkling
1 cup dried bread crumbs
½ tsp salt

¼ tsp each freshly ground black pepper, garlic powder and dried oregano
1 egg or 2 egg whites lightly beaten
2 to 3 Tbsp oil

SLICER: Wash zucchini and pat dry. Trim off ends; cut zucchini to fit feed tube. Use the center mini-tube if your processor has one. Slice zucchini, using firm pressure. Sprinkle with salt and let stand 20 minutes to remove excess moisture.

Combine crumbs, salt, pepper, garlic powder and oregano. Pat zucchini dry. Dip slices in beaten egg, then seasoned crumbs.

Heat oil in large nonstick skillet. Brown zucchini slices a few at a time on medium heat, 2 or 3 minutes per side. Watch carefully to prevent burning. Drain on paper towels. Add additional oil to pan as needed.

273 calories per serving, 31.5 g carbohydrates, 3.5 g fiber, 8 g protein, 13.1 g fat (1.7 g saturated fat), 71 mg cholesterol, 676 mg sodium, 421 mg potassium, 2 mg iron, 93 mg calcium, 141 mg phosphorus

### variations

• Add 3 to 4 Tbsp grated Parmesan cheese to bread crumb mixture.

• For crispy fried zucchini, omit egg and substitute flour for bread crumbs. Coat zucchini slices with seasoned flour. Sauté in hot oil.

## CARROT LATKES

*Different and delicious! Minis make great appetizers. Try these with zucchini (page 244) for a different twist.*

4 to 6 medium carrots
1 medium onion
3 eggs (or 2 eggs and 2 egg whites)
¾ tsp salt

dash freshly ground black pepper
½ cup flour
½ tsp baking powder
2 Tbsp oil

GRATER: Cut carrots to fit feed tube. Grate, using medium pressure. Measure 2 cups. (Any leftovers can be added to soups or salads.) *Continued*

Yield: 16 to 18 pancakes
or 5 dozen hors
d'oeuvres. Keeps 2 to
3 days in the refrigerator.
Reheats and/or freezes
well (see Chef's Tip,
page 245).

STEEL BLADE: Process onion until fine, 6 to 8 seconds. Add carrots along with remaining ingredients except oil. Process until blended, about 15 seconds.

Heat oil in large nonstick skillet. Drop carrot mixture from a spoon into hot oil and flatten patties with the back of the spoon. Brown on medium heat 2 to 3 minutes on each side, until golden. Repeat with remaining batter, adding more oil if necessary. Drain well on paper towels.

53 calories each, 5.0 g carbohydrates, 0.6 g fiber, 2 g protein, 2.8 g fat (0.4 g saturated fat), 40 mg cholesterol, 146 mg sodium, 70 mg potassium, 0 mg iron, 20 mg calcium, 30 mg phosphorus

## zucchini latkes

Replace carrots with 2 or 3 medium zucchini. After grating, salt zucchini lightly and let stand 15 minutes. Press out excess moisture. Measure 2 cups.

# BROCCOLI LATKES

Be sure to try the variations below.

Yield: About 18 small
pancakes. Keeps 2 to
3 days in the refrigerator.
Reheats and/or freezes
well (see Chef's Tip,
page 245).

| | |
|---|---|
| 1 pkg (10 oz/300 g) frozen broccoli (or ½ bunch fresh broccoli, cut in chunks) | ½ cup matzo meal or cracker crumbs |
| | ¾ tsp salt |
| | dash freshly ground black pepper |
| 1 medium onion, halved | 2 Tbsp canola oil |
| 3 eggs (or 2 eggs plus 2 egg whites) | |

Cook frozen broccoli according to package directions (or microwave fresh broccoli on High, allowing 5 to 6 minutes per lb). Drain well.

STEEL BLADE: Process onion until minced. Scrape down sides of bowl. Add eggs and broccoli and process until finely chopped, about 20 seconds. Add matzo meal or cracker crumbs, salt and pepper; process a few seconds longer, until smooth.

Heat oil in large nonstick skillet on medium-high heat. Drop mixture from a tablespoon into hot oil to make small pancakes. Flatten slightly with the back of the spoon. Brown on both sides. Drain on paper towels. Repeat with remaining batter, adding more oil as needed.

46 calories each, 4.4 g carbohydrates, 0.6 g fiber, 2 g protein, 2.5 g fat (0.4 g saturated fat), 35 mg cholesterol, 111 mg sodium, 44 mg potassium, 0 mg iron, 13 mg calcium, 24 mg phosphorus

## variations

Replace broccoli with green beans, cauliflower or spinach.

# EASY POTATO LATKES

I use Idaho (russet) potatoes, but some cooks prefer Yukon Golds or red-skinned potatoes. Serve latkes with applesauce or sour cream. For Passover, use matzo meal instead of flour.

Yield: About 2 dozen, or 5 dozen miniatures. Keeps 2 to 3 days in the refrigerator. Reheats and/or freezes well (see Chef's Tip).

4 medium potatoes, peeled or scrubbed
1 medium onion
2 eggs (or 1 egg plus 2 egg whites)
⅓ cup flour or matzo meal

1 tsp baking powder
¾ tsp salt
freshly ground black pepper to taste
¼ cup oil (approximately)

STEEL BLADE: Cut potatoes in chunks and onion in half. Place in processor with eggs. Process until puréed, 20 to 30 seconds. Add remaining ingredients except oil; process a few seconds longer to blend into a smooth mixture.

Heat 2 Tbsp oil in large nonstick skillet over medium-high heat. Drop potato mixture into hot oil by large spoonfuls to form pancakes; brown well on both sides. (Don't crowd the pan.) Drain well on paper towels. Add additional oil to pan as needed. Stir batter before cooking each new batch. Latkes can be placed on a baking sheet and kept warm in a 250°F oven.

59 calories per serving, 7.4 g carbohydrates, 0.6 g fiber, 1 g protein, 2.8 g fat (0.3 g saturated fat), 18 mg cholesterol, 100 mg sodium, 105 mg potassium, 0 mg iron, 17 mg calcium, 26 mg phosphorus

## variations

- LACY LATKES (DOUBLE PROCESSING METHOD): GRATER: Grate potatoes, using light pressure. Transfer potatoes to a colander, rinse them under cold water and drain thoroughly. Insert STEEL BLADE. Process onion until minced. Add grated potatoes, eggs, flour, baking powder, salt and pepper. Process with 2 or 3 very quick on/off pulses, just until combined. Do not overprocess. Fry or bake as directed.

- NO-FRY LATKES: Place oven racks on lowest and middle position in oven. Preheat oven to 450°F. Line 2 baking sheets with foil. Spray with nonstick spray, then brush with oil. Prepare latke mixture as directed and stir in 2 tsp oil. Drop by spoonfuls onto baking sheets; flatten slightly. Bake 10 minutes, until bottoms are browned and crispy. Turn latkes over. Transfer pan from upper rack to lower rack and vice versa. Bake 8 to 10 minutes longer. One baked latke contains 42 calories and 0.9 g fat.

## chef's tip

Freezing and reheating latkes: To save space when freezing or reheating latkes, stand them upright in a loaf pan. Reheat, uncovered, in preheated 400°F oven for about 10 minutes.

# NOODLE LATKES (PANCAKES)

Yield: 16 to 18 pancakes. Keeps 2 to 3 days in the refrigerator. Reheats and/or freezes well. To reheat, place in a single layer on foil-lined baking sheet. Bake, uncovered, in preheated 425°F oven for 10 minutes, until hot and crispy.

| | |
|---|---|
| ½ of a 12 oz (375 g) pkg fine noodles | salt and freshly ground black pepper |
| 2 eggs | to taste |
| 1 small onion | 2 Tbsp oil |

Cook noodles according to package directions. Drain well and return to saucepan.

STEEL BLADE: Process eggs with onion until blended, about 10 seconds. Add to noodles. Season with salt and pepper. Heat oil in nonstick skillet. Drop noodle mixture by large spoonfuls into hot oil to form pancakes. Brown on medium heat on both sides. Drain on paper towels. Repeat with remaining batter, adding more oil as needed.

63 calories each, 7 g carbohydrates, 0.4 g fiber, 2 g protein, 3 g fat (0.4 g saturated fat), 34 mg cholesterol, 9 mg sodium, 24 mg potassium, 1 mg iron, 7 mg calcium, 32 mg phosphorus

# VEGGIE LATKES

Idaho (russet) potatoes are higher in starch and less watery when grated. If well scrubbed, they don't need peeling.

| | |
|---|---|
| 2 medium Idaho potatoes, cut in chunks | 2 eggs |
| 1 medium onion, cut in chunks | ⅓ cup dried bread crumbs or matzo meal |
| 1 carrot, cut in chunks | 1 tsp dried basil (or 1 Tbsp fresh basil) |
| 1 medium zucchini, cut in chunks | ½ tsp salt (or to taste) |
| 1 green and 1 red bell pepper, cut in chunks | freshly ground black pepper to taste |
| | 2 Tbsp oil |

Yield: 2 dozen latkes or 4 dozen minis. Keeps 2 to 3 days in the refrigerator. Reheats and/or freezes well (see Chef's Tip, page 245).

STEEL BLADE: Process vegetables in batches until finely minced. Transfer to large mixing bowl. Add eggs, bread crumbs or matzo meal, basil, salt and pepper; mix well.

Heat oil in large nonstick skillet on medium-high heat. Drop mixture by spoonfuls into hot oil to form pancakes. Flatten slightly with the back of the spoon. Brown well on both sides. Repeat with remaining batter, adding more oil as needed. Drain on paper towels.

43 calories each, 5.7 g carbohydrates, 0.7 g fiber, 1 g protein, 1.7 g fat (0.3 g saturated fat), 18 mg cholesterol, 68 mg sodium, 129 mg potassium, 0 mg iron, 11 mg calcium, 26 mg phosphorus

VEGETABLES AND SIDE DISHES

# BAKED VEGGIE PATTIES

These scrumptious patties are a variation of my favorite veggie burgers. Everyone loves them!

Yield: 20 patties. Keeps 3 days in the refrigerator. Reheats and/or freezes well.

1 pkg (10 oz/300 g) frozen chopped spinach

3 large sweet potatoes

2 cloves garlic

2 Tbsp fresh dill

2 Tbsp fresh parsley

2 medium onions, cut in chunks

1 red bell pepper, cut in chunks

1 Tbsp extra-virgin olive oil

2 medium carrots

2 medium zucchini (unpeeled)

2 eggs

1 cup matzo meal or bread crumbs

salt and pepper to taste

1 Tbsp extra-virgin olive oil (for coating patties)

Microwave spinach on High for 5 minutes. Cool and squeeze dry. Place in a large mixing bowl.

Pierce sweet potatoes with a fork. Microwave on High for 8 to 10 minutes, until tender, turning them over halfway through cooking. Let cool. Cut in half and scoop out pulp. You should have about 3 cups. Combine with spinach.

STEEL BLADE: Drop garlic, dill and parsley through feed tube and process until minced. Empty bowl and mix garlic/herb mixture with spinach/sweet potato mixture.

STEEL BLADE: Process onions and red pepper with quick on/off pulses, until coarsely chopped. Heat oil in a large nonstick skillet on medium heat. Sauté onions and pepper for 5 minutes, until softened.

GRATER: Meanwhile, cut carrots and zucchini to fit feed tube. Grate, using medium pressure. Add to onions and pepper and cook 3 to 4 minutes longer. Cool slightly. Add to spinach/sweet potato mixture. Add eggs, matzo meal, salt and pepper; mix well.

Preheat oven to 375°F. Shape mixture into 20 patties and place on parchment-lined baking sheet(s). Oil your fingertips, then lightly oil the tops of each patty, flattening them slightly.

Bake, uncovered, for 10 minutes. Turn patties over and bake 10 to 12 minutes longer, until golden.

82 calories each, 14 g carbohydrates, 2 g fiber, 3 g protein, 2.2 g fat (0.4 g saturated fat), 21 mg cholesterol, 31 mg sodium, 242 mg potassium, 1 mg iron, 37 mg calcium, 40 mg phosphorus

# HOISIN VEGETABLE STIR-FRY

It takes more time to read this recipe than to prepare it! You can add cauliflower florets, bamboo shoots, bean sprouts and/ or baby corn for additional fiber and color.

Yield: 6 servings. If frozen, vegetables will become soggy.

1 medium onion, halved

1 red and 1 green bell pepper, halved

1 bunch broccoli, trimmed

2 cloves garlic

2 Tbsp hoisin sauce

2 Tbsp soy sauce (low-sodium or regular)

2 Tbsp honey

2 Tbsp orange juice

dash cayenne pepper

1 Tbsp oil

1 Tbsp cornstarch dissolved in 2 Tbsp water

1 tsp toasted sesame oil

SLICER: Slice onion and peppers, using medium pressure. Transfer to mixing bowl. Cut florets from broccoli and add to onion and peppers. Slice stems, using medium pressure. Add to vegetables.

STEEL BLADE: Drop garlic through feed tube while machine is running; process until minced. Add hoisin, soy sauce, honey, orange juice and cayenne. Process a few seconds longer, until blended.

Heat oil in nonstick wok. Stir-fry vegetables on high heat for 2 minutes. Add sauce mixture and bring to a boil. Stir in cornstarch mixture and sesame oil. Cook 1 to 2 minutes longer, until thickened, stirring constantly. Serve immediately.

126 calories per serving, 21.9 g carbohydrates, 3.6 g fiber, 4 g protein, 3.8 g fat (0.4 g saturated fat), 0 mg cholesterol, 300 mg sodium, 456 mg potassium, 1 mg iron, 61 mg calcium, 91 mg phosphorus

# PEA POD, PEPPER AND MUSHROOM STIR-FRY

Yield: 4 to 6 servings. Do not freeze.

2 medium onions, halved

1 green and 1 red bell pepper, halved

2 cups mushrooms

2 cloves garlic

1 cup snow peas or sugar snap peas

1 Tbsp oil

2 Tbsp soy sauce (low-sodium or regular)

1½ Tbsp cornstarch

¼ cup cold water, chicken or vegetable broth

salt and freshly ground black pepper to taste

SLICER: Slice onions and peppers, using medium pressure. Repeat with mushrooms, using light pressure. Pat dry with paper towels; set aside in a mixing bowl.

STEEL BLADE: Drop garlic through feed tube while machine is running; process until minced. Add garlic and snow peas or sugar snap peas to mixing bowl.

Heat oil in a wok on high heat. Add vegetables and stir-fry for 2 minutes. Stir in soy sauce. Dissolve cornstarch in water or broth. Stir cornstarch mixture into center of wok and cook until thickened, stirring constantly, about 1 minute. Season to taste. Serve immediately.

113 calories per serving, 17.7 g carbohydrates, 3.2 g fiber, 4 g protein, 3.9 g fat (0.3 g saturated fat), 0 mg cholesterol, 273 mg sodium, 384 mg potassium, 2 mg iron, 40 mg calcium, 84 mg phosphorus

### variations

- Stir-fry vegetables for 2 minutes. (Omit snow peas if desired.) Add ½ cup water chestnuts, ½ cup bamboo shoots and 2 cups bean sprouts; stir-fry 1 minute longer. Add soy sauce and cornstarch mixture and stir-fry until thickened. Serve over noodles.

### passover variation

- Replace snow peas with broccoli florets. Replace soy sauce with Passover duck sauce. Replace cornstarch with potato starch.

## STICKY TOFU

Natalie Frankel of Milwaukee, Wisconsin, adapted my recipe for Sticky Chicky (page 215), substituting tofu and adding vegetables and pineapple chunks. This tasty vegetarian dish is the result. Serve it over rice.

Yield: 6 servings. Keeps 2 days in the refrigerator. Do not freeze.

1½ lb (750 g) firm tofu, cut in 1-inch squares
2 Tbsp soy sauce (low-sodium or regular)
3 to 4 Tbsp sesame seeds
1 red and 1 green bell pepper quartered
4 green onions
1 can (8 oz/250 mL) water chestnuts, drained and halved

1 cup canned pineapple chunks, drained (reserve 2 Tbsp juice)
2 cloves garlic
1 Tbsp fresh ginger (or ½ tsp ground ginger)
½ cup soy sauce (low-sodium or regular)
½ cup honey
2 Tbsp vinegar or lemon juice
1 Tbsp cornstarch
1 tomato, cut in chunks

Place tofu in a sprayed casserole; sprinkle with 2 Tbsp soy sauce and 1 Tbsp of the sesame seeds. Bake, uncovered, in preheated 350°F oven for 20 minutes.

SLICER: Slice bell peppers and green onions, using medium pressure. Add to tofu along with water chestnuts and drained pineapple chunks.

STEEL BLADE: Drop garlic and ginger through feed tube while machine is running; process until minced. Add the ½ cup soy sauce, honey and vinegar or lemon juice and process until blended. Pour over tofu/vegetable mixture. Bake, uncovered, for 20 minutes longer, stirring occasionally.

Dissolve cornstarch in reserved pineapple juice. Add to casserole along with tomato. Sprinkle with remaining sesame seeds and cook 10 minutes longer.

358 calories per serving, 46.2 g carbohydrates, 6.4 g fiber, 22 g protein, 12.5 g fat (1.8 g saturated fat), 0 mg cholesterol, 676 mg sodium, 564 mg potassium, 5 mg iron, 844 mg calcium, 295 mg phosphorus

# NO-FRY FRIED RICE

My assistant Elaine Kaplan loves this dish, and so do her guests! It's great for vegetarians and is oven-ready in minutes.

Yield: 8 to 10 servings. Keeps 2 to 3 days in the refrigerator. Reheats well. May be frozen or prepared in advance.

2 cups uncooked rice
1 to 2 Tbsp oil
1 pkg (1.9 oz/54 g) dry onion soup mix
3 Tbsp soy sauce (low-sodium or regular)
1 green or red bell pepper, halved
2 cups mushrooms

1 can (8 oz/250 mL) water chestnuts
1 can (8 oz/250 mL) sliced bamboo shoots
4 cups liquid (reserved juices from canned vegetables, plus cold water)
salt and freshly ground black pepper to taste

Combine rice, oil, soup mix and soy sauce in a large sprayed casserole. Mix well.

SLICER: Slice pepper and mushrooms, using light pressure. Drain canned vegetables and reserve liquid. Slice water chestnuts, using firm pressure. Combine all ingredients in casserole and mix well.

Cover and bake in preheated 350°F oven about 1 hour, or until all liquid is absorbed. Adjust seasonings to taste.

244 calories per serving, 50 g carbohydrates, 3.3 g fiber, 5 g protein, 2.4 g fat (0.3 g saturated fat), 0 mg cholesterol, 597 mg sodium, 169 mg potassium, 2 mg iron, 26 mg calcium, 92 mg phosphorus

### variation

Replace onion soup mix with 2 chopped onions. Add ½ cup each of chopped carrots and celery. Coarsely chop vegetables on the STEEL BLADE, using quick on/off pulses. Add 1 cup firm tofu, cut in ½ inch cubes.

# LOW-CARB "FRIED RICE"

This colorful low-carb dish is ideal for vegetarians or anyone following a gluten-free diet. It's also perfect for Passover. Prepare the veggies in advance, then stir-fry them quickly in a wok or large skillet.

½ cup parsley
4 cloves garlic
1 slice ginger, peeled (1 Tbsp minced)
½ head of cauliflower
2 medium carrots
2 stalks celery
1 red onion
1 broccoli stalk, trimmed

2 cups mushrooms
2 red bell peppers, quartered
2 Tbsp oil
2 large eggs, lightly beaten (optional)
salt and pepper to taste
1 tsp instant pareve chicken soup mix
½ cup toasted sliced almonds

For machines with nested bowls, see page 251.

STEEL BLADE: Process parsley until finely minced. Remove from bowl and reserve to use as a garnish. Drop garlic and ginger through feed tube while machine is running; process until minced. Set aside.

VEGETABLES AND SIDE DISHES

Yield: 8 servings. Keeps 2 days in the refrigerator. Reheats well in the microwave. Do not freeze.

GRATER: Wash and drain cauliflower thoroughly; cut into large chunks. Grate, using medium pressure. The grated cauliflower is your "rice." Grate carrots, using medium pressure. Set aside.

SLICER: Cut celery, onion and broccoli to fit the feed tube. Slice, using medium pressure. Slice mushrooms and red peppers, using medium pressure. (Veggies can be prepared in advance, covered and refrigerated for several hours or overnight.)

Heat oil in a large nonstick wok or skillet on high heat. Stir-fry garlic and ginger for 30 seconds. Add onion, celery, broccoli, mushrooms and red peppers and stir-fry for 2 to 4 minutes. Add grated cauliflower and carrots. Stir-fry 3 to 4 minutes longer, until tender-crisp. Don't overcook veggies or they will get too soft.

If adding eggs, push the entire vegetable mixture to 1 side of the wok. On the empty side, add beaten eggs and scramble for 2 minutes or until they are just set. Mix the eggs into the "rice." Season with salt, pepper and soup mix. Remove from heat and transfer to a serving platter. Sprinkle with chopped parsley and almonds. Best served immediately.

108 calories per serving, 10.8 g carbohydrates, 3.8 g fiber, 4 g protein, 6.7 g fat (0.5 g saturated fat), 0 mg cholesterol, 86 mg sodium, 414 mg potassium, 1 mg iron, 54 mg calcium, 89 mg phosphorus

### nested bowl method

Use mini-bowl and mini-blade to mince parsley; remove from bowl. Use again to mince garlic and ginger. Use medium bowl and GRATER/SHREDDING DISC to grate cauliflower and carrots. Use large bowl and SLICER to slice remaining veggies.

### variation

To make this into a main dish, add strips of cooked chicken or turkey in the last 2 minutes of stir-frying.

## CHINESE FRIED RICE

Rice should be cold for best results. Leftover rice is ideal. It keeps for 3 or 4 days in the refrigerator.

**3 green onions, cut in chunks**
**1 stalk celery, cut in chunks**
**1 red bell pepper, cut in chunks**
**½ cup cooked chicken (optional)**
**2 eggs**
**1 to 2 Tbsp oil**

**3 cups cold cooked rice**
**½ cup frozen green peas**
**2 Tbsp soy sauce (low-sodium or regular)**
**1 tsp toasted sesame oil**
**freshly ground black pepper to taste**

Yield: 4 to 6 servings. Reheats well in the microwave. If frozen, rice has a tendency to become hard.

STEEL BLADE: Process green onions, celery and red pepper, with quick on/offs, until coarsely chopped. Empty bowl. If using chicken, coarsely chop with quick on/offs. Set chicken aside separately from vegetables. Process eggs for 2 or 3 seconds to mix.

Heat 1 tsp of the oil in large nonstick skillet or wok over medium-high heat. Add eggs and scramble them briefly. Remove eggs from pan. Add remaining oil to pan. Stir-fry onions, celery and red pepper for 1 minute. Add rice and peas and mix thoroughly, until heated through. Add remaining ingredients and stir well. Serve piping hot.

292 calories per serving, 46.7 g carbohydrates, 3.3 g fiber, 8 g protein, 7.7 g fat (1.3 g saturated fat), 106 mg cholesterol, 319 mg sodium, 210 mg potassium, 3 mg iron, 32 mg calcium, 123 mg phosphorus

---

# RICE PILAF

To substitute brown rice, increase cooking time to 45 minutes.

Yield: 6 to 8 servings. Keeps 2 to 3 days in the refrigerator. If frozen, rice has a tendency to get hard.

2 medium onions, cut in chunks
1 stalk celery, cut in chunks
1 red bell pepper, cut in chunks
1 to 2 Tbsp olive oil
1½ cups uncooked basmati or long-grain rice, rinsed and drained

3 cups chicken or vegetable broth, boiling (salt-free or regular)
salt and freshly ground black pepper to taste
½ tsp each dried dill and dried thyme
¼ cup fresh parsley
½ cup cooked chicken (optional)

STEEL BLADE: Process onions, celery and red pepper with several quick on/off pulses, until coarsely chopped.

Heat olive oil in nonstick skillet. Add vegetables and sauté on medium heat for 2 to 3 minutes. Add rice and cook 2 minutes longer, stirring. Add boiling broth, salt, pepper, dill and thyme. Cover and simmer 15 minutes for basmati rice and 20 minutes for long-grain rice.

STEEL BLADE: Process parsley until minced. Add chicken (if using). Process with quick on/offs, until coarsely chopped. Add to rice. Remove from heat and let stand, covered, for 10 minutes. Fluff with a fork.

141 calories per serving, 23.2 g carbohydrates, 1.2 g fiber, 5 g protein, 3.2 g fat (0.6 g saturated fat), 13 mg cholesterol, 74 mg sodium, 125 mg potassium, 1 mg iron, 18 mg calcium, 19 mg phosphorus

# LEEK AND RICE SKILLET CASSEROLE

Yield: 4 to 6 servings. Keeps 2 to 3 days in the refrigerator. Reheats and/or freezes well.

4 leeks
1 green or red bell pepper
2 stalks celery
1 to 2 Tbsp oil
½ to ¾ cup boiling water

1 cup tomato juice or sauce (low-sodium or regular)
1 cup cooked rice
salt and freshly ground black pepper to taste

Clean leeks thoroughly, then dry well (see below). Cut all vegetables to fit feed tube.

SLICER: Slice leeks, bell pepper and celery, using medium pressure. Sauté in oil on medium heat for about 5 minutes, until golden. Add boiling water just to cover. Simmer, covered, for 5 minutes.

Add tomato juice and bring to a boil. Add rice, salt and pepper. Cover and simmer 10 minutes.

225 calories per serving, 43.8 g carbohydrates, 3.4 g fiber, 4 g protein, 4 g fat (0.4 g saturated fat), 0 mg cholesterol, 67 mg sodium, 474 mg potassium, 3 mg iron, 55 mg calcium, 65 mg phosphorus

## preparing leeks

Leeks are difficult to clean. First, remove and discard all but 2 or 3 inches of the green part. Make 4 lengthwise cuts to within 1 inch of the roots, so that the leeks resemble a whisk broom. To remove sand and grit, swish them in cold water. Dry well, then slice or chop.

# RAPID RISOTTO

Classic risotto requires almost constant stirring. With this method, you won't go as stir-crazy!

Yield: 6 servings. Do not freeze. Keeps 2 to 3 days in the refrigerator. Risotto reheats very well in the microwave.

4½ cups vegetable broth (low-sodium or regular)
2 cloves garlic
1 large onion, cut in chunks
1 carrot, cut in chunks
1 to 2 Tbsp olive oil
1½ cups uncooked arborio rice
½ cup white wine
salt and freshly ground black pepper to taste

1 tsp each dried basil and dried thyme
1 cup frozen green peas
½ cup roasted red peppers, cut in strips (see page 53), or use store-bought
½ cup grated Parmesan cheese
chopped fresh parsley and green onions, for garnish

Heat broth until almost boiling; keep warm.

*Continued*

STEEL BLADE: Drop garlic through feed tube while machine is running; process until minced. Add onion and carrot. Process with several quick on/off pulses, until coarsely chopped.

Heat oil in large saucepan. Sauté vegetables for 5 minutes on medium heat, until softened. Stir in rice, making sure grains are lightly coated with oil. Add 1 cup hot broth and cook, stirring, until almost no liquid remains. Add wine and stir until it is nearly absorbed, about 2 minutes.

Stir in remaining broth, bring to a boil and reduce heat to simmer. Cook, covered, for 20 to 25 minutes. Add salt, pepper, basil, thyme, peas, roasted peppers and Parmesan cheese. Remove from heat and let stand 5 minutes. Risotto will be very creamy. Garnish with chopped parsley and green onions. Serve immediately.

285 calories per serving, 48.4 g carbohydrates, 4.4 g fiber, 8 g protein, 4.9 g fat (1.5 g saturated fat), 6 mg cholesterol, 229 mg sodium, 114 mg potassium, 1 mg iron, 110 mg calcium, 80 mg phosphorus

### chef's tip

Arborio is a short-grain, starchy Italian rice. It remains firm on the inside and is able to absorb large quantities of liquid. Do not rinse it before cooking or you will wash away the starch that helps create the creamy texture of risotto.

## RICE, SPINACH AND MUSHROOM BAKE

This recipe comes from my friend Katy Brass. I modified it slightly, using basmati rice and fresh dill.

Yield: 8 servings. Keeps 2 to 3 days in the refrigerator. Reheats well. Freezes well.

1½ cups uncooked basmati or long-grain rice
3 cups water
salt to taste
1 pkg (10 oz/300 g) frozen chopped spinach
2 medium onions, quartered

1 to 2 Tbsp olive or canola oil
½ lb (250 g) mushrooms
salt and freshly ground black pepper to taste
2 to 3 Tbsp fresh dill, minced (optional)

Preheat oven to 350°F.

Place rice in a strainer and rinse well. In saucepan with tight-fitting lid, bring water to a boil. Add rice and salt. Simmer, covered, for 12 to 14 minutes for basmati rice; long-grain rice will take 18 to 20 minutes. Remove from heat and let stand, covered, for 5 minutes. While rice is cooking, prepare remaining ingredients.

Pierce package of spinach in several places with a sharp knife. Place package on microwavable plate and microwave on High for 4 minutes. Cool slightly; squeeze out excess moisture.

SLICER: Slice onions, using medium pressure. Heat oil in large nonstick skillet. Add onions and sauté on medium heat until golden, about 5 minutes. Slice mushrooms and add to skillet. Sauté 5 minutes longer.

Combine all ingredients and mix well. Transfer to sprayed 2-quart casserole and bake 20 to 25 minutes. (For a crusty top, do not cover rice.)

154 calories per serving, 30.3 g carbohydrates, 2.4 g fiber, 4 g protein, 2.5 g fat (0.3 g saturated fat), 0 mg cholesterol, 376 mg sodium, 196 mg potassium, 1 mg iron, 51 mg calcium, 40 mg phosphorus

## VEGETABLE KISHKA

A vegetable stuffing shaped in a roll or ring. My original recipe called for ½ cup of fat. I reduced the fat by more than half and added dill and extra vegetables to boost the flavor. So easy!

Yield: 10 servings. (Allow for second and third helpings!) Keeps 2 to 3 days in the refrigerator. Reheats and/or freezes well.

crackers to yield 3½ cups crumbs (about 100 TamTams), or 3½ cups matzo meal
2 cloves garlic
2 medium onions, cut in chunks
2 carrots, cut in chunks (or 10 baby carrots)
2 stalks celery, cut in chunks
1 red bell pepper, cut in chunks
3 Tbsp fresh dill
salt, freshly ground black pepper and paprika to taste
3 Tbsp oil
1 cup water, or vegetable or chicken broth

STEEL BLADE: To make cracker crumbs, process crackers until finely ground, 20 to 25 seconds. Empty into a bowl. Process garlic, onions, carrots, celery, bell pepper and dill in batches until minced, emptying processor each time. Combine all ingredients and process with quick on/off pulses, until mixed.

Form 3 long rolls, each about 2 inches in diameter. (Wet your hands for easier handling.) Wrap each roll in foil that has been sprayed with nonstick spray. (You can prepare the kishka to this point and refrigerate until needed.)

Place rolls on a baking sheet and bake in preheated 350°F oven about 1 hour. Unwrap and slice. Serve hot.

202 calories per serving, 33.5 g carbohydrates, 2.2 g fiber, 5 g protein, 5 g fat (0.3 g saturated fat), 0 mg cholesterol, 215 mg sodium, 100 mg potassium, 2 mg iron, 40 mg calcium, 15 mg phosphorus

### microwave method

Instead of making long rolls, place half the mixture on a microwavable plate and shape into a ring about 2 inches wide. Wet your hands for easier handling. Cover with parchment paper, tucking ends under dish. Repeat with remaining mixture. Microwave 1 plate at a time on High for 6 to 8 minutes, until dry to the touch. Let stand, covered, for 2 minutes.

VEGETABLES AND SIDE DISHES

# POTATO KNISHES

Knishes have been called New York's favorite nosh (snack). Watching my mother make knishes was one of my first childhood memories. It's the ultimate Jewish soul food! Knishes traditionally have a potato filling, but corned beef and chicken or meat fillings (page 257) are also delicious.

Yield: 24 to 30 knishes. Keeps 3 days in the refrigerator. Reheats well, but underbake slightly. Reheat, uncovered, at 350°F for 12 to 15 minutes. Freezes well.

## KNISH DOUGH

2 eggs (or 1 egg plus 2 egg whites)
½ cup oil
½ cup warm water
2½ cups flour
2 tsp baking powder
½ tsp salt

## POTATO FILLING

8 medium potatoes, peeled and cut in
   chunks
3 or 4 medium onions, cut in chunks
¼ cup oil or margarine
2 eggs (or 1 egg plus 2 egg whites)
salt and freshly ground black pepper
   to taste

For dough: Process eggs, oil and water on the STEEL BLADE until mixed, about 5 seconds. Add remaining ingredients and process just until blended, about 8 seconds. Do not overprocess or dough will become tough. Cover dough and let stand while you prepare filling.

For filling: Cook potatoes in boiling salted water until tender, about 20 minutes. Drain well. Return saucepan to heat for about 1 minute to remove excess moisture, shaking pan to prevent scorching. Mash potatoes with a potato masher. (If done in the processor, they become gluey.)

STEEL BLADE: Process onions in 2 batches, using quick on/offs, until coarsely chopped. Sauté in oil or margarine until golden brown. Process eggs for 1 or 2 seconds, until blended.

Combine potatoes with onions, oil, eggs and seasonings. Mix well.

Assembly: Divide dough into 4 pieces. Working with 1 piece at a time on a floured surface, coat lightly on all sides with a little flour and pat into a rectangle. Roll as thin as possible into a large rectangle.

Place a row of filling about 2 inches wide along longer side of rectangle, about 1 inch from edge. Roll up into a long roll. Using the edge of your hand, press down on roll and, with a sawing motion, cut through dough completely. Repeat every 2 inches. Turn knishes on end, pressing cut edge in slightly. Repeat with remaining dough and filling.

Bake on parchment-lined baking sheet in preheated 350°F oven about 35 minutes, until golden.

175 calories each, 22.5 g carbohydrates, 1.5 g fiber, 4 g protein, 8.1 g fat (0.8 g saturated fat), 35 mg cholesterol, 103 mg sodium, 227 mg potassium, 1 mg iron, 36 mg calcium, 63 mg phosphorus

### variation

To make miniature knishes, roll dough into a 6- × 18-inch rectangle. Place a narrow band of filling (about 1 inch wide) along longer side of rectangle, about 1 inch from edge. Roll up into a long, narrow roll. Cut with the edge of your hand into 1-inch pieces. Seal ends. Bake for 20 to 25 minutes, until golden. Excellent for hors d'oeuvres!

## CORNED BEEF FILLING

Yield: About 2 cups filling. Use to fill knishes, kreplach or turnovers. Freezes well.

**1 lb (500 g) lean corned beef, smoked meat or pickled brisket**

**1 medium onion, halved**

**3 eggs**

**½ tsp dry mustard**

Cut meat in chunks; discard fat. You should have about 2 cups meat. Using the STEEL BLADE, process meat with onion in 1 or 2 batches (depending on capacity of your machine) until finely ground, about 8 seconds per batch. Add eggs and mustard. Process with 3 or 4 quick on/offs, just until mixed.

23 calories per Tbsp, 0.4 g carbohydrates, 0 g fiber, 2 g protein, 1.3 g fat (0.4 g saturated fat), 25 mg cholesterol, 104 mg sodium, 26 mg potassium, 0 mg iron, 3 mg calcium, 18 mg phosphorus

### variation

For corned beef potato filling, coarsely chop 2 medium onions on STEEL BLADE. Sauté in 2 Tbsp oil until golden. Process 2 cups cut-up corned beef until ground, about 8 seconds. In a mixing bowl, mix corned beef with onions, 2 cups mashed potatoes, 2 eggs, salt and freshly ground black pepper. Makes about 3 cups filling.

## CHICKEN OR MEAT FILLING

Yield: About 4 cups filling. May be frozen.

**2 lb (1 kg) cooked leftover chicken or meat (about 4 cups)**

**½ cup leftover gravy**

**2 eggs (or 1 egg plus 2 egg whites)**

**salt and freshly ground black pepper to taste**

STEEL BLADE: Cut chicken or meat in 1½-inch chunks. Process half the chicen until minced, 6 to 8 seconds. Add half of remaining ingredients and process 3 or 4 seconds longer, until mixed. Empty bowl and repeat with remaining ingredients.

21 calories per Tbsp, 0.1 g carbohydrates, 0 g fiber, 4 g protein, 0.6 g fat (0.2 g saturated fat), 17 mg cholesterol, 12 mg sodium, 32 mg potassium, 0 mg iron, 3 mg calcium, 29 mg phosphorus

*Continued*

VEGETABLES AND SIDE DISHES

257

### notes

- If you don't have gravy, use chicken or beef broth. Fried onion may be added for additional flavor.

- Recipe may be halved, if desired.

### freezing knishes

Place unbaked knishes on a baking sheet and freeze; transfer to resealable bags. Bake frozen knishes uncovered in preheated 350°F oven until golden. Large knishes take about 45 minutes, minis need 30 minutes. They will taste freshly baked!

## KASHA KNISH

A long roll of crispy dough filled with buckwheat groats.

Yield: 2 rolls, each making 6 slices. Keeps 3 days in the refrigerator. Reheats and/or freezes well.

1 large onion, cut in chunks

2 to 3 Tbsp oil

1 cup kasha (buckwheat groats)

2½ cups boiling water or chicken soup (approximately)

salt and freshly ground black pepper to taste

Knish Dough, ½ recipe (page 256)

STEEL BLADE: Process onion with 3 or 4 quick on/offs, until coarsely chopped. Sauté until golden in hot oil. Add kasha and stir well. Brown over medium heat, stirring often. When nicely browned, carefully add boiling liquid to cover. Season with salt and pepper, cover and simmer 8 to 10 minutes, until water is absorbed. Let cool.

Prepare dough as directed. Place half the filling along 1 side, about 1 inch from edge. Roll up, turning in ends. Do not cut. Repeat with remaining dough and filling. Place on a parchment-lined baking sheet.

Bake in preheated 350°F oven for 35 minutes, until golden. Slice to serve.

134 calories per serving, 14 g carbohydrates, 0.9 g fiber, 3 g protein, 7.7 g fat (0.7 g saturated fat), 18 mg cholesterol, 98 mg sodium, 49 mg potassium, 1 mg iron, 32 mg calcium, 43 mg phosphorus

## KREPLACH

The Jewish version of wontons, ravioli or perogies. Meat or chicken kreplach are delicious in chicken

DOUGH

2 cups flour

¼ tsp salt

2 eggs

¼ cup warm water

FILLING

2 cups filling of your choice (e.g., Chicken or Meat Filling, page 257, or Cheese Filling, page 166)

soup or with gravy
as a side dish.
Cheese kreplach are
served with sour
cream.

STEEL BLADE: Process all dough ingredients until dough is well kneaded and forms a ball on the blade, 25 to 30 seconds. Remove from bowl and wrap in plastic wrap for about 15 minutes for easier handling. Meanwhile, prepare desired filling.

Divide dough in 4 pieces. Work with 1 piece at a time; keep remainder covered. Roll on lightly floured surface into a 9-inch square about ⅛ inch thick. Cut into 3-inch squares.

Place 1 Tbsp filling in the center of each square. Moisten edges of dough with water. Fold in half to form a triangle. Pinch edges together firmly to seal tightly. Join 2 points of the triangle and press to form a little "purse." Repeat with remaining dough and filling.

Bring a large pot of salted water to a boil. Cook kreplach in 2 batches. Drop into boiling water. Once kreplach float to the surface, reduce heat to medium and cook, uncovered, for 15 minutes until tender. Remove with a slotted spoon and drain well. Sprinkle with 1 tsp oil to prevent sticking.

Yield: 2½ to 3 dozen.
Kreplach can be frozen
for 1 to 2 months.

55 calories per serving (with chicken filling), 6.5 g carbohydrates, 0.2 g fiber, 5 g protein, 0.9 g fat (0.3 g saturated fat), 27 mg cholesterol, 34 mg sodium, 44 mg potassium, 1 mg iron, 5 mg calcium, 41 mg phosphorus

### varenikas

Varenikas are made from the same dough as kreplach, but are filled with potato, kasha (buckwheat groats) or fruit. (Try canned cherry or blueberry pie filling if you are in a hurry.) Varenikas are shaped like a half-moon, rather than a triangle, and you do not join the 2 points to make a purse shape. Potato varenikas are delicious served with roast chicken or meat and gravy. Serve fruit varenikas with sour cream or yogurt. Freezes well.

## HOMEMADE PASTA

The processor whips
up pasta dough in
just 30 seconds!

| 1½ cups flour | 1½ Tbsp water |
| ½ tsp salt | 1 Tbsp oil (optional) |
| 2 eggs (or 1 egg plus 2 egg whites) | |

Yield: 3 to 4 servings,
or about ¾ lb noodles
(the equivalent of a
12 oz package).

STEEL BLADE: Process all ingredients together until dough is well kneaded and forms a ball, 25 to 30 seconds. Divide into 4 equal pieces.

To roll by hand: Work with 1 piece of dough at a time. Roll out on a floured surface as thin as possible into a 10-inch square. Let dough dry for a few minutes. Roll up jelly-roll style; cut into ½-inch strips with a sharp knife. Unroll and

*Continued*

place noodles on a lightly floured towel to dry for 1 to 2 hours. (Kids love to help unroll the dough and lay it out!) Drying is not necessary if noodles will be cooked immediately.

Bring 4 quarts of water to a boil. Add 4 tsp salt. Cook noodles for 3 to 4 minutes, until al dente (slightly firm, but done). Cooking time varies, depending on dryness of noodles. Drain immediately and combine with desired sauce. (Reserve about ½ cup of cooking water to thicken pasta sauce if necessary.)

279 calories per serving, 48 g carbohydrates, 1.7 g fiber, 11 g protein, 4.1 g fat (1.2 g saturated fat), 141 mg cholesterol, 431 mg sodium, 109 mg potassium, 3 mg iron, 27 mg calcium, 125 mg phosphorus

### notes

- Uncooked pasta can be refrigerated for 2 to 3 days or frozen for up to 1 month. Recipe can be doubled and processed in 1 batch.

- To use pasta machine: Crank each piece of dough through widest setting of machine rollers (#1 setting) 3 or 4 times, flouring and folding dough in half each time. Reset machine to #2 setting and feed each piece of pasta through once. Repeat for each setting (#3, #4 and #5), flouring dough as needed to prevent sticking, until desired thickness. If dough is too long and awkward to handle, cut it in half. To prevent sticking, let dough dry for a few minutes before cutting it into noodles.

- Change handle of machine from roller to cutter position for thin or wide noodles. Roll pasta through desired cutters. Separate noodles and let dry at least 15 minutes before cooking.

- FETTUCCINE: Cut in ½-inch strips. Cook 3 to 4 minutes.

- LASAGNA NOODLES: Make pasta but do not let it dry. Cut into rectangles about 4½ inches wide and the same length as your baking dish. (This makes it easy to assemble!) Cooking is not necessary.

- CANNELLONI AND MANICOTTI: Cut in 5-inch lengths. Cook about 1 minute. Drain well; lay flat on towels. Fill as desired.

- SPINACH NOODLES: Cook a 10 oz (300 g) package frozen spinach according to package directions; squeeze very dry. Process on STEEL BLADE until finely minced. Prepare a double recipe of pasta as directed, but add spinach to dough. Divide dough into 8 equal pieces, roll and cut as directed. Makes 1½ lb noodles.

## PEANUT BUTTER PASTA

This vegetarian
dish is delicious
hot or cold.

Yield: 6 to 8 servings as
a side dish. Leftovers
will keep 2 or 3 days
in the fridge. Reheat
in the microwave.
Do not freeze.

2 medium onions, cut in chunks
1 red and 1 green bell pepper, cut in
   chunks
1 Tbsp olive oil
2 cups mushrooms

1 pkg (12 oz/375 g) fusilli, penne or
   bow tie pasta
Peanut Butter Sauce (page 110)
salt and freshly ground black pepper
   to taste

STEEL BLADE: Process onions and bell peppers with 4 or 5 quick on/off pulses, until coarsely chopped. Heat oil in large nonstick skillet. Sauté onions and peppers on medium-high heat until tender, about 5 minutes. Process mushrooms with quick on/off pulses, until coarsely chopped. Add to skillet and sauté 3 or 4 minutes longer.

Meanwhile, cook pasta according to package directions. Reserve ½ cup of pasta cooking water. Drain pasta but do not rinse. Combine pasta with reserved cooking water, peanut butter sauce and vegetables; mix well. Season with salt and pepper.

375 calories per serving, 63.8 g carbohydrates, 3.9 g fiber, 12 g protein, 9.5 g fat (1.7 g saturated fat), 0 mg cholesterol, 415 mg sodium, 378 mg potassium, 3 mg iron, 35 mg calcium, 165 mg phosphorus

## POPCORN STUFFING MOUNDS

Thanks to my friend
Kathy Guttman for
helping me develop
this gluten-free
vegetarian dish.

Yield: 10 to 12 mounds
(about 4 cups stuffing).
Keeps 2 to 3 days in the
refrigerator. Reheats
and/or freezes well.

2 Tbsp canola oil
⅓ cup popcorn kernels (see About
   Popcorn, page 262)
2 medium onions, cut in chunks
3 stalks celery, cut in chunks
1 red bell pepper or carrot, cut in
   chunks
2 cloves garlic

2 cups mushrooms
½ cup fresh parsley
2 Tbsp fresh basil (or 1 tsp dried basil)
1 Tbsp fresh thyme (or ½ tsp dried
   thyme)
2 eggs, lightly beaten
½ tsp salt (or to taste)
freshly ground black pepper to taste

Heat 1 Tbsp of the oil in a large covered pot. Add corn kernels, cover and pop, shaking pot constantly. Cool slightly. You will have 9 to 10 cups of popcorn. Discard any unpopped kernels.

STEEL BLADE: Coarsely chop onions, celery and bell pepper or carrot, using quick on/off pulses. Sauté in remaining 1 Tbsp oil over medium heat in a large deep skillet or Dutch oven until tender, about 5 minutes. Drop garlic through feed tube and process until minced. Add mushrooms and process with quick on/off pulses, until coarsely chopped. Add to skillet and sauté 5 minutes longer. Process parsley, basil and thyme until finely minced, 10 to 15 seconds. Add to vegetable mixture.

*Continued*

Do not clean bowl before processing popcorn. Process popcorn in 1 or 2 batches until coarsely chopped, about 20 seconds. Add to vegetable mixture, along with eggs, salt and pepper, and mix well. (Can be prepared up to this point and refrigerated for 1 or 2 days.)

Scoop out the stuffing mixture with an ice cream scoop. Place mounds on a sprayed or parchment-lined baking sheet. Bake in preheated 350°F oven about 30 minutes, until crusty.

87 calories per serving, 10 g carbohydrates, 2 g fiber, 3 g protein, 4.4 g fat (0.6 g saturated fat), 42 mg cholesterol, 142 mg sodium, 181 mg potassium, 1 mg iron, 24 mg calcium, 67 mg phosphorus

### variations

- Place mixture in a sprayed 2-quart casserole. Bake at 350°F for 45 to 50 minutes. For a crusty top, bake uncovered. If you prefer a moist stuffing, cover casserole with foil.

### lighter variation

Use 9 to 10 cups air-popped popcorn (no oil needed) and use 1 Tbsp oil to sauté the vegetables. One serving contains 75 calories and 3.0 g fat.

### about popcorn

If you observe Jewish dietary laws, microwave popcorn usually has a dairy designation and should not be used to stuff meat or poultry unless you use a pareve brand. Microwave popcorn is already salted, so adjust seasonings accordingly. One bag of microwave popcorn yields about 10 cups when popped.

## STUFFING CASSEROLE

This is especially delicious made with challah (egg bread).

Yield: 6 to 8 servings. Keeps 2 to 3 days in the refrigerator. Reheats well. May be frozen.

| | |
|---|---|
| 5 cups soft bread crumbs (page 36), or 10 slices bread | 3 eggs (or 2 eggs plus 2 egg whites) |
| | 1 tsp baking powder |
| 2 Tbsp oil or margarine | 1 tsp salt (or to taste) |
| 2 medium onions, halved | ¼ tsp garlic powder |
| 1 green bell pepper, cut in chunks | dash freshly ground black pepper |
| 2 stalks celery, cut in chunks | 1 cup chicken or vegetable broth (salt-free or regular) |
| 1 cup mushrooms | |

STEEL BLADE: Make crumbs from stale bread or rolls. Tear into chunks and drop through feed tube while machine is running. Process until fine crumbs are formed. Measure 5 cups crumbs, loosely packed.

Heat oil or margarine in large nonstick skillet. Meanwhile, process onions with quick on/offs, until coarsely chopped. Add to skillet. Repeat with bell pepper, then celery, then mushrooms, adding each in turn to skillet. Brown vegetables quickly on medium-high heat. Remove from heat and cool slightly.

Process eggs for 2 or 3 seconds. Add with bread crumbs and remaining ingredients to skillet and mix well. Place in sprayed 7- × 11-inch glass baking dish. Bake, uncovered, in preheated 350°F oven for 40 to 45 minutes, until golden brown.

217 calories per serving, 26.7 g carbohydrates, 2.3 g fiber, 8 g protein, 9 g fat (1.5 g saturated fat), 110 mg cholesterol, 790 mg sodium, 263 mg potassium, 2 mg iron, 131 mg calcium, 127 mg phosphorus

### variation

To use as a stuffing for veal brisket or turkey, omit baking powder and increase mushrooms to 2 cups. Add ½ tsp each of dried sage and dried thyme.

# SUPER SALADS AND DRESSINGS
### recipe list

| | |
|---|---|
| 268 | Super Coleslaw |
| 269 | Asian Coleslaw |
| 269 | Tangy Marinated Carrot Salad |
| 270 | Marinated Fresh Vegetable Salad |
| 271 | Marinated Bean Salad |
| 271 | Carrot and Raisin Salad |
| 272 | Moroccan Pepper Salad (Salade Cuite) |
| 272 | Faux-Tato Salad |
| 273 | Caesar Salad |
| 274 | Croutons |
| 274 | Cucumber Salad |
| 275 | Farmer's Salad |
| 275 | Layered Salad |
| 276 | Salad Niçoise |
| 278 | Asian Luncheon Salad |
| 278 | Asian Spinach Salad |
| 279 | Raspberry Spinach Salad |
| 280 | Greek Salad |
| 280 | Pesto Pasta Salad |
| 281 | Bev's Colorful Couscous Salad |
| 282 | Quick Couscous Salad |
| 283 | Cranberry Quinoa Salad |
| 284 | Mediterranean Quinoa Salad |
| 285 | Tabbouleh Salad |
| 285 | Chickpea Broccoli Salad |
| 286 | Italian Salad Dressing |
| 286 | Light and Easy Italian Dressing |
| 287 | Best Vinaigrette Dressing |
| 287 | Balsamic Vinaigrette |
| 288 | Sweet and Spicy French Dressing |
| 288 | Sweet Vidalia Onion Dressing |
| 289 | Fresh Tomato Dressing |
| 289 | Russian Salad Dressing |
| 289 | Creamy Dill Salad Dressing |
| 290 | Creamy Garlic Dressing |
| 290 | Marty's Garlic Cheese Dressing |
| 291 | Green Goddess Salad Dressing or Dip |
| 291 | Low-Fat Ranch Dressing |
| 291 | Yummy Yogurt Salad Dressing |
| 292 | Asian Salad Dressing |

- Refer to the **Smart Chart** (pages 24–41) for basic processing techniques.
- Before processing, wash and dry vegetables well. Peel and core, and remove seeds and any pits to prevent damage to the processor blades.
- See Vegetables and Side Dishes chapter (starting on page 222) for vegetable processing techniques.
- Vegetables with a high water content (e.g., cucumbers, bell peppers) should be patted dry with paper towels after processing to absorb excess moisture.
- Use a salad spinner to dry salad greens, then wrap in a towel to absorb remaining moisture. Greens can be stored in a resealable plastic bag for a day or 2 in your refrigerator.
- Salad bore or salad bar? There is an amazing selection of fresh produce available today, including local and organic. Much of it is washed, trimmed and ready to serve.
- Take your pick of salad greens! Reach for arugula, Bibb/butterhead, Boston, curly leaf lettuce, endive, escarole, iceberg, romaine, mesclun/mixed salad greens, oak leaf, radicchio, spinach/baby spinach or watercress.
- To give color, texture and flavor to salads, add avocado, broccoli slaw, carrots/baby carrots, red or green cabbage, celery, cucumbers, fennel, bell peppers, onions (Spanish, Vidalia, red), green onions/scallions or chives, and alfalfa, bean or broccoli sprouts.
- Tomatoes are available in many shapes, sizes and colors, from grape tomatoes to beefsteaks to heirlooms. For maximum flavor, store them at room temperature.
- Roasted and grilled vegetables add terrific flavor to salads. Choose from bell peppers, garlic, beets, eggplant, mushrooms or zucchini.
- Lightly steamed broccoli or cauliflower florets, asparagus and green or yellow beans add crunch and flavor to salads.
- Use baked, microwaved or boiled potatoes for potato salad. When cool, remove peel. (New potatoes do not need to be peeled.) Slice or cut into cubes by hand; potatoes may crumble if sliced on the processor.
- Jarred or canned marinated artichoke hearts, olives, sun-dried tomatoes, roasted bell peppers, canned beets, kidney beans, black beans, chickpeas, lentils or corn niblets add variety with no fuss or muss.
- Use pasta, rice, bulgur, couscous, quinoa, barley, kasha or other cooked grains for a hearty salad base.

- Add color, zing and nutrients to salads with fresh fruit. Dried fruits (e.g., apricots, cranberries, raisins) make a quick, delicious addition. Pomegranate seeds are beautiful as a garnish!
- Finish off your salads with toasted sunflower seeds, sesame seeds, almonds, walnuts, flax seed, wheat germ, croutons or chow mein noodles.
- Try adding cheddar, Swiss, mozzarella, Muenster or Parmesan, crumbled feta, goat or cottage cheese to salads for flavor and extra protein.
- Add cooked chicken, turkey, cold cuts, hard-cooked egg wedges, cooked or canned fish (e.g., salmon, tuna) for hearty main-dish salads. Allow 1 to 2 cups salad per person as a main dish.
- Use the **Steel Blade** to make salad dressings. Transform dips into dressings by thinning them down with a little milk or buttermilk.
- For small quantities of salad dressings and marinades, use a mini-prep. If your processor comes with nested bowls, use the mini-bowl and mini-blade for small amounts.
- Replace part of the oil in salad dressings with fruit juice, or chicken or vegetable broth. Experi-ment with different vinegars (balsamic, cider, rice or wine vinegar) and fruit juices (lemon, lime, grapefruit, mango or orange juice). For variety, use extra-virgin olive oil, toasted sesame oil or walnut oil.
- Add salad dressing to salads just before serving; otherwise salad will become limp and watery.
- INSTANT GAZPACHO! Transform limp, left-over salad into delicious soup. Process on the **Steel Blade** until finely chopped. Combine with tomato or vegetable juice and a squeeze of fresh lemon juice. Season to taste. Serve chilled. Garnish with chopped tomatoes, bell peppers and green onions.
- NESTED BOWL METHOD: Choose the appropriate bowl and blade or disc for the task. Use the small bowl to mince garlic or herbs for salad dressings or for other small tasks. Use the medium or large bowl and appropriate disc to slice or shred/grate veggies, cheese, etc. Use the large bowl and **Steel Blade** to chop/mince vegetables and to combine ingredients.
- To shred leafy vegetables like lettuce or spinach for salads, roll leaves together and stand them up in the feed tube. Process using medium pressure.

# SUPER COLESLAW

I've made this family favorite for years—it's a winner! The hot marinade keeps the coleslaw mixture crisp. For a colorful slaw, use a mixture of red and green cabbage.

Yield: 12 to 16 servings. Keeps about 1 month in the refrigerator.

| | |
|---|---|
| 1 head cabbage (about 3 lb/1.4 kg) | 1 cup white vinegar |
| 1 green bell pepper, cut in chunks | ¾ cup canola or vegetable oil |
| 3 carrots (or 12 mini carrots) | ½ cup sugar (see below) |
| 2 cloves garlic | 1 tsp salt |
| 3 green onions, cut in chunks | ¼ tsp freshly ground black pepper |

SLICER: Discard soft, outer leaves of cabbage. Cut cabbage into wedges to fit feed tube. Discard core. Slice, using very light pressure. If too thick, chop in batches on the STEEL BLADE, using quick on/off pulses. Slice green pepper, using medium pressure. Empty into a large bowl.

GRATER: Use the mini feed tube if your machine has one. Grate carrots, using firm pressure. Add to cabbage.

STEEL BLADE: Drop garlic and green onions through feed tube while machine is running; process until minced. Add to cabbage.

Combine remaining ingredients in a saucepan or microwavable bowl. Heat until almost boiling (2 to 3 minutes on High in the microwave), stirring occasionally. Pour hot marinade over coleslaw mixture and mix well. Refrigerate.

189 calories per serving, 15.1 g carbohydrates, 2.6 g fiber, 1 g protein, 14.1 g fat (1.1 g saturated fat), 0 mg cholesterol, 219 mg sodium, 205 mg potassium, 1 mg iron, 41 mg calcium, 30 mg phosphorus

### variations

- Replace cabbage with packaged broccoli slaw, or shred peeled broccoli stems on the grater, using firm pressure. Add a handful of raisins or dried cranberries, if desired.

- Prepare coleslaw mixture. For dressing, blend 1 cup light mayonnaise (or make your own Mayonnaise, page 111), 2 Tbsp sugar (or to taste) and 2 Tbsp lemon juice or vinegar. Add salt and freshly ground black pepper to taste. One serving contains 102 calories, 10.4 g carbohydrates and 6.8 g fat.

- To boost the flavor, add 1 tsp white horseradish or 1 Tbsp Dijon mustard.

### about sweeteners

Coleslaw won't keep as long if sweetener is used instead of sugar. Some sweeteners become bitter when heated. Splenda is heat-stable and can be used with excellent results.

# ASIAN COLESLAW

This fabulous coleslaw is sure to become a favorite. It makes a great addition to your buffet table. The dressing can be made a few days in advance and refrigerated.

2 cloves garlic
¼ cup rice vinegar
¼ cup peanut butter
2 to 3 Tbsp honey (or to taste)
2 Tbsp tamari or soy sauce
1 Tbsp toasted sesame oil
¼ tsp chili powder or red pepper flakes
12 baby carrots (or 3 medium)

1 savoy or regular cabbage (about 2 lb/1 kg)
1 red bell pepper, quartered
4 green onions, cut to fit feed tube
salt and freshly ground black pepper to taste
½ cup toasted slivered almonds, for garnish
¼ cup toasted sesame seeds, for garnish

Yield: 10 to 12 servings. Keeps for 3 or 4 days in the refrigerator.

STEEL BLADE: Drop garlic through feed tube while machine is running; process until minced. Add vinegar, peanut butter, honey, tamari or soy sauce, sesame oil and chili powder or pepper flakes. Process until smooth, about 15 seconds. Transfer to a measuring cup. You will have about ¾ cup dressing. Don't bother washing the processor bowl or blade. Process carrots until finely minced. Transfer them to a large bowl.

SLICER: Cut cabbage in wedges to fit feed tube; discard core. Slice, using very light pressure. Add to carrots. Place bell pepper and green onions vertically in feed tube. Slice, using light pressure. Add to cabbage mixture.

Add dressing and mix well. Season with salt and pepper. Transfer to a serving bowl, cover and chill. At serving time, garnish with almonds and sesame seeds.

94 calories per serving, 11.8 g carbohydrates, 3.4 g fiber, 4 g protein, 4.7 g fat (0.8 g saturated fat), 0 mg cholesterol, 263 mg sodium, 284 mg potassium, 1 mg iron, 39 mg calcium, 66 mg phosphorus

### variation

For a peanut-free variation, substitute ¾ cup Asian Salad Dressing (page 292) for the coleslaw dressing above. If desired, add a 3 oz package of ramen-style noodles, broken up.

# TANGY MARINATED CARROT SALAD

Delicious hot or cold!

3 lb (1.4 kg) carrots
1 green bell pepper, cut in chunks
1 medium onion, cut in chunks
1 can (10 oz/284 mL) tomato soup
½ cup sugar
1 tsp Worcestershire sauce

1 tsp freshly ground black pepper
1 tsp dry mustard
1 tsp dried dill (or 2 Tbsp fresh dill)
¾ cup white vinegar
½ cup canola or extra-virgin olive oil

Yield: 12 servings.

Keeps 7 to 10 days

in the refrigerator.

SLICER: Cut carrots to fit feed tube. Pack tightly in an upright position. Slice, using firm pressure. Cook in boiling salted water for 1 minute. Drain well. Place in a large bowl. Slice green pepper and onion, using light pressure. Add to carrots.

STEEL BLADE: Process soup with sugar, Worcestershire sauce, pepper, mustard and dill for 5 seconds. Add vinegar and oil through feed tube while machine is running. Process 8 to 10 seconds.

Immediately pour soup mixture over carrots. Cover and marinate in the refrigerator overnight for maximum flavor. Serve chilled.

185 calories per serving, 23.5 g carbohydrates, 3.4 g fiber, 2 g protein, 9.7 g fat (0.7 g saturated fat), 0 mg cholesterol, 211 mg sodium, 3361 mg potassium, 1 mg iron, 41 mg calcium, 41 mg phosphorus

## MARINATED FRESH VEGETABLE SALAD

Yield: 10 to 12 servings.

Keeps about 10 days in

the refrigerator.

2 cups green beans, trimmed

2 cups yellow beans, trimmed

1 cup baby carrots

1 green and 1 red bell pepper, cut in
    chunks

1 Spanish or red onion, cut in chunks

2 stalks celery, cut in chunks

1 medium zucchini (optional)

2 cups cauliflower and/or broccoli
    florets

1 jar marinated artichoke hearts,
    drained (optional)

½ cup black olives (optional)

2 cloves garlic

1 cup white vinegar

¼ cup canola oil

½ cup sugar

1 tsp salt (or to taste)

Cut beans in half. Cook beans and carrots for 2 minutes in boiling water to cover. Drain well.

SLICER: Slice bell peppers, onion, celery and zucchini (if using), using medium pressure. Empty bowl as necessary. Combine with cauliflower and/or broccoli florets in large mixing bowl. Add artichoke hearts and olives (if desired).

STEEL BLADE: Drop garlic through feed tube while machine is running; process until minced. Combine with vinegar, oil, sugar and salt in a saucepan or microwavable bowl. Heat mixture until almost boiling (2 to 3 minutes on High in the microwave), stirring occasionally. Pour hot marinade over vegetables and mix well. Refrigerate.

92 calories per serving, 20.4 g carbohydrates, 3.3 g fiber, 2 g protein, 0.2 g fat (0 g saturated fat), 0 mg cholesterol, 262 mg sodium, 266 mg potassium, 1 mg iron, 44 mg calcium, 42 mg phosphorus

## MARINATED BEAN SALAD

To substitute fresh or frozen beans for the canned ones in this recipe, undercook them slightly, and drain well.

Yield: 12 servings. Keeps about 10 days in the refrigerator.

1 can (14 oz/398 mL) cut green beans

1 can (14 oz/398 mL) cut yellow beans

1 can (10 oz/284 mL) baby lima beans

1 cup canned kidney beans or chickpeas

1 green and 1 red bell pepper, halved

1 large Spanish or Vidalia onion, cut in chunks

2 cups raw cauliflower florets (optional)

⅓ cup extra-virgin olive oil or canola oil

¼ cup vinegar (white, wine or balsamic)

2 to 3 Tbsp sugar (or to taste)

1 tsp dry mustard

1 tsp Italian seasoning

salt and freshly ground black pepper to taste

Place beans in a colander, rinse and drain well.

SLICER: Slice bell peppers and onion, using medium pressure.

Combine all ingredients in a large bowl and mix well. Cover and refrigerate for at least 24 hours before serving.

121 calories per serving, 12.8 g carbohydrates, 3 g fiber, 3 g protein, 6.7 g fat (0.9 g saturated fat), 0 mg cholesterol, 142 mg sodium, 208 mg potassium, 1 mg iron, 25 mg calcium, 38 mg phosphorus

## CARROT AND RAISIN SALAD

Yield: 6 servings. Keeps 2 to 3 days in the refrigerator.

1 lb (500 g) carrots (about 5 or 6)

1 cup sultana raisins or dried cranberries

½ cup sweetened flaked coconut

2 Tbsp lemon juice

2 Tbsp honey

2 Tbsp extra-virgin olive oil

2 Tbsp minced fresh parsley (optional)

GRATER: Cut carrots to fit feed tube horizontally. Grate, using medium pressure. Transfer to mixing bowl and combine with remaining ingredients. Refrigerate for several hours to blend flavors. Serve chilled.

200 calories per serving, 36.2 g carbohydrates, 3.7 g fiber, 2 g protein, 6.9 g fat (2.6 g saturated fat), 0 mg cholesterol, 75 mg sodium, 458 mg potassium, 1 mg iron, 39 mg calcium, 59 mg phosphorus

### variation

Grated apple may be substituted for coconut. Sprinkle with lemon juice to prevent discoloration.

SUPER SALADS AND DRESSINGS

# MOROCCAN PEPPER SALAD (SALADE CUITE)

My daughter-in-law Ariane prepares this dish for me whenever I visit Montreal. She roasts and peels the peppers first, but my son Doug, who is a chef, omits this step (see Variation below). Either way, it's delicious.

Yield: 4 to 6 servings. Serve hot or cold. Keeps about 1 week in the refrigerator. Freezes well.

6 roasted red peppers (page 53)
8 Italian plum tomatoes
2 cloves garlic
1 medium onion, cut in chunks
1 Tbsp olive oil

1 cup tomato sauce
1 to 2 Tbsp sugar (or to taste)
salt and freshly ground black pepper
  to taste
few drops hot sauce (optional)

Prepare roasted peppers as directed. Peel and remove seeds, then cut into strips. Set aside.

Bring water to a boil in a large saucepan. Cut an X in the bottom of each tomato. Drop into boiling water for 30 seconds; plunge into cold water immediately. Peel tomatoes, cut in half and squeeze gently to remove seeds. Set aside.

STEEL BLADE: Drop garlic through feed tube while machine is running; process until minced. Add onion and process with quick on/off pulses, until coarsely chopped. Heat oil in large skillet. Add garlic and onion. Sauté on medium heat until tender, 5 to 7 minutes.

Process tomatoes with quick on/off pulses, until coarsely chopped. Add to skillet and cook 3 or 4 minutes longer. Add roasted peppers along with remaining ingredients. Simmer for 20 minutes, stirring occasionally. Adjust seasonings to taste.

154 calories per serving, 28.7 g carbohydrates, 5.4 g fiber, 4 g protein, 4.3 g fat (0.6 g saturated fat), 0 mg cholesterol, 333 mg sodium, 899 mg potassium, 2 mg iron, 49 mg calcium, 95 mg phosphorus

## variation

Instead of roasting the peppers, cut fresh red peppers in half; remove seeds and core. Slice on SLICER, using medium pressure. Sauté with garlic and onion until tender. Roasted red peppers from a jar can also be substituted.

# FAUX-TATO SALAD

Cauliflower replaces potatoes in this low-carb version of potato salad!

Yield: 6 servings. Keeps 2 to 3 days in the refrigerator. Do not freeze. Recipe may be doubled.

1 medium cauliflower, cut up
3 hard-cooked eggs (or 5 hard-
  cooked egg whites)
2 Tbsp fresh dill
2 stalks celery, cut in chunks
2 green onions, cut in chunks

½ cup light or regular mayonnaise
  (approximately)
½ tsp dry mustard
salt and freshly ground black pepper
  to taste

Cook cauliflower in boiling water to cover until very tender, 15 to 20 minutes. Drain well and pat dry. (Or microwave, covered, on High for 7 to 8 minutes.) You should have about 4 cups. Let cool. Eggs should be cooked in advance and cooled.

STEEL BLADE: Process dill until minced. Add celery and green onions; process with quick on/off pulses, until coarsely chopped. Add eggs and process with quick on/offs, until coarsely chopped. Transfer to a large bowl, add remaining ingredients and mix gently. Cover and refrigerate.

132 calories per serving, 7.7 g carbohydrates, 2.7 g fiber, 6 g protein, 9.5 g fat (1.9 g saturated fat), 113 mg cholesterol, 205 mg sodium, 376 mg potassium, 1 mg iron, 44 mg calcium, 97 mg phosphorus

## CAESAR SALAD

A tried-and-true favorite!

Yield: 8 servings.

| | |
|---|---|
| 2 to 3 heads romaine lettuce (depending on size) | 1 Tbsp lemon juice |
| 1 can flat anchovies (optional) | ½ tsp salt |
| ½ cup canola or extra-virgin olive oil (approximately) | freshly ground black pepper to taste |
| 1 or 2 cloves garlic | ½ tsp sugar |
| ¼ cup wine vinegar | 1 tsp Worcestershire sauce |
| | ¼ to ⅓ cup grated Parmesan cheese |
| | Croutons (page 274) |

Wash lettuce; dry thoroughly. Tear into bite-sized pieces. (May be wrapped in paper towels and stored in a plastic bag in refrigerator until serving time.)

Drain oil from anchovies into measuring cup; add oil to measure ¾ cup. (If you don't use anchovies, increase canola or olive oil to ¾ cup.)

STEEL BLADE: Drop garlic through feed tube while machine is running; process until minced. Add oil, vinegar, lemon juice, salt, pepper, sugar, Worcestershire sauce and Parmesan cheese. Process 8 to 10 seconds to blend. (May be prepared in advance and refrigerated.)

Combine approximately 1 cup dressing with lettuce, anchovies and croutons in a large salad bowl; mix well. Add additional dressing if needed. Serve immediately.

281 calories per serving, 10.4 g carbohydrates, 3.5 g fiber, 4 g protein, 26 g fat (2.4 g saturated fat), 2 mg cholesterol, 263 mg sodium, 408 mg potassium, 2 mg iron, 95 mg calcium, 75 mg phosphorus

### variation

Omit anchovies. Increase oil to 1 cup and increase Parmesan cheese to ½ cup. Process until blended. Makes about 1¾ cups dressing. Keeps about 7 to 10 days in the refrigerator. If desired, add 3 Tbsp mayonnaise to make a creamier dressing. (This will give the same texture as using a coddled egg, which was called for in my original recipe.)

93 calories per Tbsp (dressing only), 0.3 g carbohydrates, 0 g fiber, 1 g protein, 10 g fat (1 g saturated fat), 2 mg cholesterol, 78 mg sodium, 5 mg potassium, 0 mg iron, 20 mg calcium, 13 mg phosphorus

# CROUTONS

Yield: 8 servings (about
2 cups). Freezes well.

2 cups cubed stale French bread,
   crusts trimmed (freeze crusts for
   bread crumbs)

2 Tbsp canola or olive oil
1 clove garlic, minced (optional)
dried basil and oregano (optional)

Spread bread cubes on baking sheet and bake in preheated 325°F oven for 10 to 15 minutes, until dry. Cool slightly. Toss with oil, garlic and herbs (if using). Return to oven for a few minutes, until lightly toasted and completely dry and crisp. Store in refrigerator in an airtight container for up to 1 week.

54 calories per serving, 4.4 g carbohydrates, 0.2 g fiber, 1 g protein, 3.8 g fat (0.3 g saturated fat), 0 mg cholesterol, 60 mg sodium, 9 mg potassium, 0 mg iron, 13 mg calcium, 9 mg phosphorus

# CUCUMBER SALAD

For Passover, do
not use Splenda.

Yield: 8 to 10 servings.
Keeps 2 to 3 days in
the refrigerator.

¼ cup fresh dill, loosely packed
4 English cucumbers, unpeeled
1 to 2 tsp salt
1 medium onion, cut in chunks

1 small red bell pepper, cut in chunks
Best Vinaigrette Dressing (page 287)
2 to 3 Tbsp sugar or granular Splenda
   (optional)

STEEL BLADE: Process dill until minced, 6 to 8 seconds. Remove from bowl and reserve. (If your processor comes with nested bowls, mince dill in mini-bowl.)

SLICER: Cut cucumbers to fit feed tube. Slice, using medium pressure. Transfer to a colander, sprinkle with salt and mix well. Weigh down cucumbers with a heavy plate and let drain for half an hour. Press to remove excess liquid; rinse well. Pat dry with paper towels.

Slice onion and bell pepper, using light pressure. Prepare dressing as directed, adding reserved dill. In a large bowl, combine about ¾ cup dressing with all ingredients and mix well. Marinate for at least 1 hour before serving. Serve chilled.

136 calories per serving, 6.3 g carbohydrates, 1.1 g fiber, 1 g protein, 12.2 g fat (1.7 g saturated fat), 0 mg cholesterol, 320 mg sodium, 228 mg potassium, 1 mg iron, 26 mg calcium, 37 mg phosphorus

## creamy cucumber salad

Instead of Best Vinaigrette Dressing, mix dill with ¾ to 1 cup light sour cream, 1 Tbsp extra-virgin olive oil and 1 Tbsp fresh lemon juice. Omit sugar. One serving contains 65 calories and 3.6 g fat.

# FARMER'S SALAD

This is one of the few salad recipes where the lettuce is shredded on the slicing disc instead of being torn into small pieces by hand.

Yield: 4 to 6 servings.

4 green onions, cut in chunks

2 Tbsp fresh dill

1 head iceberg or romaine lettuce

1 green bell pepper, halved

½ English cucumber

6 radishes

¾ cup creamed cottage cheese (low-fat or regular)

¾ cup yogurt or sour cream (low-fat or regular)

salt and freshly ground black pepper to taste

STEEL BLADE: Drop green onions and dill through feed tube while machine is running; process until minced.

SLICER: Cut lettuce in wedges; discard core. Slice lettuce, bell pepper, cucumber and radishes, using medium pressure. Empty bowl as necessary. Combine all ingredients in large serving bowl and toss gently to mix. Best served immediately.

90 calories per serving, 11.8 g carbohydrates, 2.7 g fiber, 9 g protein, 1.2 g fat (0.6 g saturated fat), 5 mg cholesterol, 214 mg sodium, 465 mg potassium, 1 mg iron, 125 mg calcium, 142 mg phosphorus

# LAYERED SALAD

The layered look is in! Although this recipe seems complicated at first glance, you are simply processing 2 ingredients with each blade. The processor makes this salad so quick to prepare.

Yield: 12 servings.

10 oz (300 g) bag salad mix (or 1 medium head iceberg or romaine lettuce)

2 medium red bell peppers, quartered

1 cup packed fresh parsley (discard stems)

2 Tbsp fresh dill or basil

4 medium carrots (or 2 cups baby carrots)

1 cup radishes

2 medium green bell peppers, quartered

2 medium red onions, halved

1 English cucumber

6 oz (180 g) chilled cheddar or mozzarella cheese (low-fat or regular) (1½ cups grated)

As you process each vegetable, layer it in a 2½-quart glass salad bowl. Pat veggies dry with paper towels to remove excess moisture. Check that edges of each layer are visible from outside of bowl. Wipe processor bowl dry as needed.

SLICER: If using iceberg or romaine lettuce, slice using light pressure. Layer salad mix or lettuce in salad bowl. Slice red peppers, using medium pressure. Arrange over lettuce. Wipe bowl dry with paper towels.

STEEL BLADE: Process parsley with dill or basil until minced, about 10 seconds. Sprinkle over red peppers.

*Continued*

GRATER: Arrange carrots horizontally in feed tube. Grate, using medium pressure. Arrange over parsley. Grate radishes, using medium pressure. Arrange over carrots.

SLICER: Slice green peppers, using medium pressure. Arrange over radishes. Slice onions, using medium pressure. Arrange over peppers.

SLICER OR GRATER: Slice or grate cucumber, using medium pressure. Wrap in several layers of paper towels and dry very well. Arrange over onions. Wipe bowl dry before grating cheese. Grate cheese, using medium pressure. Sprinkle over cucumber. Cover with plastic wrap and refrigerate up to 24 hours.

To serve, do not mix the salad! Use long-handled salad servers so each person can taste all the layers. Serve with your favorite salad dressing (e.g., Balsamic Vinaigrette, page 287; Best Vinaigrette, page 287; Green Goddess Salad Dressing, page 291).

64 calories per serving (without dressing), 8.9 g carbohydrates, 2.6 g fiber, 5 g protein, 1.3 g fat (0.7 g saturated fat), 3 mg cholesterol, 114 mg sodium, 329 mg potassium, 1 mg iron, 95 mg calcium, 110 mg phosphorus

### variation

Layer sliced hard-cooked eggs, sliced olives, grated broccoli stems, drained chickpeas or kidney beans—use your imagination!

# SALAD NIÇOISE

DIJON VINAIGRETTE

This composed salad is my adaptation of a classic recipe that Judge Robert Carr of Winnipeg shared with me. He uses fresh tuna, but canned tuna makes for an easy alternative. Prepare everything in advance and assemble just before serving. Delicious? You be the judge!

2 cloves garlic

2 cups flat-leaf parsley, loosely packed

¾ cup mixture of tarragon and chervil leaves, loosely packed

1 cup plus 2 Tbsp extra-virgin olive oil

3 Tbsp cider vinegar

1 Tbsp Dijon mustard

salt and pepper to taste

STEEL BLADE: Drop garlic through feed tube while machine is running. Process until minced. Add parsley, tarragon and chervil; process until minced. Scrape down sides of bowl, add remaining dressing ingredients and process until blended, about 10 seconds. Refrigerate in a covered container.

70 calories per Tbsp (dressing only), 0.5 g carbohydrates, 0.1 g fiber, 0 g protein, 7.4 g fat (1 g saturated fat), 0 mg cholesterol, 13 mg sodium, 31 mg potassium, 0 mg iron, 9 mg calcium, 3 mg phosphorus

Yield: 8 to 10 main dish
servings. Recipe can be
halved easily. Vinaigrette
keeps about a week in
the refrigerator and can
be used on any salad of
your choice.

SALAD

½ red bell pepper, halved and seeded

½ yellow bell pepper, halved and seeded

1 medium sweet onion, halved

1 lb (500 g) green beans, trimmed

1 lb (500 g) yellow beans, trimmed

2 lb (1 kg) tiny new potatoes, well scrubbed

4 cans (6 oz/170 g each) solid white tuna, drained

1 can anchovy fillets, drained (optional)

4 or 5 hard-cooked eggs, quartered

6 medium red and yellow tomatoes, quartered

1 cup olives (niçoise or kalamata)

SLICER: Slice peppers, using medium pressure. Slice onion, using light pressure. Transfer to a large bowl.

Steam green beans and yellow beans over boiling water until tender-crisp, about 6 minutes. (Do this in batches if necessary.) Rinse under ice-cold water to stop cooking and preserve the color. Pat dry. Add to sliced peppers and onion along with one-third of dressing. Toss together and set aside.

Boil unpeeled potatoes in salted water until tender, about 15 minutes. Drain and cool slightly (if in a hurry, refrigerate for 15 minutes). Peel if desired. Cut each potato in half. Combine warm potatoes with one-third of dressing. Toss together and set aside.

Break tuna into large flakes and drizzle with 3 to 4 Tbsp dressing. Set aside.

Shortly before serving time, arrange beans and peppers in mounds on 2 serving platters. Top with drained anchovy fillets (if using), making an attractive design. Place egg and tomato wedges around beans and peppers. Drizzle with 2 to 3 Tbsp vinaigrette. Arrange potatoes and tuna in separate mounds on each platter. Scatter olives on top. Drizzle with remaining vinaigrette. Serve immediately.

656 calories per serving (salad with dressing), 46.9 g carbohydrates, 9 g fiber, 31 g protein, 39.4 g fat (6.3 g saturated fat), 142 mg cholesterol, 576 mg sodium, 1410 mg potassium, 6 mg iron, 158 mg calcium, 437 mg phosphorus

# ASIAN LUNCHEON SALAD

Easy and elegant.

Yield: 6 servings

2 stalks celery

4 green onions

1 can (8 oz/250 mL) water chestnuts, drained

¼ Spanish, Vidalia or sweet red onion

1 head lettuce, torn into bite-sized pieces

2 cups bean sprouts or broccoli sprouts

2 cans (6 oz/170 g each) solid white tuna, drained and flaked

½ cup mayonnaise (light or regular)

¼ cup red wine vinegar

¼ cup corn syrup or honey

1 Tbsp soy sauce (low-sodium or regular)

½ tsp ground ginger (or 1 tsp minced fresh ginger)

1 tsp toasted sesame oil

1 cup chow mein noodles, for garnish

SLICER: Cut celery and green onions to fit feed tube. Pack green onions in between celery. Arrange in an upright position in feed tube. Slice, using medium pressure. Slice water chestnuts, using firm pressure. Slice onion, using light pressure. Empty bowl as necessary.

Line a platter or individual serving plates with lettuce. Arrange sliced vegetables and sprouts attractively over the lettuce. Top with tuna. Cover and refrigerate.

STEEL BLADE: Combine mayonnaise, vinegar, syrup or honey, soy sauce, ginger and sesame oil. Process just until blended. (Can be prepared in advance and refrigerated.) At serving time, drizzle dressing over salad; garnish with chow mein noodles.

241 calories per serving, 24.5 g carbohydrates, 3.2 g fiber, 16 g protein, 9.4 g fat (1.7 g saturated fat), 31 mg cholesterol, 476 mg sodium, 450 mg potassium, 2 mg iron, 48 mg calcium, 189 mg phosphorus

### variation

Replace chow mein noodles with ⅓ cup toasted sesame seeds or ½ cup toasted slivered almonds.

# ASIAN SPINACH SALAD

So colorful; so many options.

Yield: 6 to 8 servings.

1 pkg (10 oz/300 g) fresh spinach (or baby spinach can be substituted)

Asian Salad Dressing (page 292)

1 red and 1 yellow bell pepper, quartered

4 green onions

½ cup radishes

2 carrots

2 cups bean sprouts or broccoli sprouts

salt and freshly ground black pepper

½ cup toasted slivered almonds

2 Tbsp toasted sesame seeds

Trim tough stems from spinach leaves. Wash and dry thoroughly. Tear into bite-sized pieces if using large spinach leaves. Place in large bowl. Prepare salad dressing as directed and set aside.

SLICER: Slice bell peppers, green onions and radishes, using medium pressure. Add to spinach.

GRATER: Grate carrots, using medium pressure. Add to spinach along with sprouts. (Vegetables and dressing can be prepared in advance and refrigerated separately for several hours.)

At serving time, combine vegetables with dressing and mix gently. Season with salt and pepper. Sprinkle with almonds and sesame seeds. Serve immediately.

230 calories per serving, 19.8 g carbohydrates, 3.8 g fiber, 5 g protein, 16 g fat (1.4 g saturated fat), 0 mg cholesterol, 419 mg sodium, 560 mg potassium, 3 mg iron, 81 mg calcium, 80 mg phosphorus

## variations

Add sliced water chestnuts, bamboo shoots, baby corn, snow peas and/or mandarin oranges. For a main dish salad, top with slices of cooked chicken breast.

# RASPBERRY SPINACH SALAD

This crunchy salad comes from Lisa Kaufman of Toronto. She uses raspberries but sliced strawberries are a delicious alternative.

Yield: 6 servings.

½ cup slivered almonds
½ cup sugar, divided
2 tsp water
¼ small onion (about 1 Tbsp)
2 tsp poppy seeds
¼ tsp paprika

½ cup canola oil
¼ cup raspberry or balsamic vinegar
¼ tsp Worcestershire sauce
1 lb (500 g) fresh spinach, baby spinach or mixed salad greens (mesclun)
2 cups fresh raspberries

In a heavy skillet, combine almonds with ¼ cup of the sugar and the water. Stir over medium heat until sugar melts and coats the almonds. Set aside to cool; break into small pieces.

STEEL BLADE: Process onion until minced. Add remaining ¼ cup sugar, poppy seeds, paprika, oil, vinegar and Worcestershire sauce; process for 10 to 12 seconds. (Can be made ahead and refrigerated.)

Wash and dry greens. If using large spinach leaves, remove stems. At serving time, gently toss dressing with greens. Transfer to a serving platter or bowl. Sprinkle with raspberries and almonds.

329 calories per serving, 28.5 g carbohydrates, 5.5 g fiber, 5 g protein, 23.4 g fat (1.8 g saturated fat), 0 mg cholesterol, 65 mg sodium, 565 mg potassium, 3 mg iron, 123 mg calcium, 98 mg phosphorus

## GREEK SALAD

In Detroit, cut-up cooked beets are added to Greek Salad!

Yield: 8 servings.

2 heads romaine lettuce

1 red onion or ¼ Spanish onion

1 red and 1 green bell pepper, halved

3 mini seedless cucumbers (or ½ English cucumber)

2 cups cherry or grape tomatoes or 2 large ripe tomatoes, cut in wedges

2 dozen black olives

½ lb (250 g) feta cheese

1 large clove garlic

½ cup extra-virgin olive oil

juice of 1 lemon (3 Tbsp)

½ tsp dry mustard

½ tsp dried oregano

salt and freshly ground black pepper to taste

1 can flat anchovies, drained

Wash lettuce; dry well. Tear into bite-sized pieces and place in large salad bowl.

SLICER: Slice onion, peppers and cucumbers, using medium pressure. Pat dry with paper towels. Add to salad bowl along with tomatoes and olives, reserving a few olives for garnishing.

STEEL BLADE: Process feta cheese with quick on/offs, until crumbled. Add to salad. Wipe out processor bowl and blade with paper towels.

Drop garlic through feed tube while machine is running; process until minced. Add oil, lemon juice, mustard and oregano. Process for a few seconds to blend. (Can be prepared in advance up to this point and refrigerated until serving time.)

Pour dressing over salad. Season lightly with salt and pepper and toss well. Arrange anchovies like the spokes of a wheel on top of salad. Place reserved olives between anchovies.

280 calories per serving, 12.9 g carbohydrates, 5.1 g fiber, 9 g protein, 22.7 g fat (6.6 g saturated fat), 30 mg cholesterol, 654 mg sodium, 639 mg potassium, 3 mg iron, 231 mg calcium, 182 mg phosphorus

## PESTO PASTA SALAD

I love to combine pesto with pasta. It's the best!

Yield: 8 servings.

Keeps 2 or 3 days in the refrigerator.

1 pkg (12 oz/375 g) fusilli or penne (about 4 cups cooked)

¾ cup sun-dried tomatoes

¼ cup fresh parsley

6 green onions

1 red and 1 yellow bell pepper, quartered

½ cup light or regular mayonnaise (approximately)

¼ to ⅓ cup Pesto (page 105)

¼ cup grated Parmesan cheese

salt and freshly ground black pepper to taste

Cook pasta in boiling salted water according to package directions; drain well. Place in large bowl. Cover sun-dried tomatoes with boiling water; soak for 10 minutes. (If using sun-dried tomatoes packed in oil, drain well.)

SUPER SALADS AND DRESSINGS

STEEL BLADE: Process parsley until minced, about 10 seconds. Add drained sun-dried tomatoes and process with quick on/off pulses, until coarsely chopped. (No need to empty the work bowl.)

SLICER: Slice green onions and peppers, using light pressure. Combine all ingredients with pasta and mix well. Adjust seasonings to taste. Chill before serving.

287 calories per serving, 38.5 g carbohydrates, 3.1 g fiber, 9 g protein, 11.4 g fat (2.6 g saturated fat), 10 mg cholesterol, 232 mg sodium, 354 mg potassium, 2 mg iron, 110 mg calcium, 138 mg phosphorus

## BEV'S COLORFUL COUSCOUS SALAD

This nutritious, delicious salad from my friend Bev Binder of Winnipeg is an excellent vegetarian dish for a buffet and can be made in advance.

Yield: 12 servings. Leftovers keep for 4 or 5 days in the refrigerator.

1½ cups vegetable broth (low-sodium or regular)
1 cup couscous
1 can (19 oz/540 mL) chickpeas, drained and rinsed
½ cup fresh parsley
¾ to 1 cup dried apricots
½ cup pitted prunes
½ cup dried cranberries
½ cup raisins
1 small red onion, cut in chunks
1 red bell pepper, cut in chunks
1 medium zucchini, cut in chunks

2 cloves garlic
1 slice fresh ginger (1 Tbsp minced) (optional)
⅓ cup extra-virgin olive oil or canola oil
3 Tbsp lemon juice
3 Tbsp orange juice
1 tsp ground cumin
1 tsp curry powder
salt and freshly ground black pepper to taste
½ cup toasted slivered almonds, for garnish

Combine broth with couscous in a large bowl. Cover and let stand 5 to 10 minutes, then stir with a fork. Add chickpeas.

STEEL BLADE: Process parsley until minced, about 10 seconds. Add apricots, prunes, cranberries and raisins and process with quick on/off pulses, until coarsely chopped. Add to couscous. Process onion, bell pepper and zucchini with quick on/off pulses, until coarsely chopped. Add to couscous mixture.

Drop garlic and ginger (if using) through feed tube while machine is running; process until minced. Add remaining ingredients, except almonds, and process until blended. Pour dressing over couscous mixture and mix well. Adjust seasonings to taste. Garnish with toasted almonds at serving time.

245 calories per serving, 41.8 g carbohydrates, 4.9 g fiber, 5 g protein, 7.1 g fat (1 g saturated fat), 0 mg cholesterol, 146 mg sodium, 391 mg potassium, 2 mg iron, 37 mg calcium, 85 mg phosphorus

*Continued*

- Add other dried fruits such as dates, figs, dried cherries, etc. Toasted sesame or sunflower seeds also make a nice garnish.

### passover variation

Substitute 1½ cups quinoa for couscous. Place in a fine strainer and rinse thoroughly under cold running water. Cook in 3 cups vegetable broth for 15 minutes. Remove from heat and let stand, covered, for 5 minutes. Uncover and fluff with a fork. Cool completely. Omit chickpeas, cumin and curry powder. Combine quinoa with remaining ingredients and mix well. One serving contains 223 calories, 35.5 g carbohydrates, 3.8 g fiber and 43 g sodium.

## QUICK COUSCOUS SALAD

So versatile, so easy!

Yield: 6 servings.
Keeps up to 3 days in the refrigerator.

1½ **cups couscous**
2¼ **cups water or chicken or vegetable broth**
2 **cloves garlic**
¼ **cup fresh parsley**
1 **red and 1 yellow bell pepper, cut in chunks**
4 **green onions, cut in 2-inch pieces**

2 **carrots**
2 **Tbsp extra-virgin olive oil**
3 **Tbsp lemon juice**
**salt and freshly ground black pepper to taste**
½ **tsp each chili powder, dry mustard and ground cumin**

In a large mixing bowl, combine couscous with water or broth. Cover and let stand for 10 minutes to absorb liquid. Fluff with a fork.

STEEL BLADE: Drop garlic and parsley through feed tube while machine is running; process until minced. Add bell peppers and green onions; process with quick on/off pulses, until coarsely chopped. Add to couscous.

GRATER: Grate carrots, using medium pressure. Add to couscous along with remaining ingredients. Adjust seasonings to taste. Cover and refrigerate.

238 calories per serving, 40.7 g carbohydrates, 4 g fiber, 7 g protein, 5.3 g fat (0.7 g saturated fat), 0 mg cholesterol, 30 mg sodium, 304 mg potassium, 1 mg iron, 41 mg calcium, 101 mg phosphorus

### variations

- To turn this into a main dish, add 2 cups of cooked chicken, cut in chunks.
- For a vegetarian main dish, add a can of drained chickpeas or kidney beans.
- Replace chili powder, mustard and cumin with ¼ cup each of chopped sun-dried tomatoes, minced fresh basil and parsley, if desired.

# CRANBERRY QUINOA SALAD

Quinoa (KEEN-wah) has a somewhat nutty flavor and is very high in protein. It's an excellent alternative to rice or couscous in salads and pilafs and is ideal for Passover.

Yield: 8 servings. Keeps 2 days in the refrigerator.

3 cups vegetable or chicken broth (low-sodium or regular)
1½ cups quinoa
½ cup fresh parsley or mint
¼ cup fresh basil (or 1 tsp dried)
1 medium red onion, cut in chunks
1 red bell pepper, cut in chunks
1 yellow or green bell pepper, cut in chunks

2 stalks celery, cut in chunks
¾ to 1 cup dried cranberries
2 cloves garlic
1 slice fresh ginger, peeled (or 1 Tbsp frozen or bottled minced ginger)
¼ cup extra-virgin olive oil
2 Tbsp orange juice
2 Tbsp honey
salt and pepper to taste

Bring broth to a boil in a medium saucepan over high heat. Place quinoa in a fine-mesh strainer and rinse under cold running water for 1 to 2 minutes, until water runs clear. Drain well. (Rinsing removes the bitter coating.)

Add quinoa to boiling liquid. Reduce heat to low and simmer, covered, for 15 minutes, until liquid is absorbed. Don't overcook. Remove from heat and let stand, covered, for 5 minutes. Fluff with a fork, transfer to a large bowl and let cool. (Can be done in advance.)

STEEL BLADE: Process parsley and basil until minced. Process onion, bell peppers and celery (in batches if necessary) with quick on/off pulses, until coarsely chopped. Add herbs, vegetables and cranberries to quinoa.

STEEL BLADE: Drop garlic and ginger through feed tube while machine is running. Process until minced. Add oil, orange juice and honey and process briefly to combine. Pour over quinoa mixture and mix well. Season with salt and pepper. Chill for up to 24 hours before serving.

261 calories per serving, 40.2 g carbohydrates, 4.1 g fiber, 5 g protein, 9.1 g fat (1.2 g saturated fat), 0 mg cholesterol, 66 mg sodium, 348 mg potassium, 2 mg iron, 43 mg calcium, 167 mg phosphorus

## variations

- Add 1 cup chopped mango or dried apricots. Instead of orange juice, use pomegranate, cranberry or mango juice.
- For an Asian twist, add 2 Tbsp soy sauce and 1 tsp toasted sesame oil. If desired, add sliced water chestnuts, bamboo shoots, edamame and/or toasted slivered almonds.
- Using Your Grain: Instead of quinoa, substitute 3 cups of cooked couscous, bulgur, rice or wheat berries.

*Continued*

# MEDITERRANEAN QUINOA SALAD

You can make this refreshing salad with other grains such as couscous or rice instead of quinoa, but not for Passover. To keep it dairy-free, just omit the feta cheese.

Yield: 8 servings.
Keeps 1 to 2 days in the refrigerator.

3 cups water or vegetable broth (low-sodium or regular)
1½ cups quinoa
2 cloves garlic
¼ cup fresh parsley or coriander
2 Tbsp fresh basil
2 Tbsp fresh dill
½ red onion, cut in chunks (or 4 green onions)
1 red bell pepper, cut in chunks

2 or 3 mini English cucumbers (or ½ English cucumber), cut in chunks
24 cherry tomatoes, halved
½ to ¾ cup sliced black olives
3 Tbsp extra-virgin olive oil
3 Tbsp lemon juice
salt and pepper to taste
½ cup crumbled feta cheese

Bring broth to a boil in a medium saucepan over high heat. Place quinoa in a fine-mesh strainer and rinse under cold running water for 1 to 2 minutes, until water runs clear. (Rinsing removes the bitter coating.) Drain well.

Add quinoa to boiling liquid. Reduce heat to low and simmer, covered, for 15 minutes, until liquid is absorbed. Don't overcook. Remove from heat and let stand, covered, for 5 minutes. Fluff with a fork, transfer to a large bowl and let cool. (Can be done in advance.)

STEEL BLADE: With machine running, drop garlic through feed tube and process until minced. Add parsley, basil and dill; process until minced.

SLICER or FRENCH FRY DISC: Slice onion, bell pepper and cucumber chunks, using light pressure. Pat dry with paper towels. Add to quinoa along with tomatoes, olives, oil and lemon juice. Mix gently to combine. Season with salt and pepper to taste. Crumble feta cheese overtop; cover and chill before serving.

232 calories per serving, 28.2 g carbohydrates, 4 g fiber, 7 g protein, 10.3 g fat (2.5 g saturated fat), 8 mg cholesterol, 237 mg sodium, 410 mg potassium, 2 mg iron, 94 mg calcium, 205 mg phosphorus

# TABBOULEH SALAD

This nutritious Middle Eastern salad is packed with vitamins, minerals and flavor. For best results, dry parsley and mint thoroughly before chopping them in the processor. Save the parsley stems and use them when making chicken or vegetable broth.

Yield: 6 servings. Leftovers will keep for 1 or 2 days in the refrigerator.

| | |
|---|---|
| ½ cup bulgur (cracked wheat) | 4 firm, ripe tomatoes, cored and |
| 2 cups boiling water | quartered |
| 1 large bunch flat-leaf parsley (about | 4 green onions, cut in chunks |
| 1 cup chopped) | ¼ cup extra-virgin olive oil |
| 1 small bunch mint (about ¼ cup | ¼ cup fresh lemon juice |
| chopped) | salt and freshly ground black pepper |
| | to taste |

In a medium bowl, soak bulgur in boiling water for 15 minutes. Drain in a fine mesh strainer. Soak parsley and mint in cold, salted water for 10 minutes. Drain and dry well. Trim stems from parsley and mint.

STEEL BLADE: Process tomatoes with on/off pulses, until coarsely chopped. Place in a large bowl. Add drained bulgur to tomatoes. Wipe processor bowl dry with paper towels. Process parsley with mint until finely minced. Add green onions and process with on/off pulses, until chopped. Add to bulgur mixture along with remaining ingredients and mix gently. Refrigerate at least 1 hour before serving. Serve chilled.

156 calories per serving, 15.3 g carbohydrates, 3.4 g fiber, 3 g protein, 9.8 g fat (1.3 g saturated fat), 0 mg cholesterol, 112 mg sodium, 297 mg potassium, 2 mg iron, 35 mg calcium, 31 mg phosphorus

## variations

For a grain-based tabbouleh, increase bulgur to 1 cup. If you prefer a greener tabbouleh, use only ¼ to ⅓ cup bulgur. Couscous can be substituted for the bulgur, or you can replace the soaked bulgur with 1 cup cooked quinoa. If desired, add ½ cup sliced olives and sprinkle with feta cheese.

# CHICKPEA BROCCOLI SALAD

An ideal way to use up broccoli stems!

Yield: 6 servings. Leftovers keep for 2 to 3 days (add additional seasonings).

| | |
|---|---|
| 4 green onions, cut in chunks | ¼ cup extra-virgin olive oil |
| ¼ cup fresh parsley | 3 Tbsp honey (or to taste) |
| 2 or 3 carrots | 3 Tbsp lemon juice or rice vinegar |
| 4 thick broccoli stems, peeled | ½ tsp each dried basil and dried thyme |
| (reserve florets for another time) | salt and freshly ground black pepper |
| 1 can (19 oz/540 mL) chickpeas, | to taste |
| drained and rinsed | |

STEEL BLADE: Chop green onions and parsley with quick on/off pulses.

GRATER: Grate carrots and broccoli stems, using medium pressure. Transfer to a mixing bowl. Add remaining ingredients and mix well. Refrigerate before serving.

247 calories per serving, 34.2 g carbohydrates, 6.8 g fiber, 7 g protein, 10.6 g fat (1.5 g saturated fat), 0 mg cholesterol, 277 mg sodium, 509 mg potassium, 2 mg iron, 83 mg calcium, 136 mg phosphorus

## ITALIAN SALAD DRESSING

Easy to prepare in a mini-prep. Why not double the recipe and make it in a regular processor?

Yield: About 1¼ cups. Store in a tightly closed jar in the refrigerator. Keeps about 1 month. Shake before using.

1 or 2 cloves garlic
1 cup extra-virgin olive oil
  or canola oil
¼ cup red wine vinegar
1 Tbsp lemon juice
1¼ tsp salt (or to taste)

½ tsp dry mustard
¼ tsp dried oregano
¼ tsp sugar or honey
freshly ground black pepper to taste
pinch dried thyme and dried dill

STEEL BLADE: Drop garlic through feed tube while machine is running; process until minced. (If using a mini-prep, process garlic directly in bowl.) Scrape down sides of bowl, add remaining ingredients and process until blended, about 5 seconds.

98 calories per Tbsp, 0.2 g carbohydrates, 0 g fiber, 0 g protein, 10.8 g fat (1.5 g saturated fat), 0 mg cholesterol, 140 mg sodium, 3 mg potassium, 0 mg iron, 1 mg calcium, 1 mg phosphorus

## LIGHT AND EASY ITALIAN DRESSING

This can also be prepared easily in a mini-prep.

Yield: 1 cup. Store in a covered container in the refrigerator. Keeps about 1 month. Shake before using.

¼ cup sweet onion (e.g., Vidalia or
  Spanish)
1 clove garlic
¼ cup extra-virgin olive oil
¼ cup water
¼ cup lemon juice
1 to 2 Tbsp honey (or to taste)

1 tsp Dijon mustard
½ tsp salt
freshly ground black pepper to taste
½ tsp each dried oregano and dried
  basil
¼ tsp paprika

STEEL BLADE: Drop onion and garlic through feed tube while machine is running; process until minced. (If using a mini-prep, process onion and garlic directly in bowl.) Add remaining ingredients and process until blended, about 10 seconds.

37 calories per Tbsp, 1.7 g carbohydrates, 0.1 g fiber, 0 g protein, 3.4 g fat (0.5 g saturated fat), 0 mg cholesterol, 77 mg sodium, 11 mg potassium, 0 mg iron, 2 mg calcium, 2 mg phosphorus

## BEST VINAIGRETTE DRESSING

You can make this one quickly too in a mini-prep. For Passover, do not use canola oil.

1 clove garlic
3 Tbsp fresh parsley
2 Tbsp fresh basil (or ½ tsp dried basil)

¾ cup extra-virgin olive oil or canola oil
¼ cup red wine vinegar
½ tsp salt
¼ tsp freshly ground black pepper

Yield: About 1 cup. Keeps about 10 days. Shake before using.

STEEL BLADE: Drop garlic, parsley and basil through feed tube while machine is running; process until minced. (If using a mini-prep, process garlic, parsley and basil directly in bowl.) Add remaining ingredients and process until blended. Refrigerate.

92 calories per Tbsp, 0.1 g carbohydrates, 0 g fiber, 0 g protein, 10.1 g fat (1.4 g saturated fat), 0 mg cholesterol, 70 mg sodium, 7 mg potassium, 0 mg iron, 2 mg calcium, 1 mg phosphorus

## BALSAMIC VINAIGRETTE

This is wonderful on salad greens or roasted vegetables, or as a marinade for chicken or salmon. You can process all the ingredients in a mini-prep.

2 cloves garlic
2 Tbsp fresh parsley
⅔ cup extra-virgin olive oil
⅓ cup balsamic vinegar
2 to 3 Tbsp honey (or to taste)

2 Tbsp orange juice
salt and freshly ground black pepper to taste
¼ tsp each dried basil and dried thyme

Yield: 1¼ cups. Refrigerate for up to 2 weeks. Shake before using.

STEEL BLADE: Drop garlic and parsley through feed tube while machine is running; process until minced. (If using a mini-prep, process garlic and parsley directly in bowl.) Add remaining ingredients and process for 8 to 10 seconds to blend.

73 calories per Tbsp, 2.5 g carbohydrates, 0 g fiber, 0 g protein, 7 g fat (1 g saturated fat), 0 mg cholesterol, 1 mg sodium, 12 mg potassium, 0 mg iron, 3 mg calcium, 2 mg phosphorus

## SWEET AND SPICY FRENCH DRESSING

Yield: About 2¾ cups. Keeps about 2 months in the refrigerator in a tightly closed jar.

2 cloves garlic

½ cup sugar

1½ tsp salt (or to taste)

½ tsp dry mustard

½ tsp paprika

1½ cups canola oil

½ cup vinegar

½ cup ketchup

½ tsp Worcestershire sauce

STEEL BLADE: Drop garlic through feed tube while machine is running; process until minced. Scrape down sides of bowl. Add remaining ingredients and process until blended and creamy, 25 to 30 seconds.

76 calories per Tbsp, 2.9 g carbohydrates, 0 g fiber, 0 g protein, 7.3 g fat (0.5 g saturated fat), 0 mg cholesterol, 105 mg sodium, 12 mg potassium, 0 mg iron, 1 mg calcium, 1 mg phosphorus

## SWEET VIDALIA ONION DRESSING

Try this on pasta, vegetable salads or coleslaw, or as a marinade for chicken or fish.

1 large Vidalia onion (or 1 lb/500 g mild, sweet onions)

½ cup canola oil

¾ cup white vinegar

¾ to 1 cup sugar

1 Tbsp dry mustard

1 tsp salt (or to taste)

1 tsp celery seed (or to taste)

½ tsp garlic powder

freshly ground black pepper to taste

Yield: 3 cups. Store in a jar in the refrigerator for up to 2 weeks.

Cut off a small piece (about 1 to 2 Tbsp) from 1 end of onion and reserve. Pierce skin of remaining onion in several places with a sharp knife. Place cut side down in a microwavable bowl. Microwave on High 5 to 6 minutes, until soft. Let cool; discard peel.

STEEL BLADE: Peel reserved onion piece. Process raw onion with cooked onion until puréed, 10 to 12 seconds. You should have about 1½ cups purée. Add remaining ingredients and process a few seconds longer, until blended, scraping down sides of bowl as needed. Chill before serving.

35 calories per Tbsp, 3.6 g carbohydrates, 0.1 g fiber, 0 g protein, 2.2 g fat (0.2 g saturated fat), 0 mg cholesterol, 45 mg sodium, 10 mg potassium, 0 mg iron, 3 mg calcium, 2 mg phosphorus

# FRESH TOMATO DRESSING

Light and easy! Use ripe, juicy tomatoes for best results.

Yield: 1 cup. Keeps for a day or 2 in the refrigerator.

1 clove garlic

2 ripe tomatoes, cut in chunks

¼ cup fresh basil

2 Tbsp extra-virgin olive oil

salt and freshly ground black pepper to taste

pinch sugar

STEEL BLADE: Drop garlic through feed tube while machine is running; process until minced. Add tomatoes and basil and process until finely chopped. Drizzle oil through the feed tube while machine is running; process until blended. Season with salt, pepper and sugar.

16 calories per Tbsp, 0.6 g carbohydrates, 0.2 g fiber, 0 g protein, 1.5 g fat (0.2 g saturated fat), 0 mg cholesterol, 1 mg sodium, 33 mg potassium, 0 mg iron, 3 mg calcium, 4 mg phosphorus

# RUSSIAN SALAD DRESSING

Yield: About 1⅓ cups. Keeps about 1 week in a tightly covered container in the refrigerator.

1 cup Mayonnaise (page 111) or Tofu Mayonnaise (page 112)

¼ small onion

2 Tbsp chives or green onions

⅓ cup chili sauce or ketchup

STEEL BLADE: Prepare mayonnaise as directed. Drop onion through feed tube while machine is running; process until minced. Add remaining ingredients and process until combined.

81 calories per Tbsp, 1.3 g carbohydrates, 0 g fiber, 0 g protein, 8.5 g fat (0.7 g saturated fat), 15 mg cholesterol, 74 mg sodium, 4 mg potassium, 0 mg iron, 2 mg calcium, 6 mg phosphorus

### thousand island dressing

Add 3 Tbsp relish or 2 small minced gherkins.

# CREAMY DILL SALAD DRESSING

Yield: About ⅔ cup. Keeps about 1 week. Recipe may be doubled.

1 or 2 cloves garlic (or ¼ tsp garlic powder)

2 Tbsp fresh dill (or ½ tsp dried dill)

½ cup mayonnaise (light or regular)

3 Tbsp vinegar

salt and freshly ground black pepper to taste

STEEL BLADE: Drop garlic and dill through feed tube while machine is running; process until minced. Add remaining ingredients and process until blended, about 5 seconds. Refrigerate.

*Continued*

36 calories per Tbsp, 1 g carbohydrates, 0 g fiber, 0 g protein, 3.5 g fat (0.6 g saturated fat), 4 mg cholesterol, 72 mg sodium, 6 mg potassium, 0 mg iron, 2 mg calcium, 4 mg phosphorus

## CREAMY GARLIC DRESSING

Yield: About 1¼ cups.
Keeps 4 to 5 days in the refrigerator.

**2 cloves garlic**

**2 Tbsp fresh parsley (or 1 tsp dried parsley)**

**1 cup 1% cottage cheese**

**¼ cup buttermilk**

**2 Tbsp white vinegar**

**salt and freshly ground black pepper to taste**

**pinch dried tarragon**

STEEL BLADE: Drop garlic and parsley through feed tube; process until minced. Add remaining ingredients and process until smooth and creamy, about 30 seconds, scraping down bowl once or twice. Refrigerate.

9 calories per Tbsp, 0.5 g carbohydrates, 0 g fiber, 1.4 g protein, 0.1 g fat (0.1 g saturated fat), 1 mg cholesterol, 45 mg sodium, 16 mg potassium, 0 mg iron, 11 mg calcium, 17 mg phosphorus

## MARTY'S GARLIC CHEESE DRESSING

The verdict's in—this creamy, garlicky dressing from Toronto lawyer Marty Kaplan is a winner!

Yield: About 2 cups.
Keeps about 2 weeks in the refrigerator. If too thick, thin with a little water.

**3 or 4 large cloves garlic**

**4 oz (125 g) chilled low-fat mozzarella or brick cheese**

**2 to 4 Tbsp grated Parmesan cheese**

**1 cup extra-virgin olive oil or canola oil**

**½ cup red wine vinegar**

**1 tsp lemon juice**

**½ tsp Worcestershire sauce**

**½ tsp Italian seasoning**

**salt to taste**

**freshly ground black pepper (or mixed peppercorns) to taste**

STEEL BLADE: Drop garlic through feed tube while machine is running; process until minced. Cut mozzarella or brick cheese in 1-inch chunks. Process until finely chopped, 20 to 25 seconds. Add remaining ingredients and process until combined, about 15 seconds longer.

Store in a jar in the refrigerator. Wait a few hours before serving to allow flavors to blend. Shake very well before serving.

72 calories per Tbsp, 0.3 g carbohydrates, 0.1 g fiber, 1 g protein, 7.3 g fat (1.1 g saturated fat), 2 mg cholesterol, 31 mg sodium, 4 mg potassium, 0 mg iron, 35 mg calcium, 3 mg phosphorus

## GREEN GODDESS SALAD DRESSING OR DIP

Yield: 1½ cups. Keeps about 10 days in the refrigerator.

1 or 2 cloves garlic
4 green onions, cut in chunks
¼ cup fresh parsley
1 can anchovies, drained
½ cup sour cream or yogurt (light or regular)

½ cup mayonnaise (light or regular)
3 Tbsp white wine vinegar
2 to 3 Tbsp lemon juice
freshly ground black pepper to taste

STEEL BLADE: Drop garlic through feed tube while machine is running; process until minced. Add green onions, parsley and anchovies. Process until minced. Add remaining ingredients and process until blended, scraping down sides of bowl once or twice. Refrigerate.

23 calories per Tbsp, 0.9 g carbohydrates, 0.1 g fiber, 1 g protein, 1.9 g fat (0.5 g saturated fat), 4 mg cholesterol, 87 mg sodium, 29 mg potassium, 0 mg iron, 12 mg calcium, 10 mg phosphorus

## LOW-FAT RANCH DRESSING

Yield: 1 cup. Keeps for 5 or 6 days in the refrigerator.

½ cup light mayonnaise
¼ cup skim milk
¼ cup fat-free or low-fat yogurt
2 tsp white vinegar

1 tsp Dijon mustard
1 tsp honey
½ tsp dried basil

STEEL BLADE: Process all ingredients until blended, about 10 seconds.

27 calories per Tbsp, 1.4 g carbohydrates, 0 g fiber, 0 g protein, 2.3 g fat (0.4 g saturated fat), 3 mg cholesterol, 58 mg sodium, 19 mg potassium, 0 mg iron, 11 mg calcium, 11 mg phosphorus

## YUMMY YOGURT SALAD DRESSING

Yield: 1¼ cups. Keeps about 10 days in a tightly covered container in the refrigerator.

½ small onion
2 Tbsp fresh parsley (or 2 tsp dried parsley)
1 cup yogurt (fat-free or low-fat)
2 to 3 Tbsp canola oil
1 Tbsp white vinegar

½ tsp salt
¼ tsp each dried oregano, dried basil and garlic powder
dash freshly ground black pepper
pinch dried tarragon

STEEL BLADE: Process onion with parsley until minced. Add remaining ingredients and process about 10 seconds longer. Chill for 1 hour before serving to blend flavors.

*Continued*

19 calories per Tbsp, 1.1 g carbohydrates, 0.1 g fiber, 1 g protein, 1.3 g fat (0.1 g saturated fat), 0 mg cholesterol, 66 mg sodium, 39 mg potassium, 0 mg iron, 20 mg calcium, 17 mg phosphorus

### variations

Omit dried tarragon and dried basil. Add 2 Tbsp fresh basil and/or dill. Add 2 Tbsp chili sauce or ketchup, if desired.

## ASIAN SALAD DRESSING

Use this on spinach, mixed greens or coleslaw.

Yield: 1¼ cups. Keeps about a month in the refrigerator.

2 cloves garlic
½ cup rice vinegar
¼ cup canola oil
¼ cup soy sauce (low-sodium or regular)

2 Tbsp toasted sesame oil
3 to 4 Tbsp honey (or to taste)
2 Tbsp toasted sesame seeds

STEEL BLADE: Drop garlic through feed tube while machine is running; process until minced. Add remaining ingredients and process until blended, about 10 to 15 seconds. Store in a jar in the refrigerator. Shake well before using.

46 calories per Tbsp, 2.6 g carbohydrates, 0.1 g fiber, 0 g protein, 4 g fat (0.3 g saturated fat), 0 mg cholesterol, 91 mg sodium, 7 mg potassium, 0 mg iron, 3 mg calcium, 4 mg phosphorus

# YEAST DOUGHS, QUICK BREADS AND MUFFINS
## recipe list

301 Challah
302 Streusel Topping
302 Challah (Double Recipe for Large Processors)
303 Heavenly Holiday Challah (for 16-Cup Processors)
305 Cranberry or Raisin Challah
306 Crusty French Bread
306 Homemade White Bread
308 Pareve White Bread
309 100% Whole Wheat Bread
310 Old-Fashioned Rye Bread
311 Pumpernickel Bread
312 Wholesome Oatmeal Bread
313 Confetti Bread
314 Pizza Pinwheels
316 Focaccia
317 Potato and Onion Focaccia
317 Pita Bread
318 Bagels
319 Best-Ever Onion Rolls
320 Garlic Buns
321 Bialies
321 All-Purpose Pareve Dough
322 Norene's Yummy Yeast Dough

323 Cinnamon Buns or Kuchen
324 Almond Tea Ring
325 Bubble Ring Coffee Cake
325 Chocolate Babka
326 Decadent Chocolate Glaze
326 Chocolate Shmear
327 Chocolate Danish
328 Brioche
329 Croissants
330 Criss-Cross Buns
331 Stollen
332 I Can't Believe It's Broccoli Bread!
333 Orange Corn Bread
333 Best Banana Bread
334 Nana's Zucchini Bread
335 One-Banana Muffins
335 Mom's Blueberry Muffins
336 Honey Bran Muffins
337 Sugar-Free Bran Muffins
337 Cottage Cheese Muffins
338 Morning Glorious Muffins
339 Fudgy Chocolate Muffins
339 Oatmeal Raisin Muffins
340 Scones

- Although I have a bread machine and a heavy-duty mixer, I love making yeast dough in my food processor. I can make several batches, shaping them any way I like. If I am busy, I can refrigerate the dough for a few hours (or even days), then take it out and continue when I have time.

- Since my first food processor was a 7-cup Cuisinart, my yeast dough recipes were based on approximately 3 cups of flour and made 1 loaf of bread. I always used the **Steel Blade** to mix and knead the dough, with excellent results. I now use a 14-cup model that can make enough dough for 2 loaves at a time.

- Today's models are much more powerful than earlier ones. Many models come with a **Dough Blade** (either plastic or stainless steel). The more powerful, larger models also feature a **Dough Cycle** that works in conjunction with the **Dough Blade** at a slightly reduced speed. These features prevent the dough from over-heating, help preserve nutrients and produce wonderful artisanal-style breads.

- Note: On models that come with nested bowls, the **Dough Blade** can only be used in the large bowl.

- Even if you have an older model that doesn't include a **Dough Cycle** or **Dough Blade**, you can still make excellent breads with your food processor.

- Each yeast dough recipe in this book gives step-by-step instructions for mixing, kneading, rising, shaping and baking. You can convert your favorite yeast recipes for the food processor using the following guidelines, so stop loafing around and let's get started!

- CAPACITY: The recommended maximum amount of flour in a standard (7-cup) processor is 3 to 3¼ cups all-purpose flour or 2½ to 3 cups whole-grain flour. In a large (14-cup) processor, the recommended maximum amount is 6 cups all-purpose flour or 4 cups whole-grain flour (e.g., oats, rye). (Refer to your manual for capacity guidelines.) If your recipe calls for more flour than recommended, divide the recipe in half. Process in batches, then combine the batches and knead together by hand.

- FLOUR POWER: When a recipe calls for flour, use all-purpose flour (preferably unbleached) unless otherwise indicated. Do not use self-rising or pastry flour. I often replace some of the flour with whole wheat flour. Instead of all-purpose flour, you can use bread flour, as it has a higher protein content and gives breads a chewy texture. For rye breads, use light or medium rye flour, and for pumpernickel, use dark rye flour. These and other specialty flours are available from King Arthur Flour and can be ordered online. I especially like their white whole-wheat flour—it looks and tastes like you've used all-purpose white flour.

- As a general guideline when substituting other flours, you can replace up to half the flour called for in a recipe with whole wheat, rye, spelt or other specialty flours.

- The weather will affect the amount of flour you need to add to yeast doughs. When it is hot and humid, you will need to add more flour.

- Vital wheat gluten helps improve the rising and texture of heavier breads, especially those that rise slowly and that are made with rye flour or whole grains. Add 1 tsp for each cup of all-purpose flour and 2 tsp for each cup of whole grain or rye flour.

- YEAST COMES IN SEVERAL FORMS: active dry (also called traditional yeast), instant (also known as fast-rising, rapid rise or bread machine yeast) and fresh cake yeast. Always check the expiry date before using yeast. I buy active dry yeast and instant yeast in a jar rather than individual packages and refrigerate or freeze it for 3 or 4 months.

- YEAST SUBSTITUTION GUIDE: 1 Tbsp active dry yeast = 2½ tsp instant or bread machine yeast = ¾ ounce fresh yeast.

- I like to proof the yeast first (i.e., test if it is good). Dissolve active dry yeast in warm water (105°F to 115°F) with a pinch of sugar or flour. If the yeast is good, it will become foamy and creamy within 10 minutes. Stir to dissolve.

- If using fresh cake yeast, the water should be 85°F. If it is too hot, it will kill the yeast. If it's too cool, the dough will take longer to rise. An instant-read thermometer is an excellent way to ensure that the water is the correct temperature.

- Using instant or bread machine yeast? Instead of dissolving it in warm liquid, add yeast to the dry ingredients in the processor bowl. Combine the total amount of liquid called for in the recipe and heat to 90°F to 100°F; set aside briefly.

- Next, insert the **Dough Blade** and select the **Dough Cycle** if your machine has these features. First press the DOUGH button, then the ON button—otherwise the machine won't start! If your machine does not have a **Dough Blade** and **Dough Cycle**, insert the **Steel Blade** and press the ON button or lever.

- Process the dry ingredients (e.g., flour, salt, sugar, herbs) until mixed, about 10 seconds. If using instant or bread machine yeast, process it with the dry ingredients. If the recipe calls for solid butter or margarine, cut it in chunks and process with the dry ingredients. Increase processing time to 20 seconds. If using oil, add with liquid ingredients.

- Next, add the dissolved yeast mixture to the dry ingredients; process for 10 seconds.

- Combine the liquid ingredients (oil, water/milk, eggs) in a large measuring cup. Always start the food processor before adding liquid. Add liquid through the feed tube in a slow, steady stream directly onto the flour mixture, as fast as the flour can absorb it. Do not pour liquid directly onto the bottom of the work bowl. If the liquid sloshes or splatters, either stop adding it or drizzle it in more slowly.

- Process until the dough gathers together and forms a mass around the blades, 30 to 45 seconds. The dough will pull away from the sides of the bowl and should be slightly sticky. Add nuts, raisins, herbs, etc., a few seconds before you stop processing, or add them when kneading by hand.
- If the dough is too sticky, the motor may slow down, so have ¼ cup flour handy. Dump flour through feed tube while the machine is running and the motor will return to normal speed. If you are worried about adding too much flour, add it a tablespoon or 2 at a time. Sometimes, when the dough is extremely sticky, it may go under the blade and push it up. Simply reinsert the blade, then immediately add 2 Tbsp flour through the feed tube. If the dough is too dry, just add more water, a Tbsp or 2 at a time.
- Transfer the dough to a lightly floured surface and let it rest briefly while you wash the bowl and blade. Be careful—the blade is very sharp! See technique described in "Self-Cleaning Processor" (page 7).
- Technical difficulties? If the motor stops while kneading the dough, turn the machine off and let it cool down for 10 to 15 minutes. Excessive strain may have caused the motor to overheat. Divide the dough into 2 batches and process each batch until well kneaded.
- On Cuisinart Elite models, if the large pusher moves when processing dough or other heavy loads, pull out the pusher lock feature, which is located above the handle. (Some vibration is normal.)
- I like to knead the dough by hand on a lightly floured surface for 1 to 2 minutes, until smooth and elastic. It should be dimpled, like a baby's bottom.
- Place the dough in a large bowl greased with about 1 tsp of oil. Turn the dough over so that all the surfaces are greased. Make sure the bowl is large enough for the dough to rise at least double in size. Cover the bowl tightly with plastic wrap (not a towel) to prevent the dough from drying out.

### RISING

- Let dough rise once or twice before shaping, then once after shaping. It can rise either at room temperature or in the refrigerator.
- At room temperature (80°F), the dough will take 1 to 1½ hours to double. Multigrain breads take slightly longer, 1½ to 2 hours. A second rising takes about half the time, ¾ to 1 hour. Rising time varies, depending on the temperature and humidity. Don't let the dough get too warm during rising or it will develop a yeasty taste.
- If you're letting it rise in the refrigerator, make sure there is enough room between the shelves for the dough to rise. If the dough is made with butter or margarine, let it rise at room temperature for 1 hour before refrigerating.
- If you are busy, refrigerate the dough (or a shaped loaf) at any point to slow down the rising process. Dough made with water will keep 4 to 5 days in the fridge. Dough made with milk will keep 3 to 4 days. Remove dough from the refrigerator and let stand at room temperature for about half an hour before completing the recipe.
- THE FINGER TEST: To test if the dough has risen enough, poke your finger into it. If the dough slowly springs back but not completely, it is ready. If it springs back right away, it isn't ready. If the dent remains, the dough is over-risen.
- Punch down the dough by plunging your fist into the center. Fold the outside edges into the center to release gases and redistribute the yeast. If you have time, let the dough rise a second time for a finer texture.

- **SHAPING:** Punch down the dough before shaping. Let it rest for about 5 minutes for easier handling. (If you don't, the dough will be very springy when you try to roll it out.)

- **BRAIDING:** Divide dough into 3 equal pieces. Roll each piece into a long rope, then line up the ropes parallel to each other. Start at the middle and braid towards you; press ends together and tuck them under. Turn the loaf around and braid towards you once again. Press ends together and tuck them under.

- **PREPARING BAKING PANS:** Spray loaf pans with nonstick spray. Line baking sheets with parchment paper—it's considered oven-safe to 400°F. (I've even used it in a 425°F oven if the baking time is 15 minutes or less.) Many bakers like to use a nonstick silicone baking mat (Silpat)—it's oven-safe to 500°F. If the oven temperature called for in a recipe is higher than 400°F, you can line baking sheets with aluminum foil, then spray with nonstick spray. Line muffin pans with paper baking liners for easy cleanup.

- **RISE AND SHINE!** Place the shaped dough in/on prepared baking pans. Cover dough with a towel and let rise at room temperature until doubled (about 1 hour for room-temperature dough, 2 to 3 hours for refrigerated dough). Or put the baking pan into a large plastic food-safe bag, closing it loosely. (Garbage bags are not food-safe as they've been treated with chemicals.) Glazing is best done after shaping and rising.

- If yeast breads rise for too long, the gluten strands will break and the bread will collapse. Once the breads have been shaped, they should not rise to more than double in size before baking.

- **GLAZING OPTIONS:** Brush the dough with egg glaze (1 egg yolk mixed with 1 to 2 tsp water) just before baking. Coffee cakes and buns can be brushed with juice from canned fruit 10 minutes before baking is completed. Baker's Glaze (page 311) will give a lovely sheen to rye and pumpernickel breads.

- Bake yeast breads in the middle or lower third of a preheated oven. There will be a final expansion known as "oven spring" in the first few minutes of baking.

- **FULL STEAM AHEAD!** Many bread bakers like to add steam to the oven, as it softens the crust and lets yeast dough rise quickly to its maximum size. After placing the loaf in the oven, spray the walls quickly with water 8 to 10 times. Avoid spraying the oven light, heating coils and fan. Repeat spraying twice during the first 10 minutes of baking time. Open the oven door partway, spray quickly, then shut the door.

- When done, yeast dough will be evenly browned and sound hollow when the crust is tapped lightly. Test by inserting an instant-read thermometer into the center of the loaf. A sandwich loaf reaches 195°F to 200°F, a rustic loaf reaches 200°F to 210°F, a whole-grain loaf reaches 210°F, and a sweet bread reaches 200°F. If the dough is browning too quickly during baking, cover it loosely with foil.

- Remove breads from pans immediately after baking. Cool on a wire rack away from drafts.

- **FILL UP ON FIBER!** Add ¼ cup wheat germ or ground flax seeds to your favorite bread doughs and muffins. You can also sprinkle whole flax seeds or sunflower, sesame or poppy seeds on top of loaves after brushing them with egg glaze.

- **FREEZE WITH EASE!** Immediately after shaping, wrap unbaked dough airtight and freeze it for up to 1 month. When needed, remove it from the freezer. Place it on a sprayed baking sheet, cover and defrost at room temperature until it doubles in size, 6 to 7 hours. Bake as directed. Another option is to defrost dough in the refrigerator, then let it rise at room temperature until doubled. Baked breads, rolls, coffee cakes and muffins can be frozen for about 4 months if well wrapped.

- Store bread in a plastic bag at room temperature or freeze it. Store crusty, artisanal-style bread in a paper bag—it loses its crispness if stored in plastic. Don't store breads in the refrigerator. It draws out the moisture and the bread becomes stale faster. Wrap bread well in a plastic freezer bag, press out air and freeze for up to 3 months.

- TO REFRESH STALE OR FROZEN BREAD, spray it with water, wrap in foil and warm in a 400°F oven for 10 to 15 minutes. Let cool before unwrapping.

## QUICK BREADS AND MUFFINS

- Quick breads don't contain yeast. Instead, they use baking powder, baking soda or a combination of both for the leavening. Although quick breads are usually baked in a loaf pan, they can also be baked in a square or oblong pan. To bake the batter in muffin pans, bake at 375°F to 400°F about 20 to 25 minutes.

- Overmixing will make quick breads and muffins tough. Combine the wet and dry ingredients quickly and don't mix any longer than necessary. Don't insert the pusher in the feed tube. Process with quick on/off pulses just until flour disappears, scraping down sides of work bowl as needed.

- Quick breads and muffins will freeze for up to 3 months.

- NESTED WORK BOWLS: Choose the appropriate bowl and blade or disc for the task. For recipes that require using multiple bowls, begin with the smallest one to minimize cleanups. Use the mini or medium bowl to prep ingredients. Chop nuts, dried fruit or chocolate in the small bowl with the mini-blade. Use the medium or large bowl and appropriate disc to grate cheese, veggies, etc. Use the large bowl and **Steel Blade** to combine dry ingredients and process batters for muffins and quick breads. Use the large bowl and **Steel Blade** or **Dough Blade** for kneading yeast doughs (some models have a **Dough Cycle**).

- On Cuisinart Elite models, the **Steel Blade** can also be used in the medium bowl. The **Steel Blade** locks into place and the nested bowls have pouring spouts, so pouring batters into baking pans is much easier.

- An easy way to fill muffin pans is to use an ice cream scoop or a 1/3 cup dry measure. Fill empty muffin compartments one-third full with water to prevent pan from discoloring or burning.

# CHALLAH

A delectable braided egg bread that is served on the Sabbath, Jewish holidays and special ceremonial occasions.

Yield: 1 large loaf (12 to 16 slices). Freezes well.

1 tsp sugar

½ cup warm water (105°F to 115°F)

1 pkg active dry yeast (1 Tbsp)

3 cups flour (approximately) (part whole wheat can be used)

2 to 3 Tbsp sugar or honey

1 tsp salt

⅓ cup oil

2 eggs (or 1 egg plus 2 egg whites)

¼ cup lukewarm water

1 egg yolk beaten with 1 tsp water

poppy or sesame seeds, or Streusel Topping (page 302) (optional)

In a measuring cup, dissolve 1 tsp sugar in ½ cup warm water. Sprinkle yeast over and let stand for 8 to 10 minutes, until foamy. Stir to dissolve.

STEEL BLADE OR DOUGH BLADE: (Use DOUGH CYCLE if your machine has one.) Place flour, sugar or honey and salt in processor. Pour dissolved yeast mixture over and process 12 to 15 seconds. While machine is running, add oil and eggs through feed tube and process until blended, about 10 seconds. Add water through feed tube while machine is running, drizzling it directly onto flour mixture; process until dough gathers and forms a mass around the blades. (Have an additional ¼ cup flour ready in case machine begins to slow down; add it through feed tube if necessary.) Process 45 seconds longer; dough will be sticky.

Turn out onto lightly floured surface. Knead by hand for 1 to 2 minutes, until smooth and elastic, adding just enough flour to prevent dough from sticking.

Place dough in large greased bowl; turn dough over so all surfaces are lightly greased. Cover bowl with plastic wrap and let rise in warm place until doubled, 1½ to 2 hours. (Dough may also rise in refrigerator; it will keep up to 3 days before shaping and baking.) Punch down. For a lighter texture, let dough rise again until doubled; punch down.

To shape: Divide dough into 3 equal portions. Roll into 3 long strands. Place on parchment-lined baking sheet. Braid loosely; tuck ends under. Cover with a towel and let rise until doubled, about 1 hour. Brush with egg glaze; sprinkle with seeds or topping (if desired).

Bake in preheated 400°F oven for 30 minutes, until golden brown. Dough will sound hollow when tapped with your fingers. Cool away from drafts.

198 calories per slice, 26.6 g carbohydrates, 1 g fiber, 5 g protein, 7.9 g fat (0.9 g saturated fat), 53 g cholesterol, 206 mg sodium, 57 mg potassium, 2 mg iron, 12 mg calcium, 62 mg phosphorus

## variations

HONEY RAISIN CHALLAH: Use 3 Tbsp honey instead of sugar. Add ¾ cup sultana raisins to dough about 20 seconds after it gathers into a mass around the blades. Process 10 seconds longer. Knead and let rise

*Continued*

as directed. To shape, roll dough into a long thick rope. Place on parchment-lined baking sheet. Coil up like a snail, starting from the center and working outwards. Tuck end under. Cover with a towel and let rise. When doubled, brush with egg glaze, sprinkle with seeds or topping and bake as directed.

- CHALLAH ROLLS (BULKAS): Divide dough into 12 equal pieces (or 24 smaller pieces). Roll each piece into a rope and tie in a knot. Place on parchment-lined baking sheet, cover with a towel and let rise. When doubled, brush with egg glaze and sprinkle with seeds or topping. Bake at 400°F for 15 to 18 minutes, until golden.

## STREUSEL TOPPING

Diane Plant of Toronto shared this scrumptious topping with me.

Yield: Enough topping for 1 or 2 challas or babkas. Freezes well.

½ cup flour

½ cup icing sugar

¼ cup canola oil, butter or tub margarine

STEEL BLADE: Process flour, icing sugar and oil until fine crumbs are formed, 15 to 20 seconds.

80 calories per Tbsp, 9 g carbohydrates, 0.1 g fiber, 0 g protein, 4.8 g fat (0.4 g saturated fat), 0 g cholesterol, 0 mg sodium, 6 mg potassium, 0 mg iron, 1 mg calcium, 6 mg phosphorus

## CHALLAH (DOUBLE RECIPE FOR LARGE PROCESSORS)

A food processor with a 14-cup capacity, dough cycle and dough blade can mix 2 loaves at a time, using up to 6 cups of flour. If desired, replace half the flour with whole wheat flour. You can still make this recipe without a dough

1 tsp sugar

½ cup warm water (105°F to 115°F)

2 pkgs active dry yeast (2 Tbsp)

½ cup canola oil

2 eggs, lightly beaten

¾ to 1 cup water (room temperature)

5 cups flour (approximately) (part whole wheat can be used)

½ cup sugar

2 tsp salt

cornmeal for the baking pan

1 egg yolk beaten with 2 tsp water

sesame or poppy seeds

In a 2-cup glass measure, dissolve 1 tsp sugar in ½ cup warm water. Sprinkle yeast over and let stand 8 to 10 minutes, until foamy. Stir to dissolve. Add oil and eggs to dissolved yeast mixture; mix well. Measure 1 cup of water in a separate cup. (You may only need to add about ¾ cup. See "Chef's Secrets: Processing Bread Dough," page 304.)

cycle. The liquid
ingredients are
combined with the
dissolved yeast
mixture and are
added to the dry
ingredients in one
easy step!

Yield: 2 loaves (12 to
16 slices per loaf).
Freezes well.

DOUGH BLADE OR STEEL BLADE: (Use DOUGH CYCLE if your machine has one.) Process flour, ½ cup sugar and salt for 10 seconds, until combined. Start machine and gradually pour yeast mixture through small feed tube, then gradually add ¾ to 1 cup water directly onto flour mixture as fast as flour will absorb it. If you hear a sloshing, splattering sound, pour liquid in more slowly. Continue to process until dough cleans sides of processor bowl. Process 45 seconds longer, until well kneaded. If dough is too sticky and machine begins to slow down, add a couple Tbsp of flour, using just enough to make a soft, sticky dough.

Turn out onto a lightly floured surface. Knead for 2 minutes by hand, until smooth and elastic, adding just enough flour to keep dough from sticking.

Place dough in large greased bowl, turning to grease all surfaces. Cover bowl with plastic wrap and let rise in warm place until doubled, 1½ to 2 hours. (Dough may also rise in refrigerator. It will keep up to 3 days before shaping and baking.) Punch down. For a lighter loaf, let dough rise again until doubled; punch down.

To shape: Divide dough in half. Divide each half in 3 equal pieces. Roll into 3 long strands. Braid loosely, tucking ends under (see Variation). Repeat with remaining dough to form a second loaf. Place on parchment-lined baking sheet that has been sprinkled with cornmeal. Cover with a towel and let rise until doubled, about 1 hour. Brush with egg glaze; sprinkle with seeds.

Bake in preheated 400°F oven for 25 to 30 minutes, until golden brown.

164 calories per slice, 24.5 g carbohydrates, 0.8 g fiber, 4 g protein, 5.6 g fat (0.6 g saturated fat), 27 g cholesterol, 201 mg sodium, 46 mg potassium, 1 mg iron, 8 mg calcium, 46 mg phosphorus

## variation

For a more festive loaf, divide each half into 4 equal pieces. Roll 3 pieces into long strands and form a large braid. Divide remaining piece into 3 smaller strands and form a smaller braid. Place smaller braid on top of large braid. Pinch in several places to join the 2 braids.

# HEAVENLY HOLIDAY CHALLAH (FOR 16-CUP PROCESSORS)

Sandy Glazier used
to make the dough
for this coiled and
braided challah
in her heavy-duty
mixer but found it
much faster

1 tsp sugar

¼ cup warm water (105°F to 115°F)

2 pkgs active dry yeast (2 Tbsp)

¼ cup canola oil

2 eggs, lightly beaten

1½ cups lukewarm water

7 cups all-purpose flour

½ cup sugar

2 tsp salt

zest of 1 lemon (about 2 tsp)

2 cups raisins

1 egg beaten with 2 tsp water

sesame or poppy seeds (optional)

to make in her Cuisinart Elite 16-cup processor. This model can process yeast doughs made with 7 cups all-purpose flour or 5 cups whole wheat flour. To make this in a smaller food processor, see Chef's Tip (below).

Yield: 1 extra-large coiled loaf (28 to 30 servings). Freezes well.

In a 2-cup glass measure, dissolve 1 tsp sugar in ¼ cup warm water. Sprinkle yeast overtop and let stand 8 to 10 minutes, until foamy. Stir to dissolve. Add oil and eggs to dissolved yeast mixture; mix well. Measure 1½ cups lukewarm water in a separate cup.

DOUGH BLADE/DOUGH CYCLE: Process flour, sugar, salt and lemon zest for 10 seconds, until combined. Start machine and gradually pour yeast mixture through feed tube directly onto flour mixture; gradually add water as fast as flour will absorb it. If you hear a sloshing, splattering sound, pour in liquid more slowly. Continue to process until dough cleans sides of bowl. Process 45 seconds longer, until well kneaded. If dough is too sticky and machine begins to slow down, add a couple of Tbsp of flour, using just enough to make a soft, sticky dough.

Turn out onto a lightly floured surface. Knead for 2 minutes by hand, until smooth and elastic, adding just enough flour to keep dough from sticking. Gradually knead in raisins, about ½ cup at a time.

Place dough in large greased bowl, turning dough to grease all surfaces. Cover bowl with plastic wrap and let rise in a warm place until doubled, 1½ to 2 hours. (Dough may also rise in refrigerator. It will keep up to 3 days before shaping and baking.) Punch down. For a lighter loaf, let dough rise again until doubled; punch down.

To shape: Divide dough into 4 equal pieces. Roll 3 pieces into very long, equal strands, braid them and form into a coil. Divide remaining piece into 3 smaller strands and form a smaller braid. Coil it and place it on top of the larger coil. Place on parchment-lined baking sheet, cover with a towel and let rise until doubled, about 1 hour.

Brush with egg glaze and sprinkle with sesame or poppy seeds (if using). Bake in preheated 400°F oven for 15 minutes, then reduce heat to 350°F and bake 30 to 45 minutes longer, until golden brown.

189 calories per serving, 36 g carbohydrates, 1.7 g fiber, 5 g protein, 3.1 g fat (0.4 g saturated fat), 30 g cholesterol, 177 mg sodium, 137 mg potassium, 2 mg iron, 12 mg calcium, 60 mg phosphorus

### chef's tip

For a 7- or 11-cup processor, make 2 batches of Challah dough (page 301). Combine both batches of dough and knead together on a lightly floured surface for 2 minutes. Knead in raisins and continue as directed above.

### chef's secrets: processing bread dough

• When pouring liquid through the feed tube, aim it towards the outside walls of the bowl where the flour is gathered. Do not pour liquid towards the center or directly onto the bottom of the bowl or the dough may not mix properly when using the dough blade.

- If the liquid sloshes or splatters, don't turn off the machine. Either add the liquid more slowly, or stop adding it, wait until the ingredients in the bowl have mixed and then slowly add the remaining liquid.

- The amount of water needed will vary, depending on the moisture content of the flour. If the dough is too dry, add a little more water. If the dough is too wet, add a little more flour.

## CRANBERRY OR RAISIN CHALLAH

This is a wonderful bread to serve at Thanksgiving.

**Challah dough (page 301 or 302)**
**1 cup dried cranberries or raisins**
**1 egg yolk mixed with 1 tsp water**

**¼ cup sliced almonds**
**½ tsp ground cinnamon mixed with**
**2 to 3 Tbsp sugar**

Yield: 1 loaf (12 to 16 servings). Freezes well.

(If you use the Double Recipe for Large Processors, page 302, use *half* of the dough to make this bread.) Remove dough from processor, knead in cranberries or raisins by hand, adding ⅓ cup at a time.

Transfer dough to large greased bowl, turning dough to grease all surfaces. Cover bowl with plastic wrap and let dough rise until doubled.

Shape as directed. Place on parchment-lined baking sheet, cover with a towel and let rise. When doubled, brush with egg glaze; sprinkle with almonds and cinnamon/sugar mixture.

Bake in preheated 400°F oven 25 to 30 minutes, until golden. Dough will sound hollow when tapped with your fingers.

248 calories per serving, 37.6 g carbohydrates, 1.8 g fiber, 5 g protein, 9 g fat (1 g saturated fat), 53 g cholesterol, 207 mg sodium, 75 mg potassium, 2 mg iron, 19 mg calcium, 73 mg phosphorus

### chocolate chip challah

Prepare dough and let rise as directed, replacing dried cranberries with chocolate chips and omitting almonds. Don't add chocolate chips until you are ready to braid challah. Divide dough into 3 equal portions. Roll into 3 long strands. Flatten each strand with your fingertips. Top with chocolate chips. Pinch edges of dough together to form 3 long ropes, encasing chocolate chips in each rope. Braid loosely, tucking ends under. Transfer to parchment-lined baking sheet and cover with a towel. When doubled, brush with egg glaze and sprinkle with cinnamon/sugar mixture. Bake as directed.

# CRUSTY FRENCH BREAD

Bread has never been so easy to make. It takes less than a minute to prepare the dough in the processor!

Yield: 2 round or long loaves (10 servings per loaf). These are best eaten the same day—and probably will be! They also freeze well. To reheat, place on baking sheet, sprinkle with a few drops of water and heat at 350°F about 10 minutes, until crusty.

| | |
|---|---|
| 1½ tsp active dry yeast | 2 tsp salt |
| ⅓ cup warm water (105°F to 115°F) | 1 cup lukewarm water |
| 3½ cups flour (about 1 lb/500 g) | cornmeal for the baking sheet |

In a measuring cup, combine yeast with ⅓ cup warm water. Add a pinch of flour and let stand 8 to 10 minutes, until foamy; stir to dissolve.

STEEL BLADE OR DOUGH BLADE: (Use DOUGH CYCLE if your machine has one.) Place flour, salt and dissolved yeast mixture in processor. Start machine and slowly pour remaining water through feed tube directly onto flour mixture, adding it as quickly as flour will absorb it. Process until dough cleans sides of bowl and becomes soft and somewhat sticky. Process 45 seconds longer, until well kneaded. If dough seems too dry, add a couple of Tbsp of water. If dough is too sticky and your processor begins to slow down or "walk" along your counter, quickly add a couple of Tbsp of additional flour through feed tube.

Transfer dough to large greased bowl, cover bowl with plastic wrap and let rise until doubled, 1½ to 2 hours. Punch down. If you have time, let dough rise once again until doubled, or shape it at this point.

To shape: Divide dough in half, cover and let rest 15 minutes. This makes it easier to shape. Dust dough with a little flour. For round loaves, form each piece into a ball. For baguettes, form each piece into an elongated loaf. Line baking sheet with foil and spray with nonstick spray (or line with a silicone mat); sprinkle with cornmeal. Place loaves on baking sheet. Cover with a towel and let rise about 45 minutes, until doubled.

Sprinkle top of each loaf with a little flour. For round loaves, cut 4 slashes in top of each loaf with serrated knife, making tic-tac-toe design. For long loaves, cut 3 or 4 parallel slashes diagonally across each loaf.

Bake in preheated 450°F oven for 30 to 35 minutes, until browned and crusty. Loaves should sound hollow when lightly tapped. Cool completely.

81 calories per serving, 16.8 g carbohydrates, 0.7 g fiber, 2 g protein, 0.2 g fat (0 g saturated fat), 0 g cholesterol, 234 mg sodium, 30 mg potassium, 1 mg iron, 4 mg calcium, 28 mg phosphorus

# HOMEMADE WHITE BREAD

You can replace half the flour with whole wheat flour for scrumptious, healthy bread.

| | |
|---|---|
| ¾ cup milk (1%) or water | 3 cups flour (half whole wheat flour |
| 1 tsp sugar | may be used) |
| ½ cup warm water (105°F to 115°F) | 4 tsp sugar |
| 1 pkg active dry yeast (1 Tbsp) | 1½ tsp salt |
| | 1 Tbsp tub margarine or oil |

Yield: 1 loaf (12 to 16 servings). Freezes well.

Heat milk or water for 1 minute on High in the microwave. Let cool for 5 minutes, until lukewarm. Meanwhile, dissolve 1 tsp sugar in ½ cup warm water. Sprinkle yeast over and let stand for 8 to 10 minutes, until foamy. Stir to dissolve.

STEEL BLADE OR DOUGH BLADE: (Use DOUGH CYCLE if your machine has one.) Process flour, 4 tsp sugar, salt and margarine or oil for 6 to 8 seconds. Add dissolved yeast and process for 12 to 15 seconds. While machine is running, add milk or water through feed tube directly onto flour mixture as quickly as flour will absorb it. Process until dough gathers and forms a mass around the blades, then process 30 to 40 seconds longer.

Turn out onto lightly floured surface. Knead by hand for 1 to 2 minutes, until smooth and elastic.

Place dough in large greased bowl; turn dough over so all surfaces are lightly greased. Cover bowl with plastic wrap and let rise until doubled. Punch down. (For a lighter texture, let dough rise a second time; punch down. First rising will take 1 to 1½ hours; second rising will take half the time.)

To shape: Roll dough on lightly floured surface into 9- × 12-inch rectangle. Roll up jelly-roll style from shorter side. Seal ends by pressing down with edge of your hand. Place seam side down in sprayed 9- × 5-inch loaf pan or on baking sheet that has been lined with foil and sprayed. Cover with a towel and let rise until doubled, about 1 hour.

Bake in preheated 425°F oven for 25 to 30 minutes. Remove from pan and let cool.

137 calories per serving, 26.6 g carbohydrates, 1 g fiber, 4 g protein, 1.4 g fat (0.3 g saturated fat), 1 g cholesterol, 307 mg sodium, 68 mg potassium, 2 mg iron, 24 mg calcium, 56 mg phosphorus

## variations

- DINNER ROLLS: Divide dough into 12 equal pieces. Form into round balls and place on parchment-lined baking sheet; cover with a towel and let rise until doubled. Bake in preheated 375°F oven about 20 minutes, until golden brown. Makes 1 dozen.

- VIENNA OR KAISER ROLLS: Divide dough into 10 equal pieces. Roll each piece into a flat circle about ⅓-inch thick and place on parchment-lined baking sheet. Cover with a towel and let rise. When doubled, cut a fairly deep X into each roll. Brush with egg glaze; sprinkle with poppy or sesame seeds. Bake in preheated 375°F oven about 20 minutes. Makes 10 rolls.

# PAREVE WHITE BREAD

This dairy-free bread is slightly sweeter and richer than Homemade White Bread (page 306). Excellent for dinner rolls, hamburger or hot dog buns.

Yield: 1 loaf (12 to 16 servings). Freezes well.

| | |
|---|---|
| 1 tsp sugar | 3 Tbsp sugar |
| ½ cup warm water (105°F to 115°F) | 1 tsp salt |
| 1 pkg active dry yeast (1 Tbsp) | ½ cup lukewarm water |
| 2¾ cups flour | 3 Tbsp oil |

In a measuring cup, dissolve 1 tsp sugar in ½ cup warm water. Sprinkle yeast over and let stand 8 to 10 minutes, until foamy. Stir to dissolve.

STEEL BLADE OR DOUGH BLADE: (Use DOUGH CYCLE if your machine has one.) Process flour, 3 Tbsp sugar and salt for 5 seconds. Pour dissolved yeast over flour mixture; process 10 seconds longer. Combine ½ cup lukewarm water with oil. Start machine and gradually add liquid through feed tube directly onto flour mixture while machine is running. Process until dough forms a mass around the blades. Process 30 to 40 seconds longer.

Turn out onto lightly floured surface. Knead by hand for 1 to 2 minutes, until smooth and elastic.

Place dough in large greased bowl; turn dough over so all surfaces are lightly greased. Cover bowl with plastic wrap and let rise until doubled in bulk, 1 to 1½ hours. Punch down.

To shape: Roll dough on lightly floured surface into 9- × 12-inch rectangle. Roll up jelly-roll style from shorter side. Seal ends by pressing down with edge of your hand. Place seam side down in sprayed 9- × 5-inch loaf pan. Cover with a towel and let rise until doubled, about 1 hour.

Bake in preheated 400°F oven for 20 minutes. Remove from pan immediately. Cool away from drafts.

151 calories per serving, 25.6 g carbohydrates, 0.9 g fiber, 3 g protein, 3.8 g fat (0.3 g saturated fat), 0 g cholesterol, 195 mg sodium, 42 mg potassium, 1 mg iron, 5 mg calcium, 39 mg phosphorus

## variations

- PAREVE WHOLE WHEAT BREAD: Use 1½ cups all-purpose flour and 1¼ cups whole wheat flour. One serving contains 146 calories, 24.7 g carbohydrates and 2.1 g fiber.

- CINNAMON RAISIN BREAD: Roll dough into large rectangle. Sprinkle ¼ cup brown sugar, ½ tsp cinnamon and ¾ cup raisins evenly over dough to within 1 inch of edges. Roll up jelly-roll style from shorter side. Seal ends. Cover with a towel, let rise and bake as directed. One serving contains 195 calories, 37.3 g carbohydrates and 1.6 g fiber.

# 100% WHOLE WHEAT BREAD

This fiber-packed loaf is "dough" good!

Yield: 1 loaf (12 to 16 servings). Freezes well.

½ cup milk (1%) or water

1 tsp sugar

½ cup warm water (105°F to 115°F)

1 pkg active dry yeast (1 Tbsp)

3¼ cups whole wheat flour (approximately)

1 tsp salt

2 Tbsp honey

2 Tbsp oil

2 eggs (or 1 egg plus 2 whites), lightly beaten

Heat milk or water until steaming, about 45 seconds on High in the microwave. Let cool for 5 minutes, until lukewarm. Meanwhile, dissolve 1 tsp sugar in ½ cup warm water. Sprinkle yeast overtop and let stand for 8 to 10 minutes, until foamy. Stir to dissolve.

STEEL BLADE OR DOUGH BLADE: (Use DOUGH CYCLE if your machine has one.) Reserve ¼ cup flour. Process 3 cups flour, salt and honey in processor for 5 seconds. Add dissolved yeast mixture and process 10 seconds longer. In a measuring cup, combine lukewarm milk with oil and eggs. Start machine and slowly add milk mixture through feed tube directly onto flour mixture while machine is running. Batter will be very sticky. Add reserved ¼ cup flour as machine begins to slow down. Process until well kneaded, 30 to 40 seconds. (If necessary, add 1 to 2 Tbsp additional flour.) Batter will *not* form a ball on the blades.

Turn out onto well-floured surface. Flour surface of dough lightly. Knead by hand about 2 minutes, until smooth and elastic, adding flour as necessary to prevent dough from sticking.

Place dough in large greased bowl; turn dough over so all surfaces are lightly greased. Cover bowl with plastic wrap and let rise until doubled. Punch down. For a lighter texture, let dough rise once again until doubled; punch down.

To shape: Roll on lightly floured surface into 9- × 12-inch rectangle. Roll up jelly-roll style from shorter side. Seal ends by pressing down with edge of your hand. Place seam side down in sprayed 9- × 5-inch loaf pan or on parchment-lined baking sheet. Cover with a towel and let rise until doubled.

Bake in preheated 375°F oven for 35 to 40 minutes. Remove from pan and cool.

162 calories per serving, 27.6 g carbohydrates, 4.1 g fiber, 6 g protein, 4 g fat (0.6 g saturated fat), 36 g cholesterol, 211 mg sodium, 171 mg potassium, 2 mg iron, 28 mg calcium, 144 mg phosphorus

## variation

For rolls, divide dough into 12 pieces. Shape each piece into a ball. Baking time will be about 20 minutes.

# OLD-FASHIONED RYE BREAD

For best results, use light or medium rye flour.

Yield: 1 large loaf (16 servings). Freezes well.

½ **tsp sugar**

½ **cup warm water (105°F to 115°F)**

**1 pkg active dry yeast (1 Tbsp)**

**1¾ cups all-purpose flour**

    **(approximately)**

**1¼ cups rye flour**

**2 Tbsp granulated or brown sugar**

**1½ tsp salt**

**1 Tbsp oil**

⅔ **cup lukewarm water**

**2 Tbsp caraway seeds**

**2 Tbsp cornmeal for baking pan**

GLAZE

(or use Baker's Glaze, page 311)

**1 tsp instant coffee dissolved in 1 Tbsp**
    **boiling water**

**1 egg yolk beaten with 1 tsp water**

In a measuring cup, dissolve ½ tsp sugar in ½ cup warm water. Sprinkle yeast over and let stand for 8 to 10 minutes, until foamy. Stir to dissolve.

STEEL BLADE OR DOUGH BLADE: (Use DOUGH CYCLE if your machine has one.) Process flours, 2 Tbsp sugar and salt for 5 seconds. Pour dissolved yeast mixture overtop and process for 12 to 15 seconds. Combine oil and lukewarm water. Start machine and slowly pour liquid through feed tube directly onto flour mixture while machine is running; process dough 15 to 20 seconds longer. If processor begins to slow down, add up to ¼ cup all-purpose flour through feed tube.

Turn out onto well-floured surface. Dough will be somewhat sticky. Flour surface of dough lightly. Knead by hand for about 2 minutes, until smooth and elastic, adding just enough flour to prevent dough from sticking. Knead in caraway seeds.

Place dough in large greased bowl; turn dough over so all surfaces are lightly greased. Cover bowl with plastic wrap and let rise until doubled, about 2 hours; punch down. If you have time, let dough rise a second time. Punch down once again.

To shape: Roll on lightly floured surface into 12- × 18-inch rectangle. Roll up jelly-roll style from the longer side. Seal ends by pressing down with edge of your hand. Place seam side down on parchment-lined baking sheet that has been sprinkled with cornmeal. Cover with a towel and let rise until doubled, about 2 hours. Brush with coffee mixture, then with egg glaze. (Omit this step if using Baker's Glaze.)

Bake in preheated 375°F oven about 45 minutes, or until well browned and bread sounds hollow when tapped lightly. (If using Baker's Glaze, brush it overtop of loaf the last 10 minutes of baking, then brush again the last 3 minutes.) Cool on a wire rack.

104 calories per serving, 19.6 g carbohydrates, 2 g fiber, 3 g protein, 1.7 g fat (0.2 g saturated fat), 13 g cholesterol, 220 mg sodium, 67 mg potassium, 1 mg iron, 12 mg calcium, 49 mg phosphorus

## variations

- **ONION RYE BREAD**: Roll dough into 1 large or 2 smaller rectangles. Spread onion filling for Best-Ever Onion Rolls (page 319) over dough to within 1 inch of edges. Roll up jelly-roll style; seal ends. Transfer to parchment-lined baking sheet, cover with a towel and let rise. When doubled, glaze and bake as directed. One loaf takes 45 minutes, 2 loaves take 35 to 40 minutes at 375°F.

- **RYE CRESCENTS**: Divide dough in half. Roll out each piece on a floured surface into a 12-inch circle; cut each circle into 8 wedges. Beginning at outer edge, roll up. Place on a parchment-lined baking sheet and curve into crescents. Cover with a towel and let rise. When doubled, glaze and bake as directed. Baking time will be 20 to 25 minutes. Makes 16 crescents.

- **BAKER'S GLAZE**: In a small saucepan, whisk together 1 Tbsp cornstarch and ½ cup water. Heat on medium-low for 1 to 2 minutes, just until mixture bubbles slightly and begins to thicken. Remove from heat; cool completely. Brush glaze on top of rye or pumpernickel loaves or rolls the last 10 minutes of baking, then brush again in the last 3 minutes. Makes ½ cup.

# PUMPERNICKEL BREAD

*Yield: 1 large or 2 small loaves (16 servings). Freezes well.*

½ tsp sugar

½ cup warm water (105°F to 115°F)

1 pkg active dry yeast (1 Tbsp)

1 Tbsp unsweetened cocoa powder

⅔ cup boiling water

3 Tbsp molasses

2 Tbsp oil

1¾ cups all-purpose flour
   (approximately)

1½ cups rye flour

1½ tsp salt

1 to 2 Tbsp caraway seeds

2 Tbsp cornmeal for baking pan

GLAZE

(or use Baker's Glaze, above)

1 tsp instant coffee dissolved in 1 Tbsp
   boiling water

1 egg yolk beaten with 1 tsp water

In measuring cup, dissolve ½ tsp sugar in ½ cup warm water. Sprinkle yeast overtop and let stand for 8 to 10 minutes, until foamy. Stir to dissolve. Dissolve cocoa in boiling water. Add molasses and oil; stir well. Cool until lukewarm.

STEEL BLADE OR DOUGH BLADE: (Use DOUGH CYCLE if your machine has one.) Reserve ¼ cup all-purpose flour. Process remaining all-purpose flour,

*Continued*

rye flour and salt for 5 seconds. Add dissolved yeast mixture and process for 12 to
15 seconds. Start machine and add cocoa mixture through feed tube while machine
is running, drizzling it directly over flour mixture. As machine slows down, add
reserved all-purpose flour through feed tube and process 10 seconds longer. Dough
will be quite sticky.

Turn out onto well-floured surface. Flour surface of dough lightly. Knead by
hand 2 to 3 minutes, until smooth and elastic, adding just enough flour to keep
dough from sticking. Knead in caraway seeds.

Place dough in large greased bowl; turn dough over so all surfaces are lightly
greased. Cover bowl with plastic wrap and let rise in warm place until doubled in
bulk, about 2 hours; punch down. If you have time, let dough rise a second time;
punch down once again.

To shape: Shape into 1 large or 2 smaller balls. Place on parchment-lined baking
sheet that has been sprinkled with cornmeal. Cover with a towel and let rise until
doubled, about 2 hours. Brush with coffee mixture, then with egg glaze. (Omit
this step if using Baker's Glaze.)

Bake in preheated 375°F oven about 45 minutes for a large loaf or 35 to 40 minutes for smaller loaves. (If using Baker's Glaze, brush it overtop of loaf the last
10 minutes of baking, then brush again the last 3 minutes.) Cool on a wire rack.

121 calories per serving, 22.1 g carbohydrates, 2.2 g fiber, 3 g protein, 2.6 g fat (0.3 g saturated fat), 13 g
cholesterol, 222 mg sodium, 128 mg potassium, 1 mg iron, 18 mg calcium, 54 mg phosphorus

### variation

For rolls, divide dough into 12 pieces. Shape each piece into a ball and
flatten slightly. Cover with a towel and let rise until doubled. Glaze and
bake as directed. Baking time will be 20 to 25 minutes.

## WHOLESOME OATMEAL BREAD

This is a very heavy
batter, so you need
to use a processor
with a strong motor
to handle the
kneading.

Yield: 1 loaf (16 servings).
Freezes well.

| | |
|---|---|
| 1 tsp granulated sugar | 1½ tsp salt |
| ¼ cup warm water (105°F to 115°F) | 1 cup hot water |
| 1 pkg active dry yeast (1 Tbsp) | ¼ cup molasses or honey |
| ½ cup rolled oats | 2 Tbsp tub margarine or oil |
| 2 Tbsp brown sugar | 2¾ cups flour divided |

In a measuring cup, dissolve 1 tsp sugar in ¼ cup warm water. Sprinkle yeast overtop and let stand for 8 to 10 minutes, until foamy. Stir to dissolve.

STEEL BLADE OR DOUGH BLADE: (Use DOUGH CYCLE if your machine
has one.) Place remaining ingredients except flour in processor bowl. Process with

a few quick on/off pulses to mix. Let stand until cool. Add yeast mixture plus 1 cup of flour. Process for 4 or 5 seconds. Add remaining flour and process until dough forms a mass around the blades. If machine begins to slow down, add up to ¼ cup additional flour through feed tube while machine is running. Process 30 to 40 seconds longer.

Turn out onto lightly floured surface. Knead dough by hand for 1 or 2 minutes, until smooth and elastic.

Place dough in large greased bowl; turn dough over so all surfaces are lightly greased. Cover bowl with plastic wrap and let rise until doubled, 1½ to 2 hours. Punch down and let rise until doubled once again. Punch down.

To shape: Roll dough on lightly floured surface into 9- × 12-inch rectangle. Roll up jelly-roll style from the shorter side. Seal ends by pressing down with edge of your hand. Place seam side down in sprayed 9- × 5-inch loaf pan or on a parchment-lined baking sheet. Cover with a towel and let rise until doubled, about 2 hours.

Bake in preheated 350°F oven about 45 minutes, until bread sounds hollow when tapped. Remove from pan and cool.

125 calories per serving, 24.1 g carbohydrates, 1 g fiber, 3 g protein, 1.8 g fat (0.3 g saturated fat), 0 g cholesterol, 234 mg sodium, 114 mg potassium, 2 mg iron, 17 mg calcium, 35 mg phosphorus

## CONFETTI BREAD

What a wonderful way to eat your veggies! This dough is also excellent for Focaccia (page 316).

Yield: 1 loaf (12 to 16 servings). Freezes well.

1 tsp sugar
¾ cup warm water (105°F to 115°F)
1 pkg active dry yeast (1 Tbsp)
1 medium carrot (½ cup grated)
½ small zucchini (½ cup grated)
¼ small red onion (¼ cup grated)
¼ red bell pepper (¼ cup grated)

3¼ cups flour (approximately)
2 Tbsp extra-virgin olive oil
1 tsp salt
1 additional tsp sugar
½ tsp dried thyme
½ tsp dried basil

In a measuring cup, dissolve 1 tsp sugar in warm water. Sprinkle yeast over and let stand for 8 to 10 minutes, until foamy. Stir to dissolve.

GRATER: Grate vegetables, using medium pressure. Transfer to measuring cup. You need about 1½ cups of vegetables.

STEEL BLADE OR DOUGH BLADE: (Use DOUGH CYCLE if machine has one.) Place flour, oil, salt, remaining 1 tsp sugar, thyme and basil in processor. Process 10 seconds, until combined. Start machine and add dissolved yeast mixture through feed tube while machine is running, drizzling it directly over flour mixture. Process until dough gathers together around the blades. Add grated vegetables

*Continued*

313

and let machine knead dough about 30 to 40 seconds longer. If machine slows down because dough is too sticky, add a few Tbsp of flour through feed tube; if dough is too dry, add a few Tbsp of water.

Turn out onto a lightly floured surface. Knead by hand for 1 to 2 minutes, until smooth and elastic, adding just enough flour to prevent dough from sticking to your hands.

Place dough in large greased bowl, turning to grease all surfaces. Cover bowl with plastic wrap and let rise in warm place until doubled, about 1½ hours. Punch down. If you have time, let rise a second time; punch down once again.

To shape: On lightly floured surface, roll dough into 9- × 12-inch rectangle. Roll up like a jelly-roll from the shorter side. Seal ends by pressing down with edge of your hand. Place seam side down in sprayed 9- × 5-inch loaf pan. Cover with a towel and let rise until doubled, about 1 hour.

Bake in preheated 425°F oven for 25 to 30 minutes, until golden brown. Bread should sound hollow when tapped with your fingertips. Remove from pan and let cool.

154 calories per slice, 27.8 g carbohydrates, 1.4 g fiber, 4 g protein, 2.7 g fat (0.4 g saturated fat), 0 g cholesterol, 199 mg sodium, 90 mg potassium, 2 mg iron, 10 mg calcium, 54 mg phosphorus

## PIZZA PINWHEELS

These "wheels" are a favorite of my grandson Max. They're perfect for a lunchbox. For a cute party presentation, serve them on wooden skewers. Fun buns!

Yield: About 32 medium or 24 large pinwheels. Reheats and/or freezes well.

DOUGH

3 cups flour (part whole wheat can be used)
2 tsp instant or bread machine yeast (see Note on page 315)
1½ tsp salt
1¼ cups lukewarm water (100°F)
2 Tbsp olive oil

FILLING

8 oz (250 g) chilled low-fat mozzarella cheese (2 cups grated)
1 cup tomato or pizza sauce (unsalted or regular)

STEEL BLADE OR DOUGH BLADE: (Use DOUGH CYCLE if your machine has one.) Place flour, yeast and salt in processor. Process for 6 to 8 seconds to combine. While machine is running, slowly drizzle water and oil through feed tube directly over flour mixture. Continue processing until dough gathers together and forms a mass around the blades. If dough seems dry, add 1 to 2 Tbsp water. Let machine knead dough 30 to 40 seconds longer; it should be slightly sticky.

Turn out onto lightly floured surface and knead for 1 to 2 minutes, until smooth and elastic.

Rub surface of dough lightly with oil and place in large resealable plastic bag or bowl. Let rise at room temperature until doubled, 1½ to 2 hours. (You can refrigerate it for up to 4 days or freeze for up to 1 month. Bring to room temperature before shaping.)

GRATER: Grate cheese, using medium pressure.

Assembly: Punch down dough and divide in half. Working with 1 piece at a time, roll out thinly on a lightly floured surface into a long, narrow rectangle (7 × 15 inches for smaller pinwheels, 9 × 12 inches for larger ones). If dough is too elastic, let rest a few minutes for easier rolling. Spread half the tomato sauce to within 1 inch of edges of dough. Sprinkle with half the cheese. Roll up from long edge into a tight log and pinch seam firmly to seal. Gently stretch log to elongate it. Cut with a serrated knife into 1-inch slices (12 to 16 slices per log, depending on size).

Place slices cut side up on parchment-lined baking sheets, about 2 inches apart. Repeat with remaining dough and filling. Cover with a towel and let rise for 20 to 30 minutes.

Bake 1 batch at a time in preheated 375°F oven until golden. Smaller pinwheels take 12 to 15 minutes; larger pinwheels take 15 to 18 minutes. Cool slightly, then use a sharp knife to trim off any filling that leaks out during baking.

76 calories per pinwheel, 10 g carbohydrates, 0.5 g fiber, 3 g protein, 2.4 g fat (1 g saturated fat), 4 g cholesterol, 148 mg sodium, 52 mg potassium, 1 mg iron, 55 mg calcium, 55 mg phosphorus

### note

If using active dry yeast, don't add it to flour mixture. Sprinkle yeast over ¼ cup of lukewarm water called for in the recipe. Let stand 5 to 10 minutes, then stir to dissolve.

### variations

- Substitute dough for Make-and-Bake Pizza (page 69) or Focaccia (page 316).

- SNEAKY CUISINE: Purée some cooked veggies or legumes (e.g., carrots, squash, spinach, chickpeas) into the tomato sauce to boost nutrients and fiber.

# FOCACCIA

This addictive Italian flatbread is also delicious using the dough for Confetti Bread (page 313). Focaccia is wonderful with soups and salads, for sandwiches, or as an hors d'oeuvre.

Yield: 8 servings. Reheats and/or freezes well.

## DOUGH

1 tsp sugar
½ cup warm water (105°F to 115°F)
1 pkg active dry yeast (1 Tbsp)
3 cups flour
1 tsp salt
½ tsp each of dried basil, thyme and rosemary
2 Tbsp olive oil
¾ cup lukewarm water

## TOPPING

2 Tbsp olive oil
2 or 3 cloves garlic, crushed
fresh or dried basil, thyme and rosemary to taste
kosher (coarse) salt and pepper to taste

For dough: In measuring cup, dissolve 1 tsp sugar in ½ cup warm water. Sprinkle yeast overtop and let stand 8 to 10 minutes, until foamy. Stir to dissolve.

STEEL BLADE OR DOUGH BLADE: (Use DOUGH CYCLE if your machine has one.) Place flour, salt, herbs and oil in processor. Process for 10 seconds, until combined. Add dissolved yeast and process 10 seconds. While machine is running, add lukewarm water slowly through feed tube directly onto flour mixture. Process until dough gathers together and forms a mass around the blades. Let machine knead dough 30 to 40 seconds longer.

Turn out onto lightly floured surface and knead for 1 to 2 minutes, until smooth and elastic.

Place dough in large greased bowl, turning to grease all surfaces. Cover bowl with plastic wrap and let rise until doubled, 1 to 1½ hours. Punch down.

To shape: Transfer dough to parchment-lined baking sheet and pat into a large rectangle or 8 smaller ovals about ½ inch thick. Cover with a towel and let rise for 45 minutes, or until doubled.

For topping: Combine olive oil with garlic. Poke your fingers into surface of dough to give it a dimpled appearance. Brush top of dough with garlic oil. Sprinkle with desired herbs and salt. Let rise briefly while oven is preheating.

Bake in preheated 375°F oven for 25 to 30 minutes, until crisp and golden.

242 calories per serving, 37.2 g carbohydrates, 1.7 g fiber, 6 g protein, 7.5 g fat (1.1 g saturated fat), 0 g cholesterol, 294 mg sodium, 86 mg potassium, 3 mg iron, 14 mg calcium, 72 mg phosphorus

### variations

Brush top of dough with garlic oil. Top with 1 cup each of thinly sliced zucchini, red onions and roasted red pepper strips (from a jar or home-made, page 53). Sautéed onions also make a delicious topping. Sprinkle with dried or fresh herbs, salt and pepper. If desired, top with ½ cup grated Parmesan. For hors d'oeuvres, cut baked Focaccia in 2-inch squares.

# POTATO AND ONION FOCACCIA

Paper-thin slices of potatoes and onions make a terrific topping for this savory flatbread!

Yield: 8 servings. Reheats and/or freezes well.

**Focaccia Dough (page 316)**
**2 to 3 Tbsp olive oil, divided**
**4 cloves garlic**
**2 medium onions, halved**

**2 medium potatoes, peeled**
**kosher salt and pepper to taste**
**¾ cup grated Parmesan cheese (optional)**

Prepare dough and let rise as directed (see Focaccia, page 316).

To shape: Punch down dough. Transfer to parchment-lined baking sheet and pat into a 9- × 15-inch rectangle. Cover with a towel and let rise for 45 minutes.

STEEL BLADE: Drop garlic through feed tube and process until minced. Brush dough with most of oil, then sprinkle with garlic.

THIN OR MEDIUM SLICER (2 or 4 mm): Slice onions and potatoes, using very light pressure. Spread evenly over dough and brush with a little more oil. Sprinkle with salt, pepper and Parmesan cheese (if using). Let rise briefly while oven is preheating.

Bake in preheated 375°F oven for 25 to 30 minutes, until crisp and golden.

308 calories per serving, 47.9 g carbohydrates, 2.7 g fiber, 8 g protein, 9.1 g fat (2 g saturated fat), 4 g cholesterol, 373 mg sodium, 265 mg potassium, 3 mg iron, 76 mg calcium, 132 mg phosphorus

# PITA BREAD

Pita is also known as "pocket bread." This fat-free Middle Eastern bread is popular for falafel, sandwiches and wraps.

Yield: 16 pitas. Store in plastic bags. These will keep for 1 or 2 days at room temperature. Freezes well.

**1 tsp sugar**
**¼ cup warm water (105°F to 115°F)**
**1 pkg active dry yeast (1 Tbsp)**

**3¼ cups flour**
**1 tsp salt**
**1 cup lukewarm water**

In measuring cup, dissolve 1 tsp sugar in ¼ cup warm water. Sprinkle yeast over and let stand for 8 to 10 minutes, until foamy. Stir to dissolve.

STEEL BLADE OR DOUGH BLADE: (Use DOUGH CYCLE if your machine has one.) Place flour and salt in processor. Add dissolved yeast and process 8 to 10 seconds to mix. Start machine and drizzle lukewarm water through feed tube directly onto flour mixture while machine is running. Process until dough is well kneaded and forms a mass around the blades. Process 30 to 40 seconds longer.

Turn out onto lightly floured surface. Knead dough by hand for 2 minutes, until smooth and elastic. (Optional: Place dough in large greased bowl and turn it to grease all surfaces. Cover bowl with plastic wrap and let dough rise for half an hour.)    *Continued*

To shape: Divide into 16 balls about 2 inches in diameter. Use a rolling pin to roll each ball to ¼-inch thickness. If dough is too elastic, let it rest for a few minutes for easier rolling.) Cover with a towel and let rise for half an hour. Roll once again and let rise half an hour longer.

Preheat oven to 500°F. Place pitas on baking sheet that has been lined with foil and sprayed (or line baking sheet with a silicone mat). Bake about 8 minutes, or until puffed and golden.

97 calories per pita, 19.9 g carbohydrates, 0.8 g fiber, 3 g protein, 0.3 g fat (0 g saturated fat), 0 g cholesterol, 147 mg sodium, 42 mg potassium, 1 mg iron, 5 mg calcium, 37 mg phosphorus

## variations

- WHOLE WHEAT PITAS: Use 1¾ cups flour and 1½ cups whole wheat flour. You can make these with white whole wheat flour.

- PITA CHIPS: Split each pita crosswise into 2 rounds. Brush with olive oil and minced garlic; sprinkle with oregano, basil and salt. Cut in wedges. Bake in preheated 400°F oven for 10 minutes, until crisp and golden. Serve with Hummus (page 56) or your favorite dip.

## BAGELS

Here's how to mix, shape and bake your own bagels— the hole story!

Yield: 10 to 12 bagels.

Freezes well.

DOUGH

| | |
|---|---|
| 1 tsp sugar | ¾ cup lukewarm water |
| ½ cup warm water (105°F to 115°F) | 1 Tbsp canola oil |
| 1 pkg active dry yeast (1 Tbsp) | |
| 3¼ cups flour (part whole wheat flour may be used) | 6 cups water |
| | 1 tsp salt |
| 4 tsp sugar | 1 tsp honey |
| 1½ tsp salt | ¾ to 1 cup sesame or poppy seeds for dipping (or half and half) |

In a 2-cup glass measure, dissolve 1 tsp sugar in ½ cup warm water. Sprinkle yeast over and let stand for 8 to 10 minutes, until foamy. Stir to dissolve.

STEEL BLADE OR DOUGH BLADE: (Use DOUGH CYCLE if your machine has one.) Process flour, remaining 4 tsp sugar and salt for 6 to 8 seconds. Add dissolved yeast and process for 12 to 15 seconds. While machine is running, gradually add lukewarm water and oil through feed tube directly onto flour mixture as quickly as flour will absorb it. Process until dough gathers and forms a mass around the blades, then process 30 to 40 seconds longer.

Turn out onto lightly floured surface. Knead by hand for 1 to 2 minutes, until smooth and elastic. Cover dough with a towel or plastic wrap and let rest for 20 minutes.

To shape: Divide dough into 10 to 12 equal pieces. Roll each piece between the palms of your hands into an 8-inch rope. Join ends to form a ring. Let rise for 20 to 30 minutes, until slightly puffy.

In large pot, bring water to a rolling boil. Add salt and honey. Drop 3 or 4 bagels at a time into boiling water. Cook for 30 seconds, turn bagels over and remove from water immediately with a perforated skimmer. Place on clean towel. Repeat with remaining bagels.

Put sesame or poppy seeds in a shallow bowl. Dip each bagel in seeds to coat all sides, then transfer to parchment-lined baking sheet. Bake in preheated 400°F oven about 25 minutes, until well browned. It may be necessary to turn bagels over for even browning.

234 calories per bagel, 36.1 g carbohydrates, 2.6 g fiber, 7 g protein, 7.2 g fat (0.9 g saturated fat), 0 g cholesterol, 353 mg sodium, 119 mg potassium, 4 mg iron, 113 mg calcium, 127 mg phosphorus

### notes

- For sweeter bagels, use 2 Tbsp white sugar and 2 tsp brown sugar in dough. Add ¼ cup honey to boiling water.

- If baking bagels becomes a habit, buy glazed ceramic tiles from your local ceramic dealer. Place tiles on bottom rack of your oven so they touch each other. Preheat oven. Bake bagels directly on the hot tiles to produce a crisp crust. This method is excellent for pizzas or any crusty types of bread.

## BEST-EVER ONION ROLLS

The name says it all!

Yield: 15 to 18 rolls.

Freezes well.

**Challah dough (page 301)**
**2 medium onions, cut in chunks**
**¾ cup bread crumbs**
**3 Tbsp oil**
**1 Tbsp poppy seeds**

**1 tsp salt**
**dash freshly ground black pepper**
**1 tsp caraway seeds (optional)**
**1 egg yolk beaten with 1 tsp water**

Prepare dough and let rise as directed.

STEEL BLADE: Chop onions with 3 or 4 quick on/off pulses. Add remaining ingredients except egg glaze; process with 2 or 3 quick on/offs to mix. Reserve about ½ cup filling as a topping.

To shape: Roll dough on floured surface into large rectangle about ¼ inch thick. Cut into 3-inch squares. Place about 1 Tbsp of filling on each square. Gather up edges and pinch together tightly to seal. Place on parchment-lined baking sheet. Brush each roll with egg glaze and sprinkle with about 1 tsp reserved onion filling. Cover with a towel and let rise until doubled.

Bake in preheated 375°F oven for 18 to 20 minutes, until golden.

217 calories per roll, 26.6 g carbohydrates, 1.3 g fiber, 5 g protein, 10 g fat (1.1 g saturated fat), 57 g cholesterol, 361 mg sodium, 82 mg potassium, 2 mg iron, 32 mg calcium, 74 mg phosphorus

## GARLIC BUNS

If you like garlic bread, you'll love these garlicky buns! When baked, they're almost like a pull-apart loaf.

Yield: 20 buns.

Freezes well.

Challah dough (page 301)
1 cup fresh parsley
10 cloves garlic
¼ cup olive oil
1 tsp kosher salt
¼ cup grated Parmesan cheese (optional)
1 egg yolk mixed with 1 tsp water
sesame seeds or kosher salt for sprinkling

Prepare dough and let rise as directed. Spray two 10-inch round glass pie plates or a 9 × 13 inch glass baking dish with nonstick spray.

STEEL BLADE: Process parsley until minced. Set aside. With machine running, drop garlic through feed tube and process until minced. Heat oil in a small skillet on medium heat. Sauté garlic for 2 minutes, until fragrant. Remove from heat and let cool.

Roll out dough on a lightly floured surface into a large rectangle about 12 × 20 inches. Spread with garlic/oil mixture, then sprinkle with salt, parsley and Parmesan cheese (if using). Roll up from the longer side into a jelly roll. Cut with a serrated knife into twenty 1-inch slices.

Place slices cut side down in prepared pan(s). Cover with a towel and let rise until doubled, about 45 to 60 minutes. Brush with egg glaze and sprinkle with sesame seeds or kosher salt.

Bake in preheated 375°F oven 25 to 30 minutes, until golden brown.

147 calories per bun, 16.5 g carbohydrates, 0.6 g fiber, 3 g protein, 7.5 g fat (0.9 g saturated fat), 32 g cholesterol, 241 mg sodium, 46 mg potassium, 1 mg iron, 11 mg calcium, 40 mg phosphorus

## BIALIES

This recipe was inspired by Mimi Sheraton's *The Bialy Eaters*, which describes her quest for the perfect bialy and the long-lost bakers of Bialystok. It is impossible to duplicate a bakery-style bialy in a home oven, but I hope you'll enjoy my version.

**Crusty French Bread dough (page 306)**
**1 medium onion, cut in chunks**
**3 Tbsp bread crumbs**
**2 Tbsp poppy seeds**
**cornmeal for baking pan**

Prepare dough and let rise as directed.

STEEL BLADE: Process onion until finely chopped, using quick on/off pulses. Add bread crumbs and poppy seeds. Process with quick on/off pulses, just until mixed.

To shape: Divide dough into 10 equal pieces. Shape into slightly flattened balls. Place on baking sheet that has been lined with foil and sprayed, then dusted with cornmeal. Cover with a towel and let rise until doubled, about 45 minutes.

Using your fingertips or the bottom of a small glass, gently press a deep indentation into the center of each roll, leaving a 1-inch rim. Brush tops of each roll lightly with a few drops of water. Fill the indentation with a spoonful of onion mixture.

Bake in preheated 450°F oven for 18 to 20 minutes, until brown and crusty.

Yield: 10 bialies.
Freezes well.

182 calories per bialy, 36.5 g carbohydrates, 1.9 g fiber, 5 g protein, 1.3 g fat (0.2 g saturated fat), 0 g cholesterol, 483 mg sodium, 91 mg potassium, 2 mg iron, 38 mg calcium, 76 mg phosphorus

### note

To simulate a baker's oven, place a baking stone (available in kitchenware shops) on the lower rack of your oven. Preheat oven to desired temperature. Carefully slide unbaked loaves (or rolls) directly onto the hot baking stone. If you place a pan filled with boiling water or ice cubes on the bottom rack of your oven during baking, the steam will help produce a chewy crust.

## ALL-PURPOSE PAREVE DOUGH

Excellent for cinnamon buns, rolls and coffee cakes, and free of meat and dairy products.

**1 tsp sugar**
**¼ cup warm water (105°F to 115°F)**
**1 pkg active dry yeast (1 Tbsp)**
**3 cups flour**
**½ tsp salt**
**⅓ cup sugar**
**⅓ cup oil**
**2 eggs (or 1 egg plus 2 egg whites)**
**⅓ cup lukewarm water or soy milk**

Yield: Enough dough for 12 to 18 servings, depending on recipe.

In measuring cup, dissolve 1 tsp sugar in ¼ cup warm water. Sprinkle yeast over and let stand for 8 to 10 minutes, until foamy. Stir to dissolve.

STEEL BLADE OR DOUGH BLADE: (Use DOUGH CYCLE if your machine has one.) Place flour, salt and remaining ⅓ cup sugar in processor. Add dissolved yeast

*Continued*

mixture and process for 12 to 15 seconds. While machine is running, add oil and eggs through feed tube and process until blended, about 10 seconds. Slowly add lukewarm water or soy milk directly onto flour mixture and process until dough forms a mass on the blades. Process 30 to 40 seconds longer. Turn out onto lightly floured surface. Knead by hand for 1 to 2 minutes, until smooth and elastic, adding just enough flour to keep dough from sticking.

Place dough in large greased bowl; turn dough over so all surfaces are lightly greased. Cover bowl with plastic wrap. *Either* let dough rise at room temperature until doubled in bulk (about 2 hours) *or* refrigerate and let rise overnight. (Dough will keep in refrigerator for 3 or 4 days.) Punch down and shape as desired.

To shape: Refer to specific recipes for shaping, baking times and yield. Dough may be frozen before or after baking (see "Freeze with Ease," page 299).

206 calories per serving ($\frac{1}{12}$ of recipe), 30.1 g carbohydrates, 1 g fiber, 5 g protein, 7.4 g fat
(0.8 g saturated fat), 35 g cholesterol, 109 mg sodium, 56 mg potassium,
2 mg iron, 10 mg calcium, 56 mg phosphorus

## NORENE'S YUMMY YEAST DOUGH

This versatile dough has become a favorite with families all over the world! It's wonderful for cinnamon buns, Danish or your favorite sweet yeast breads.

Yield: Enough dough for 12 to 18 servings, depending on recipe.

| | |
|---|---|
| 1 tsp sugar | ⅓ cup sugar |
| ¼ cup warm water (105°F to 115°F) | ½ tsp salt |
| 1 pkg active dry yeast (1 Tbsp) | ½ cup butter or tub margarine, cut in |
| ⅓ cup milk (2%) or water | chunks |
| 3 cups flour | 2 eggs (or 1 egg plus 2 egg whites) |

In a measuring cup, dissolve 1 tsp sugar in ¼ cup warm water. Sprinkle yeast over-top and let stand for 8 to 10 minutes, until foamy. Stir to dissolve. Meanwhile, heat milk until steaming (about 30 to 40 seconds in the microwave). Let cool for 5 minutes, until lukewarm.

STEEL BLADE OR DOUGH BLADE: (Use DOUGH CYCLE if your machine has one.) Process flour, remaining ⅓ cup sugar, salt and butter for 20 seconds, until no large pieces of butter remain. Add dissolved yeast mixture and process another 5 seconds. Start machine and add eggs and lukewarm milk through feed tube directly onto flour mixture while machine is running. If machine begins to slow down, add up to an additional ¼ cup flour through feed tube. Once dough has formed a mass around the blades, process 30 to 40 seconds longer.

Knead dough by hand on lightly floured surface for 1 to 2 minutes, until smooth and elastic. Small bubbles will begin to form under the surface of the dough, and it will not cling to your hands or the work surface.

Place dough in large greased bowl; turn dough over so all surfaces are lightly greased. Cover bowl with plastic wrap and let rise until doubled, about 2 hours at room temperature. Punch down. If desired, let rise until doubled once again; punch down.

To shape: Refer to specific recipes for shaping, baking times and yield. Dough may be frozen before or after baking (see "Freeze with Ease," page 299).

222 calories per serving (1/12 of recipe), 30.5 g carbohydrates, 1 g fiber, 5 g protein, 9 g fat (5.2 g saturated fat), 56 g cholesterol, 166 mg sodium, 68 mg potassium, 2 mg iron, 20 mg calcium, 64 mg phosphorus

### lighter variation

Use ¼ cup margarine or oil. Replace milk with water.

## CINNAMON BUNS OR KUCHEN

Yield: 20 buns.

Freezes well.

Norene's Yummy Yeast Dough
(page 322) or All-Purpose Pareve
Dough (page 321)
2 Tbsp soft butter or tub margarine

½ cup Cinnamon-Sugar Mixture
(page 324)
½ cup raisins and/or chopped nuts
(optional)
1 egg yolk beaten with 2 tsp water

Prepare dough and let rise as directed.

To shape: On a lightly floured surface, roll dough into 12- × 20-inch rectangle. Spread with butter or margarine. Sprinkle with cinnamon-sugar mixture, raisins and/or nuts (if using). Roll lightly with a rolling pin, pressing sugar mixture into dough. Roll up like a jelly roll, pinching edges firmly to seal seams. Cut with a serrated knife into twenty 1-inch slices. Place cut side down in sprayed 9- × 13-inch glass baking dish. Cover with a towel and let rise until doubled. Brush with egg glaze.

Bake in preheated 375°F oven 25 to 30 minutes, until golden brown.

167 calories per serving, 23.6 g carbohydrates, 0.8 g fiber, 3 g protein, 6.8 g fat (3.9 g saturated fat), 47 g cholesterol, 108 mg sodium, 44 mg potassium, 1 mg iron, 17 mg calcium, 43 mg phosphorus

### sticky pecan buns

In small saucepan, melt ¼ cup butter or tub margarine. Add ½ cup firmly packed brown sugar and 1 Tbsp water; mix well. Drizzle mixture into well-sprayed 9- × 13-inch glass baking dish; spread evenly. Sprinkle with 1 cup coarsely chopped pecans. Place buns in pan, cover with a towel and let rise until doubled, about 1 hour. Bake at 375°F for 25 to 30 minutes. Cool in pan 2 or 3 minutes. Invert pan onto serving platter so sugar mixture glazes buns. *Continued*

323

246 calories per serving, 29.8 g carbohydrates, 1.3 g fiber, 4 g protein, 13 g fat (5.7 g saturated fat), 53 g cholesterol, 126 mg sodium, 74 mg potassium, 1 mg iron, 26 mg calcium, 59 mg phosphorus

### cinnamon-sugar mixture

Process 2 Tbsp cinnamon with 1 cup white or brown sugar on the STEEL BLADE. Use quick on/off pulses to start, then let machine run until well mixed. Makes 1 cup.

## ALMOND TEA RING

Yield: 1 large or 2 small rings (16 servings). Freezes well, but glaze after thawing.

Norene's Yummy Yeast Dough (page 322) or All-Purpose Pareve Dough (page 321)
1½ cups almonds
¾ cup sugar
1 Tbsp lemon juice

1 egg yolk
⅓ to ½ cup strawberry or apricot jam
White Glaze (page 381)
½ cup toasted slivered almonds, for garnish

Prepare dough and let rise as directed.

STEEL BLADE: Process almonds with sugar until finely ground, about 30 seconds. Add lemon juice and egg yolk; process 5 seconds longer.

To shape: Roll out dough on floured surface into 1 large (9- × 18-inch) or 2 smaller (8- × 12-inch) rectangles. Spread with jam to within 1 inch of edges; sprinkle with almond mixture. Roll up like a jelly roll. Join ends together to form a ring; pinch to seal. Place seam side down on parchment-lined baking pan. Using a sharp knife or scissors, cut in 1-inch slices to within ¾ inch of inside of ring. (Inside of ring will still be attached.) Turn each slice on its side, cut side up, slightly overlapping slices. Cover with a towel and let rise until doubled.

Bake in preheated 375°F oven 25 to 30 minutes for a large ring, or 20 to 25 minutes for smaller rings. When cool, drizzle with glaze. Garnish with toasted almonds.

322 calories per serving, 46.9 g carbohydrates, 2.2 g fiber, 6 g protein, 12.9 g fat (4.5 g saturated fat), 55 g cholesterol, 126 mg sodium, 140 mg potassium, 2 mg iron, 50 mg calcium, 112 mg phosphorus

# BUBBLE RING COFFEE CAKE

This is also known as Monkey Bread and is ideal for any festive occasion. Absolutely impressive!

Yield: 12 servings. If freezing, glaze after thawing.

**Norene's Yummy Yeast Dough (page 322) or All-Purpose Pareve Dough (page 321)**
**1 cup pecans or walnuts**
**⅓ cup melted butter**

**¾ cup brown sugar mixed with**
**1 Tbsp ground cinnamon**
**¼ to ½ cup raisins or dried cranberries**
**White Glaze (page 381) (optional)**

Prepare dough and let rise as directed.

STEEL BLADE: Process nuts with 6 to 8 quick on/off pulses, until coarsely chopped.

To shape: Form dough into forty 1-inch balls. Roll in melted butter, then in cinnamon-sugar mixture. Arrange in sprayed 12-cup fluted tube pan, sprinkling nuts and raisins or cranberries between layers. Reserve 2 Tbsp nuts to garnish baked cake. Cover with a towel and let rise until doubled.

Bake in preheated 375°F oven 30 to 35 minutes, until done. Loosen edges with a spatula and let stand 15 minutes before inverting and removing from pan. When cool, drizzle with glaze (if desired). Sprinkle with reserved nuts.

387 calories per serving (without glaze), 48 g carbohydrates, 2.3 g fiber, 6 g protein, 20 g fat (9 g saturated fat), 70 g cholesterol, 207 mg sodium, 150 mg potassium, 2 mg iron, 46 mg calcium, 92 mg phosphorus

# CHOCOLATE BABKA

This yeast coffee cake is a combination of 2 of my favorite foods—bread and chocolate! Instead of glazing the babka after baking, you can sprinkle it with Streusel Topping (page 302) just before baking.

Yield: 12 to 16 servings. Freezes well, but glaze after thawing.

**Norene's Yummy Yeast Dough (page 322) or All-Purpose Pareve Dough (page 321)**
**¾ cup chocolate chips**
**2 Tbsp unsweetened cocoa powder**
**¼ cup sugar**

**¼ cup almonds or pecans (optional)**
**1 egg yolk blended with 1 tsp water**
**Decadent Chocolate Glaze (page 326) or Streusel Topping (page 302)**

Prepare dough and let rise as directed.

STEEL BLADE: Process chocolate chips, sugar, nuts (if using) and cocoa until coarsely ground, 20 to 25 seconds.

To shape: On a lightly floured surface, roll out dough into large rectangle about 9 x 16 inches. Sprinkle filling over dough, leaving ½-inch border around edges. Roll up from longer side, jelly-roll style, pinching edges to seal. Place seam side down in sprayed 12-cup fluted tube pan and join ends to form a ring. Cover pan with plastic wrap or a towel and let rise until doubled, about 1 hour. Brush with egg glaze. (If using Streusel Topping, sprinkle it on now.) *Continued*

Bake in preheated 375°F oven 30 to 35 minutes, until golden. Babka should sound hollow when tapped with your fingers. Loosen edges with a spatula and let stand 15 minutes. Invert onto a platter then invert onto another platter so the top side is facing up. Cool completely. (If you didn't use Streusel Topping, drizzle Decadent Chocolate Glaze on top of babka.)

325 calories per serving (with glaze), 46.3 g carbohydrates, 2.1 g fiber, 6 g protein, 14 g fat (8.1 g saturated fat), 74 g cholesterol, 168 mg sodium, 141 mg potassium, 2 mg iron, 26 mg calcium, 92 mg phosphorus

### variation

Prepare dough and let rise as directed. Instead of sprinkling dough with chocolate/nut mixture, spread with Chocolate Shmear (below).

## DECADENT CHOCOLATE GLAZE

Yield: Enough glaze for 1 large or 2 medium loaves or about 16 buns. Glaze after thawing if loaves or buns have been frozen.

2 squares semisweet chocolate (2 oz/60 g)
1 Tbsp honey
1½ Tbsp hot water
½ tsp pure vanilla extract

Melt chocolate in microwave on Medium (50%) for about 2 minutes, stirring once or twice. Add honey, hot water and vanilla extract; blend well. Drizzle over babka or use as glaze for brownies and cakes.

54 calories per Tbsp, 8.1 g carbohydrates, 0.6 g fiber, 0 g protein, 2.8 g fat (1.7 g saturated fat), 0 g cholesterol, 1 mg sodium, 36 mg potassium, 0 mg iron, 3 mg calcium, 13 mg phosphorus

## CHOCOLATE SHMEAR

This nut-free shmear makes a decadent filling for babkas and yeast buns.

1½ cups chocolate chips (or semisweet chocolate, broken into chunks)
¼ cup unsweetened cocoa powder
½ tsp ground cinnamon
½ cup sugar
3 Tbsp butter or tub margarine, cut in chunks

Yield: Enough filling for a large Chocolate Babka (page 325) or about 16 buns.

STEEL BLADE: Combine all ingredients and process for 25 to 30 seconds, making a spreadable paste.

72 calories per Tbsp, 9.8 g carbohydrates, 1 g fiber, 1 g protein, 4 g fat (2.4 g saturated fat), 3 g cholesterol, 10 mg sodium, 34 mg potassium, 0 mg iron, 4 mg calcium, 12 mg phosphorus

# CHOCOLATE DANISH

Yield: 2 loaves or about 16 buns. Freezes well but glaze after thawing.

Norene's Yummy Yeast Dough (page 322) or All-Purpose Pareve Dough (page 321)

½ cup brown sugar, packed

⅓ cup walnuts or pecans

2 Tbsp unsweetened cocoa powder

1 tsp ground cinnamon

2 Tbsp tub margarine

Chocolate Glaze (page 381) or White Glaze (page 381) (optional)

Prepare dough and let rise as directed.

STEEL BLADE: Process brown sugar, nuts, cocoa and cinnamon with several on/off pulses, until nuts are finely chopped.

To shape: Divide dough in half. Working with 1 piece at a time, roll out on floured surface into 9- × 12-inch rectangle. Spread with half the margarine. Sprinkle with half the filling. Roll up like a jelly roll; pinch edges firmly to seal. If making a loaf, seal ends. For individual buns, cut in 1-inch pieces. Repeat with remaining dough and filling. Line a baking sheet with parchment paper or foil; spray foil with nonstick spray. Place loaf or buns on baking sheet, cover with a towel and let rise until doubled.

Bake in preheated 375°F oven 25 to 30 minutes for a loaf, or 18 to 20 minutes for buns. Glaze when cooled (if desired).

223 calories per serving, 30.5 g carbohydrates, 1.2 g fiber, 4 g protein, 9.8 g fat (4.4 g saturated fat), 42 g cholesterol, 138 mg sodium, 82 mg potassium, 2 mg iron, 26 mg calcium, 62 mg phosphorus

## cheese danish

Replace nut filling with Cheese Filling (page 166). To shape, roll out half of dough into a rectangle. Spread half of filling in a 2-inch band along bottom edge of dough. (Dough can be sprinkled first with a little cinnamon, sugar and raisins, if desired.) Roll up, sealing edges well. Repeat with remaining dough and filling. Let rise and bake as directed. If desired, sprinkle with Streusel Topping (page 302) just before baking. Do not glaze.

200 calories per serving, 27.2 g carbohydrates, 0.7 g fiber, 7 g protein, 7.1 g fat (4.1 g saturated fat), 57 g cholesterol, 215 mg sodium, 92 mg potassium, 1 mg iron, 40 mg calcium, 105 mg phosphorus

# BRIOCHE

This sweet, buttery yeast bread is delicious toasted and topped with jam. Leftovers make fabulous French toast or bread pudding!

Yield: 1 loaf (10 to 12 servings). Freezes well.

**1 tsp sugar**
**¼ cup warm milk (1%) (105°F to 115°F)**
**1 pkg active dry yeast (1 Tbsp)**
**2½ cups flour (approximately)**
**3 Tbsp sugar**

**½ tsp salt**
**¾ cup (1½ sticks) frozen butter, cut in pieces**
**3 eggs**
**1 egg yolk beaten with 1 tsp milk or water**

In a measuring cup, dissolve 1 tsp sugar in warm milk. Sprinkle yeast over and let stand for 8 to 10 minutes, until foamy. Stir to dissolve.

STEEL BLADE OR DOUGH BLADE: (Use DOUGH CYCLE if your machine has one.) Process flour, remaining 3 Tbsp sugar, salt and butter for 20 to 25 seconds, until blended. Add dissolved yeast mixture and process another 5 seconds. Start machine and add eggs through feed tube directly onto flour mixture while machine is running. Process until dough forms a mass around the blades. If machine begins to slow down, add up to another ¼ cup flour. Process 30 seconds longer.

Turn out onto lightly floured surface. Knead by hand for 1 to 2 minutes, until smooth and elastic.

Place dough in large greased bowl; turn dough over so all surfaces are lightly greased. Cover bowl with plastic wrap and let rise until doubled, 1½ to 2 hours. Punch down. Cover and refrigerate overnight. (Dough must be chilled for best results.)

To shape: Form three-quarters of dough into a ball; place in sprayed brioche mold or 6-cup round casserole. Using 3 fingers, make a hole about 2 inches wide and 2 inches deep in center of ball. Form remaining piece of dough into a pear shape. Fit it into the hole, narrow end down. Cover loosely with plastic wrap and let rise until doubled, about 2 hours. Brush top of brioche lightly with egg glaze, making sure it does not drip down sides of pan. Just before putting it into the oven, use scissors to make 4 or 5 cuts between the "head" (small ball) and "shoulders" (large ball)—this helps the brioche rise.

Bake in preheated 350°F oven 35 to 45 minutes, or until nicely browned and loaf sounds hollow when tapped. Remove from pan onto wire rack and let cool.

286 calories per serving, 28.8 g carbohydrates, 1 g fiber, 6 g protein, 16.3 g fat (9.5 g saturated fat), 122 g cholesterol, 237 mg sodium, 81 mg potassium, 2 mg iron, 26 mg calcium, 87 mg phosphorus

# CROISSANTS

These croissants are light and flaky. Well worth the effort!

Yield: 18 croissants. Freezes well. To thaw: Place frozen croissants on parchment-lined baking sheet and heat at 400°F for about 5 minutes.

| | |
|---|---|
| ½ tsp sugar | 2 Tbsp butter |
| ¼ cup warm water (105°F to 115°F) | 1 Tbsp sugar |
| 1 pkg active dry yeast (1 Tbsp) | ½ tsp salt |
| 1 cup milk (1%) | ½ cup chilled butter, cut in chunks |
| 2½ cups flour | 1 egg yolk plus 2 tsp water |

In measuring cup, dissolve ½ tsp sugar in warm water. Sprinkle yeast over and let stand for 8 to 10 minutes, until foamy. Stir to dissolve. Microwave milk until steaming, about 1½ minutes on High; cool to lukewarm.

STEEL BLADE OR DOUGH BLADE: (Use DOUGH CYCLE if your machine has one.) Process flour with 2 Tbsp butter, 1 Tbsp sugar and salt for 10 seconds. Add dissolved yeast mixture and process 5 or 6 seconds longer. Start machine and add milk through feed tube directly onto flour mixture while machine is running; process until dough forms a mass around the blades. Process for 30 to 40 seconds longer.

Turn dough out onto lightly floured surface and knead by hand 1 to 2 minutes, until smooth and elastic.

Place dough in large greased bowl; turn dough over so all surfaces are lightly greased. Cover bowl with plastic wrap and let rise 1½ hours, or until doubled. Punch down. Refrigerate dough for half an hour.

STEEL BLADE: Process ½ cup chilled butter until lump-free and smooth, about 45 seconds, scraping down sides of bowl as needed. Refrigerate butter while you roll out dough.

Rolling/Folding Technique: On floured surface, roll dough into a rectangle about 9 × 15 inches. Working from the shorter side, spread lower two-thirds of dough with butter, leaving a ½-inch border around edges. Start from the top and fold dough in 3, as if you were folding a business letter. Rotate dough 90 degrees, so that it resembles a book you are going to open. Roll out once again into a large rectangle, adding flour as needed to prevent dough from sticking. Fold into 3 as

*Continued*

before. You have now completed 2 "turns." Repeat twice, turning dough a quarter turn (90 degrees) each time. You will have completed 4 turns in all. Place in a large resealable plastic bag and refrigerate at least 2 hours or overnight.

To shape: Roll dough on floured surface into a 12-inch square. Cut into 9 squares. Cut each square in half diagonally to make 18 triangles. Starting at the base of each triangle, roll up, stretching dough slightly. Shape into crescents. Place 3 inches apart on parchment-lined baking sheet with the point of the triangle underneath. Cover with a towel and let rise for about 1 hour at room temperature. Brush with egg glaze.

Bake in preheated 425°F oven 12 to 15 minutes, until puffed and golden.

134 calories per croissant, 15 g carbohydrates, 0.6 g fiber, 3 g protein, 7 g fat (4.3 g saturated fat), 30 g cholesterol, 117 mg sodium, 50 mg potassium, 1 mg iron, 22 mg calcium, 43 mg phosphorus

## CRISS-CROSS BUNS

Small, sweet festive yeast buns filled with raisins or currants.

Yield: 15 buns. Freezes well, but glaze after thawing.

| | |
|---|---|
| 1 tsp sugar | ¼ tsp nutmeg |
| ¼ cup warm water (105°F to 115°F) | ¼ cup butter, cut in chunks |
| 1 pkg active dry yeast (1 Tbsp) | 2 eggs |
| ¾ cup milk (1%) | 3 Tbsp candied mixed fruit (optional) |
| 3¼ cups flour | ¾ cup raisins or currants |
| ¼ cup brown sugar, lightly packed | 1 egg yolk blended with 2 tsp water |
| 1 tsp ground cinnamon | White Glaze (page 381) |
| ½ tsp salt | |

Dissolve 1 tsp sugar in warm water. Sprinkle yeast overtop and let stand for 8 to 10 minutes, until foamy. Stir to dissolve. Meanwhile, heat milk until steaming, about 1¼ minutes on High in the microwave. Cool to lukewarm.

STEEL BLADE OR DOUGH BLADE: (Use DOUGH CYCLE if your machine has one.) Place flour, brown sugar, cinnamon, salt, nutmeg and butter in processor. Process for 20 to 25 seconds, until no large pieces of butter remain. Add dissolved yeast mixture and process 10 seconds. Start machine and add milk and eggs through feed tube directly onto flour mixture while machine is running. Process until dough forms a mass around blades. Process 30 to 40 seconds longer. If machine begins to slow down, add up to ¼ cup flour through feed tube. Dough will be somewhat sticky and quite elastic.

Turn out onto lightly floured surface. Knead in candied fruit (if desired), and raisins or currants. Knead for 1 to 2 minutes, until smooth and elastic.

Place dough in large greased bowl; turn dough so all surfaces are lightly greased. Cover bowl with plastic wrap and let rise until doubled, about 2 hours at room temperature. Punch down.

To shape: Divide dough into 15 balls, making sure dried fruit and raisins are covered by dough. Place on parchment-lined baking sheet, barely touching each other. Cover with a towel and let rise until doubled, about 1 hour. Brush with egg glaze.

Bake in preheated 375°F oven 18 to 20 minutes, until golden brown. When cool, mark an X on each bun with White Glaze.

216 calories per bun, 39.4 g carbohydrates, 1.4 g fiber, 5 g protein, 4.6 g fat (2.4 g saturated fat), 51 g cholesterol, 118 mg sodium, 136 mg potassium, 2 mg iron, 34 mg calcium, 72 mg phosphorus

## STOLLEN

You'll love this rich holiday loaf filled with dried fruit and decorated with candied cherries.

Yield: 2 loaves (10 servings per loaf). If freezing, decorate after thawing.

1 tsp sugar
¼ cup warm water (105°F to 115°F)
1 pkg yeast (1 Tbsp)
½ cup milk (1%)
½ cup butter, cut in chunks
3¼ cups flour
½ cup sugar
2 eggs

¾ cup candied mixed fruit
¾ cup raisins and/or currants
½ cup candied cherries, halved
¾ cup slivered almonds
White Glaze (page 381)
candied red and green cherries and whole almonds, for garnish

In a measuring cup, dissolve 1 tsp sugar in warm water. Sprinkle yeast over and let stand for 8 to 10 minutes, until foamy. Stir to dissolve. Meanwhile, heat milk until steaming, about 1 minute on High in the microwave. Stir in butter until melted. Cool to lukewarm.

STEEL BLADE OR DOUGH BLADE: (Use DOUGH CYCLE if your machine has one.) Process flour, remaining ½ cup sugar and dissolved yeast mixture for 10 to 12 seconds, until mixed. Start machine and add eggs and lukewarm milk and butter mixture through feed tube directly onto flour mixture. Process until dough forms a mass around the blades, then process 30 to 40 seconds longer; dough will be somewhat sticky. If machine begins to slow down, add up to ¼ cup additional flour through the feed tube.

Turn dough out onto floured surface and let rest for 2 minutes. Knead in candied fruit, raisins or currants, cherries and almonds by hand. Knead for about 2 minutes, adding just enough flour to keep dough from sticking. Fruit and nuts should be evenly distributed throughout dough.

Place dough in large greased bowl; turn dough over so all surfaces are lightly greased. Cover bowl with plastic wrap and let rise in a warm place until doubled. Punch down. *Continued*

To shape: Divide dough in half. On floured surface, roll each piece of dough into 12- × 7-inch oval. Fold in half lengthwise; press edges firmly to seal. Place on parchment-lined baking sheet and shape into a crescent. Cover with a towel and let rise until doubled.

Bake in preheated 375°F oven about 30 minutes, until golden brown. When cool, drizzle with White Glaze. Decorate with red and green candied cherries and almonds to form flowers and leaves. Use half a red cherry for the center, almonds for the petals and strips of green cherries to form stems and leaves.

252 calories per serving, 45.9 g carbohydrates, 1.7 g fiber, 4 g protein, 6.6 g fat (3.1 g saturated fat), 13 g cholesterol, 55 mg sodium, 120 mg potassium, 1 mg iron, 28 mg calcium, 57 mg phosphorus

## I CAN'T BELIEVE IT'S BROCCOLI BREAD!

None of my taste testers could guess the mystery ingredient! This is a wonderful way to use broccoli stems. If you don't have enough broccoli, add grated carrots. Use the florets in your favorite stir-fry.

Yield: 1 loaf (12 servings). Freezes well.

| | |
|---|---|
| 1½ cups flour (part whole wheat can be used) | 1 cup brown sugar, packed |
| 1½ tsp ground cinnamon | 1 egg |
| ½ tsp baking powder | ¼ cup canola oil |
| ½ tsp baking soda | ½ tsp pure vanilla extract |
| pinch salt | 1 tsp orange zest |
| 2 or 3 thick broccoli stems, trimmed and peeled (1 cup grated) | 2 Tbsp orange juice |
| | ½ to ¾ cup fresh or dried cranberries |
| | ½ cup slivered almonds (optional) |

STEEL BLADE: Process flour, cinnamon, baking powder, baking soda and salt for 5 to 10 seconds, until blended. Transfer to a bowl and set aside.

GRATER: Grate broccoli, using medium pressure. Measure 1 cup loosely packed and set aside.

STEEL BLADE: Process brown sugar, egg, oil, vanilla extract and orange zest until mixed, about 30 seconds. Do not insert pusher in feed tube. Add grated broccoli and process 1 minute longer, until well blended. Add flour mixture, orange juice, cranberries and almonds (if using). Process with quick on/off pulses, just until flour mixture disappears, scraping down bowl as necessary.

Spread batter in sprayed 9- × 5-inch loaf pan. Bake in preheated 350°F oven for 50 to 60 minutes, or until a wooden toothpick inserted in the center comes out clean.

181 calories per serving, 31.6 g carbohydrates, 1 g fiber, 2.4 g protein, 5.3 g fat (0.5 g saturated fat), 18 g cholesterol, 98 mg sodium, 75 mg potassium, 1 mg iron, 38 mg calcium, 34 mg phosphorus

# ORANGE CORN BREAD

This recipe has traveled as far away as Israel, to rave reviews. Serve it warm or toasted with butter or preserves. Delicious!

Yield: 1 loaf (12 servings). Freezes well.

1 cup plus 3 Tbsp flour
¾ cup cornmeal
4 tsp baking powder
½ tsp salt
1 medium seedless orange (unpeeled)

3½ Tbsp sugar
½ cup tub margarine or butter, cut in chunks
1 egg
1¼ cups milk (1%) or soy milk
¾ cup raisins (optional)

STEEL BLADE: Process flour, cornmeal, baking powder and salt until blended, about 5 seconds. Empty bowl.

Cut orange in quarters. Process on STEEL BLADE for 20 seconds. Add sugar and margarine or butter and process for 1 minute. Add egg and milk through feed tube while machine is running. Process for 3 seconds. Add dry ingredients. Process, using 3 or 4 quick on/off pulses, just until blended. If adding raisins, process 2 seconds longer.

Pour into sprayed 9- × 5-inch loaf pan or 8-inch square pan. Bake in preheated 375°F oven about 45 minutes, until cake tester comes out clean.

181 calories per serving, 22.2 g carbohydrates, 1.4 g fiber, 4 g protein, 8.9 g fat (1.7 g saturated fat), 19 g cholesterol, 339 mg sodium, 105 mg potassium, 1 mg iron, 132 mg calcium, 99 mg phosphorus

# BEST BANANA BREAD

The large amount of baking soda and long baking time at a low temperature give this delicious banana bread its dark color.

Yield: 1 loaf (12 servings). Freezes well. If your processor has a large (14-cup) bowl, you can double the recipe.

3 medium very ripe bananas (the blacker the better)
1 cup sugar
3 tsp baking soda
dash salt
2 eggs (or 1 egg plus 2 egg whites)
¼ cup canola oil

1½ cups flour
1 tsp lemon juice plus milk (1%) to equal ½ cup (or substitute ½ cup buttermilk for the lemon-milk mixture)
2 Tbsp ground flax seed or wheat germ (optional)

STEEL BLADE: Process bananas until puréed, 15 to 20 seconds. Measure 1 cup banana purée. Add sugar, baking soda and salt to banana purée and process for 30 seconds. Add eggs and oil and process until blended, about 10 seconds. Pour flour overtop, then add sour milk or buttermilk. Process 8 to 10 seconds longer, until smooth, scraping down bowl as necessary. Blend in flax seed or wheat germ (if using).

Line 9- × 5-inch loaf pan with buttered parchment paper or aluminum foil. Pour in batter. Bake on middle rack in preheated 275°F oven about 2½ hours, or until loaf tests done. *Continued*

197 calories per serving, 33.6 g carbohydrates, 0.9 g fiber, 3 g protein, 5.9 g fat (0.7 g saturated fat), 36 g cholesterol, 343 mg sodium, 111 mg potassium, 1 mg iron, 20 mg calcium, 45 mg phosphorus

## NANA'S ZUCCHINI BREAD

To escape the summer heat, Evelyn Laederer (called Nana by close friends and family) used to cook and bake downstairs in her laundry room, using her toaster oven and slow cooker. I'm sure she would have loved my lighter variation of her famous zucchini bread.

Yield: 2 loaves (12 servings per loaf). Freezes well.

| | |
|---|---|
| 1½ cups walnuts | 1 tsp salt |
| 1 cup raisins, currants or chocolate chips | 1 tsp baking powder |
| | ¾ tsp baking soda |
| 3 cups flour | 2 medium zucchini (2 cups grated) |
| 1½ cups sugar | 3 eggs |
| 1 tsp ground cinnamon | 1 cup canola oil |

For machines with nested bowls, see method below.

STEEL BLADE: Chop nuts coarsely with several quick on/offs. Reserve ½ cup nuts to sprinkle on top of loaves. Combine remaining nuts with raisins in a small bowl; set aside.

Process flour with sugar, cinnamon, salt, baking powder and baking soda for 10 seconds, until blended. Transfer to a large mixing bowl.

GRATER: Discard tips of zucchini. Grate, using medium pressure. Measure 2 cups loosely packed. Add to flour mixture.

STEEL BLADE: Blend eggs with oil until light, about 45 seconds. Add to flour mixture. Stir with wooden spoon just until moistened. Stir in raisin/nut mixture.

Pour into two sprayed 9- × 5-inch loaf pans. Sprinkle with reserved nuts. Bake in preheated 350°F oven 50 to 60 minutes, until a toothpick inserted in center comes out clean. Cool for 15 minutes before removing from pans.

266 calories per serving, 31.1 g carbohydrates, 1.6 g fiber, 4 g protein, 15 g fat (1.4 g saturated fat), 27 g cholesterol, 167 mg sodium, 145 mg potassium, 1 mg iron, 29 mg calcium, 68 mg phosphorus

### nested bowl method

Use mini-bowl and mini-blade to chop nuts. Use medium bowl and GRATER/SHREDDING DISC for zucchini. Use large bowl and STEEL BLADE for remaining processing tasks.

### variations

Helaine Finkelstein of Israel substitutes spelt flour, and uses 1 cup sugar and 1¼ tsp baking powder. She also adds ½ cup pumpkin seeds or pistachios. Add ½ to 1 cup chocolate chips instead of raisins or nuts. One serving contains 169 calories, 23 g carbohydrates and 1.6 g fiber.

Reduce nuts to ⅓ cup; do not sprinkle loaves with nuts. Use 2 eggs plus 2 egg whites. Reduce sugar to 1⅓ cups and replace half the oil with unsweetened applesauce. One serving contains 183 calories, 29.5 g carbohydrates, 1.3 g fiber and 6.4 g fat.

### zucchini muffins

• Pour batter into paper-lined or sprayed muffin tins. Bake in preheated 350°F oven about 25 minutes. Makes 24 to 30 muffins.

## ONE-BANANA MUFFINS

Although these muffins are made with just 1 banana, they are moist and delicious.

Yield: About 18 muffins. Freezes well.

½ cup tub margarine or butter, cut in chunks

2 eggs (or 1 egg plus 2 whites)

1 tsp pure vanilla extract

1¼ cups sugar

1 medium banana

1 tsp baking soda

¾ cup buttermilk (or 2 tsp lemon juice plus milk to make ¾ cup)

2 cups flour

1 tsp baking powder

cinnamon sugar for sprinkling (optional)

STEEL BLADE: Process margarine or butter, eggs, vanilla extract and sugar for 2 minutes, scraping down bowl once or twice. Do not insert pusher in feed tube. Break banana into 2-inch pieces and add through feed tube while machine is running. Dissolve baking soda in buttermilk or sour milk. Add through feed tube while machine is running and process for 3 seconds. Add flour and baking powder; process with 3 or 4 quick on/off pulses, just until flour disappears.

Fill paper-lined or sprayed muffin tins two-thirds full. Sprinkle with cinnamon sugar (if desired). Bake in preheated 400°F oven for 18 to 20 minutes.

171 calories per muffin, 26.8 g carbohydrates, 0.5 g fiber, 3 g protein, 6 g fat (1.2 g saturated fat), 24 g cholesterol, 155 mg sodium, 66 mg potassium, 1 mg iron, 35 mg calcium, 40 mg phosphorus

## MOM'S BLUEBERRY MUFFINS

When you're in a blue mood, these will make you "berry" happy! Try using a combination of blueberries and raspberries.

½ cup tub margarine or butter, cut in chunks

¾ cup sugar

2 eggs

1 tsp baking soda

1 Tbsp white vinegar plus milk (1%) to equal 1 cup

2 cups flour

2 tsp baking powder

1½ cups fresh or frozen blueberries (do not thaw)

335

Yield: About 2 dozen muffins. Freezes well.

STEEL BLADE: Process margarine or butter, sugar and eggs for 2 minutes, scraping down bowl once or twice. Do not insert pusher in feed tube. Dissolve baking soda in vinegar-milk mixture. Add through feed tube while machine is running and process for 3 seconds. Add flour and baking powder. Process with 3 or 4 quick on/off pulses, just until flour disappears. Carefully stir in berries with a rubber spatula.

Pour into paper-lined or sprayed muffin tins. Bake in preheated 375°F oven for 25 to 30 minutes.

152 calories per muffin, 22.3 g carbohydrates, 0.8 g fiber, 3 g protein, 6 g fat (1.2 g saturated fat), 24 g cholesterol, 179 mg sodium, 55 mg potassium, 1 mg iron, 51 mg calcium, 50 mg phosphorus

### lighter variation

Reduce margarine to ⅓ cup. Use 1 egg plus 2 egg whites; use skim milk. One muffin contains 132 calories, 22.2 g carbohydrates, 0.8 g fiber, 3.9 g fat.

## HONEY BRAN MUFFINS

Grated carrots are the secret to these moist muffins.

Yield: About 18 to 24 muffins. Freezes well.

| | |
|---|---|
| 1½ cups whole wheat flour | ¼ cup canola oil |
| 1½ cups wheat bran | 1½ cups milk (1%) or orange juice |
| 1½ tsp baking soda | ½ cup honey |
| 1 tsp ground cinnamon | ¼ cup molasses |
| ½ tsp nutmeg | 2 Tbsp vinegar |
| ¼ tsp salt | ½ cup raisins or dried cranberries |
| 2 or 3 medium carrots (1 cup grated) | (optional) |
| 2 eggs (or 1 egg plus 2 egg whites) | |

STEEL BLADE: Process flour, bran, baking soda, cinnamon, nutmeg and salt for 4 or 5 seconds. Transfer to large mixing bowl. Cut carrots in 1-inch chunks. Process until fine, scraping down sides of bowl as necessary. Measure 1 cup and add to mixing bowl.

Process eggs and oil for 3 seconds. Add with remaining ingredients to mixing bowl and stir with a wooden spoon just until blended. Do not overmix.

Divide batter among paper-lined or sprayed muffin cups. Bake in preheated 375°F oven for 20 to 25 minutes.

134 calories per muffin, 23.1 g carbohydrates, 3.6 g fiber, 4 g protein, 4.3 g fat (0.6 g saturated fat), 25 g cholesterol, 160 mg sodium, 225 mg potassium, 1 mg iron, 47 mg calcium, 117 mg phosphorus

### variation

Reduce flour to 1¼ cups and add ¼ cup ground flax seed or wheat germ.

# SUGAR-FREE BRAN MUFFINS

These muffins are moist, light and delicious.

Yield: 1 dozen muffins.

Freezes well.

1 cup flour (part whole wheat, if desired)
1 tsp baking soda
1 tsp baking powder
¼ tsp salt
⅓ cup pitted dates (about 10)

½ cup granular Splenda
1 cup bran cereal (e.g., bran flakes)
1 egg (or 2 egg whites)
1 cup buttermilk (or 1 Tbsp lemon juice plus skim milk to equal 1 cup)
2 Tbsp canola oil

STEEL BLADE: Place flour, baking soda, baking powder, salt, dates and sugar substitute in processor. Start with 3 or 4 quick on/off pulses, then process 6 to 8 seconds longer, until dates are coarsely chopped. Add remaining ingredients and process with 3 or 4 quick on/off pulses, just until mixed. Do not overprocess.

Spoon batter into sprayed muffin cups. Bake in preheated 400°F oven for 20 to 25 minutes, until nicely browned.

101 calories per muffin, 16.3 g carbohydrates, 1.2 g fiber, 3 g protein, 3.1 g fat (0.4 g saturated fat), 19 g cholesterol, 245 mg sodium, 97 mg potassium, 2 mg iron, 54 mg calcium, 62 mg phosphorus

### nutrition note

If made with sugar, 1 muffin contains 130 calories and 23.7 g carbohydrates.

### variation

Raisins, dried cranberries or dried cherries may be substituted for dates. Processing time for dry ingredients will be about 5 seconds.

# COTTAGE CHEESE MUFFINS

These muffins are so quick to make and a perfect choice for breakfast or a snack. The recipe is from my Auntie Fay Rykiss of Winnipeg—her grandchildren love them.

½ cup tub margarine or butter, melted and cooled
4 eggs
3 Tbsp sugar

1 lb (500 g) dry cottage cheese (1%)
1 cup flour
2 tsp baking powder

STEEL BLADE: Process margarine, eggs and sugar for 2 minutes, until well blended. Don't insert pusher in feed tube. Add cottage cheese and process a few seconds longer, until blended, scraping down sides of bowl as needed. Add flour and baking powder; process with 4 or 5 quick on/offs to combine.

*Continued*

337

Yield: 12 muffins.

Freezes well.

Spoon batter into sprayed muffin cups, filling them three-quarters full. Bake in preheated 400°F oven for 20 to 25 minutes, until nicely browned.

153 calories per muffin, 12.4 g carbohydrates, 0.3 g fiber, 4 g protein, 9.5 g fat (1.9 g saturated fat), 72 g cholesterol, 204 mg sodium, 51 mg potassium, 1 mg iron, 66 mg calcium, 80 mg phosphorus

### lighter variation

Substitute 4 egg whites for 2 of the eggs. Substitute granular Splenda for sugar. One muffin contains 135 calories, 9.6 g carbohydrates and 8.6 g fat.

## MORNING GLORIOUS MUFFINS

These moist, marvelous muffins are packed with glorious goodness! They taste even better a day after baking.

Yield: 24 muffins.

Freezes well.

½ cup pecans or walnuts

3 carrots, cut in chunks (about 1½ cups)

1 large apple, peeled, cored and cut in chunks

3 eggs (or 2 eggs plus 2 egg whites)

1¼ cups sugar

½ cup canola oil

½ cup unsweetened applesauce

1 tsp pure vanilla extract

2 cups flour (you can use half whole wheat)

1 Tbsp ground cinnamon

2 tsp baking soda

1 tsp baking powder

1 cup crushed pineapple, well drained

¾ cup raisins, dried cherries or cranberries

½ cup shredded coconut (unsweetened or sweetened)

For machines with nested bowls, see page 339.

STEEL BLADE: Process nuts with 3 or 4 quick on/offs, until coarsely chopped. Set aside. Process carrots and apple until minced, 12 to 15 seconds. Transfer to a large measuring cup. You should have about 2 cups firmly packed.

STEEL BLADE: Process eggs, sugar, oil, applesauce and vanilla for 2 minutes. Don't insert pusher in feed tube. Add carrots and apple to processor; process 10 seconds longer, until blended. Add flour, cinnamon, baking soda and baking powder. Process with 4 or 5 quick on/offs, just until flour disappears. Scrape down sides of bowl as needed. Add pineapple, raisins, coconut and nuts; process with quick on/offs, just until combined.

Divide batter among paper-lined or sprayed muffin pans, filling them three-quarters full. Bake in preheated 375°F oven for 25 to 30 minutes.

186 calories per muffin, 26.8 g carbohydrates, 1.7 g fiber, 3 g protein, 8.2 g fat (1.7 g saturated fat), 27 g cholesterol, 141 mg sodium, 123 mg potassium, 1 mg iron, 27 mg calcium, 44 mg phosphorus

## nested bowl method

Use mini-bowl and mini-blade to chop nuts. Use large bowl and STEEL BLADE for all other processing tasks.

# FUDGY CHOCOLATE MUFFINS

Oats add fiber to these crusty-topped muffins, making them a guilt-free chocolate-studded treat.

Yield: 12 muffins.
Freezes well.

½ cup unsweetened applesauce
½ cup quick-cooking oats
1 cup sugar
¼ cup tub margarine
1 egg
1 tsp pure vanilla extract

¾ cup flour
¼ cup unsweetened cocoa powder
½ tsp baking powder
½ tsp baking soda
¾ cup chocolate chips

In a small bowl, mix applesauce with oats. Set aside.

STEEL BLADE: Process sugar, margarine, egg and vanilla extract until well mixed, about 2 minutes, scraping down sides of bowl as needed. Add applesauce/oat mixture and process just until blended. Add flour, cocoa, baking powder and baking soda. Process with 3 or 4 quick on/off pulses, just until combined. Do not overprocess. Stir in chocolate chips with a rubber spatula.

Spoon batter into paper-lined or sprayed muffin tins. Bake in preheated 375°F oven for 20 to 25 minutes.

207 calories per muffin, 34.1 g carbohydrates, 1.9 g fiber, 3 g protein, 8 g fat (2.8 g saturated fat), 18 g cholesterol, 111 mg sodium, 89 mg potassium, 1 mg iron, 24 mg calcium, 48 mg phosphorus

## variation

Add 2 tsp instant espresso coffee powder and 1 tsp cinnamon with dry ingredients. If desired, replace chocolate chips with butterscotch chips.

# OATMEAL RAISIN MUFFINS

"Oat" cuisine made easy!

Yield: 12 muffins.
These freeze well.

1 cup flour (part whole wheat, if desired)
1 tsp ground cinnamon
1 tsp baking powder
½ tsp baking soda
¼ tsp salt
1 cup quick-cooking oats

1 Tbsp white vinegar plus milk (1%) to equal 1 cup (or 1 cup buttermilk)
1 egg
½ cup sugar (granulated or brown)
½ cup canola oil
¾ cup raisins

STEEL BLADE: Process flour, cinnamon, baking powder, baking soda and salt until blended, about 5 seconds. Transfer to large mixing bowl. Place oats and sour milk or buttermilk in processor and let stand 2 or 3 minutes. Add egg, sugar and oil; process for 10 seconds. Add to flour mixture along with raisins. Stir with a wooden spoon just enough to moisten.

Spoon into paper-lined or sprayed muffin tins. Bake in preheated 400°F oven for 18 to 20 minutes, until golden.

223 calories per muffin, 29.5 g carbohydrates, 1.8 g fiber, 4 g protein, 10.6 g fat (1 g saturated fat), 19 g cholesterol, 158 mg sodium, 121 mg potassium, 1 mg iron, 59 mg calcium, 52 mg phosphorus

### lighter variation

Substitute 2 egg whites for 1 egg. Use skim milk. Replace half the oil with unsweetened applesauce. Use only ½ cup raisins or dried cranberries. One muffin contains 169 calories, 27.7 g carbohydrates and 5.3 g fat.

## SCONES

Scones are rich biscuits made with cream. You can use milk, but they won't be as light and flaky. They are best eaten the same day they're made, but since unbaked scones freeze well, it's easy to enjoy them fresh from the oven.

Yield: 12 scones.
Freezes well.

| | |
|---|---|
| 2 cups flour | 1 cup whipping cream (35%), light |
| 2 Tbsp sugar | cream or milk |
| 1 Tbsp baking powder | ¾ cup currants or raisins |
| ½ tsp salt | 1 Tbsp additional cream for brushing |
| 2 tsp grated orange zest | 1 Tbsp sugar for sprinkling |
| 5 Tbsp butter, cut in chunks | |

Preheat oven to 400°F. Line a baking sheet with parchment paper. Arrange oven rack on middle rack.

STEEL BLADE: Process flour, sugar, baking powder, salt and orange zest for 10 to 12 seconds. Add butter and process with 8 to 10 quick on/off pulses, until butter is the size of small peas. With the machine running, add cream through the feed tube and process briefly, just until combined. Don't overmix. Add currants and pulse with 2 or 3 quick on/offs.

Turn out dough onto a lightly floured surface and knead gently 8 to 10 times, just until it comes together into a rough, sticky ball. Divide dough in half. Working with 1 piece at a time, pat into a circle about 5 inches in diameter. Cut in 6 wedges and place on baking sheet. Or cut in 2-inch rounds with a biscuit cutter or glass; gather up scraps and repeat. (Unbaked scones can be frozen at this point. Scones taste best when eaten the same day they're baked.)

Brush top of each scone with cream and sprinkle lightly with sugar. Bake for 20 minutes, or until tops are golden. (If frozen, don't thaw before baking; just add about 2 minutes to baking time.) Transfer to a rack to cool. Delicious with butter and homemade jam.

230 calories per scone, 26.7 g carbohydrates, 1.2 g fiber, 3 g protein, 12.9 g fat (8 g saturated fat), 42 g cholesterol, 262 mg sodium, 121 mg potassium, 1 mg iron, 94 mg calcium, 74 mg phosphorus

### variations

- Instead of currants or raisins, substitute dried cranberries or mini chocolate chips.
- You can cut the dough in squares to avoid re-rolling dough scraps.

### cheese scones

Omit sugar, orange zest and currants. Add ¼ tsp cayenne to flour mixture. Add 1 cup grated cheddar cheese to flour mixture after butter has been cut in. If desired, add 3 to 4 Tbsp chopped green onions. One scone contains 230 calories, 17 g carbohydrates, 0.6 g fiber and 16 g fat.

# CAKES AND FROSTINGS
recipe list

351 Apple Lover's Cake
351 Apple Coffee Cake
352 Family Apple Cake
353 Lattice Apple Cake
354 Applesauce Date and Nut Cake
355 Banana Yogurt Cake
356 Banana Cranberry Chocolate Chip Cake
357 Chocolate Banana Streusel Cake
358 Family Blueberry Cake
358 Blueberry Crumble Cake
359 Genie's Birthday Cake
360 Carrot Honey Loaf
360 Nutritious Carrot Cake
361 Burnt Sugar Cake
362 Fluffy Burnt Sugar Frosting
362 Honey Cola Cake
363 Honey Apple Cake
364 Cockeyed Cake
364 Pareve Chocolate Cake
365 Root Beer Cake
366 Root Beer Glaze

366 Sour Cream Fudge Cake
367 Flourless "Chick"-olate Cake
368 Favorite Chocolate Chip Cake
368 Secret Chocolate Chip Cake
369 Pistachio Marble Cake
369 Basic Pareve Cake
370 Pareve Coffee Cake
371 Best Coffee Cake
371 Marbled Streusel Coffee Cake
373 Toffee Coffee Cake
374 Cinnamon Marble Cake
374 Marble Marvel Cake
375 Zesty Orange Loaf
376 Poppy Seed Cake
376 Mom's Old-Fashioned Crumb Cake
377 Raisin Spice Cake
378 Zucchini Spice Cake
379 Dark Rich Fruitcake
380 Chocolate Ganache
381 Chocolate Glaze

381 White Glaze
382 Banana Frosting
382 Butter Frosting
382 Chocolate Frosting
383 One-Two-Three Mint Frosting
383 Chocolate Cocoa Frosting
383 Chocolate Fudge Frosting
384 Cinnamon Frosting
384 Cream Cheese Frosting

384 Orange Frosting
385 Peanut Butter Frosting
385 Peppermint Butter Frosting
386 Chocolate Buttercream
386 Koko-Moko Buttercream
386 Mocha Buttercream
387 Whipped Cream
387 Genie's Icing

- You can whip up cakes in the food processor in about a third of the time it usually takes in an electric mixer or by hand. They will be light and delicious, although they may be slightly smaller than and not quite as light as those made with an electric mixer.
- Almost all the cakes in this book can be made in a standard-sized (7-cup) processor. The thicker the batter, the more you can process in 1 batch. Check your manual for recommended quantities.
- A general guideline is to make cakes not exceeding 2 to 2½ cups of flour or 1 package (18.5 oz/517 g) cake mix. When converting a recipe, the total volume of ingredients should not exceed 6½ cups. Calculate each egg as ¼ cup liquid.
- Refer to "How Much Food Can I Process at a Time?" (page 13–14). New food processors (e.g., Cuisinart Elite) are able to process larger batches because of improvements in design.
- NESTED WORK BOWLS: If your machine comes with nested bowls, choose the appropriate bowl and blade or disc for the task. For recipes that require multiple bowls, begin with the smallest one to minimize cleanups. Chop nuts, dried fruit or chocolate in the small bowl with the mini-blade. Use the medium or large bowl and **Grater/Shredding Disc** or **Slicer** to grate or slice fruits and veggies. Use the large bowl and **Steel Blade** to combine dry ingredients and to process cake batters.
- On Cuisinart Elite 14-cup models, the **Steel Blade** can also be used in the medium bowl. The **Steel Blade** locks into place and the nested bowls have pouring spouts, so pouring batters into baking pans is much easier. The nested bowls include a locking feature to prevent them from coming out of position when pouring. You can also use the **Steel Blade** in the medium bowl (e.g., when combining dry ingredients). However, since most brands don't have this capability, I didn't suggest this in my recipes.

## MIXING METHOD (STEEL BLADE)

- Combine dry ingredients by processing for 5 to 10 seconds, until blended—insert pusher in feed tube or cover opening with your hand. Empty mixture into another bowl. (If your machine comes with nested bowls, leave mixture in processor bowl unless otherwise indicated.)

- When creaming ingredients, do not insert the pusher, so that more air can be incorporated into the batter.
- Cut chilled butter or margarine in chunks. Process with sugar, eggs and flavoring for about 2 minutes, until well mixed. (Or process butter and sugar for 45 seconds. Add eggs 1 at a time; process for 15 seconds after each addition. Add flavoring.)
- Stop the machine once or twice to scrape down the sides of the bowl with a rubber spatula.
- Add the liquids; process for 3 seconds. Add them either through the feed tube or directly into the processor bowl.
- Add the combined dry ingredients over the top of the batter and process with 3 or 4 quick on/off pulses. If necessary, scrape down the sides of the bowl once again.
- Process just until the flour mixture disappears. Do not overprocess or your cakes will be tough and heavy.
- SPIN THE BLADE! To clean batter off the blade, empty most of the batter from the bowl. Put the bowl and blade back onto the base of the machine, replace the cover, then turn on the processor. Centrifugal force will spin your blade clean in seconds!
- SELF-CLEANING PROCESSOR: For an easy way to clean the bowl, blade and cover when making cake batters and frostings, see technique on page 7.
- Too much batter? If the amount of batter is too large for your processor, process all the ingredients except the flour and baking powder/soda. Then place all the ingredients in a large mixing bowl and stir with a wooden spoon for about 45 seconds, just until the batter is blended.
- When using packaged cake mixes, begin with the dry ingredients; add liquids through feed tube while machine is running. Process about 1½ minutes.

- For sponge and chiffon cakes, use an electric mixer. These cakes rely on egg whites for volume and a mixer will produce superior results.

## FLOUR POWER

- The recipes in this book are made with all-purpose or whole wheat flour (either bleached or unbleached). To substitute cake flour for all-purpose flour, add 2 Tbsp more per cup. To substitute all-purpose flour for cake flour, subtract 2 Tbsp. You can replace 1 cup all-purpose flour with ½ cup whole wheat flour or whole wheat pastry flour and ½ cup all-purpose flour; the texture may be slightly heavier. You can also use 2 Tbsp wheat germ or soy flour, ½ cup whole wheat flour, plus enough all-purpose flour to equal 1 cup.
- To measure flour, use dry measuring cups, not a glass measuring cup. Stir the flour before measuring. Dip the cup into the flour and fill to overflowing. Level off with the straight edge of a knife. Never bang the cup on the counter or you will end up using too much flour, causing heavy or dry cakes, or cracks on the top.

## GLUTEN-FREE BAKING

- I've added some delicious gluten-free cake and cookie recipes to this edition—and they taste like the real thing! Refer to the index for a listing of gluten-free recipes.
- Packaged gluten-free flour (e.g., Bob's Red Mill) is convenient to use and can replace all-purpose flour in most baking recipes. It has a slightly beany taste and is somewhat expensive. If you do a lot of gluten-free baking, consider making your own gluten-free flour.
- GLUTEN-FREE FLOUR MIX: For 1 cup all-purpose flour, combine ½ cup rice flour, ¼ cup tapioca starch and ¼ cup cornstarch or potato starch. Make a big batch and store it in

a well-sealed container in the refrigerator or freezer. It will keep for several months.

- Xanthan gum is the glue that holds gluten-free baked goods together. Although it's expensive, a little goes a long way. As a general guideline, add ½ tsp xanthan gum per cup of gluten-free flour for cakes, ¼ tsp per cup for cookies, and ¾ tsp per cup for muffins and quick breads. Guar gum can be substituted for xanthan gum. Use 1½ tsp guar gum for 1 tsp xanthan gum.
- Xanthan gum and guar gum are not kosher for Passover.

### LEAVENING

- Baking powder and baking soda should be stirred before measuring.
- Baking powder loses its strength after a year. To test if it is still good, add ½ tsp baking powder to ½ cup hot water. If it fizzes, it's fine.
- Regular baking powder and baking soda contain cornstarch, whereas Passover versions contain potato starch.

### HOW SWEET IT IS

- To measure brown sugar, pack it firmly into a measuring cup. Level with a straight-edge knife.
- For 1 cup of brown sugar, you can use 1 cup granulated sugar plus 2 Tbsp molasses.
- How low can you go? You can reduce the amount of sugar called for in recipes by up to 25%. However, the moisture, texture and color of baked goods may be affected.
- You can usually replace up to half the sugar in baked goods with granular Splenda with excellent results. To replace brown sugar in recipes, use half the amount of Splenda Brown Sugar Blend. However, artificial sweeteners don't add texture or bulk to baked goods. If you substitute granular Splenda completely for sugar, your baked products will be lower in volume, drier and paler in color.

- Baking time is usually shorter with Splenda than with sugar. Check cakes 7 to 10 minutes before the completion of a recipe's expected baking time.

### FAT FACTS

- Butter and margarine are generally interchangeable. Use directly from refrigerator unless otherwise indicated. I use tub margarine in my recipes unless otherwise indicated. Fleischmann's makes dairy-free, salt-free tub margarine. Diet margarine is not suitable for baking but is fine for streusel toppings.
- Use the water method to measure butter or margarine. Fill a 2-cup glass measuring cup with 1 cup of cold water. To measure ½ cup butter, for example, add butter until the water level reaches 1½ cups. You will then have 1 cup of water and ½ cup butter. Spill out the water. (Or you can press butter or margarine into a nested measuring cup; press firmly so there are no air spaces underneath.)
- PRUNE PURÉE. Combine 2 cups pitted prunes with 1 cup hot water in the processor; let it stand for 5 minutes. Process until smooth, about 1 minute. Scrape down the sides of the bowl as needed. Makes 2 cups of Prune Purée. Refrigerate up to 3 months or freeze. (One Tbsp contains only 20 calories and is fat-free!)
- Lighten up! To replace ½ cup fat in cakes, quick breads and muffins, use ¼ cup fat and ¼ cup applesauce or Prune Purée. Use applesauce in light-colored cakes and Prune Purée in dark-colored cakes.

### DAIRY REPLACEMENTS

- For dairy-free baking, replace milk with water, apple or orange juice, coffee, soy milk, rice milk, or nondairy creamer diluted with water. Use dairy-free margarine or canola oil.

- BUTTERMILK/SOUR MILK/PAREVE
  BUTTERMILK: For 1 cup, measure 1 Tbsp vinegar or lemon juice in a glass measuring cup. Add milk, soy milk or rice milk to equal 1 cup. Another substitute is ½ cup yogurt mixed with ½ cup milk. I use 1% milk in my recipes unless otherwise indicated.
- Sour cream and yogurt are interchangeable in baking. I use light sour cream and fat-free yogurt unless otherwise indicated. Greek yogurt is thick like sour cream and is very high in protein. When dissolving baking soda in yogurt, be sure to use a large enough container—the mixture will nearly double in volume.

## ABOUT CHOCOLATE

- One square (1 oz) of unsweetened chocolate in baking can be replaced with 3 Tbsp unsweetened cocoa powder plus ½ Tbsp canola oil. A great lower-fat alternative!
- To melt chocolate in the microwave, microwave uncovered on Medium (50%). For 1 to 2 oz chocolate or 1 cup chocolate chips, allow 2 to 3 minutes, stirring every minute. For 8 to 16 oz, allow 3 to 4 minutes. Stir after 2 minutes, then again every minute.
- Container must be dry and chocolate should not be covered. Otherwise it can seize (get thick and lumpy).
- CHOCOLATE RESCUE: If chocolate seizes, add oil 1 tsp at a time; stir until smooth. Another remedy is to add an equal volume of hot liquid (cream, milk or coffee) plus a few drops of vanilla extract or liqueur—instant chocolate sauce! Another scrumptious solution is to make Chocolate Truffles (page 425).

## ABOUT NUTS AND DRIED FRUIT

- Soak raisins or other dried fruit (e.g., cranberries, apricots) in hot water for 3 to 4 minutes to make them plump and juicy. Drain and dry well.

- To prevent nuts, raisins, dates or currants from sinking to the bottom of the batter, mix them with a little of the flour called for in the recipe before adding them to the batter. After the dry ingredients have been added to the batter, mix nuts or dried fruits in with on/off pulses.
- Store nuts and coconut in the freezer for up to 1 year. There's no need to defrost them before you use them.

## ABOUT BAKING WITH EGGS

- To replace 1 egg in baking, use 2 egg whites (or ¼ cup liquid egg whites) or ¼ cup egg substitute, or use reduced-cholesterol eggs. Don't replace more than half the eggs in a recipe with just whites or the texture could be affected.
- Vegans can replace each egg with ¼ cup mashed banana, tofu, soy/imitation sour cream or soy yogurt. Baked goods may be more dense and heavy.
- To replace 1 egg with flax seed, combine 1 Tbsp ground flax seed with 3 Tbsp water. Let stand until thick, 2 to 3 minutes. You can replace up to 2 regular eggs in baked goods without any noticeable change to the final product. If you use more, the texture may be compromised. A coffee grinder does a better job of grinding flax seed; see page 39.
- I don't use the processor to whip egg whites for meringues. They will only increase 4 times in volume (instead of 7) and will not be as stiff. Use an electric mixer or a wire whisk for best results.
- For maximum volume, egg whites should be at room temperature before beating. To warm them quickly, place them in a bowl; immerse in another bowl filled with warm water. Stir to warm evenly. Egg whites will not whip to maximum volume if they contain any particles of egg yolk, or if bowl or beaters are greasy or moist.
- Use a stainless steel, glass or copper bowl; don't use plastic. Add ¼ tsp cream of tartar or 1 tsp

lemon juice for every 4 whites for maximum volume. (Omit if using a copper bowl.) Add cream of tartar and flavoring when egg whites become frothy. Beat until stiff but not dry. To test if they are stiff enough, turn the bowl upside down; egg whites should not fall out!

- For meringues, begin adding sugar when whites form soft peaks. Add sugar 1 Tbsp at a time, beating until you cannot feel sugar when you rub the meringue between your fingertips. It should look like marshmallow cream.
- When adding beaten egg whites into a batter, stir about one-quarter of the whites into the batter to lighten it. Then add the remaining egg whites to the top of the batter. Using the edge of your spatula like a knife, gently cut down from the top center of the mixture to the bottom of the bowl. Pull the spatula across the bottom of the bowl towards you, until you reach the edge of the bowl, then up and out. Rotate the bowl a quarter turn after each cut-and-fold movement. This should take no more than 1 minute; don't be too thorough or the whites will deflate.

### BAKE SOMEONE HAPPY

- Preheat the oven to the required temperature before placing the cake batter in the oven. Do not open the oven door for the first 15 minutes of baking.
- Incorrect oven temperatures often cause poor results. If the temperature is too low, the cake may rise too much before it sets. If the temperature is too high, the top crust will set before the cake has finished rising, causing it to crack. An oven thermometer is an excellent investment. If your temperature is incorrect, adjust it according to your thermometer.
- Lower the temperature by 25°F if using dark or glass baking pans.

- Spray cake pans with nonstick spray. Butter or margarine may cause sticking.
- Place cake pans on the center rack or in the lower third of the oven. Pans should not touch each other or the sides of the oven for proper heat circulation.

### READY OR NOT?

- When the cake is completely baked, it will shrink slightly from the sides of the pan and will feel firm to the touch. The top of the cake should spring back; a toothpick inserted in the center will come out dry.
- Let cakes cool in the pan for a few minutes. Allow 5 minutes for layers, 10 minutes for square or rectangular cakes and 15 to 20 minutes for large cakes. If the cake is left in the pan too long, it may stick or be difficult to remove. If the cake is removed too soon, it may break when inverted.
- Loosen the edges with a flexible spatula or knife and invert onto a rack.

### FROSTINGS

- Frost cakes when they are completely cool. Dip a knife in hot water as often as necessary to help spread the frosting easily.
- Most frostings are easily made in the processor. Use the **Steel Blade** to process all ingredients until smooth and blended, usually 10 or 15 seconds. Scrape down the sides of the bowl with a rubber spatula as necessary.

### FREEZE WITH EASE

- Unfrosted cakes can be frozen for 4 to 6 months. Frosted cakes will keep for 2 to 3 months. It's best to freeze frosted cakes first, then wrap them so that they are airtight.
- It takes 1 to 3 hours to thaw a cake, depending on its size. Keep cakes wrapped while defrosting to prevent them from drying out.

- Cakes become stale more quickly if they have been frozen.
- If necessary, cakes can be frozen a second time, but they will be drier.
- Whipped cream cakes freeze very well. Thaw them overnight in the refrigerator, not at room temperature. Keep chilled.

## PORTIONS, PORTIONS!

- Many of my readers are concerned with healthier eating. In response to their requests, I've reduced the serving size when I felt it was necessary, used lighter versions of ingredients and offered many tips on how to lighten up recipes. Please use the nutrient analysis as a guide to help you make healthier choices and save rich desserts for special occasions!

## BAKING FAULTS

| | |
|---|---|
| **Cracked or peaked surface** | Oven too hot; too much flour; batter overmixed; not enough liquid; cake batter not spread right into corners. |
| **Sunken** | Too much sugar, fat or baking powder; underbaked; opening oven door too soon; not enough eggs or flour. |
| **Poor volume** | Not enough baking powder; batter overmixed; uneven oven temperature (too hot at top); too much fat or liquid; ingredients too cold or too warm. |
| **Too pale** | Too little sugar; underbaked. |
| **Too brown** | Overbaked; oven temperature too high; too much sugar. |
| **Tunnels and holes inside** | Batter overmixed after flour is added; too much flour; too much baking powder; undercreaming fat and sugar. |
| **Heavy, rubbery layer on bottom** | Too much liquid; batter undermixed. |
| **Dry** | Insufficient fat or sugar; overbaked; too much flour or not enough liquid; cake not covered when completely cooled. |
| **Tough** | Overmixed; overbaked; insufficient fat. |
| **Compact and heavy** | Too much sugar, liquid, fat or flour. |
| **Cake breaks when removed from pan** | Undergreasing of pan; removed from pan too soon. A good guide is 10 minutes for small cakes, 15 to 20 minutes for large cakes. Sponge and chiffon cakes should cool inverted for at least 1 hour. (Do not grease pan.) |
| **Cake sticks to pan** | Undergreasing of pan; butter or margarine used to grease pan; cake left in pan too long. |
| **Uneven height** | Oven temperature not even; batter spread unevenly in pan. |

## CAKE PANS, BAKING TEMPERATURES AND TIMES

| USE: | INSTEAD OF: |
|------|-------------|
| 9-inch square pan<br>350°F for 40 to 45 minutes | 7- × 11-inch pan<br>350°F for 40 to 50 minutes |
| Two 8-inch round layer pans<br>350°F for 25 to 30 minutes | 7- × 11-inch or 9-inch-square pan<br>350°F for 40 to 50 minutes |
| Two 9-inch round layer pans<br>350°F for 30 to 35 minutes | 9- × 13-inch pan<br>350°F for 40 to 50 minutes |
| 9- × 5-inch loaf pan<br>350°F for 40 to 50 minutes | 8-inch square pan<br>350°F for 35 to 40 minutes |
| Two 9- × 5-inch loaf pans<br>350°F for 40 to 50 minutes | 9- × 13-inch pan<br>350°F for 40 to 50 minutes |
| Two 9- × 5-inch loaf pans<br>350°F for 40 to 50 minutes | 12-cup fluted tube pan<br>325°F for 50 to 60 minutes |
| 9- × 13-inch pan<br>350°F for 40 to 50 minutes | 12-cup fluted tube pan<br>325°F for 50 to 60 minutes |

## CUPCAKES

Any cake batter may be baked in muffin tins. Line cups with paper liners and fill them two-thirds full. Bake at 400°F for 18 to 20 minutes. (Note: When baking cupcakes or muffins, fill empty muffin cups one-third full with water to prevent the pan from discoloring or burning.)

| PAN | YIELD |
|-----|-------|
| 8-inch square or 9- × 5-inch loaf pan | 12 to 14 cupcakes |
| 9-inch square or 7- × 11-inch pan | 18 to 20 cupcakes |
| 12-cup fluted tube or 9- × 13-inch pan | 24 to 30 cupcakes |

# APPLE LOVER'S CAKE

Delicious served warm with ice cream or frozen yogurt.

Yield: 12 to 15 servings. Cake gets soggy if frozen, but it's unlikely there will be leftovers!

14 to 16 apples, peeled, quartered and cored

⅓ to ½ cup sugar (or to taste)

2 tsp ground cinnamon

½ cup additional sugar

½ cup canola oil

½ cup unsweetened applesauce

1 tsp pure vanilla extract (or 1 Tbsp brandy)

2 eggs (or 1 egg plus 2 egg whites)

1 cup flour (half whole wheat flour can be used)

1 tsp baking powder

¼ tsp salt

Preheat oven to 350°F.

SLICER: Slice apples, using medium pressure. Place in sprayed 9- × 13-inch glass baking dish, filling it nearly to the top. (Apples will shrink during baking.) Sprinkle with ⅓ to ½ cup sugar and cinnamon and mix well; spread evenly in pan.

STEEL BLADE: Process additional ½ cup sugar, oil, applesauce, vanilla extract and eggs for 1 minute, until well blended. Add flour, baking powder and salt; process with 3 or 4 quick on/offs, until blended. Pour batter evenly over apples. Bake about 1 hour, or until golden.

284 calories per serving, 47.7 g carbohydrates, 3.1 g fiber, 3 g protein, 10.6 g fat (1 g saturated fat), 35 g cholesterol, 100 mg sodium, 201 mg potassium, 1 mg iron, 43 mg calcium, 56 mg phosphorus

### note

For a small family, make half the recipe in a 7- × 11-inch baking dish and bake 45 to 50 minutes.

# APPLE COFFEE CAKE

Yield: 12 servings.

Freezes well.

TOPPING

½ cup brown sugar, packed

½ cup walnuts

1 tsp ground cinnamon

BATTER

2 large apples, peeled, cored and cut in chunks

½ cup tub margarine or butter, cut in chunks

½ cup granulated sugar

½ cup brown sugar, packed

1 egg

½ cup buttermilk

1½ cups flour

1 tsp baking powder

½ tsp baking soda

½ tsp ground cinnamon

¼ tsp nutmeg

⅛ tsp cloves

Preheat oven to 350°F. Process all ingredients on the STEEL BLADE. For machines with nested bowls, see method on page 352. *Continued*

For topping: Process topping ingredients with 4 quick on/off pulses, until nuts are coarsely chopped. Transfer to a small bowl.

For batter: Process apples with several quick on/offs, until coarsely chopped. Remove from bowl. Process margarine or butter, both sugars and egg for 2 minutes, until well mixed. Do not insert pusher in feed tube. Stop machine once or twice to scrape down sides of bowl. Add buttermilk to creamed mixture and process for 3 seconds. Add remaining ingredients and blend in with 3 or 4 quick on/off pulses, just until flour almost disappears. Add apples and process with 2 or 3 quick on/offs to mix. Do not overprocess.

Pour batter into sprayed 8-inch square baking pan. Sprinkle with topping. Bake for 40 to 45 minutes.

288 calories per serving, 44.6 g carbohydrates, 1.4 g fiber, 3 g protein, 11.5 g fat (1.9 g saturated fat), 18 g cholesterol, 177 mg sodium, 119 mg potassium, 1 mg iron, 65 mg calcium, 64 mg phosphorus

### nested bowl method

Use mini-bowl and mini-blade to process topping; set aside. Use large bowl and STEEL BLADE for all other processing tasks.

### pareve variation

Replace buttermilk with 1½ tsp lemon juice plus soy or rice milk to equal ½ cup.

## FAMILY APPLE CAKE

Sure to become a favorite with your family!

Yield: 18 servings. May be frozen, but cake will become very moist. Reheat, uncovered, at 350°F for 10 minutes.

### FILLING

8 or 9 apples, peeled, cored and halved (6 cups sliced)
½ cup brown sugar, packed
2 Tbsp flour
1 Tbsp ground cinnamon
½ cup raisins (optional)

### BATTER

1 cup tub margarine, cut in chunks
4 eggs (or 2 eggs plus 4 egg whites)
1¾ cups granulated sugar
1 tsp pure vanilla extract
½ cup apple juice or whiskey
2¾ cups flour
4 tsp baking powder

Preheat oven to 350°F.

For filling: Insert SLICER. Slice apples, using firm pressure. Transfer to a large bowl and mix with remaining filling ingredients. Wipe processor bowl with paper towels.

For batter: Process margarine with eggs, sugar and vanilla extract on the STEEL BLADE for 2 minutes, scraping down bowl once or twice. Do not insert pusher in feed tube. Add juice or whiskey and process for 3 seconds. Add flour and baking powder. Process with about 6 quick on/off pulses, just until flour mixture disappears. Do not overprocess. Scrape down sides of bowl as necessary.

Spread one-third of batter in sprayed 12-cup fluted tube pan. Arrange half of apple filling over batter. Do not allow filling to touch sides of pan. Repeat layers, ending with batter.

Bake for 70 to 75 minutes, or until cake tests done. Cool for 20 minutes before removing from pan. Dust with icing sugar when cool.

319 calories per serving, 51.6 g carbohydrates, 1.7 g fiber, 4 g protein, 11.6 g fat (2.2 g saturated fat), 47 g cholesterol, 208 mg sodium, 120 mg potassium, 1 mg iron, 83 mg calcium, 73 mg phosphorus

lighter variation

Use ½ cup margarine and ½ cup unsweetened applesauce in batter. Also use 2 eggs and 4 egg whites. One serving contains 272 calories and 6 g fat.

## LATTICE APPLE CAKE

Yield: 16 to 18 servings.

Freezes well.

| | |
|---|---|
| 1 medium seedless orange, cut in chunks (do not peel) | 7 or 8 apples, peeled, cored and halved |
| 1 cup granulated sugar | ½ to ¾ cup granulated or brown sugar, packed |
| 3 eggs (or 2 eggs plus 2 egg whites) | 1 Tbsp ground cinnamon |
| 1 tsp pure vanilla extract | ½ cup sultana raisins (optional) |
| ¾ cup canola oil | icing sugar, for garnish |
| 3 cups flour | |
| 2 tsp baking powder | |

Preheat oven to 350°F.

STEEL BLADE: Process orange until fine, 20 to 25 seconds. Add the 1 cup sugar, eggs, vanilla extract, oil, flour and baking powder. Process until mixed, 12 to 15 seconds, scraping down sides of bowl if necessary. Press two-thirds of dough into the bottom and 1 inch up the sides of sprayed 10-inch springform pan (or 9- × 13-inch baking pan). Reserve remaining dough for topping.

SLICER: Slice apples, using firm pressure. Transfer to a bowl and mix with remaining ¾ cup sugar, cinnamon and raisins (if using). Spread evenly over dough in pan.

Flour your hands for easier handling. Roll pieces of reserved dough between your palms into thin ropes. Arrange in a criss-cross design to form latticework over filling. Bake for about 1 hour, until golden. Cool completely. Sprinkle with icing sugar. *Continued*

306 calories per serving, 47.6 g carbohydrates, 2 g fiber, 4 g protein, 11.8 g fat (1.1 g saturated fat), 40 g cholesterol, 73 mg sodium, 118 mg potassium, 1 mg iron, 54 mg calcium, 64 mg phosphorus

### variation

Use 4 apples, 2 cups blueberries (well drained) and ¼ cup flour instead of 7 or 8 apples. Omit raisins.

# APPLESAUCE DATE AND NUT CAKE

To make this recipe nut-free, replace nuts with chocolate chips.

Yield: 18 servings. Freezes well.

| | |
|---|---|
| 1 cup walnuts | ¼ tsp each nutmeg and ground cloves |
| 1 cup pitted dates | ½ cup tub margarine, cut in chunks |
| 2 cups plus 2 Tbsp flour | 1½ cups brown sugar, packed |
| 2 tsp ground cinnamon | 4 eggs (or 2 eggs plus 4 egg whites) |
| 1 tsp baking powder | 2 tsp pure vanilla extract |
| 1 tsp baking soda | 1 cup unsweetened applesauce |

Preheat oven to 350°F. For machines with nested bowls, see method below.

STEEL BLADE: Process nuts until coarsely chopped, 6 to 8 seconds. Empty into small bowl. Process dates with 2 Tbsp of the flour until coarsely chopped, about 8 seconds. Add to nuts. Place remaining 2 cups flour, cinnamon, baking powder, baking soda, nutmeg and cloves in processor. Process until blended, 6 to 8 seconds. Transfer to large bowl.

Process margarine, sugar, eggs and vanilla extract for 2 minutes. Do not insert pusher in feed tube. Add applesauce and process for 3 seconds. Add flour mixture and process with 3 or 4 quick on/offs, just until blended. Do not overprocess. Add nuts and dates. Mix in with 2 or 3 quick on/offs. Scrape down bowl as necessary.

Pour batter into sprayed 12-cup fluted tube pan. Bake for 55 to 60 minutes, until cake tests done. (Or bake in 2 sprayed 9- × 5-inch loaf pans for 45 to 50 minutes.)

263 calories per serving, 39.4 g carbohydrates, 1.8 g fiber, 4 g protein, 10.7 g fat (1.7 g saturated fat), 47 g cholesterol, 158 mg sodium, 154 mg potassium, 1 mg iron, 53 mg calcium, 65 mg phosphorus

### nested bowl method

Use mini-bowl and mini-blade to process nuts, then dates. Use large bowl and STEEL BLADE for remaining processing tasks.

### applesauce streusel cake

Process ¼ cup tub margarine or butter, ¾ cup flour, ½ cup brown or white sugar and ½ tsp ground cinnamon until crumbly. (Can be done with mini-bowl/mini-blade.) Set topping aside. Prepare batter as directed and pour into sprayed 9- × 13-inch pan. Sprinkle with topping. Bake at 350°F for 45 to 50 minutes. One serving contains 328 calories, 49.5 g carbohydrates, 2 g fiber and 13.2 g fat.

## BANANA YOGURT CAKE

My son Doug, who is a chef, loves this banana cake!

Yield: 12 servings.
Freezes well.

½ cup butter or tub margarine, cut in chunks
1½ cups sugar
2 eggs (or 1 egg plus 2 egg whites)
1 tsp pure vanilla extract
2 large ripe bananas

1 tsp baking soda
¾ cup fat-free yogurt or light sour cream
2 cups flour (part whole wheat may be used)
1 tsp baking powder

Preheat oven to 350°F.

STEEL BLADE: Process butter or margarine, sugar, eggs and vanilla extract for 2 minutes, scraping down bowl once or twice. Do not insert pusher in feed tube. While machine is running, drop chunks of banana through feed tube. Process until blended.

Meanwhile, dissolve baking soda in yogurt in 2-cup glass measuring cup. Let stand 1 to 2 minutes, until nearly double in volume. Add to batter and process for 3 seconds. Add flour and baking powder. Process with 3 or 4 quick on/off pulses, just until flour mixture disappears. Do not overprocess.

Spread batter evenly in sprayed 9-inch square or 7- × 11-inch baking pan. Bake for 50 minutes, until cake tests done. Cool 10 minutes before removing from pan. If desired, frost with Banana Frosting (page 382) or Chocolate Frosting (page 382) when completely cool.

285 calories per serving, 47.6 g carbohydrates, 1.2 g fiber, 4 g protein, 9.1 g fat (5.3 g saturated fat), 57 g cholesterol, 222 mg sodium, 153 mg potassium, 1 mg iron, 62 mg calcium, 75 mg phosphorus

### variations

• For a pareve/nondairy variation, substitute orange juice for yogurt. Do not dissolve baking soda in juice. Decrease baking soda to ½ tsp, increase baking powder to 2 tsp and add to batter along with flour.

*Continued*

- For chocolate-flaked cake, cut 1 or 2 squares of semisweet chocolate in half (or use ¼ to ½ cup chocolate chips). Process on STEEL BLADE until finely ground, 25 to 30 seconds. Remove from bowl. Prepare batter as directed, adding chocolate along with dry ingredients. One serving contains 300 calories, 49.6 g carbohydrates, 1.3 g fiber and 10 g fat.

### lighter variation

- Use ¼ cup tub margarine or canola oil, 1 cup sugar, 1 egg plus 2 egg whites and 3 bananas. One serving contains 224 calories, 41.9 g carbohydrates, 1.4 g fiber and 4.6 g fat.

# BANANA CRANBERRY CHOCOLATE CHIP CAKE

Bonnie Tregobov of Winnipeg sent me a version of this delicious cake that was higher in fat. I reduced the fat and added dried cranberries for more fiber. It makes a healthy snack in a slice!

Yield: 18 servings.

Freezes well.

| | |
|---|---|
| 2 large bananas (1 cup mashed) | 1 cup quick-cooking oats |
| ½ cup tub margarine | 1 tsp baking powder |
| 1 cup sugar | 1 tsp baking soda |
| 2 eggs (or 1 egg plus 2 egg whites) | 1 cup fat-free yogurt |
| 1 tsp pure vanilla extract | ¾ cup dried cranberries (dried |
| 1 cup all-purpose flour | cherries can be substituted) |
| 1 cup whole wheat flour | ½ cup chocolate chips |

Preheat oven to 350°F.

STEEL BLADE: Process bananas until puréed, about 20 seconds. Measure 1 cup and set aside. Process margarine, sugar, eggs and vanilla extract for 2 minutes, scraping down sides of bowl once or twice. Do not insert pusher in feed tube. Add banana purée and process 3 or 4 seconds to combine. Add both flours, oats, baking powder, baking soda and yogurt. Process with 4 or 5 quick on/off pulses, just until flour mixture disappears. Do not overprocess. Stir in cranberries and chocolate chips with a rubber spatula.

Spray a 12-cup fluted tube pan or 9- × 13-inch baking pan with nonstick spray. Spread batter evenly in pan. Bake for 55 to 60 minutes for tube pan or 35 to 40 minutes for 9- × 13-inch baking pan.

222 calories per serving, 36.1 g carbohydrates, 2.4 g fiber, 4 g protein, 7.7 g fat (2 g saturated fat), 24 g cholesterol, 157 mg sodium, 151 mg potassium, 1 mg iron, 54 mg calcium, 77 mg phosphorus

# CHOCOLATE BANANA STREUSEL CAKE

Chocolate chips, chocolate banana cake and a scrumptious streusel topping—who could ask for anything more?

Yield: 12 servings.
Freezes well.

### TOPPING

¼ cup flour
¼ cup quick-cooking oats
¼ cup brown sugar, firmly packed
1 tsp unsweetened cocoa powder
1 tsp ground cinnamon
1½ Tbsp canola oil

### BATTER

3 large ripe bananas (1⅓ cups mashed)
1½ cups granulated sugar
⅓ cup canola oil
2 eggs (or 1 egg plus 2 egg whites)
1 tsp pure vanilla extract
1¾ cups flour
¼ cup unsweetened cocoa powder
1 tsp baking soda
1 tsp baking powder
½ cup orange juice
½ to ¾ cup chocolate chips

Preheat oven to 325°F. Process all ingredients on the STEEL BLADE. For machines with nested bowls, see method below.

For topping: Process topping ingredients for 6 to 8 seconds, just until mixed. Set aside. Wipe out bowl with paper towels.

For batter: Cut bananas in chunks. Process until smooth, about 20 seconds. Measure 1⅓ cups and set aside. Process sugar, oil, eggs and vanilla extract for 2 to 3 minutes, until light. Do not insert pusher in feed tube. Add 1⅓ cups bananas and blend until smooth, about 10 seconds. Add flour, cocoa, baking soda, baking powder and juice. Process with quick on/off pulses, just until flour disappears. Do not overprocess.

Spread batter evenly in sprayed 7- × 11-inch glass baking dish. Sprinkle with chocolate chips; gently stir into batter with a rubber spatula. Sprinkle topping evenly over batter. Bake for 50 to 55 minutes. Insert a wooden toothpick and test for doneness in 2 or 3 places since melted chocolate chips may cling to toothpick even though cake is completely baked.

356 calories per serving, 61.5 g carbohydrates, 2.8 g fiber, 5 g protein, 11.7 g fat (2.3 g saturated fat), 35 g cholesterol, 159 mg sodium, 239 mg potassium, 2 mg iron, 45 mg calcium, 78 mg phosphorus

### nested bowl method

Use mini-bowl and mini-blade for topping. Use large bowl and STEEL BLADE for all other processing tasks.

### cupcakes

Fill 12 paper-lined or sprayed muffin cups two-thirds full. Sprinkle with chocolate chips and reserved topping. Bake at 375°F for 20 to 25 minutes.

# FAMILY BLUEBERRY CAKE

Berry delicious!

Yield: 18 servings.

Freezes well.

¾ cup tub margarine or butter,
  cut in chunks

1½ cups sugar

3 eggs (or 2 eggs plus 2 egg whites)

1 tsp pure vanilla extract

1½ tsp baking soda

4 tsp vinegar plus milk (1%) or soy
  milk to equal 1½ cups

3 cups flour

3 tsp baking powder

2 cups fresh or frozen blueberries
  (unthawed)

icing sugar, for dusting cake (optional)

Preheat oven to 325°F.

STEEL BLADE: Process margarine or butter, sugar, eggs and vanilla extract for 2 minutes, scraping down bowl once or twice. Do not insert pusher in feed tube. Dissolve baking soda in vinegar-milk mixture. Pour in through feed tube while machine is running and process for 3 seconds. Add flour and baking powder. Process with 4 or 5 quick on/off pulses, just until flour disappears. Do not over-mix. Carefully stir in blueberries with a rubber spatula.

Pour batter into sprayed 12-cup fluted tube pan. Bake for 1 hour, or until cake tests done. Let cool 15 minutes. Invert and remove from pan. Dust with icing sugar (if desired).

240 calories per serving, 36.5 g carbohydrates, 1 g fiber, 4 g protein, 8.9 g fat (1.8 g saturated fat), 36 g cholesterol, 268 mg sodium, 77 mg potassium, 1 mg iron, 77 mg calcium, 75 mg phosphorus

# BLUEBERRY CRUMBLE CAKE

An all-time family favorite! This is a winner. It's also delicious with raspberries.

Yield: 12 servings.

Delicious warm or at room temperature.

Freezes well.

2¼ cups flour

1¼ cups sugar

¾ cup butter or tub margarine,
  cut in chunks

1 tsp baking soda

1 cup light sour cream or yogurt

1 tsp baking powder

2 eggs

1½ cups fresh blueberries

Preheat oven to 375°F.

STEEL BLADE: Process flour, sugar and butter or margarine until fine crumbs are formed, 12 to 15 seconds. Remove 1 cup of crumb mixture from processor and set aside. Dissolve baking soda in sour cream or yogurt. Add to processor along with baking powder and eggs. Process for 6 to 8 seconds, just until blended, scraping down sides of bowl with a rubber spatula as necessary. Do not overprocess. Stir in blueberries by hand.

Spread batter evenly in sprayed 9-inch square baking pan. Sprinkle with reserved crumb mixture. Bake for 40 to 45 minutes, until done.

# GENIE'S BIRTHDAY CAKE

An old-time Winnipeg favorite. This was the cake I had for my birthday parties when I was a little girl. Too bad a genie can't make the calories magically disappear!

Yield: 12 servings. Freezes well.

## BASE

⅓ cup soft shortening or tub margarine

1 cup flour

¼ cup icing sugar

½ tsp baking powder

1 tsp pure vanilla extract

## BATTER

½ cup soft shortening or tub margarine

¾ cup sugar

2 eggs

1 tsp pure vanilla extract

½ cup milk (1%)

1⅓ cups flour

2 tsp baking powder

½ tsp salt

Genie's Icing (page 387)

chocolate sprinkles or grated chocolate (optional)

Preheat oven to 350°F. Use STEEL BLADE to process all ingredients.

For base: Process all ingredients for base until blended, about 10 seconds. Spray an 8-inch square baking pan with nonstick spray, then line with parchment paper, leaving about 1 inch of paper extending beyond top of pan on either side. Press dough firmly into bottom of pan. Bake for 12 to 15 minutes. When cool, remove from pan. Place on serving plate and peel off paper.

For batter: Process shortening or margarine, sugar, eggs and vanilla extract on the STEEL BLADE for 2 minutes. Do not insert pusher in feed tube. Add milk and process 3 seconds. Add dry ingredients and process with 3 or 4 quick on/off pulses, just until flour disappears. Do not overprocess. Scrape down bowl as necessary.

Pour batter into sprayed 8-inch square pan. Bake for 35 to 40 minutes. Cool 10 minutes, then remove from pan.

Assembly: Prepare Genie's Icing (page 387). Spread base with a thin layer of icing. Cover with cooled cake. Frost completely, reserving about ½ cup icing. Add a few drops of food coloring to reserved icing; pipe leaves and flowers with a cake decorating set. Coat sides of cake with chocolate sprinkles or grated sweet chocolate (if desired).

## CARROT HONEY LOAF

My original recipe called for ¾ cup of oil. This moist, low-fat variation uses only ¼ cup of oil and is low in saturated fat. Make several loaves as gifts for the holidays.

Yield: 1 loaf (12 servings). Freezes well.

1 cup junior baby food carrots (or 1 cup Carrot Purée, below)

1 cup sugar

2 eggs (or 1 egg plus 2 egg whites)

¼ cup canola oil

¼ cup honey

1½ cups flour (or 1 cup all-purpose plus ½ cup whole wheat)

1 tsp baking powder

1 tsp baking soda

¾ tsp ground cinnamon

2 Tbsp wheat germ (optional)

½ cup raisins or dried cranberries (optional)

Preheat oven to 350°F.

STEEL BLADE: Process carrots with sugar, eggs, oil and honey for 1 minute, until well blended. Add flour, baking powder, baking soda, cinnamon and wheat germ (if using). Process with 3 or 4 quick on/off pulses, just until flour disappears. Do not overprocess. If using dried fruit, add to batter with 2 or 3 quick on/off pulses.

Pour batter into sprayed 9- × 5-inch loaf pan. Bake for 60 to 65 minutes, until loaf tests done. Cool 15 minutes, then remove from pan.

205 calories per serving, 36.2 g carbohydrates, 1 g fiber, 3 g protein, 5.8 g fat (0.6 g saturated fat), 35 g cholesterol, 160 mg sodium, 96 mg potassium, 1 mg iron, 38 mg calcium, 45 mg phosphorus

### carrot purée

Peel and trim 3 large carrots. Cut into chunks. Place in saucepan with 1 cup boiling water and a tiny pinch of salt. Cover and simmer about 20 minutes, until very soft. Process on the STEEL BLADE until puréed, 25 to 30 seconds, adding a little cooking water for desired consistency. This makes about 1 cup purée.

## NUTRITIOUS CARROT CAKE

This well-loved cake was in my original processor book, and it's back again due to popular demand, but in a lighter, healthier version. For a more

3 medium carrots, scraped and trimmed

1 medium apple, peeled and cored

3 eggs (or 2 eggs plus 2 egg whites)

1¼ cups sugar

½ cup canola oil

½ cup unsweetened applesauce

2 cups flour (you can use half whole wheat)

2 Tbsp wheat germ

2 tsp ground cinnamon

2 tsp baking soda

1 tsp baking powder

¾ to 1 cup chocolate chips or raisins

icing sugar for sprinkling (optional)

decadent version, frost it with Cream Cheese Frosting (page 384).

Yield: 18 servings.

Freezes well.

GRATER: Cut carrots and apple to fit feed tube. Grate, using medium pressure. Transfer to a large measuring cup. You should have about 2 cups lightly packed. (If there are any large pieces, don't worry—just add them along with the grated carrot/apple mixture to the batter.)

STEEL BLADE: Process eggs, sugar, oil and applesauce for 2 minutes. Don't insert pusher in feed tube. Add carrots and apples to processor; process 10 seconds longer, until blended. Add flour, wheat germ, cinnamon, baking soda and baking powder. Process with 4 or 5 quick on/offs, just until flour disappears. Scrape down sides of bowl as necessary. Sprinkle chocolate chips or raisins over batter and give 1 or 2 more quick on/offs.

Pour batter into sprayed 12-cup fluted tube pan or 9- × 13-inch baking pan. Bake in preheated 350°F oven for 40 to 50 minutes, until cake tests done. Cool for 20 minutes before removing from pan. Sprinkle cooled cake with icing sugar.

221 calories per serving, 32.7 g carbohydrates, 1.5 g fiber, 3 g protein, 9.5 g fat (2 g saturated fat), 35 g cholesterol, 186 mg sodium, 105 mg potassium, 1 mg iron, 31 mg calcium, 56 mg phosphorus

### carrot muffins

Divide batter among 18 paper-lined muffin cups. Fill empty compartments one-third full with water. Bake in preheated 375°F oven for 25 minutes.

# BURNT SUGAR CAKE

This recipe was a specialty of my late mother-in-law, Rella Gilletz. It's an oldie but a goodie, with a wonderful caramel flavor. It's very high in carbs, so be careful with portion sizes.

Yield: 12 servings.

If freezing cake, do not frost.

| | |
|---|---|
| ½ cup sugar | 3 eggs |
| ½ cup boiling water | 1 cup milk (1%) |
| ½ cup tub margarine or butter, cut in chunks | 2⅓ cups flour |
| 1⅓ cups sugar | 2½ tsp baking powder |
| 1 tsp pure vanilla extract | ½ tsp salt |
| | Fluffy Burnt Sugar Frosting (page 362) |

Preheat oven to 350°F.

Melt ½ cup sugar in heavy skillet on medium heat until clear and dark brown, stirring constantly to prevent sugar from burning. Remove from heat and slowly and carefully stir in boiling water, or mixture may splatter. Return mixture to heat and simmer until lumps melt and mixture is syrupy. Let cool.

STEEL BLADE: Process margarine or butter, 1⅓ cups sugar, vanilla extract and eggs for 2 minutes, scraping down bowl once or twice. Do not insert pusher in feed tube. Add milk and ¼ cup of the burnt sugar syrup (reserve remainder for frosting). Process for 3 seconds. Add remaining ingredients, except frosting. Process

*Continued*

with 4 quick on/off pulses, just until flour disappears. Do not overprocess. Scrape down bowl as necessary.

Pour batter into two 9-inch sprayed layer pans. Bake for 30 to 35 minutes. Cool and frost with Fluffy Burnt Sugar Frosting.

364 calories per serving (with frosting), 65.6 g carbohydrates, 0.7 g fiber, 5 g protein, 9.4 g fat (1.9 g saturated fat), 54 g cholesterol, 302 mg sodium, 96 mg potassium, 2 mg iron, 100 mg calcium, 90 mg phosphorus

## FLUFFY BURNT SUGAR FROSTING

Yield: Fills and frosts two 9-inch layers (12 servings). Do not freeze.

| | |
|---|---|
| **2 Tbsp burnt sugar syrup** | **¼ cup corn syrup** |
| **½ cup brown sugar, packed** | **2 egg whites** |
| **1 Tbsp water** | **1 tsp pure vanilla extract** |

Blend burnt sugar syrup, brown sugar, water and corn syrup in a saucepan. Cover and bring to a boil. Uncover and cook until mixture reaches 242°F on a candy thermometer, or spins a 6- to 8-inch thread when dropped from a fork. Beat egg whites with an electric mixer until stiff peaks form. Pour syrup slowly in a thin stream into egg whites. Beat until mixture holds stiff peaks. Add vanilla extract.

72 calories per serving, 17.6 g carbohydrates, 0 g fiber, 1 g protein, 0 g fat (0 g saturated fat), 0 g cholesterol, 18 mg sodium, 34 mg potassium, 0 mg iron, 11 mg calcium, 11 mg phosphorus

## HONEY COLA CAKE

Quick, easy and delicious. Perfect for the Jewish high holidays!

Yield: 15 servings. Freezes well.

| | |
|---|---|
| **2¼ cups flour** | **3 eggs (or 2 eggs plus 2 egg whites)** |
| **2 tsp baking powder** | **1 cup liquid honey** |
| **1 tsp baking soda** | **¾ cup canola oil** |
| **2 tsp ground cinnamon** | **½ cup cola (diet or regular)** |
| **¾ cup brown sugar, packed** | |

Preheat oven to 325°F.

STEEL BLADE: Process flour, baking powder, baking soda and cinnamon until blended, about 10 seconds. Empty into another bowl. Process brown sugar with eggs for 30 seconds. Do not insert pusher in feed tube. Add honey and oil; process 1½ minutes longer. Remove cover and add dry ingredients. Pour cola on top. Process with 4 or 5 quick on/off pulses, just until batter is blended. Do not overprocess.

Immediately remove processor bowl from base and pour batter into sprayed 12-cup fluted tube pan. Bake for about 1 hour, until cake tests done. Let cool for 20 minutes before removing from pan. This cake keeps very well.

294 calories per serving, 43.9 g carbohydrates, 0.7 g fiber, 4 g protein, 12.4 g fat (1.2 g saturated fat), 42 g cholesterol, 166 mg sodium, 61 mg potassium, 1 mg iron, 58 mg calcium, 54 mg phosphorus

### variations

Replace cola with strong tea, coffee, orange juice or club soda. For a darker color, add 1 or 2 Tbsp unsweetened cocoa powder with dry ingredients. If desired, add ½ cup sultana raisins or chopped nuts. To prevent raisins or nuts from sinking to the bottom of the cake, combine them with ¼ cup of the flour called for in the recipe. Process with quick on/off pulses. (Do this before mixing up the batter to save on cleanup.)

## HONEY APPLE CAKE

This moist and delicious cake combines apples and honey, 2 traditional foods that represent good wishes for a sweet and healthy New Year! Use a large (14-cup) processor to make this cake (see Note on page 364).

Yield: 18 servings. Freezes well.

| | |
|---|---|
| 3¼ cups flour | 3 eggs plus 2 egg whites (or 4 eggs) |
| 2 tsp baking powder | 1 cup sugar |
| 2 tsp ground cinnamon | 1 cup liquid honey |
| 1 tsp baking soda | ½ cup canola oil |
| ¼ tsp ground ginger | ¾ cup cold tea |
| 2 medium apples, peeled and cut in chunks | ¼ cup brandy |

Preheat oven to 325°F.

STEEL BLADE: Process flour, baking powder, cinnamon, baking soda and ginger for 10 seconds, until blended. Transfer to large mixing bowl. Process apples until finely minced, 8 to 10 seconds. Measure 1 cup firmly packed and set aside.

Process eggs and egg whites, sugar, honey and oil for 2 to 3 minutes, until light. Do not insert pusher in feed tube. Add dry ingredients to batter alternately with tea and brandy. Process with quick on/off pulses, just until blended. Do not overprocess. Add apples and process with quick on/off pulses, just until mixed.

Pour batter into sprayed 12-cup fluted tube pan. Bake for 1 hour and 10 minutes, until cake tests done. A wooden skewer inserted into the center should come out dry. If necessary, cover top of cake with foil to prevent overbrowning. Let cake cool in pan for 20 minutes. Carefully loosen with a flexible spatula; invert cake onto a serving plate. *Continued*

271 calories per serving, 47.6 g carbohydrates, 1 g fiber, 4 g protein, 7.4 g fat (0.8 g saturated fat), 35 g cholesterol, 142 mg sodium, 72 mg potassium, 1 mg iron, 43 mg calcium, 54 mg phosphorus

### note

If you don't have a large processor, add beaten egg mixture to dry ingredients in mixing bowl alternately with tea and brandy. Mix with a wooden spoon until blended, about 45 seconds. Stir in apples.

## COCKEYED CAKE

Fast and fudgy. This cake contains no eggs or baking powder. It's excellent for anyone with egg allergies.

Yield: 12 servings.
Freezes well.

| | |
|---|---|
| 1½ cups flour | 5 Tbsp canola oil |
| 1 cup sugar | 1 Tbsp vinegar |
| ⅓ cup unsweetened cocoa powder | 1 tsp pure vanilla extract |
| 1 tsp baking soda | 1 cup cold water |
| ½ tsp salt | |

Preheat oven to 350°F.

STEEL BLADE: Process flour, sugar, cocoa, baking soda and salt for 10 seconds, until blended. Add remaining ingredients and process 6 to 8 seconds longer, just until blended. Do not overprocess.

Pour into sprayed 8-inch square baking pan. Bake for 30 minutes.

180 calories per serving, 30.1 g carbohydrates, 1.2 g fiber, 2 g protein, 6.3 g fat (0.6 g saturated fat), 0 g cholesterol, 203 mg sodium, 54 mg potassium, 1 mg iron, 6 mg calcium, 35 mg phosphorus

### variation

Replace vanilla extract with peppermint extract. Immediately after removing cake from oven, top with a 7 oz (200 g) package of chocolate mint patties. As they melt, spread evenly with a spatula. One serving contains 244 calories, 43.5 g carbohydrates and 7.5 g fat.

## PAREVE CHOCOLATE CAKE

Big, moist, dark and delicious, this dairy-free cake is a family favorite all over the world. I've reduced the

| | |
|---|---|
| 2¼ cups flour | ½ tsp salt |
| 2 cups sugar | 1½ cups orange juice or water |
| ⅔ cup unsweetened cocoa powder | 3 eggs (or 2 eggs plus 2 egg whites) |
| 1½ tsp baking powder | 1¼ cups canola oil |
| 1½ tsp baking soda | Pareve Chocolate Ganache (page 381) |
| 1½ tsp instant coffee powder | (optional) |

serving size from my original recipe so you won't feel as guilty if you have a second helping!

Yield: 18 servings. Freezes well.

Preheat oven to 350°F.

STEEL BLADE: Combine flour, sugar, cocoa, baking powder, baking soda, coffee powder and salt in processor. Process until blended, about 10 seconds. Add orange juice or water and eggs. Start processor and add oil through feed tube while machine is running. Process batter for 45 seconds. Do not insert pusher in feed tube and do not overprocess.

Pour batter into sprayed 12-cup fluted tube pan or 9- × 13-inch baking pan. Bake for 55 to 60 minutes, until cake tests done. Cool for 20 minutes before removing cake from pan. Place on serving platter. When completely cooled, drizzle with Ganache (if desired). (If baked in a 9- × 13-inch pan, frost cake with your favorite chocolate frosting.)

311 calories per serving, 38.5 g carbohydrates, 1.5 g fiber, 3 g protein, 17.1 g fat (1.7 g saturated fat), 35 g cholesterol, 222 mg sodium, 121 mg potassium, 1 mg iron, 36 mg calcium, 67 mg phosphorus

### note

This amount of batter may be too large for some processors. For a smaller version, use 2 cups flour, 1½ cups sugar, ½ cup unsweetened cocoa powder, 1 tsp baking powder, 1 tsp baking soda, 1 tsp instant coffee, dash salt, 1¼ cups orange juice, water or milk, 3 eggs and ¾ cup canola oil. Bake at 325°F for 55 to 60 minutes. Makes 15 servings.

- HIGH SKOR CHOCOLATE CAKE: Bake batter in 4 sprayed 9-inch layer pans at 350°F about 25 minutes. Whip 2 cups nondairy topping or whipping cream with an electric mixer until nearly stiff. Beat in ¼ cup icing sugar and 1 Tbsp chocolate liqueur. Fold in 1 cup toffee bits. Fill and frost cooled layers. Sprinkle with additional toffee bits. Refrigerate. Serves 18.

414 calories per serving, 50.1 g carbohydrates, 1.5 g fiber, 4 g protein, 23 g fat (5.2 g saturated fat), 40 g cholesterol, 280 mg sodium, 121 mg potassium, 1 mg iron, 36 mg calcium, 67 mg phosphorus

## ROOT BEER CAKE

Chocolate cake with a deep, dark secret ingredient: root beer!

| | |
|---|---|
| 1½ cups regular root beer (not diet) | 1½ tsp baking soda |
| 2¼ cups flour | ¼ tsp salt |
| 1¼ cups sugar | 3 eggs |
| ½ cup brown sugar, packed | 1 cup canola oil |
| ¾ cup unsweetened cocoa powder | 1 tsp pure vanilla extract |
| 1½ tsp baking powder | Root Beer Glaze (page 366) |

Yield: 18 servings. Cake
freezes well. Glaze may
crack slightly if frozen.

Preheat oven to 350°F. Pour root beer into a measuring cup and let stand 5 minutes.

STEEL BLADE: Combine flour, sugars, cocoa, baking powder, baking soda and salt in processor. Process until blended, about 10 seconds. Start processor and gradually add root beer, eggs, oil and vanilla through feed tube while machine is running. Process batter for 45 seconds, scraping down sides of bowl once or twice. Do not insert pusher in feed tube and do not overprocess.

Pour batter into sprayed 12-cup fluted tube pan. Bake for 55 to 60 minutes, until cake tests done. Let cool for 20 minutes, then invert cake onto a serving platter. When completely cool, drizzle with Root Beer Glaze.

324 calories per serving (with glaze), 47.5 g carbohydrates, 1.9 g fiber, 4 g protein, 14.8 g fat (2 g saturated fat), 35 g cholesterol, 196 mg sodium, 104 mg potassium, 2 mg iron, 41 mg calcium, 73 mg phosphorus

## ROOT BEER GLAZE

Yield: About ¾ cup.

| | |
|---|---|
| 1 square (1 oz/30 g) unsweetened chocolate, melted and cooled | 2 Tbsp root beer |
| 1½ cups icing sugar | ½ tsp pure vanilla extract |

STEEL BLADE: Combine all ingredients and process 6 to 8 seconds to blend, scraping down sides of bowl once or twice. Drizzle glaze over cooled cake.

54 calories per Tbsp, 11.9 g carbohydrates, 0.3 g fiber, 0 g protein, 0.9 g fat (0.6 g saturated fat), 0 g cholesterol, 1 mg sodium, 15 mg potassium, 0 mg iron, 2 mg calcium, 7 mg phosphorus

## SOUR CREAM FUDGE CAKE

This cake does not
contain baking
powder.

| | |
|---|---|
| ¼ cup butter or tub margarine | 2 squares (2 oz) unsweetened chocolate, melted and cooled |
| 1 cup sugar | ¾ tsp baking soda |
| 2 eggs | ¾ cup sour cream (light or regular) |
| 1 tsp pure vanilla extract | 1 cup less 2 Tbsp flour |

Yield: 9 to 12 servings.
Freezes well.

Preheat oven to 350°F.

STEEL BLADE: Process butter or margarine, sugar, eggs and vanilla extract for 2 minutes. Do not insert pusher in feed tube. Add melted chocolate and process until blended, about 10 seconds. Scrape down sides of bowl with rubber spatula as necessary. Dissolve baking soda in sour cream; add to batter and process 3 seconds. Add flour and process with 3 or 4 quick on/off pulses, just until blended. Do not overprocess.

Pour batter into sprayed 8-inch square baking pan. Bake for about 45 minutes, until cake tests done. Frost with your favorite chocolate frosting.

254 calories per serving, 35.2 g carbohydrates, 1.4 g fiber, 4 g protein, 11.9 g fat (7 g saturated fat), 68 g cholesterol, 172 mg sodium, 126 mg potassium, 2 mg iron, 45 mg calcium, 74 mg phosphorus

# FLOURLESS "CHICK"-OLATE CAKE

Chickpeas are the mystery ingredient in this gluten-free chocolate cake that contains no added fat! Steve Silbert of Richmond, Virginia, shared his scrumptious recipe, which he makes for his wife, Debbie, who is gluten-intolerant.

Yield: 12 servings. Freezes well.

| | |
|---|---|
| 1½ cups sugar | 1 can (15 oz/425 g) chickpeas |
| ½ cup unsweetened cocoa powder | (1½ cups), drained and rinsed |
| 2 Tbsp cornstarch or potato starch | 4 eggs (or 3 eggs plus 2 egg whites) |
| ¾ tsp baking powder | 2 tsp pure vanilla extract |
| ¼ tsp baking soda | icing sugar for sprinkling (optional) |
| ¼ tsp salt | |

Preheat oven to 350°F. Spray the inside of a 9-inch round cake pan with nonstick spray. Cut parchment paper into a circle to cover bottom of pan and place it inside. (Otherwise, spray a 7- × 11-inch baking pan with nonstick spray. If serving cake directly from pan, there's no need to line it with parchment.)

STEEL BLADE: Process sugar, cocoa powder, cornstarch, baking powder, baking soda and salt until blended, 10 to 12 seconds. Empty into another bowl.

STEEL BLADE: Process chickpeas for 25 to 30 seconds, until ground. Add eggs and vanilla extract and process 1 minute longer, stopping machine once or twice to scrape down sides of bowl. Add cocoa mixture and process 25 to 30 seconds longer, until blended. Pour batter into prepared pan.

Bake for 50 to 55 minutes, or until a sharp knife inserted into the center comes out almost clean, with just a few crumbs clinging to it. Remove from oven and cool for 10 to 15 minutes before removing from pan. Invert onto a serving plate and carefully peel off parchment. Cool completely. Sprinkle with icing sugar (if desired). Store in the refrigerator.

175 calories per serving, 35.6 g carbohydrates, 2.5 g fiber, 4 g protein, 2.6 g fat (0.9 g saturated fat), 71 g cholesterol, 216 mg sodium, 129 mg potassium, 1 mg iron, 40 mg calcium, 89 mg phosphorus

### variation

Omit icing sugar. Frost cake with your favorite chocolate frosting or pour Chocolate Glaze (page 381) overtop.

# FAVORITE CHOCOLATE CHIP CAKE

Thanks to Marilyn Elias for this easy, delicious recipe!

Yield: 12 servings. Freezes well.

1⅓ cups flour
1½ tsp baking powder
1 tsp baking soda
1 tsp ground cinnamon
6 Tbsp butter or tub margarine

1 cup sugar
2 eggs
1 cup light sour cream or yogurt
½ to ¾ cup chocolate chips

Preheat oven to 350°F.

STEEL BLADE: Process flour, baking powder, baking soda and cinnamon for 5 seconds. Empty into a bowl. Process butter or margarine, sugar and eggs for 2 minutes, scraping down bowl once or twice. Do not insert pusher in feed tube. Add sour cream or yogurt and process for 3 seconds. Add dry ingredients. Process with 4 quick on/off pulses, just until flour disappears. Do not overprocess.

Pour batter into sprayed 9-inch square or 7- × 11-inch baking pan. Sprinkle chocolate chips evenly over batter. Bake for 35 to 40 minutes, until cake tests done.

242 calories per serving, 33.7 g carbohydrates, 0.9 g fiber, 4 g protein, 11.1 g fat (6.5 g saturated fat), 58 g cholesterol, 233 mg sodium, 98 mg potassium, 1 mg iron, 76 mg calcium, 68 mg phosphorus

# SECRET CHOCOLATE CHIP CAKE

If you don't tell them you used a mix, they'll never know!

Yield: 18 servings. Freezes well.

1 pkg (18.25 oz/517 g) chocolate or white cake mix
1 pkg instant chocolate pudding (4-serving size)
1 cup light sour cream or yogurt

4 eggs (or 1 cup egg substitute)
½ cup canola oil
1 cup chocolate chips
Chocolate Glaze (page 381)

Preheat oven to 325°F.

STEEL BLADE: Place cake mix, pudding and sour cream or yogurt in processor. Add eggs and oil through feed tube while machine is running. Process for 2 minutes. Do not insert pusher in feed tube. Stop machine once or twice to scrape down batter. Sprinkle chocolate chips over batter. Process with 2 or 3 quick on/off pulses to mix.

Pour batter into sprayed 12-cup fluted tube pan. Bake for 50 to 60 minutes, until cake tests done. Cool for 15 to 20 minutes before removing cake from pan. Drizzle cooled cake with Chocolate Glaze.

329 calories per serving, 43.6 g carbohydrates, 1.7 g fiber, 4 g protein, 17.2 g fat (4.9 g saturated fat), 52 g cholesterol, 345 mg sodium, 202 mg potassium, 2 mg iron, 76 mg calcium, 132 mg phosphorus

## PISTACHIO MARBLE CAKE

This retro recipe is back in style again!

Yield: 18 servings.

Freezes well.

| | |
|---|---|
| 1 pkg (18.25 oz/517 g) yellow or white cake mix | ½ cup water |
| 1 pkg instant pistachio pudding (4-serving size) | 4 eggs (or 1 cup egg substitute) |
| ½ cup orange juice | ½ cup canola oil |
| | ¾ cup canned chocolate syrup |
| | icing sugar for sprinkling (optional) |

Preheat oven to 350°F.

STEEL BLADE: Combine all ingredients except chocolate syrup and icing sugar in processor bowl. Process for 2 minutes. Do not insert pusher in feed tube. Stop machine once or twice to scrape down sides of bowl.

Pour three-quarters of batter into sprayed 12-cup fluted tube pan. Add chocolate syrup to remaining batter and process a few seconds longer, just until mixed. Pour chocolate batter over batter in pan and cut through in a swirl design with a spatula.

Bake for 50 to 60 minutes, until cake tests done. Cool for 15 to 20 minutes before removing cake from pan. Place on a serving platter. Sprinkle cooled cake with icing sugar (if desired).

263 calories per serving, 37.7 g carbohydrates, 0.7 g fiber, 3 g protein, 11.1 g fat (1.4 g saturated fat), 48 g cholesterol, 299 mg sodium, 81 mg potassium, 1 mg iron, 49 mg calcium, 130 mg phosphorus

## BASIC PAREVE CAKE

This versatile cake is moist and dairy-free.

Yield: 12 servings.

Freezes well.

| | |
|---|---|
| 2 eggs | ¾ cup orange or apple juice |
| 1 cup sugar | 2 cups flour |
| 1 tsp pure vanilla extract | 3 tsp baking powder |
| ½ cup canola oil | ¼ tsp salt |

Preheat oven to 350°F.

STEEL BLADE: Process eggs with sugar and vanilla extract for 1 minute. Do not insert pusher in feed tube. Add oil and process 1 minute longer. While machine is running, add juice through feed tube and process for 3 seconds. Add remaining ingredients. Process with 4 quick on/off pulses, just until flour disappears. Do not overprocess.                                        *Continued*

CAKES AND FROSTINGS

Pour into sprayed 9-inch square or 7- × 11-inch baking pan. Bake for 40 to 50 minutes, until cake tests done. Delicious with Chocolate Cocoa Frosting (page 383) or Peanut Butter Frosting (page 385).

245 calories per serving, 34.8 g carbohydrates, 0.6 g fiber, 3 g protein, 10.5 g fat (1 g saturated fat), 35 g cholesterol, 181 mg sodium, 65 mg potassium, 1 mg iron, 77 mg calcium, 65 mg phosphorus

## PAREVE COFFEE CAKE

Yield: 12 servings.

Freezes well.

½ cup walnuts

½ cup brown sugar, packed

2 tsp ground cinnamon

⅛ tsp each ground cloves and allspice (optional)

¼ cup flour

3 Tbsp melted margarine

Basic Pareve Cake batter (page 369)

Preheat oven to 350°F. For machines with nested bowls, see method below.

STEEL BLADE: For topping, process nuts, sugar, cinnamon, cloves and allspice (if using), flour and margarine with 4 quick on/off pulses, until nuts are finely chopped. Empty bowl and wipe out with paper towels.

Prepare cake batter as directed. Pour half the batter into sprayed 9-inch square or 7- × 11-inch baking pan. Sprinkle with half the topping. Repeat with remaining batter and topping. Bake for 45 to 55 minutes, until cake tests done.

348 calories per serving, 46.8 g carbohydrates, 1.2 g fiber, 4 g protein, 16.5 g fat (1.8 g saturated fat), 35 g cholesterol, 207 mg sodium, 104 mg potassium, 2 mg iron, 94 mg calcium, 85 mg phosphorus

### nested bowl method

Use mini-bowl and mini-blade for topping. Use large bowl and STEEL BLADE for batter.

### variation

Use topping from Best Coffee Cake (page 371). One serving contains 396 calories, 54.2 carbohydrates, 2.5 g fiber and 19.6 g fat.

# BEST COFFEE CAKE

The name says it all!

Yield: 12 servings.

Freezes well.

**TOPPING**

¾ cup pecans or almonds

½ cup brown sugar, packed

1 Tbsp unsweetened cocoa powder

2 tsp ground cinnamon

1 cup chocolate chips

**BATTER**

6 Tbsp butter or tub margarine

1 cup granulated sugar

2 eggs

1 tsp pure vanilla extract

1 tsp baking soda

1 cup light sour cream or yogurt

1⅓ cups flour

1½ tsp baking powder

Preheat oven to 350°F. Process all ingredients on the STEEL BLADE. For machines with nested bowls, see method below.

For topping: Process nuts, brown sugar, cocoa and cinnamon with 6 to 8 quick on/off pulses, until nuts are coarsely chopped. Transfer to small bowl. Stir in chocolate chips. Wipe processor bowl clean with paper towels.

For batter: Process butter or margarine, sugar, eggs and vanilla extract for 2 minutes, scraping down sides of bowl as needed. Do not insert pusher in feed tube. Dissolve baking soda in sour cream or yogurt. Add to batter and process for 3 seconds. Add flour and baking powder. Process with 4 quick on/off pulses, just until flour disappears. Do not overprocess. Scrape down bowl if necessary.

Pour half the batter into sprayed 9-inch square or 7- × 11-inch baking pan. Sprinkle with half the topping. Repeat with remaining batter and topping. Bake for 40 to 45 minutes, until cake tests done. When cool, invert cake onto a plate, then invert again onto another plate so that nut topping is on top.

356 calories per serving, 48.5 g carbohydrates, 2.2 g fiber, 5 g protein, 17.7 g fat (8.2 g saturated fat), 58 g cholesterol, 236 mg sodium, 169 mg potassium, 2 mg iron, 93 mg calcium, 98 mg phosphorus

## nested bowl method

Use mini-bowl and mini-blade for topping. Use large bowl and STEEL BLADE for batter.

# MARBLED STREUSEL COFFEE CAKE

This is a favorite of my nephew Marshall Matias.

**TOPPING**

1 cup walnuts or pecans

½ cup sweetened flaked coconut (optional)

½ cup brown sugar, packed

2 Tbsp unsweetened cocoa powder

2 tsp ground cinnamon

**BATTER**

| | |
|---|---|
| ¾ **cup tub margarine or butter** | 1½ **tsp baking soda** |
| 1½ **cups granulated sugar** | 1½ **tsp baking powder** |
| 3 **eggs (or 2 eggs plus 2 egg whites)** | ¼ **tsp salt** |
| 2 **tsp pure vanilla extract** | 1 **square (1 oz/30 g) semisweet** |
| 3 **cups flour** | **chocolate, melted and cooled** |
| 4 **tsp vinegar plus milk (1%) or soy** | |
| **milk to make 1½ cups** | |

Preheat oven to 350°F. Process all ingredients on the STEEL BLADE. For machines with nested bowls, see method below.

For topping: Chop nuts coarsely, using several quick on/off pulses. Remove ½ cup nuts and set aside. Add remaining topping ingredients to processor. Process for a few seconds to mix. Empty bowl and wipe with paper towels.

For batter: Process margarine or butter, sugar, eggs and vanilla extract for 2 minutes. Do not insert pusher in feed tube. Add half the flour and process with 2 or 3 on/off pulses, until nearly blended. Add vinegar/milk mixture, remaining flour, baking soda, baking powder and salt. Process with several quick on/offs, just until blended. Do not overprocess. Mix in reserved nuts with 1 or 2 quick on/offs.

Pour half the batter into sprayed 12-cup fluted tube pan. Drizzle half the melted chocolate over batter and cut through with a knife. Sprinkle with three-quarters of the topping. Add remaining batter and drizzle with remaining chocolate. Cut through second layer of batter with a knife. Sprinkle with remaining topping.

Bake for 55 to 60 minutes. Let cool in pan for 15 minutes. Invert cake onto a plate, then turn cake over so that nut mixture is on top.

307 calories per serving, 42.5 g carbohydrates, 1.4 g fiber, 5 g protein, 13.7 g fat (2.5 g saturated fat), 36 g cholesterol, 262 mg sodium, 118 mg potassium, 2 mg iron, 69 mg calcium, 94 mg phosphorus

### nested bowl method

Use mini-bowl and mini-blade for topping. Use large bowl and STEEL BLADE for batter.

### lighter variation

For batter, combine equal parts of margarine and unsweetened applesauce to make ¾ cup. Reduce sugar to 1¼ cups and use 2 eggs and 2 egg whites. Use skim milk; omit semisweet chocolate. For topping, combine ½ cup sugar, 2 tsp cinnamon and ½ cup chopped nuts. One serving contains 209 calories, 37.6 g carbohydrates, 0.8 g fiber and 4.7 g fat.

### chocolate melt-away coffee cake

For topping, use ¾ cup pecans, ½ cup packed brown sugar and 8 oz chilled semisweet chocolate, cut in chunks. Process on the STEEL BLADE, using several quick on/off pulses, until coarsely chopped. Prepare batter for Marbled Streusel Coffee Cake. Assemble and bake as directed. One serving contains 355 calories, 49.8 g carbohydrates, 2.0 g fiber and 16.4 g fat.

## TOFFEE COFFEE CAKE

My helpers loved this addictive cake so much, they barely left any for taste testing.

Yield: 15 servings.

Freezes well.

TOPPING

¾ cup pecans

¼ cup brown sugar, lightly packed

1 cup toffee bits (or 4 Skor bars, 1.4 oz/39 g each, broken up)

BATTER

½ cup margarine or butter, cut in chunks

1 cup granulated sugar

2 eggs

1½ tsp pure vanilla extract

1 tsp baking soda

1 cup yogurt or sour cream (low-fat or regular)

1¾ cups flour

1 tsp baking powder

¼ tsp salt

Preheat oven to 350°F. Process all ingredients on the STEEL BLADE. For machines with nested bowls, see method on page 374.

For topping: Coarsely chop nuts, brown sugar and toffee bits, using 10 to 12 on/off pulses. (If using Skor bars, processing time will take slightly longer.) Remove from bowl and reserve. Wipe out bowl with paper towels.

For batter: Process margarine or butter, sugar, eggs and vanilla extract for 2 minutes, until well mixed. Do not insert pusher in feed tube. Add baking soda to yogurt or sour cream; stir to dissolve. Add to processor and process 5 seconds. Add flour, baking powder and salt. Process with 4 or 5 quick on/off pulses, just until flour disappears. Do not overprocess.

Spread half the batter in sprayed 12-cup fluted tube pan. Sprinkle with half the topping. Add remaining batter, then sprinkle with remaining topping. Bake for 50 to 55 minutes, until cake tests done. Cool in pan for 20 minutes. Loosen edges with a flexible spatula, invert cake onto a platter, then invert it onto another platter so the topping is on top. Let cool—if you can control yourself!

315 calories per serving, 39.9 g carbohydrates, 0.9 g fiber, 5 g protein, 15.5 g fat (3.9 g saturated fat), 35 g cholesterol, 290 mg sodium, 90 mg potassium, 1 mg iron, 60 mg calcium, 72 mg phosphorus

*Continued*

## CINNAMON MARBLE CAKE

I love anything made with cinnamon! This cake contains no baking powder; baking soda is the leavening agent. It is delicious frosted with Cinnamon Frosting (page 384).

Yield: 12 servings.
Freezes well.

| | |
|---|---|
| ½ cup tub margarine or butter, cut in chunks | 2 cups flour |
| 1¼ cups sugar | 1 tsp baking soda |
| 2 eggs plus 2 egg whites (or 3 eggs) | ¼ cup brandy or rum |
| ¾ cup yogurt (fat-free or regular) | 1 Tbsp ground cinnamon |
| | 2 Tbsp sugar |

Preheat oven to 350°F.

STEEL BLADE: Process margarine or butter with 1¼ cups sugar, eggs and egg whites for 2 minutes. Do not insert pusher in feed tube. Add yogurt and process for 3 seconds. Add flour, baking soda and brandy or rum. Process with 4 quick on/off pulses, just until blended. Do not overprocess. Scrape down bowl if necessary.

Pour into sprayed 9-inch square baking pan. Combine cinnamon with 2 Tbsp sugar. Sprinkle over cake. Cut through with a knife to give a marbled effect. Smooth out surface of cake with a rubber spatula. Bake for 45 minutes, until cake tests done.

272 calories per serving (without frosting), 42.7 g carbohydrates, 0.9 g fiber, 5 g protein, 8.7 g fat (1.7 g saturated fat), 36 g cholesterol, 199 mg sodium, 86 mg potassium, 1 mg iron, 45 mg calcium, 63 mg phosphorus

## MARBLE MARVEL CAKE

Chocolate syrup added to the batter makes this marble cake fudgy and delicious. Ice it with your favorite

| | |
|---|---|
| ¾ cup margarine or butter, cut in chunks | 2½ cups flour |
| 1½ cups sugar | 2 tsp baking powder |
| 3 eggs (or 2 eggs plus 2 egg whites) | ¼ tsp salt |
| 1½ tsp pure vanilla extract | ½ cup chocolate syrup |
| ¾ cup milk (1%) or orange juice | ¼ tsp baking soda |

chocolate frost-
ing, glaze with
Chocolate Glaze
(page 381) or
sprinkle lightly with
icing sugar—the
choice is yours.

Yield: 18 servings.

Freezes well.

Preheat oven to 325°F.

STEEL BLADE: Process margarine or butter, sugar, eggs and vanilla extract for 2 minutes, scraping down bowl once or twice. Do not insert pusher in feed tube. Add milk or juice through feed tube while machine is running. Process for 3 or 4 seconds. Add flour, baking powder and salt. Process with 4 or 5 quick on/off pulses, scraping down bowl once or twice, just until mixed. Do not overprocess.

Pour two-thirds of batter into sprayed 12-cup fluted tube pan. Add chocolate syrup and baking soda to remaining batter. Process for a few seconds, just until blended. Scrape down bowl as necessary. Pour chocolate batter over white batter. Cut through batters in a swirl design with a spatula or fork.

Bake for 60 to 70 minutes, until cake tests done. Cool for 20 minutes before removing from pan.

238 calories per serving, 36.5 g carbohydrates, 0.7 g fiber, 3 g protein, 8.8 g fat (1.8 g saturated fat), 36 g cholesterol, 188 mg sodium, 66 mg potassium, 1 mg iron, 51 mg calcium, 66 mg phosphorus

## ZESTY ORANGE LOAF

This tastes even
better the next day!

Yield: 1 loaf (12 servings).

Freezes well.

| | |
|---|---|
| 1 Tbsp grated orange zest | ¾ cup sugar |
| 1¾ cups flour | ½ cup fat-free yogurt |
| 1½ tsp baking powder | ¼ cup fresh orange juice |
| ½ tsp baking soda | |
| 2 eggs (or 1 egg plus 2 egg whites) | ORANGE SYRUP |
| ½ cup applesauce | ¼ cup fresh orange juice |
| ¼ cup tub margarine | ¼ cup sugar |

Preheat oven to 350°F.

STEEL BLADE: Process orange zest, flour, baking powder and baking soda for 10 seconds, until mixed. Empty bowl.

Process eggs, applesauce, margarine and ¾ cup sugar, until light, about 2 minutes. Do not insert pusher in feed tube. Add yogurt and orange juice. Process for 3 seconds to blend. Add dry ingredients and process with quick on/off pulses, just until flour disappears. Do not overprocess.

Spread batter in sprayed 9- × 5-inch loaf pan. Bake for 40 to 45 minutes. Loaf will crack slightly down the center.

For syrup: Combine orange juice with ¼ cup sugar and heat until steaming hot; stir well. Poke holes all over the top of loaf with wooden skewer. Slowly drizzle hot syrup all over loaf, letting it soak up the liquid. Remove from pan when cooled.

194 calories per serving, 34.1 g carbohydrates, 0.7 g fiber, 4 g protein, 4.9 g fat (1 g saturated fat), 36 g cholesterol, 163 mg sodium, 87 mg potassium, 1 mg iron, 64 mg calcium, 65 mg phosphorus

## POPPY SEED CAKE

Yield: 18 servings.

Freezes well.

½ cup poppy seeds

1 cup buttermilk (or 1 Tbsp lemon
    juice plus 1% milk or soy milk to
    equal 1 cup)

1 cup margarine or butter, cut in
    chunks

1½ cups sugar

4 eggs (or 2 eggs plus 4 egg whites)

2 tsp pure vanilla extract

2½ cups flour

2 tsp baking powder

1 tsp baking soda

Soak poppy seeds in buttermilk for at least half an hour. Preheat oven to 325°F.

STEEL BLADE: Process margarine or butter, sugar, eggs and vanilla extract for 2 minutes. Do not insert pusher in feed tube. Remove cover and add poppy seed/ milk mixture to batter. Process for 3 or 4 seconds to blend. Add remaining ingredients and process with 5 or 6 quick on/off pulses. Mix with a rubber spatula if batter is not completely blended.

Pour batter into sprayed 12-cup fluted tube pan. Bake for 50 to 60 minutes, until cake tests done. Cool for 15 minutes before removing from pan.

264 calories per serving, 32.2 g carbohydrates, 1.2 g fiber, 4 g protein, 13.3 g fat (2.5 g saturated fat), 48 g cholesterol, 234 mg sodium, 87 mg potassium, 1 mg iron, 112 mg calcium, 93 mg phosphorus

### variation

Pour half of batter into pan. Mix together ⅓ cup brown sugar, 1 tsp cinnamon and 2 tsp unsweetened cocoa powder; sprinkle over batter. Sprinkle with ½ cup chocolate chips. Top with remaining batter. One serving contains 303 calories, 39.4 g carbohydrates, 1.6 g fiber and 14.7 g fat.

## MOM'S OLD-FASHIONED CRUMB CAKE

This cake takes less
than a minute to mix
up in the processor.

Yield: 12 servings.

Freezes well.

2¼ cups flour

1 cup sugar

½ cup tub margarine or butter, cut
    in chunks

2 tsp baking powder

½ tsp baking soda

1 tsp ground cinnamon

½ tsp ground cloves (optional)

2 eggs

1 Tbsp lemon juice plus milk (1%) to
    equal 1 cup

1 cup raisins, rinsed in hot water and
    drained

Preheat oven to 350°F.

STEEL BLADE: Process flour, sugar and margarine or butter until fine crumbs are formed, 10 to 12 seconds. Remove ¾ cup of mixture and reserve for topping. Add remaining ingredients except raisins to processor. Process 10 to 15 seconds longer, until blended. Add raisins and process with 2 or 3 quick on/off pulses.

Pour batter into sprayed 7- × 11-inch glass baking dish; sprinkle with reserved topping. Bake for 40 to 45 minutes, until cake tests done.

276 calories per serving, 45.8 g carbohydrates, 1.6 g fiber, 5 g protein, 9 g fat (1.8 g saturated fat), 36 g cholesterol, 219 mg sodium, 169 mg potassium, 2 mg iron, 82 mg calcium, 84 mg phosphorus

### cupcakes

Omit raisins. Fold 1 cup of fresh or frozen cranberries into batter. Fill 12 sprayed or paper-lined muffin tins two-thirds full. Sprinkle with reserved topping. Bake at 375°F for 20 to 25 minutes.

# RAISIN SPICE CAKE

Perfect with a cup of coffee or a glass of milk!

Yield: 12 servings.

Freezes well.

| | |
|---|---|
| 2 cups flour | 1 cup sugar |
| 1 tsp baking powder | 2 eggs |
| 2 tsp ground cinnamon | 1 tsp pure vanilla extract |
| ¼ tsp each ground cloves and allspice | 1 tsp baking soda |
| ½ cup raisins | 1 cup sour cream (light or regular) |
| ½ cup tub margarine or butter, cut in chunks | |

Preheat oven to 350°F.

STEEL BLADE: Process flour, baking powder, cinnamon, cloves and allspice for about 5 seconds, until blended. Transfer to a bowl; stir in raisins.

Process margarine or butter, sugar, eggs and vanilla extract for 2 minutes, scraping down bowl once or twice. Do not insert pusher in feed tube. Meanwhile, stir baking soda into sour cream. Add to creamed mixture and process for 3 seconds. Add dry ingredients; process with 4 or 5 quick on/off pulses, just until flour mixture disappears. Do not overprocess.

Spread batter evenly in sprayed 7- × 11-inch baking pan. Bake for 45 to 50 minutes, until cake tests done.

270 calories per serving, 39.6 g carbohydrates, 1.2 g fiber, 4 g protein, 10.9 g fat (3 g saturated fat), 43 g cholesterol, 235 mg sodium, 132 mg potassium, 1 mg iron, 66 mg calcium, 65 mg phosphorus

*Continued*

## ZUCCHINI SPICE CAKE

I once had a cooking student whose children hated her cooking. When she made this cake, her son asked, "What are the green flecks?" She replied "Pistachio nuts." He exclaimed, "If you made it, it's probably mold!" Believe it or not, he loved the cake!

Yield 18 servings. Freezes well.

| | |
|---|---|
| 1 cup walnuts or shelled pistachios | 3 eggs (or 2 eggs plus 2 egg whites) |
| 2 cups flour | 1½ to 2 cups sugar (or 1½ cups brown |
| 2 tsp baking soda | sugar, packed) |
| 1 tsp baking powder | 1 cup canola oil |
| ½ tsp salt | 2 tsp pure vanilla extract |
| 1 Tbsp ground cinnamon | 1 cup raisins or chocolate chips |
| ¼ tsp allspice (optional) | Cream Cheese Frosting (page 384) or |
| 2 medium zucchini (2 cups grated) | White Glaze (page 381) (optional) |

Preheat oven to 350°F. For machines with nested bowls, see method below.

STEEL BLADE: Process nuts until chopped, about 6 seconds; set aside. Process flour, baking soda, baking powder, salt, cinnamon and allspice (if using) for 10 seconds to blend. Empty into large mixing bowl.

GRATER: Grate unpeeled zucchini, using medium pressure. Measure 2 cups loosely packed.

STEEL BLADE: Process eggs with sugar for 1 minute. Do not insert pusher in feed tube. While machine is running, add oil and vanilla extract through feed tube. Process for about 45 seconds. Add zucchini and process for 10 seconds. Remove cover and add dry ingredients. Process with 3 or 4 quick on/off pulses, just until flour disappears. Sprinkle nuts and raisins or chocolate chips over batter. Mix in with quick on/off pulses. (See Note on page 379.)

Pour batter into sprayed 9- x 13-inch pan or 12-cup fluted tube pan. Bake for 55 to 60 minutes, until cake tests done. Cool 20 minutes before removing cake from pan. If desired, frost oblong cake with Cream Cheese Frosting or drizzle White Glaze over fluted cake.

311 calories per serving, 35.9 g carbohydrates, 1.8 g fiber, 4 g protein, 17.8 g fat (1.6 g saturated fat), 35 g cholesterol, 247 mg sodium, 181 mg potassium, 1 mg iron, 38 mg calcium, 72 mg phosphorus

### nested bowl method

Use mini-bowl and mini-blade to chop nuts; set aside. Use medium bowl and GRATER/SHREDDING DISC for zucchini; measure 2 cups. Use large bowl and STEEL BLADE for all other processing tasks.

## note

Batter will almost fill bowl of standard-sized processor, but will not over-flow. If amount of batter is too much for your processor, reverse proce-dure and add zucchini mixture to dry ingredients in mixing bowl. Mix with a wooden spoon until blended, about 45 seconds. Stir in nuts and raisins.

### lighter variation

Reduce nuts and raisins to ½ cup each. Instead of 1 cup oil, use ½ cup oil and ½ cup unsweetened applesauce. One serving contains 226 calories, 33.1 g carbohydrates, 1.4 g fiber and 9.4 g fat.

### carrot pineapple cake

Replace zucchini with 4 medium carrots (or 3 carrots plus 1 apple, peeled and cored). Measure 2 cups loosely packed. Add ¾ cup well-drained crushed pineapple to batter with nuts and raisins. One serving contains 318 calories, 37.7 g carbohydrates, 2.1 g fiber and 17.8 g fat.

# DARK RICH FRUITCAKE

This is a variation of the fruitcake my mother made for my wedding. Fruitcake will last for several years if properly stored. Sometimes it lasts even longer than the marriage!

Yield: 8 lb fruitcake or 3 loaves (about 40 servings). Freezes well.

| | |
|---|---|
| 1 lb (500 g) sultana raisins | 1 tsp each nutmeg and ground cloves |
| 1 lb (500 g) dried cranberries | 1 seedless thin-skinned orange, |
| 1 lb (500 g) candied mixed fruits | quartered (unpeeled) |
| 1 lb (500 g) shelled nuts (almonds, | 1 cup tub margarine, cut in chunks |
| pecans, walnuts, etc. or a | 1½ cups sugar |
| combination) | 6 eggs |
| 1 lb (500 g) candied cherries | ½ cup grape or apple jelly |
| 3½ cups flour | ¼ cup brandy |
| 1 tsp baking powder | ½ cup corn syrup (optional) |
| ½ tsp baking soda | ¼ cup water (optional) |
| 2 Tbsp unsweetened cocoa powder | |
| 2 tsp ground cinnamon | |

Preheat oven to 275°F.

Pour boiling water over raisins and cranberries to cover completely. Let stand for 5 minutes. Drain well; pat dry. Place in a very large mixing bowl. Add candied mixed fruits.

STEEL BLADE: Chop nuts in batches of 1 to 2 cups at a time. Use on/off pulses, until coarsely chopped. Add to mixing bowl. Coarsely chop cherries with ¼ cup

*Continued*

flour in 2 batches, using quick on/off pulses. Add to mixing bowl with an additional 1 cup flour. Mix well.

Process remaining flour, baking powder, baking soda, cocoa, cinnamon, nutmeg and cloves for 10 seconds. Add to mixing bowl. Process orange until fine, about 20 seconds. Add to mixing bowl.

Process margarine, sugar and eggs for 2 minutes, until well blended. Do not insert pusher in feed tube. Add jelly and process 10 seconds to blend. Add brandy and process 2 or 3 seconds longer. Add to mixing bowl.

Stir with a wooden spoon until well mixed. Batter will be very heavy. Line three 9- × 5-inch loaf pans with well-greased parchment paper or aluminum foil. Fill three-quarters full. Bake for about 3 hours, until done. Cool in pans for half an hour. Remove from pans; cool completely.

For a shiny glaze, combine corn syrup and water in a saucepan. Bring to a boil, remove from heat and cool to lukewarm. Pour over cooled fruitcakes.

For long-term storage, wrap fruitcakes in brandy-soaked cheesecloth, then in foil. Store in a cool place to ripen. If cheesecloth is remoistened occasionally, fruitcakes will keep at least 2 or 3 years.

351 calories per serving, 59.8 g carbohydrates, 3.3 g fiber, 5 g protein, 11.8 g fat (1.6 g saturated fat), 32 g cholesterol, 88 mg sodium, 238 mg potassium, 2 mg iron, 59 mg calcium, 101 mg phosphorus

> **note**
> For gift giving, bake fruitcakes in small foil pans about 2 hours.

## CHOCOLATE GANACHE

This dark and shiny glaze is true decadence! It's fabulous on cakes, tortes and brownies.

Yield: Enough glaze for a 9-inch pan of brownies or a large fluted cake (12 to 18 servings).

¾ cup whipping cream (35%)

8 oz (250 g) chilled semisweet or
   bittersweet chocolate, cut in chunks

2 tsp almond, coffee or orange liqueur

Microwave whipping cream, uncovered, on High for 1½ minutes, until almost boiling.

STEEL BLADE: Process chocolate with several on/off pulses, then let machine run until chocolate is finely ground, about 30 seconds. Pour hot cream through feed tube while machine is running. Process until chocolate is melted. Blend in liqueur.

Cover and refrigerate for 30 minutes, until cooled and slightly thickened. Drizzle over your favorite cake or torte or pour over brownies. Refrigerate after glazing.

63 calories per Tbsp, 5.5 g carbohydrates, 0.5 g fiber, 1 g protein, 4.8 g fat (2.9 g saturated fat), 9 g cholesterol, 3 mg sodium, 35 mg potassium, 0 mg iron, 7 mg calcium, 15 mg phosphorus

## variations

- **PAREVE CHOCOLATE GANACHE:** Replace whipping cream with ¾ cup boiling water plus 2 Tbsp dairy-free margarine. One Tbsp contains 45 calories, 5 g carbohydrates and 3.1 g fat.
- **PAREVE MOCHA GANACHE:** Replace whipping cream with ½ cup non-dairy topping plus ¼ cup brewed coffee. One Tbsp contains 55 calories, 7 g carbohydrates and 3.4 g fat.

## CHOCOLATE GLAZE

Yield: About ¾ cup. Do not freeze.

**1½ cups icing sugar**

**2 Tbsp milk (1%) or water**

**1 square (1 oz/30 g) unsweetened chocolate, melted and cooled**

STEEL BLADE: Combine all ingredients and process for 6 to 8 seconds to blend, scraping down sides of bowl once or twice. Drizzle over your favorite cake. Excellent on Marble Marvel Cake (page 374).

54 calories per Tbsp, 11.9 g carbohydrates, 0.3 g fiber, 0 g protein, 1 g fat (0.6 g saturated fat), 0 g cholesterol, 1 mg sodium, 18 mg potassium, 0 mg iron, 4 mg calcium, 9 mg phosphorus

## WHITE GLAZE

Yield: About ½ cup. Do not freeze.

**1 cup icing sugar**

**2 Tbsp milk (1%) or water**

**½ tsp pure vanilla extract**

STEEL BLADE: Process all ingredients until smooth, 6 to 8 seconds. Scrape down sides of bowl as necessary. Drizzle over your favorite cake or sweet yeast breads. If desired, decorate with chopped nuts.

48 calories per Tbsp, 11.9 g carbohydrates, 0 g fiber, 0 g protein, 0 g fat (0 g saturated fat), 0 g cholesterol, 2 mg sodium, 5 mg potassium, 0 mg iron, 4 mg calcium, 3 mg phosphorus

## variations

For lemon or orange glaze, replace milk or water with lemon or orange juice. Add 1 tsp lemon or orange zest. For almond glaze, replace vanilla extract with almond extract.

## BANANA FROSTING

Yield: For a 9-inch square
cake (12 servings).

Freezes well.

2 Tbsp butter or tub margarine

2-inch piece of banana
   (about 2 Tbsp)

½ tsp lemon juice

1¼ cups icing sugar (approximately)

pinch salt

STEEL BLADE: Process butter or margarine with banana for several seconds, until blended. Add remaining ingredients and process until smooth. Add a little extra icing sugar if frosting is too loose.

68 calories per serving, 13 g carbohydrates, 0.1 g fiber, 0 g protein, 1.9 g fat (1.2 g saturated fat), 5 g cholesterol, 27 mg sodium, 10 mg potassium, 0 mg iron, 1 mg calcium, 1 mg phosphorus

## BUTTER FROSTING

Yield: For two 9-inch
layers or a 9- × 13-inch
cake (12 to 18 servings).

Freezes well.

¼ cup butter or tub margarine

2 cups icing sugar

dash salt

2 to 3 Tbsp hot milk (1%) or light
   cream

1 tsp pure vanilla extract (or desired
   flavoring)

STEEL BLADE: Combine all ingredients and process until smooth and blended, 10 to 15 seconds. Scrape down sides of bowl as necessary.

114 calories per serving, 20.1 g carbohydrates, 0 g fiber, 0.1 g protein, 3.9 g fat (2.5 g saturated fat), 10 g cholesterol, 42 mg sodium, 6 mg potassium, 0 mg iron, 4 mg calcium, 7 mg phosphorus

### variations

Substitute various flavorings for vanilla extract (maple, almond, butterscotch, etc.).

## CHOCOLATE FROSTING

Yield: For a 9-
inch square cake
(12 servings). Double the
recipe for a large cake.

Freezes well.

1 square (1 oz/30 g) unsweetened
   chocolate, melted and cooled

¼ cup soft tub margarine or butter

1½ cups icing sugar

2 to 3 Tbsp milk (1%), cream, sour
   cream or boiling water

½ tsp pure vanilla extract

STEEL BLADE: Process all ingredients until smooth and blended, about 10 seconds. Scrape down sides of bowl as necessary.

106 calories per serving, 15.8 g carbohydrates, 0.4 g fiber, 0 g protein, 5.1 g fat (1.5 g saturated fat), 0 g cholesterol, 33 mg sodium, 25 mg potassium, 0 mg iron, 6 mg calcium, 12 mg phosphorus

## ONE-TWO-THREE MINT FROSTING

Yield: For a 9-inch square cake (12 servings).

1 pkg (7 oz/200 g) chocolate mint patties

Place chocolate mint patties in a single layer on top of chocolate cake or brownies immediately upon removal from oven. As patties melt, spread evenly with a spatula.

64 calories per serving, 13.4 g carbohydrates, 0.3 g fiber, 0 g protein, 1.2 g fat (0.7 g saturated fat), 0 g cholesterol, 5 mg sodium, 18 mg potassium, 0 mg iron, 2 mg calcium, 0 mg phosphorus

## CHOCOLATE COCOA FROSTING

Yield: For a 9-inch square cake (12 servings).

Freezes well.

| | |
|---|---|
| 1 cup icing sugar | 2 Tbsp unsweetened cocoa powder |
| pinch salt | 2 Tbsp milk (1%), soy milk or hot water |
| 2 Tbsp soft tub margarine or butter | ½ tsp pure vanilla extract |

STEEL BLADE: Process all ingredients until smooth and blended, about 10 seconds. Scrape down sides of bowl as necessary.

59 calories per serving, 10.6 g carbohydrates, 0.3 g fiber, 0 g protein, 2.1 g fat (0.4 g saturated fat), 0 g cholesterol, 30 mg sodium, 18 mg potassium, 0 mg iron, 4 mg calcium, 9 mg phosphorus

note

Recipe may be doubled for a large cake.

## CHOCOLATE FUDGE FROSTING

Yield: To fill and frost two 9-inch layers, or frost a 9- × 13-inch cake (12 to 18 servings). Freezes well.

| | |
|---|---|
| 1 cup chocolate chips | dash salt |
| 3 Tbsp butter or tub margarine | ½ cup milk (1%) (scant) |
| 3 cups icing sugar | 1 tsp pure vanilla extract |

Melt chocolate chips with butter or margarine on low heat (or microwave on Medium [50%] for 2 to 3 minutes, stirring every minute). Let cool.

STEEL BLADE: Combine all ingredients in processor, using slightly less than ½ cup milk. Process until smooth and blended, about 15 seconds. If frosting seems too thick, add a few more drops of milk. If frosting is too loose, add 1 or 2 Tbsp more icing sugar. Frosting will thicken somewhat upon standing.

215 calories per serving, 39.3 g carbohydrates, 0.8 g fiber, 1 g protein, 7.2 g fat (4.4 g saturated fat), 8 g cholesterol, 40 mg sodium, 68 mg potassium, 0 mg iron, 18 mg calcium, 29 mg phosphorus

## CINNAMON FROSTING

Yield: For a 9-inch square cake (12 servings). To frost a 9- × 13-inch cake, make 1½ times the recipe. Freezes well.

1 cup icing sugar
½ tsp ground cinnamon
2 Tbsp soft butter or tub margarine
½ tsp pure vanilla extract
2 Tbsp sour cream (light or regular)

STEEL BLADE: Process all ingredients until smooth, about 10 seconds. Scrape down sides of bowl as necessary.

60 calories per serving, 10.3 g carbohydrates, 0.1 g fiber, 0 g protein, 2.2 g fat (1.4 g saturated fat), 6 g cholesterol, 16 mg sodium, 7 mg potassium, 0 mg iron, 5 mg calcium, 3 mg phosphorus

## CREAM CHEESE FROSTING

Yield: To fill and frost two 9-inch layers or frost a 9- × 13-inch cake (12 to 18 servings). Freezes well.

2 cups icing sugar
¼ tsp salt
½ cup softened cream cheese (light or regular)
¼ cup soft butter or tub margarine
½ tsp pure vanilla extract

STEEL BLADE: Process all ingredients until smooth, about 10 seconds.

130 calories per serving, 20.5 g carbohydrates, 0 g fiber, 1 g protein, 5.2 g fat (3.3 g saturated fat), 15 g cholesterol, 121 mg sodium, 2 mg potassium, 0 mg iron, 31 mg calcium, 1 mg phosphorus

## ORANGE FROSTING

Yield: To fill and frost two 9-inch layers or frost a 9- × 13-inch

2 cups icing sugar
dash salt
¼ cup butter or tub margarine
2 to 3 Tbsp orange juice
½ tsp pure vanilla extract
1 tsp grated orange zest (optional)

cake (12 to 18 servings). Freezes well.

STEEL BLADE: Combine all ingredients and process until smooth and blended, about 15 seconds. Scrape down sides of bowl as necessary. For a deeper orange color, add a few drops each of red and yellow food coloring.

113 calories per serving, 20.2 g carbohydrates, 0 g fiber, 0 g protein, 3.9 g fat (2.4 g saturated fat), 10 g cholesterol, 40 mg sodium, 7 mg potassium, 0 mg iron, 2 mg calcium, 2 mg phosphorus

### variation

Substitute lemon juice for orange juice, and lemon zest for orange zest.

## PEANUT BUTTER FROSTING

Yield: For a 9-inch square cake (12 servings). Freezes well.

1½ cups icing sugar

6 Tbsp peanut butter

4 to 5 Tbsp milk (1%) or hot water

STEEL BLADE: Process all ingredients until smooth and blended, about 10 seconds. Scrape down sides of bowl as necessary.

108 calories per serving, 17.1 g carbohydrates, 0.5 g fiber, 2 g protein, 4 g fat (0.8 g saturated fat), 0 g cholesterol, 41 mg sodium, 55 mg potassium, 0 mg iron, 11 mg calcium, 32 mg phosphorus

## PEPPERMINT BUTTER FROSTING

Yield: To fill and frost two 9-inch layers or frost a large cake (12 to 18 servings). Freezes well.

1 peppermint candy cane (about ⅓ cup crushed candy)

3 cups icing sugar

6 Tbsp soft butter

½ tsp peppermint extract

few drops red food coloring

4 to 5 Tbsp hot milk or cream

STEEL BLADE: Break peppermint candy into 1-inch pieces. Start machine and drop candy through feed tube while machine is running. Process for a few seconds, until coarsely crushed. (It will be very noisy.) Empty bowl and set aside.

Combine remaining ingredients and process until smooth and blended, 10 to 12 seconds, scraping down sides of bowl as necessary. Delicious on chocolate cake. Use crushed candy as a garnish for top of cake.

201 calories per serving, 36.3 g carbohydrates, 0 g fiber, 0 g protein, 5.8 g fat (3.7 g saturated fat), 16 g cholesterol, 43 mg sodium, 10 mg potassium, 0 mg iron, 8 mg calcium, 7 mg phosphorus

# CHOCOLATE BUTTERCREAM

Yield: To fill and frost two or three 9-inch layer cakes or to frost a large cake (12 to 18 servings). Freezes well.

2 cups icing sugar

½ cup unsweetened cocoa powder

1 cup soft butter, cut in chunks

¼ cup milk (1%) or cream

¼ tsp pure vanilla extract

STEEL BLADE: Process all ingredients until smooth and blended, 15 to 20 seconds. Scrape down sides of bowl once or twice.

224 calories per serving, 22.3 g carbohydrates, 1.2 g fiber, 1 g protein, 15.9 g fat (10.1 g saturated fat), 41 g cholesterol, 112 mg sodium, 67 mg potassium, 1 mg iron, 15 mg calcium, 36 mg phosphorus

# KOKO-MOKO BUTTERCREAM

Yield: To fill and frost two or three 9-inch layer cakes or to frost a large cake (12 to 18 servings). Freezes well.

2 cups icing sugar

⅓ cup unsweetened cocoa powder

1 tsp instant coffee or espresso powder

1 cup soft butter, cut in chunks

2 to 3 Tbsp milk (1%) or cream

1 Tbsp boiling water

¼ tsp pure vanilla extract

Dissolve coffee in boiling water. Process all ingredients on STEEL BLADE until smooth and blended, 15 to 20 seconds. Scrape down sides of bowl once or twice.

221 calories per serving, 21.5 g carbohydrates, 0.8 g fiber, 1 g protein, 15.7 g fat (9.9 g saturated fat), 41 g cholesterol, 111 mg sodium, 48 mg potassium, 0 mg iron, 11 mg calcium, 25 mg phosphorus

# MOCHA BUTTERCREAM

Yield: To fill and frost two 9-inch layers or a 9-inch square (12 servings). Freezes well.

1½ cups icing sugar

½ cup soft butter or tub margarine

2 tsp instant coffee dissolved in 4 tsp boiling water

STEEL BLADE: Process all ingredients until blended, 10 to 15 seconds. Scrape down sides of bowl if necessary.

127 calories per serving, 15.0 g carbohydrates, 0 g fiber, 0 g protein, 7.7 g fat (4.9 g saturated fat), 20 g cholesterol, 55 mg sodium, 9 mg potassium, 0 mg iron, 3 mg calcium, 3 mg phosphorus

# WHIPPED CREAM

**2 cups chilled whipping cream**          **¼ cup granulated or icing sugar**

STEEL BLADE: Place a heavy book under back part of processor base so machine is tipped forward. Whip cream until texture of sour cream, about 35 seconds. Do not insert pusher in feed tube. Add sugar and process about 10 seconds longer, or until stiff. Do not overprocess. (See Whipping Cream in the **Smart Chart** on page 41.)

154 calories per serving, 5.3 g carbohydrates, 0 g fiber, 1 g protein, 14.8 g fat (9.2 g saturated fat), 55 g cholesterol, 15 mg sodium, 30 mg potassium, 0 mg iron, 26 mg calcium, 25 mg phosphorus

## variations

- CHOCOLATE WHIPPED CREAM: Increase sugar to ½ cup and add ¼ cup unsweetened cocoa powder along with sugar. One serving contains 175 calories, 10.6 g carbohydrates and 15 g fat.
- MOCHA WHIPPED CREAM: Increase sugar to ½ cup. Add 2 tsp instant coffee and 2 Tbsp unsweetened cocoa powder along with sugar. One serving contains 173 calories, 10.1 g carbohydrates and 14.9 g fat.

# GENIE'S ICING

*Yield: For one 8-inch square cake or two 9-inch layers (12 servings). Freezes well.*

**1 cup sugar**

**2 Tbsp cornstarch**

**1 cup milk (1%)**

**1 cup unsalted butter or shortening, softened**

STEEL BLADE: Place sugar and cornstarch in processor. Add milk through feed tube while machine is running. Blend until smooth. Transfer to a saucepan and cook on medium heat, stirring often, until mixture comes to a boil. Cook 1 minute longer. Remove from heat and cover surface of mixture with waxed paper. Cool thoroughly.

Using an electric mixer, cream butter or shortening until light and fluffy. Add cooled mixture and beat at high speed for at least 5 minutes. Add a few drops of food coloring, if desired.

214 calories per serving, 19 g carbohydrates, 0 g fiber, 1 g protein, 15.6 g fat (9.9 g saturated fat), 42 g cholesterol, 11 mg sodium, 35 mg potassium, 0 mg iron, 29 mg calcium, 24 mg phosphorus

## note

Icing may be processed with the STEEL BLADE for about 2 minutes. However, it will not have the same light, fluffy texture as when beaten with an electric mixer. Taste will not be affected.

# DESSERTS AND TORTES
## recipe list

393 Strawberry Dream Cheesecake

393 Easy Cheesecake

395 Chocolate Cheesecake

396 Dreamy Creamy Chocolate Cheesecake

397 Basic Torte Layers

398 Cinnamon Torte

398 Sour Cream Torte

399 Napoleon Torte

399 Chocolate Layer Torte

400 Chocolate Fantasy Torte

401 Grasshopper Torte

402 Hazelnut (Filbert) Torte

402 Linzertorte

403 Malakov Cream Cake

404 Top Skor Torte

404 Milles-Feuilles Dessert

405 Terrific Trifle

407 Heavenly Chocolate Trifle

407 Lemon Trifle

408 Light 'n' Lemony Cheese Dessert

409 Strawberry Yogurt Delight

409 Strawberry Mousse

410 Tofu Smoothie

410 Chocolate Tofu Mousse

411 Victorian Chocolate Mousse

412 Dark and Decadent Chocolate Pâté

412 Pudding Parfait

413 Frozen Peach Dessert

414 Berry Good Sherbet

414 Strawberry Swirl Popsicles

415 Biscuit Tortoni

415 Apple Chips

416 Easy Apple Crumble

417 Blueberry Streusel Dessert

417 English Plum Pudding with Brandy Hard Sauce

418 Brandy Hard Sauce

- Processors are classified according to their dry ingredient capacity, ranging from 3 to 20 cups. As a general guideline, the liquid capacity is about half the dry ingredient capacity. Refer to your manual for guidelines.
- The thicker the liquid, the more you can process in one batch. If liquid leaks out between the bowl and cover when the machine is running, you've added too much liquid. Some models have a maximum liquid fill line on the bowl, indicating the maximum amount of liquid that can be processed at a time.
- To prevent liquids from leaking from the bottom of the bowl, remove the bowl and **Steel Blade** together as soon as you've finished processing. Do not remove the blade first, especially if liquids in the bowl are above the hub of the blade. Otherwise, liquids will leak out from the center opening in the bowl when you remove the blade.
- NESTED WORK BOWLS: If your machine comes with nested bowls, choose the appropriate bowl and blade or disc for the task. For recipes that require multiple bowls, begin with the smallest one to minimize cleanups. Use the mini-bowl and mini-blade to chop nuts. Use the medium bowl and **Slicer** for fruit (e.g., apples, strawberries). Use the **Grater/Shredding Disc** for chocolate. Use the large bowl and **Steel Blade** for cheesecakes, tortes, mousses, smoothies, sherbets and fruit crisps.
- The Cuisinart Elite 14-cup model can process larger amounts in one batch (8 to 10 cups, depending on thickness of liquid). The **Steel Blade** locks into place and the nested bowls have convenient pouring spouts. The nested bowls also include a locking feature to prevent them from coming out of position when pouring. You can also use the **Steel Blade** in the medium bowl (e.g., to make a crust for cheesecake), which minimizes cleanup. However, since most brands don't have this capability, I didn't suggest doing this in my recipes.
- See "Quick Cleanups" (pages 7–8) for additional tips.
- When a dessert recipe calls for sugar, you can usually reduce it by up to 25%.
- Artificial sweeteners work best in dishes that don't depend on sugar for color, texture or moistness (e.g., fruit crisps, crumb

crusts, smoothies, sherbets and mousses). Replace 1 cup sugar with ½ cup sugar and ½ cup granular Splenda. Brown sugar can be replaced with half the amount of Splenda Brown Sugar Blend.

- SUPERFINE/FRUIT SUGAR: Process granulated sugar for 1 to 2 minutes on the **Steel Blade**. Excellent in meringues to prevent them from weeping!

- WHIPPING CREAM (35% CREAM): Whipping cream will turn to butter if it is warmer than 35°F when being whipped. To avoid this, chill whipping cream (and even the **Steel Blade** and work bowl) in the freezer for a few minutes before whipping. Whipped cream continues to stiffen as you work with it, so underwhip it slightly. Processor whipped cream is excellent as a garnish. However, it only increases 1½ times in volume and is firmer than cream that is whipped with an electric mixer, which doubles in volume.

- Dessert topping can be whipped in the processor, but it won't double in volume. See the **Smart Chart** entry for whipping cream (page 41) for method. Nondairy topping needs to be whipped with an electric mixer.

- You can use frozen light whipped topping instead of whipping cream to reduce calories and fat. It is convenient to use because it's already whipped but it contains artificial ingredients.

- ALMOST WHIPPING CREAM: Process 1 cup curd cottage cheese or ricotta cheese (low-fat or regular) on the **Steel Blade** for 2 to 3 minutes, until silky smooth. Add 2 Tbsp icing or granulated sugar (to taste) and ¼ tsp pure vanilla extract or orange liqueur. Chill; serve with fresh berries or cut-up fruit.

- YOGURT CHEESE: To make yogurt cheese, use plain yogurt without added gelatin, starches or stabilizers. Line a strainer with a double layer of cheesecloth and place over a large bowl. Spoon 3 cups low-fat or fat-free yogurt into strainer, wrap with cheesecloth and refrigerate. Let drain 2 to 24 hours—the longer it drains, the firmer the cheese. After 2 to 3 hours, you'll have 2 cups soft yogurt cheese. After 24 hours, you'll have 1½ cups firm yogurt cheese.

- Use soft yogurt cheese instead of whipped cream (no whipping necessary). Blend in 3 to 4 Tbsp icing sugar or granular Splenda and ½ tsp pure vanilla extract. Use firm yogurt cheese instead of cream cheese or cottage cheese in sweet or savory dishes. Use the drained whey instead of buttermilk or yogurt in cakes, muffins and smoothies.

- Blended Tofu (see **Smart Chart**, page 36) can replace uncooked eggs in mousses or is delicious in smoothies (e.g., Tofu Smoothie, page 410).

- Keep frozen fruit handy for sherbets, smoothies or fruit purées. Your processor will whip them up in moments!

- STRAWBERRY OR RASPBERRY PURÉE: Thaw 2 packages (10 oz/284 mL each) of frozen strawberries or raspberries; drain, reserving juice. (Or use 2 cups of fresh, ripe berries.) Purée briefly on the **Steel Blade**. Raspberries should be strained to remove seeds. If necessary, thin with some of the reserved juices. Sweeten with 2 to 3 Tbsp sugar or honey. Serve chilled.

- For fruit coulis or purées, cut peeled and pitted fruit in chunks (e.g., peaches, nectarines, mangoes, apricots). Process on the **Steel Blade** until smooth. Add a few drops of lemon juice to prevent discoloration. Sweeten with honey or sugar. Serve chilled. Canned, drained fruits also make delicious purées. Don't fill the bowl more than one-third to one-half full. For larger quantities, process food in batches.

- Cookies or wafers broken into chunks, then processed on the **Steel Blade** until fine, are ideal for cookie crumb crusts. See the **Smart Chart** under "Crumbs (Cookies, Crackers, Corn Flakes)" (page 37) for yields.

- Process nuts on the **Steel Blade** with quick on/off pulses (see "Nuts" in the **Smart Chart**, page 40). You can also "chop" nuts with the **Grater**, using medium pressure.

- Grind cookie crumbs (and nuts) for cheesecake in your processor, then process with remaining crust ingredients. Wipe out the processor bowl with paper towels. (If you have the Cuisinart 14-Cup Elite, you can use the medium bowl and **Steel Blade** to make the crust, then make the cheesecake batter in the large bowl.) It will take less than a minute to whip up your cheesecake!

- To prevent cheesecake from cracking, place a pie plate half filled with water on the bottom rack of the oven. Place the cheesecake on the middle rack and bake as directed in your recipe.

- DAIRY-FREE CHEESECAKE: Substitute Tofutti imitation cream cheese for cream cheese or dry cottage cheese. Use imitation sour cream instead of sour cream or yogurt in the filling or topping. Use margarine instead of butter in the crust. Delicious!

- Chop chocolate for mousses, sauces and desserts on the **Steel Blade** or grate on the **Grater** (see "Chocolate" in the **Smart Chart**, page 39). For melted chocolate, pour hot liquid called for in your recipe through feed tube while machine is running; chopped chocolate will melt instantly! See also "About Chocolate" (page 347) in the Cakes and Frostings chapter.

- CHOCOLATE CURLS: Temperature is the key. If the chocolate is cold, you will get flakes or small curls. For larger curls, the surface of the chocolate should be slightly warm. Place it briefly under a desk lamp or quickly pass a blow dryer across the surface. Do not melt the chocolate. Then take long strokes along the flat side of the chocolate with a sharp knife, vegetable peeler, melon baller or spoon. Lift the curls carefully with a metal spatula or toothpick.

- PORTIONS, PORTIONS! To keep calories, carbohydrates and fat content more reasonable, I've reduced the serving size in many of my dessert recipes, used lighter versions of ingredients and offered tips on ways to lighten up recipes. Please use the nutrient analysis as a guide to help you make healthier choices and save rich desserts for special occasions!

# STRAWBERRY DREAM CHEESECAKE

Light and refreshing, yet low in fat and sugar!

Yield: 16 servings.

Do not freeze.

15 single graham wafers (about 1¼ cups crumbs)

¼ cup margarine, cut in chunks

2 Tbsp brown sugar (or sugar substitute)

3 oz (85 g) pkg strawberry gelatin (regular or sugar-free)

1 cup boiling water

2 cups marshmallows

1 pint fresh strawberries, hulled

4 cups (2 lb/1 kg) dry cottage cheese or light cream cheese

3 Tbsp granulated sugar (or sugar substitute)

whole strawberries, for garnish

Preheat oven to 375°F. For machines with nested bowls, see method below.

STEEL BLADE: Break wafers into pieces. Process to make coarse crumbs, about 20 seconds. Add margarine and brown sugar and process until blended, 5 or 6 seconds longer. Press into sprayed 10-inch springform pan. Bake for 6 to 8 minutes, until golden. Cool.

Dissolve gelatin in boiling water in a saucepan. Add marshmallows and stir over low heat until melted. Refrigerate for 1 hour, or place in freezer for half an hour, until thickened.

SLICER: Slice berries, using gentle pressure. Set aside.

Process cheese for 1 to 2 minutes, until smooth and creamy. Add gelatin mixture and granulated sugar. Process until blended, about 15 seconds, scraping down bowl as necessary. Fold berries into cheese mixture by hand. Pour over crust. Chill overnight. Garnish with whole strawberries.

140 calories per serving, 22.7 g carbohydrates, 0.6 g fiber, 5 g protein, 3.7 g fat (0.7 g saturated fat), 3 g cholesterol, 211 mg sodium, 91 mg potassium, 0 mg iron, 38 mg calcium, 81 mg phosphorus

## nested bowl method

Use medium bowl and SLICER to slice strawberries. Use large bowl for remaining tasks.

# EASY CHEESECAKE

I've been making this recipe for years, with rave reviews! You can substitute chocolate or vanilla wafers in the crust.

CRUST

18 single graham wafers (about 1½ cups crumbs)

6 Tbsp soft tub margarine or butter, cut in small chunks

2 Tbsp sugar (granulated or brown)

½ tsp ground cinnamon

Yield: 16 servings. If
frozen, crust won't be as
crisp. For best results,
add topping when
cheesecake has thawed.

FILLING

4 cups (2 lb/1 kg) cream cheese,
   cut in chunks (light or regular)

1½ cups sugar

4 eggs (or 2 eggs plus 4 egg whites)

1 Tbsp pure vanilla extract (or 2 Tbsp
   lemon juice)

topping of your choice (optional; see
   below)

Preheat oven to 350°F.

For crust: Break wafers into chunks. Process on STEEL BLADE until coarse crumbs are formed. Add remaining crust ingredients and process until blended, 5 or 6 seconds. Press into sprayed 10-inch springform pan. Wipe bowl and blade with paper towels.

For filling: Process cheese with sugar until blended, about 15 seconds. Add eggs and vanilla extract. Process until smooth and creamy, 20 to 30 seconds longer. Pour over crust.

Place a pie plate half filled with water on lowest rack of oven. Place cheesecake on middle rack. Bake for 40 to 45 minutes. When done, edges will be set but center will jiggle slightly. Turn off heat and let cheesecake cool in oven with door partly open for about 1 hour. It will firm up during this time. Refrigerate. Add desired topping and chill for 3 to 4 hours before serving. (Can be made a day or 2 ahead.)

279 calories per serving (without topping), 30.4 g carbohydrates, 0.3 g fiber, 7 g protein, 14.4 g fat
(6.6 g saturated fat), 80 g cholesterol, 364 mg sodium, 29 mg potassium,
1 mg iron, 187 mg calcium, 30 mg phosphorus

### lighter variation

Use granular Splenda instead of sugar. Use half cream cheese and half dry cottage cheese, 2 eggs and 4 eggs whites. One serving contains 171 calories, 12.5 g carbohydrates and 9.8 g fat.

### cheesecake toppings

One serving with any of the following toppings contains approximately 315 calories, 40 g carbohydrates and 1 g fiber. Numbers vary slightly depending on topping used.

- **FRESH STRAWBERRY TOPPING:** Hull 4 cups of strawberries; cut in half lengthwise. Arrange cut side down in an attractive design over cooled cheesecake. Microwave ½ cup apricot preserves on High for 45 seconds, until melted. Gently brush glaze over fruit.

- MANDARIN ORANGE TOPPING: Drain three 10 oz (285 mL) cans mandarin oranges. Pat dry. Arrange in an attractive design over cooled cheesecake. Microwave ½ cup apricot preserves on High for 45 seconds, until melted. Gently brush glaze over fruit.
- GLAZED FRESH FRUIT TOPPING: Use topping for Glazed Fruit Cheesecake (page 517).
- CANNED PIE FILLING: Spoon a 19 oz (540 mL) can of cherry, blueberry or pineapple pie filling evenly over cheesecake.

### mini cheesecakes

Prepare filling for Easy Cheesecake as directed. Omit crust. Line muffin pans with 24 paper cupcake liners. Place a vanilla wafer in each liner. Top with cheesecake mixture. Bake in preheated 350°F oven for 10 to 12 minutes, until set. When cooled, top each cheesecake with a large strawberry or a spoonful of thick jam. One mini contains 154 calories, 18.9 g carbohydrates and 6.8 g fat.

# CHOCOLATE CHEESECAKE

This delicious cheesecake is extremely rich, so serve very small portions.

Yield: 16 small servings. Freezes well. Thaw overnight in refrigerator.

| | |
|---|---|
| 8 oz (250 g) pkg chocolate wafers (about 1¾ cups crumbs) | ¾ cup granulated sugar |
| ½ cup butter or margarine, melted | 4 eggs |
| 2 Tbsp granulated or brown sugar | ½ cup sour cream (light or regular) |
| ½ tsp ground cinnamon | ½ cup chilled whipping cream |
| 2 cups chocolate chips | 1 Tbsp icing sugar |
| 2 cups (1 lb/500 g) cream cheese, cut in chunks (light or regular) | Chocolate Curls (page 392), for garnish |

DESSERTS AND TORTES

Preheat oven to 350°F.

STEEL BLADE: Break wafers in chunks. Drop through feed tube while machine is running; process until fine crumbs are formed. Add butter or margarine, 2 Tbsp sugar and cinnamon; process a few seconds longer to blend. Press into sprayed 9-inch springform pan, reserving ⅓ cup crumb mixture for topping. Wash and dry bowl and blade.

Melt chocolate chips (2 to 3 minutes on Medium [50%] in the microwave), stirring once or twice.

STEEL BLADE: Process cheese with the ¾ cup sugar for 30 seconds. Do not insert pusher in feed tube. Add eggs and process until well blended, scraping down

*Continued*

sides of bowl as necessary. Add melted chocolate and sour cream; process about 20 seconds longer.

Pour chocolate mixture over crust and sprinkle with reserved crumbs. Place a pie plate half filled with water on bottom rack of oven. Place cheesecake on middle rack. Bake for 50 to 55 minutes. When done, edges of cake will be set, but center will be somewhat soft. Turn off oven and let cake cool inside for half an hour with the door partly open. When completely cooled, place cheesecake on a serving plate. Remove sides of pan.

Place a thick book under back of processor base so that machine is tipped forward. Do not insert pusher in feed tube. Whip cream on the STEEL BLADE until thick, 35 to 40 seconds. Add icing sugar and process a few seconds longer, until stiff. Pipe rosettes of whipped cream around edges of cheesecake. Garnish with Chocolate Curls. Refrigerate until serving time.

367 calories per serving, 37.7 g carbohydrates, 1.8 g fiber, 7 g protein, 23 g fat (13.3 g saturated fat), 95 g cholesterol, 282 mg sodium, 147 mg potassium, 1 mg iron, 124 mg calcium, 80 mg phosphorus

### passover variation

Make crust for Glazed Fruit Cheesecake (page 517), using chocolate macaroons.

## DREAMY CREAMY CHOCOLATE CHEESECAKE

This scrumptious unbaked cheesecake is a breeze to prepare! However, it's very rich, and even the lighter variation is not so light!

Yield: 16 servings. Freezes well. Thaw overnight in refrigerator.

1 square (1 oz/30 g) chilled
   semisweet chocolate, for garnish
8 oz (250 g) pkg chocolate wafers
½ cup melted butter or margarine
2 envelopes dessert topping mix
1 cup cold milk (1%)
2 cups (1 lb/500 g) cream cheese,
   cut in chunks (light or regular)

2 Tbsp coffee or chocolate liqueur
⅔ cup sugar
2 cups chocolate chips, melted
1 cup chilled whipping cream (or
   1 envelope dessert topping plus
   ½ cup cold milk)

GRATER: Grate chocolate, using firm pressure. Set aside. (Or make Chocolate Curls, page 392.)

STEEL BLADE: Break wafers in chunks. Drop wafers through feed tube while machine is running. Process until fine crumbs are formed. Add butter or margarine and process a few seconds longer to blend. Press into ungreased 10-inch springform pan. Bake in preheated 350°F oven for 7 to 8 minutes. Cool. Wash and dry bowl and blade; replace blade in bowl.

Place a thick book under the back of processor base so the machine is tipped forward. Do not insert pusher in feed tube. Process dessert topping with milk for 2 minutes, until stiff. Remove book from under machine. Add chunks of cream cheese through feed tube while machine is running. Process until smooth. Add liqueur, sugar and melted chocolate. Process until smooth and light, about 2 minutes. Scrape down sides of bowl as necessary. Pour mixture over crust. Wash bowl and blade.

Tip processor forward once again, using a thick book underneath the base. Process whipping cream until stiff, 35 to 40 seconds (2 minutes for dessert topping). Pipe rosettes of whipped cream around edges of cake; sprinkle with reserved grated chocolate. Refrigerate for 6 to 8 hours, or overnight.

395 calories per serving, 41.5 g carbohydrates, 1.8 g fiber, 5 g protein, 24.3 g fat (14.5 g saturated fat), 50 g cholesterol, 271 mg sodium, 150 mg potassium, 1 mg iron, 130 mg calcium, 74 mg phosphorus

### lighter variation

Decrease chocolate chips to 1½ cups and omit whipping cream. One serving contains 318 calories, 37.8 g carbohydrates and 17.2 g fat.

### note

Recipe may be halved, if desired, using a 9-inch pie plate. Decrease crumbs to 1¼ cups and butter to ⅓ cup. Do not decrease whipping cream for topping.

## BASIC TORTE LAYERS

A torte is a rich, multilayered dessert that is absolutely delicious but very high in calories. A sliver goes a long way!

Yield: 5 to 6 layers. May be prepared in advance and frozen until needed.

| | |
|---|---|
| 1 cup butter, cut in chunks | 2 cups flour |
| ½ cup sugar | 1 tsp baking powder |
| 2 eggs | |

Preheat oven to 350°F.

STEEL BLADE: Process butter, sugar and eggs until well blended, about 1 minute. Add flour and baking powder. Process just until mixed, using on/off pulses. Do not overprocess.

Divide dough into 5 or 6 equal portions. Roll out each piece into an 8-inch circle. Place on inverted 8-inch layer pans. (Greasing is not necessary.) Bake until light brown, 10 to 12 minutes. Remove from pans immediately and let cool. Fill and assemble as directed in torte recipes (pages 398–99).

309 calories per serving (¹⁄₁₀ of recipe), 29.4 g carbohydrates, 0.7 g fiber, 4 g protein, 19.7 g fat (12 g saturated fat), 91 g cholesterol, 193 mg sodium, 45 mg potassium, 1 mg iron, 41 mg calcium, 60 mg phosphorus

# CINNAMON TORTE

Sinful but absolutely
scrumptious!

Yield: 10 servings.

Do not freeze.

**Basic Torte Layers (page 397)**

**1½ Tbsp ground cinnamon**

**3 cups chilled whipping cream**

**⅓ cup icing sugar**

**1 tsp ground cinnamon**

**½ tsp pure vanilla extract**

**Chocolate Curls (page 392), for garnish**

**pecan halves, for garnish**

Prepare Basic Torte Layers as directed, adding 1½ Tbsp cinnamon to batter along with dry ingredients.

Cream may be whipped with either an electric mixer or processor, using the STEEL BLADE. (Electric mixer will yield a larger volume.) Place a thick book under back of processor base so machine is tipped forward. Do not insert pusher in feed tube. Pour cream through feed tube while machine is running. Whip until texture of sour cream, 30 to 40 seconds. Add sugar, cinnamon and vanilla extract. Process about 10 seconds longer, or until cream is stiff. Do not overprocess.

Spread whipped cream between torte layers, ending with cream. Garnish with Chocolate Curls and pecans.

577 calories per serving, 36.6 g carbohydrates, 1.4 g fiber, 6 g protein, 46.4 g fat (28.6 g saturated fat), 190 g cholesterol, 220 mg sodium, 106 mg potassium, 2 mg iron, 103 mg calcium, 105 mg phosphorus

# SOUR CREAM TORTE

Yield: 10 servings.

Do not freeze.

**Basic Torte Layers (page 397)**

**1½ cups walnuts (or your favorite nuts)**

**1½ cups sour cream (light or regular)**

**1 tsp pure vanilla extract**

**½ cup icing sugar (or to taste)**

**additional icing sugar, for garnish**

Prepare Basic Torte Layers as directed.

STEEL BLADE: Process nuts until finely chopped, 15 to 20 seconds; do not overprocess. Add sour cream, vanilla extract and ½ cup icing sugar. Process a few seconds longer to mix. Spread filling between torte layers. Refrigerate at least 24 hours before serving. Sprinkle generously with sifted icing sugar at serving time.

499 calories per serving, 40.5 g carbohydrates, 1.9 g fiber, 8 g protein, 35.1 g fat (15.6 g saturated fat), 104 g cholesterol, 219 mg sodium, 202 mg potassium, 2 mg iron, 111 mg calcium, 147 mg phosphorus

# NAPOLEON TORTE

Yield: 10 servings.

Do not freeze.

Basic Torte Layers (page 397)

1 pkg (6-serving size) vanilla
    pudding (not instant)

2⅓ cups milk (1%)

1 cup chilled whipping cream
    (or 1 envelope dessert topping
    plus ½ cup cold milk)

icing sugar, for garnish

Prepare Basic Torte Layers as directed.

Cook pudding according to package directions, using 2⅓ cups milk. Cover surface of cooked pudding with waxed paper; refrigerate until completely cold.

STEEL BLADE: Place a thick book under processor base so machine is tipped forward. Do not insert pusher in feed tube. Process whipping cream until stiff, about 45 seconds (2 minutes for dessert topping). Add chilled pudding and process until smooth, about 20 seconds.

Spread cream filling between layers. Sprinkle top of torte with icing sugar. Refrigerate for at least 24 hours before serving. Cut with very sharp knife.

453 calories per serving, 45.3 g carbohydrates, 0.8 g fiber, 7 g protein, 27.8 g fat (17 g saturated fat), 121 g cholesterol, 325 mg sodium, 156 mg potassium, 1 mg iron, 126 mg calcium, 129 mg phosphorus

### fruit variation

Arrange sliced bananas (sprinkled with lemon juice to prevent darkening) between layers along with pudding mixture. Other fruits may be substituted (e.g., peaches, mandarin oranges, mangoes, kiwis, strawberries).

# CHOCOLATE LAYER TORTE

Yield: 10 servings.

Freezes well.

Basic Torte Layers (page 397)

½ cup water

¼ cup flour

¼ cup granulated sugar

1 square (1 oz/30 g) semisweet
    chocolate

1 cup chilled butter or tub margarine,
    cut in chunks

1 cup icing sugar

2 Tbsp unsweetened cocoa powder

½ cup sliced or slivered almonds,
    toasted (page 407)

Prepare Basic Torte Layers as directed.

STEEL BLADE: Combine water, flour and sugar in a heavy saucepan. Cook over medium heat, stirring constantly, until thick, 2 to 3 minutes. Add chocolate and stir until melted. Remove from heat and cool completely.

STEEL BLADE: Process butter or margarine with icing sugar until well creamed, about 1 minute. Add cocoa and cooled chocolate mixture. Process until well blended, about 20 seconds, scraping down bowl as necessary. *Continued*

Spread filling thinly between torte layers, ending with filling. Sprinkle toasted almonds on top of torte. Refrigerate for 24 hours before serving.

592 calories per serving, 52.2 g carbohydrates, 1.8 g fiber, 6 g protein, 41.5 g fat (24.5 g saturated fat), 140 g cholesterol, 324 mg sodium, 113 mg potassium, 2 mg iron, 62 mg calcium, 103 mg phosphorus

## CHOCOLATE FANTASY TORTE

Decadent and delicious! If you have concerns about using raw eggs, refer to Egg Safety (page 401) for other alternatives.

Yield: 16 servings.
Do not freeze.

1 cup pecans
3 squares (3 oz/85 g) unsweetened chocolate
1¼ cups chocolate or vanilla wafer crumbs (see Smart Chart, page 37)
¼ cup melted butter or tub margarine
2 Tbsp granulated sugar

½ cup chilled butter, cut in chunks
1½ cups icing sugar
3 eggs
1½ cups chilled whipping cream
½ cup maple syrup
4 cups cut-up or mini marshmallows
Chocolate Curls (page 392), for garnish

For machines with nested bowls, see method below.

STEEL BLADE: Chop pecans coarsely, using several quick on/off pulses. Empty bowl and set aside. Microwave chocolate on Medium (50%) for 2 to 3 minutes, until melted, stirring every minute. (Chopping chocolate first on the STEEL BLADE until fine will make it melt more quickly.)

Process crumbs with ¼ cup melted butter or margarine and granulated sugar until blended, about 8 seconds. Press mixture into sprayed 10-inch springform pan. Bake in preheated 375°F oven for 7 to 8 minutes. Wash and dry bowl and blade.

Process ½ cup chilled butter with icing sugar and eggs for 45 seconds, until mixed. Do not insert pusher in feed tube. Add melted chocolate and process until blended, about 20 seconds. Scrape down sides of bowl as necessary. Pour mixture over crust. Place in freezer while preparing topping.

Use an electric mixer for maximum volume. Whip cream with maple syrup until thick. Fold in marshmallows and pecans. Spread over chilled chocolate layer. Garnish with Chocolate Curls. Refrigerate overnight.

396 calories per serving, 39.3 g carbohydrates, 1.9 g fiber, 4 g protein, 27 g fat (13.5 g saturated fat), 94 g cholesterol, 145 mg sodium, 144 mg potassium, 2 mg iron, 42 mg calcium, 86 mg phosphorus

### nested bowl method

Use mini-bowl and mini-blade to chop pecans. Use large bowl and STEEL BLADE for remaining processor tasks.

# GRASSHOPPER TORTE

*This tastes almost like ice cream!*

*Yield: 12 servings. Serve frozen. Let stand at room temperature for 5 to 10 minutes before serving.*

**8 oz (250 g) pkg chocolate or vanilla wafers**
**½ cup melted tub margarine**
**3 cups marshmallows**

**¼ cup milk (1%)**
**¼ cup mint liqueur**
**2 cups chilled whipping cream**

STEEL BLADE: Break wafers into chunks; process to make fine crumbs, about 30 seconds. Add melted margarine and process a few seconds longer, until mixed. Reserve ½ cup mixture for topping. Press remaining crumbs into ungreased 9-inch springform pan. Chill while preparing filling.

Combine marshmallows with milk in 3-quart microwavable bowl. Microwave, uncovered, on High for 2 to 3 minutes, until puffy and melted, stirring once or twice. Stir in liqueur. Cool, stirring occasionally.

Whip cream until stiff. (Use an electric mixer for maximum volume.) Fold into marshmallow mixture. Pour over crust. Top with reserved crumbs, wrap with aluminum foil and freeze overnight, or until needed.

348 calories per serving, 28.2 g carbohydrates, 0 g fiber, 3 g protein, 25 g fat (11.2 g saturated fat), 58 g cholesterol, 172 mg sodium, 42 mg potassium, 1 mg iron, 33 mg calcium, 32 mg phosphorus

## variations

- Replace mint liqueur with ¼ cup milk plus 1 tsp peppermint extract and a few drops green food coloring.

- For a pareve (nondairy) version, replace marshmallows and milk with 9 oz jar of marshmallow cream. Replace whipping cream with nondairy topping.

### lighter variation

Instead of whipping cream, substitute 4 cups frozen light whipped topping, partially thawed. One serving contains 265 calories, 33 g carbohydrates and 13.5 g fat.

# HAZELNUT (FILBERT) TORTE

Yield: 12 servings.

Freezes well.

2 squares (2 oz/60 g) chilled
   semisweet chocolate
¾ cup hazelnuts
¾ cup tub margarine or butter,
   cut in chunks
¾ cup sugar

2 eggs
¾ cup flour
¾ tsp baking powder
Mocha Buttercream (page 386) or
   Chocolate Buttercream (page 386)
additional nuts, for garnish

Preheat oven to 350°F. For machines with nested bowls, see method below.

STEEL BLADE: Divide each square of chocolate in half. Process chocolate with nuts until ground, 35 to 40 seconds. Empty bowl. Process margarine or butter with sugar for 30 seconds. Add eggs and process 1 minute longer. Add flour and baking powder. Process with 3 or 4 quick on/offs. Add chocolate and nuts. Process for 5 seconds, just until mixed. Do not overprocess.

Spread batter evenly into 2 sprayed 9-inch round layer pans. Bake for 30 to 35 minutes, until golden. Wait 10 minutes, then remove from pans. Cool completely.

Spread Mocha or Chocolate Buttercream on bottom layer. Add second layer; spread top and sides with remaining buttercream. Garnish with additional nuts.

394 calories per serving, 38.2 g carbohydrates, 1.3 g fiber, 3 g protein, 26.6 g fat (8.4 g saturated fat), 56 g cholesterol, 190 mg sodium, 105 mg potassium, 1 mg iron, 37 mg calcium, 63 mg phosphorus

## nested bowl method

Use mini-bowl and mini-blade to process chocolate and nuts. Use large bowl and STEEL BLADE for remaining processing tasks.

# LINZERTORTE

This scrumptious, lattice-topped jam and nut delight originated in Austria.

¾ cup almonds
1½ cups flour
½ cup butter or tub margarine,
   cut in chunks
½ cup icing sugar

1 tsp grated lemon zest
1 egg
1¼ cups raspberry jam (or strawberry,
   peach or apricot)

Yield: 10 to 12 servings.

Freezes well.

Preheat oven to 350°F.

STEEL BLADE: Process nuts with ¼ cup flour until finely chopped, about 30 seconds. Empty bowl. Process remaining flour with butter or margarine and icing sugar, until crumbly, about 10 seconds. Add nut-flour mixture, lemon zest and egg. Process until blended, 10 to 15 seconds.

Press three-quarters of dough into bottom and ¼ inch up sides of lightly sprayed 9-inch springform pan to form a shallow shell about ¼ inch thick. Spread shell evenly with jam. Roll out remaining dough on lightly floured surface; cut in strips ½ inch wide. Arrange strips in latticework design on top of torte. Bake for 45 minutes. Cool completely. Fill any spaces between latticework with more jam. Dust with additional icing sugar.

321 calories per serving, 47.9 g carbohydrates, 1.4 g fiber, 4 g protein, 13.3 g fat (6.3 g saturated fat), 46 g cholesterol, 72 mg sodium, 78 mg potassium, 1 mg iron, 27 mg calcium, 65 mg phosphorus

## MALAKOV CREAM CAKE

This rich, creamy dessert can be doubled for a crowd, using a 10-inch springform pan. If you have concerns about using raw egg yolks, refer to Egg Safety (page 401) for alternatives.

Yield: 10 servings.
Do not freeze.

3 squares (3 oz/85 g) unsweetened chocolate
1 cup unsalted butter, cut in chunks
1¾ cups icing sugar
3 egg yolks
¼ cup milk
2 Tbsp rum, brandy or Cognac
16 oz (500 g) sponge cake, cut in 1-inch squares

1 to 1½ cups chilled whipping cream
2 Tbsp granulated sugar or icing sugar
whole almonds and strawberries, for garnish
Chocolate Curls (page 392), for garnish

Microwave chocolate on medium for 2 to 3 minutes, until melted, stirring every minute. (Chopping chocolate first on the STEEL BLADE until fine will make it melt more quickly.) Cool completely.

STEEL BLADE: Process butter and 1¾ cups icing sugar until well creamed and light, about 1 minute. Add egg yolks and process another 20 seconds, until well blended. Scrape down sides of bowl as necessary. Blend in milk and rum for a few seconds. Add melted chocolate and process 10 seconds longer, scraping down sides of bowl once or twice.

Arrange half the cake pieces in sprayed 9-inch pie plate, leaving spaces between. Pour half the chocolate mixture over cake. Repeat with remaining cake and chocolate. Cover with plastic wrap and weigh down with a heavy plate. (I usually put several jars on top to help force chocolate mixture between cake pieces.) Refrigerate overnight, or freeze until needed, then thaw overnight in the refrigerator.

STEEL BLADE: Place a thick book under back of processor base so machine is tipped forward. Do not insert pusher in feed tube. Process whipping cream until the texture of sour cream, about 35 seconds. Add 2 Tbsp sugar and process until stiff, about 10 seconds longer. Spread most of whipped cream over chocolate layer. Pipe whipped cream rosettes around edges. Garnish with almonds, strawberries and Chocolate Curls. Chill until serving time. *Continued*

541 calories per serving, 56 g carbohydrates, 1.7 g fiber, 5 g protein, 34.7 g fat (20.9 g saturated fat), 192 g cholesterol, 130 mg sodium, 156 mg potassium, 3 mg iron, 76 mg calcium, 148 mg phosphorus

## variation

Omit chocolate. Process ¼ lb (125 g) toasted almonds on STEEL BLADE until finely ground, about 30 seconds. Empty bowl. Prepare buttercream mixture as directed, adding ground almonds with quick on/off pulses. Replace milk and liqueur with ⅓ cup strong coffee. One serving contains 555 calories and 36.1 g fat.

## TOP SKOR TORTE

You'll score points with your guests with this updated version of an old favorite. It's very decadent, so save it for special occasions.

Yield: 16 servings.
Do not freeze.

8 chilled Skor bars (1.4 oz/39 g each), broken up
2 cups chilled whipping cream
¼ cup icing sugar
4 to 5 dozen Chocolate Chip Cookies (page 430) (or use a 2 lb/900 g pkg)
⅔ cup milk (1%)
⅔ cup coffee- or chocolate-flavored liqueur

STEEL BLADE: Process Skor bars with quick on/off pulses to start, then let machine run until coarsely chopped. Set aside.

Whip cream and sugar with an electric mixer until stiff. Set aside, reserving ½ cup to make rosettes. (Processor may be used, but will not yield enough volume.)

Dip cookies quickly into milk, then into liqueur. Arrange in single layer in bottom of ungreased 10-inch springform pan. Fill in spaces with pieces of cookies that have also been dipped. Spread a layer of whipped cream over cookies; sprinkle with ¾ cup of chopped Skor bars. Repeat twice, ending with whipped cream. Pipe rosettes of whipped cream around edge of torte. Sprinkle with remaining Skor bars. Refrigerate overnight.

492 calories per serving, 51.7 g carbohydrates, 1.4 g fiber, 4 g protein, 29.9 g fat (14.6 g saturated fat), 70 g cholesterol, 251 mg sodium, 151 mg potassium, 1 mg iron, 46 mg calcium, 80 mg phosphorus

## MILLES-FEUILLES DESSERT

A favorite family or company dessert. A popular restaurant chain has added

18 double graham wafers (approximately)
2 pkgs instant pudding (4-serving size)
2 cups light sour cream or yogurt
2 cups milk (1% or 2%)
2 cups chilled whipping cream plus 2 Tbsp icing sugar (or 2 envelopes dessert topping mix plus 1 cup cold 1% milk)

this dessert to
its menu!

2½ cups icing sugar

6 Tbsp milk

½ tsp pure vanilla extract

2 squares (2 oz/60 g) semisweet
chocolate, melted (or ¼ cup
chocolate syrup)

Yield: About 18 servings.
Keeps about 3 days
in the refrigerator.
Do not freeze.

Arrange half the wafers closely together in the bottom of ungreased 9- × 13-inch glass baking dish. Fill any spaces with pieces of broken wafers.

STEEL BLADE: Process pudding with sour cream or yogurt for a few seconds. Gradually add 2 cups milk through feed tube while machine is running, stopping machine once or twice to scrape down sides of bowl. Process for about 20 seconds, until smooth. Immediately pour over graham wafer base. Refrigerate for about 15 minutes, until thickened. Wash and dry bowl and blade.

STEEL BLADE: Place a thick book under back of processor base so machine is tipped forward. Do not insert pusher in feed tube. Process whipping cream with 2 Tbsp icing sugar (or dessert topping with milk) until stiff. Spread carefully over pudding. Top with remaining wafers.

Process 2½ cups icing sugar with 6 Tbsp milk and vanilla extract until blended, 6 to 8 seconds. Spread carefully over wafers.

Drizzle parallel lines of chocolate over icing about 1 inch apart, down length of dessert. Draw the dull side of a knife across width of dessert, cutting through chocolate lines about every 2 inches to make a decorative pattern. Chill for several hours before serving. Cut in oblongs about 2 × 3 inches. May be prepared in advance.

302 calories per serving, 40 g carbohydrates, 0.4 g fiber, 3 g protein, 15.1 g fat (9.1 g saturated fat), 48 g cholesterol, 245 mg sodium, 153 mg potassium, 0 mg iron, 99 mg calcium, 157 mg phosphorus

### note

Recipe may be halved and prepared in an 8-inch square pan. Makes 8 servings (about 2- × 4-inch pieces).

## TERRIFIC TRIFLE

This easy dessert is
great for a crowd!

Yield: 18 to 20 servings.
Do not freeze and do not
make more than 1 day in
advance. Leftovers will
keep 2 or 3 days.

1 pint strawberries, hulled

2 bananas

1 Tbsp lemon juice

1 pkg vanilla instant pudding
(6-serving size)

1½ cups light sour cream or yogurt

1½ cups milk (1%)

1 sponge cake, cut in 1-inch chunks

¼ cup rum or orange liqueur

2 cups chilled whipping cream

¼ cup granulated sugar or icing
sugar

grated semisweet chocolate,
for garnish

SLICER: Reserve several strawberries for garnish. Slice remaining strawberries, using gentle pressure. Transfer to a bowl. Cut bananas to fit feed tube. Slice, using light pressure. Sprinkle with lemon juice. Transfer to another bowl.

STEEL BLADE: Process pudding with sour cream or yogurt for a few seconds. Slowly add milk through feed tube while machine is running. Process for 20 seconds, until blended. Scrape down sides of bowl as necessary.

Place one-third of the cake in 3-quart glass serving bowl. Sprinkle with 2 Tbsp rum or liqueur. Arrange strawberries over cake and cover with half the pudding. Repeat with cake, liqueur and bananas. Top with remaining pudding and cake. Wash bowl and blade.

STEEL BLADE: Place a thick book underneath processor base so machine is tipped forward. Do not insert pusher in feed tube. Whip cream until it's the texture of sour cream, 35 to 40 seconds. Add sugar and process a few seconds longer, until stiff. Garnish trifle with whipped cream, grated chocolate and strawberries. Chill for several hours or overnight.

270 calories per serving, 34.5 g carbohydrates, 0.8 g fiber, 4 g protein, 13.1 g fat (7.9 g saturated fat), 71 g cholesterol, 212 mg sodium, 195 mg potassium, 1 mg iron, 93 mg calcium, 149 mg phosphorus

## variations

- For a large crowd, use 2 packages (4-serving size) vanilla instant pudding, 2 cups light sour cream or yogurt, 2 cups 1% milk, extra cake and 3 different kinds of fruit. Makes 25 to 30 servings.

- For a small crowd, use 1 package (4-serving size) pudding, 1 cup light sour cream or yogurt and 1 cup 1% milk. Decrease the amount of cake and fruit slightly. Makes 12 servings.

## passover trifle

Omit sour cream and milk. Combine 1 package Passover instant vanilla pudding, 1 cup nondairy topping, ½ cup water, ½ cup juice from canned fruit and 2 tsp lemon juice. Process until blended. Alternate layers of Passover sponge cake, pudding mixture and fresh or canned drained fruit. Use Passover liqueur or wine to sprinkle on cake. Garnish with whipped nondairy topping. Makes 12 servings.

STEEL BLADE: Process tofu until very smooth, 1 to 2 minutes, scraping down sides of bowl as needed. Add remaining ingredients and process until blended, about 20 seconds. Pour into dessert dishes and chill until serving time.

149 calories per serving, 31.6 g carbohydrates, 6 g fiber, 6 g protein, 1.9 g fat (0.9 g saturated fat), 0 g cholesterol, 66 mg sodium, 195 mg potassium, 2 mg iron, 40 mg calcium, 131 mg phosphorus

### notes

- With Splenda, 1 serving contains 64 calories and 9.5 g carbohydrates. Excellent for diabetics.
- Some brands of tofu come in a 12 oz (340 g) package. Use 2 packages and make one-and-a-half times the recipe. This amount will be perfect for filling a baked 9-inch Graham Wafer Crust (page 473).

## VICTORIAN CHOCOLATE MOUSSE

My original recipe called for 4 egg yolks and less chocolate. Because of health concerns with using uncooked egg yolks, I replaced the yolks with Blended Tofu or Almost Sour Cream! No one will ever know!

Yield: 8 servings.

Do not freeze.

2 cups chilled whipping cream (or 2 envelopes dessert topping plus 1 cup cold 1% milk)

1 cup chocolate chips

½ cup Blended Tofu (page 36) or Almost Sour Cream! (page 145)

3 Tbsp sugar

STEEL BLADE: Place a thick book underneath processor base to tip machine forward. Do not insert pusher in feed tube. Whip cream or dessert topping until stiff peaks form, about 45 seconds for whipping cream or 2 minutes for dessert topping. Empty bowl.

Microwave chocolate chips on Medium (50%) for 2 to 3 minutes, until melted, stirring every minute. Cool slightly.

Process Blended Tofu or Almost Sour Cream! with sugar and melted chocolate for 45 seconds. Reserve about ¼ cup of the whipped cream for garnish. Blend remaining cream into chocolate with several quick on/offs, scraping down bowl as necessary.

Pour into 8 parfait glasses and refrigerate until set, about 1 hour. Garnish with reserved whipped cream. Sprinkle with a few chocolate chips, if desired.

360 calories per serving, 20.7 g carbohydrates, 1.8 g fiber, 6 g protein, 30.6 g fat (17.8 g saturated fat), 82 g cholesterol, 28 mg sodium, 178 mg potassium, 1 mg iron, 207 mg calcium, 110 mg phosphorus

### lighter variation

Replace whipping cream with dessert topping and 1% milk. One serving contains 269 calories, 30 g carbohydrates and 15.8 g fat.

DESSERTS AND TORTES

# DARK AND DECADENT CHOCOLATE PÂTÉ

Thanks to Ricki Heller, who shared this no-bake gluten-free dessert from her cookbook, *Sweet Freedom*. This is her husband's favorite dessert! Ricki uses 70% dark chocolate, but chocolate chips also work.

Yield: 6 servings. Freezes well. Thaw, wrapped in plastic, in refrigerator overnight.

scant ½ cup packed avocado purée (from 1 small barely ripe avocado)

1 tsp pure vanilla extract

pinch fine sea salt

9 oz (255 g) good-quality dark chocolate, chopped (or 1½ cups chocolate chips)

¼ cup freshly squeezed orange juice

1 Tbsp pure maple syrup

Line a miniature loaf pan (about 6 × 3 inches) with plastic wrap and set aside.

STEEL BLADE: Process avocado, vanilla and salt until smooth. Leave mixture in processor.

In a heavy-bottomed pot, combine chocolate, orange juice and maple syrup. Using lowest heat possible, stir constantly until melted and smooth, about 5 minutes. Immediately add to avocado mixture. Blend until smooth and glossy, scraping down bowl as necessary. Pour mixture into prepared pan and smooth the top.

Refrigerate, uncovered, until top is firm and dry. Cover top with plastic wrap and refrigerate until entire loaf is firm, 4 to 6 hours or overnight.

To unmold, remove plastic from top of loaf. Invert over a serving dish and remove pan, then carefully peel away plastic wrap. Serve with fresh berries.

300 calories per serving, 24.4 g carbohydrates, 5.9 g fiber, 4 g protein, 21 g fat (10.8 g saturated fat), 1 g cholesterol, 59 mg sodium, 424 mg potassium, 5 mg iron, 37 mg calcium, 143 mg phosphorus

## nutrition note

Heart-healthy flavonoids from the dark chocolate and monounsaturated fats from the avocado make this cholesterol-free indulgence good for you!

# PUDDING PARFAIT

Great for kids!

Yield: 8 servings.
Do not freeze.

1½ to 2 cups fresh strawberries, hulled

1 envelope dessert topping mix

2 cups cold milk (1%), divided

1 pkg instant vanilla pudding (4-serving size)

1 cup graham wafer crumbs or granola (approximately)

For machines with nested bowls, see method on page 413.

SLICER: Reserve 8 strawberries for garnish. Slice remaining berries, using light pressure. Set aside. Wash and dry bowl.

STEEL BLADE: Place a thick book underneath processor base to tip machine forward. Do not insert pusher in feed tube. Process topping with ½ cup of the milk until stiff, about 2 minutes. Add pudding to whipped topping. Start machine and slowly pour remaining 1½ cups milk through feed tube. Process until smooth, 20 to 30 seconds, scraping down sides of bowl as necessary.

Spoon half of pudding mixture into 8 parfait glasses. Sprinkle each parfait with 1 Tbsp crumbs or granola; top with sliced strawberries. Repeat layers. Garnish with a whole strawberry. Chill about 1 hour before serving.

171 calories per serving, 33.8 g carbohydrates, 0.9 g fiber, 3 g protein, 1.8 g fat (0.6 g saturated fat), 3 g cholesterol, 269 mg sodium, 151 mg potassium, 1 mg iron, 81 mg calcium, 163 mg phosphorus

### nested bowl method

Use medium bowl and SLICER for strawberries. Use large bowl and STEEL BLADE for remaining processing tasks.

### variation

Substitute chocolate pudding and chocolate wafer crumbs. Garnish with rosettes of whipped cream, if desired.

## FROZEN PEACH DESSERT

Quick, easy and refreshing—almost like ice cream.

| | |
|---|---|
| 1 can (19 oz/540 mL) peaches | ⅛ tsp almond extract |
| ⅓ cup sugar | 1 cup whipping cream |
| ⅓ to ½ cup peach brandy | |

Yield: 8 servings. Keeps for about 1 month in the freezer.

Drain peaches, reserving ½ cup peach juice. Measure 2 cups drained peaches.

STEEL BLADE: Process peaches with reserved peach juice, sugar, brandy and extract. Purée until smooth. Meanwhile, whip cream with electric mixer until stiff. Add whipped cream to peach purée. Blend in with 3 or 4 on/off pulses.

Pour mixture into 1-quart mold. Freeze until firm. To unmold, dip mold in hot water for about 5 seconds, then shake to loosen. Repeat if necessary. Freeze until 15 minutes before serving time. Let stand to soften slightly.

195 calories per serving, 20.9 g carbohydrates, 0.7 g fiber, 1 g protein, 11.2 g fat (6.9 g saturated fat), 41 g cholesterol, 15 mg sodium, 79 mg potassium, 0 mg iron, 23 mg calcium, 27 mg phosphorus

### variations

Substitute canned apricots and apricot brandy. Also delicious with 2 cups puréed mango and ½ cup mango juice.

# BERRY GOOD SHERBET

Keep frozen fruit on hand to make this easy, refreshing dessert in moments.

2 cups frozen unsweetened strawberries, raspberries or mixed berries

¼ cup sugar or honey

⅓ cup fat-free yogurt, buttermilk or soy milk

1 tsp lemon juice

Yield: 3 servings. Recipe can be doubled easily. Keeps for about 1 month in the freezer.

STEEL BLADE: Process berries with sugar or honey until mixture reaches the texture of snow. Add yogurt, buttermilk or soy milk and lemon juice. Process until smooth. Serve immediately, or transfer to a serving bowl and freeze until half an hour before serving.

116 calories per serving, 28.1 g carbohydrates, 2.1 g fiber, 2 g protein, 0.2 g fat (0 g saturated fat), 1 g cholesterol, 23 mg sodium, 219 mg potassium, 1 mg iron, 70 mg calcium, 56 mg phosphorus

## notes

- Buy packages of frozen fruit or prepare your own by cutting up ripe fruit and freezing it in a single layer on a cookie sheet. Transfer frozen fruit to freezer bags in 2-cup quantities.
- For a tropical-flavored sherbet, use a combination of mango, papaya and cantaloupe or honeydew instead of berries.

# STRAWBERRY SWIRL POPSICLES

Keep these treats on hand in the freezer. What a cool way to get kids to eat more fruit!

2½ cups fresh strawberries, hulled

¼ cup sugar

2 tsp lemon juice

2 cups vanilla yogurt (low-fat or regular)

Yield: 4 to 6 popsicles.

STEEL BLADE: Process strawberries with sugar and lemon juice until puréed, 12 to 15 seconds.

Fill popsicle molds with spoonfuls of strawberry purée and yogurt, alternating them to make a swirled design. Cover and insert wooden sticks if necessary. Freeze 6 to 8 hours, until completely frozen.

Remove molds from freezer and dip in hot water for a few seconds. Remove popsicles from molds and serve immediately. Store extras in a resealable freezer bag.

157 calories per popsicle, 28.6 g carbohydrates, 1.9 g fiber, 7 g protein, 2.2 g fat (1.2 g saturated fat), 7 g cholesterol, 87 mg sodium, 434 mg potassium, 1 mg iron, 240 mg calcium, 199 mg phosphorus

## BISCUIT TORTONI

An elegant and easy frozen dessert.

Yield: About 8 servings. Keeps for about 1 month in the freezer.

½ cup almonds

6 to 8 macaroons (to yield ¾ cup crumbs)

2 cups chilled whipping cream

2 Tbsp rum or sherry

¼ cup icing sugar

maraschino cherries, for garnish

STEEL BLADE: Process almonds until fine, about 20 seconds. Empty into a bowl. Process macaroons for 6 to 8 seconds to make crumbs. Add to almonds. Set aside about ⅓ cup almond/macaroon mixture as garnish. Add ¾ cup of whipping cream and rum or sherry to remaining almonds and macaroons; stir to moisten.

STEEL BLADE: Place a thick book underneath back of processor base to tip machine forward. Do not insert pusher in feed tube. Process remaining 1¼ cups whipping cream until it's the texture of sour cream, about 35 seconds. Add sugar and process a few seconds longer, until stiff.

Pour almond mixture over whipped cream. Blend in with 3 or 4 quick on/off pulses. Spoon into paper cups (or paper cupcake liners). Sprinkle with reserved crumb mixture and garnish with half a cherry. Freeze until firm, about 4 hours.

354 calories per serving, 20.1 g carbohydrates, 1.3 g fiber, 4 g protein, 29 g fat (16.2 g saturated fat), 82 g cholesterol, 67 mg sodium, 138 mg potassium, 1 mg iron, 63 mg calcium, 87 mg phosphorus

## APPLE CHIPS

Perfect for kids of all ages. This nutritious snack makes a terrific addition to the lunchbox. The thinner the slice, the crisper the chip. Chip chip hooray!

2 medium apples, cored (do not peel) (e.g., Gala, Granny Smith, Honeycrisp)

2 Tbsp sugar mixed with 1 tsp ground cinnamon

Preheat oven to 200°F.

SLICER: Use thin slicing disc (2 mm), if your processor comes with one. If your processor doesn't have a wide-mouth feed tube, cut apples to fit feed tube. Slice apples, using light pressure. Arrange slices in a single layer on 2 parchment-lined baking pans; don't let slices overlap. Sprinkle with cinnamon sugar.

*Continued*

Bake in upper and lower third of oven until apples are dry and crisp, about 2 hours, switching position of pans halfway through baking. Remove from oven. Apple chips will crisp up as they cool. Transfer to an airtight container and store at room temperature for 4 or 5 days. (They're so delicious, they probably won't last that long!)

147 calories per serving, 38.8 g carbohydrates, 5.1 g fiber, 1 g protein, 0.3 g fat (0.1 g saturated fat), 0 g cholesterol, 2 mg sodium, 201 mg potassium, 0 mg iron, 24 mg calcium, 21 mg phosphorus

## EASY APPLE CRUMBLE

TOPPING

½ cup tub margarine or butter,
  cut in chunks
1 cup flour or gluten-free flour
  (e.g., Bob's Red Mill)
½ cup brown sugar, packed
2 tsp ground cinnamon

FILLING

6 medium apples, peeled,
  cored and halved
¼ cup granulated sugar
3 Tbsp flour or gluten-free flour
1 tsp ground cinnamon

For machines with nested bowls, see method below.

For topping: Process topping ingredients on the STEEL BLADE for 8 to 10 seconds, until crumbly. Empty bowl.

For filling: Insert SLICER. Slice apples, using medium pressure. Empty into sprayed deep 9-inch glass pie plate or 10-inch ceramic quiche dish. Combine with remaining filling ingredients and mix well.

Sprinkle crumb mixture over apples; pat down evenly. Bake in preheated 375°F oven 35 to 45 minutes (or microwave on High for 10 to 12 minutes, rotating dish ¼ turn halfway through cooking).

306 calories per serving, 50.3 g carbohydrates, 2.6 g fiber, 2 g protein, 11.7 g fat (2.1 g saturated fat), 0 g cholesterol, 98 mg sodium, 154 mg potassium, 1 mg iron, 31 mg calcium, 35 mg phosphorus

### nested bowl method

Use medium bowl and SLICER for apples. Use large bowl and STEEL BLADE for topping.

### lighter variation

For topping, use ¼ cup canola oil or melted margarine. Reduce flour to ½ cup and add ½ cup quick-cooking rolled oats. One serving contains 258 calories, 47.6 g carbohydrates, 2.9 g fiber and 7.6 g fat. (If you replace sugar with granular Splenda, 1 serving contains 190 calories and 30 g carbohydrates.)

## BLUEBERRY STREUSEL DESSERT

Delicious served warm with ice cream or frozen yogurt. Substitute your favorite berries in season. Sliced peaches, nectarines or plums can replace part of the berries.

Yield: 8 servings. Freezes well.

3 cups fresh or frozen blueberries
½ cup granulated sugar
⅓ cup water
2 Tbsp cornstarch
2 Tbsp orange juice

1 cup flour or gluten-free flour
   (e.g., Bob's Red Mill)
½ cup icing sugar or brown sugar
¼ cup tub margarine, cut in chunks
½ tsp ground cinnamon

Preheat oven to 350°F. Combine blueberries, granulated sugar and water in 2-quart microwavable bowl. Microwave, uncovered, on High for 8 to 10 minutes, or until bubbling, stirring once or twice. Dissolve cornstarch in orange juice; stir into blueberry mixture. Microwave 1 to 2 minutes longer, until thick and shiny. Pour into sprayed deep 9-inch pie plate or 10-inch ceramic quiche dish.

STEEL BLADE: Process remaining ingredients for 10 seconds, until crumbly. Sprinkle streusel topping over hot blueberry mixture. Bake for 30 minutes, or until golden.

227 calories per serving, 42.4 g carbohydrates, 1.9 g fiber, 2 g protein, 6 g fat (1.1 g saturated fat), 0 g cholesterol, 48 mg sodium, 70 mg potassium, 1 mg iron, 9 mg calcium, 25 mg phosphorus

## ENGLISH PLUM PUDDING WITH BRANDY HARD SAUCE

Make this 2 to 3 weeks ahead so it can mellow. Serve this in slivers, not slices, as it is very rich. Oddly, plum pudding rarely contains plums!

Yield: 10 servings. Freezes well.

4 or 5 slices white bread (2 cups
   fresh bread crumbs)
½ cup almonds, walnuts or pecans
1 cup sultana raisins
1 cup mixed candied peel
½ cup flour
¾ cup brown sugar, packed
1 tsp ground cinnamon
¼ tsp nutmeg
pinch ground cloves

½ cup candied cherries
1 apple, peeled, cored and
   cut in chunks
2 eggs
½ cup orange juice (part brandy may
   be used)
1 Tbsp lemon juice
⅓ cup canola oil
Brandy Hard Sauce (page 418)

STEEL BLADE: Tear bread in chunks. Process until fine crumbs are formed, about 20 seconds. Transfer to large mixing bowl. Chop nuts coarsely, using 6 to 8 on/off pulses. Add to bowl along with raisins and candied peel. Process flour, brown sugar, cinnamon, nutmeg, cloves and cherries with 3 or 4 quick on/off pulses, until cherries are coarsely chopped. Add to bowl and mix well. Process apple until fine, about 15 seconds. Add to bowl. Process eggs, orange and lemon juice and oil for 5 seconds. Add to bowl and mix well. *Continued*

Spread evenly in lightly sprayed 6-cup casserole. Cover with a double layer of greased aluminum foil and tie securely with string. Place on rack in steamer or Dutch oven. Add enough boiling water to come halfway up sides of pot. Cover pot tightly and simmer for 6 hours. Add boiling water as needed to maintain water level.

Remove pudding from steamer and cool 15 to 20 minutes. Loosen edges with a spatula and unmold. Cool completely; wrap in foil and refrigerate or freeze. (May also be wrapped in cheesecloth moistened with brandy, then wrapped tightly with foil.)

To serve: Thaw if frozen. Return pudding to greased casserole; cover tightly with foil. Steam 1½ to 2 hours. Serve with the sauce.

368 calories per serving (without sauce), 65.2 g carbohydrates, 2.6 g fiber, 4 g protein, 11.4 g fat (1.2 g saturated fat), 42 g cholesterol, 90 mg sodium, 235 mg potassium, 10 mg iron, 59 mg calcium, 76 mg phosphorus

## BRANDY HARD SAUCE

Yield: 1⅓ cups.

Freezes well.

1½ cups icing sugar

1 Tbsp lemon or orange zest

½ cup butter, cut in chunks

3 Tbsp brandy (or 1 Tbsp brandy and 2 Tbsp milk)

1 tsp pure vanilla extract

½ tsp nutmeg (optional)

STEEL BLADE: Process all ingredients until smooth, about 20 seconds. Pour over steamed pudding.

70 calories per Tbsp, 8.4 g carbohydrates, 0 g fiber, 0 g protein, 3.9 g fat (2.5 g saturated fat), 10 g cholesterol, 28 mg sodium, 2 mg potassium, 0 mg iron, 2 mg calcium, 1 mg phosphorus

# CHOCOLATES, COOKIES AND SQUARES
## recipe list

425 Chocolate Truffles
425 Oh Henrys
426 Fast Fudge
427 Easy Rum Balls
427 Yummy Rum Balls
428 Peanut Butter Krispies
429 Old-Fashioned Peanut Butter Cookies
429 Almond Crescents
430 Chocolate Chip Cookies
430 Reverse Chocolate Chip Cookies
431 Reverse Chocolate Chip Cookies (Gluten-Free)
432 Chocolate Chip Cookies (Gluten-Free)
432 Chocolate Turtle Cookies
433 Debbie's Decadent Delights
434 Banana Chocolate Chip Drops
434 Meringue Horns
435 Coconut Oatmeal Bar Cookies

435 Kathy's Swiss Mocha Hazelnut Cookies
436 Melting Moments
437 Orange Pecan Butter Balls
437 Tom Thumb Cookies
438 Shortbread Cookies
439 Butterscotch Toffee Dreams
439 Sesame Crescents
440 Holiday Cookies
440 Gingerbread Cookies
441 Sugar Cookies
442 Cinnamon Twists
443 Sesame Nothings (Kichel)
444 Basic Oil Dough
444 Mandel Bread (Mandelbroit)
445 Chocolate Almond Biscotti
446 Hamentaschen
446 Apricot Raisin Filling
447 Prune Filling
447 Date Filling
447 Chocolate Hamentaschen Kisses

448 Roly Poly

449 Chocolate Rogelach

450 Cinnamon Nut Rogelach

450 French Unbaked Cake

451 Nanaimo Crunch Bars

452 Almond Crisp Bars

452 Apricot Almond Triangles

453 Peanut Butter Squares

453 Basic Brownies

454 Butterscotch Brownies

455 Marbled Cheesecake Brownies

456 Easy Cheese Dreams

457 Brownie Bites

457 Butter Tart Slice

458 By Cracky Bars

459 Chocolate Chip Nut Chews

459 Crumbly Jam Squares

460 Halfway Squares

460 Heavenly Squares

461 Hello Dolly Squares

462 Lemon Squares

462 Lime Coconut Bars

463 Pecan Jam Squares

463 Raspberry Chocolate Chip Squares

- With the help of your processor and the quick tips and techniques in this book, you can whip up easy and delicious chocolate treats, cookies and squares in a fraction of the time!
- Use the **Steel Blade** to mix up your cookie dough, make crumb mixtures, chop dried fruits or mince citrus zest. Chop or grate nuts and chocolate with the **Steel Blade** or **Grater**. Refer to the **Smart Chart** (pages 24–41) for basic techniques.
- Many baking tips for cakes (pages 344–350) and desserts (pages 390–392) also apply. Refer to "Gluten-Free Baking" (page 345), "How Sweet It Is" (page 346) and "Dairy Replacements" (page 346) in the Cakes and Frostings chapter.
- As a general guideline, cookie recipes using 2 to 2½ cups of flour can be made in a standard-sized processor. A large processor will handle up to twice the amount.
- NESTED WORK BOWLS: If your machine comes with nested bowls, choose the appropriate bowl and blade or disc for the task. For recipes that require multiple bowls, begin with the smallest one to minimize cleanups.

- If a recipe calls for chopped ingredients (e.g., nuts, chocolate, orange zest), chop them first while the processor bowl is clean and dry (or use mini-bowl and mini-blade), then set them aside until needed.
- If your usual recipe calls for sifting dry ingredients together, process on the **Steel Blade** for 8 to 10 seconds to combine. If you have a Cuisinart Elite 14- or 16-cup model, you can also use the **Steel Blade** in the medium bowl.
- Next, prepare the cookie dough. This usually takes 2 or 3 minutes. Add chopped nuts, chocolate chips, etc., using quick on/off pulses to prevent overprocessing. Some recipes call for mixing them in with a spatula or wooden spoon.
- To process sticky fruits (e.g., dates, prunes, raisins, candied fruits), freeze them for 10 minutes. Then add some of the flour called for in the recipe (2 to 4 Tbsp) and process with quick on/off pulses, until the desired texture is reached. This helps prevent fruit from sticking to the **Steel Blade**.
- To chop nuts, use on/off pulses, until the desired texture is reached (see **Smart Chart**, page 40). To prevent overprocessing and

creating nut butter, add some of the flour or sugar called for in the recipe to the nuts before processing (up to ½ cup for each cup of nuts).

- Chill chocolate before processing. Otherwise, the heat from the speed of the blades may melt the chocolate. Chocolate can be chopped or ground on the **Steel Blade**, or grated on the **Grater**. See **Smart Chart** under "Chocolate" (page 39), and "About Chocolate" (page 347) in the Cakes and Frostings chapter.

- BATTER UP! Process butter or margarine with sugar on the **Steel Blade** until well creamed, 1 to 2 minutes. Eggs are either processed with butter and sugar or added through the feed tube. Blend in flour and dry ingredients with quick on/off pulses, just until blended. In some recipes, dough is processed just until it forms a ball.

- See "Quick Cleanups" (pages 7–8) for more tips.

- Butter and margarine are interchangeable in most recipes. Don't bake with light margarine; it contains too much water. I use tub margarine in most of my recipes unless otherwise indicated. Earth Balance Buttery Sticks are dairy-free and work well.

- If dough is too soft, refrigerate until firm enough to handle. Work with small amounts at a time. Keep the rest refrigerated.

- SIZE DOES COUNT! For even baking, cookies should be uniform in size. A small cookie scoop works perfectly! Leave 1 to 2 inches between cookies as some doughs spread during baking.

- For best results, use shiny, heavy-quality aluminum cookie sheets. Dark pans absorb too much heat and the bottoms of the cookies may burn. You can insulate lightweight pans by lining them with heavy-duty foil, or by placing one pan on top of another.

- TO GREASE OR NOT TO GREASE? I used to grease and flour my pans. Now I use nonstick spray or line pans with parchment paper or foil.

Greasing or spraying is not necessary if cookies are high in fat (e.g., shortbread).

- Parchment paper is oven-safe to 400°F. (I've even used it in a 425°F oven if the baking time is 15 minutes or less.) Many bakers like to use a nonstick silicone baking mat (Silpat)—it's oven-safe to 500°F. If the oven temperature called for in a recipe is higher than 400°F, line baking sheets with aluminum foil; spray if directed.

- Not enough cookie sheets? While the first batch of cookies is in the oven, place the next batch on parchment paper or foil. When the first batch is baked, slide the parchment or foil (and cookies) off the pan. Cool the pan slightly, then replace with the next batch. (Lining pans with foil or parchment also saves on cleanups.)

- Cookies can spread or flatten if placed on hot cookie sheets, so cool pans between batches.

- Preheat oven for best results. Make sure your oven temperature is accurate. An oven thermometer is helpful.

- POSITION IS EVERYTHING! Bake cookies on the middle rack of your oven. If baking 2 pans at once, place racks so they divide the oven evenly into thirds. For even browning, switch pans (top to bottom and front to back) for the last few minutes of baking.

- Use a timer for accurate results. Check a few minutes before the end of baking time to prevent overbaking.

- READY OR NOT? When checking for doneness, open and close the door quickly so the oven won't lose too much heat. Some cookies will still be soft when ready, but will firm up after a few minutes. If the bottoms are too brown, remove the cookies from the pan immediately to prevent continued baking.

- Let cookies cool on baking pans for a few minutes, then transfer to cooling racks.

- To prevent sticking, always cool cookies before transferring them to your cookie jar. If sprinkling cookies with icing sugar, cool them first so the sugar doesn't melt.
- For that just-baked taste, microwave 2 or 3 cookies for 10 seconds on High.
- DIP TIP! Microwave 4 oz (125 g) semisweet or white chocolate on Medium (50%) for 3 to 4 minutes, stirring every minute, until melted. Stir in 2 tsp canola or vegetable oil. Dip cookies halfway into melted chocolate. Place on waxed paper to dry.
- CHOCOLATE MELTDOWN! When melting chocolate, the bowl and mixing spoon must be completely dry to prevent chocolate from seizing (lumping and clumping). If this happens, see "Chocolate Rescue" (page 347) in the Cakes and Frostings chapter.
- SWEETENED CONDENSED MILK: It's so easy to make your own. (See recipe on page 427.) Sweetened condensed milk and evaporated milk are **not** interchangeable in recipes.
- Unbaked cookies can be frozen for several months. Shape, then freeze. Transfer to freezer containers when frozen. No need to defrost them before baking! Take out as many as you need and bake, increasing cooking time slightly.
- Cookies and squares freeze well. They take about 15 minutes to defrost, depending on size. Most can be eaten directly from the freezer—I know from experience!
- That's the way the cookie crumbles! Process leftover or broken cookies on the **Steel Blade** until fine. Use to make cookie crumb crusts for squares and desserts.
- Substitute granola for half the graham wafer crumbs in cookies and squares for an interesting taste and texture.
- THE BAR SCENE! Bars and squares are a great timesaver and use only 1 pan. Cool bar cookies in the pan, then cut with a sharp knife. For entertaining or gift giving, cut into small squares and place in pretty paper baking cups.
- Reduce oven temperature by 25°F when baking in glass pans.

# CHOCOLATE TRUFFLES

The ultimate in chocolate ecstasy!

Yield: About 3 dozen. Serve chilled as they soften quite quickly at room temperature. Keep about 1 week in fridge or 1 to 2 months in the freezer.

¼ cup unsweetened cocoa powder
2 Tbsp icing sugar
¾ cup whipping cream
2 Tbsp butter
8 oz (250 g) semisweet or bittersweet chocolate, broken into chunks
1 Tbsp rum, cognac or your favorite liqueur

STEEL BLADE: Process cocoa and icing sugar for 3 or 4 seconds to blend. Transfer to pie plate. Microwave whipping cream and butter on High for 1½ minutes, until almost boiling.

Process chocolate with several on/off pulses to start, then let machine run until chocolate is fine, about 30 seconds. Pour hot cream through feed tube while machine is running; process just until chocolate is melted and mixture is smooth. Blend in liqueur.

Transfer mixture to bowl. Cover and refrigerate until firm, about 3 hours or overnight. (Or freeze about 1 hour, stirring several times.)

Drop 1-inch mounds of chocolate into cocoa mixture. Roll into balls, coating truffles completely with cocoa. Wash and dry your hands as necessary. Licking is not allowed! Place truffles in paper candy cups. Refrigerate or freeze until needed.

57 calories each, 4.9 g carbohydrates, 0.6 g fiber, 1 g protein, 4.5 g fat (2.7 g saturated fat), 9 g cholesterol, 7 mg sodium, 36 mg potassium, 0 mg iron, 6 mg calcium, 16 mg phosphorus

## variations

- Roll truffles in grated semisweet chocolate, chocolate sprinkles, finely chopped nuts or toffee bits.

- For white chocolate truffles, use ½ cup whipping cream, 2 Tbsp butter and 8 oz white chocolate. Flavor truffle mixture with 1 Tbsp almond or orange liqueur. Roll in ¾ cup finely ground almonds or hazelnuts. Makes 2½ dozen. One truffle contains 112 calories, 9.9 carbohydrates and 8.1 g fat.

# OH HENRYS

No baking required—quick to make and quicker to disappear.

Yield: About 3½ dozen.

1 cup walnuts, Brazil nuts or salted peanuts
1 cup chocolate chips
1 cup butterscotch chips
3 oz (85 g) can chow mein noodles

STEEL BLADE: Chop walnuts or Brazil nuts with several quick on/off pulses, until coarsely chopped. Peanuts do not need chopping. *Continued*

In large microwavable bowl, melt chocolate and butterscotch chips on Medium (50%) for 3 to 4 minutes. Stir after 2 minutes, then every minute. Stir in noodles and nuts. Drop from a teaspoon onto parchment-lined baking sheet. Refrigerate or freeze.

76 calories each, 7.8 g carbohydrates, 0.5 g fiber, 1 g protein, 4.9 g fat (2.5 g saturated fat), 0 g cholesterol, 13 mg sodium, 28 mg potassium, 0 mg iron, 4 mg calcium, 17 mg phosphorus

### variation

Replace any of the nuts with slivered blanched almonds. Do not chop.

## FAST FUDGE

So quick and easy! Great for gifts.

Yield: 1½ lb or 25 squares. Freezes well.

1 cup walnuts, almonds, pecans or cashews

2 cups chocolate chips

2 squares (2 oz/60 g) unsweetened chocolate

1 Tbsp tub margarine or butter

14 oz (398 mL) can sweetened condensed milk (or see page 427)

1 tsp pure vanilla extract

STEEL BLADE: Process nuts with quick on/off pulses, until coarsely chopped. Set aside.

Combine chocolate chips, chocolate, margarine or butter and milk in 2-quart microwavable bowl. Microwave on High for 2 minutes, stir well. Microwave 1 minute longer, until melted. Mixture should be smooth and shiny. Stir in nuts and vanilla extract.

Spread mixture evenly in sprayed 8-inch-square pan and chill until firm. Cut into squares. Serve in small paper cups.

158 calories per square, 18.4 g carbohydrates, 1.4 g fiber, 3 g protein, 9.7 g fat (4.3 g saturated fat), 5 g cholesterol, 26 mg sodium, 145 mg potassium, 1 mg iron, 56 mg calcium, 81 mg phosphorus

### variations

- Stir 2 cups cut-up or miniature marshmallows into fudge along with chopped nuts. One square contains 170 calories and 21.6 g carbohydrates.

- Drop mixture by small spoonfuls into pretty paper baking cups instead of spreading it in a pan. No cutting required!

> ### make your own sweetened condensed milk
>
> Combine 6 Tbsp butter, 1 cup plus 2 Tbsp sugar, ½ cup water and 1½ cups instant skim milk powder in 3-quart microwavable bowl. Mix well. Microwave on High for 5 to 6 minutes, until boiling and thickened. Stir well 2 or 3 times during cooking. Mixture will thicken upon standing. Let cool. Store in refrigerator for 2 to 3 weeks. Makes equivalent of a 14 oz (398 mL) can of sweetened condensed milk.

## EASY RUM BALLS

*This is a great way to use up stale cake.*

*Yield: 5 dozen. Delicious right from the freezer!*

2 cups almonds or hazelnuts

4 cups stale chocolate or white cake, cut in chunks

2 cups icing sugar

3 Tbsp unsweetened cocoa powder

¼ cup tub margarine or butter

¼ cup milk (1%)

2 Tbsp rum (or chocolate, orange or almond liqueur)

STEEL BLADE: Process nuts until finely ground, about 30 seconds. Empty bowl. Process cake until finely ground, about 30 seconds. Measure 4 cups. Process icing sugar with cocoa, margarine or butter, milk and rum until blended, 15 to 20 seconds. Add cake crumbs and ½ cup of the ground nuts; process until well mixed.

Roll mixture into 1-inch balls. Roll in reserved nuts. Place on parchment-lined cookie sheets and refrigerate or freeze until firm. Serve in paper cups.

80 calories each, 9.1 g carbohydrates, 0.8 g fiber, 2 g protein, 4.4 g fat (0.8 g saturated fat), 4 g cholesterol, 31 mg sodium, 51 mg potassium, 0 mg iron, 18 mg calcium, 34 mg phosphorus

> ### passover variation
>
> PASSOVER "YUM" BALLS: Replace rum with Passover chocolate liqueur or wine; use stale Passover sponge cake. For a pareve version, replace milk with nondairy creamer.

## YUMMY RUM BALLS

*Yield: 3½ to 4 dozen balls. Freezes well.*

1 cup pecans or walnuts

½ cup sultana raisins

¼ cup rum

8 oz (250 g) pkg vanilla wafers

2 Tbsp unsweetened cocoa powder

½ cup corn syrup

2 Tbsp butter or tub margarine

½ cup chocolate chips

chocolate sprinkles, coconut and/or chopped nuts for coating

For machines with nested bowls, see method below.

STEEL BLADE: Chop nuts with 6 or 8 quick on/off pulses. Set aside. Process raisins until ground, about 8 to 10 seconds. Combine in a small bowl with rum and let soak half an hour.

Break wafers in chunks. Drop through feed tube while machine is running and process to make fine crumbs. Add cocoa, corn syrup, nuts and raisins. Process with on/off pulses to blend thoroughly. Wet your hands and roll crumb mixture into 1-inch balls. Place on a parchment-lined cookie sheet and refrigerate for 20 minutes, or until firm.

Melt butter with chocolate chips on low heat (or microwave on Medium [50%] about 1 minute). Dip balls in cooled chocolate mixture, then in sprinkles, coconut and/or chopped nuts. Refrigerate or freeze. Let stand about 5 minutes (if you can wait that long!) before serving. Serve in tiny paper cups.

75 calories each, 10.3 g carbohydrates, 0.5 g fiber, 1 g protein, 3.6 g fat (1 g saturated fat), 2 g cholesterol, 30 mg sodium, 34 mg potassium, 0 mg iron, 4 mg calcium, 13 mg phosphorus

## nested bowl method

Use mini-bowl and mini-blade for nuts. Empty bowl, then process raisins. Use large bowl and STEEL BLADE for remaining processing tasks.

# PEANUT BUTTER KRISPIES

Another quick, no-bake recipe.

Yield: About 3 dozen. Freezes well.

| | |
|---|---|
| 2 cups peanuts | 1 cup icing sugar |
| 1 cup smooth peanut butter | 2 Tbsp milk (1%) (approximately) |
| 2 Tbsp tub margarine or butter | 3 cups Rice Krispies or Cheerios |

STEEL BLADE: Process peanuts with 6 or 8 quick on/off pulses, until coarsely chopped. Transfer to a pie plate.

Process peanut butter, margarine or butter, icing sugar and milk until smooth and blended, stopping machine once or twice to scrape down sides of bowl.

Place cereal in large mixing bowl. Stir in peanut butter mixture. Shape into 1-inch balls and roll in chopped peanuts. Store in refrigerator in covered container.

115 calories each, 8.4 g carbohydrates, 1.1 g fiber, 4 g protein, 8.2 g fat (1.4 g saturated fat), 0 g cholesterol, 57 mg sodium, 99 mg potassium, 1 mg iron, 9 mg calcium, 56 mg phosphorus

# OLD-FASHIONED PEANUT BUTTER COOKIES

These cookies bring back childhood memories.

Yield: About 3½ dozen cookies. Freezes well.

½ cup tub margarine or butter

½ cup peanut butter (smooth or chunky)

½ cup granulated sugar

½ cup brown sugar, packed

1 egg

1¼ cups flour

½ tsp baking powder

½ tsp baking soda

½ cup chocolate chips (optional)

Preheat oven to 375°F.

STEEL BLADE: Process margarine or butter, peanut butter, sugars and egg until well creamed, about 1 minute. Add flour, baking powder and baking soda. Process with quick on/off pulses, just until blended. Do not overprocess.

Form into 1-inch balls and place about 3 inches apart on parchment-lined cookie sheets. Flatten in a crisscross design with a fork that has been dipped in flour. If desired, press 3 or 4 chocolate chips into each cookie.

Bake for 10 to 12 minutes, until golden. (Cookies will spread during baking.) Cool slightly before removing from pan.

72 calories each, 8.6 g carbohydrates, 0.3 g fiber, 1 g protein, 3.8 g fat (0.7 g saturated fat), 5 g cholesterol, 55 mg sodium, 28 mg potassium, 0 mg iron, 8 mg calcium, 18 mg phosphorus

# ALMOND CRESCENTS

Marty Kaplan's late mother, Zelda, was famous for these cookies. When Marty, a Toronto lawyer, tasted my gluten-free version, he couldn't tell the difference. He immediately added a 1 lb cookie surcharge to all his future legal bills to me!

1 cup almonds

1 cup soft butter, cut in chunks

⅓ cup sugar

1 tsp pure vanilla extract

1 Tbsp water

2 cups flour (all-purpose or Bob's Red Mill gluten-free)

⅓ cup icing sugar for sprinkling

Preheat oven to 350°F. For machines with nested bowls, see method on page 430.

STEEL BLADE: Process almonds with quick on/off pulses, until finely chopped. Set aside.

STEEL BLADE: Process butter, sugar and vanilla extract for 1 to 2 minutes, until well blended. Sprinkle water and flour on top. Process with several quick on/offs, just until mixed. Scrape down sides of bowl as needed. Sprinkle almonds on top and process with 3 or 4 on/off pulses to combine. Do not overprocess.

Form into 1-inch balls, then shape each ball into a crescent. Place about 2 inches apart on parchment-lined baking sheets. If dough is sticky, flour your hands lightly for easier handling.

Bake for 15 to 18 minutes, until golden. When cool, sprinkle generously with icing sugar.

*Continued*

79 calories each, 6.8 g carbohydrates, 0.5 g fiber, 1 g protein, 5.4 g fat (2.6 g saturated fat), 10 g cholesterol, 27 mg sodium, 28 mg potassium, 0 mg iron, 10 mg calcium, 21 mg phosphorus

### nested bowl method

Use mini-bowl and mini-blade to chop nuts. Use large bowl and STEEL BLADE for remaining processing tasks.

## CHOCOLATE CHIP COOKIES

These are my granddaughter Lauren Sprackman's favorite cookies! I sometimes like to press five M&M chocolate candies onto each cookie (reducing the heat to 350°F and baking for 10 minutes). For a soft, chewy cookie, reduce flour to 2 cups (also baking at 350°F for 10 minutes).

½ to 1 cup pecans (optional)
1 cup tub margarine or butter, cut in chunks
¾ cup granulated sugar
¾ cup brown sugar, packed
2 eggs
1 tsp pure vanilla extract or 1 Tbsp coffee liqueur

2¼ cups flour
1 tsp baking soda
½ tsp salt
2 cups chocolate chips or chunks (or 1 cup white chocolate chips and 1 cup semisweet chocolate chips)

Preheat oven to 375°F.

STEEL BLADE: Process nuts (if using) until coarsely chopped, 8 to 10 seconds. Empty bowl. Process margarine or butter, sugars, eggs and vanilla extract or liqueur for 1 minute. Add flour, baking soda and salt, and process with several quick on/off pulses, just until blended. Do not overprocess. Stir in chips and nuts with a rubber spatula. (If desired, transfer dough to a large bowl, cover and refrigerate for 24 to 36 hours before baking.)

Drop by small spoonfuls onto parchment- or foil-lined cookie sheets. Bake for 10 to 12 minutes, until lightly browned. Cool 10 minutes before removing from pan.

78 calories each, 10.3 g carbohydrates, 0.4 g fiber, 1 g protein, 4.1 g fat (1.3 g saturated fat), 6 g cholesterol, 57 mg sodium, 27 mg potassium, 0 mg iron, 5 mg calcium, 13 mg phosphorus

## REVERSE CHOCOLATE CHIP COOKIES

My catering clients loved these. They're truly addictive!

1 cup tub margarine or butter, cut in chunks
¾ cup granulated sugar
¾ cup brown sugar, packed
2 eggs
1 tsp pure vanilla extract

1½ cups plus 2 Tbsp flour
½ cup unsweetened cocoa powder
1 tsp baking soda
⅛ tsp salt
2 cups white chocolate chips

Preheat oven to 350°F.

STEEL BLADE: Process margarine or butter, sugars, eggs and vanilla extract for 1 minute. Add flour, cocoa, baking soda and salt, and process with several quick on/off pulses, just until blended. Do not overprocess. Stir in chocolate chips with a rubber spatula.

Drop by small spoonfuls onto parchment- or foil-lined cookie sheets. Bake for 10 minutes.

68 calories each, 8.3 g carbohydrates, 0.2 g fiber, 1 g protein, 3.7 g fat (1.3 g saturated fat), 6 g cholesterol, 27 mg sodium, 27 mg potassium, 0 mg iron, 11 mg calcium, 16 mg phosphorus

### variation

Substitute 2 cups peanut butter chips for the white chocolate chips. Kids love them!

## REVERSE CHOCOLATE CHIP COOKIES (GLUTEN-FREE)

Joni Brinder-Frydrych, vice-president of the Canadian Celiac Association (Toronto) for 13 years, is an expert on gluten-free recipes. I've adapted her recipe for these scrumptious cookies, using my processor to speed up preparation. I use potato starch, but Joni uses tapioca starch.

Yield: About 36 cookies. Freezes well—if they last that long after you bake them!

| | |
|---|---|
| 1 cup potato starch or tapioca starch (tapioca flour) | ¼ tsp salt |
| ½ cup unsweetened cocoa powder (gluten-free) | ½ cup butter or tub margarine, cut in chunks |
| 1 tsp xanthan gum (or 2 tsp unflavored gelatin) | ½ cup granulated sugar |
| ½ tsp baking soda | ½ cup brown sugar, packed |
| ¼ tsp baking powder | 1 egg |
| | 2 tsp pure vanilla extract |
| | 1 cup white chocolate chips |

Preheat oven to 350°F.

STEEL BLADE: Process potato starch, cocoa, xanthan gum, baking soda, baking powder and salt to combine, about 10 seconds. Set aside.

STEEL BLADE: Process butter, sugars, egg and vanilla extract for 2 minutes, until well blended. Add dry ingredients and blend in with several quick on/offs. Scrape down sides of bowl as necessary. Add white chocolate chips and process with 2 or 3 quick on/offs, just until mixed. Don't overprocess.

Drop batter by rounded teaspoonfuls about 2 inches apart onto parchment-lined baking pan(s). Flatten cookies slightly.

Bake 1 pan at a time 10 to 12 minutes, until tops are slightly cracked. Let cool 5 to 10 minutes before removing from pan. Cookies will firm up as they cool.

90 calories each, 13 g carbohydrates, 0.5 g fiber, 1 g protein, 4.4 g fat (2.7 g saturated fat), 14 g cholesterol, 62 mg sodium, 39 mg potassium, 0 mg iron, 17 mg calcium, 21 mg phosphorus

# CHOCOLATE CHIP COOKIES (GLUTEN-FREE)

Joni Brinder-Frydrych makes these addictive gluten-free cookies for her daughter, Haley, who has celiac disease. Haley loves these cookies and you will, too!

Yield: 48 cookies.
Freezes well.

2 cups gluten-free flour (use 1½ cups tapioca starch or potato starch and ½ cup rice flour)

1 tsp xanthan gum

¾ tsp baking soda

½ tsp salt

¾ cup butter or shortening, cut in chunks

1¼ cups brown sugar, packed

1 egg

2 to 3 tsp pure vanilla extract (to taste)

1½ cups semisweet chocolate chips

½ cup M&Ms (optional) (Smarties may contain wheat)

STEEL BLADE: Process gluten-free flour mixture, xanthan gum, baking soda and salt for 10 seconds, until combined. Set aside.

STEEL BLADE: Process butter, brown sugar, egg and vanilla extract for 2 minutes, until light. Add flour mixture and process with quick on/offs, just until combined. Scrape down sides of bowl as necessary. Stir in chocolate chips and M&Ms (if using) with a rubber spatula. Refrigerate batter for 30 minutes. Preheat oven to 375°F.

Drop batter by rounded teaspoonfuls about 2 inches apart onto parchment-lined baking sheets. With wet hands, pat cookies down gently to flatten.

Bake one pan at a time, about 8 minutes for a soft cookie and 12 minutes for a crispy cookie. Cool for 10 minutes before removing cookies from pan. They will firm up as they cool.

92 calories each, 13.3 g carbohydrates, 0.4 g fiber, 1 g protein, 4.6 g fat (2.8 g saturated fat), 12 g cholesterol, 68 mg sodium, 29 mg potassium, 0 mg iron, 8 mg calcium, 10 mg phosphorus

### note

Since gluten-free flour is harder to bake with, you may have to add a little more "flour" if cookies spread too much during baking. Bake half the cookies at a time in case you need to add more "flour" to the second batch. If the first batch spreads too much, they'll be flatter but still delicious. Tapioca starch and potato starch are interchangeable.

# CHOCOLATE TURTLE COOKIES

Turtles may move slowly, but these cookies disappear in a flash.

½ cup butter or margarine, cut in chunks

½ cup brown sugar, lightly packed

1 egg

1 egg, separated (reserve egg white)

1 tsp pure vanilla extract

1½ cups flour

¼ **tsp baking soda**

¼ **tsp salt**

**2 cups pecan halves, split
in half lengthwise**

**Chocolate Fudge Frosting,
½ recipe (page 383)**

Preheat oven to 350°F.

STEEL BLADE: Process butter or margarine, sugar, egg, egg yolk and vanilla extract for 2 minutes. Add flour, baking soda and salt and process just until dough is mixed and begins to gather in a ball around the blades. On/off pulses help prevent overprocessing dough.

Line cookie sheets with parchment paper. Arrange pecan pieces in groups to resemble head, tail and legs of a turtle. Shape dough into 1-inch balls; flatten slightly. Dip bottoms into lightly beaten egg white; press gently onto nuts. Tips of nuts should be visible.

Bake for 10 to 12 minutes, until golden. Remove from pans; cool. Frost tops of cookies with chocolate frosting.

132 calories each, 14.3 g carbohydrates, 0.8 g fiber, 2 g protein, 8.1 g fat (2.8 g saturated fat), 20 g cholesterol, 54 mg sodium, 48 mg potassium, 1 mg iron, 12 mg calcium, 32 mg phosphorus

## DEBBIE'S DECADENT DELIGHTS

Debbie Brass bakes the best cookies. You can't have just one, but don't worry—the oats take away the guilt!

**1 cup butter, cut in chunks**

**1 cup brown sugar, lightly packed**

**½ cup granulated sugar**

**1 egg**

**1 tsp pure vanilla extract**

**1½ cups flour**

**1½ cups quick-cooking oats**

**1 tsp baking soda**

**1 cup chocolate chips**

**1 cup dried cranberries**

**1 cup toffee bits (or 4 Skor bars
(1.4 oz/39 g each), chopped)**

Preheat oven to 350°F.

STEEL BLADE: Process butter, sugars, egg and vanilla extract for 2 minutes. Add flour, oats and baking soda; process with several quick on/off pulses, just until mixed. Do not overprocess. Scrape down sides of bowl as needed. Mix in chocolate chips, cranberries and toffee bits with a rubber spatula.

Drop by rounded spoonfuls onto parchment-lined cookie sheets. Bake for 10 minutes, until golden.

134 calories each, 18 g carbohydrates, 0.7 g fiber, 1 g protein, 6.8 g fat (3.9 g saturated fat), 18 g cholesterol, 77 mg sodium, 27 mg potassium, 1 mg iron, 9 mg calcium, 12 mg phosphorus

# BANANA CHOCOLATE CHIP DROPS

A soft, cake-like cookie. Great for kids!

Yield: 6 dozen.

Freezes well.

| | |
|---|---|
| ⅔ cup tub margarine, cut in chunks | 2½ cups flour |
| ½ cup granulated sugar | 2 tsp baking powder |
| ½ cup brown sugar, packed | ¼ tsp baking soda |
| 2 eggs | ⅛ tsp salt |
| ½ tsp pure vanilla extract | 1 cup chocolate chips |
| 2 large ripe bananas (about 1 cup) | |

Preheat oven to 400°F.

STEEL BLADE: Process margarine, sugars, eggs and vanilla extract for 2 minutes, scraping down sides of bowl as necessary. While machine is running, drop in chunks of banana and process until blended. Add flour, baking powder, baking soda and salt. Process just until flour disappears, using quick on/off pulses. Do not overprocess. Dough will be very soft, like a thick cake batter. Sprinkle chocolate chips over batter and mix in with 3 or 4 quick on/offs.

Drop from a teaspoon onto parchment-lined cookie sheets. Bake for 10 to 12 minutes, until golden.

59 calories each, 8.6 g carbohydrates, 0.4 g fiber, 1 g protein, 2.6 g fat (0.8 g saturated fat), 6 g cholesterol, 38 mg sodium, 31 mg potassium, 0 mg iron, 11 mg calcium, 14 mg phosphorus

# MERINGUE HORNS

Yield: 4 dozen.

Freezes well.

DOUGH

| | |
|---|---|
| 2 tsp sugar | |
| ¼ cup warm water (105°F–115°F) | |
| 1 pkg active dry yeast (2¼ tsp) | |
| 1 cup butter or tub margarine, cut in chunks | |
| 2 cups flour | |
| 2 egg yolks | |

FILLING

| | |
|---|---|
| 2 squares (2 oz/60 g) semisweet chocolate | |
| 2 egg whites | |
| ½ cup sugar | |
| ¾ to 1 cup sweetened flaked coconut or sesame seeds | |
| icing sugar, to garnish | |

For dough: Dissolve sugar in warm water. Sprinkle yeast overtop and let stand 8 to 10 minutes. Stir to dissolve.

STEEL BLADE: Process butter with flour until crumbly, about 10 seconds. Add egg yolks and yeast mixture. Process until a soft dough is formed, about 15 seconds. Wrap dough in plastic wrap and refrigerate overnight.

For filling: Insert GRATER in processor. Grate chocolate, using firm pressure. (Or grate chocolate on the STEEL BLADE; process for 20 to 25 seconds, until fine.)

Using electric mixer, beat egg whites at high speed until soft peaks form. Gradually add sugar and beat until stiff.

Divide dough into 6 balls. Roll each ball of dough on a floured board or pastry cloth into a circle about ⅛ inch thick. Cut into 8 wedges. Spread with meringue and sprinkle with grated chocolate. Beginning at outer edge, roll up. Roll in coconut or sesame seeds. Place on a parchment-lined cookie sheet, point side down.

Bake at 350°F for 18 to 20 minutes. Cool. Sprinkle with icing sugar.

79 calories each, 7.4 g carbohydrates, 0.4 g fiber, 1 g protein, 5.3 g fat (3.4 g saturated fat), 19 g cholesterol, 34 mg sodium, 27 mg potassium, 1 mg iron, 5 mg calcium, 19 mg phosphorus

## COCONUT OATMEAL BAR COOKIES

Easy and delicious.

Yield: About 5 dozen cookies. Freezes well.

½ cup walnuts
⅔ cup rolled oats
½ cup sweetened flaked coconut
1⅓ cups flour

1 cup tub margarine or butter, cut in chunks
⅔ cup brown sugar, packed

Preheat oven to 300°F.

STEEL BLADE: Process nuts until coarsely chopped, 6 to 8 seconds. Empty into a large mixing bowl; add rolled oats and coconut to nuts. Process flour, margarine or butter and sugar until mixed, about 20 seconds. Add to mixing bowl. Mix to a crumbly mass with your fingertips.

Pat onto a lightly sprayed rimmed baking sheet (10 × 15 × 1 inch). Bake for 40 to 45 minutes. When cool, cut into squares with a sharp knife.

59 calories each, 5.6 g carbohydrates, 0.3 g fiber, 1 g protein, 3.9 g fat (0.8 g saturated fat), 0 g cholesterol, 28 mg sodium, 13 mg potassium, 0 mg iron, 4 mg calcium, 7 mg phosphorus

## KATHY'S SWISS MOCHA HAZELNUT COOKIES

This fabulous cookie is adapted from Kathy Guttman's collection of recipes and anecdotes from the arts and crafts community of the Smoky Mountains in Tennessee, titled *Whop Biscuits &*

2 oz (60 g) chilled semisweet chocolate
½ cup toasted hazelnuts (see Note on page 436)
¼ tsp ground cinnamon
1 Tbsp sugar

½ cup soft butter
⅓ cup additional sugar
1 Tbsp instant coffee powder (e.g., Swiss Mocha)
2 Tbsp hot water
1 cup flour

Preheat oven to 325°F. For machines with nested bowls, see method on page 436.

STEEL BLADE: Process chocolate, nuts and cinnamon until ground, about 25 seconds. Transfer to a bowl. Remove 3 Tbsp of mixture to a small bowl, add

*Continued*

*Fried Apple Pie.*
It contains her
favorite flavors:
chocolate, coffee
and hazelnuts!

Yield: 2 dozen.

Freezes well.

1 Tbsp sugar to it, and set aside to use as a topping. (No need to wash the processor bowl or blade.)

Process butter with ⅓ cup sugar until creamed, about 25 seconds, scraping down sides of bowl as needed. Dissolve instant coffee in hot water. Add to batter and process for 20 seconds. Add flour and process 35 seconds longer, until well mixed. Add chocolate/hazelnut mixture (except for reserved topping) to processor. Process for 15 seconds.

Empty mixture onto waxed paper. If necessary, press or knead to bring together. Form into 1-inch balls. Press each ball into reserved topping, flattening slightly. Place on ungreased or parchment-lined cookie sheets.

Bake for 15 to 17 minutes. Cookies will be slightly soft. Cool for 5 minutes before removing from pan.

96 calories each, 9.3 g carbohydrates, 0.6 g fiber, 1 g protein, 6.3 g fat (3 g saturated fat), 10 g cholesterol, 28 mg sodium, 40 mg potassium, 0 mg iron, 6 mg calcium, 15 mg phosphorus

### nested bowl method

Use mini-bowl and mini-blade to process chocolate/nut mixture. Use large bowl and STEEL BLADE for remaining processing tasks.

### note

Hazelnuts may be toasted in the microwave on High for 1½ minutes. If desired, replace hazelnuts with almonds.

## MELTING MOMENTS

¾ cup butter or tub margarine,
  cut in chunks
⅓ cup brown sugar, packed
1 tsp pure vanilla extract

1½ cups flour
1 cup pecans or walnuts
⅓ cup icing sugar for sprinkling
  cookies

Preheat oven to 350°F.

STEEL BLADE: Process butter or margarine, brown sugar and vanilla extract for 1 minute, or until well creamed. Sprinkle flour and nuts on top. Process with several on/off pulses, just until mixed. Do not overprocess.

Form into 1-inch balls. Place on parchment-lined cookie sheets. Bake for 18 to 20 minutes. When cool, sprinkle generously with icing sugar.

58 calories each, 3.5 g carbohydrates, 0.2 g fiber, 0 g protein, 5 g fat (2.2 g saturated fat), 9 g cholesterol, 24 mg sodium, 14 mg potassium, 0 mg iron, 4 mg calcium, 8 mg phosphorus

# ORANGE PECAN BUTTER BALLS

Yield: 5 dozen.

Freezes well.

1 cup pecans

1 cup soft butter, cut in chunks

1 cup icing sugar

2 tsp grated orange zest

1 tsp pure vanilla extract

¼ cup orange juice

2 cups flour

pinch salt

Preheat oven to 325°F. For machines with nested bowls, see method below.

STEEL BLADE: Process nuts with 6 quick on/off pulses, until coarsely chopped. Empty bowl. Process butter, icing sugar, orange zest and vanilla extract for 2 minutes. Add orange juice and process 3 seconds longer. Add flour, salt and chopped nuts. Process just until mixture gathers in a ball around the blades. Do not over-process. Chill dough in freezer for 20 minutes for easier handling.

Form into 1-inch balls. Place 2 inches apart on parchment-lined cookie sheets. Bake for 20 minutes, until golden.

62 calories each, 5.5 g carbohydrates, 0.3 g fiber, 1 g protein, 4.3 g fat (2.1 g saturated fat), 8 g cholesterol, 25 mg sodium, 15 mg potassium, 0 mg iron, 3 mg calcium, 10 mg phosphorus

## nested bowl method

Use mini-bowl and mini-blade for nuts. Use large bowl and STEEL BLADE for remaining processing tasks.

## variations

• POPPY SEED BUTTER BALLS: Omit nuts and increase flour to 2¼ cups. Add ⅓ cup poppy seeds to batter along with flour and salt. Sprinkle cooled cookies with icing sugar. One cookie contains 58 calories, 5.9 g carbohydrates and 3.5 g fat.

• WALNUT BRANDY COOKIES: Replace pecans with walnuts. Replace orange juice with brandy. Omit orange zest. One cookie contains 64 calories, 5.4 g carbohydrates and 4.3 g fat.

# TOM THUMB COOKIES

Yield: 4 dozen.

Freezes well.

¾ cup almonds or walnuts

1½ cups flour, divided

½ cup butter or tub margarine, cut in chunks

½ to ¾ cup icing sugar

½ tsp almond extract

1 egg

½ cup raspberry or strawberry jam

Preheat oven to 350°F.

STEEL BLADE: Process nuts with ¼ cup of the flour until very finely chopped. Empty bowl. Process remaining 1¼ cups flour with butter or margarine and icing sugar for about 10 seconds, until crumbly. Add nut/flour mixture, almond extract and egg. Process until blended, about 15 seconds.

Shape dough into 1-inch balls. Place on parchment-lined cookie sheets. Press your thumb into the center of each cookie to make an indentation. Fill with a dab of jam (see Chef's Tip below). Bake for 15 to 18 minutes, until golden.

59 calories each, 6.8 g carbohydrates, 0.4 g fiber, 1 g protein, 3.2 g fat (1.3 g saturated fat), 10 g cholesterol, 15 mg sodium, 22 mg potassium, 0 mg iron, 7 mg calcium, 17 mg phosphorus

### chef's tip

Fill a resealable plastic bag with jam and seal well. Cut a small opening on bottom corner of bag. Squeeze a dab of jam into indentation of each cookie. Easy-squeezy!

## SHORTBREAD COOKIES

These melt-in-your-mouth cookies are great for gift giving.

Yield: About 4 dozen. Freezes well.

| | |
|---|---|
| 1 cup butter, cut in chunks | 1½ cups flour |
| ½ cup icing sugar | ½ cup cornstarch or potato starch |
| ½ tsp pure vanilla extract | |

Preheat oven to 350°F.

STEEL BLADE: Process butter, icing sugar and vanilla extract until well creamed, about 1 minute. Add flour and cornstarch or potato starch. Process with several on/off pulses, just until dough is well mixed and begins to gather in a ball around the blades. Do not overprocess.

Shape rounded teaspoonfuls of dough into small balls. Place on parchment-lined cookie sheets. Flatten in a crisscross pattern with a fork. Bake for 12 to 15 minutes, or until edges are slightly browned.

58 calories each, 5.5 g carbohydrates, 0.1 g fiber, 0 g protein, 3.9 g fat (2.4 g saturated fat), 10 g cholesterol, 28 mg sodium, 5 mg potassium, 0 mg iron, 2 mg calcium, 6 mg phosphorus

### variations

• Mix 1 cup chopped nuts into dough. If desired, dip cookies halfway in melted semisweet chocolate. One cookie contains 74 calories, 5.8 g carbohydrates and 5.5 g fat.

## BUTTERSCOTCH TOFFEE DREAMS

These easy, elegant shortbread cookies taste like a dream.

Yield: 5 dozen.

Freezes well.

| | |
|---|---|
| 1 cup butter or tub margarine, cut in chunks | 1½ cups flour |
| | ½ cup cornstarch |
| ½ cup brown sugar, packed | ¾ cup toffee bits |
| ½ cup granulated sugar | ½ cup butterscotch chips |

Preheat oven to 350°F.

STEEL BLADE: Process butter or margarine and sugars until well creamed, about 1 minute. Add flour and cornstarch. Process with several on/off pulses, just until blended. Do not overprocess. Sprinkle toffee bits and butterscotch chips over batter. Stir in with a wooden spoon.

Shape dough into 1-inch balls (a small cookie scoop works well). Place on parchment-lined cookie sheets. Bake for 12 to 15 minutes, until edges are golden. Cool slightly before removing from pan.

83 calories each, 10.0 g carbohydrates, 0.1 g fiber, 1 g protein, 4.5 g fat (2.9 g saturated fat), 9 g cholesterol, 36 mg sodium, 7 mg potassium, 0 mg iron, 3 mg calcium, 5 mg phosphorus

## SESAME CRESCENTS

Yield: About 3½ dozen cookies. Freezes well.

| | |
|---|---|
| ½ cup butter or tub margarine, cut in chunks | 1½ cups flour |
| | ¼ tsp baking soda |
| ½ cup brown sugar, packed | ½ cup sesame seeds (approximately) |
| 1 egg plus 1 egg yolk | 3 Tbsp sugar |
| 1 tsp pure vanilla extract | |

Preheat oven to 375°F.

STEEL BLADE: Process butter or margarine, brown sugar, egg, egg yolk and vanilla extract for 2 minutes. Add flour and baking soda and process just until dough is mixed and begins to gather in a ball around the blades. Do not overprocess.

Use 1 tsp of dough for each cookie; shape into crescents. Roll in a mixture of sesame seeds and sugar. Place on parchment-lined cookie sheets. Bake for 10 minutes, until golden. *Continued*

63 calories each, 7.3 g carbohydrates, 0.3 g fiber, 1 g protein, 3.3 g fat (1.6 g saturated fat), 16 g cholesterol, 26 mg sodium, 19 mg potassium, 1 mg iron, 21 mg calcium, 20 mg phosphorus

### variation

Replace sesame seeds with chopped nuts or granola.

## HOLIDAY COOKIES

*These thin, crisp cookies can be cut into all sorts of holiday shapes. Great all year round—just use your favorite cookie cutters and have the kids help!*

*Yield: About 5 dozen. Freezes well.*

¾ cup chilled butter, cut in chunks
1 cup sugar
2 eggs
1 tsp pure vanilla extract
  or lemon juice

2½ cups flour
1 tsp baking powder
¼ tsp salt

Preheat oven to 400°F.

STEEL BLADE: Process butter, sugar, eggs and vanilla extract or lemon juice for 2 minutes, until well creamed. Scrape down sides of bowl as needed. Add remaining ingredients and process with 3 or 4 on/off pulses, just until mixed. Do not overprocess. Divide dough into 4 pieces. Flour surface of dough lightly and wrap in plastic wrap. Chill until firm enough to roll, 1 to 2 hours.

Roll out dough ⅛-inch thick on lightly floured surface. Cut into various shapes. (Save all the scraps until the end, then gather them together and re-roll.) Place on ungreased or parchment-lined baking sheets. Bake for 6 to 8 minutes, until golden.

55 calories each, 7.4 g carbohydrates, 0.1 g fiber, 1 g protein, 2.5 g fat (1.5 g saturated fat), 13 g cholesterol, 36 mg sodium, 9 mg potassium, 0 mg iron, 7 mg calcium, 11 mg phosphorus

### note

If desired, brush unbaked cookies with lightly beaten egg white and decorate with sprinkles, chopped nuts or sugar.

## GINGERBREAD COOKIES

*Yield: About 2 dozen, depending on size.*

*Freezes well.*

1 egg
½ cup cold butter, cut in chunks
½ cup light brown sugar, packed
¼ cup molasses
2¼ cups flour
1 tsp ground ginger
1 tsp ground cinnamon

½ tsp baking soda
½ tsp ground cloves
¼ tsp salt
White Glaze (page 381)
raisins and candied cherries, for
  decorating (optional)

Preheat oven to 375°F.

STEEL BLADE: Process egg, butter and brown sugar for 1 minute. Add molasses and process 1 minute longer. (If you spray the measuring cup with nonstick spray, molasses will slide right out.) Add half the flour along with remaining ingredients except White Glaze and dried fruit. Process with 3 or 4 on/off pulses to blend. Add remaining flour and process 5 seconds longer, just until dough gathers into a sticky mass. Do not overprocess.

Remove from bowl and knead in a little extra flour to make a dough that is soft, yet firm enough to roll. Divide in half, wrap well and refrigerate for 2 hours for easier handling.

Roll out dough ⅛ inch thick (see Baker's Secret, below). Cut with floured ginger-bread boy/girl cookie cutters. Transfer with a spatula to parchment-lined cookie sheets. Bake for 10 minutes, until set.

Cool completely. Frost with White Glaze. Decorate with raisins and bits of candied cherries (if desired).

128 calories each, 21.2 g carbohydrates, 0.4 g fiber, 2 g protein, 4.2 g fat (2.5 g saturated fat), 19 g cholesterol, 84 mg sodium, 75 mg potassium, 1 mg iron, 18 mg calcium, 20 mg phosphorus

### baker's secret

For easier handling, roll out cookie dough directly on parchment-lined cookie sheets; place in freezer until firm. Cut into desired shapes. Remove scraps with a floured spatula. Re-roll scraps for more cookies.

## SUGAR COOKIES

These easy, versatile cookies are fun to make with the kids.

Yield: 4 to 5 dozen.

Freezes well.

2 eggs
¾ cup sugar
½ cup canola oil
¼ cup orange juice or water

3 cups flour
2 tsp baking powder
additional sugar for dipping

Preheat oven to 375°F.

STEEL BLADE: Process eggs with sugar, oil and juice or water until blended, about 5 seconds. Add flour and baking powder. Process just until mixed, using on/off pulses. Do not overprocess.

Divide dough into 4 pieces. Roll each piece on a lightly floured surface into a rectangle about ⅛ inch thick. Using assorted cookie cutters, cut in different shapes. Dip each cookie lightly in sugar. Place sugar side up on parchment-lined cookie sheets. Bake for 8 to 10 minutes, until golden. *Continued*

65 calories each, 9.3 g carbohydrates, 0.2 g fiber, 1 g protein, 2.6 g fat (0.3 g saturated fat), 9 g cholesterol, 23 mg sodium, 14 mg potassium, 0 mg iron, 14 mg calcium, 16 mg phosphorus

### haman's hats

Add ¼ cup poppy seeds with dry ingredients. Roll out dough thinly, then cut in triangles using a fluted pastry wheel or pizza cutter. Dip in sugar and bake as directed. Perfect for Purim! One cookie contains 70 calories, 9.5 g carbohydrates and 3 g fat.

## CINNAMON TWISTS

My grandmother and mother made these cookies for my sister Rhonda and me when we were children, and now we make them for our children and grandchildren.

Yield: 4 to 5 dozen. Freezes well, if you can put them away quickly enough!

½ cup sugar

1 Tbsp ground cinnamon

3 eggs

1 cup granulated or brown sugar, lightly packed

¾ cup canola oil

3 cups flour

2 tsp baking powder

Preheat oven to 375°F.

STEEL BLADE: Process ½ cup sugar and cinnamon with several quick on/off pulses, then let machine run until well mixed. Empty mixture into a small bowl.

Process eggs, 1 cup sugar and oil until blended, about 5 seconds. Add flour and baking powder. Process with several on/off pulses, just until flour disappears. Do not overprocess.

Using about 1 Tbsp dough for each cookie, roll between your palms to form a pencil-shaped roll. Shape into twists, crescents, rings, the letter S, or any initial you wish. Kids love to make their own designs. Roll in cinnamon-sugar mixture.

Place on parchment-lined cookie sheets. Bake for 12 to 15 minutes, until nicely browned. (Baking time depends on size of cookies, which can vary if the children are assisting you.)

89 calories each, 12.5 g carbohydrates, 0.3 g fiber, 1 g protein, 3.9 g fat (0.4 g saturated fat), 13 g cholesterol, 24 mg sodium, 13 mg potassium, 0 mg iron, 16 mg calcium, 18 mg phosphorus

### lighter variation

For coating, use 2 tsp cinnamon and ⅓ cup sugar. In batter, reduce oil to ½ cup and use 2 eggs plus 2 egg whites. One cookie contains 76 calories, 11.7 g carbohydrates and 2.7 g fat.

# SESAME NOTHINGS (KICHEL)

It only takes
2 minutes to mix
up this batter in
the processor,
compared to
20 minutes with
an electric mixer.
They're excellent
for diabetics, as
they can be made
sugar-free.

Yield: About 40 cookies.
Freezes well.

3 eggs

2 Tbsp sugar or granular Splenda

dash salt

½ cup canola oil

1 cup flour

¾ cup sesame seeds or poppy seeds

2 additional Tbsp sugar or granular
Splenda

Preheat oven to 500°F. (See Hot Stuff, below.)

STEEL BLADE: Process eggs with 2 Tbsp sugar and salt for 30 to 60 seconds, until light. While machine is running, pour oil through feed tube in a steady stream. Process 1 minute longer. Add flour by heaping spoonfuls through feed tube while machine is running. Process 30 to 40 seconds longer. (Processor may shut off automatically after about 40 seconds because batter is very sticky. If you have an inexpensive processor, don't let machine shut itself off or you may require a service call!)

Combine sesame seeds with 2 Tbsp sugar on a flat plate. Take a scant tsp of dough and use another spoon to push it off into sesame seed mixture. Roll dough in sesame seeds.

Stretch dough to about 3 inches in length, then twist it to make a long, twisted finger shape. Roll again in sesame seeds. Place on sprayed foil-lined cookie sheets, leaving 3 inches between cookies for expansion.

Reduce heat to 400°F. Place cookies on middle rack of oven and bake for 7 to 8 minutes. Reduce heat to 300°F and bake 10 to 12 minutes longer. Turn off heat and leave cookies in oven 10 minutes longer to dry.

62 calories each, 4.3 g carbohydrates, 0.4 g fiber, 1 g protein, 4.6 g fat (0.5 g saturated fat), 16 g cholesterol, 9 mg sodium, 21 mg potassium, 1 mg iron, 29 mg calcium, 27 mg phosphorus

## variations

- If you use Splenda, 1 cookie contains 58 calories and 3.2 g carbohydrates.
- Instead of shaping batter into fingers, drop from a teaspoon onto sprayed cookie sheets, leaving about 3 inches between cookies. If desired, sprinkle lightly with sugar before baking.

## hot stuff

Newer ovens are better insulated, so they hold the heat better. If you have a newer oven, you may have to reduce the heat and baking time to prevent cookies from burning. If your oven door has a window, peek and check, but don't open the door!

## cute tip

A cotton swab will remove the sticky dough from the hole on the underside of the STEEL BLADE.

443

# BASIC OIL DOUGH

This dough is
excellent for Mandel
Bread (below),
Hamentaschen
(page 446)
or Roly Poly
(page 448). The
chocolate variation
can be used to
make Chocolate
Hamentaschen
Kisses (page 447).

1 medium seedless orange
  (thin-skinned)

2 eggs

¾ cup sugar

½ cup canola oil

2¾ cups flour (approximately)

2 tsp baking powder

STEEL BLADE: Cut orange in quarters, but do not peel. Process until fine, about 25 seconds. Add eggs, sugar and oil. Process for 10 seconds. Add flour and baking powder. Process with several on/off pulses, just until flour is blended into dough. Do not overprocess. Dough will be fairly sticky. Remove from bowl with a rubber spatula onto a lightly floured surface. Use as directed.

64 calories per serving, 9.1 g carbohydrates, 0.3 g fiber, 1 g protein, 2.6 g fat (0.3 g saturated fat), 9 g cholesterol, 23 mg sodium, 15 mg potassium, 0 mg iron, 15 mg calcium, 16 mg phosphorus

Yield: Enough dough for
about 48 cookies. Use
as directed in recipes.
Freezes well.

## chocolate oil dough

Increase sugar to 1 cup. Reduce flour to 2½ cups and add ½ cup unsweetened cocoa powder.

# MANDEL BREAD (MANDELBROIT)

These crisp, crunchy
cookies are the
Jewish version of
biscotti! "Mandel"
means "almond"
in Yiddish.

1 cup whole almonds

Basic Oil Dough (above)

Preheat oven to 350°F.

STEEL BLADE: Chop almonds coarsely, 12 to 15 seconds. Empty bowl. Prepare dough as directed, but add nuts to dough along with flour and baking powder.

Shape into 3 rolls, flouring your hands for easier handling. Place on parchment-lined cookie sheets. Smooth the tops and make edges neat with a rubber spatula. Bake for 25 minutes. Dough will be cake-like and not quite baked.

Remove from oven and let cool for 5 minutes. Reduce oven temperature to 250°F. Slice rolls diagonally into ½-inch slices with a sharp knife. Place cut side down on cookie sheets. Return cookies to oven for ¾ to 1 hour, until dry and crisp.

Yield: About 4 dozen.
These keep very
well stored in cookie
tins. Freezes well.

81 calories each, 9.6 g carbohydrates, 0.6 g fiber, 2 g protein, 4.1 g fat (0.4 g saturated fat), 9 g cholesterol, 23 mg sodium, 37 mg potassium, 1 mg iron, 22 mg calcium, 30 mg phosphorus

## baker's secret

- For slices that are uniform in width, bake Mandel Bread in metal ice cube trays sprayed with nonstick spray!

- **KOMISH BROIT:** Bake and slice rolls as directed. Combine ½ cup sugar and 1 Tbsp cinnamon in a small bowl. Dip each slice into sugar mixture, coating both sides. Dry at 250°F for ¾ to 1 hour. One cookie contains 89 calories and 11.8 g carbohydrates.

- **CHOCOLATE CHIP MANDEL BREAD:** Reduce almonds to ½ cup. Add 1 cup chocolate chips. Bake and slice rolls as directed. Dry at 300°F for 30 minutes. One cookie contains 98 calories and 13.8 g carbohydrates.

- **CHOCOLATE MANDEL BREAD:** Use Chocolate Oil Dough (page 444) and 1 cup chopped almonds. Bake and slice rolls as directed. Dry at 250°F for ¾ to 1 hour. One cookie contains 78 calories and 10.5 g carbohydrates.

# CHOCOLATE ALMOND BISCOTTI

Chocolate lovers will adore these.

Yield: About 42. Store in an airtight container for a few weeks. Freezes well.

| | |
|---|---|
| 1 cup almonds | 3 eggs |
| 1¾ cups flour | ¼ cup canola oil |
| 1 cup sugar | 1½ tsp pure vanilla extract |
| ¼ cup unsweetened cocoa powder | ½ tsp almond extract |
| 1 tsp baking soda | 1 cup chocolate chips |
| ⅛ tsp salt | 1 egg white (for glazing) |

Preheat oven to 350°F.

STEEL BLADE: Process almonds with quick on/off pulses, until coarsely chopped. Do not overprocess. Remove from bowl and set aside. Process flour, sugar, cocoa, baking soda and salt for 10 seconds, until combined. Add eggs, oil, vanilla extract and almond extract. Process to make a sticky dough, 20 to 25 seconds longer. Add almonds and chocolate chips and process a few seconds longer. Don't worry if they are not completely mixed in.

Empty bowl onto a floured surface. Flour your hands for easier handling. Gather dough into a ball. Divide into 4 long, narrow rolls. Place on parchment-lined baking sheet(s). Leave at least 3 inches between logs as they will spread during baking. Smooth the tops and make the edges neat with a rubber spatula. Brush with egg white. Bake for 25 minutes.

Remove from oven and let cool for 5 minutes. Reduce oven temperature to 300°F. Slice rolls diagonally into ½-inch slices with a sharp knife. Place cut side down on cookie sheets. Bake for about 30 minutes, until dry and crisp.

96 calories each, 12.3 g carbohydrates, 0.9 g fiber, 2 g protein, 4.8 g fat (1.1 g saturated fat), 15 g cholesterol, 43 mg sodium, 58 mg potassium, 1 mg iron, 13 mg calcium, 37 mg phosphorus

# HAMENTASCHEN

Hamentaschen are triangular pastries stuffed with various sweet fillings. They are a traditional treat for the Jewish holiday of Purim.

Yield: About 4 dozen.

Freezes well.

**Basic Oil Dough (page 444) or double recipe of Cream Cheese Pastry (page 472)**

**filling of your choice (see pages 446–447)**

**1 egg yolk beaten with 2 tsp water**

Prepare desired dough and filling as directed. (Can be prepared in advance and refrigerated or frozen.)

Divide dough into 4 pieces. Flour each piece of dough lightly. Roll out on a floured surface to ¼-inch thickness. Cut into 3-inch circles. (A small juice glass is ideal.) Place a spoonful of filling on each circle. Bring up 3 sides to meet, then pinch edges of dough together to form a triangle. Repeat with remaining dough and filling.

Place on sprayed foil-lined cookie sheets. Brush with egg glaze. If using Cream Cheese Pastry, preheat oven to 400°F and bake for about 15 minutes. If using Basic Oil Dough, preheat oven to 350°F and bake for 25 to 30 minutes.

94 calories each (using Basic Oil Dough and Apricot Raisin Filling), 16.8 g carbohydrates, 0.8 g fiber, 1 g protein, 2.8 g fat (0.3 g saturated fat), 13 g cholesterol, 24 mg sodium, 109 mg potassium, 1 mg iron, 21 mg calcium, 27 mg phosphorus

### notes

- Haman's Hats (page 442) are a delicious alternative if your children don't like fruit fillings.
- For Purim, make Apricot Almond Triangles (page 452). No dough to roll, no filling to make, no need to pinch the dough together into triangles.

# APRICOT RAISIN FILLING

Yield: 2 cups filling (enough for 4 dozen Hamentaschen).

Freezes well.

**1 medium seedless orange**

**8 oz (250 g) pkg dried apricots**

**1½ cups sultana raisins**

**3 to 4 Tbsp sugar**

STEEL BLADE: Cut orange in quarters, but do not peel. If you have a standard-sized processor, process filling in 2 batches. Process orange until fine, about 20 seconds. Add remaining ingredients and process 15 seconds longer, until fine.

29 calories per tsp, 7.7 g carbohydrates, 0.6 g fiber, 0 g protein, 0 g fat (0 g saturated fat), 0 g cholesterol, 1 mg sodium, 94 mg potassium, 0 mg iron, 6 mg calcium, 9 mg phosphorus

### variations

- Use only ¾ cup raisins and add ¾ cup dried cranberries.
- Use ½ cup raisins and 1 cup dried cherries. Reduce sugar to 2 Tbsp.

# PRUNE FILLING

Yield: 2½ cups filling

(enough for 5 dozen

Hamentaschen).

Freezes well.

**1 medium seedless orange**

**12 oz (340 g) pkg pitted prunes**

**1½ cups raisins**

**¼ cup walnuts (optional)**

**2 Tbsp sugar (optional)**

STEEL BLADE: Cut orange in quarters, but do not peel. If you have a standard-sized processor, process filling in 2 batches. Process orange until fine, about 20 seconds. Add remaining ingredients and process 15 to 20 seconds, until fine.

25 calories per tsp, 6.6 g carbohydrates, 0.7 g fiber, 0 g protein, 0.1 g fat (0 g saturated fat), 0 g cholesterol, 1 mg sodium, 76 mg potassium, 0 mg iron, 5 mg calcium, 8 mg phosphorus

### it's the pits!

Feel prunes with your fingertips to make sure they don't contain pits, or you could damage the blade!

# DATE FILLING

Yield: 2 cups filling

(enough for 4 dozen

Hamentaschen).

**2 cups pitted dates**

**¼ cup walnuts**

**½ cup sultana raisins**

**1 tsp grated lemon rind (optional)**

**½ tsp ground cinnamon**

If dates are packaged in a solid block, they need to be rehydrated. Cut them into chunks, cover with boiling water and soak for 20 minutes, until softened. Drain well.

STEEL BLADE: Chop walnuts coarsely, about 5 seconds. Empty bowl. Process dates with raisins, lemon rind (if using) and cinnamon until minced, 15 to 20 seconds. Add nuts with 1 or 2 quick on/off pulses.

28 calories per tsp, 6.6 g carbohydrates, 0.6 g fiber, 0 g protein, 0.3 g fat (0 g saturated fat), 0 g cholesterol, 0 mg sodium, 57 mg potassium, 0 mg iron, 5 mg calcium, 3 mg phosphorus

# CHOCOLATE HAMENTASCHEN KISSES

These triangular

chocolate treats

will become a new

Purim tradition!

**Chocolate Cream Cheese Pastry**
  **(page 472)**

**¾ cup peanut butter (approximately)**

**4 dozen chocolate kisses**

**icing sugar, for dusting**

Preheat oven to 375°F.

Prepare dough as directed and refrigerate for ½ hour. Flour each piece of dough lightly. Roll out on floured surface to ¼-inch thickness. Cut 3-inch circles with a small juice glass or cookie cutter.

Place a dab of peanut butter on each circle. Top with a chocolate kiss. Bring up 3 sides to meet, then pinch edges of dough together to form a triangle. Repeat with remaining dough and filling.

Place on parchment-lined baking sheets. To prevent burning, double up 2 baking sheets, placing 1 inside the other. Bake for 18 to 20 minutes. When completely cooled, dust with icing sugar.

117 calories each, 9.9 g carbohydrates, 0.7 g fiber, 2 g protein, 8 g fat (4.2 g saturated fat), 13 g cholesterol, 73 mg sodium, 55 mg potassium, 1 mg iron, 29 mg calcium, 34 mg phosphorus

## variations

These are also delicious using Chocolate Oil Dough (page 444). Instead of chocolate kisses, use chocolate hazelnut spread. (There are several brands available, including a kosher one from Israel.) Kids also love peanut butter mixed with chocolate chips. Drop rounded spoonfuls of filling onto dough. Shape and bake as directed.

## ROLY POLY

Basic Oil Dough (page 444)

1½ cups jam (raspberry, strawberry or apricot)

1½ cups chopped walnuts or pecans

1½ cups raisins, dried cranberries or cherries

1 cup sweetened flaked coconut

1 cup chocolate chips or grated chocolate

jelly candies or gummy bears, cut in pieces (optional)

1 egg beaten with 2 tsp water

This strudel-type cookie is traditionally made with an oil dough, but it's also excellent with Flaky Ginger Ale Pastry (page 471) or Cream Cheese Pastry (page 472).

Yield: Makes 3 rolls (about 45 pieces).

Keeps for several weeks.

Freezes well.

Preheat oven to 350°F.

Prepare dough and divide into 3 pieces. Flour dough lightly. Working with 1 piece at a time, roll out on a lightly floured surface into a rectangle about ⅛ inch thick.

Spread a thin layer of jam on dough (about ½ cup) to within 1 inch of edges. Sprinkle with one-third of nuts, raisins, coconut, chocolate and candies (if using). Roll up like a jelly roll, turning in ends. Place rolls seam side down on parchment-lined cookie sheets. Repeat twice with remaining dough and filling to make 3 rolls. Brush with egg glaze.

Bake for 25 to 30 minutes, until golden. When cool, wrap in aluminum foil and store in a cool place. Slice as needed, using a sharp serrated knife.

## CHOCOLATE ROGELACH

I usually double this recipe because they disappear so quickly. The variations are equally delicious.

Yield: 2 dozen.
Freezes well.

**Cream Cheese Pastry (page 472) or Flaky Ginger Ale Pastry (page 471)**
**¼ cup sugar (granulated or brown)**
**½ tsp ground cinnamon**
**⅓ cup chocolate chips**
**⅓ cup walnuts or almonds**
**icing sugar (optional)**

Preheat oven to 375°F.

Prepare dough as directed. Divide into 2 balls. (Flaky Ginger Ale Pastry should be chilled first.) Flour dough lightly. Roll out 1 portion of dough on a lightly floured surface into a circle about ⅛ inch thick.

STEEL BLADE: Process sugar, cinnamon, chocolate chips and nuts until finely chopped, 25 to 30 seconds.

Sprinkle dough with ¼ cup of filling. Cut with a sharp knife or pastry wheel into 12 wedges. Roll up from the outside edge towards the center. Place on parchment-lined cookie sheets. Repeat with remaining dough and filling. Bake for 18 to 20 minutes, until lightly browned. If desired, dust with icing sugar when cooled.

92 calories each, 8.1 g carbohydrates, 0.4 g fiber, 1 g protein, 6.3 g fat (3.4 g saturated fat), 12 g cholesterol, 50 mg sodium, 23 mg potassium, 0 mg iron, 20 mg calcium, 16 mg phosphorus

### note

Ingredients for filling may be doubled. Extra filling freezes well.

### variations

- For the filling, process ½ cup brown sugar, 1 tsp cinnamon, 2 Tbsp unsweetened cocoa powder and ¼ cup walnuts on the STEEL BLADE for 12 to 15 seconds. Sprinkle rolled-out dough with ¼ cup of filling. Cut into 12 wedges. Place 4 chocolate chips at outer edge of each wedge (about ¼ cup total). Roll up and bake as directed. One cookie contains 97 calories, 10.4 g carbohydrates and 5.9 g fat.

- Use Chocolate Cream Cheese Pastry (page 472). Prepare a double batch of desired filling. Roll out dough, sprinkle with filling and shape as directed. One cookie contains 101 calories, 10.9 g carbohydrates and 6.4 g fat.

- These are also delicious filled with chocolate hazelnut paste (e.g., Nutella).

# CINNAMON NUT ROGELACH

These nut-crusted crescents were always a favorite with my catering clients and students.

Yield: 2 dozen.

Freezes well.

| | |
|---|---|
| **Cream Cheese Pastry (page 472) or** | ⅓ **cup sugar** |
| **Flaky Ginger Ale Pastry (page 471)** | **1 tsp ground cinnamon** |
| ⅔ **cup walnuts or pecans** | **1 egg white, lightly beaten** |

Preheat oven to 375°F.

Prepare dough as directed. Divide into 2 balls. (Flaky Ginger Ale Pastry should be chilled first.) Flour dough lightly. Roll out 1 portion of dough on a floured surface into a circle about ⅛ inch thick.

STEEL BLADE: Process nuts, sugar and cinnamon for 12 to 15 seconds, until nuts are fairly fine.

Sprinkle dough with about ¼ cup of filling. Cut with a sharp knife or pastry wheel into 12 wedges. Roll up from the outside edge towards the center. Repeat with remaining dough and filling.

Dip rogelach in egg white, then in cinnamon/nut mixture. Place on parchment-lined cookie sheets. Bake for 18 to 20 minutes, until lightly browned.

95 calories each, 7.6 g carbohydrates, 0.4 g fiber, 2 g protein, 6.7 g fat (3.1 g saturated fat), 12 g cholesterol, 52 mg sodium, 24 mg potassium, 0 mg iron, 21 mg calcium, 18 mg phosphorus

### note

Ingredients for filling may be doubled. Extra filling freezes well.

### variation

Spread each piece of rolled-out dough with ½ cup apricot or seedless raspberry preserves, then with nut mixture. Do not dip rogelach in egg white/nut mixture. Bake as directed. Dust cooled cookies with icing sugar.

# FRENCH UNBAKED CAKE

Good anytime, but especially in the summer when you don't want to turn on the oven.

Yield: About 25 squares.

Freezes well, but cut into squares before freezing.

| | |
|---|---|
| ½ **cup walnuts** | ¼ **cup butter or tub margarine** |
| **1 egg** | ½ **tsp pure vanilla extract** |
| ¼ **cup brown sugar, lightly packed** | **16 double graham wafers** |
| **2 Tbsp unsweetened cocoa powder** | **Chocolate Cocoa Frosting (page 383)** |

STEEL BLADE: Chop nuts with several quick on/off pulses. Empty bowl. Process egg, brown sugar and cocoa for a few seconds, until mixed. Melt butter in a heavy-bottomed saucepan. Add chocolate mixture to saucepan. Cook on medium heat, stirring constantly, just until thickened, like custard. Do not boil or mixture will curdle. Stir in vanilla extract.

Break up wafers into chunks about the size of corn flakes. Place in a large mixing bowl. Add half the nuts. Pour chocolate mixture over wafers and mix with a wooden spoon until wafers are well coated. Spread evenly in a sprayed 8-inch square glass baking dish.

Spread frosting over chocolate/wafer mixture and swirl with a knife. (You can double the recipe for a thicker layer of frosting.) Sprinkle with reserved nuts and refrigerate. Cut into squares.

109 calories per square, 14.7 g carbohydrates, 0.7 g fiber, 1 g protein, 5.3 g fat (1.7 g saturated fat), 13 g cholesterol, 85 mg sodium, 42 mg potassium, 1 mg iron, 10 mg calcium, 28 mg phosphorus

# NANAIMO CRUNCH BARS

These delicious squares are sure to be a favorite with your family! No baking required.

Yield: 2 dozen. Freezes well, but cut into squares before freezing.

## BASE

½ cup butter or tub margarine

⅓ cup unsweetened cocoa powder

¼ cup granulated sugar

1 egg

1 tsp pure vanilla extract

½ cup walnuts or pecans

1½ cups graham wafer crumbs
    or granola cereal

1 cup sweetened flaked coconut

## FILLING

¼ cup soft butter or tub margarine

3 Tbsp milk (1%)

2 cups icing sugar

2 Tbsp vanilla pudding powder or
    custard powder

## GLAZE

4 squares (4 oz/125 g) semisweet
    chocolate

1 Tbsp butter or margarine

For base: In a large microwavable bowl, microwave butter or margarine on High until melted, about 1 minute. Blend in cocoa, sugar, egg and vanilla extract. Microwave, uncovered, for 1 minute, stirring after 30 seconds. Mixture will resemble custard. Chop nuts on the STEEL BLADE with 6 or 8 quick on/off pulses. Add nuts, graham wafer crumbs or granola and coconut to microwaved mixture; stir well. Press evenly into a sprayed 9-inch square pan.

For filling: Process all filling ingredients until well mixed, 15 to 20 seconds. Scrape down sides of bowl as needed. Spread filling evenly over base. Chill for 15 minutes.

For glaze: Microwave chocolate and butter or margarine on Medium (50%) for 2 to 3 minutes, until melted, stirring after each minute. Let cool for 10 minutes. Pour glaze over filling. Tilt pan back and forth so that glaze coats evenly. Chill. Cut into squares.

198 calories per square, 23.9 g carbohydrates, 1.2 g fiber, 2 g protein, 11.8 g fat (6.7 g saturated fat), 26 g cholesterol, 91 mg sodium, 78 mg potassium, 1 mg iron, 14 mg calcium, 42 mg phosphorus

# ALMOND CRISP BARS

Warning—these may become habit-forming!

Yield: About 25 squares.

Freezes well.

½ cup butter or tub margarine,
   cut in chunks
¼ cup granulated sugar
¼ cup brown sugar, lightly packed
½ tsp pure vanilla or almond extract
1 egg yolk

½ cup flour
½ cup rolled oats or granola
¾ cup chocolate chips
1 Tbsp additional butter
¼ cup almonds

Preheat oven to 350°F.

STEEL BLADE: Process the ½ cup butter or margarine with sugars, vanilla or almond extract and egg yolk for 45 seconds. Add flour and process for 5 seconds to mix. Add oats or granola and process with several quick on/off pulses to mix.

Spread mixture with rubber spatula in sprayed 8-inch square baking pan. Bake for 25 minutes, until golden. Melt chocolate chips with the 1 Tbsp butter (about 2 minutes on Medium [50%] in the microwave). Stir well; spread over base.

Process almonds until fine, about 15 seconds. Sprinkle over chocolate. Cut into squares while still warm.

103 calories per bar, 10.6 g carbohydrates, 0.7 g fiber, 1 g protein, 6.7 g fat (3.6 g saturated fat), 20 g cholesterol, 31 mg sodium, 36 mg potassium, 0 mg iron, 11 mg calcium, 21 mg phosphorus

### note

Recipe may be doubled and baked in sprayed 10- × 15-inch jelly roll pan. Increase baking time slightly.

# APRICOT ALMOND TRIANGLES

These are *jam* good. You'll go nuts over them!

Yield: 48 triangles.

Freezes well.

1 cup butter or tub margarine,
   cut in chunks
2½ cups flour
¾ cup finely ground almonds
   or Almond Flour (page 41)
½ cup sugar

1 tsp pure vanilla extract
1½ cups apricot jam
2 Tbsp lemon juice
½ cup slivered almonds

Preheat oven to 350°F. Spray a 9- × 13-inch baking pan with nonstick spray.

For base: Using STEEL BLADE, process butter or margarine, flour, ground almonds, sugar and vanilla until crumbly, about 20 seconds. Reserve 1½ cups of crumb mixture for topping. Press remaining mixture evenly into prepared pan. Bake for 20 minutes, until golden.

For topping: Mix apricot jam with lemon juice; spread over base. Crumble reserved crumb mixture over jam layer, and then sprinkle with slivered almonds.

Bake 30 minutes longer, until golden. Cool completely. Cut with a sharp knife into 24 squares, then cut each 1 in half diagonally to form 48 triangles.

105 calories each, 14.1 g carbohydrates, 0.5 g fiber, 1 g protein, 5.2 g fat (2.5 g saturated fat), 10 g cholesterol, 31 mg sodium, 35 mg potassium, 0 mg iron, 11 mg calcium, 21 mg phosphorus

## PEANUT BUTTER SQUARES

Yield: 3 to 4 dozen.

Freezes well.

1 cup butter or tub margarine, cut in chunks

2 cups flour

¼ cup brown sugar, packed

¾ cup smooth peanut butter

1 cup chocolate chips

chopped peanuts (optional)

Preheat oven to 375°F.

STEEL BLADE: Process butter or margarine with flour and brown sugar until well blended, 15 to 20 seconds. Press evenly into sprayed 9- × 13-inch baking pan. Bake for 15 to 20 minutes, until golden. Cool.

Melt peanut butter with chocolate chips (2 to 3 minutes on Medium [50%] in the microwave). Stir well to blend. Spread over cooled base. Cover and refrigerate until firm. Cut into squares or fingers. If desired, sprinkle with chopped peanuts.

130 calories per square, 11 g carbohydrates, 0.8 g fiber, 2 g protein, 9.2 g fat (4.6 g saturated fat), 14 g cholesterol, 63 mg sodium, 60 mg potassium, 1 mg iron, 8 mg calcium, 33 mg phosphorus

## BASIC BROWNIES

These brownies are moist and fudgy. Your lips won't be sorry, but maybe your hips will.

Yield: 25 brownies.

Freezes well.

⅓ cup butter or tub margarine

⅔ cup sugar

2 Tbsp water

1 cup chocolate chips

2 eggs

¾ cup flour

½ tsp baking powder

1 tsp pure vanilla or peppermint extract

¾ cup walnuts

Chocolate Frosting (page 382)

chopped walnuts, for sprinkling on top

Preheat oven to 350°F.

Combine butter or margarine, sugar and water in saucepan and bring to a boil, stirring constantly.

STEEL BLADE: Process hot butter mixture with chocolate chips until smooth and blended, 15 to 20 seconds. Add eggs through feed tube while machine is running and process a few seconds longer. Add flour, baking powder, vanilla or

*Continued*

peppermint extract and the ¾ cup walnuts, and process with 3 or 4 quick on/off pulses, just until nuts are chopped. Do not overprocess. Scrape down sides of bowl as necessary.

Spread batter evenly in sprayed 8-inch square baking pan. Bake for 25 to 30 minutes. Let cool. Frost and sprinkle with chopped nuts. Cut into squares.

166 calories each, 20.6 g carbohydrates, 0.9 g fiber, 2 g protein, 9.3 g fat (3.8 g saturated fat), 24 g cholesterol, 49 mg sodium, 60 mg potassium, 1 mg iron, 17 mg calcium, 39 mg phosphorus

## variations

- **PEPPERMINT PATTY BROWNIES:** As soon as you remove brownies from oven, place a layer of chocolate mint patties directly on top. Spread evenly with a spatula. The white cream filling in the patties will blend in with the chocolate as it melts. Cool before cutting. One brownie contains 139 calories and 18 g carbohydrates.

- **CHOCOLATE MARSHMALLOW BROWNIES:** Bake Basic Brownies as directed. Remove from oven and immediately top with a layer of marshmallows that have been cut in half (or top with 2 cups miniature marshmallows). Return pan to oven for 5 minutes, until marshmallows are melted and puffy. Cool completely before frosting with Chocolate Frosting. One brownie contains 178 calories and 23.8 g carbohydrates.

- **TWO-TONE MINT BROWNIES:** Bake Basic Brownies as directed. Prepare Butter Frosting (page 382), replacing vanilla with peppermint extract. If desired, add a few drops of green food coloring. Spread icing over brownies. Drizzle 2 oz melted semisweet chocolate over icing in a crisscross design. When firm, cut into squares. One brownie contains 184 calories and 24.5 g carbohydrates.

# BUTTERSCOTCH BROWNIES

Yield: 25 squares.

Freezes well.

| | |
|---|---|
| ½ cup walnuts | 1 tsp pure vanilla extract |
| 1 cup brown sugar, packed | ¾ cup flour |
| 1 egg | 1 tsp baking powder |
| ¼ cup butter or tub margarine, melted | dash salt |

Preheat oven to 350°F.

STEEL BLADE: Process nuts until coarsely chopped, about 5 seconds. Empty bowl. Process brown sugar, egg, butter or margarine and vanilla extract for 30 seconcds, until blended. Add flour, baking powder and salt; process a few seconds longer to blend. Sprinkle with nuts and mix in with 2 or 3 quick on/off pulses.

Spread mixture evenly in sprayed 8-inch square baking pan. Bake for 25 minutes. Edges will pull away from sides of pan. Do not overbake. Cut into squares while warm.

80 calories each, 11.9 g carbohydrates, 0.2 g fiber, 1 g protein, 3.4 g fat (1.4 g saturated fat), 13 g cholesterol, 44 mg sodium, 28 mg potassium, 0 mg iron, 22 mg calcium, 19 mg phosphorus

### variation

Add ½ cup butterscotch chips, ½ cup chocolate chips and ½ cup shredded sweetened coconut to batter. One brownie contains 131 calories, 18.1 g carbohydrates and 6.3 g fat.

## MARBLED CHEESECAKE BROWNIES

Cheesecake and brownies are combined in 1 luscious recipe!

Yield: 48 squares. Freezes for up to 2 months if well wrapped and well hidden!

| CHEESECAKE BATTER | BROWNIE BATTER |
| --- | --- |
| 1 cup (8 oz/250 g) cream cheese (light or regular) | 1 cup butter or tub margarine, melted |
| ⅓ cup granulated sugar | 1 cup granulated sugar |
| 1 egg | 1 cup brown sugar, lightly packed |
| ½ tsp pure vanilla extract | ¾ cup unsweetened cocoa powder |
| | 3 eggs |
| | 1 tsp pure vanilla extract |
| | 1 cup flour |
| | ½ tsp baking powder |
| | ⅛ tsp salt |

Preheat oven to 350°F. For machines with nested bowls, see method on page 456.

For cheesecake batter: Process cream cheese with sugar on the STEEL BLADE until blended, about 20 seconds. Add egg and vanilla extract; process until smooth and creamy, about 30 seconds longer. Scrape down sides of bowl as needed. Transfer mixture to a 2-cup measuring cup. (No need to wash the bowl or blade.)

For brownie batter: Process butter or margarine, sugars, cocoa, eggs and vanilla extract until well mixed, about 1 minute. Scrape down sides of bowl. Add flour, baking powder and salt; process with quick on/off pulses, just until blended. Do not overprocess.

Pour half the brownie batter into sprayed 9- × 13-inch baking pan. Drizzle half the cheesecake batter over brownie batter. Repeat layers. With a knife, cut through batters in a swirl design to make a marbled effect. *Continued*

Bake for 30 minutes. When done, a toothpick inserted into the center will come out clean. Cool completely. Cut into squares and refrigerate.

101 calories each, 13.3 g carbohydrates, 0.3 g fiber, 2 g protein, 5.2 g fat (3.1 g saturated fat), 30 g cholesterol, 67 mg sodium, 36 mg potassium, 0 mg iron, 27 mg calcium, 22 mg phosphorus

### nested bowl method

Use mini-bowl and mini-blade for cheesecake batter. No need to empty bowl. Use large bowl and STEEL BLADE for brownie batter.

### polka dot brownies

Omit cheesecake batter. Prepare brownie batter, adding 1 cup white chocolate or peanut butter chips. Bake as directed. Frost cooled brownies with your favorite chocolate frosting. Top with additional chips to make polka dots. One brownie without frosting contains 104 calories and 13.6 g carbohydrates.

## EASY CHEESE DREAMS

Yield: 2 dozen.

Freezes well.

BASE

½ cup walnuts or pecans

¼ cup brown sugar, lightly packed

6 Tbsp butter or tub margarine, cut in chunks

¾ cup flour

TOPPING

1 cup (8 oz/250 g) cream cheese, cut in chunks (light or regular)

¼ cup granulated sugar

1 egg

2 Tbsp milk (1%)

1 Tbsp lemon juice

1 tsp almond extract

Preheat oven to 350°F.

STEEL BLADE: Process nuts, brown sugar, butter or margarine and flour with several on/off pulses, until crumbly. Press mixture into sprayed 8-inch-square baking pan. Bake for 15 minutes. Remove from oven.

Process remaining ingredients until well blended, about 30 seconds. Scrape down sides of bowl as needed. Spread over base. Return pan to oven and bake 25 minutes longer. When cool, cut into squares. Refrigerate.

92 calories per square, 8.4 g carbohydrates, 0.2 g fiber, 2 g protein, 5.8 g fat (2.9 g saturated fat), 21 g cholesterol, 69 mg sodium, 23 mg potassium, 0 mg iron, 38 mg calcium, 17 mg phosphorus

### variation

Reserve about ½ cup crumbly mixture from base. Sprinkle over cheese topping and bake as directed.

# BROWNIE BITES

Thanks to my friend Helene Medjuck for inspiring these yummy treats. These round brownies are excellent for the lunchbox or as a snack. Bet you can't stop at just one bite!

Yield: 28 to 30 bites. Freezes well.

½ cup tub margarine

½ cup granulated sugar

½ cup brown sugar, packed

6 Tbsp unsweetened cocoa powder

1 egg plus 1 egg white

½ tsp pure vanilla extract

½ cup flour

¼ tsp baking powder

Chocolate Frosting (page 382) or Chocolate Glaze (page 381), optional

Preheat oven to 350°F. Spray miniature muffin pans with nonstick spray.

Process margarine, sugars, cocoa, egg plus egg white and vanilla extract until well mixed, about 1 minute. Scrape down sides of bowl. Add flour and baking powder; process with quick on/off pulses, just until blended. Do not overprocess.

Spoon batter into muffin pans, filling them three-quarters full. Fill any empty compartments half full with water. Bake for 14 to 16 minutes; tops will spring back when lightly touched. When cooled, frost or glaze (if desired).

68 calories each (unfrosted), 9.2 g carbohydrates, 0.4 g fiber, 1 g protein, 3.4 g fat (2.1 g saturated fat), 15 g cholesterol, 31 mg sodium, 28 mg potassium, 0 mg iron, 9 mg calcium, 15 mg phosphorus

# BUTTER TART SLICE

No need to make individual tarts. Fabulous!

Yield: 25 squares. Freezes well.

BASE

½ cup butter or tub margarine, cut in chunks

1½ cups flour

2 Tbsp icing sugar or brown sugar

TOPPING

1½ cups brown sugar, lightly packed

¼ cup butter, melted

2 eggs

1 Tbsp vinegar

1 tsp pure vanilla extract

1 cup raisins

Preheat oven to 350°F.

For base: Process butter or margarine, flour and icing sugar on the STEEL BLADE until blended, about 20 seconds. Press into bottom of sprayed 9-inch square baking pan. Bake for 10 minutes.

For topping: Combine all ingredients for topping except raisins. Process until well mixed. Add raisins and blend in with 2 quick on/off pulses. Pour over base. Bake 30 to 35 minutes longer, until golden. When cool, cut into squares.

153 calories per square, 23.9 g carbohydrates, 0.6 g fiber, 2 g protein, 6.1 g fat (3.7 g saturated fat), 32 g cholesterol, 50 mg sodium, 80 mg potassium, 1 mg iron, 17 mg calcium, 22 mg phosphorus

*Continued*

- Omit raisins. Sprinkle ¾ cup pecan halves or pieces over baked base before adding topping. Bake as directed. One square contains 156 calories, 19.8 g carbohydrates and 8.2 g fat.

- My friend Debbie Shawn bakes this recipe in a 9- × 13-inch pan, making 48 squares. She uses the same base so the crust is thinner. For the topping, she doubles the ingredients, but only uses 2½ cups brown sugar. One square contains 118 calories, 19.4 g carbohydrates and 4.4 g fat.

# BY CRACKY BARS

These luscious triple-layer squares from the late 1950s come from my friend Roz Brown's recipe collection.

Yield: About 3 dozen.

Freezes well.

| | |
|---|---|
| ½ cup walnuts or pecans | 1½ cups flour |
| 1 cup sugar | ¼ tsp baking soda |
| ¾ cup butter or tub margarine, cut in chunks | 1 square (1 oz/30 g) unsweetened chocolate, melted |
| 2 eggs | 15 to 18 single graham wafers |
| 1 tsp pure vanilla extract | 1 cup chocolate chips |
| ⅓ cup milk (1%) | |

Preheat oven to 350°F.

STEEL BLADE: Process nuts until chopped, 6 to 8 seconds. Empty bowl. Process sugar, butter or margarine, eggs and vanilla extract for 1 minute. Add milk through feed tube while machine is running. Process 3 seconds. Add flour and baking soda. Process with 3 or 4 quick on/off pulses, just until blended. Do not overprocess.

Remove half the batter and set aside. Add melted chocolate and nuts to batter in processor. Process with quick on/off pulses, just until blended, scraping down sides of bowl as needed. Do not overprocess.

Spread chocolate/nut batter evenly in sprayed 9- × 13-inch baking pan. Arrange wafers over batter to cover. Mix chocolate chips into remaining batter and spread evenly over wafers. Bake for 30 to 35 minutes, until a cake tester comes out dry. When cool, cut into squares.

128 calories per square, 15.4 g carbohydrates, 0.7 g fiber, 2 g protein, 7.2 g fat (3.8 g saturated fat), 22 g cholesterol, 59 mg sodium, 48 mg potassium, 1 mg iron, 10 mg calcium, 31 mg phosphorus

# CHOCOLATE CHIP NUT CHEWS

Yield: 25 squares.

Freezes well.

### BASE

½ cup butter or tub margarine,
    cut in chunks

1 cup flour

½ cup sugar (granulated or brown)

1 cup chocolate chips

### TOPPING

1 cup walnuts, pecans or peanuts

1 cup brown sugar, packed

2 eggs

½ tsp pure vanilla extract

½ cup sweetened flaked coconut

2 Tbsp flour

½ tsp baking powder

Preheat oven to 350°F.

For base: Process butter or margarine, flour and sugar on the STEEL BLADE for 20 seconds, until blended. Press into lightly sprayed 8-inch square pan. Bake for 15 minutes. Remove from oven and sprinkle with chocolate chips.

For topping: Process nuts until coarsely chopped, 6 to 8 seconds. Empty bowl. Process brown sugar, eggs and vanilla extract for 30 seconds. Add remaining ingredients and mix in with 2 or 3 quick on/off pulses. Spread over chocolate chips. Bake about 25 minutes longer. When cool, cut into squares.

176 calories per square, 22.7 g carbohydrates, 0.9 g fiber, 2 g protein, 9.4 g fat (4.5 g saturated fat), 27 g cholesterol, 49 mg sodium, 73 mg potassium, 1 mg iron, 23 mg calcium, 41 mg phosphorus

# CRUMBLY JAM SQUARES

Quick and
scrumptious.

Yield: 25 squares.

Freezes well.

4 oz (125 g) chilled low-fat cheddar
    cheese (1 cup grated)

½ cup butter or tub margarine,
    cut in chunks

1½ cups flour

3 Tbsp sugar

1 tsp baking powder

1 cup apricot jam or orange
    marmalade

Preheat oven to 350°F.

STEEL BLADE: Cut cheese into chunks. Process until fine, about 15 seconds. Add butter or margarine and process 30 seconds longer, scraping down sides of bowl as needed. Add flour, sugar and baking powder. Process 10 to 15 seconds longer, until crumbly.

Press half the mixture into ungreased 8-inch square pan. Spread with jam. Sprinkle remaining crumbs overtop. Bake for about 30 minutes. When cool, cut into squares.

115 calories per square, 15.6 g carbohydrates, 0.2 g fiber, 2 g protein, 5.3 g fat (3.3 g saturated fat), 15 g cholesterol, 79 mg sodium, 24 mg potassium, 1 mg iron, 48 mg calcium, 37 mg phosphorus

CHOCOLATES,
COOKIES AND SQUARES

459

# HALFWAY SQUARES

They're half
gone before you
turn around!

Yield: 25 squares.

Do not freeze.

⅓ cup butter, cut in chunks

1 egg, separated

¼ cup granulated sugar

¼ cup brown sugar, packed

1 cup flour

¾ tsp baking powder

½ tsp pure vanilla extract

¾ cup chocolate chips

½ cup additional brown sugar, packed

Preheat oven to 375°F.

For base: Process butter, egg yolk, granulated sugar and ¼ cup brown sugar on the STEEL BLADE for 45 seconds, until blended. Add flour, baking powder and vanilla extract. Process with several on/off pulses, until mixed. Press into sprayed 8-inch square pan. Sprinkle with chocolate chips.

Using an electric mixer or whisk, beat egg white until soft peaks form. Gradually add ½ cup brown sugar and beat until stiff. Carefully spread meringue over chocolate layer. Bake for about 25 minutes. When cool, cut into squares.

101 calories per square, 15.6 g carbohydrates, 0.4 g fiber, 1 g protein, 4.2 g fat (2.5 g saturated fat), 15 g cholesterol, 37 mg sodium, 36 mg potassium, 1 mg iron, 18 mg calcium, 20 mg phosphorus

# HEAVENLY SQUARES

These scrumptious
squares live up to
their name!

Yield: About 25 squares.

Freezes well.

| BASE | TOPPING |
| --- | --- |
| ¾ cup flour | 1 cup pitted dates |
| ½ cup walnuts | 5 Tbsp flour, divided |
| ¼ cup brown sugar, lightly packed | ¼ cup maraschino cherries, drained |
| 6 Tbsp butter or tub margarine, cut in chunks | 2 eggs |
| | 1 cup brown sugar, lightly packed |
| | ½ tsp baking powder |
| | 1¼ cups sweetened flaked coconut |
| | ½ cup chocolate chips |

Preheat oven to 350°F.

For base: Process base ingredients with quick on/off pulses, until crumbly. Press into lightly sprayed 8-inch square pan. Bake for 15 minutes. Remove from oven.

For topping: Process dates with 2 Tbsp of the flour until coarsely chopped, 6 to 8 seconds. Empty bowl. Pat cherries dry with paper towels. Process cherries with 1 Tbsp of the flour, using 2 quick on/off pulses. Add to dates. Process eggs, brown sugar, baking powder and remaining 2 Tbsp flour until well blended, about 30 seconds. Add dates, cherries, coconut and chocolate chips. Mix in with several quick on/off pulses. Scrape down sides of bowl as needed.

Spread mixture over base. Bake 25 to 30 minutes longer, until golden. Cut into squares while warm.

166 calories per square, 25.4 g carbohydrates, 1.2 g fiber, 2 g protein, 7.2 g fat (4.1 g saturated fat), 24 g cholesterol, 50 mg sodium, 105 mg potassium, 1 mg iron, 26 mg calcium, 32 mg phosphorus

## HELLO DOLLY SQUARES

My daughter Jodi adores these!

Yield: About 4 dozen.

Freezes well.

½ cup walnuts, slivered almonds or pecans

1¼ cups graham wafer crumbs (or 15 single graham wafers)

½ cup butter or margarine

1½ cups chocolate chips

1½ cups sweetened flaked coconut

½ cup raisins (optional)

14 oz (398 mL) can sweetened condensed milk (or make your own—see page 427)

Preheat oven to 350°F.

STEEL BLADE: Process nuts until coarsely chopped, 6 to 8 seconds. Empty bowl. If using graham wafers, break in chunks and process to make fine crumbs, 25 to 35 seconds.

Place butter or margarine in 9- × 13-inch baking pan and place in oven to melt. Mix in crumbs; spread evenly in pan. Sprinkle with chocolate chips, coconut, raisins (if using) and nuts. Drizzle condensed milk evenly overtop. Bake for 25 to 30 minutes, until golden. Cool and cut into squares.

109 calories per square, 12.6 g carbohydrates, 0.6 g fiber, 2 g protein, 6.4 g fat (3.8 g saturated fat), 9 g cholesterol, 49 mg sodium, 78 mg potassium, 0 mg iron, 36 mg calcium, 45 mg phosphorus

### variations

- Substitute 1½ cups granola or any leftover cookies for graham wafer crumbs.

- Combine melted butter with graham wafer crumbs; spread evenly in pan. Instead of 1½ cups chocolate chips, sprinkle crumb mixture with 1 cup chocolate chips, 1 cup Skor bar pieces, coconut and nuts. If desired, add ½ cup glazed cherries, halved. Drizzle condensed milk over mixture. Bake as directed. One square contains 124 calories, 13.8 g carbohydrates and 7.4 g fat.

# LEMON SQUARES

This is a favorite of Elaine Kaplan, who worked tirelessly by my side to guide the creation of this cookbook.

**BASE**

1 cup butter or tub margarine, cut in chunks

2 cups flour

½ cup sugar

**TOPPING**

4 eggs

¼ to ⅓ cup lemon juice (preferably fresh)

2 cups sugar

¼ cup flour

1 tsp baking powder

Yield: About 48 squares.

Freezes well.

Preheat oven to 350°F.

For base: Process base ingredients on the STEEL BLADE until crumbly, about 20 seconds. Press into sprayed 9- × 13-inch baking pan. Bake for 18 to 20 minutes, until golden.

For topping: Process topping ingredients until blended, about 10 seconds. Pour over base. Bake 25 to 30 minutes longer, until golden. Cut into squares when cool.

103 calories per square, 15.2 g carbohydrates, 0.2 g fiber, 1 g protein, 4.3 g fat (2.6 g saturated fat), 28 g cholesterol, 43 mg sodium, 15 mg potassium, 0 mg iron, 10 mg calcium, 17 mg phosphorus

# LIME COCONUT BARS

You put the lime with the coconut and eat these all up!

**BASE**

1 cup butter or tub margarine, cut in chunks

2 cups flour

½ cup icing sugar

**TOPPING**

4 eggs

¼ cup lime juice (bottled or fresh)

2 cups sugar

¼ cup flour

1 tsp baking powder

1 cup sweetened flaked coconut

Yield: 48 squares.

Freezes well.

Preheat oven to 350°F.

For base: Process base ingredients on the STEEL BLADE until crumbly, about 20 seconds. Press evenly into sprayed 9- × 13-inch baking pan. Bake for 18 to 20 minutes, until golden.

For topping: Process eggs, lime juice, sugar, flour and baking powder until blended, about 10 seconds. Pour over base. Sprinkle evenly with coconut. Bake 25 to 30 minutes longer, until golden. Cut into squares when cool.

109 calories per square, 15.2 g carbohydrates, 0.3 g fiber, 1 g protein, 5 g fat (3.2 g saturated fat), 28 g cholesterol, 48 mg sodium, 21 mg potassium, 0 mg iron, 10 mg calcium, 19 mg phosphorus

# PECAN JAM SQUARES

Yield: About 25 squares.

Freezes well.

BASE

½ cup butter or tub margarine,
   cut in chunks

1 cup flour

½ cup brown sugar, packed

½ cup strawberry or raspberry jam

TOPPING

1 cup pecans or almonds

2 eggs

1 tsp pure vanilla extract

1 cup brown sugar, packed

1 Tbsp flour

¼ tsp baking powder

2 Tbsp icing sugar for dusting
   (optional)

Preheat oven to 350°F.

For base: Process butter or margarine, flour and brown sugar on the STEEL BLADE for 20 seconds, until blended. Press into lightly sprayed 8-inch square pan. Bake for 15 minutes. Spread with jam.

For topping: Process nuts until coarsely chopped, 8 to 10 seconds. Empty bowl and set aside. Process remaining topping ingredients, except icing sugar, until mixed, 12 to 15 seconds. Mix in nuts with 2 or 3 quick on/off pulses. Spread over base. Bake about 25 minutes longer. Cool completely. Dust with icing sugar (if desired). Cut into squares.

152 calories per square, 21.8 g carbohydrates, 0.5 g fiber, 2 g protein, 7 g fat (2.7 g saturated fat), 27 g cholesterol, 40 mg sodium, 46 mg potassium, 1 mg iron, 20 mg calcium, 26 mg phosphorus

# RASPBERRY CHOCOLATE CHIP SQUARES

These scrumptious squares with their shortbread crust will "shortly" disappear!

1 cup butter or tub margarine,
   cut in chunks

2½ cups flour

½ cup brown sugar, packed

¾ cup pecans

1½ cups raspberry preserves

1½ cups sweetened flaked coconut

1 cup chocolate chips

Yield: 4 dozen squares.

Freezes well.

Preheat oven to 350°F. Spray a 9- × 13-inch baking pan with nonstick spray.

For base: Using STEEL BLADE, process butter, flour, brown sugar and pecans until crumbly, about 20 seconds. Reserve 1½ cups crumb mixture for topping. Press remaining mixture evenly into prepared pan. Bake for 20 minutes, until golden.

For topping: Spread raspberry preserves over base. Sprinkle with coconut and chocolate chips. Crumble reserved crumb mixture evenly overtop.

Bake 30 minutes longer, until golden. When cool, cut with a sharp knife into squares.

135 calories each, 17.6 g carbohydrates, 0.7 g fiber, 1 g protein, 7.2 g fat (4.1 g saturated fat), 10 g cholesterol, 36 mg sodium, 41 mg potassium, 1 mg iron, 7 mg calcium, 21 mg phosphorus

# PIES AND PASTRIES
### recipe list

470 Standard Butter Pastry

470 Pareve Pie Crust (Basic Pastry)

471 Flaky Ginger Ale Pastry

472 Cream Cheese Pastry

472 Chocolate Cream Cheese Pastry

473 Sour Cream Pastry

473 Graham Wafer Crust

474 Family Apple Pie

475 Crumbly Apple Pie

475 Apple Crostata

476 Apple Flan

477 Apple Strudel

478 Berry Hand Pies

479 Ruby-Red Rhubarb Pie

479 Fresh Strawberry Flan

480 Pumpkin Pie

481 Pecan Pie

482 Choc' Full of Pecan Pie

482 Miniature Pecan Tarts

483 Butter Tarts

483 Lemon Meringue Pie

484 Key Lime Pie

485 Chocolate Cream Pie

485 Chocolate Marshmallow Pie

486 Fudge Ribbon Baked Alaska Pie

487 Cream Puffs (Choux Pastry)

488 Crème Pâtissière (Pastry Cream)

- Making pastry dough is as easy as pie! For the best results when making pastry, measure accurately and use cold ingredients. Freeze butter or shortening in advance and use ice-cold water.
- Cut shortening and/or butter into 1-inch pieces and place in the processor bowl. Add flour and salt. Process on the **Steel Blade** with several quick on/off pulses, until the mixture resembles coarse oatmeal.
- Add cold water through the feed tube in a thin stream while the machine is running. In 12 to 15 seconds, the dough will begin to gather around the blades. Do not overprocess or the dough will be tough.
- If the dough is too dry, add extra liquid a few drops at a time. Use on/off pulses, just until the dough begins to hold together.
- If the dough is too sticky, remove it from the processor and gently knead in a little more flour. Do not overhandle.
- Shape the dough into 1 or 2 round discs (like a large, thick hamburger).

## ROLL IT RIGHT!

- Chill dough before rolling for easier handling.

Wrap well and refrigerate for at least half an hour or place it in the freezer for 15 minutes.
- A floured surface prevents the dough from sticking. The less flour used, the flakier the pastry.
- A lightly floured pastry cloth and stockinette rolling pin cover make rolling dough easy. Anchor the pastry cloth by tucking it under your pastry board.
- Rolling dough on parchment or waxed paper is an excellent alternative. Wet the countertop so the paper won't slip.
- Roll dough equally in all directions, like the spokes of a wheel. This helps keep the pastry round. Take your time! Use light strokes and a lifting motion. Flour the rolling pin or stockinette cover from time to time to prevent sticking.
- If the dough begins to stick, lift it up carefully with a floured spatula and add a little more flour.
- Roll the pastry into a large circle about 2 inches larger than your pie plate when inverted. Mend cracks as they form.

- Fold the dough in half carefully, then in half again to make a pie-shaped wedge. Transfer to an ungreased pie plate, placing the point at the center of the plate. Unfold carefully. Do not stretch the dough or it will shrink during baking.

### EASY DOUGHS IT!

- For a single prebaked 9-inch pie shell, roll out the dough and place it in the pie plate. Trim the edge, leaving a ½-inch overhang. Fold the edge under to form a rim. Flute the edge, then press firmly against the pie plate. Prick the bottom of the pastry all over with a fork. Chill for half an hour before baking; this prevents the crust from shrinking. Bake at 425°F for about 10 minutes, until golden.

- For a partially baked pie shell, prepare the pastry shell as above, then line it with aluminum foil. Weigh the foil down with dried beans or uncooked rice. Bake at 400°F for 10 minutes. Remove the foil and beans. (Careful—don't spill the beans!) Bake 5 minutes longer.

- For a 2-crust pie, roll out the bottom crust and place it in the pan. Trim the overhanging edges. Fill as desired. Roll out the top crust and fold it in half. Place the top crust over the filling and unfold it carefully. Trim the top pastry, leaving a 1-inch overhang around the rim. Fold the edge of the top crust under the bottom crust (not under the pan). Press the edges together to seal, using 1 of the following methods. Cut several slits in the top crust to release steam while the pie is baking. (Don't cut the slits if you're freezing the unbaked pie.)

- FORK EDGE: Dip the tines of a fork in flour, then press firmly to make a decorative edge.

- SPOON EDGE: Press the rounded tip of a teaspoon into the edge to form a scalloped design.

- RUFFLED EDGE: Place your thumb and index finger about ½ inch apart along the rim of the pie plate, pointing towards the center. With the index finger of the opposite hand, pull the pastry gently towards the center. Repeat every inch or so, forming a rounded, ruffled edge.

- Save the scraps of dough. Roll them out and cut out shapes with tiny cookie cutters. Brush the bottoms of the cut-outs with water and arrange them attractively on top of the pie.

- FOR A SHINY TOP, brush the crust with milk before baking. For a glazed top, brush with beaten egg. For a sugary top, brush with water, then sprinkle with sugar.

- TO MAKE A LATTICE TOP, use a sharp knife or pastry wheel to cut dough into twelve ½-inch strips. (Use a ruler to keep the strips straight.) Carefully lay half the strips 1 inch apart across the top of the filled pie. Arrange the remaining strips at right angles. (To create a woven effect, lift every other strip as you arrange the strips at right angles.) Trim the ends even with the edge of the pie. Press the ends of the strips into the rim of the crust. Fold the bottom pastry over the latticework. Seal and flute.

- If the edges of the pie start to brown too quickly, cover the edge with strips of foil.

- SLICE AND ROLL TECHNIQUE: For hand pies and turnovers, make a double recipe of Cream Cheese Pastry (page 472) or Flaky Ginger Ale Pastry (page 471), but use butter. Shape dough into a log about 8 inches long, wrap well and chill until needed. With a sharp knife, cut dough into ¾-inch slices, then, on a lightly floured surface, roll each slice into a circle. Fill, fold in half and crimp edges to seal.

### PAN-TASTIC!

- Glass or aluminum pie plates are best for baking pies. Disposable foil pans are handy for freezing.

- A 9-inch pie plate holds 4 cups of filling and

serves 8 people. An 8-inch pie plate holds 3 cups of filling and serves 6 people. You can replace a 9-inch pie plate with a 10-inch or 11-inch quiche pan, which serves 10 people.

- When using a quiche pan with a fluted or rippled sharp edge, roll your rolling pin over the edge. The excess pastry will automatically be cut away!
- TO GREASE OR NOT TO GREASE? Pastry is high in fat, so don't grease the pie plate. For cookie crumb crusts, spray the pie plate first with nonstick spray to prevent sticking.
- To prevent spillovers in your oven, place a foil-lined baking sheet under fruit or custard-type pies before baking.

### FREEZE WITH EASE

- Fruit pies freeze well, but don't freeze those with a custard base.
- Don't freeze pies in glass pie plates. They may crack from extreme temperature changes when baking or reheating.
- Disposable foil pie plates are great for freezing. However, pies baked in foil pie plates do not brown evenly. To offset this, place the foil pie plate on a heavy-duty baking sheet and bake on the middle rack.
- Unbaked pastry can be frozen for 1 to 2 months. Baked pie shells can be frozen for 2 to 4 months. Baked pies can be frozen for about 3 months. Wrap them well.
- To defrost baked pies, place the frozen pie in a 425°F oven for 20 to 25 minutes. To pre-

vent overbrowning, cover loosely with foil. To defrost in the microwave, transfer the frozen pie to a microwavable glass pie plate. Microwave on Medium (50%) for 8 to 12 minutes. Let stand for 5 to 10 minutes to complete thawing.

- To bake a frozen unbaked pie, bake at 450°F for 15 minutes. Cut slits in the top crust, reduce the heat to 375°F and bake 45 minutes longer.

### PORTIONS, PORTIONS!

Pies and pastries are high in calories, carbs and fat—no doubt about it. Here are some easy ways to lighten them up:

- Omit the top or bottom crust or make a thinner crust.
- Creamy fillings can often be served in parfait glasses, minus the crust.
- Use less topping or simply omit it (e.g., whipped cream).
- Make individual medium or miniature tarts for portion control.
- Instead of using a 9-inch pie plate that serves 8, use an 11-inch quiche pan to make a thinner, larger pie that serves 10.
- By dividing a pie or tart into 10 servings instead of 8, you will reduce the calories substantially—by about 100 calories or more per serving—as well as the carbs and fat!
- Please use the nutrient analysis as a guide to help you make smarter choices and save rich desserts for special occasions!

| | |
|---|---|
| **Dough dry and hard to work with** | Insufficient liquid; dough is too cold; dough was not shaped into round disc and flattened before chilling and rolling. |
| **Baked pastry is hard** | Too much water; overmixing; excess flour on pastry board; dough overhandled. |
| **Baked pastry is tough** | Insufficient shortening; overmixing shortening and flour; dough over-handled; oven temperature too low. |
| **Too pale** | Oven temperature too low; underbaked. |
| **Too dark** | Oven temperature too high; overbaked. |
| **Soggy lower crust** | Pastry overhandled; too much filling; filling too moist; pastry not put in oven soon enough; pie baked too high up in oven; oven temperature too low. (To help prevent a soggy pie shell, brush with unbeaten egg white before adding filling.) |
| **Crust thick and doughy** | Insufficient fat; too much water; water not cold enough; pastry rolled too thick; oven temperature too low. |
| **Crust shrinks while baking** | Pastry rolled too thin or not chilled before baking; pastry overhandled or stretched when fitted in pan; too much water; oven temperature too low. |
| **Baked pie shell has bumps and does not lie flat in pan** | Pastry not pricked enough; oven temperature too low. |
| **Apple pie has large air space under top crust of pie** | Apples not packed tightly into shell; apples sliced too thick; apples not mounded high enough in center. |

# STANDARD BUTTER PASTRY

A simple, delicious dough that's perfect for any pie!

¼ lb (125 g) frozen butter (½ cup/ 1 stick)
¼ cup frozen shortening

2 cups flour
½ tsp salt
½ cup ice water

Yield: Two 9-inch crusts or 12 medium tart shells. Freezes well.

STEEL BLADE: Cut butter and shortening into 6 or 8 pieces; place in processor. Add flour and salt. Turn machine on and off quickly 4 or 5 times (2 or 3 seconds each time), until mixture looks like coarse oatmeal. Add water in slow stream through feed tube while machine is running. Process just until dough begins to gather around the blades, 10 to 12 seconds once all the liquid is added. Do not overprocess.

Remove dough from machine, press into a ball and divide in 2 equal pieces. (Dough should look like a large, thick burger.) Wrap in plastic wrap. Chill in refrigerator for at least half an hour (or in freezer for 15 minutes) while you prepare filling.

Roll out dough on lightly floured surface (or use a pastry cloth and rolling pin stockinette cover). Use a light, lifting motion. Roll equally in all directions, making sure to keep dough circular and mending cracks as they form. Roll about 2 inches larger than pie plate, about ⅛ inch thick. Use as directed.

181 calories per tart shell, 15.9 g carbohydrates, 0.6 g fiber, 2 g protein, 12.1 g fat (6 g saturated fat), 20 g cholesterol, 152 mg sodium, 25 mg potassium, 1 mg iron, 6 mg calcium, 25 mg phosphorus

note

Dough may be refrigerated for 3 or 4 days. For easier rolling, let dough stand at room temperature for a few minutes to soften slightly.

# PAREVE PIE CRUST (BASIC PASTRY)

This easy, versatile pastry contains no dairy or meat products.

⅔ cup frozen shortening, cut in chunks
2 cups flour
½ tsp salt

1 tsp vinegar
scant ½ cup ice water or orange juice (about 3½ oz)

Yield: Two 9-inch pie crusts or 12 medium tart shells. Freezes well.

STEEL BLADE: Place shortening, flour and salt in processor. Process with 5 or 6 quick on/off pulses, stopping to check texture, until mixture begins to look like coarse oatmeal. Add vinegar. With machine running, add liquid in a steady stream through feed tube just until dough begins to gather around the blades, about 10 seconds after all the liquid is added. Do not overprocess.

Remove dough from machine, press into a ball and divide in 2 equal pieces. (Dough should look like a large, thick burger.) Wrap in plastic wrap. Chill dough in refrigerator for at least 1 hour before rolling out. (May be made 2 or 3 days in advance.)

Roll out dough on lightly floured surface (or use a pastry cloth and rolling pin stockinette cover); use a light lifting motion. Roll equally in all directions, making sure to keep dough circular and mending cracks as they form. Roll about 2 inches larger than pie plate, about ⅛ inch thick. Use as directed.

177 calories per tart shell, 15.9 g carbohydrates, 0.6 g fiber, 2 g protein, 11.6 g fat (2.9 g saturated fat), 0 g cholesterol, 98 mg sodium, 22 mg potassium, 1 mg iron, 4 mg calcium, 23 mg phosphorus

### variation

Use 1 egg plus enough ice water to equal a scant ½ cup. This crisp, golden pastry is ideal for turnovers or pies.

## FLAKY GINGER ALE PASTRY

Versatile, easy and dairy-free! Excellent for Mushroom Turnovers (page 74), Tuna Strudel (page 136), Roly Poly (page 448), Rogelach (pages 449–450), or Apple Crostata (page 475).

Yield: One large or two 8-inch circles (enough for 24 cookies) or one 9-inch pie crust. Doubles easily. Freezes well.

1 cup plus 1 Tbsp flour

½ cup frozen stick margarine, cut in 6 or 8 pieces (see Note, below)

¼ cup ginger ale (regular or diet) or soda water

1½ tsp vinegar or lemon juice

STEEL BLADE: Process flour and margarine with 4 or 5 on/off pulses (2 to 3 seconds each time), until mixture looks like coarse oatmeal. Add liquids through feed tube while machine is running. Process just until dough begins to gather in a mass around the blades, 8 to 10 seconds. Do not overprocess.

Remove dough from machine, divide into 2 balls and wrap in plastic wrap. Chill in the refrigerator at least 1 hour or overnight. The colder the dough, the easier it is to roll.

Roll out on lightly floured surface (or on a pastry cloth, using a rolling pin stockinette cover for easier rolling). Use as directed. Also see "Slice and Roll Technique" (page 467).

55 calories per serving, 4.5 g carbohydrates, 0.1 g fiber, 1 g protein, 3.8 g fat (0.7 g saturated fat), 0 g cholesterol, 44 mg sodium, 7 mg potassium, 0 mg iron, 1 mg calcium, 6 mg phosphorus

### note

This dough works well with Earth Balance Buttery Sticks. If you use tub margarine, the dough will be soft and difficult to roll out, so increase flour to 1 cup plus 2 Tbsp. This dough is also delicious when made with butter, but then it won't be dairy-free.

# CREAM CHEESE PASTRY

Quick and easy! Use for Spinach Cheese Turnovers (page 75), Roly Poly (page 448), Hamentaschen (page 446), Rogelach (pages 449–450), Miniature Pecan Tarts (page 482), or Spinach Borekas (page 154).

½ cup chilled butter or margarine, cut in chunks

½ cup chilled cream cheese or pressed dry cottage cheese (light or regular), cut in chunks

1 cup flour

2 Tbsp sugar (optional)

STEEL BLADE: Combine all ingredients in processor. Process until dough forms a ball on the blades, 18 to 20 seconds. Chilling is not necessary. Roll out on lightly floured surface (or on a pastry cloth, using a rolling pin stockinette cover for easier rolling).

Use as directed. Also see "Slice and Roll Technique" (page 467).

62 calories per serving, 4.3 g carbohydrates, 0.1 g fiber, 1 g protein, 4.6 g fat (2.9 g saturated fat), 12 g cholesterol, 50 mg sodium, 7 mg potassium, 0 mg iron, 17 mg calcium, 7 mg phosphorus

Yield: One large or two 8-inch circles (enough for 24 cookies or miniature tarts) or one 9-inch pie crust. Doubles easily. Freezes well.

## dairy-free variation

Use dairy-free margarine and Tofutti imitation cream cheese. For best results, freeze margarine first. Earth Balance Buttery Sticks are dairy-free and produce excellent results.

## tart shells

Instead of rolling out dough, shape into 1-inch balls and press into the bottom and up the sides of ungreased mini muffin tins.

# CHOCOLATE CREAM CHEESE PASTRY

Use for Chocolate Rogelach (page 449) or Chocolate Hamentaschen Kisses (page 447).

Yield: Four 8-inch circles (enough for 48 cookies.) Freezes well.

1 cup chilled cream cheese (light or regular), cut in chunks

1 cup chilled butter or margarine, cut in chunks

2 cups flour

6 Tbsp sugar

¼ cup unsweetened cocoa powder

STEEL BLADE: Combine all ingredients in processor. Process until dough forms a ball on the blades, 18 to 20 seconds. Divide dough into 4 balls, wrap in plastic wrap and refrigerate for half an hour for easier rolling. Roll out on lightly floured surface (or on a pastry cloth, using a rolling pin stockinette cover for easier rolling).

Use as directed.

69 calories per serving, 6.1 g carbohydrates, 0.3 g fiber, 1 g protein, 4.6 g fat (2.9 g saturated fat), 12 g cholesterol, 50 mg sodium, 14 mg potassium, 0 mg iron, 17 mg calcium, 10 mg phosphorus

# SOUR CREAM PASTRY

Rich and flaky, almost like a mock puff pastry. It is excellent for Butter Tarts (page 483), Apple Strudel (page 477), cheese bagels, knishes and borekas.

Yield: Two 9-inch pie crusts or 24 medium tart shells. Freezes well. Dough will keep in refrigerator for 5 days.

1 cup chilled butter, cut in 1-inch chunks

1½ cups flour

½ cup cold sour cream (light or regular)

STEEL BLADE: Process butter and flour with 6 to 8 on/off pulses, until it is the consistency of coarse oatmeal. Add sour cream and process just until pastry begins to cling together around the blades and form a ball. You will have to scrape down the sides of the bowl once or twice. Do not overprocess.

Divide dough in half, wrap in plastic wrap and refrigerate at least 4 hours or overnight. For easier rolling, let dough stand at room temperature for 5 to 10 minutes to remove the chill. Roll out on lightly floured surface (or on a pastry cloth, using a rolling pin stockinette cover for easier rolling).

103 calories per tart shell, 6.3 g carbohydrates, 0 g fiber, 1 g protein, 8.3 g fat (5.2 g saturated fat), 22 g cholesterol, 58 mg sodium, 22 mg potassium, 0 mg iron, 11 mg calcium, 14 mg phosphorus

### tart shells

Cut dough into 3½-inch circles with a round cookie cutter. Fit dough into ungreased muffin cups. Unfilled tart shells should be baked in a preheated 425°F oven for 10 minutes or until golden. Cool before filling.

# GRAHAM WAFER CRUST

Yield: One 9-inch pie crust (8 servings). If frozen, crust will not be as crisp.

18 single graham wafers (1½ cups crumbs)

¼ cup melted butter or tub margarine

3 Tbsp granulated or brown sugar

½ tsp ground cinnamon (optional)

STEEL BLADE: Break wafers into chunks. Process until coarse crumbs are formed. Add remaining ingredients and process a few seconds longer. Pat into bottom and up sides of sprayed 9-inch glass pie plate. Bake at 375°F for 7 to 8 minutes, or microwave on High for 2 minutes, until set.

136 calories per serving, 16.8 g carbohydrates, 0.4 g fiber, 1 g protein, 7.3 g fat (3.9 g saturated fat), 15 g cholesterol, 136 mg sodium, 23 mg potassium, 1 mg iron, 6 mg calcium, 18 mg phosphorus

*Continued*

# FAMILY APPLE PIE

I've taught this scrumptious pie recipe for years in my cooking classes. I usually use Cortland or Spartan apples, but most apples will work well.

Yield: 8 servings. Freezes well.

| | |
|---|---|
| Standard Butter Pastry (page 470) | ½ to 1 cup sugar (or to taste) |
| 2 Tbsp bread crumbs | ¼ cup flour |
| 8 large apples, peeled and cored | 1 tsp ground cinnamon |

Preheat oven to 425°F.

Prepare pastry and chill as directed. Roll out 1 portion into a large circle and place in ungreased 9-inch pie plate. Trim off overhanging edges. Sprinkle with bread crumbs.

SLICER: Cut apples to fit feed tube. Slice, using medium pressure. You should have 6 to 7 cups. Combine apples in large bowl with sugar, flour and cinnamon; mix well.

Fill shell, mounding apples higher in the center. Roll out remaining dough and cut several slits. Place over apple filling. Trim away edges, leaving ½-inch border all around. Tuck under bottom crust. Flute edges.

Bake for 45 to 50 minutes, until golden.

446 calories per serving, 68.5 g carbohydrates, 4 g fiber, 5 g protein, 18.6 g fat (9 g saturated fat), 31 g cholesterol, 241 mg sodium, 240 mg potassium, 2 mg iron, 27 mg calcium, 68 mg phosphorus

variations

- PEACH PIE: Replace apples with 8 large peaches. Pour boiling water over peaches, then immerse in cold water. Peel, cut in half and remove pits. Slice, using medium pressure. One serving contains 411 calories and 57.6 g carbohydrates.
- BLUEBERRY APPLE PIE: Use 3 to 4 peeled, sliced apples, 1½ cups blueberries, ¾ to 1 cup sugar, ⅓ cup flour and 1 tsp cinnamon. One serving contains 426 calories and 62.6 g carbohydrates.

## CRUMBLY APPLE PIE

Your willpower will
crumble after 1 bite!
Beware, this pie is
high in carbs!

**Family Apple Pie (page 474),
omitting top crust**
**1 cup flour**

**½ cup brown sugar, packed**
**½ cup chilled butter, cut in 1-inch
pieces**
**½ tsp ground cinnamon**

Yield: 10 servings.

Freezes well.

Preheat oven to 400°F. Prepare ingredients for Family Apple Pie as directed, but omit the top crust. Roll out chilled dough on a floured surface into a large circle. Transfer to an ungreased 11-inch quiche pan with removable bottom. Trim away excess edges of dough. Fill with apple filling.

STEEL BLADE: Process flour, sugar, butter and cinnamon for 10 seconds, until crumbly. Sprinkle over filling. Bake for 45 to 50 minutes. Serve warm or cold.

417 calories per serving, 65.7 g carbohydrates, 3.3 g fiber, 4 g protein, 17 g fat (9.5 g saturated fat), 37 g cholesterol, 170 mg sodium, 209 mg potassium, 2 mg iron, 38 mg calcium, 56 mg phosphorus

### variations

Other fruits may be substituted for the apple filling (e.g., peaches, pears, blueberries, plums, nectarines).

### sugar-free variation

Instead of ½ cup sugar in the filling, use ½ cup granular Splenda. Instead of ½ cup brown sugar in the topping, use ¼ cup Splenda Brown Sugar Blend. One serving contains 362 calories and 51.4 g carbohydrates.

## APPLE CROSTATA

A crostata is a
single-crust, free-
form tart with the
filling piled on top.
Easier than pie!

**Flaky Ginger Ale Pastry (page 471)**

TOPPING
**¼ cup brown sugar, packed**
**¼ cup flour**
**¼ cup chilled tub margarine or
butter, cut in chunks**
**½ tsp ground cinnamon**

FILLING
**6 large apples, peeled, cored and
halved (e.g., Granny Smith or
Cortland)**
**1 Tbsp lemon juice**
**½ cup sugar**
**2 Tbsp flour**
**1 tsp ground cinnamon**

Yield: 8 servings.

Freezes well.

For machines with nested bowls, see method on page 476.

Prepare pastry as directed and press into a large ball. Wrap well and chill for 1 hour or overnight.

STEEL BLADE: Process topping ingredients until crumbly, about 10 to 12 seconds. Set aside.

*Continued*

SLICER: For filling, slice apples, using medium pressure. Place in a mixing bowl and sprinkle with lemon juice. Add sugar, flour and cinnamon; mix well.

Roll chilled pastry into a 12-inch circle on lightly floured parchment paper. Slide parchment (with pastry on it) onto a large baking sheet. Spoon filling evenly onto pastry, leaving a 2-inch border. Carefully fold border up over filling to form a 2-inch rim, pleating and folding pastry as necessary. Make sure to seal any cracks in pastry. Sprinkle reserved topping over filling.

Bake in preheated 400°F about 35 minutes, until golden. Apples should be tender when pierced with a knife. Delicious warm or at room temperature.

370 calories per serving, 53.3 g carbohydrates, 2.4 g fiber, 3 g protein, 17.3 g fat (3.3 g saturated fat), 0 g cholesterol, 201 mg sodium, 151 mg potassium, 1 mg iron, 21 mg calcium, 39 mg phosphorus

### nested bowl method

Use mini-bowl and mini-blade for topping. Use medium bowl and SLICER for apples. Use large bowl and STEEL BLADE for pastry.

### variations

- Try other fruit fillings such as strawberry-rhubarb, blueberry-apple, peaches, pears, nectarines or plums.

- Omit streusel topping. Brush edges of pastry with beaten egg and sprinkle with coarse sugar before baking.

### sugar-free variation

Use diet ginger ale or club soda in pastry. Substitute granular Splenda for sugar in filling and topping. One serving contains 301 calories and 35.5 g carbohydrates.

## APPLE FLAN

Yield: 10 servings.

Freezes well.

**Standard Butter Pastry, ½ recipe (page 470)**
**3 Tbsp bread crumbs**
**6 to 8 large apples, peeled and cored**
**¼ cup sugar**
**2 Tbsp butter or tub margarine**
**¾ cup apple jelly**

Preheat oven to 400°F.

Prepare pastry as directed. Roll out chilled dough on floured pastry cloth or surface into large circle. Transfer to 11-inch quiche pan with removable bottom. Trim away excess edges. Sprinkle with crumbs. Chill while you prepare filling.

SLICER: Cut apples to fit feed tube. Slice, using medium pressure. Arrange attractively in pie shell. Sprinkle with sugar and dot with butter or margarine.

Bake for about 1 hour, until well browned. Melt apple jelly in small saucepan (or microwave on High for 1 minute). Brush over apples.

279 calories per serving, 48.2 g carbohydrates, 2.1 g fiber, 2 g protein, 9.9 g fat (5.1 g saturated fat), 18 g cholesterol, 122 mg sodium, 136 mg potassium, 1 mg iron, 14 mg calcium, 33 mg phosphorus

## APPLE STRUDEL

*Delicious served warm and topped with ice cream.*

*Yield: 2 strudels (12 servings).*

*Freezes well.*

Sour Cream Pastry (page 473)
6 apples, peeled and cored
½ cup granulated sugar
2 Tbsp flour
1 tsp ground cinnamon

½ cup raisins or dried cranberries
½ cup chopped walnuts (optional)
2 Tbsp fine dry bread crumbs
icing sugar, for dusting

Preheat oven to 375°F.

Prepare pastry as directed. Roll out half the dough as thinly as possible into a large rectangle (about 8 × 15 inches).

SLICER: Cut apples to fit feed tube. Slice, using light pressure. Transfer to a bowl. Add sugar, flour, cinnamon, raisins or cranberries and walnuts (if using). Mix well.

Sprinkle dough with 1 Tbsp bread crumbs. Spread half the filling over dough to within 1 inch of edges. Roll up, turning in ends. Place seam side down on parchment-lined baking sheet. Repeat with remaining dough, crumbs and filling.

Bake for 35 to 45 minutes, until golden. When cool, dust with icing sugar.

305 calories per serving, 38.1 g carbohydrates, 2.1 g fiber, 3 g protein, 16.8 g fat (10.5 g saturated fat), 44 g cholesterol, 127 mg sodium, 170 mg potassium, 1 mg iron, 32 mg calcium, 46 mg phosphorus

### lighter variation

Instead of Sour Cream Pastry, use 3 sheets of phyllo dough for each strudel (you need 6 sheets in total). Brush each sheet of dough lightly with 1 to 2 tsp oil and place 1 on top of the other. Prepare filling. Sprinkle 2 Tbsp crumbs over top layer of dough. Top with filling. Roll up and place seam side down on foil. Repeat with remaining phyllo dough, crumbs and filling. Reduce baking time slightly. One serving contains 152 calories, 31.2 g carbohydrates and 3.2 g fat.

# BERRY HAND PIES

Thanks to food writer Melissa Trainer of Seattle for sharing her terrific slice-and-roll technique for these portable pies— It's a wonderful way to teach children how to roll out dough. Berry delicious!

Yield: 1 dozen.

Freezes well.

**double recipe of Cream Cheese Pastry (page 472) or Flaky Ginger Ale Pastry (page 471)**

**2 cups blueberries, fresh or frozen**

**2 cups strawberries, hulled and halved**

**⅔ cup sugar**

**1 tsp lemon zest**

**2 Tbsp cornstarch**

**2 Tbsp orange juice or water**

**1 egg, lightly beaten**

**cinnamon sugar for sprinkling**

Prepare pastry as directed. Form into a log about 8 inches long, wrap well and chill.

In a medium saucepan, combine berries with sugar and lemon zest. Cook over medium heat, stirring occasionally, until mixture comes to a boil. Dissolve cornstarch in orange juice or water; stir into berry mixture. Continue cooking until juices have thickened, about 1 minute. Remove from heat and cool to room temperature.

Preheat oven to 375°F. Line baking pan(s) with parchment paper.

Put pastry log on a lightly floured surface. With a sharp knife, slice a ¾-inch disc and roll it into a 5-inch circle. Place a dollop of berry filling slightly off center on dough—don't overfill. Fold dough over filling, crimping edges to seal well. Place on baking sheet. Repeat with remaining dough and filling. Cut vents in top of pastry with a sharp knife to allow steam to escape. Brush with beaten egg and sprinkle with cinnamon sugar.

Bake about 25 minutes, or until pastry is golden brown and juices are bubbling. Serve at room temperature.

185 calories each, 23.6 g carbohydrates, 1.4 g fiber, 3 g protein, 9.7 g fat (5.9 g saturated fat), 42 g cholesterol, 105 mg sodium, 82 mg potassium, 1 mg iron, 42 mg calcium, 30 mg phosphorus

## chef's tips

- Use whatever fruits are in season (e.g., rhubarb, apples, peaches). Filling must be cooked first or the crust will get soggy. Don't overfill hand pies or they may burst.

- Cool completely before serving or you may end up wearing the filling instead of eating it!

- Unbaked hand pies can be frozen after assembling. When needed, bake them from frozen, adding 5 minutes to baking time.

- For savory hand pies, fill with Potato Filling (page 256) or Spinach Borekas filling (page 154). If using Chicken or Meat Filling (page 257), use Flaky Ginger Ale Pastry, which is dairy-free.

# RUBY-RED RHUBARB PIE

Rhubarb roots and leaves are poisonous, so be sure to trim the stalks carefully and wash them well.

Yield: 8 servings. Freezes well.

Standard Butter Pastry (page 470) or any pastry for a 2-crust pie

2 Tbsp bread crumbs

8 stalks rhubarb, peeled and trimmed (4 cups sliced)

1¼ cups sugar (or to taste)

⅓ cup flour

1 Tbsp butter or margarine

Preheat oven to 425°F.

Prepare pastry and chill as directed. Roll out 1 portion into a large circle and transfer to ungreased 9-inch pie plate. Trim off overhanging edges. Sprinkle with bread crumbs.

SLICER: Cut rhubarb to fit feed tube. Slice, using firm pressure. Measure 4 cups. Mix with sugar and flour. Fill pastry shell with rhubarb filling; dot with butter or margarine. Roll out remaining pastry and place over filling. Trim away edges, leaving ½-inch border all around. Tuck top crust under bottom crust. Flute edges. Cut several slits in crust and sprinkle lightly with sugar.

Bake for 40 to 50 minutes, until golden.

445 calories per serving, 63.3 g carbohydrates, 2.2 g fiber, 5 g protein, 19.9 g fat (9.9 g saturated fat), 34 g cholesterol, 253 mg sodium, 223 mg potassium, 2 mg iron, 65 mg calcium, 55 mg phosphorus

## variations

- Substitute 2 to 3 cups sliced strawberries for half the rhubarb. One serving contains 452 calories and 65.1 g carbohydrates.

- Replace rhubarb with 4 cups pitted cherries. If using drained canned cherries, baking time will be 35 to 45 minutes. One serving contains 481 calories and 72.9 g carbohydrates.

# FRESH STRAWBERRY FLAN

Very berry good!

Yield: 8 servings. Best served the same day. Do not freeze.

Standard Butter Pastry, ½ recipe (page 470)

Crème Pâtissière (page 488) or 1 pkg (4-serving size) vanilla pudding (not instant)

½ cup red currant jelly or apricot jam

1 pint strawberries, hulled and cut in half lengthwise

Preheat oven to 400°F.

Prepare pastry as directed. Roll out chilled pastry on floured pastry cloth into 12-inch circle. Transfer to 11-inch flan pan with removable bottom. Roll the rolling pin over edges of pan to cut away excess dough. Line pastry with aluminum foil; fill with uncooked rice or beans to weigh down pastry. *Continued*

Bake for 10 minutes. Remove foil and rice or beans. Bake 5 minutes longer, until golden. Cool completely.

Prepare Crème Pâtissière or pudding according to directions. Place a piece of waxed paper directly on surface to prevent skin from forming; cool completely. (May be prepared in advance up to this point.)

Heat jelly or jam on low heat until melted (or microwave on High for 45 seconds). Brush bottom of pie shell lightly with jelly. Allow to set for 5 minutes, then add Crème Pâtissière. Do not fill more than ½ inch thick. Arrange berries attractively overtop. Brush with remaining jelly. (If using apricot jam, first press it through a sieve.) Refrigerate flan for 2 to 3 hours before serving.

292 calories per serving, 39.8 g carbohydrates, 1.3 g fiber, 4 g protein, 12.9 g fat (6.2 g saturated fat), 100 g cholesterol, 141 mg sodium, 134 mg potassium, 1 mg iron, 56 mg calcium, 92 mg phosphorus

### variations

- Use a colorful combination of fresh or canned fruits arranged in an attractive design (e.g., sliced kiwis, apricots, seedless grapes, berries, mandarin oranges). If using canned fruits, drain well and pat dry.

- Instead of Crème Pâtissière, process 1 cup light cream cheese or Yogurt Cheese (page 391), 2 Tbsp 1% milk, 2 Tbsp sugar and 1 tsp vanilla extract on the STEEL BLADE until smooth, about 15 seconds. One slice of flan contains 266 calories, 32.9 g carbohydrates and 13.2 g fat.

## PUMPKIN PIE

A Thanksgiving tradition that's good any time of year! If using fresh pumpkin purée, drain it well.

Yield: 8 servings. Can be frozen for up to 1 month.

Standard Butter Pastry, ½ recipe (page 470)
1½ cups canned or fresh Pumpkin Purée (page 101)
¾ cup brown sugar, packed
2 eggs
1¼ tsp ground cinnamon

½ tsp ground ginger
¼ tsp each nutmeg and ground cloves
dash salt
1¼ cups whipping cream
¼ cup orange liqueur
8 pecan halves, for garnish

Preheat oven to 425°F.

Prepare pastry as directed. Roll out chilled dough on floured pastry cloth about 2 inches larger than pie plate. Carefully transfer to deep 9-inch pie plate. Trim off overhanging edges, leaving about ½ inch excess. Turn edges under and make a decorative fluted edge.

STEEL BLADE: Process pumpkin, brown sugar, eggs, spices and salt for 30 seconds, until blended. Scrape down sides of bowl as necessary. Pour whipping cream and liqueur through feed tube while machine is running; process a few seconds longer to blend. Pour filling into unbaked pie shell.

Bake for 15 minutes, then reduce heat to 325°F and bake 40 to 45 minutes longer. When done, knife inserted into center of pie will come out clean.

Place pecans in a circular design around edge of warm pie and press lightly into filling.

413 calories per serving, 40.4 g carbohydrates, 1.3 g fiber, 5 g protein, 25.5 g fat (13.7 g saturated fat), 120 g cholesterol, 151 mg sodium, 209 mg potassium, 1 mg iron, 65 mg calcium, 83 mg phosphorus

### pareve (nondairy) variation

Use Pareve Pie Crust (page 470). Replace whipping cream with nondairy creamer. One serving contains 388 calories, 41.4 g carbohydrates and 22.4 g fat.

## PECAN PIE

*They'll go nuts over this! This is extremely rich, so eat a sliver, not a slice.*

*Yield: 10 servings. Freezes well.*

**Standard Butter Pastry, ½ recipe (page 470)**
**1 cup sugar**
**4 eggs**
**1 cup dark corn syrup**
**1 tsp pure vanilla or rum extract**
**½ tsp salt**
**1½ cups pecans**

Preheat oven to 350°F.

Prepare and chill pastry as directed. Roll out on floured surface about 2 inches larger than pie plate. Carefully transfer to deep ungreased 9-inch pie plate. Trim off overhanging edges, leaving about ½ inch excess. Turn edges under and make a decorative fluted edge.

STEEL BLADE: Process sugar, eggs, corn syrup, vanilla or rum extract and salt for 8 to 10 seconds, until blended. Add pecans and mix in with 1 or 2 very quick on/off pulses. Pour filling into pie shell.

Bake for 55 to 60 minutes, or until knife inserted in center of pie comes out clean.

424 calories per serving, 57.1 g carbohydrates, 1.9 g fiber, 5 g protein, 21.2 g fat (5.2 g saturated fat), 97 g cholesterol, 282 mg sodium, 122 mg potassium, 1 mg iron, 31 mg calcium, 98 mg phosphorus

### chef's tip

- To catch spillovers, place a foil-lined cookie sheet under the pie before baking it.

# CHOC' FULL OF PECAN PIE

Easy as pie.

Yield: 10 servings.

Freezes well.

**Standard Butter Pastry, ½ recipe (page 470)**

**2 squares (2 oz/60 g) unsweetened chocolate**

**2 Tbsp butter or margarine**

**1½ cups pecans**

**3 eggs**

**1¼ cups sugar**

Preheat oven to 375°F.

Prepare and chill pastry as directed. Roll out on floured surface about 2 inches larger than pie plate. Carefully transfer to ungreased 9-inch pie plate. Trim off overhanging edges, leaving about ½ inch excess. Turn edges under and make a decorative fluted edge.

Melt chocolate and butter or margarine (2 to 3 minutes on Medium [50%] in the microwave). Let cool.

STEEL BLADE: Process pecans with 5 or 6 quick on/off pulses, until coarsely chopped. Empty bowl and set aside. Process eggs and sugar for 5 seconds. Add melted chocolate mixture and process 8 to 10 seconds longer, until blended. Add nuts with 1 or 2 very quick on/off pulses. Pour mixture into unbaked pie shell.

Bake for 35 to 45 minutes, just until set. Pie will firm up when cooled.

391 calories per serving, 38.9 g carbohydrates, 2.8 g fiber, 6 g protein, 25.9 g fat (8.4 g saturated fat), 82 g cholesterol, 186 mg sodium, 149 mg potassium, 2 mg iron, 29 mg calcium, 109 mg phosphorus

# MINIATURE PECAN TARTS

No need to roll out the dough for these luscious tarts.

Yield: 2 dozen.

Freezes well.

**Cream Cheese Pastry (page 472)**

**¾ cup pecans**

**1 egg**

**¾ cup brown sugar, packed**

**1 Tbsp butter or margarine**

**1 tsp pure vanilla extract**

Preheat oven to 350°F.

Prepare dough as directed. Divide into 24 equal pieces. Press into the bottom and up the sides of miniature muffin pans.

STEEL BLADE: Process pecans with quick on/off pulses, until coarsely chopped. Empty bowl and set aside. Process egg with brown sugar, butter or margarine and vanilla extract until well blended, about 1 minute.

Divide half the pecans among the tart shells. Fill three-quarters full with batter. Top with remaining pecans. Bake for 18 to 20 minutes, until set. Cool slightly. Loosen with a flexible spatula and carefully remove from pans.

117 calories each, 11.5 g carbohydrates, 0.4 g fiber, 2 g protein, 7.5 g fat (3.4 g saturated fat), 23 g cholesterol, 58 mg sodium, 32 mg potassium, 0 mg iron, 26 mg calcium, 19 mg phosphorus

# BUTTER TARTS

*Gooey and good!*

*Yield: 2 dozen tarts.*

*Freezes well.*

**Sour Cream Pastry (page 473)**
**½ cup butter, cut in chunks**
**1½ cups brown sugar, lightly packed**
**2 eggs**

**1 Tbsp lemon juice**
**½ tsp pure vanilla extract**
**½ cup raisins**

Preheat oven to 375°F.

Prepare dough as directed. Roll out and cut into 24 circles. Fit into ungreased muffin cups.

STEEL BLADE: Process butter with brown sugar and eggs for 1 minute, scraping down sides of bowl once or twice. Mixture should be well creamed. Add lemon juice and vanilla extract and process a few seconds longer. Divide raisins evenly among tart shells. Fill about three-quarters full with creamed mixture.

Bake until golden, 18 to 20 minutes. Let stand for 2 minutes. Loosen tarts from pan with a flexible metal spatula. Cool completely.

206 calories each, 22.4 g carbohydrates, 0.4 g fiber, 2 g protein, 12.6 g fat (7.8 g saturated fat), 50 g cholesterol, 96 mg sodium, 72 mg potassium, 1 mg iron, 26 mg calcium, 26 mg phosphorus

# LEMON MERINGUE PIE

*The processor makes superfine sugar, which helps prevent the meringue from weeping. It also does a great job of grinding the lemon rind.*

*Yield: 8 servings.*

*Do not freeze.*

**Standard Butter Pastry, ½ recipe**
 **(page 470), or a baked Graham**
 **Wafer Crust (page 473)**
**6 Tbsp sugar (for meringue)**
**2 lemons, well-scrubbed**
**1 cup additional sugar**
**3 Tbsp flour**

**3 Tbsp cornstarch**
**dash salt**
**1½ cups boiling water**
**3 egg yolks**
**1 Tbsp butter or margarine**
**3 egg whites**
**¼ tsp cream of tartar**

Prepare and chill pastry as directed. Roll out on floured surface about 2 inches larger than pie plate. Carefully transfer to ungreased 9-inch pie plate. Trim off overhanging edges, leaving about ½ inch excess. Turn edges under and make a decorative fluted edge. Prick bottom of pastry all over with a fork. Chill for ½ hour. Bake in preheated 400°F oven for 10 minutes, until golden. Cool completely. Reduce oven to 350°F.

STEEL BLADE: Process 6 Tbsp sugar until fine, about 1 to 2 minutes. Remove from bowl and reserve for meringue.

Peel the lemon rind, being careful not to include any of the bitter white pith. Squeeze lemons and measure ⅓ cup juice; set aside. *Continued*

Process lemon rind with 1 cup sugar, starting with quick on/off pulses then processing about 30 seconds, until fine. Combine with flour, cornstarch and salt in 8-cup microwavable bowl. Slowly blend in boiling water. Microwave on High for 3 to 4 minutes, until thickened and boiling, stirring twice.

Process egg yolks with reserved lemon juice for 5 seconds. Add half of hot mixture and process for 10 seconds. Whisk egg yolk mixture back into remaining hot mixture. Microwave on High 1 to 2 minutes longer, until boiling and thickened, stirring once or twice. Stir in butter or margarine. Pour hot filling into pie shell.

Using an electric mixer, beat egg whites with cream of tartar until foamy. Slowly beat in the reserved 6 Tbsp sugar a little at a time. Beat until stiff and shiny. Pile meringue onto hot pie filling. Seal meringue onto edge of crust to prevent it from shrinking.

Bake for 8 to 10 minutes, until golden. Cool away from drafts.

337 calories per serving, 52.8 g carbohydrates, 0.6 g fiber, 4 g protein, 12.6 g fat (6 g saturated fat), 99 g cholesterol, 169 mg sodium, 75 mg potassium, 1 mg iron, 18 mg calcium, 56 mg phosphorus

## KEY LIME PIE

This should be made with the small, tart key limes from the Florida Keys, but you can substitute bottled or fresh juice from regular limes if necessary.

Yield: 8 servings. Delicious frozen!

Graham Wafer Crust (page 473)
1 can (14 oz/398 mL) sweetened condensed milk (or make your own—see page 127)

4 egg yolks
½ cup key lime juice

Preheat oven to 350°F. Prepare crust and press firmly into bottom and up sides of sprayed 9-inch glass pie dish.

STEEL BLADE: Process condensed milk with egg yolks and lime juice until smooth and blended, 25 to 30 seconds, scraping down sides of bowl as needed. Pour filling carefully into unbaked crust.

Bake for 15 minutes, until set. Cool completely. Refrigerate or freeze.

329 calories per serving, 45.2 g carbohydrates, 0.5 g fiber, 7 g protein, 14.2 g fat (7.4 g saturated fat), 139 g cholesterol, 203 mg sodium, 233 mg potassium, 1 mg iron, 160 mg calcium, 186 mg phosphorus

# CHOCOLATE CREAM PIE

This is delicious and so easy. Chocoholics will love it.

Yield: 8 servings.

Do not freeze.

Cookie Crumb Crust (page 474)

½ cup sugar

¼ cup unsweetened cocoa powder

3 Tbsp cornstarch

⅛ tsp salt

2 cups milk (1%)

½ cup chocolate chips

1 tsp pure vanilla extract or 1 Tbsp almond or chocolate liqueur

½ cup sweetened whipped cream

grated chocolate, for garnish

Prepare crust as directed, using 1½ cups chocolate wafer crumbs. Either bake at 375°F for 7 to 8 minutes, or microwave on High for 2 minutes, or until set. Let cool.

Combine sugar, cocoa, cornstarch and salt in 8-cup microwavable bowl. Gradually whisk in milk. Microwave on High for 6 to 7 minutes, stirring every 2 minutes, until boiling and thickened. Add chocolate chips and flavoring; stir until melted.

Pour mixture into pie shell. Chill thoroughly. Garnish with whipped cream rosettes and grated chocolate.

330 calories per serving, 46.8 g carbohydrates, 2.3 g fiber, 5 g protein, 15.6 g fat (8.7 g saturated fat), 29 g cholesterol, 231 mg sodium, 223 mg potassium, 2 mg iron, 93 mg calcium, 126 mg phosphorus

### chocolate pudding

Omit crust. Prepare filling, but omit chocolate chips. Pour into 4 dessert dishes and refrigerate. One serving contains 187 calories, 40 g carbohydrates and 1.9 g fat.

# CHOCOLATE MARSHMALLOW PIE

When frozen, this tastes like ice cream pie. If refrigerated, it's more like a chiffon pie. Try it both ways!

Yield: 10 servings.

Freezes well.

Cookie Crumb Crust (page 474)

24 marshmallows (about 3 cups)

½ cup milk (1%)

2 squares (2 oz/60 g) semisweet chocolate, halved

1½ cups chilled whipping cream

2 Tbsp icing sugar

chocolate curls (page 392), for garnish

Prepare and bake crust as directed. (I like it best with chocolate wafer crumbs.) Cool completely.

Combine marshmallows, milk and chocolate in 3-quart microwavable bowl. Microwave on High for 3 to 4 minutes, until marshmallows and chocolate are melted, stirring twice. Cool to room temperature.

You can whip cream in the processor (although an electric mixer will produce a lighter texture). Insert STEEL BLADE and tip processor forward by placing a thick

*Continued*

485

book underneath base. Process whipping cream until it becomes the texture of sour cream, about 35 seconds. Add icing sugar and process about 10 seconds longer, until stiff. Measure 2 cups whipped cream and fold into chocolate mixture. Pour into crust.

Place remaining whipped cream in a pastry bag fitted with a star tube; garnish edges of pie. Garnish with chocolate curls. Refrigerate until set, about 4 hours or overnight. (Or wrap well and freeze until needed. Let frozen pie stand 5 to 10 minutes at room temperature before serving.)

354 calories per serving, 37.8 g carbohydrates, 1 g fiber, 3 g protein, 22.7 g fat (13.3 g saturated fat), 63 g cholesterol, 164 mg sodium, 110 mg potassium, 1 mg iron, 48 mg calcium, 69 mg phosphorus

## variation

For chocolate marshmallow parfaits, omit crust. Alternate layers of marshmallow mixture with chocolate wafer crumbs (about 1 cup) in 8 parfait glasses. Garnish with whipped cream. Chill 1 to 2 hours before serving. One parfait contains 275 calories, 30 g carbohydrates and 17.3 g fat.

# FUDGE RIBBON BAKED ALASKA PIE

Yield: 10 servings.

Freezes well.

Standard Butter Pastry, ½ recipe (page 470)

peppermint stick candy (⅓ to ½ cup crushed)

¾ cup sugar

½ cup evaporated milk (not condensed milk)

1 cup chocolate chips

1 tsp pure vanilla extract

1 quart/litre (4½ cups) vanilla ice cream, slightly softened

3 egg whites

¼ tsp cream of tartar

6 Tbsp sugar (see Chef's Tips, page 487)

Prepare and chill pastry as directed. Roll out on floured surface about 2 inches larger than pie plate. Carefully transfer to ungreased 9-inch pie plate. Trim off overhanging edges, leaving about ½ inch excess. Turn edges under and make a decorative fluted edge. Prick bottom of pastry all over with a fork. Chill for half an hour. Preheat oven to 400°F. Bake crust for 10 minutes, until golden. Cool completely.

STEEL BLADE: Drop peppermint stick candy through feed tube while machine is running. Process until crushed. Set aside.

Combine the ¾ cup sugar and evaporated milk in saucepan. Simmer until sugar is dissolved, stirring occasionally.

Process chocolate chips until finely chopped, about 30 seconds. Pour hot milk mixture and vanilla extract through feed tube while machine is running;

process until chocolate is melted and mixture is blended. Cool chocolate sauce completely.

Reserve 2 Tbsp candy for garnish and stir remainder into ice cream. Press half of ice cream into pie shell. Cover with half of cooled chocolate sauce. Repeat with remaining ice cream and sauce. Wrap well and freeze until firm.

Preheat oven to 475°F about 15 minutes before serving. Using an electric mixer, beat egg whites with cream of tartar until soft peaks form. Gradually beat in the 6 Tbsp sugar. Continue beating until whites are stiff and no sugar can be felt when you rub the meringue between your fingertips. Spread meringue over frozen filling, sealing edges well. Swirl meringue to make decorative peaks. Place on baking sheet and bake for 3 to 5 minutes, until golden. Sprinkle reserved candy over meringue. Serve immediately.

466 calories per serving, 68.0 g carbohydrates, 1.7 g fiber, 6 g protein, 18.9 g fat (10.7 g saturated fat), 39 g cholesterol, 164 mg sodium, 247 mg potassium, 1 mg iron, 109 mg calcium, 118 mg phosphorus

### variation

Omit peppermint candy. Substitute your favorite flavor of ice cream or frozen yogurt.

### chef's tips

- To prevent meringue from weeping, process the 6 Tbsp sugar on the STEEL BLADE until fine, about 1 to 2 minutes, before beating it into the egg whites.
- Dip knife into water before cutting pie to prevent meringue from sticking to knife. Repeat as needed.

## CREAM PUFFS (CHOUX PASTRY)

Fill cream puffs with sweetened whipped cream or Crème Pâtissière (page 488) and dust the tops with icing sugar. Also delicious filled with ice cream and served with hot chocolate sauce!

**½ cup butter or tub margarine**
**1 cup water**
**1 Tbsp sugar (use ½ tsp for savory fillings)**
**½ tsp salt**
**1 cup flour**
**4 eggs**

Preheat oven to 425°F.

Combine butter or margarine, water, sugar and salt in saucepan. Bring to a boil, stirring occasionally. As soon as butter is melted, remove from heat and dump in flour all at once. Stir vigorously with a wooden spoon until mixture pulls away from sides of pan and forms a ball. Cool 5 minutes.

*Continued*

Yield: 15 medium or
30 miniature puffs.

Freezes well.

STEEL BLADE: Transfer mixture from saucepan to processor. Process for 5 seconds. Drop eggs through feed tube 1 at a time while machine is running. Process 25 to 30 seconds longer after you have added all the eggs. Mixture should be smooth and shiny.

Transfer dough to pastry bag fitted with ¼-inch or ½-inch plain tube. Pipe mounds of dough onto lightly sprayed baking sheet. (See Chef's Tip, below.) If desired, brush the cream puffs with a little beaten egg before baking.

Bake for 10 minutes, then reduce heat to 375°F and bake 20 to 25 minutes longer, depending on size. Puffs should be golden. Remove from oven and cut 1-inch slit in each puff so steam can escape. Cool completely. Pull out soft insides of each puff before filling.

109 calories each, 7.4 g carbohydrates, 0.2 g fiber, 3 g protein, 7.6 g fat (4.3 g saturated fat), 73 g cholesterol, 139 mg sodium, 28 mg potassium, 1 mg iron, 10 mg calcium, 34 mg phosphorus

### chef's tip

- If you don't have a pastry bag and plain tube, drop mixture by rounded tablespoons onto sprayed baking sheet. Or put the dough into a freezer bag, snip off a corner and pipe away!

### variations

- Puffs can be filled with sautéed vegetables, chicken or seafood, but be sure to use only ½ tsp of sugar in pastry. Miniatures are excellent as hors d'oeuvres.

- For éclairs, shape into 3-inch fingers and fill with sweetened whipped cream or Crème Pâtissière (below); frost with chocolate icing.

## CRÈME PÂTISSIÈRE (PASTRY CREAM)

Yield: About 1¼ cups.
This amount will fill
an 11-inch flan, which
serves 8 to 10. Recipe
can be doubled to fill
tart shells or cream
puffs. Freezes well.

1 cup milk (1% or 2%)

3 egg yolks

¼ cup sugar

¼ cup flour

1 Tbsp butter

1 Tbsp orange liqueur or cherry brandy (or 1 tsp pure vanilla extract)

Microwave milk in 4-cup glass measuring cup until steaming, about 2 minutes on High.

STEEL BLADE: Process egg yolks with sugar and flour until well mixed, 15 to 20 seconds.

Add hot milk through feed tube while machine is running. Process until smooth. Pour mixture back into measuring cup and microwave on High for 2 minutes, until very thick, whisking every 30 seconds to prevent lumping. Whisk in butter and liqueur or brandy. Cover surface of mixture with waxed paper or parchment to prevent skin from forming. May be prepared 3 to 4 days in advance and refrigerated until needed.

94 calories per serving, 11.9 g carbohydrates, 0.1 g fiber, 3 g protein, 3.7 g fat (1.7 g saturated fat), 85 g cholesterol, 27 mg sodium, 57 mg potassium, 0 mg iron, 46 mg calcium, 64 mg phosphorus

## variations

- Whip 1 cup whipping cream until stiff. Fold into chilled pastry cream and serve in parfait glasses. This variation is also excellent as a filling for cream pies. One serving contains 197 calories, 12.8 g carbohydrates and 14.8 g fat.

- For a quick trifle, alternate layers of sponge cake, pastry cream and fruit, sprinkling each layer with rum or liqueur.

- To make chocolate pastry cream, substitute chocolate liqueur for orange liqueur. Stir ½ cup chocolate chips into hot mixture along with butter and liqueur. Whip 1 cup whipping cream until stiff. Fold into chilled pastry cream. One serving contains 247 calories, 19.4 g carbohydrates and 18.0 g fat.

# PASSOVER
### recipe list

495 Charoset
495 Charoset Truffles
496 Knaidlach for a Crowd
496 Quick Soup Dumplings
497 Passover Cranberry Sweet
and Sour Meatballs
497 Passover Wacky Franks
498 Stuffed Shoulder Steak
Rolls
499 Stuffed Chicken Breasts
499 Mostly Vegetable Stuffing
500 Quick Matzo Meal Stuffing
500 Cheryl's Vegetable
Casserole
501 Rainbow Quinoa, Two
Ways
502 Passover Knishes
503 Farfel Apple Pudding
503 Farfel, Chicken and
Vegetable Kugel
504 Farfel Apricot Pudding
505 Passover Blintzes
506 Egg Roll Blintzes
506 Grate and Bake

507 Sweet Potato Bake
508 Passover Carrot Kugel
508 Passover Carrot Tsimmis
509 Matzo Meal Latkes
509 Passover Cheese Latkes
510 Passover Cupcake
Blintzes
510 Florentine Cupcake
Blintzes
511 Crustless Passover Tuna
Quiche
512 Salmon Mediterranean
512 Passover Lasagna
(Matzagna)
513 Passover Rolls or Bagels
514 Homemade Matzo
515 Passover Pie Crust
515 Upsy-Downsy Pie Crust or
Topping
516 Passover Apple Crumb
Pie
516 Passover Fruit Crisp
517 Passover Cheese Pie
517 Glazed Fruit Cheesecake

519 Passover Apple Cake

519 Another Passover Apple Cake

520 Passover Banana Cake

521 My Mother's Passover Cake

521 Passover Cream Puffs

522 Farfel Marshmallow Treats

523 Chocolate Matzo Bark

523 Passover Brownies

524 Fudgy Brownies

525 Passover Mud Cookies

525 Mustachudos

526 Coconut Almond Macaroons

527 Passover Mandelbroit

- During the 8 days of Passover, it is forbidden to eat *chametz*: wheat, barley, oats, rye or spelt, or any form of these grains to which a leavening agent has been added, such as their flour, or that has come into contact with water or other liquids containing water, and has been left alone for 18 minutes or longer.
- Matzo is made from special wheat flour, but it must be prepared and baked in less than 18 minutes, under special supervision. *Shmurah* matzo, which is handmade and round, is served by many families.
- Some Jews refrain from eating *gebrochts* (matzo or matzo meal combined with water or other liquids) on the first 7 days of Passover, but do eat it on the 8th day. Potato starch or ground almonds are often used as a replacement for matzo meal and cake meal.
- Ashkenazic (Eastern European) Jews will not eat *kitniyot*, which includes legumes (beans, chickpeas, lentils, peanuts, soybeans), corn, sugar snap peas, snow peas, string beans, rice, buckwheat/kasha, millet, mustard, seeds (poppy, sesame, sunflower) or soy products. Many Sephardic Jews eat legumes and rice. Fresh fruits, herbs and most vegetables are kosher for Passover.
- In addition to the recipes in this chapter, many recipes throughout this book are suitable for Passover or can be adapted easily. Other recipes include Passover variations. Use Passover ingredients manufactured under strict supervision or substitute as necessary. Sephardic and Ashkenazic Jews follow different customs. When in doubt, consult your Rabbi. Also check out www.kashrut.com/Passover for up-to-date information.
- Availability of Passover products varies from year to year.
- Refer to "Passover" in the index for a full listing of recipes.
- Replace canola oil with olive oil for cooking or vegetable oil for cooking or baking.
- To replace rice in recipes, substitute quinoa. Rinse thoroughly in a fine-mesh strainer to remove the bitter coating; drain well. Cook, covered, in double the amount of boiling water for 15 minutes. Let stand, covered, for 5 minutes, then fluff with a fork. Also excellent as a cereal for breakfast.

- Replace maple syrup with honey.
- Splenda is not certified as "kosher for Passover" as it contains *kitniyot*. There is an industrial "kosher for Passover Splenda" available to food manufacturers but it is not available to consumers. Instead of Splenda, you can use Passover sugar substitute (e.g., Gefen Sweet 'N Low) (or just use granulated sugar or brown sugar). One packet of sugar substitute is equal to 2 tsp sugar or granular Splenda. Passover sweeteners are not heat-stable.
- To replace bread crumbs, substitute an equal amount of matzo meal or ground mandlen (Passover soup nuts). Ground almonds or potato starch can be used as a coating for fish or chicken.
- To make 1 cup of matzo meal, process 2 cups matzo farfel or 3 matzos, broken up, on the **Steel Blade** until fine.
- ALMOST BREAD CRUMBS: To make 1 cup of crumbs, process 3 cups mandlen (1¾ oz package) on the **Steel Blade** until fine, 15 to 20 seconds. Use in stuffing mixtures, as a coating for chicken or fish, or as a topping for casseroles.
- Instead of using matzo meal in ground meat mixtures, process 1 medium potato on the **Steel Blade** until fine, about 10 seconds. This amount is enough to bind 2 lb of ground meat or poultry.
- Potato starch can be used to thicken gravies, sauces and puddings/kugels. Substitute 1 Tbsp potato starch for 1 Tbsp cornstarch or 2 Tbsp flour/matzo meal. Potato starch and ground almonds can be used as a coating for fish or chicken and are gluten-free.
- To replace 1 cup flour in baking, use ⅝ to ¾ cup (10 to 12 Tbsp) potato starch or cake meal (or a combination sifted together). Another option is to use ¾ cup ground almonds and ¼ cup potato starch for each cup of flour. However, some experimentation may be necessary to achieve the desired results.
- To replace 1 cup cake meal in Passover sponge cakes, use 1 cup of finely ground almonds.
- To make your own cookie crumbs, process Passover cookies (e.g., egg kichel, mandel bread, macaroons) on the **Steel Blade**. Use quick on/off pulses to start, then process until fine. Use in crumb crusts and streusel toppings.
- Replace ⅛ tsp cream of tartar with 1 tsp lemon juice.
- Replace 1 square (1 oz/30 g) of unsweetened chocolate with 1½ ounces (45 g) dark, semi-sweet or bittersweet chocolate. Reduce sugar in recipe by 2 Tbsp.
- Replace 1 cup chocolate chips with 6 ounces (175 g) dark, semisweet or bittersweet chocolate, broken up. Passover dark chocolate usually comes in 100 g packages.
- Replace 1 tsp vanilla extract with 1 Tbsp Passover liqueur. Pure vanilla extract for Passover is not available, and artificial vanilla extract is inferior in flavor, although I do use it occasionally.
- TO MAKE VANILLA SUGAR, bury vanilla beans in granulated sugar, using 1 bean per lb. Store in an airtight container for a week, then remove the bean. (It can be reused for up to 6 months.) Use vanilla sugar in recipes instead of granulated sugar and vanilla extract. Packaged vanilla sugar is also available.
- PASSOVER ICING SUGAR: Process 1 cup granulated sugar with ½ Tbsp potato starch on the **Steel Blade** for 2 to 3 minutes, until pulverized. (Texture will be grainier than icing sugar.) Makes 1 cup icing sugar.
- Passover baking powder and baking soda are now available. Passover versions contain potato starch whereas regular baking powder and baking soda contain cornstarch.

- Do not use your processor to make Passover sponge cakes. An electric mixer is superior for whipping egg whites.
- Lighter Butter or Margarine (page 39) makes a great spread for matzo, or use it as a topping for veggies. It has half the calories and fat! Do not use it for baking.
- Prune Purée (page 346) is fat-free, high in fiber and makes a delicious spread for matzo. Use it to replace up to half the fat in your favorite Passover brownies.
- QUICK MATZO PIZZA: Spread matzo with 2 to 3 Tbsp tomato sauce. Sprinkle with ¼ cup grated mozzarella cheese, chopped mushrooms and bell peppers. Microwave on Medium (50%) for 2 to 2½ minutes, until cheese melts. For miniatures, use matzo crackers. An easy lunch or snack for the kids!
- Make your own Horseradish (page 110) a few weeks in advance and refrigerate it in tightly sealed jars. It lasts for months!

- Recycle those leftovers! Grind cooked chicken, turkey or brisket on the **Steel Blade** and use in Passover Blintzes (page 505) or Passover Knishes (page 502). Leftover meat or poultry can be thinly sliced and used in a stir-fry or kugel. Try the Passover variation of Mandarin Chicken Meatballs (page 194).
- Refrigerate leftover wine, or freeze it in ice cube trays, then store the cubes in freezer bags. Wine adds flavor to meats, poultry, gravies and sauces.
- Extra bowls and blades are available on some processor models. Check with your manufacturer for availability. Many people purchase an inexpensive food processor just for Passover use.
- NESTED WORK BOWLS: If your machine comes with nested bowls, choose the appropriate bowl and blade or disc for the task. For recipes that require multiple bowls, begin with the smallest one to minimize cleanups.

## CHAROSET

Charoset is a sweet mixture of fruits, nuts and spices served at Passover Seders all over the world. Different communities and families have their own special recipes.

Yield: About 2½ cups. Refrigerate mixture until serving time. Do not freeze.

½ cup walnuts

3 large apples, peeled, cored and cut in chunks

2 or 3 Tbsp sugar or honey

1 tsp ground cinnamon

⅓ cup sweet red wine

⅛ tsp ground ginger (optional)

STEEL BLADE: Process nuts for 6 to 8 seconds, until coarsely chopped. Empty bowl. Process apples until minced, about 10 seconds. Add remaining ingredients, including nuts. Process with quick on/offs, just until mixed. Do not overprocess.

20 calories per Tbsp, 2.4 g carbohydrates, 0.3 g fiber, 0 g protein, 1.1 g fat (0.1 g saturated fat), 0 g cholesterol, 0 mg sodium, 20 mg potassium, 0 mg iron, 3 mg calcium, 7 mg phosphorus

### chef's tips

If anyone has nut allergies, substitute Passover Cheerios-style cereal or Passover soup nuts (mandlen), or just omit the nuts. Leftover charoset makes a delicious topping for baked apples or a tasty spread on matzo.

## CHAROSET TRUFFLES

My daughter-in-law Ariane's mother, Matla Cohen, makes charoset the Sephardic way and rolls the mixture into tiny balls. Our grandson Sam loves these as a healthy treat.

Yield: 2½ to 3 dozen (10 to 12 servings), depending on size. Freezes well.

½ cup almonds (optional)

2 cups pitted dates

1 tsp ground cinnamon

1 to 2 Tbsp sweet red wine or grape juice (approximately)

¼ cup Cinnamon-Sugar Mixture (page 324), for coating

STEEL BLADE: Process nuts (if using) with 6 to 8 quick on/off pulses, until chopped. Remove from bowl. Check that dates don't contain any pits. Process with on/off pulses to start, then process until smooth, 25 to 30 seconds. Add cinnamon and 1 Tbsp wine. Process until blended, scraping down sides of bowl as needed. If mixture seems dry, add a few more drops of wine. Mix in nuts with 2 or 3 quick on/off pulses.

Sprinkle cinnamon sugar on foil. Drop mixture by small spoonfuls onto foil, roll into small balls and coat with Cinnamon Sugar. To blend flavors, refrigerate several hours or overnight before serving. Serve in foil or paper candy cups.

40 calories per serving, 10.4 g carbohydrates, 0.9 g fiber, 0 g protein, 0 g fat (0 g saturated fat), 0 g cholesterol, 0 mg sodium, 71 mg potassium, 0 mg iron, 8 mg calcium, 0 mg phosphorus

## KNAIDLACH FOR A CROWD

If you don't need such a large quantity, make Matzo Balls (page 88).

**3¼ cups matzo meal**

**1½ tsp salt**

**¼ tsp freshly ground black pepper**

**9 or 10 large eggs (measure 2 cups eggs)**

**1 cup oil**

**1 cup water (or ½ cup water and ½ cup club soda)**

Yield: About 2½ dozen. To freeze, add matzo balls to chicken soup and freeze in freezer-safe containers, leaving 2 inches at the top for expansion.

STEEL BLADE: Place matzo meal, salt and pepper in processor. Add eggs and process for 10 to 15 seconds. Pour oil and water through feed tube while machine is running. Process for 20 to 30 seconds, until fairly smooth. Mixture will be quite loose.

Transfer to large bowl and refrigerate for at least 4 hours or overnight. Mixture will thicken.

Fill 2 large soup pots half full with water. Add ½ tsp salt to each pot. Bring to a boil. Wet your hands and shape mixture into 2-inch balls. Drop into boiling liquid. Cover partially and simmer for 45 to 55 minutes, until light, puffed and cooked through.

139 calories each, 11.9 g carbohydrates, 0.4 g fiber, 3 g protein, 9.2 g fat (1 g saturated fat), 64 g cholesterol, 136 mg sodium, 19 mg potassium, 0 mg iron, 8 mg calcium, 26 mg phosphorus

### matzo balls lyonnaise

Slice leftover matzo balls ½-inch thick. Sauté 1 or 2 sliced onions in a little oil until golden. Add matzo balls, sprinkle with salt, pepper and paprika. Brown on both sides until golden. (Also delicious if you add mushrooms.)

## QUICK SOUP DUMPLINGS

These are an easy alternative to matzo balls. Kids love these!

**2 eggs**

**⅔ cup matzo meal**

**½ tsp salt**

**dash freshly ground black pepper**

**½ cup water**

Yield: 8 to 10 servings. Do not freeze.

STEEL BLADE: Process all ingredients until smooth, about 10 seconds. Drop from a teaspoon into simmering soup. Cover and cook for 4 to 5 minutes.

58 calories per serving, 9.1 g carbohydrates, 0.3 g fiber, 3 g protein, 1.4 g fat (0.4 g saturated fat), 53 g cholesterol, 162 mg sodium, 16 mg potassium, 0 mg iron, 7 mg calcium, 22 mg phosphorus

# PASSOVER CRANBERRY SWEET AND SOUR MEATBALLS

Yield: 12 servings as an appetizer or 6 as a main course. Keeps 2 days in the refrigerator. Reheats and/or freezes well.

2 lb (1 kg) extra-lean ground beef, veal or chicken (or see Grind Your Own, page 36)

2 cloves garlic

1 egg (or 2 egg whites)

½ tsp salt (or to taste)

¼ tsp freshly ground black pepper

½ tsp dried basil

¼ cup matzo meal (or 1 small grated potato)

2 cans (14 oz/398 mL each) cranberry sauce

½ tsp ground cinnamon

2 cups tomato sauce (or 2 cans [10 oz/285 mL each] tomato-mushroom sauce)

STEEL BLADE: Place meat in large mixing bowl. Drop garlic through feed tube while machine is running; process until minced. Add egg, salt, pepper and basil; process a few seconds. Mix into meat along with matzo meal or grated potato. (Potato can be grated on the STEEL BLADE.)

Place cranberry sauce and cinnamon in processor. Add tomato sauce through feed tube while machine is running. Process for 10 to 15 seconds. To avoid leakage from bottom of bowl, immediately remove bowl and blade from base of machine. Pour sauce into large pot and heat to simmering.

Form meat mixture into tiny meatballs, wetting your hands for easier handling. Drop meatballs into simmering sauce. Cover and simmer about 1½ hours.

269 calories per serving (appetizer), 36.2 g carbohydrates, 1.6 g fiber, 17 g protein, 6.4 g fat (2.5 g saturated fat), 59 g cholesterol, 388 mg sodium, 386 mg potassium, 2 mg iron, 18 mg calcium, 153 mg phosphorus

# PASSOVER WACKY FRANKS

Hot dog and bun, all baked in one!

Yield: 12 servings. Keeps 2 days in the refrigerator. Reheats and/or freezes well.

½ cup oil

1 cup water

2 cups matzo or cake meal

1 Tbsp sugar

½ to 1 tsp salt (to taste)

4 eggs

12 hot dogs, frozen (beef, chicken or veal)

12 wooden skewers

Preheat oven to 375°F.

Combine oil and water in saucepan and bring to a boil. Add matzo or cake meal, sugar and salt and mix well, until mixture pulls away from sides of pan. Transfer mixture into processor bowl.

STEEL BLADE: Process mixture for 5 seconds. Add eggs 1 at a time through feed tube while machine is running. Process 30 to 40 seconds longer, until smooth.

*Continued*

Mold mixture around frozen hot dogs, oiling hands slightly for easier handling. Place on sprayed foil-lined baking sheet. Bake for 50 minutes. Remove from oven and insert wooden skewers.

336 calories each, 20.3 g carbohydrates, 0.7 g fiber, 9 g protein, 24.9 g fat (6.8 g saturated fat), 96 g cholesterol, 581 mg sodium, 80 mg potassium, 1 mg iron, 14 mg calcium, 92 mg phosphorus

# STUFFED SHOULDER STEAK ROLLS

Yield: 4 servings. Keeps 2 days in the refrigerator. Reheats and/or freezes well.

STUFFING

2 medium onions, quartered
1 Tbsp oil
1 cup mushrooms
1 stalk celery, cut in chunks
1 large carrot, cut in chunks
1 cup matzo meal
2 eggs (or 1 egg plus 2 egg whites)
2 Tbsp water
¾ tsp salt
dash freshly ground black pepper

MEAT ROLLS

4 shoulder steaks, ¼ inch thick
  (2 lb/1 kg)
salt, freshly ground black pepper and
  paprika to taste
¼ cup potato starch
2 to 3 Tbsp oil
¾ cup red wine (part chicken broth
  may be used)

Preheat oven to 350°F.

For stuffing: Coarsely chop onions on the STEEL BLADE, using quick on/off pulses. Heat oil in large nonstick skillet on medium heat. Add onions and sauté for 5 minutes. Process mushrooms with 3 or 4 quick on/offs. Add to onions and sauté 2 to 3 minutes longer. Process celery and carrot until fine, 8 to 10 seconds. Add matzo meal, eggs, water, salt, pepper and sautéed vegetables to processor. Process with on/off pulses, just until mixed.

For meat rolls: Trim excess fat from meat. Pound to flatten slightly. Sprinkle lightly on both sides with salt, pepper and paprika. Spread stuffing evenly over meat to within ¼ inch of edges. Roll up like a jelly roll. Coat meat on all sides with potato starch. (Note: If you are very careful, it is not necessary to tie the meat rolls.)

Heat oil in large nonstick skillet on medium-high heat. Add meat rolls and brown on all sides. Remove to ovenproof casserole. Add wine to skillet and, using a wooden spoon, scrape up any browned bits sticking to the pan. Cook mixture until it is reduced to about half; pour over meat rolls. (May be prepared in advance up to this point.)

Cover and bake for 1½ to 2 hours, until tender.

639 calories per serving, 43.2 g carbohydrates, 2.4 g fiber, 49 g protein, 26.4 g fat (6.6 g saturated fat), 291 g cholesterol, 597 mg sodium, 680 mg potassium, 3 mg iron, 70 mg calcium, 415 mg phosphorus

# STUFFED CHICKEN BREASTS

This festive dish
is sure to impress
your Passover
guests—and they
won't feel stuffed!

Yield: 8 servings. Keeps
2 days in the refrigerator.
Doubles easily. Reheats
and/or freezes well.

Mostly Vegetable Stuffing
(below)
8 single boneless, skinless chicken
breasts
salt and pepper to taste
dried basil and thyme to taste

MARINADE

2 cloves garlic
¼ cup fresh parsley
2 Tbsp fresh basil (or 1 tsp dried)
¼ cup balsamic vinegar
2 Tbsp olive oil
2 Tbsp honey
paprika to taste

Prepare stuffing as directed, substituting thyme for oregano.

Rinse chicken and pat dry. Trim excess fat. Cut horizontally through the middle of each breast, leaving it hinged on 1 side so that it opens flat like a book. Sprinkle lightly with salt, pepper, basil and thyme. Spread ¼ cup of stuffing on 1 side, then fold the other side over to cover stuffing. Place chicken in a single layer in a sprayed 9- × 13-inch baking dish.

STEEL BLADE: Drop garlic through feed tube while machine is running; process until minced. Add parsley, basil, vinegar, oil and honey; process 12 to 15 seconds. Drizzle marinade over chicken and sprinkle with paprika. Marinate for 1 hour (or cover and refrigerate up to 24 hours, basting occasionally).

Roast, uncovered, in preheated 375°F oven for 35 to 40 minutes, basting occasionally with marinade. Juices should run clear when pierced with a fork.

294 calories per serving, 24.1 g carbohydrates, 1.7 g fiber, 31 g protein, 8.1 g fat (1.8 g saturated fat), 126 g cholesterol, 312 mg sodium, 377 mg potassium, 2 mg iron, 39 mg calcium, 241 mg phosphorus

# MOSTLY VEGETABLE STUFFING

A delicious way to
increase your intake
of vegetables.

Yield: For a 10 to 12 lb
(4.5 to 5.5 kg) turkey,
a large veal brisket or
2 chickens (8 servings).
Keeps 2 days in the
refrigerator. Freezes well.

2 medium onions
2 large or 3 medium carrots
1 medium zucchini, unpeeled
2 eggs (or 1 egg plus 2 egg whites)
1 cup matzo meal

¾ tsp salt
freshly ground black pepper to taste
½ tsp each dried oregano and paprika
¼ tsp dried basil

GRATER: Cut vegetables to fit feed tube. Grate, using medium pressure. Push vegetables to 1 side with a rubber spatula. Insert STEEL BLADE in processor bowl, pushing blade all the way down. Add remaining ingredients and process just until mixed, 8 to 10 seconds.

96 calories per serving, 18.2 g carbohydrates, 1.7 g fiber, 4 g protein, 1.6 g fat (0.4 g saturated fat), 53 g cholesterol, 246 mg sodium, 141 mg potassium, 1 mg iron, 21 mg calcium, 42 mg phosphorus

## QUICK MATZO MEAL STUFFING

The processor mixes up this stuffing in no time!

Yield: Enough stuffing for a large veal brisket or capon (8 servings). Double the recipe to stuff a 10 to 12 lb (4.5 to 5.5 kg) turkey. Keeps 2 days in the refrigerator. See Chef's Tips (below) for freezing information.

| | |
|---|---|
| 2 Tbsp fresh dill and/or fresh parsley | 1¾ cups matzo meal |
| 1 or 2 cloves garlic (or ¼ tsp garlic powder) | 2 eggs (or 1 egg plus 2 egg whites) |
| 1 medium onion, quartered | ⅔ cup chicken broth or water |
| 1 stalk celery, cut in chunks | 2 Tbsp oil |
| 1 large or 2 medium carrots, cut in chunks | salt and freshly ground black pepper to taste |

STEEL BLADE: Process dill and/or parsley, garlic, onion, celery and carrot until minced, 10 to 12 seconds. Add remaining ingredients and process until well mixed. Scrape down sides of bowl as needed.

165 calories per serving, 26.3 g carbohydrates, 1.5 g fiber, 5 g protein, 5.2 g fat (0.7 g saturated fat), 53 g cholesterol, 94 mg sodium, 96 mg potassium, 1 mg iron, 16 mg calcium, 37 mg phosphorus

### chef's tips

- If you have extra stuffing, wrap it in greased foil and bake it separately for 40 to 45 minutes at 350°F. It can also be baked in a sprayed casserole. Bake uncovered for a crusty top. Freezes well.

- Stuff meat or poultry just before cooking. Pack loosely as stuffing expands during cooking. Remove stuffing before refrigerating or freezing leftovers.

## CHERYL'S VEGETABLE CASSEROLE

My friend Cheryl Goldberg makes this scrumptious dish every year for Passover. Her vegetarian husband, Len, loves it as a main dish, and the nonvegetarians at her table love it as a side dish!

| | |
|---|---|
| 1 long, slim Japanese eggplant (¾ lb/375 g), unpeeled | ¾ cup mushrooms |
| salt for sprinkling | 3 tomatoes, cut in chunks |
| 3 or 4 medium potatoes, peeled | 2 Tbsp fresh dill |
| 1 large or 2 medium onions, cut in chunks | 2 to 3 Tbsp oil |
| 2 medium carrots, cut in chunks | salt and pepper to taste |
| 2 medium zucchini, cut in chunks (do not peel) | 2 tsp instant pareve chicken or onion soup mix |
| | ⅓ to ½ cup matzo meal |
| | 1 egg, lightly beaten |
| | paprika to garnish |

Yield: 8 servings. Keeps 2 to 3 days in the refrigerator. Reheats well. Do not freeze.

Cut eggplant into thick slices. Place in a colander, salting each layer. Let stand for 30 minutes. Rinse well and pat dry. Cut in chunks; set aside.

SLICER: Slice potatoes, using medium pressure. Parboil in boiling salted water for 5 minutes; do not overcook. Drain well and set aside. (Potatoes will be used as a topping.)

STEEL BLADE: Coarsely chop eggplant, onion, carrots, zucchini, mushrooms and tomatoes in batches, using quick on/off pulses. Transfer to a large bowl. Process dill until fine.

Heat oil in a large pot on medium heat. Add veggies and dill to pot and stir well. Season with soup mix, salt and pepper. Sauté for 15 minutes, until tender, stirring occasionally. Add a little more oil or a few Tbsp of water if necessary.

Remove pot from heat. Add matzo meal and egg; mix well. Spread mixture evenly in a sprayed 2-quart round casserole. Top with sliced potatoes and sprinkle with paprika.

Bake, uncovered, in preheated 350°F oven for 40 to 45 minutes, until golden.

158 calories per serving, 27.1 g carbohydrates, 4.1 g fiber, 4 g protein, 4.6 g fat (0.8 g saturated fat), 27 g cholesterol, 211 mg sodium, 539 mg potassium, 1 mg iron, 30 mg calcium, 83 mg phosphorus

## RAINBOW QUINOA, TWO WAYS

Some like it hot, some like it cold! Serve quinoa cold as a colorful salad or hot as a pilaf (see page 502).

Yield: 8 servings. Keeps 2 days in the refrigerator. Do not freeze.

3 cups vegetable or chicken broth (low-sodium or regular)
1½ cups quinoa
2 cloves garlic
½ cup fresh parsley
¼ cup fresh basil or dill
4 green onions, cut in chunks
1 red and 1 yellow bell pepper, cut in chunks

½ cup baby carrots (or 1 medium carrot)
1 cup canned mandarin oranges, well drained
¾ cup dried cranberries
¼ cup extra virgin olive oil
¼ cup orange juice
salt and pepper to taste

Place broth in a medium saucepan and bring to a boil over high heat. Place quinoa in a fine-meshed strainer and rinse under cold running water for 1 to 2 minutes; drain well. (Rinsing removes the bitter coating.) Add quinoa to boiling liquid. Reduce heat to low and simmer, covered, for 15 minutes. Remove from heat and let stand, covered, for 5 minutes. Fluff with a fork, transfer to a large bowl and let cool.

STEEL BLADE: Process garlic, parsley and basil or dill until minced, about 10 seconds. Add to quinoa. Process green onions, peppers and carrots with several quick on/offs, until coarsely chopped. Add to quinoa along with mandarins and dried cranberries. Add oil, orange juice, salt and pepper. Mix gently to combine. Cover and refrigerate up to 1 day in advance. Adjust seasonings to taste before serving.

255 calories per serving, 38.1 g carbohydrates, 4.7 g fiber, 6 g protein, 9.3 g fat (1.2 g saturated fat), 0 g cholesterol, 65 mg sodium, 362 mg potassium, 2 mg iron, 50 mg calcium, 168 mg phosphorus

*Continued*

## quinoa pilaf

Cook quinoa as directed and keep warm. Reduce oil to 2 Tbsp and heat in a large, deep skillet or pot. Add coarsely chopped green onions, peppers and carrots and sauté on medium heat for 5 to 7 minutes, until tender. Add cooked quinoa to skillet along with remaining ingredients (don't add any more oil). Mix gently, cover and cook 5 to 10 minutes, until heated through. Add a little orange juice or broth to prevent sticking, if necessary. Reheats and/or freezes well. One serving contains 224 calories and 5.8 g fat.

# PASSOVER KNISHES

These are also delicious filled with chopped liver.

Yield: 8 to 10 knishes. Keeps 2 to 3 days in the refrigerator. Reheats and/or freezes well.

4 potatoes, peeled, boiled
  and mashed (about 3 cups)
2 Tbsp tub margarine or oil
1 egg (or 2 egg whites)
½ cup matzo meal

salt and freshly ground black pepper
  to taste
1¼ cups cooked brisket or chicken
leftover gravy or broth, if needed

Preheat oven to 400°F.

Combine mashed potatoes with margarine or oil, egg, matzo meal, salt and pepper; mix well.

STEEL BLADE: Trim fat from meat or chicken; cut in chunks. Process until minced, about 10 seconds. If mixture is dry, moisten with a little gravy or broth. Season to taste.

Oil the palms of your hands and shape potato mixture into flat patties. Place about 2 Tbsp meat filling in center of each patty; wrap potato mixture around filling to enclose it. Flatten slightly and make an indentation in center of each knish with your finger. Place on parchment-lined or sprayed baking sheet and bake for about 35 minutes, until golden brown.

225 calories each, 23.7 g carbohydrates, 1.8 g fiber, 9 g protein, 10.4 g fat (3 g saturated fat), 61 g cholesterol, 438 mg sodium, 334 mg potassium, 1 mg iron, 13 mg calcium, 89 mg phosphorus

## variation

For a vegetarian alternative, substitute cooked chopped broccoli, spinach or sautéed mushrooms and onions. Use sweet potatoes instead of regular potatoes.

# FARFEL APPLE PUDDING

Yield: 8 servings. Keeps
2 to 3 days in the
refrigerator. Reheats
and/or freezes well.
Recipe may be doubled
for a large crowd.

3 cups matzo farfel

cold water (about 2 cups)

3 eggs (or 2 eggs plus 2 egg whites)

¾ cup sugar

1 tsp ground cinnamon

½ tsp salt

¼ cup walnuts

3 apples, peeled and cored

½ cup raisins

2 Tbsp oil

Preheat oven to 375°F.

Combine farfel with cold water to cover. Drain immediately, pressing out excess moisture. Place farfel in large mixing bowl. Add eggs, sugar, cinnamon and salt; mix lightly.

STEEL BLADE: Chop nuts with several quick on/off pulses. Add to farfel.

GRATER: Cut apples to fit feed tube. Grate, using medium pressure. Add apples, raisins and oil to farfel; mix well. Spread evenly in sprayed 7- × 11-inch glass baking dish. Bake for 35 to 45 minutes, until nicely browned.

242 calories per serving, 40.6 g carbohydrates, 2 g fiber, 4 g protein, 8.1 g fat (1.1 g saturated fat), 80 g cholesterol, 174 mg sodium, 179 mg potassium, 1 mg iron, 26 mg calcium, 65 mg phosphorus

# FARFEL, CHICKEN AND VEGETABLE KUGEL

Yield: 8 to 10 servings.
Keeps 2 days in the
refrigerator. Reheats
and/or freezes well.
Recipe may be doubled
for a large crowd.

3 cups matzo farfel

2½ cups hot chicken broth
   (low-sodium or regular)

2 medium onions

2 stalks celery

1 cup mushrooms

½ green or red bell pepper

2 cups cooked chicken (discard
   skin and bones)

1 to 2 Tbsp oil

2 Tbsp each fresh parsley
   and fresh dill

2 cloves garlic

3 eggs (or 2 eggs plus 2 egg whites)

salt, freshly ground black pepper and
   paprika to taste

Preheat oven to 375°F.

Combine farfel and broth in mixing bowl and let soak for 5 to 10 minutes. Drain excess liquid.

SLICER: Cut vegetables to fit feed tube. Slice, using medium pressure. Slice chicken with sharp knife or on the processor, using firm pressure. (If chicken is cold, it will slice more easily. Check carefully that you've removed all tiny bones.)

Heat oil in large nonstick skillet. Add vegetables and brown quickly over medium-high heat. Add chicken and cook 1 to 2 minutes longer, stirring to mix well.

*Continued*

STEEL BLADE: Process parsley, dill and garlic until minced, 8 to 10 seconds. Add to farfel along with remaining ingredients; mix well.

Spread mixture evenly in sprayed 7- × 11-inch glass baking dish. Bake for 45 minutes, until golden.

162 calories per serving, 11.4 g carbohydrates, 1.1 g fiber, 16 g protein, 5.7 g fat (1.3 g saturated fat), 109 g cholesterol, 84 mg sodium, 321 mg potassium, 2 mg iron, 45 mg calcium, 164 mg phosphorus

### variation

Bake in sprayed muffin tins for 25 to 30 minutes, until golden. Muffins make a delicious lunch for the kids. Makes 12 to 15 muffins. One muffin contains 108 calories, 7.6 g carbohydrates and 3.8 g fat.

# FARFEL APRICOT PUDDING

Thanks to Lori Schankerman of Indianapolis for sharing this scrumptious dairy kugel. What a delicious way to use up your leftover matzo farfel!

Yield: 12 servings. Keeps 2 to 3 days in the refrigerator. Reheats and/or freezes well.

TOPPING
¾ cup chopped walnuts
2 Tbsp sugar
1 tsp ground cinnamon

FARFEL MIXTURE
3 cups matzo farfel
2½ cups cold water (approximately)

5 eggs (or 3 eggs plus 4 egg whites)
⅓ cup sugar
3 cups creamed cottage cheese (low-fat is fine)
¾ cup apricot preserves
⅓ cup melted tub margarine
1½ cups light sour cream
¾ cup raisins or dried cranberries

Preheat oven to 350°F. Spray a 9- × 13-inch baking dish with nonstick spray.

For topping: Process nuts with sugar and cinnamon on STEEL BLADE with quick on/off pulses. Set aside.

Combine farfel with cold water in a large mixing bowl and let soak for 5 minutes. Drain well, pressing out excess moisture.

STEEL BLADE: Process eggs with sugar, cottage cheese, preserves and margarine until well mixed, about 1 minute, scraping down sides of bowl once or twice. Add to farfel along with sour cream and raisins or dried cranberries. Mix well.

Spread mixture evenly in prepared pan and sprinkle with nut mixture. Bake, uncovered, for 1 hour, until golden.

332 calories per serving, 36.8 g carbohydrates, 1.4 g fiber, 13 g protein, 16.1 g fat (4.5 g saturated fat), 101 g cholesterol, 330 mg sodium, 270 mg potassium, 1 mg iron, 105 mg calcium, 171 mg phosphorus

# PASSOVER BLINTZES

Yield: About 16 blintzes. Keeps 2 to 3 days in the refrigerator. Reheats and/or freezes well.

**3 eggs**
**1 cup water**
**¼ cup potato starch**
**2 Tbsp cake meal**
**1 Tbsp oil**
**½ tsp salt**

**filling of your choice, such as Chicken or Meat Filling (page 257), Cheese Filling (page 166), or the filling for Spinach Borekas (page 154)**
**2 Tbsp oil or tub margarine, for frying**

STEEL BLADE: Combine eggs, water, potato starch, cake meal, 1 Tbsp oil and salt. Process until smooth, about 15 seconds.

Grease crêpe pan or nonstick skillet lightly for the first blintz. Pour about 3 Tbsp batter (just enough to cover bottom of pan) into skillet and cook for about 45 seconds on 1 side only, until top surface is dry. Flip and cook for 5 seconds on second side. Turn out onto a clean tea towel. Repeat with remaining batter. (Blintz leaves may be prepared in advance and refrigerated or frozen until needed.)

Place about 3 Tbsp desired filling on each blintz and roll up, turning in ends. Brown in oil or margarine on all sides, until golden.

(To bake, arrange filled blintzes seam side down in single layer in sprayed shallow casserole. Drizzle with melted margarine or oil. Bake, uncovered, at 400°F until golden, about 20 minutes, turning blintzes over halfway through cooking.)

118 calories each (with chicken filling), 3.1 g carbohydrates, 0 g fiber, 13 g protein, 5.6 g fat (1.1 g saturated fat), 96 g cholesterol, 121 mg sodium, 116 mg potassium, 1 mg iron, 14 mg calcium, 109 mg phosphorus

### note

- With Cheese Filling, 1 blintz contains 82 calories, 7.3 g carbohydrates and 4 g fat. (Use sugar or Passover sweetener.)
- With Spinach Boreka filling, 1 blintz contains 84 calories, 4.5 g carbohydrates and 5.7 g fat.

### gluten-free blintzes

Process 2 eggs, ⅛ tsp salt, 1 cup water, ½ cup potato starch and 1 Tbsp oil. Be sure to use a gluten-free filling! Makes 12.

# EGG ROLL BLINTZES

For a vegetarian version, omit chicken from filling.

Yield: About 16 blintzes. Keeps 2 days in the refrigerator. Reheats and/or freezes well.

**Passover Blintzes (page 505)**

FILLING

**2 medium onions, cut in chunks**

**2 stalks celery, cut in chunks**

**2 cups mushrooms**

**2 Tbsp oil**

**½ medium-sized cabbage, cut in wedges to fit feed tube**

**1 cup cooked chicken, skin and bones discarded (optional)**

**2 cloves garlic, crushed**

**¼ tsp ground ginger**

**salt and freshly ground black pepper to taste**

**1 Tbsp potato starch, if needed**

**2 Tbsp oil, for frying or baking blintzes**

Prepare blintz leaves as directed, but do not fill or cook. Cover and set aside while you prepare the egg roll filling.

STEEL BLADE: Process onions and celery with 3 or 4 quick on/off pulses, until coarsely chopped. Empty bowl. Repeat with mushrooms. Brown quickly in 2 Tbsp hot oil in large nonstick skillet.

GRATER: Grate cabbage, using firm pressure. Add to skillet and cook a few minutes longer, stirring often.

SLICER: Slice chicken (if using), using firm pressure. Add to skillet with garlic, ginger, salt and pepper. Mixture should be fairly dry. If it isn't, sprinkle with potato starch to absorb excess moisture. Cool mixture before filling blintzes.

Place about 3 Tbsp filling on each blintz and roll up, turning in ends. (May be prepared in advance and refrigerated or frozen until needed. Thaw before continuing.) Brown blintzes in hot oil on all sides, until golden.

(To bake, preheat oven to 400°F. Pour oil in 9- × 13-inch glass baking dish. Place in oven and heat until oil is piping hot, about 5 minutes. Carefully arrange blintzes seam side down in baking dish. Bake, uncovered, until golden, about 20 minutes, turning blintzes over halfway through cooking.)

80 calories each, 6.5 g carbohydrates, 1.1 g fiber, 2 g protein, 5.5 g fat (0.6 g saturated fat), 40 g cholesterol, 95 mg sodium, 118 mg potassium, 0 mg iron, 22 mg calcium, 35 mg phosphorus

# GRATE AND BAKE

This scrumptious vegetarian dish comes from Cheryl Goldberg of Toronto.

**2 Tbsp fresh dill**

**6 medium potatoes, peeled**

**4 carrots**

**2 medium zucchini, unpeeled**

**2 eggs**

**2 to 3 Tbsp mayonnaise (light or regular)**

**salt and freshly ground black pepper to taste**

**matzo meal, if needed**

Preheat oven to 350°F.

STEEL BLADE: Process dill until minced.

GRATER: Cut potatoes, carrots and zucchini to fit feed tube. Grate, using medium pressure. Transfer to large mixing bowl. If necessary, drain liquid from vegetables. Add eggs, mayonnaise and seasonings; mix well. Add 2 or 3 Tbsp matzo meal if mixture is too wet. Spread mixture evenly in sprayed 2-quart baking dish. Bake for 40 to 45 minutes, until golden brown.

203 calories per serving, 38.2 g carbohydrates, 4.5 g fiber, 6 g protein, 3.7 g fat (0.9 g saturated fat), 72 g cholesterol, 82 mg sodium, 753 mg potassium, 1 mg iron, 37 mg calcium, 124 mg phosphorus

### note

You can substitute or add other vegetables (e.g., sweet potatoes, celery). However, you may have to add an extra egg and a little more mayonnaise to bind the vegetable mixture. If mixture is too wet, drain off liquid or add a little matzo meal. To double the recipe, use a 9- × 13-inch glass baking dish and bake for 65 to 75 minutes.

*Yield: 6 to 8 servings. Keeps 2 to 3 days in the refrigerator. Reheats and/or freezes well.*

## SWEET POTATO BAKE

*Thanks to Omi Cantor of Boston for suggesting this easy company casserole. I modified her recipe by reducing the fat, changing a few ingredients and simplifying the preparation.*

**½ cup dried apricots**

**3 cups Passover apricot nectar (or 2¾ cups orange juice plus ¼ cup apricot jam)**

**1 cup chicken or vegetable broth**

**2 to 3 Tbsp tub margarine or olive oil**

**1½ tsp salt**

**½ tsp ground cinnamon**

**½ tsp freshly ground black pepper**

**8 or 9 sweet potatoes, peeled**

Preheat oven to 375°F.

STEEL BLADE: Process apricots with 6 to 8 quick on/off pulses, until coarsely chopped. Place in large microwavable bowl with remaining ingredients except sweet potatoes. Heat until boiling, 8 to 10 minutes on High.

SLICER: Cut sweet potatoes to fit feed tube. Slice, using medium pressure. Empty processor bowl as necessary. Spread sweet potatoes evenly in sprayed 9- × 13-inch glass baking dish. Carefully pour hot liquid over sweet potatoes. Cover with foil.

Bake, covered, for 30 minutes. Remove foil and bake about 1 hour longer, until tender and well browned. Let stand 10 to 15 minutes before serving.

*Yield: 12 servings. Keeps 2 to 3 days in the refrigerator. Reheats well. Do not freeze.*

177 calories per serving, 37.7 g carbohydrates, 4.8 g fiber, 3 g protein, 2.3 g fat (0.4 g saturated fat), 0 g cholesterol, 358 mg sodium, 723 mg potassium, 1 mg iron, 55 mg calcium, 81 mg phosphorus

*Continued*

## PASSOVER CARROT KUGEL

This kugel becomes gluten-free if made with ground almonds instead of matzo meal.

6 to 8 medium carrots
2 large apples, peeled and cored
1 lemon (unpeeled), cut in chunks (discard seeds)
6 eggs (or 4 eggs plus 4 egg whites)

½ cup sweet red wine or apple juice
1 cup sugar
½ cup potato starch
2 Tbsp matzo meal or ground almonds

Yield: 8 servings. Keeps 2 to 3 days in the refrigerator. Reheats and/or freezes well.

Preheat oven to 375°F.

GRATER: Cut carrots to fit feed tube horizontally. Grate, using firm pressure. Measure 2 cups firmly packed. Empty into large mixing bowl. Grate apples, using medium pressure. Measure 1 cup firmly packed. Add to carrots.

STEEL BLADE: Scrub lemon well. Process until fine. Add to mixing bowl. Process eggs for 3 or 4 seconds. Add with remaining ingredients to mixing bowl and mix well. Spread mixture evenly in sprayed 2-quart casserole. Bake for 50 to 60 minutes, until golden brown.

236 calories per serving, 44 g carbohydrates, 2.1 g fiber, 5 g protein, 4.1 g fat (1.2 g saturated fat), 159 g cholesterol, 68 mg sodium, 196 mg potassium, 1 mg iron, 40 mg calcium, 84 mg phosphorus

## PASSOVER CARROT TSIMMIS

An easy and delicious holiday favorite.

2 lb (1 kg) carrots
½ cup honey (or to taste)
1 Tbsp oil
1 Tbsp potato starch
¼ cup orange juice or cold water

2 Tbsp minced fresh dill
salt and freshly ground black pepper to taste
ground ginger to taste

Yield: 6 servings. Keeps 3 days in the refrigerator. Reheats and/or freezes well. Recipe can be doubled for a crowd.

Preheat oven to 375°F.

SLICER: Cut carrots to fit feed tube. Slice, using firm pressure. You should have about 6 cups sliced. Cook in boiling salted water for 15 to 20 minutes, until tender. Drain, reserving about ½ cup cooking liquid. Add honey and oil; mix well. Dissolve potato starch in juice or cold water and stir into carrots. Add dill, salt, pepper and ginger.

Bake, uncovered, for about 30 minutes, stirring occasionally.

164 calories per serving, 36.5 g carbohydrates, 4.2 g fiber, 1 g protein, 2.6 g fat (0.2 g saturated fat), 0 g cholesterol, 82 mg sodium, 363 mg potassium, 1 mg iron, 45 mg calcium, 45 mg phosphorus

### variation

Simmer tiny matzo balls in boiling water for 20 minutes. Drain well; add to boiled carrots. Bake as directed, stirring occasionally. Be careful not to break the matzo balls.

## MATZO MEAL LATKES

These make a great side dish with meat or chicken. You can also serve them as a main dish or for breakfast topped with syrup or yogurt and fresh fruit—just omit the pepper, garlic and onion powder.

Yield: About 18. Keeps 2 to 3 days in the refrigerator. Reheats and/or freezes well.

1½ cups matzo meal
4 eggs
1¼ cups cold water
1 tsp salt
⅛ tsp each freshly ground black pepper, garlic powder and onion powder (optional)
¼ cup oil for frying

STEEL BLADE: Combine all ingredients, except oil for frying, in processor. Process until blended, about 10 seconds. Let mixture stand for a few minutes to thicken.

Heat oil in large skillet. Drop mixture from large spoon into hot oil and flatten slightly with back of spoon. Fry on both sides until brown and crispy. Drain well on paper towels. If batter becomes too thick, thin with a little water.

83 calories each, 9.2 g carbohydrates, 0.3 g fiber, 2 g protein, 4.4 g fat (0.6 g saturated fat), 47 g cholesterol, 145 mg sodium, 15 mg potassium, 0 mg iron, 6 mg calcium, 19 mg phosphorus

### lighter variation

Replace 2 of the eggs with 4 egg whites. Brown in nonstick skillet, using as little oil as possible. One latke contains 58 calories and 1.5 g fat.

## PASSOVER CHEESE LATKES

Quick and luscious for lunch or brunch. Serve with yogurt or sour cream and fresh fruit, or drizzle with honey.

1 cup (½ lb/250 g) dry or pressed cottage cheese
3 eggs (or 2 eggs plus 2 egg whites)
¼ cup sour cream (light or regular)
1 Tbsp melted butter or oil
½ cup matzo or cake meal
2 Tbsp sugar
½ tsp ground cinnamon
¼ tsp salt
2 Tbsp butter and/or oil, for frying

STEEL BLADE: Combine all ingredients, except butter or oil for frying, in processor and process until smooth and blended, 20 to 25 seconds. Scrape down sides of bowl as necessary. *Continued*

509

Heat butter and/or oil in large nonstick skillet. When bubbling, drop cheese mixture from large spoon into skillet. Brown on medium heat on both sides until golden. Repeat with remaining cheese mixture, adding more butter and/or oil to skillet as necessary.

88 calories each, 8 g carbohydrates, 0.2 g fiber, 4 g protein, 4.8 g fat (2.6 g saturated fat), 63 g cholesterol, 128 mg sodium, 45 mg potassium, 0 mg iron, 26 mg calcium, 49 mg phosphorus

## PASSOVER CUPCAKE BLINTZES

These are quick and easy to make—perfect for Passover or any time. Serve them with sour cream or yogurt and berries.

Yield: 12 cupcake blintzes. Keeps 2 to 3 days in the refrigerator. Reheats and/or freezes well.

2 cups (1 lb/500 g) creamed or pressed cottage cheese (low-fat is fine)

¾ cup sugar (or sugar substitute)

1 Tbsp lemon juice

4 eggs (or 1 cup egg substitute, if available)

¼ cup melted margarine or butter

½ cup cake meal (scant)

Preheat oven to 350°F.

STEEL BLADE: Process cottage cheese, sugar and lemon juice until smooth and creamy, 30 to 60 seconds. Add remaining ingredients and process until blended, 15 to 20 seconds.

Fill sprayed muffin tins three-quarters full. Bake for 40 to 45 minutes, until golden. Loosen with a flexible spatula and remove carefully.

160 calories each, 18 g carbohydrates, 0.2 g fiber, 6 g protein, 7.1 g fat (1.8 g saturated fat), 77 g cholesterol, 180 mg sodium, 60 mg potassium, 0 mg iron, 38 mg calcium, 85 mg phosphorus

## FLORENTINE CUPCAKE BLINTZES

These are a savory version of Passover Cupcake Blintzes. Spinach done light!

Yield: 12 cupcake blintzes. Keeps 2 to 3 days in the refrigerator. Reheats and/or freezes well.

half of a 10 oz (300 g) pkg frozen spinach, thawed and squeezed dry

2 green onions, cut in chunks

2 Tbsp fresh dill

2 cups (1 lb/500 g) creamed cottage cheese (low-fat is fine)

4 eggs (or 2 eggs plus 4 egg whites)

1 Tbsp oil

⅓ cup cake meal

¼ cup grated Parmesan cheese

¾ tsp salt

¼ tsp freshly ground black pepper

½ tsp dried basil

Preheat oven to 350°F.

STEEL BLADE: Process spinach, green onions, dill, cottage cheese and eggs until smooth and blended, 30 to 45 seconds, scraping down sides of bowl as needed. Add remaining ingredients and process 15 to 20 seconds longer, until well mixed.

Fill sprayed muffin tins three-quarters full. Bake for 40 to 45 minutes, until golden and set. Cool slightly. Loosen with a flexible spatula and remove carefully.

94 calories each, 5 g carbohydrates, 0.5 g fiber, 7 g protein, 5 g fat (1.5 g saturated fat), 78 g cholesterol, 328 mg sodium, 94 mg potassium, 1 mg iron, 72 mg calcium, 102 mg phosphorus

## CRUSTLESS PASSOVER TUNA QUICHE

This makes an excellent dairy meal during Passover or all year round.

Yield: 8 servings. Keeps 2 to 3 days in the refrigerator. Reheats and/or freezes well.

| | |
|---|---|
| 1 medium onion, cut in chunks | 1 cup milk (skim or 1%) |
| 2 cups mushrooms | 2 Tbsp fresh dill or fresh basil (or |
| ½ red bell pepper, cut in chunks | ½ tsp dried dill or dried basil) |
| 1 Tbsp oil | 2 cans (7 oz/213 g each) tuna, well |
| 6 oz (180 g) chilled Swiss or | drained |
| cheddar cheese (1½ cups grated) | 4 Tbsp matzo or cake meal, divided |
| (low-fat is fine) | ½ tsp salt |
| 3 eggs (or 2 eggs plus 2 egg whites) | freshly ground black pepper to taste |

Preheat oven to 350°F. For machines with nested bowls, see method below.

STEEL BLADE: Process onion, mushrooms and red pepper with quick on/off pulses, until coarsely chopped. Heat oil in large nonstick skillet. Sauté vegetables until golden, 6 to 8 minutes. Cool slightly.

GRATER: Grate cheese, using medium pressure. Remove from bowl and reserve.

STEEL BLADE: Process eggs, milk and dill or basil for 5 to 10 seconds. Add tuna, half of the matzo or cake meal, salt, pepper, sautéed vegetables and cheese. Process with 3 or 4 very quick on/off pulses, until combined. Do not overprocess.

Sprinkle remaining matzo or cake meal in bottom of sprayed 10-inch ceramic quiche dish. Add quiche mixture and spread evenly. Bake for about 45 minutes, until set and golden.

155 calories per serving, 8.2 g carbohydrates, 0.7 g fiber, 21 g protein, 5.3 g fat (1.5 g saturated fat), 100 g cholesterol, 256 mg sodium, 272 mg potassium, 1 mg iron, 251 mg calcium, 270 mg phosphorus

### nested bowl method

Use medium bowl and GRATER/SHREDDING DISC for cheese. Use large bowl and STEEL BLADE for all other processing tasks.

## SALMON MEDITERRANEAN

This dish is great
for guests when
you're pressed for
time. It's delicious
either hot or cold—
Mediterrane-yumm!

Yield: 8 to 10 servings.
Keeps 2 to 3 days in the
refrigerator. Reheats and
or/freezes well.

1 salmon fillet with skin (3 lb/1.4 kg),
  or 8 individual salmon fillets

salt, pepper and dried basil to taste

2 cloves garlic

3 medium Roma tomatoes, quartered

1 yellow or red pepper, cut in chunks

1 medium zucchini, cut in chunks

4 green onions, cut in chunks

2 Tbsp olive oil

2 Tbsp lemon juice

2 tsp honey

¼ cup fresh basil (or 1 tsp dried)

½ cup sliced black olives (optional)

Line a baking sheet with foil and spray with nonstick spray. Place salmon on baking sheet and sprinkle lightly with salt, pepper and basil.

STEEL BLADE: Drop garlic through feed tube while machine is running; process until minced. Add remaining ingredients except olives. Process with quick on/off pulses, until coarsely chopped. Season with salt and pepper. Spread mixture evenly over salmon and marinate for 30 to 60 minutes.

Preheat oven to 425°F. Bake, uncovered, for 12 to 15 minutes, until salmon flakes when gently pressed. If desired, top with olives before serving.

370 calories per serving, 5.7 g carbohydrates, 1.1 g fiber, 35 g protein, 22.5 g fat (4.3 g saturated fat), 96 g cholesterol, 98 mg sodium, 760 mg potassium, 1 mg iron, 42 mg calcium, 408 mg phosphorus

## PASSOVER LASAGNA (MATZAGNA)

This tastes just like
lasagna that's made
with pasta!

Yield: 8 to 10 servings.
Keeps 3 days in the
refrigerator. Reheats
and/or freezes well.

2 medium onions, cut in chunks

1 red bell pepper, cut in chunks

2 cups mushrooms

2 cloves garlic, crushed

1 Tbsp oil

12 oz (375 g) chilled low-fat
  mozzarella cheese
  (3 cups grated)

3 cups pressed dry cottage cheese or
  creamed cottage cheese (low-fat
  is fine)

4 cups Passover tomato sauce (low-
  sodium or regular)

salt and freshly ground black pepper
  to taste

dried basil and dried oregano to taste

7 matzos (approximately)

Preheat oven to 375°F. For machines with nested bowls, see method on page 513.

SLICER: Slice onions, pepper and mushrooms, using medium pressure. Combine in microwavable bowl with garlic and oil. Microwave on High for 5 minutes, until softened.

GRATER: Grate mozzarella cheese, using medium pressure. Set aside.

STEEL BLADE: If dry cottage cheese isn't available, process creamed cottage cheese until smooth, 1 to 2 minutes, scraping down sides of bowl as needed.

Season tomato sauce with salt, pepper, basil and oregano. Spread one-third of the sauce in sprayed 9- × 13-inch glass baking dish. Briefly rinse matzos with hot water; drain. Arrange a layer of matzos over sauce, trimming matzos to fit. Spread half of the cottage cheese over matzos. Top with half the vegetables. Sprinkle with one-third of the mozzarella cheese. Repeat, layering sauce, matzos, cottage cheese, vegetables, and mozzarella cheese. Top with matzos and tomato sauce. Sprinkle with mozzarella cheese. (Can be made in advance up to this point and refrigerated.)

Bake, uncovered, for 40 to 45 minutes. Let stand for 10 minutes for easier cutting.

340 calories per serving, 39.4 g carbohydrates, 2.6 g fiber, 22 g protein, 10.9 g fat (5.7 g saturated fat), 27 g cholesterol, 425 mg sodium, 258 mg potassium, 2 mg iron, 389 mg calcium, 371 mg phosphorus

### nested bowl method

Use medium bowl and SLICER for vegetables. Use GRATER/SHREDDING DISC to grate mozzarella. Use large bowl and STEEL BLADE for creamed cottage cheese.

### variations

- Add sautéed or steamed vegetables (e.g., asparagus, broccoli, carrots, zucchini) between lasagna layers.

- Prepare Tortilla Lasagna Florentine (page 140), but replace tortillas with 7 matzos. Moisten matzos with hot water. Assemble lasagna in sprayed 9- × 13-inch glass baking dish. Bake in preheated 375°F oven for 40 to 45 minutes. (Do not make the variation using tofu for Passover.) One serving contains 361 calories, 36 g carbohydrates and 11.4 g fat.

## PASSOVER ROLLS OR BAGELS

These are great for sandwiches, or you can shape them into hot dog rolls as a treat for the kids.

Yield: 10 to 12 rolls or bagels, depending on size. Keeps 1 to 2 days in a loosely covered container. Freezes well.

| | |
|---|---|
| 1 cup water | 1 tsp salt |
| ½ cup oil | 2 cups matzo meal or cake meal |
| 2 tsp sugar | 4 eggs |

Preheat oven to 400°F.

Combine water, oil, sugar and salt in large saucepan. Bring to a boil. Remove from heat and add matzo meal or cake meal all at once. Stir vigorously until mixture pulls away from sides of pan. Let cool for 5 minutes.

STEEL BLADE: Transfer mixture from saucepan to processor bowl. Process for 5 seconds. Drop eggs through feed tube 1 at a time while machine is running. Process about 20 seconds longer, until smooth. *Continued*

Drop mixture from large spoon onto sprayed baking sheet. Wet your hands and shape mixture into rolls. To form bagels, poke a hole in the center of each roll with your thumb. Leave about 2 inches between rolls for expansion during baking. Bake for 50 to 60 minutes, until nicely browned.

225 calories each, 22.7 g carbohydrates, 0.8 g fiber, 5 g protein, 13.5 g fat (1.5 g saturated fat), 85 g cholesterol, 260 mg sodium, 25 mg potassium, 1 mg iron, 11 mg calcium, 34 mg phosphorus

### passover onion rolls

Sauté 1 cup chopped onions in 1 Tbsp oil in nonstick skillet until golden. Add onions to processor once all the eggs have been added and mixture is smooth. Process with 2 or 3 quick on/off pulses, until mixed. Bake as directed. One roll contains 243 calories, 24.0 g carbohydrates and 14.9 g fat.

## HOMEMADE MATZO

Fun to make with children. Matzo must be mixed, shaped and baked within 18 minutes to prevent leavening, so teamwork helps!

Yield: 8 matzos. Store in airtight containers.

**2 cups flour**        **¾ cup cold water (approximately)**

Preheat oven to 475°F. Place 2 large baking sheets in oven to heat up. (Oven racks should be on second and fourth positions from bottom.) Dust work surface with flour and have a rolling pin ready. Place flour in processor bowl. Measure water. Set your timer for 18 minutes. Ready, set, go forth and make matzo!

STEEL BLADE: Gradually add water to flour through feed tube while machine is running. Process until dough forms a ball, 20 to 30 seconds. Drizzle in a little extra water if dough seems dry.

Remove dough from processor and divide into 8 balls. Flatten each ball between your hands. Roll out each piece of dough into a circle with a rolling pin. Roll a second time into a 7- or 8-inch circle, rolling dough as thinly as possible. Armed with a fork in each hand, quickly prick dough all over to make at least 100 holes, then turn dough over and pierce another 100 times. (Truly a "holy" experience!) Hopefully you still have at least 5 minutes left on your timer!

Carefully transfer matzos to baking sheets using tongs. Bake for 2 to 3 minutes per side, until lightly browned and crisp. Cool on a rack.

114 calories per serving, 23.8 g carbohydrates, 0.8 g fiber, 3 g protein, 0.3 g fat (0 g saturated fat), 0 g cholesterol, 2 mg sodium, 33 mg potassium, 2 mg iron, 5 mg calcium, 34 mg phosphorus

### note

To make true Passover matzo, you need "kosher for Passover" flour, which may be available at a bakery that makes Passover matzo.

## PASSOVER PIE CRUST

Yield: One 9-inch pie
crust (8 servings).
Freezes well.

**1 cup matzo meal**

**3 Tbsp sugar**

**1 tsp ground cinnamon**

**⅓ cup butter or tub margarine, melted**

Preheat oven to 375°F.

STEEL BLADE: Combine all ingredients and process until well blended, 12 to 15 seconds. Press into bottom and up sides of sprayed 9-inch pie plate. Bake for 18 to 20 minutes, until golden. Cool completely. Fill as desired.

145 calories per serving, 18.5 g carbohydrates, 0.7 g fiber, 2 g protein, 7.8 g fat (4.9 g saturated fat), 20 g cholesterol, 56 mg sodium, 4 mg potassium, 0 mg iron, 6 mg calcium, 3 mg phosphorus

### variation

Replace matzo meal with 20 to 24 Passover macaroons. Omit sugar. Process macaroons until finely ground. Add remaining ingredients and process a few seconds longer.

## UPSY-DOWNSY PIE CRUST OR TOPPING

Use this versatile
crumb mixture
as a pie crust or
as a topping for
a fruit crisp! The
ingredients are
the same but the
method is slightly
different.

Yield: 8 servings.
Freezes well.

**3 cups Passover soup nuts (mandlen)**

**1 cup pecans**

**¼ cup oil or melted tub margarine**

**½ cup sugar**

**1 tsp ground cinnamon**

**Pie Crust:** Process mandlen on STEEL BLADE until ground, 15 to 20 seconds. Empty bowl. Process pecans until finely crushed, 25 to 30 seconds. Add ground mandlen, oil or margarine, sugar and cinnamon. Process 8 to 10 seconds to blend. Press mixture into bottom and up sides of sprayed 9-inch pie plate. Bake in preheated 375°F oven for 7 to 8 minutes (or microwave on High for 2 minutes, until set). When cool, fill as desired.

**Crumb Topping:** Process mandlen on STEEL BLADE until ground, 15 to 20 seconds. Add pecans and process until coarsely chopped, 8 to 10 seconds. Add remaining ingredients and process 6 to 8 seconds to blend. (Can be prepared in advance and refrigerated or frozen until needed.) Makes enough topping for a 9-inch fruit crisp.

225 calories per serving, 17.8 g carbohydrates, 1.4 g fiber, 2 g protein, 17.5 g fat (1.3 g saturated fat), 24 g cholesterol, 0 mg sodium, 52 mg potassium, 0 mg iron, 12 mg calcium, 35 mg phosphorus

*Continued*

## PASSOVER APPLE CRUMB PIE

Easy to make and sure to please!

Yield: 8 servings. Can be frozen, but crust may get soggy. Reheat, uncovered, at 350°F for 10 minutes.

**CRUST**

2 cups matzo meal

6 Tbsp sugar

2 tsp ground cinnamon

¾ cup butter or tub margarine, cut in chunks

**FILLING**

5 or 6 apples, peeled and cored

¼ cup sugar

1 tsp ground cinnamon

Preheat oven to 375°F.

For crust: Process all ingredients on the STEEL BLADE until well blended, 20 to 25 seconds. Reserve about 1¼ cups of crumb mixture for topping. Press remaining crumbs into bottom and up sides of sprayed 9-inch glass pie plate.

For filling: Cut apples to fit feed tube. Slice on SLICER, using firm pressure. Mix apples with sugar and cinnamon. Fill crust; top with reserved crumbs. Bake for 40 to 45 minutes.

379 calories per serving, 56.4 g carbohydrates, 2.8 g fiber, 4 g protein, 17.7 g fat (11 g saturated fat), 46 g cholesterol, 125 mg sodium, 100 mg potassium, 1 mg iron, 20 mg calcium, 17 mg phosphorus

## PASSOVER FRUIT CRISP

A delicious, easy dessert for a crowd!

Yield: 15 servings. Reheats and/or freezes well.

**FILLING**

6 to 7 apples, peeled and cored

2 cups strawberries, hulled

3 cups blueberries (fresh or frozen)

½ cup sugar

6 Tbsp cake meal

2 tsp ground cinnamon

**TOPPING**

2 cups matzo meal

½ cup sugar

2 tsp ground cinnamon

½ cup melted margarine

Preheat oven to 375°F.

For filling: Cut apples to fit feed tube. Slice on SLICER, using medium pressure. Slice strawberries, using light pressure. Combine all filling ingredients in large mixing bowl; mix well. Spread evenly in sprayed 9- × 13-inch glass baking dish.

For topping: Process ingredients on STEEL BLADE until combined, 12 to 15 seconds. Sprinkle evenly over filling. Bake for 50 to 60 minutes, until golden.

235 calories per serving, 45.2 g carbohydrates, 3 g fiber, 3 g protein, 6.5 g fat (1.1 g saturated fat), 0 g cholesterol, 52 mg sodium, 116 mg potassium, 1 mg iron, 16 mg calcium, 16 mg phosphorus

## PASSOVER CHEESE PIE

Rich and creamy.

Yield: 8 servings. Garnish with fresh strawberries. Do not freeze.

**Passover Pie Crust (page 515)**
**2 cups (1 lb) cream cheese (light or regular), cut in chunks**
**2 eggs**
**½ cup sugar**

**1 Tbsp Passover liqueur or orange juice**
**1 cup light sour cream**
**2 Tbsp sugar**
**½ tsp Passover liqueur or orange juice**
**fresh strawberries, for garnish**

Preheat oven to 350°F.

Prepare crust as directed; press into bottom and up sides of sprayed 9-inch pie plate. Do not bake.

STEEL BLADE: Process cream cheese with eggs, ½ cup sugar and the 1 Tbsp liqueur or orange juice for 25 to 30 seconds, until well blended, scraping down sides of bowl as needed. Pour filling into crust. Bake for 30 minutes, until set.

Process sour cream, 2 Tbsp sugar and the ½ tsp liqueur or orange juice for 5 seconds to blend. Spread over cheese pie and bake 5 minutes longer. When cool, refrigerate.

Garnish with strawberries at serving time.

380 calories per serving, 41 g carbohydrates, 0.7 g fiber, 10 g protein, 20.4 g fat (12.6 g saturated fat), 111 g cholesterol, 359 mg sodium, 86 mg potassium, 0 mg iron, 233 mg calcium, 46 mg phosphorus

## GLAZED FRUIT CHEESECAKE

This creamy cheesecake is perfect for Passover or anytime! For non-Passover use, substitute your favorite cookie crust.

CRUST
**½ lb (250 g) pkg Passover mandelbroit cookies (or chocolate macaroons)**
**¼ cup melted margarine**

CHEESECAKE MIXTURE
**1 lb (500 g) cream cheese, cut in chunks (light or regular)**
**1 lb (500 g) pressed cottage cheese, cut in chunks (low-fat is fine)**
**1¼ cups sugar**
**4 eggs**
**juice of ½ lemon**

Yield: 16 servings.

Do not freeze.

TOPPING

½ cup apricot jam (approximately)
1 pint firm strawberries, hulled and
halved lengthwise

3 to 4 firm chilled kiwis, peeled
1 to 2 cups blueberries

Preheat oven to 350°F. Fill baking pan half full of water and place it on bottom rack of oven. (The steam helps prevent cheesecake from cracking.)

For crust: Process cookies on the STEEL BLADE to make fine crumbs, 20 to 25 seconds. Add margarine and process just until combined, 6 to 8 seconds. Press into sprayed 10-inch springform pan. Wipe out bowl with paper towels.

For cheesecake mixture: Process cream cheese, cottage cheese and sugar until creamy, about 30 seconds. Add eggs and lemon juice. Process until well mixed, about 30 seconds longer. Pour over crust.

Bake on middle rack for 45 to 50 minutes. When done, center of cheesecake will jiggle slightly when you shake the pan but won't stick when touched lightly with your fingertips. Remove cheesecake from oven and immediately place in refrigerator to cool. (This helps prevent cracks from forming.) When completely cool, cover and refrigerate until ready to add topping. Carefully remove sides of pan, but don't remove base. Place cheesecake on serving plate.

For topping: Microwave jam on High for 45 seconds, until melted. Strain, if necessary. Brush top of cheesecake with thin layer of jam. Arrange strawberry halves around outside edge. Slice kiwis on SLICER, using gentle pressure. Pat dry between paper towels. Arrange an inner circle of kiwi slices. Place blueberries in center. Use a pastry brush to gently brush fruit with jam. Refrigerate until serving time.

287 calories per serving, 38.9 g carbohydrates, 1.6 g fiber, 9 g protein, 11.3 g fat (4.8 g saturated fat), 81 g cholesterol, 315 mg sodium, 131 mg potassium, 1 mg iron, 123 mg calcium, 71 mg phosphorus

### marbled cheesecake

Omit fruit topping. Prepare crust and cheesecake mixture as directed. Remove 2 cups of cheesecake mixture and blend with 2 oz melted semisweet chocolate. Pour most of white cheesecake mixture over crust, drizzle chocolate mixture on top, then add remaining white mixture. Cut through carefully with a knife to create a marbled effect. Bake for 45 to 50 minutes. One serving contains 260 calories, 29.8 g carbohydrates and 12.2 g fat.

# PASSOVER APPLE CAKE

Yield: 9 servings. If frozen, cake may become soggy. Reheat, uncovered, at 350°F for 10 minutes.

**FILLING**

4 large apples, peeled, cored and halved

½ cup sugar (or to taste)

1 Tbsp potato starch

1 tsp ground cinnamon

**BATTER**

3 eggs (or 2 eggs plus 2 egg whites)

¾ cup sugar

½ cup oil

¾ cup cake meal

¼ cup potato starch

1 tsp ground cinnamon

¼ cup orange or lemon juice

Preheat oven to 375°F.

For filling: Slice apples on the SLICER, using firm pressure. Transfer to large mixing bowl; mix with remaining filling ingredients.

For batter: Process eggs with sugar on the STEEL BLADE for 1 minute, until light. Add oil through feed tube while machine is running and process another 30 seconds. Uncover and add cake meal, potato starch and cinnamon; drizzle juice over dry ingredients. Process with 3 or 4 quick on/off pulses, until smooth. Let batter stand for 2 minutes to thicken slightly.

Pour half the batter into sprayed 8-inch square baking pan. Cover with apples. Top with remaining batter. Bake for 45 to 50 minutes, until nicely browned.

350 calories per serving, 55.1 g carbohydrates, 1.9 g fiber, 3 g protein, 14.4 g fat (1.5 g saturated fat), 71 g cholesterol, 22 mg sodium, 124 mg potassium, 1 mg iron, 20 mg calcium, 41 mg phosphorus

## lighter variation

Replace ½ cup oil in batter with ¼ cup oil and ¼ cup applesauce. Use 2 eggs and 2 egg whites. One serving contains 293 calories, 55.8 g carbohydrates and 7.6 g fat.

# ANOTHER PASSOVER APPLE CAKE

Why is this apple cake different from all the others? Because it's gluten-free! It uses potato starch to thicken the batter and contains kosher for Passover

**FILLING**

6 large apples, peeled, cored and cut in quarters

⅓ to ½ cup sugar (white or brown)

1½ tsp ground cinnamon

**BATTER**

2 eggs

1 cup sugar

½ cup oil

1 cup plus 2 Tbsp potato starch

1½ tsp Passover baking powder

¼ cup apple juice

icing sugar for sprinkling (optional)

PASSOVER

baking powder
(see page 493).
Use regular baking
powder the rest of
the year.

Preheat oven to 350°F. Spray a 7- × 11-inch glass baking dish with nonstick spray.

SLICER: For filling, slice apples, using medium pressure. Transfer to large mixing bowl; mix with sugar and cinnamon.

STEEL BLADE: Process eggs with sugar for 1 minute, until light. Add oil through feed tube while machine is running and process 30 seconds longer. Uncover and add potato starch and baking powder; drizzle apple juice over dry ingredients. Process with 4 or 5 quick on/off pulses, until smooth, scraping down sides of bowl as needed. Let batter stand for 2 minutes to thicken slightly.

Yield: 12 servings.
If frozen, cake may
become soggy. Reheat,
uncovered, at 350°F for
10 minutes.

Pour half the batter in prepared pan. Spread apples evenly over batter; top with remaining batter. Some apples may poke out—that's okay.

Bake for 50 to 60 minutes, until nicely browned. When cooled, sprinkle with icing sugar (if desired).

282 calories per serving, 49.3 g carbohydrates, 1.6 g fiber, 1 g protein, 10.4 g fat (1 g saturated fat), 35 g cholesterol, 72 mg sodium, 116 mg potassium, 0 mg iron, 47 mg calcium, 39 mg phosphorus

### lighter variation

Replace ½ cup oil in batter with ¼ cup oil and ¼ cup applesauce. Use 1 egg and 2 egg whites. One serving contains 240 calories, 49.9 g carbohydrates and 5.3 g fat.

## PASSOVER BANANA CAKE

An electric mixer is
needed to make the
batter for this cake.

| | |
|---|---|
| ½ cup walnuts or almonds | 1½ cups sugar, divided |
| 2 large, ripe bananas | 1 Tbsp lemon juice |
| 8 eggs, separated | ½ cup potato starch |
| ¼ tsp salt | ½ cup cake meal |

Yield: 15 servings.
Freezes well.

Preheat oven to 350°F.

STEEL BLADE: Process nuts for 6 to 8 seconds, until finely chopped. Empty bowl. Process bananas until puréed, 15 to 20 seconds.

In large bowl of electric mixer, beat egg yolks with salt for 1 minute. Add half the sugar gradually, then beat for 3 minutes. Slowly add bananas and lemon juice. Beat 3 minutes longer. Sift potato starch and cake meal together. Fold in very carefully with a rubber spatula.

Wash beaters thoroughly and dry well. Beat egg whites in another bowl until foamy. Gradually add remaining sugar, continuing to beat until egg whites are stiff but not dry. Fold egg whites gently into batter. Fold in nuts. Pour batter gently into ungreased 10-inch tube pan.

Bake for 1 hour. Reduce heat to 300°F and bake 10 minutes longer. Invert immediately and cool completely.

193 calories per serving, 33.1 g carbohydrates, 0.9 g fiber, 5 g protein, 5.5 g fat (1.1 g saturated fat), 113 g cholesterol, 72 mg sodium, 117 mg potassium, 1 mg iron, 18 mg calcium, 63 mg phosphorus

## MY MOTHER'S PASSOVER CAKE

You need an electric mixer to make this cake, but use your processor to grate the chocolate. You will also need 2 large mixing bowls for this recipe.

Yield: 15 servings.

Freezes well.

3 oz (85 g) chilled bittersweet chocolate bar
½ cup almonds (optional)
9 eggs, separated
1½ cups sugar
½ cup cold water
½ cup potato starch
½ cup cake meal
½ tsp salt

Preheat oven to 350°F.

STEEL BLADE: Break chocolate into 1-inch chunks. Process until fine, about 30 seconds. Add almonds (if using). Process until almonds are finely chopped, 12 to 15 seconds longer.

In large mixing bowl, beat egg yolks with electric mixer until light, 3 to 4 minutes. Add sugar and water and beat on high speed for 8 to 10 minutes. Combine potato starch and cake meal. Sprinkle over yolk mixture a little at a time (a sifter or strainer will help) and fold in carefully. Then fold in grated chocolate and nuts. Wash beaters thoroughly and dry well.

In another large mixing bowl, beat egg whites with salt until stiff but not dry. Carefully fold into batter. Pour gently into ungreased 10-inch tube pan. Batter should come to within 1½ inches of top of pan. If necessary, make a 2-inch collar of foil around top of pan.

Bake for 1 hour, then reduce heat to 300°F for 15 minutes. Invert immediately and cool completely.

184 calories per serving, 31.2 g carbohydrates, 0.5 g fiber, 5 g protein, 5.6 g fat (2.2 g saturated fat), 127 g cholesterol, 115 mg sodium, 38 mg potassium, 1 mg iron, 16 mg calcium, 52 mg phosphorus

## PASSOVER CREAM PUFFS

Yield: 15 medium or 30 miniature puffs.

Unfilled cream puffs freeze well.

½ cup orange juice
½ cup water
¼ cup butter or tub margarine
2 Tbsp sugar
¼ tsp salt
1 cup cake meal
4 eggs

Preheat oven to 425°F.

Combine juice, water, butter or margarine, sugar and salt in saucepan. Bring to a boil, stirring occasionally. As soon as butter is melted, remove from heat and dump in cake meal all at once. Stir vigorously until mixture pulls away from sides of pan. Cool for 5 minutes.

STEEL BLADE: Transfer mixture from saucepan into processor. Process for 5 seconds. Add eggs through feed tube 1 at a time while machine is running. Process 25 to 30 seconds longer once all the eggs have been added. Mixture should be smooth and shiny.

Drop rounded tablespoons of mixture onto sprayed baking sheet. Leave about 2 inches between puffs to allow for expansion during baking.

Bake for 10 minutes. Reduce heat to 375°F and bake 25 to 30 minutes longer. Remove from oven and cut 1-inch slit in each puff to allow steam to escape. Cool completely. Pull out soft insides of each puff before filling.

89 calories each, 9.9 g carbohydrates, 0.3 g fiber, 3 g protein, 4.6 g fat (2.4 g saturated fat), 65 g cholesterol, 78 mg sodium, 34 mg potassium, 0 mg iron, 9 mg calcium, 25 mg phosphorus

### notes

- Fill these with vanilla pudding. Prepare according to package directions, using 1¾ cups milk or nondairy creamer and ¼ cup orange juice. Stir in 1 tsp grated orange rind. One filled cream puff contains 131 calories and 18.8 g carbohydrates.

- Sweetened whipped cream or nondairy whipped topping can also be used as a filling.

# FARFEL MARSHMALLOW TREATS

Guaranteed to please the kids, both big and small!

Yield: 4 dozen squares. Freezes well.

| | |
|---|---|
| ¼ cup butter or tub margarine | 5 cups matzo farfel |
| 5 cups Passover marshmallows | ½ tsp ground cinnamon |
| 1 cup walnuts or almonds | 1 cup chocolate chips, melted |

Melt butter or margarine on low heat in large pot. Add marshmallows and stir until melted. Remove from heat.

STEEL BLADE: Chop nuts with quick on/off pulses, until finely chopped. Add half the nuts to marshmallow mixture. Reserve remaining nuts for garnish. Stir in matzo farfel and cinnamon. Mix well. Spread evenly in sprayed 9- × 13-inch pan. Wet your hands and pat down evenly.

Drizzle melted chocolate over farfel mixture. Sprinkle with reserved nuts. Cool until chocolate is set. Cut into squares.

80 calories each, 11.1 g carbohydrates, 0.5 g fiber, 1 g protein, 3.7 g fat (1.4 g saturated fat), 3 g cholesterol, 15 mg sodium, 29 mg potassium, 0 mg iron, 5 mg calcium, 17 mg phosphorus

## CHOCOLATE MATZO BARK

Absolutely addictive! The original recipe was made using either graham wafers or soda crackers. You'll love this Passover version— matzo never tasted so good!

Yield: 25 to 30 servings— but probably less, because once you taste this, you can't stop! Freezes well.

| | |
|---|---|
| 6 matzos | 1 cup unsalted butter or margarine |
| 1 cup pecans or almonds | 1¼ cups brown sugar, packed |
| 12 oz (340 g) bittersweet chocolate | |
| (or 2 cups chocolate chips) | |

Preheat oven to 350°F. Line a 12- × 18-inch jelly roll pan completely with aluminum foil. Spray foil very well with nonstick spray. Arrange matzos in single layer, breaking pieces to fit.

STEEL BLADE: Process nuts with several quick on/off pulses, until coarsely chopped. Remove from bowl and set aside. If using bittersweet chocolate, chop with quick on/off pulses, then let processor run until chopped, 25 to 30 seconds. (Omit this step if using chocolate chips.)

Melt butter or margarine in 2-quart saucepan. Stir in brown sugar and bring to a boil. Reduce heat to medium and boil 2 to 3 minutes, stirring constantly. Carefully pour mixture over matzos.

Bake for 10 minutes. Remove from oven and sprinkle evenly with chocolate. Return pan to oven for 3 to 4 minutes to melt chocolate. Remove from oven and spread chocolate evenly over matzos with a spatula. Sprinkle with nuts.

When cool, place in freezer or refrigerator until chocolate has set. Cut or break into small pieces. Store in an airtight container in refrigerator.

270 calories per serving, 29.1 g carbohydrates, 2.3 g fiber, 2 g protein, 17.4 g fat (8.7 g saturated fat), 21 g cholesterol, 5 mg sodium, 67 mg potassium, 1 mg iron, 17 mg calcium, 30 mg phosphorus

## PASSOVER BROWNIES

Yield: 48 small squares. Freezes well.

| | |
|---|---|
| 1 cup walnuts | 1 cup cake meal |
| 4 eggs | ½ cup unsweetened cocoa powder |
| 1½ cups sugar | 1 Tbsp potato starch |
| ⅔ cup oil | 1 Tbsp orange juice |

Preheat oven to 350°F.

STEEL BLADE: Chop nuts coarsely with 6 or 8 quick on/off pulses. Empty bowl. Process eggs with sugar for 1 minute, until light. Add oil through feed tube while machine is running. Process 30 seconds longer. Uncover and sprinkle cake

*Continued*

meal, cocoa and potato starch over batter; drizzle with orange juice. Process with 3 or 4 quick on/off pulses. Add nuts and mix in quickly with 1 or 2 more pulses.

Pour batter into sprayed 9- × 13-inch baking pan. Bake for about 25 minutes. Cool completely. Cut into squares.

87 calories each, 9.6 g carbohydrates, 0.5 g fiber, 1 g protein, 5.3 g fat (0.6 g saturated fat), 18 g cholesterol, 6 mg sodium, 30 mg potassium, 0 mg iron, 6 mg calcium, 22 mg phosphorus

### variations

- Place a layer of chocolate-covered Passover mint patties (½ lb/227 g) over hot brownies and spread quickly to frost brownies. One brownie contains 105 calories and 13.5 g carbohydrates.

- Cut marshmallows in half and place cut side down on top of hot brownies (or top with 4 cups miniature marshmallows). Bake 5 minutes longer, until puffy. Cool completely. Frost with Chocolate Fudge Frosting (page 383). One brownie contains 154 calories, 22.9 g carbohydrates and 7.1 g fat.

### notes

- Icing sugar contains cornstarch and cannot be used for Passover. If Passover icing sugar is not available, it's easy to make your own (see page 493). Use for your favorite chocolate icing.

- Pure vanilla extract for Passover is not available, so substitute Passover vanilla.

## FUDGY BROWNIES

These gluten-free, nut-free brownies are excellent for Passover—or any time of year!

Yield: 48 squares. These freeze well—if they last that long!

4 eggs
1¾ cups sugar
1 cup oil
1 cup potato starch
¾ cup unsweetened cocoa powder
¼ tsp salt

Preheat oven to 350°F. Spray a 9- × 13-inch baking pan with nonstick spray.

STEEL BLADE: Process eggs and sugar for 1 minute, until light. Add oil through feed tube while machine is running. Process 30 seconds longer. Uncover and sprinkle potato starch, cocoa and salt over mixture. Blend in with several quick on/off pulses, just until combined. Pour into prepared pan and spread evenly.

Bake for 30 to 35 minutes. Cool completely. Frost with Chocolate Fudge Frosting (page 383), if desired.

89 calories each, 10.8 g carbohydrates, 0.4 g fiber, 1 g protein, 5.3 g fat (0.6 g saturated fat), 18 g cholesterol, 18 mg sodium, 26 mg potassium, 0 mg iron, 4 mg calcium, 17 mg phosphorus

Five minutes before end of baking, sprinkle 4 cups miniature marshmallows evenly over brownies. Return pan to oven and bake 5 minutes longer. Cool completely. Prepare Decadent Chocolate Glaze (page 326) using Passover vanilla. Drizzle over marshmallow topping in a zigzag design. One brownie contains 110 calories, 15.3 g carbohydrates and 5.6 g fat.

## PASSOVER MUD COOKIES

These gluten-free cookies are so good! Sandra Phillips of Montreal got the recipe from Sandy Schreter, who got it from her sister, Aviva Yalovsky. These taste best right from the freezer.

Yield: 4 dozen small or 2 dozen large cookies. Freezes well.

4 cups pecans or walnuts

3½ cups Passover icing sugar (page 493)

6 Tbsp unsweetened cocoa powder

4 egg whites

2 tsp Passover vanilla or 1 Tbsp Passover liqueur

Preheat oven to 350°F.

STEEL BLADE: Place nuts in food processor first, followed by remaining ingredients. Pulse until mixture is moist but not overprocessed. It should look like rocks and mud. Drop from a teaspoon onto parchment-lined baking sheets.

Bake 10 to 14 minutes, depending on size, not more. Remove from pan, cool and place in freezer on a tray. When frozen, store in plastic freezer bags.

100 calories each, 10.4 g carbohydrates, 1.1 g fiber, 1 g protein, 6.6 g fat (0.6 g saturated fat), 0 g cholesterol, 5 mg sodium, 52 mg potassium, 0 mg iron, 8 mg calcium, 31 mg phosphorus

## MUSTACHUDOS

This gluten-free cookie is perfect all year round. Thanks to Helen Berg of Australia and the late Raya Tarab of Israel for their tips on this Turkish delight.

Yield: 4 to 5 dozen. Freezes well.

3 cups almonds (or a mixture of walnuts and pecans)

1 cup sugar

2 eggs

1 tsp ground cinnamon

Preheat oven to 350°F.

STEEL BLADE: Process almonds using on/off pulses, until coarsely chopped, about 30 seconds. (Walnuts and pecans will take less time.) Don't grind nuts too fine or you will have nut butter! Empty bowl. Process sugar with eggs and cinnamon until well mixed, 25 to 30 seconds. Add nuts and process 10 to 15 seconds longer to combine. Mixture will be like a thick paste.

Drop by teaspoonfuls onto parchment-lined baking sheets, leaving 1 inch between cookies. Bake for 12 to 15 minutes. When done, cookies will be oatmeal-

*Continued*

colored with lightly browned edges. However, they will be slightly soft and not look fully baked. Do not remove cookies from pan until completely cooled. They will firm up as they cool. If baked until firm, they will be too hard when they cool completely.

53 calories each, 5.5 g carbohydrates, 0.7 g fiber, 2 g protein, 3.1 g fat (0.3 g saturated fat), 9 g cholesterol, 3 mg sodium, 44 mg potassium, 0 mg iron, 17 mg calcium, 31 mg phosphorus

## COCONUT ALMOND MACAROONS

Shirley Millett, my devoted office manager, adores these cookies.

Yield: About 4 dozen.
Freezes well.

1½ cups almonds

3 egg whites

1 Tbsp lemon juice

1 cup sugar

1½ cups coconut

Preheat oven to 350°F.

STEEL BLADE: Process almonds until finely ground, about 30 seconds. Remove from bowl and set aside. Wash bowl and blade thoroughly. Dry well.

Process egg whites with lemon juice for 1 minute. Gradually add sugar through feed tube while machine is running; process 1 minute longer. Add almonds and coconut and process 10 seconds longer, just until combined.

Drop from a teaspoon onto parchment-lined baking sheets. Bake for 12 to 15 minutes, until set and oatmeal-colored. Cool completely.

49 calories each, 6.3 g carbohydrates, 0.5 g fiber, 1 g protein, 2.5 g fat (1 g saturated fat), 0 g cholesterol, 11 mg sodium, 34 mg potassium, 0 mg iron, 8 mg calcium, 17 mg phosphorus

### variation

Add 2 Tbsp unsweetened cocoa powder to meringue mixture along with ground almonds and coconut. Bake as directed. When cooled, dip cookies halfway into 3 oz (85 g) melted bittersweet chocolate and place on parchment paper to dry. One cookie contains 58 calories, 7.3 g carbohydrates and 3.2 g fat.

# PASSOVER MANDELBROIT

These crisp, gluten-free cookies are the Jewish version of biscotti—and they're absolutely addictive! Bake them in loaf pans because they'll spread too much if you try to bake them on a cookie sheet. Mandelbroit is the Jewish word for "almond bread," but if you make them with chocolate chips, they'll become "Chips-cotti!"

Yield: 3 dozen large slices (see Note). Freezes well.

3 eggs

1 cup sugar

¾ cup oil

2 Tbsp orange juice

2¾ cups potato starch

2 tsp Passover baking powder

1 cup slivered almonds or chocolate chips (or ¾ cup of each)

⅓ cup sugar mixed with 2 tsp ground cinnamon

Preheat oven to 350°F. Spray two 9- × 5-inch loaf pans with nonstick spray.

STEEL BLADE: Process eggs and sugar for 1 minute. Drizzle oil and orange juice through feed tube while machine is running. Process 45 seconds longer. Remove cover and sprinkle potato starch and baking powder on top of batter. Process with 4 or 5 quick on/off pulses to combine. Add nuts and/or chocolate chips; mix in with 2 or 3 quick on/off pulses. Mixture will be sticky; don't overprocess. Divide mixture evenly between loaf pans.

Bake for 45 to 55 minutes, until golden. Cool for 10 minutes. Carefully remove from pans and transfer to a cutting board. Reduce heat to 275°F.

Slice with a sharp knife into ½-inch slices. Place in a single layer on parchment-lined baking sheets. Sprinkle generously on both sides with cinnamon sugar.

Bake at 275°F for 35 to 45 minutes, until lightly toasted.

131 calories each, 18.2 g carbohydrates, 0.4 g fiber, 1 g protein, 6.6 g fat (0.6 g saturated fat), 18 g cholesterol, 32 mg sodium, 29 mg potassium, 0 mg iron, 27 mg calcium, 26 mg phosphorus

## note

For smaller slices, bake mixture in three 8- × 4-inch loaf pans. Makes about 4 dozen. One cookie contains 99 calories, 13.7 g carbohydrates and 4.9 g fat.

# ACKNOWLEDGMENTS

No cookbook is ever written alone, and this completely revised edition of *The Food Processor Bible* is no exception. It's been an immense undertaking to update this cookbook, which originated over 30 years ago with *The Pleasures of Your Processor*. My gratitude and appreciation go to the many special people who generously contributed their knowledge, suggestions and treasured recipes. You helped make this the best food processor cookbook ever. My heartfelt thanks go to:

Robert McCullough of Whitecap Books, who has a passion for cookbooks, kitchen toys and knishes! His vision, enthusiasm, wisdom and support helped make this 30th anniversary edition of *The Food Processor Bible* a reality.

The Whitecap Bunch, especially Taryn Boyd and Michelle Furbacher and their teams (Cameron Johnson, Grace Yaginuma, Viola Funk, Mauve Pagé, Setareh Ashrafologhalai and Paula Ayer) for their professional expertise, guidance and patience.

Stephanie Von Hirschberg, my literary agent, for her warmth, encouragement and efforts on my behalf.

Elaine Kaplan, who diligently organized and fine-tuned the manuscript for the first edition of *The Food Processor Bible*, then helped take this revised and updated edition to new heights. She pushed me to write a better book than I could have ever written on my own. Her dedication, especially in the final stages of proofing, was extraordinary.

Shirley Millett, who runs my office and keeps my life organized, for her commitment, caring and attention to the tiniest of details. She proofread the revised manuscript, and often provided the perfect phrase when I was at a loss for words. She nagged me when I procrastinated and always kept my coffee cup filled. She keeps me balanced in more ways than one, and I am blessed to have her in my life.

Erin Temple, Amna Malik and Millie Khondkar, my nutrition students, who volunteered their time and worked so diligently on the nutritional analysis of my recipes. Thanks to Raquel Duchen for setting up the guidelines for this project.

Dietician Ilana Kobric for her excellent nutritional guidance and also for setting up a focus group of moms, babies and toddlers who provided feedback for the baby food section of this book.

Maria Sullivan, who whipped the huge index into shape.

Rhonda Matias and Bruce Rykiss, my sister and brother, for their encouragement, love and support, and my wonderful children, Jodi and Paul Sprackman, Steven and Cheryl Gilletz, and Doug and Ariane Gilletz, who are always there for me. They are all excellent cooks who follow our family tradition of cooking great food.

My granddaughters, Lauren and Camille Sprackman, and my grandsons, Max, Sam and Zak Gilletz, who represent the future generation of cooks and eaters! I wish we all lived closer to each other so they could enjoy my cooking more often.

My devoted dog, Maizie, who prefers "people food" and turns her nose up at dog food.

My wonderful friends and family, both near and far, for sharing their favorite recipes, providing encouragement and valuable feedback, and making sure that I never went hungry when I was too tired to cook. Special thanks go to Helene Medjuck, who was always ready to lend a helping hand and an extra pair of eyes. Carole Alexander and Faye Zeidman provided valuable feedback and Cheryl Goldberg always had room for me at her table for her scrumptious Friday night dinners. Thanks to Laya Crust for sharing her Passover adaptations of many of my recipes.

Rachel Litner, who always found answers to my many questions about Cuisinart's newest generation of food processors so I could provide you with accurate and updated information.

Special thanks to Seattle food writer Melissa Trainer for her valuable knowledge and advice and her helpful feedback.

My cooking students, readers and visitors to my website (www.gourmania.com) for their wonderful letters, phone calls and e-mails over the years. Thanks for letting me know how much pleasure my recipes have brought you. Your loyalty makes it all worthwhile.

Thank you, one and all!

# INDEX

Recipes that are suitable for Passover, have a Passover variation, or can be easily modified, are in orange. Refer to pages 492–94 for specific substitutions/modifications.

acorn squash
   how to process, 33
almond flour
   Apricot Almond Triangles, 452–53
   how to process, 41
almonds
   Almond Crescents, 429–30
   Almond Crisp Bars, 452
   Almond Tea Ring, 324
   Apricot Almond Triangles, 452–53
   Biscuit Tortoni, 415
   Chocolate Almond Biscotti, 445
   Coconut Almond Macaroons, 526
   Cranberry or Raisin Challah, 305
   Fish Fillets Amandine, 128
   ground almonds in Passover cooking/baking, 492, 493
   Linzertorte, 402–3
   Mandel Bread (Mandelbroit), 444–45, 527
   Mushroom Almond Chicken Stir-Fry, 206–7
   Mustachudos, 525–26
   Panko-Crusted Chicken Fingers, 214–15
   toasting, 128, 407
   See also nuts
appetizers, 49–79
   Asparagus Cheese Rolls, 67–68
   Bruschetta, 68
   Carrot Latkes, 243–44
   Chicken Guy Kew, 208
   Chicken or Meat Turnovers, 75
   Easy Nachos, 51
   Easy Potato Latkes, 245
   Falafel, 78
   Focaccia, 316–17

Gefilte Fish, 118–19
Gougères (French Cheese Puffs), 72
Herbed Cheese Log, 64–65
Lox and Cheese Ring, 64
Make-and-Bake Pizza, 69–70
Mango Quesadillas, 67
Mom's Caponata, 232–33
Mushroom Turnovers, 74–75
Party Meatballs, 78–79
Pita Chips, 318
Pizza Pinwheels, 314–15
Pizza Tarts, 70–71
Potato Knishes, 256–57
Ratatouille, 233
Roasted Red Pepper Crescents, 73
Salmon or Tuna Mousse, 63
Salmon Tortilla Pinwheels, 66
Sesame Cheese Straws, 71
Spanakopita (Phyllo Triangles), 73–74
Spinach Cheese Turnovers, 75
Stuffed Italian Mushrooms, 75–76
Sweet and Sour Eggplant, 231
tips, 50–51
Veggie Latkes, 246
Zucchini Puffs, 242–43
See also dips; egg rolls; Passover appetizers and spreads; spreads
apples
   Another Passover Apple Cake, 519–20
   Apple Chips, 415–16
   Apple Coffee Cake, 351–52
   Apple Crostata, 475–76
   Apple Flan, 476–77
   Apple Lover's Cake, 351
   Apple Strudel, 477
   Blueberry Apple Pie, 474
   Crumbly Apple Pie, 475
   Easy Apple Crumble, 416
   Family Apple Cake, 352–53
   Family Apple Pie, 474
   Farfel Apple Pudding, 503
   Honey Apple Cake, 363–64
   how to process, 24

Lattice Apple Cake, 353–54
Passover Apple Cake, 519
Passover Apple Crumb Pie, 516
applesauce
   Applesauce Date and Nut Cake, 354–55
   Applesauce Streusel Cake, 355
   as fat substitute, 346
   how to process, 24
apricots
   Apricot Almond Triangles, 452–53
   Apricot Raisin Filling, 446
   Farfel Apricot Pudding, 504
   how to process, 24, 25, 26
artichoke hearts
   Broccoli Cheese Squares, 153
Asian cuisine
   Asian Coleslaw, 269
   Asian Green Bean Bake, 227
   Asian Luncheon Salad, 278
   Asian Salad Dressing, 292
   Asian Spinach Salad, 278–79
   See also Chinese foods; stir-fries; teriyaki
asparagus
   Asparagus Cheese Rolls, 67–68
   Roasted Asparagus with Portobello Mushrooms, 226
avocados
   Dark and Decadent Chocolate Pâté, 412
   Egg and Avocado Spread, 55
   Guacamole, 54–55
   how to process, 24

baby food, 16–21
   Baby Food Chart, 19–21
   tips, 16–18
bagels, 318–19
   Bagel, Salmon and Broccoli Casserole, 149
   Passover Rolls or Bagels, 513–14
baked Alaska
   Fudge Ribbon Baked Alaska Pie, 486–87
baking
   baking faults, 349
   oven temperatures, 44, 348, 350

pan capacity, 43
pan substitutions, 350
baking powder
tips, 346, 349
bananas
Banana Chocolate Chip Drops, 434
Banana Cranberry Chocolate Chip Cake, 356
Banana Frosting, 382
Banana Yogurt Cake, 355–56
Best Banana Bread, 333–34
Chocolate Banana Streusel Cake, 357
Chocolate Banana Streusel Cupcakes, 357
how to process, 25
One-Banana Muffins, 335
Passover Banana Cake, 520–21
barbecued foods
Barbecued Lyonnaise Potatoes, 236
Easy Barbecue Sauce, 105
Marinated Barbecued Chicken, 210–11
Orange Teriyaki Grilled Salmon, 123–24
Salmon Burgers, 134–35
Tangy Orange Barbecue Chicken, 210
Teriyaki Steak, 181
wood chip tips, 124
bars. See squares
basil
how to process, 30
Pesto, 105–6
batters
Basic Crêpe Batter, 162–63
Deep-Fry Beer Batter, 128
how to process, 37
tips, 13, 14, 344–50, 423
beans
Asian Green Bean Bake, 227
French-Cut Green Beans, 226
how to process, 27
Marinated Bean Salad, 271
Marinated Fresh Vegetable Salad, 270
Salad Niçoise, 276–77
Vegetarian Chopped Liver, 57–58

See also chickpeas
Béchamel (White) Sauce, 103–4
beef
Chicken or Meat Filling, 257–58
Chicken or Meat Turnovers, 75
Chili, 197
Chopped Liver, 58–59
Corned Beef Filling, 257
food safety, 173
grinding: Grind Your Own, 36
Hamburgers à la Dutch, 196–97
how to process, 35–36
Meatball Soup, 86
Moist and Spicy Meat Loaf, 201
Oven Stew, 188
Passover Wacky Franks, 497–98
Potato Kugel Meat Loaf, 201–2
Shipwreck, 203
Sneaky Spaghetti Sauce, 200
Stew Italiano, 189–90
Stir-Fried Beef and Broccoli, 203–4
Stuffed Shoulder Steak Rolls, 498
Super Spaghetti Sauce, 199
Teriyaki Chuck Roast, 180–81
Teriyaki Steak, 181
tips and techniques, 172–74
See also brisket; meatballs; ribs
beets
Dairy Beet Borscht, 85–86
Horseradish, 110–11
how to process, 27
bell peppers. See peppers
berries
Berry Good Sherbet, 414
Berry Hand Pies, 478
how to process, 26
See also blueberries; cranberries; raspberries; strawberries
biscotti
Chocolate Almond Biscotti, 445
See also mandel bread
biscuits
Biscuit Tortoni, 415
Scones, 340–41
blades, 4
cleaning, 7–8
how to use them, 9–12
safety, 6–7

Smart Chart, 24–41
blintzes
Blintz Soufflé, 166
Cheese Blintzes, 165
Crazy Blintz Soufflé, 167
Egg Roll Blintzes, 506
Florentine Cupcake Blintzes, 510–11
Gluten-Free Blintzes, 505
Passover Blintzes, 505
Passover Cupcake Blintzes, 510
See also crêpes
blueberries
Berry Hand Pies, 478
Blueberry Apple Pie, 474
Blueberry Crumble Cake, 358–59
Blueberry Streusel Dessert, 417
Family Blueberry Cake, 358
how to process, 26
Mom's Blueberry Muffins, 335–36
borekas
Spinach Borekas, 154–55
borscht
Dairy Beet Borscht, 85–86
Vegetarian Cabbage Soup, 86
brandy
Brandy Hard Sauce, 418
English Plum Pudding with Brandy Hard Sauce, 417–18
Walnut Brandy Cookies, 437
bran muffins
Honey Bran Muffins, 336
Sugar-Free Bran Muffins, 337
bread crumbs. See crumbs—bread
breads—quick breads, 295, 300, 332–35
Best Banana Bread, 333–34
I Can't Believe It's Broccoli Bread!, 332
Nana's Zucchini Bread, 334–35
Orange Corn Bread, 333
See also muffins
breads—yeast breads and doughs, 295–331
100% Whole Wheat Bread or Rolls, 309
All-Purpose Pareve Dough, 321–22
Almond Tea Ring, 324

breads—yeast breads and doughs
  (*continued*)
  Asparagus Cheese Rolls, 67–68
  Bagels, 318–19
  Baker's Glaze, 311
  Best-Ever Onion Rolls, 319–20
  Bialies, 321
  Bread Stuffing, 182–83
  Brioche, 328–29
  Bubble Ring Coffee Cake, 325
  Cheddar Cheese Puff, 148
  Chocolate Babka, 325–26
  Chocolate or Cheese Danish, 327
  Chocolate Shmear, 326
  Cinnamon Buns or Kuchen,
    323–24
  Cinnamon Raisin Bread, 308
  Cinnamon-Sugar, 324
  Confetti Bread, 313–14
  Criss-Cross Buns, 330–31
  Croissants, 329–30
  Crusty French Bread, 306
  Decadent Chocolate Glaze, 326
  Dinner Rolls, 307
  Do-Ahead (Pizza) Dough, 70
  Focaccia, 316–17
  freezing, 299–300
  Homemade White Bread, 306–7
  how to process dough, 38, 304–5
  Kaiser or Vienna Rolls, 307
  Make-and-Bake Pizza, 69–70
  Norene's Yummy Yeast Dough,
    322–23
  Old-Fashioned Rye Bread, 310–11
  Onion Rye Bread, 311
  Pareve White Bread, 308
  Pareve Whole Wheat Bread, 308
  Passover Onion Rolls, 514
  Pita Bread, 317–18
  Pizza Pinwheels, 314–15
  Potato and Onion Focaccia, 317
  Pumpernickel Bread, 311–12
  Rye Crescents, 311
  Sticky Pecan Buns, 323–24
  Stollen, 331–32
  Streusel Topping, 302
  tips, 296–300, 304–5, 319, 321
  Vienna or Kaiser Rolls, 307
  Wholesome Oatmeal Bread,
    312–13

*See also* challah; Danish
brioche, 328–29
brisket
  how to process, 35
  Marinated Brisket, 176–77
  Oven-Roasted Pickled Brisket,
    180
  Overnight Roast, 179
  Savory Brisket or Top Rib,
    178–79
  Super Roast Brisket, 177–78
  Veal Brisket with Stuffing, 182
broccoli
  Bagel, Salmon and Broccoli
    Casserole, 149
  Broccoli Cheese Squares, 153
  Broccoli Latkes, 244
  Broccoli Lentil Soup, 97–98
  Broccoli-Stuffed Fillets with
    Mushroom Sauce, 130–31
  Cheesy Broccoli Casserole, 152
  Chickpea Broccoli Salad, 285–86
  Easy Broccoli Bake, 227–28
  Herbed Cauliflower or Broccoli
    Soup, 98
  Hoisin Vegetable Stir-Fry, 248
  how to process, 27
  I Can't Believe It's Broccoli
    Bread!, 332
  Pasta Vegetable Medley, 141–42
  Stir-Fried Beef and Broccoli,
    203–4
  Stir-Fried Chicken and Broccoli,
    204
broth
  alternatives to homemade, 82
  *See also* soups
brownies
  Basic Brownies, 453–54
  Brownie Bites, 457
  Butterscotch Brownies, 454–55
  Chocolate Marshmallow
    Brownies, 454
  Fudgy Brownies, 524–25
  Marbled Cheesecake Brownies,
    455–56
  Passover Brownies, 523–24
  Peppermint Patty Brownies, 454
  Polka Dot Brownies, 456
  Rocky Roads, 525

  Two-Tone Mint Brownies, 454
brown sugar
  how to process, 41
bruschetta, 68
bulgur
  Chickpea Chili, 234
  Tabbouleh Salad, 285
burgers
  Hamburgers à la Dutch, 196–97
  Salmon Burgers, 134–35
butter
  Almond Crescents, 429–30
  Butter Tarts, 483
  Dill Butter, 66
  Garlic Butter, 65–66
  Homemade Butter, 41
  how to process, 39
  Lighter Butter, 39
  Standard Butter Pastry, 470
buttermilk
  Buttermilk Noodle Kugel, 143
  Buttermilk Pancakes, 161–62
  substitute, 347
butternut squash
  "Gourd for You" Hummus, 56
  how to process, 33
  Sweet Potato Squash Soup,
    99, 100
  tips, 100
butterscotch
  Butterscotch Brownies, 454–55
  Butterscotch Toffee Dreams, 439
  *See also* toffee/Skor bits

cabbage
  Asian Coleslaw, 269
  how to process, 27
  Super Coleslaw, 268
  Vegetarian Cabbage Soup, 86
Caesar Salad, 273
cake mixes
  how to process, 37
cakes, 342–79, 519–21
  Another Passover Apple Cake,
    519–20
  Apple Lover's Cake, 351
  Applesauce Date and Nut Cake,
    354–55
  Applesauce Streusel Cake, 355

cakes (*continued*)

baking faults, 349

Banana Cranberry Chocolate Chip Cake, 356

Banana Yogurt Cake, 355–56

Basic Pareve Cake, 369–70

Blueberry Crumble Cake, 358–59

Burnt Sugar Cake, 361–62

cake pans, temperatures and times, 350

Carrot Honey Loaf, 360

Carrot Pineapple Cake, 379

Chocolate Banana Streusel Cake, 357

Cinnamon Marble Cake, 374

Cockeyed Cake, 364

Dark Rich Fruitcake, 379–80

Family Apple Cake, 352–53

Family Blueberry Cake, 358

Favorite Chocolate Chip Cake, 368

Flourless "Chick"-olate Cake, 367

freezing, 348–49

Genie's Birthday Cake, 359

Gluten-Free Flour Mix, 345–46

High Skor Chocolate Cake, 365

Honey Apple Cake, 363–64

Honey Cola Cake, 362–63

Hot Cheese Cake, 147

how to process, 344–45

Lattice Apple Cake, 353–54

Malakov Cream Cake, 403–4

Marble Marvel Cake, 374–75

Mom's Old-Fashioned Crumb Cake, 376–77

My Mother's Passover Cake, 521

Nutritious Carrot Cake, 360–61

Pareve Chocolate Cake, 364–65

Passover Apple Cake, 519

Passover Banana Cake, 520–21

Passover cakes, 519–21

Pistachio Marble Cake, 369

Poppy Seed Cake, 376

Prune Purée, 346

Raisin Spice Cake, 377–78

Root Beer Cake, 365–66

Root Beer Glaze, 366

Secret Chocolate Chip Cake, 368–69

Sour Cream Fudge Cake, 366–67

tips, 344–50

Zesty Orange Loaf, 375

Zucchini Spice Cake, 378–79

*See also* cheesecakes; coffee cakes; cupcakes; frostings; glazes

candy

how to process, 39

*See also* chocolate and chocolate chips; fudge; marshmallows; peppermint; toffee/Skor bits

cannelloni

Cheese Cannelloni (Crêpes Italiano), 164–65

caponata

Mom's Caponata, 232–33

carrots

Apricot Candied Carrots, 228

Baked Veggie Patties, 247

Carrot and Raisin Salad, 271

Carrot and Sweet Potato Soup, 95–96

Carrot Honey Loaf, 360

Carrot Kugel, 239–40

Carrot Latkes, 243–44

Carrot Muffins, 361

Carrot Pineapple Cake, 379

Carrot Purée, 20, 360

Carrot Ring, 229

Carrot Soufflé, 229–30

Carrot Soup, 96

Cheryl's Vegetable Casserole, 500–501

Honey-Glazed Roasted Roots, 235

how to process, 27

Morning Glorious Muffins, 338

Nutritious Carrot Cake, 360–61

Passover Carrot Kugel, 508

Passover Carrot Tsimmis, 508–9

Pineapple Carrots, 228

Tangy Marinated Carrot Salad, 269–70

casseroles

Bagel, Salmon and Broccoli Casserole, 149

Baked Halibut and Potato Casserole, 124

Cheesy Broccoli Casserole, 152

Cheryl's Vegetable Casserole, 500–501

Favorite Tuna Casserole, 137–38

Leek and Rice Skillet Casserole, 253

Stuffing Casserole, 262–63

*See also* lasagnas

caster sugar

how to process, 41

cauliflower

Faux-Tato Salad, 272–73

Herbed Cauliflower or Broccoli Soup, 98

how to process, 28

Low-Carb "Fried Rice," 250–51

celery and celery root

how to process, 28

challah, 301–5

Challah (Double Recipe for Large Processors), 302–3

Challah Rolls (Bulkas), 302

Chocolate Chip Challah, 305

Cranberry or Raisin Challah, 305

Garlic Buns, 320

Heavenly Holiday Challah (for 16-Cup Processors), 303–5

Honey Raisin Challah, 301–2

charoset, 495

Charoset Truffles, 495

cheater chop, 15, 225

cheddar cheese. *See* cheese— cheddar, swiss, mozzarella cheese

cheese—cheddar, swiss, mozzarella cheese

Asparagus Cheese Rolls, 67–68

Broccoli Cheese Squares, 153

Broiled Cheesy Fillets, 129

Cheddar Cheese Puff, 148

Cheese Cannelloni (Crepes Italiano), 164–65

Cheese Fondue, 168

Cheese Sauce, 104

Cheese Scones, 341

Cheesy Broccoli Casserole, 152

Easy Broccoli Bake, 227–28

Easy Nachos, 51

Eggplant Italiano, 230

Favorite Tuna Casserole, 137–38

cheese—cheddar, swiss, mozzarella cheese (*continued*)

Fish Italian Style, 131–32

Gougères (French Cheese Puffs), 72

how to process, 34, 117

Italian Cheese Puff, 148

Layered Salad, 275–76

Make-and-Bake Pizza, 69–70

Marty's Garlic Cheese Dressing, 290

No-Fry Eggplant Parmesan, 231–32

nutritional analysis, 47

Onion Soup au Gratin, 103

Passover Eggplant Parmesan, 232

Penne with Roasted Tomatoes and Garlic au Gratin, 142–43

Sesame Cheese Straws, 71

Sole Mornay, 132

Spinach Cheese Bake, 154

Swiss Tuna Bake, 137

Three-Cheese Sweet Kugel, 146

tips, 116–17

Vegetable Cheese Chowder, 101–2

*See also* cheesecakes; lasagnas; quiches

cheese—cream cheese, cottage cheese, ricotta cheese

Almost Sour Cream!, 145–46

Blintz Soufflé, 166

Buttermilk Noodle Kugel, 143

Cheese Blintzes, 165

Cheese Cannelloni (Crêpes Italiano), 164–65

Cheese Filling, 166

Cheese Filling for Spinach Cheese Phyllo Puff, 150

Cheese Knishes, 156

Cheesy Broccoli Casserole, 152

Chocolate Cream Cheese Pastry, 472

Cookie's Hot Milk Cheese Kugel, 144

Cottage Cheese Muffins, 337–38

Crazy Blintz Soufflé, 167

Cream Cheese Frosting, 384

Cream Cheese Pastry, 472

Creamy Garlic Dressing, 290

Easy Cheese Dreams, 456

Easy Cottage Cheese Pancakes, 161

Farmer's Salad, 275

Flavored Cheese Spreads, 117

Florentine Crêpes, 163

Florentine Cupcake Blintzes, 510–11

Florentine Noodle Kugel, 144–45

Herbed Cheese Log, 64–65

Hot Cheese Cake, 147

how to process, 34, 117

Kreplach, 258–59

Light 'n' Lemony Cheese Dessert, 408–9

Lox and Cheese Ring, 64

Lox and Cheese Spread, 63–64

No-Crust Cheese and Spinach Pie, 159

No-Dough Cheese Knishes, 155

nutritional analysis, 47

Passover Cheese Latkes, 509–10

Passover Cheese Pie, 517

Pineapple Noodle Kugel, 145

Spanakopita (Phyllo Triangles), 73–74

Spinach Cheese Phyllo Puff, 149–50

Spinach Cheese Turnovers, 75

Three-Cheese Sweet Kugel, 146

tips, 116–17

Yogurt Cheese, 391

*See also* cheesecakes; lasagnas

cheese—feta cheese

Greek Salad, 280

Spinach Borekas, 154–55

cheese—Parmesan cheese

Caesar Salad, 273

Easy Fish Bake, 126–27

Florentine Crêpes, 163

how to process, 34

No-Fry Eggplant Parmesan, 231–32

Onion Soup au Gratin, 103

Passover Eggplant Parmesan, 232

Stuffed Fish Fillets au Gratin, 129–30

Swiss Tuna Bake, 137

cheesecakes, 387, 392–97, 517–18

Chocolate Cheesecake, 395–96

Dairy-Free Cheesecake, 392

Dreamy Creamy Chocolate Cheesecake, 396–97

Easy Cheesecake, 393–95

Fresh Strawberry Topping, 394

Glazed Fresh Fruit Topping, 395

Glazed Fruit Cheesecake, 518

Hot Cheese Cake, 147

Mandarin Orange Topping, 395

Marbled Cheesecake, 518

Marbled Cheesecake Brownies, 455–56

Marbled Variation, 455, 518

Mini Cheesecakes, 395

Strawberry Dream Cheesecake, 393

tips, 392

toppings, 394–95

cherries, dried

how to process, 25

chicken

Baked Crunchy Sesame Chicken, 213

Chicken and Vegetable Bake, 211

Chicken Chili, 198

Chicken Guy Kew, 208

Chicken in Pineapple-Orange Sauce, 209

Chicken Meatball Soup, 88–89

Chicken or Meat Filling, 257–58

Chicken or Meat Turnovers, 75

Chicken or Turkey Salad Spread, 59

Chinese Chicken Dinner-in-a-Dish, 208–9

Chinese Chicken Liver Stir-Fry, 204–5

Cranberry Chicken Meatballs, 193

Crunchy Sesame Chicken, 213

Farfel, Chicken and Vegetable Kugel, 503–4

food safety, 173

grinding: Grind Your Own, 36

Hamburgers à la Dutch, 196–97

Heavenly Chicken, 211–12

how to process, 35–36

Italian Seasoned Chicken with
Potatoes, 212–13

Mandarin Chicken Meatballs,
194

Maple-Glazed Garlic Chicken
Breasts, 215

Marinated Barbecued Chicken,
210–11

Moo Goo Guy Kew, 207

Mushroom Almond Chicken
Stir-Fry, 206–7

Panko-Crusted Chicken Fingers,
214–15

Passover Chicken or Turkey
Schnitzel, 213

Passover Wacky Franks, 497–98

Phony Minestrone, 92–93

Pineapple Chicken Meatballs, 195

Potato-Crusted Chicken, 214

Slow Cooker Chicken Soup, 90

slow cookers, 173–74

Sneaky Spaghetti Sauce, 200

Sticky Chicky, 215–16

Stir-Fried Chicken and Broccoli,
204

Stuffed Chicken Breasts, 499

Tangy Orange Barbecue
Chicken, 210

Teriyaki Turkey or Chicken Stir-
Fry, 205–6

tips, 172–74

See also beef; meatballs; turkey;
veal

chicken wings

Baked Crunchy Sesame Chicken,
213

chickpeas

Bev's Colorful Couscous Salad,
281–82

Chickpea Broccoli Salad, 285–86

Chickpea Chili, 234

Falafel, 78

Flourless "Chick"-olate Cake,
367

"Gourd for You" Hummus, 56

Hummus, 56

Roasted Red Pepper Hummus,
56

See also beans

chili, 197–98

Chicken Chili, 198

Chickpea Chili, 234

Chinese foods

Cantonese Marinade, 109

Cantonese Short Ribs, 186–87

Chicken Guy Kew, 208

Chinese Chicken Dinner-in-a-
Dish, 208–9

Chinese Chicken Liver Stir-Fry,
204–5

Chinese Fried Rice, 251–52

Chinese Marinade, 109

Chinese Sweet and Sour Sauce,
108

Low-Carb "Fried Rice," 250–51

Mandarin Chicken Meatballs,
194

Moo Goo Guy Kew, 207

See also Asian cuisine

chocolate and chocolate chips,
420–27

about chocolate, 347

Banana Chocolate Chip Drops,
434

Banana Cranberry Chocolate
Chip Cake, 356

Brownie Bites, 457

Choc' Full of Pecan Pie, 482

Chocolate Almond Biscotti, 445

Chocolate Babka, 325–26

Chocolate Banana Streusel Cake,
357

Chocolate Banana Streusel
Cupcakes, 357

Chocolate Buttercream, 386

Chocolate Cheesecake, 395–96

Chocolate Chip Challah, 305

Chocolate Chip Cookies, 430

Chocolate Chip Cookies
(Gluten-Free), 432

Chocolate Chip Nut Chews, 459

Chocolate Cocoa Frosting, 383

Chocolate Cream Cheese Pastry,
472

Chocolate Cream Pie, 485

Chocolate Curls, 392

Chocolate Danish, 327

Chocolate Fantasy Torte,
400–401

Chocolate Frostings, 382–84, 386

Chocolate Fudge Frosting,
383–84

Chocolate Ganache, 380–81

Chocolate Glaze, 381

Chocolate Hamentaschen Kisses,
447–48

Chocolate Layer Torte, 399–400

Chocolate Marshmallow Parfaits,
486

Chocolate Marshmallow Pie,
485–86

Chocolate Matzo Bark, 523

Chocolate Melt-Away Coffee
Cake, 373

Chocolate Mint Frosting, 383

Chocolate Peanut Butter, 40

Chocolate Pudding, 485

Chocolate Rogelach, 449

Chocolate Shmear, 326

Chocolate Tofu Mousse, 410–11

Chocolate Truffles, 425

Chocolate Turtle Cookies, 432–33

Cockeyed Cake, 364

Dark and Decadent Chocolate
Pâté, 412

Debbie's Decadent Delights, 433

Decadent Chocolate Glaze, 326

Dreamy Creamy Chocolate
Cheesecake, 396–97

Easy Rum Balls, 427

Fast Fudge, 426–27

Favorite Chocolate Chip Cake,
368

Flourless "Chick"-olate Cake,
367

Frostings, 382–84, 386

Fudge Ribbon Baked Alaska Pie,
486–87

Fudgy Brownies, 524–25

Fudgy Chocolate Muffins, 339

Heavenly Chocolate Trifle, 407

how to process, 39

Malakov Cream Cake, 403–4

chocolate and chocolate chips,
(*continued*)
  Marbled Cheesecake, 518
  Marbled Cheesecake Brownies,
    455–56
  Nanaimo Crunch Bars, 451
  Oh Henrys, 425–26
  One-Two-Three Mint Frosting,
    383
  Pareve Chocolate Cake, 364–65
  Pareve Chocolate Ganache, 381
  Pareve Mocha Ganache, 381
  Passover Brownies, 523
  Passover Mud Cookies, 525
  Raspberry Chocolate Chip
    Squares, 463
  Reverse Chocolate Chip Cookies,
    430–31
  Reverse Chocolate Chip Cookies
    (Gluten-Free), 431
  Rocky Roads, 525
  Root Beer Cake, 365–66
  Root Beer Glaze, 366
  Secret Chocolate Chip Cake,
    368–69
  Sour Cream Fudge Cake, 366–67
  tips, 392, 424
  Top Skor Torte, 404
  Victorian Chocolate Mousse, 411
  White Chocolate Truffles, 425
  Yummy Rum Balls, 427–28
  *See also* brownies; cakes; cookies;
    desserts; fudge; pies; squares
    and bars
chowder
  Manhattan Fish Chowder, 102
  Vegetable Cheese Chowder,
    101–2
cilantro
  how to process, 30
cinnamon
  Cinnamon Buns or Kuchen,
    323–24
  Cinnamon Frosting, 384
  Cinnamon Marble Cake, 374
  Cinnamon Nut Rogelach, 450
  Cinnamon Raisin Bread, 308
  Cinnamon-Sugar, 324
  Cinnamon Torte, 398

Cinnamon Twists, 442
cinnamon candy
  how to process, 39
cleanups
  hints on, 7–8
coconut
  Coconut Almond Macaroons,
    526
  Coconut Oatmeal Bar Cookies,
    435
  how to process, 25
  Lime Coconut Bars, 462
  Raspberry Chocolate Chip
    Squares, 463
coffee
  Caffé Latte, 39
  how to process, 39
  Kathy's Swiss Mocha Hazelnut
    Cookies, 435–36
  Koko-Moko Buttercream, 386
  Mocha Buttercream, 386
coffee cakes
  Apple Coffee Cake, 351–52
  Best Coffee Cake, 371
  Chocolate Melt-Away Coffee
    Cake, 373
  Marbled Streusel Coffee Cake,
    371–73
  Pareve Coffee Cake, 370
  Toffee Coffee Cake, 373–74
coleslaw
  Asian Coleslaw, 269
  Super Coleslaw, 268
condensed milk, 424
  Make Your Own Sweetened
    Condensed Milk, 427
cookies, 420–24, 429–45, 525–27
  Almond Crescents, 429–30
  Apricot Raisin Filling, 446
  Banana Chocolate Chip Drops,
    434
  Basic Oil Dough, 444
  Butterscotch Toffee Dreams, 439
  Chocolate Almond Biscotti, 445
  Chocolate Chip Cookies, 430
  Chocolate Chip Cookies
    (Gluten-Free), 432
  Chocolate Hamentaschen Kisses,
    447–48

Chocolate Oil Dough, 444
Chocolate Rogelach, 449
Chocolate Turtle Cookies, 432–33
Cinnamon Nut Rogelach, 450
Cinnamon Twists, 442
Coconut Almond Macaroons,
  526
Coconut Oatmeal Bar Cookies,
  435
Cookie Crumb Crust, 474
Date Filling, 447
Debbie's Decadent Delights, 433
freezing, 424
Gingerbread Cookies, 440–41
Haman's Hats, 442
Hamentaschen, 446–48
Hamentaschen fillings, 446–48
Holiday Cookies, 440
Kathy's Swiss Mocha Hazelnut
  Cookies, 435–36
Macaroon Crust, 474
Mandel Bread (Mandelbroit),
  444–45, 527
Melting Moments, 436
Meringue Horns, 434–35
Mustachudos, 525–26
Old-Fashioned Peanut Butter
  Cookies, 429
Orange Pecan Butter Balls, 437
Passover Mud Cookies, 525
Peanut Butter Krispies, 428
Poppy Seed Butter Balls, 437
Potato Chip Cookies, 439
Prune Filling, 447
Reverse Chocolate Chip Cookies,
  430–31
Reverse Chocolate Chip Cookies
  (Gluten-Free), 431
Roly Poly, 448–49
Sesame Crescents, 439–40
Sesame Nothings (Kichel), 443
Shortbread Cookies, 438–39
Sugar Cookies, 440, 441–42
tips, 422–24
Tom Thumb Cookies, 437–38
Walnut Brandy Cookies, 437
*See also* rum balls
coriander
  how to process, 30

cottage cheese. *See* cheese—cream cheese, cottage cheese, ricotta cheese

couscous
Bev's Colorful Couscous Salad, 281–82
Quick Couscous Salad, 282

cranberries
Banana Cranberry Chocolate Chip Cake, 356
Cranberry Chicken Meatballs, 193
Cranberry or Raisin Challah, 305
Cranberry Quinoa Salad, 283–84
Cranberry Relish, 220
Debbie's Decadent Delights, 433
how to process, 25, 26
Marinated Roast Turkey with Cranberry Relish, 218–20
Passover Cranberry Sweet and Sour Meatballs, 497

cream cheese. *See* cheese—cream cheese, cottage cheese, ricotta cheese

cream puffs
Cream Puffs (Choux Pastry), 487–88
Crème Pâtissière, 488–89
Passover Cream Puffs, 521–22

crêpes
Basic Crêpe Batter, 162–63
Cheese Cannelloni (Crêpes Italiano), 164–65
Florentine Crêpes, 163
Salmon Crêpes, 164
shaping, 162
*See also* blintzes

croissants, 329–30
croutons, 274

crumble
Blueberry Crumble Cake, 358–59
Easy Apple Crumble, 416

crumbs—bread
Almost Bread Crumbs, 493
Bread Stuffing, 182–83
Buttered Crumbs, 36
Crumb Topping, 36
how to process, 36–37
Italian Seasoned Crumbs, 36

Panko-Crusted Chicken Fingers, 214–15

crumbs—cookies, crackers, corn flakes
how to process, 37, 493
*See also* pie crusts

crumbs—matzo meal. *See* matzo and matzo meal

cucumbers
Creamy Cucumber Salad, 274
Cucumber Salad, 274
how to process, 28
Mediterranean Quinoa Salad, 284

cupcakes
Chocolate Banana Streusel Cupcakes, 357
Florentine Cupcake Blintzes, 510–11
Miniature Pecan Tarts, 482
Mini Cheesecakes, 395
Mom's Old-Fashioned Crumb Cupcakes, 377
Passover Cupcake Blintzes, 510
tips, 350
*See also* muffins

dairy dishes, 114–17, 129–68, 391–97, 455–57, 509–11
tips, 117
*See also* cheese; eggs; fish; noodles; vegetarian

dairy-free. *See* pareve dishes

Danish
Cheese Danish, 327
Chocolate Danish, 327

dates
Applesauce Date and Nut Cake, 354–55
Charoset Truffles, 495
Date Filling, 447
Heavenly Squares, 460–61
how to process, 25

desserts, 389–418, 515–27
Almost Whipping Cream, 391
Apple Chips, 415–16
Berry Good Sherbet, 414
Biscuit Tortoni, 415
Blueberry Streusel Dessert, 417

Brandy Hard Sauce, 418
Cheese Cannelloni (Crêpes Italiano), 164–65
Chocolate Marshmallow Parfaits, 486
Dark and Decadent Chocolate Pâté, 412
Easy Apple Crumble, 416
Frozen Peach Dessert, 413
Light 'n' Lemony Cheese Dessert, 408–9
Milles-Feuilles Dessert, 404–5
Strawberry or Raspberry Purée, 391
Strawberry Swirl Popsicles, 414–15
Strawberry Yogurt Delight, 409
tips, 390–92
Tofu Smoothie, 410
Yogurt Cheese, 391
*See also* cakes; cheesecakes; mousse; Passover baked goods and desserts; pudding; tortes; trifles

dessert topping
how to process, 41
tips, 391, 392, 394–95

dill
Creamy Dill Salad Dressing, 289–90
Dill Butter, 66
how to process, 30

dips
Best Vegetable Dip, 52
Curry Dip, 52
"Gourd for You" Hummus, 56
Green Goddess Salad Dressing or Dip, 291
Guacamole, 54–55
Hummus, 56
Olive Tapenade, 54
Roasted Red Pepper Dip, 53
Roasted Red Pepper Hummus, 56
Simply Salsa, 55–56
tips, 50–51

doughs
Basic Oil Dough, 444
blade for, 12

doughs (*continued*)
    Chocolate Oil Dough, 444
    cookie dough tips, 422–24
    how to process, 37–38
    pastry dough tips, 466–69
    yeast dough tips, 296–300
    *See also* batters; breads—yeast
        breads and doughs; pastry;
        phyllo dough
dressings. *See* salad dressings;
    stuffings
dried fruit. *See* fruits—dried or
    candied
dumplings
    Quick Soup Dumplings, 496
duxelles
    Mushroom Duxelles, 235

eggplant
    Cheryl's Vegetable Casserole,
        500–501
    Eggplant Italiano, 230
    Eggplant Spread, 57
    how to microwave, 57
    how to process, 28
    Mom's Caponata, 232–33
    No-Fry Eggplant Parmesan,
        231–32
    Passover Eggplant Parmesan, 232
    Ratatouille, 233
    Sneaky Spaghetti Sauce, 200
    Sweet and Sour Eggplant, 231
    Vegetarian Spaghetti Sauce, 106
egg rolls
    Egg Roll Blintzes, 506
    Egg Roll Filling, 77
    Vegetarian Egg Rolls, 76–77
eggs
    Baked Frittata, 151–52
    Chopped Egg Spread, 60
    Egg and Avocado Spread, 55
    food safety, 116
    how to process, 34–35
    nutritional analysis, 47
    Roulade, 151
    safety, 401
    substitutions, 347
    tips, 116, 347–48

    *See also* blintzes; mayonnaise;
        pancakes; quiches; soufflés
egg whites
    how to process, 35
    tips, 347–48, 487
    *See also* meringue

falafel, 78
farfel
    Farfel, Chicken and Vegetable
        Kugel, 503–4
    Farfel Apple Pudding, 503
    Farfel Apricot Pudding, 504
    Farfel Marshmallow Treats,
        522–23
    *See also* matzo and matzo meal
fat
    substitutes in baking, 346
fennel
    Honey-Glazed Roasted Roots,
        235
    how to process, 28–29
feta cheese. *See* cheese—feta cheese
fiber
    nutritional analysis, 47
fillings
    Apricot Raisin Filling, 446
    Cheese Filling, 166
    Cheese Filling for Spinach
        Cheese Phyllo Puff, 150
    Chicken or Meat Filling, 257–58
    Chocolate Shmear, 326
    Corned Beef Filling, 257
    Date Filling, 447
    Potato Knish Filling, 256
    Prune Filling, 447
fish, 114, 116, 118–39, 511–12
    Balsamic Baked Fish with
        Onions and Mushrooms, 123
    Broccoli-Stuffed Fillets with
        Mushroom Sauce, 130–31
    Broiled Cheesy Fillets, 129
    Easy Fish Bake, 126–27
    Fish Fillets Amandine, 128
    Fish Italian Style, 131–32
    Fish Patties, 132–33
    Gefilte Fish, 118–19
    how to process, 35
    Manhattan Fish Chowder, 102

    Oven-Fried Fish, 127
    Poached Fish, 125–26
    Quick Fish Salad, 126
    Sardine Spread, 62
    Stuffed Fish Fillets au Gratin,
        129–30
    Sweet and Sour Fish Patties, 133
    tips, 116
    Tricolor Gefilte Fish Mold, 119
    *See also* halibut; salmon; sole
        fillets; tuna
flanken. *See* ribs
flans. *See* pies and tarts
flax seed
    how to process, 39
    tips, 267, 299, 347
florentine. *See* spinach
flour
    how to process, 41
    tips, 296–97, 345, 349
focaccia, 316–17
food safety, 83, 116, 117, 173, 401
    eggs, 116
freezing
    Cakes, 348–49
    Cookies, 424
    Knishes, 258
    Latkes, 245
    Pastry, 468
    Soups, 83
    tips, 42
    Yeast doughs, 299–300
    *See also individual recipes*
french fry disc
    tips and techniques, 12
French-style green beans
    French-Cut Green Beans, 226
    how to process, 27
fries
    Skinny No-Fries, 237
    Sweet Potato Bake, 507–8
    Sweet Potato No-Fries, 237
frittata
    Baked Frittata, 151–52
frostings, 342–43, 348, 380–87
    Banana Frosting, 382
    Butter Frosting, 382
    Chocolate Buttercream, 386
    Chocolate Cocoa Frosting, 383

Chocolate Frosting, 382–83
Chocolate Fudge Frosting, 383–84
Chocolate Mint Frosting, 383
Cinnamon Frosting, 384
Cream Cheese Frosting, 384
Fluffy Burnt Sugar Frosting, 362
Genie's Icing, 387
Koko-Moko Buttercream, 386
Mocha Buttercream, 386
One-Two-Three Mint Frosting, 383
Orange Frosting, 384–85
Passover Icing Sugar, 493
Peanut Butter Frosting, 385
Peppermint Butter Frosting, 385
Rocky Road Frosting, 383
tips, 348
Whipped Cream, 387
See also glazes
frozen desserts
Berry Good Sherbet, 414
Frozen Peach Dessert, 413
Strawberry Swirl Popsicles, 414–15
See also ice cream
fruits—dried or candied
Dark Rich Fruitcake, 379–80
how to process, 25
tips, 347, 422
fruits—fresh, frozen, canned
Berry Good Sherbet, 414
cheesecake toppings, 394–95
Glazed Fresh Fruit Topping, 395
Glazed Fruit Cheesecake, 518
how to process, 24–26
how to purée, 26, 391–92
Instant Fruit Sauce, 16
Passover Fruit Crisp, 516–17
Smart Chart, 24–26
tips, 14–16
Tofu Smoothie, 410
See also individual fruits
fruit sugar
how to process, 41
fudge
Chocolate Fudge Frosting, 383–84
Fast Fudge, 426–27

Fudge Ribbon Baked Alaska Pie, 486–87
Sour Cream Fudge Cake, 366–67

ganache. See glazes
garlic
Creamy Garlic Dressing, 290
Garlic Buns, 320
Garlic Butter, 65–66
Honey Garlic Ribs, 187
Honey Garlic Sparerib Sauce, 110
how to process, 29
Maple-Glazed Garlic Chicken Breasts, 215
Marty's Garlic Cheese Dressing, 290
Sautéed Garlic Mushrooms, 234
See also gremolata
gazpacho, 85, 267
gefilte fish, 118–19
Tricolor Gefilte Fish Mold, 119
ginger
how to process, 29
glazes, 380–81
Baker's Glaze, 311
Chocolate Ganache, 380–81
Chocolate Glaze, 381
Decadent Chocolate Glaze, 326
Pareve Chocolate Ganache, 381
Pareve Mocha Ganache, 381
Root Beer Glaze, 366
White Glaze, 381
gluten-free foods
Almond Crescents, 429–30
Another Passover Apple Cake, 519–20
Apple Chips, 415–16
Apricot Candied Carrots, 228
Béchamel (White) Sauce, 103–4
Berry Good Sherbet, 414
Blueberry Streusel Dessert, 417
Carrot Kugel, 239–40
Chocolate Chip Cookies (Gluten-Free), 432
Coconut Almond Macaroons, 526
Cranberry Quinoa Salad, 283–84
Dark and Decadent Chocolate Pâté, 412
Easy Apple Crumble, 416

Flourless "Chick"-olate Cake, 367
Fudgy Brownies, 524–25
Gefilte Fish, 118–19
Glazed Fruit Cheesecake, 518
Gluten-Free Blintzes, 505
Gluten-Free Flour Mix, 345–46
Hamburgers à la Dutch, 196–97
Light 'n' Lemony Cheese Dessert, 408–9
Low-Carb "Fried Rice," 250–51
Mustachudos, 525–26
Passover Carrot Kugel, 508
Passover Carrot Tsimmis, 508–9
Passover Icing Sugar, 493
Passover Mandelbroit, 527
Passover Mud Cookies, 525
Popcorn Stuffing Mounds, 261–62
Rainbow Quinoa, Two Ways, 501–2
Reverse Chocolate Chip Cookies (Gluten-Free), 431
Spinach Cheese Bake, 154
Strawberry Mousse, 409–10
Strawberry Swirl Popsicles, 414–15
Strawberry Yogurt Delight, 409
Sweet Potato Bake, 507–8
Victorian Chocolate Mousse, 411
Gougères (French Cheese Puffs), 72
graham wafers
By Cracky Bars, 458
French Unbaked Cake, 450–51
Graham Wafer Crust, 473–74
Milles-Feuilles Dessert, 404–5
See also crumbs
gravy
potato starch to thicken, 493
tips, 83
Turkey Gravy, 219–20
vegetables to thicken, 83
green onions
how to process, 29, 32
gremolata, 185
Lamb Shanks with Classic Gremolata, 175–76
Rozie's Osso Bucco with Gremolata, 184–85

grilled foods. *See* barbecued foods
guacamole, 54–55

halibut
  Baked Halibut and Potato
    Casserole, 124
  Fish Italian Style, 131–32
  Poached Fish, 125–26
  Salsa Just for the Halibut!, 125
  *See also* fish
Hamburgers à la Dutch, 196–97
hamentaschen, 446
  Apricot Raisin Filling, 446
  Chocolate Hamentaschen Kisses,
    447–48
  Date Filling, 447
  fillings, 446–48
  Prune Filling, 447
hard candy
  how to process, 39
hard sauce, 418
  English Plum Pudding with
    Brandy Hard Sauce, 417
hazelnuts
  Hazelnut (Filbert) Torte, 402
  Kathy's Swiss Mocha Hazelnut
    Cookies, 435–36
  toasting, 436
  *See also* nuts
heavy cream. *See* whipping cream
herbs, fresh
  Herbed Rack of Lamb, 175
  how to process, 29, 30
herring
  Chopped Herring, 61–62
honey
  Carrot Honey Loaf, 360
  Honey Apple Cake, 363–64
  Honey Bran Muffins, 336
  Honey Cola Cake, 362–63
  Honey Garlic Ribs, 187
  Honey Garlic Sparerib Sauce, 110
  Honey-Glazed Roasted Roots,
    235
horseradish, 110–11
hot peppers. *See* peppers
hubbard squash
  how to process, 33
hummus, 56

ice, 40
ice cream
  Frozen Peach Dessert, 413
  Fudge Ribbon Baked Alaska Pie,
    486–87
  Strawberry Mousse, 409–10
icings. *See* frostings

jam
  Crumbly Jam Squares, 459
  Heavenly Chicken, 211–12
  Linzertorte, 402–3
  Pecan Jam Squares, 463
jicama
  how to process, 29
julienne strips
  disk for, 12, 15
  how to process, 32, 35
  tips and techniques, 15

kasha
  Kasha Knish, 258
kichel, 443
kids' cuisine, 22–24
  Sneaky Cuisine (for kids), 22–23,
    200, 315
  tips, 22–24
  *See also* baby food
kishka
  Vegetable Kishka, 255
kiwis
  how to process, 25
knaidlach
  Knaidlach for a Crowd, 496
  *See also* matzo balls
knishes
  Cheese Knishes, 156
  freezing, 258
  Kasha Knish, 258
  No-Dough Cheese Knishes, 155
  Passover Knishes, 502
  Potato Knishes, 256–57
kreplach, 258–59
kugels
  Buttermilk Noodle Kugel, 143
  Carrot Kugel, 239–40
  Cookie's Hot Milk Cheese Kugel,
    144
  Farfel, Chicken and Vegetable
    Kugel, 503–4

Florentine Noodle Kugel, 144–45
Lokshin Kugel (Noodle
  Pudding), 240–41
Mini Potato Zucchini Kugels,
  242
Onion Kugel, 241
Passover Carrot Kugel, 508
Pineapple Noodle Kugel, 145
Potato Kugel, 238–39
Potato Kugel Meat Loaf, 201–2
Sweet Potato Kugel, 239
Three-Cheese Sweet Kugel, 146

lamb
  Herbed Rack of Lamb, 175
  how to process, 35–36
  Lamb Shanks with Classic
    Gremolata, 175–76
lasagnas
  Luscious Vegetarian Lasagna,
    139–40
  Passover Lasagna (Matzagna),
    512–13
  Tortilla Lasagna Florentine,
    140–41
  Tuna and Mushroom Lasagna,
    138–39
latkes
  Broccoli Latkes, 244
  Carrot Latkes, 243–44
  Easy Potato Latkes, 245
  freezing and reheating, 245
  Lacy Latkes, 245
  Matzo Meal Latkes, 509
  No-Fry Latkes, 245
  Noodle Latkes (Pancakes), 246
  Passover Cheese Latkes, 509–10
  Veggie Latkes, 246
  Zucchini Latkes, 244
leeks
  how to prepare, 253
  how to process, 29
  Leek and Rice Skillet Casserole,
    253
  Parmentier Soup, 94–95
  Vichyssoise, 95
leftovers
  Potato Chip Cookies, 439
  tips, 51, 82–83, 172–73, 494, 496

Luscious Vegetarian Lasagna, 139–40
Pasta Vegetable Medley, 141–42
Peanut Butter Pasta, 261
Penne with Roasted Tomatoes and Garlic au Gratin, 142–43
Pesto Pasta Salad, 280–81
tips, 225
Tuna and Mushroom Lasagna, 138–39
*See also* noodles
pastry, 465–89
Berry Hand Pies, 478
Chicken or Meat Turnovers, 75
Chocolate Cream Cheese Pastry, 472
Cream Cheese Pastry, 472
Crème Pâtissière, 488–89
Flaky Ginger Ale Pastry, 471
how to process, 38
Mushroom Turnovers, 74–75
Pareve Pie Crust (Basic Pastry), 470–71
Pastry Cream, 488–89
pastry problems, 469
Sour Cream Pastry, 473
Spinach Cheese Turnovers, 75
Standard Butter Pastry, 470
Tart Shells, 473
tips, 466–69
*See also* cream puffs; phyllo dough; pie crusts; pies and tarts
peaches
Frozen Peach Dessert, 413
how to process, 26
Peach Pie, 474
peanut butter
Asian Coleslaw, 269
Chocolate Hamentaschen Kisses, 447–48
Chocolate Peanut Butter, 40
how to process, 40
Old-Fashioned Peanut Butter Cookies, 429
Peanut Butter Frosting, 385
Peanut Butter Krispies, 428
Peanut Butter Pasta, 261
Peanut Butter Sauce, 110

Peanut Butter Squares, 453
pea pods
Pea Pod, Pepper and Mushroom Stir-Fry, 248–49
pears
how to process, 26
pecans
Choc' Full of Pecan Pie, 482
Chocolate Fantasy Torte, 400–401
Chocolate Turtle Cookies, 432–33
Miniature Pecan Tarts, 482
Morning Glorious Muffins, 338
Orange Pecan Butter Balls, 437
Panko-Crusted Chicken Fingers, 214–15
Passover Mud Cookies, 525
Pecan Jam Squares, 463
Pecan Pie, 481
*See also* nuts
peppermint
how to process peppermint sticks, 39
Peppermint Butter Frosting, 385
Peppermint Patty Brownies, 454
pepperoni
how to process, 35
Super Spaghetti Sauce, 199
peppers
how to process, 31
Mango Quesadillas, 67
Moroccan Pepper Salad (Salade Cuite), 272
Pea Pod, Pepper and Mushroom Stir-Fry, 248–49
Rina's Red Pepper Sauce, 107
Roasted Red Pepper Crescents, 73
Roasted Red Pepper Dip, 53
Roasted Red Pepper Hummus, 56
Roasted Red Pepper Mayonnaise, 112
Roasted Red Peppers, 53
Salad Niçoise, 276–77
Sneaky Spaghetti Sauce, 200
Turkey Cutlets with Peppers and Mushrooms, 217–18

pesto, 105–6
Pesto Pasta Salad, 280–81
phyllo dough
Spanakopita (Phyllo Triangles), 73–74
Spinach Cheese Phyllo Puff, 149–50
tips, 74
pickles
how to process, 31
pie crusts
Cookie Crumb Crust, 474
Corn Flake Crumb Crust, 474
Graham Wafer Crust, 473–74
Macaroon Crust, 474
Pareve Pie Crust (Basic Pastry), 470–71
*See also* pastry
pies and tarts, 465–69, 474–87, 515–17
Apple Crostata, 475–76
Apple Flan, 476–77
Berry Hand Pies, 478
Blueberry Apple Pie, 474
Butter Tarts, 483
Butter Tart Slice, 457–58
Choc' Full of Pecan Pie, 482
Chocolate Cream Pie, 485
Chocolate Marshmallow Pie, 485–86
Crumbly Apple Pie, 475
Family Apple Pie, 474
freezing, 468
Fresh Strawberry Flan, 479–80
Fudge Ribbon Baked Alaska Pie, 486–87
Key Lime Pie, 484
Lemon Meringue Pie, 483–84
Miniature Pecan Tarts, 482
Passover Pies, 159–60, 515–17
Peach Pie, 474
Pecan Pie, 481
pie plates, 467–68
Pumpkin Pie, 480–81
Ruby-Red Rhubarb Pie, 479
Tart Shells, 473
tips, 466–69
*See also* pie crusts; quiches; strudels

pilaf
Quinoa Pilaf, 502
Rice Pilaf, 252
pineapple
Cantonese Short Ribs, 186–87
Carrot Pineapple Cake, 379
Chicken in Pineapple-Orange
Sauce, 209
Hawaiian Meatballs, 191–92
how to process, 26
Pineapple Carrots, 228
Pineapple Chicken Meatballs, 195
Pineapple Noodle Kugel, 145
pita
Pita Bread, 317–18
Pita Chips, 318
Pitas, Wraps and Roll-ups, 51
Whole Wheat Pita, 318
See also spreads
pizza
Do-Ahead Dough, 70
Make-and-Bake Pizza, 69–70
Pizza Pinwheels, 314–15
Pizza Tarts, 70–71
Quick Matzo Pizza, 494
plums
how to process, 26
popcorn
about popcorn, 262
Popcorn Stuffing Mounds,
261–62
Turkey Popcorn Shepherd's Pie,
202
poppy seeds
Haman's Hats, 442
Poppy Seed Butter Balls, 437
Poppy Seed Cake, 376
potatoes
Baked Halibut and Potato
Casserole, 124
Barbecued Lyonnaise Potatoes,
236
Best-Ever Scalloped Potatoes,
236–37
Cheryl's Vegetable Casserole,
500–501
Easy Potato Latkes, 245
Grate and Bake, 506–7
how to process, 31–32

Italian Seasoned Chicken with
Potatoes, 212–13
Mini Potato Zucchini Kugels,
242
Parmentier Soup, 94–95
Passover Knishes, 502
Potato and Onion Focaccia, 317
Potato Chip Cookies, 439
Potato-Crusted Chicken, 214
Potato Knishes, 256–57
Potato Kugel, 238–39
Potato Kugel Meat Loaf, 201–2
Potato Mushroom Soup, 94
Quick Potato Soup, 92
Rescued Mashed Potatoes, 225
Rösti Potatoes, 238
Salad Niçoise, 276–77
Skinny No-Fries, 237
Vichyssoise, 95
Zucchini and Two Potato Soup,
96
poultry, 170–220, 497–99, 503–5
tips, 172–74
See also chicken; meatballs;
Passover meat and poultry
dishes; turkey
prunes
how to process, 25, 26
Prune Filling, 117
Prune Purée, 346
pudding
Chocolate Pudding, 485
English Plum Pudding with
Brandy Hard Sauce, 417–18
Farfel Apple Pudding, 503
Farfel Apricot Pudding, 504
Lokshin Kugel (Noodle
Pudding), 240–41
Pistachio Marble Cake, 369
Pudding Parfait, 412–13
pumpkin
Cream of Pumpkin Soup,
100–101
"Gourd for You" Hummus, 56
Pumpkin Pie, 480–81
Pumpkin Purée, 101
Roasted Pumpkin Seeds, 101
purées
Carrot Purée, 20, 360

Fruit Purée, 26, 391–92
how to process, 26, 32, 82
Prune Purée, 346
Pumpkin Purée, 101
quantities, 13
Strawberry or Raspberry Purée,
391
vegetables, 32

quesadillas
Mango Quesadillas, 67
quiches
Crustless Passover Tuna Quiche,
511
No-Crust Zucchini Quiche,
159–60
Onion Cheese Quiche, 156–67
Pareve Vegetable Quiche, 158–59
Sour Cream Tuna Quiche, 158
quick breads. See breads—quick
breads
quinoa
Cranberry Quinoa Salad, 283–84
Mediterranean Quinoa Salad,
284
Quinoa Pilaf, 502
Rainbow Quinoa, Two Ways,
501–2

radishes
how to process, 32
raisins
Carrot and Raisin Salad, 271
Cinnamon Raisin Bread, 308
Cranberry or Raisin Challah, 305
Dark Rich Fruitcake, 379–80
how to process, 25
Oatmeal Raisin Muffins, 339–40
Raisin Spice Cake, 377–78
Roly Poly, 448–49
raspberries
Berry Good Sherbet, 414
Raspberry Chocolate Chip
Squares, 463
Raspberry Spinach Salad, 279
Strawberry or Raspberry Purée,
391
Ratatouille, 233

red peppers. *See* peppers
reheating
    tips, 42, 245
    *See also individual recipes*
rhubarb
    how to process, 26
    Ruby-Red Rhubarb Pie, 479
ribs and short ribs
    Cantonese Short Ribs, 186–87
    Flanken and Barley Soup, 84
    Honey Garlic Ribs, 187
    Savory Brisket or Top Rib,
      178–79
    Spicy Short Ribs/Miami Ribs,
      188
rice and risotto
    about arborio rice, 254
    Chinese Fried Rice, 251–52
    Leek and Rice Skillet Casserole,
      253
    Low-Carb "Fried Rice," 250–51
    No-Fry Fried Rice, 250
    Rapid Risotto, 253–54
    Rice, Spinach and Mushroom
      Bake, 254–55
    Rice Pilaf, 252
ricotta cheese. *See* cheese—cream
    cheese, cottage cheese, ricotta
    cheese
risotto. *See* rice and risotto
roasted peppers. *See* peppers
rogelach
    Chocolate Rogelach, 449
    Cinnamon Nut Rogelach, 450
rolls. *See* breads—yeast breads and
    doughs
root beer
    Root Beer Cake, 365–66
    Root Beer Glaze, 366
rum balls
    Easy Rum Balls, 427
    Passover "Yum" Balls, 427
    Yummy Rum Balls, 427–28

safety
    equipment safety tips, 4, 6–7
    food safety, 83, 116, 117, 173, 401
salad dressings, 265, 267, 286–92
    Asian Salad Dressing, 292

Balsamic Vinaigrette, 287
Best Vinaigrette Dressing, 287
Creamy Dill Salad Dressing,
    289–90
Creamy Garlic Dressing, 290
Fresh Tomato Dressing, 289
Green Goddess Salad Dressing or
    Dip, 291
Italian Salad Dressing, 286
Light and Easy Italian Dressing,
    286–87
Low-Fat Ranch Dressing, 291
Marty's Garlic Cheese Dressing,
    290
Russian Salad Dressing, 289
Sweet and Spicy French
    Dressing, 288
Sweet Vidalia Onion Dressing,
    288
Tahini Dressing, 108
Thousand Island Dressing, 289
tips, 267
Yummy Yogurt Salad Dressing,
    291–92
*See also* mayonnaise; Passover
    salads and dressings
salads, 265–86, 501–2
    Asian Coleslaw, 269
    Asian Luncheon Salad, 278
    Asian Spinach Salad, 278–79
    Bev's Colorful Couscous Salad,
      281–82
    Caesar Salad, 273
    Carrot and Raisin Salad, 271
    Chickpea Broccoli Salad, 285–86
    Cranberry Quinoa Salad, 283–84
    Creamy Cucumber Salad, 274
    Croutons, 274
    Cucumber Salad, 274
    Farmer's Salad, 275
    Faux-Tato Salad, 272–73
    Greek Salad, 280
    Instant Gazpacho!, 267
    Layered Salad, 275–76
    Marinated Bean Salad, 271
    Marinated Fresh Vegetable Salad,
      270
    Mediterranean Quinoa Salad,
      284

Moroccan Pepper Salad (Salade
    Cuite), 272
Pesto Pasta Salad, 280–81
Quick Couscous Salad, 282
Quick Fish Salad, 126
Rainbow Quinoa, Two Ways,
    501–2
Raspberry Spinach Salad, 279
Salad Niçoise, 276–77
Super Coleslaw, 268
Tabbouleh Salad, 285
Tangy Marinated Carrot Salad,
    269–70
tips, 266–67
*See also* Passover salads and
    dressings; salad dressings
salami
    how to process, 35
    Super Spaghetti Sauce, 199
salmon
    Bagel, Salmon and Broccoli
      Casserole, 149
    Baked Salmon with Mango Salsa,
      122–23
    Baked Salmon with Mushroom
      Stuffing, 121
    Balsamic Baked Fish with
      Onions and Mushrooms, 123
    Dishwasher Salmon, 120–21
    Lox and Cheese Ring, 64
    Lox and Cheese Spread, 63–64
    Mushroom Stuffing, 122
    Orange Teriyaki Grilled Salmon,
      123–24
    Pickled Salmon, 120
    Salmon Burgers, 134–35
    Salmon Crêpes, 164
    Salmon Mediterranean, 512
    Salmon or Tuna Mousse, 63
    Salmon Patties, 134
    Salmon Spread, 62
    Salmon Tortilla Pinwheels, 66
    *See also* fish; lox
salsa
    Baked Salmon with Mango Salsa,
      122–23
    Easy Nachos, 51
    Mango Salsa, 107
    Salsa Just for the Halibut!, 125
    Simply Salsa, 55–56

salt
  nutritional analysis, 47
sardine spread, 62
sauces, 80–83, 103–12
  Béchamel (White) Sauce, 103–4
  Brandy Hard Sauce, 418
  Cheese Sauce, 104
  Chinese Sweet and Sour Sauce,
    108
  Cranberry Relish, 220
  Easy Barbecue Sauce, 105
  Honey Garlic Sparerib Sauce, 110
  Instant Fruit Sauce, 16
  Mushroom Sauce, 104
  Peanut Butter Sauce, 110
  Quick Tomato Sauce, 105
  Rina's Red Pepper Sauce, 107
  Super Spaghetti Sauce, 199
  Tartar Sauce, 112
  Teriyaki Sauce, 109
  tips, 82–83
  Vegetarian Spaghetti Sauce, 106
  See also marinades; salad
    dressings; salsa; spaghetti
    sauce
scallions. See green onions
scones, 340–41
  Cheese Scones, 341
sesame seeds
  Baked Crunchy Sesame Chicken,
    213
  Crunchy Sesame Chicken, 213
  Sesame Cheese Straws, 71
  Sesame Crescents, 439–40
  Sesame Nothings (Kichel), 443
shallots
  how to process, 32
Shepherd's Pie
  Turkey Popcorn Shepherd's Pie,
    202
sherbet
  Berry Good Sherbet, 414
short ribs. See ribs and short ribs
side dishes, 222–63
  tips, 224–25
Skor bits. See toffee/Skor bits
slow cooker preparation
  Cantonese Short Ribs, 186–87

Chicken Chili, 198
Chickpea Chili, 234
Chili, 197
conversion times, 83, 174
Cranberry Chicken Meatballs,
  193
Marinated Brisket, 176–77
meat and poultry, 173–74
Mmm-Good Meatballs, 192–93
Overnight Roast, 179
Rozie's Osso Bucco with
  Gremolata, 184–85
Savory Brisket or Top Rib,
  178–79
Slow Cooker Chicken Soup, 90
Sneaky Spaghetti Sauce, 200
soups and, 83
Spicy Short Ribs/Miami Ribs,
  188
Stew Italiano, 189–90
Super Roast Brisket, 177–78
Super Spaghetti Sauce, 199
tips, 83
smart chart, 24–41
smoothies
  how to process, 40
  Tofu Smoothie, 410
sneaky cuisine (for kids), 22–23,
  200, 315
sodium
  nutritional analysis, 47
soft cheese. See cheese—cream
  cheese, cottage cheese, ricotta
  cheese
sole fillets
  Broccoli-Stuffed Fillets with
    Mushroom Sauce, 130–31
  Broiled Cheesy Fillets, 129
  Easy Fish Bake, 126–27
  Fish Fillets Amandine, 128
  Fish Patties, 132–33
  Manhattan Fish Chowder, 102
  Oven-Fried Fish, 127
  Sole Mornay, 132
  Stuffed Fish Fillets au Gratin,
    129–30
  See also fish
soufflés
  Blintz Soufflé, 166

Carrot Soufflé, 229–30
Crazy Blintz Soufflé, 167
Spinach Soufflé, 150–51
soups, 80–103
  As-You-Like-It Vegetable Soup,
    87
  Broccoli Lentil Soup, 97–98
  Carrot and Sweet Potato Soup,
    95–96
  Carrot Soup, 96
  Chicken Meatball Soup, 88–89
  Cream of Pumpkin Soup,
    100–101
  Dairy Beet Borscht, 85–86
  Easy Lentil Vegetable Soup, 90
  Flanken and Barley Soup, 84
  freezing, 83
  Gazpacho, 85, 267
  Herbed Cauliflower or Broccoli
    Soup, 98
  Instant Gazpacho!, 267
  Manhattan Fish Chowder, 102
  Meatball Soup, 86
  Minestrone, 91–93
  Mom's Vegetable Soup with
    Matzo Balls, 87–88
  Onion Soup au Gratin, 103
  Parmentier Soup, 94–95
  Penny's Tomato Bisque, 93
  Phony Minestrone, 92–93
  Potato Mushroom Soup, 94
  Puréed Soups, 32
  Quick Potato Soup, 92
  Quick Vegetable Broth, 84
  Roasted Squash Soup, 99
  Slow Cooker Chicken Soup, 90
  Sweet Potato Squash Soup,
    99–100
  tips, 82–83
  Vegetable Cheese Chowder,
    101–2
  Vegetarian Cabbage Soup, 86
  Vegetarian Minestrone, 91
  Vichyssoise, 95
  Zucchini and Two Potato Soup,
    96
  Zucchini Noodle Soup, 97
  See also chili

sour cream
  Almost Sour Cream!, 145–46
  nutritional analysis, 47
  Sour Cream Fudge Cake, 366–67
  Sour Cream Pastry, 473
  Sour Cream Torte, 398
  Sour Cream Tuna Quiche, 158
sour milk—substitutions, 347
spaghetti sauce
  Sneaky Spaghetti Sauce, 200
  Super Spaghetti Sauce, 199
  Vegetarian Spaghetti Sauce, 106
Spanakopita (Phyllo Triangles),
  73–74
spinach
  Asian Spinach Salad, 278–79
  Florentine Crêpes, 163
  Florentine Cupcake Blintzes,
  510–11
  Florentine Noodle Kugel, 144–45
  how to process, 32–33
  No-Crust Cheese and Spinach
  Pie, 159
  Raspberry Spinach Salad, 279
  Rice, Spinach and Mushroom
  Bake, 254–55
  Roulade, 151
  Spanakopita (Phyllo Triangles),
  73–74
  Spinach Borekas, 154–55
  Spinach Cheese Bake, 154
  Spinach Cheese Phyllo Puff,
  149–50
  Spinach Cheese Turnovers, 75
  Spinach Soufflé, 150–51
  Tortilla Lasagna Florentine,
  140–41
  to use in Pesto, 105–6
spreads
  Antipasto Spread, 61
  Chicken or Turkey Salad Spread,
  59
  Chopped Egg Spread, 60
  Chopped Herring, 61–62
  Chopped Liver, 58–59
  Dill Butter, 66
  Egg and Avocado Spread, 55
  Eggplant Spread, 57

  Garlic Butter, 65–66
  Hummus, 56
  Lighter Butter (or margarine), 39
  Lox and Cheese Ring, 64
  Lox and Cheese Spread, 63–64
  Olive Tapenade, 54
  Salmon Spread, 62
  Sardine Spread, 62
  Sun-Dried Tomato Spread, 53
  Tuna Spread, 60–61
  Vegetarian Chopped Liver, 57–58
  See also Passover appetizers and
    spreads
squares and bars, 420–24, 445–63
  Almond Crisp Bars, 452
  Apricot Almond Triangles,
    452–53
  Butter Tart Slice, 457–58
  By Cracky Bars, 458
  Chocolate Chip Nut Chews, 459
  Crumbly Jam Squares, 459
  Easy Cheese Dreams, 456
  French Unbaked Cake, 450–51
  Halfway Squares, 460
  Heavenly Squares, 460–61
  Hello Dolly Squares, 461
  Lemon Squares, 462
  Lime Coconut Bars, 462
  Nanaimo Crunch Bars, 451
  Peanut Butter Squares, 453
  Pecan Jam Squares, 463
  Raspberry Chocolate Chip
    Squares, 463
  tips, 422–24
  See also brownies
squash
  "Gourd for You" Hummus, 56
  how to process, 33
  Roasted Squash Soup, 99
  Sweet Potato Squash Soup,
    99–100
stews
  Oven Stew, 188
  Spicy Short Ribs, 188
  Stew Italiano, 189–90
  Tasty Meatball Stew, 190–91
stir-fries
  Chinese Chicken Liver Stir-Fry,
    204–5

  Hoisin Vegetable Stir-Fry, 248
  Moo Goo Guy Kew, 207
  Mushroom Almond Chicken
    Stir-Fry, 206–7
  Pea Pod, Pepper and Mushroom
    Stir-Fry, 248–49
  Stir-Fried Beef and Broccoli,
    203–4
  Stir-Fried Chicken and Broccoli,
    204
  Teriyaki Turkey or Chicken Stir-
    Fry, 205–6
  tips, 173
stollen, 331–32
strawberries
  Berry Good Sherbet, 414
  Berry Hand Pies, 478
  Fresh Strawberry Flan, 479–80
  Fresh Strawberry Topping, 394
  how to process, 26
  Pudding Parfait, 412–13
  Strawberry Dream Cheesecake,
    393
  Strawberry Mousse, 409–10
  Strawberry or Raspberry Purée,
    391
  Strawberry Purée, 391
  Strawberry Swirl Popsicles,
    414–15
  Strawberry Yogurt Delight, 409
  Tofu Smoothie, 410
streusel
  Applesauce Streusel Cake, 355
  Blueberry Streusel Dessert, 417
  Chocolate Banana Streusel Cake,
    357
  Chocolate Banana Streusel
    Cupcakes, 357
  Marbled Streusel Coffee Cake,
    371–73
  Streusel Topping, 302
strudels
  Apple Strudel, 477
  Roly Poly, 448–49
  Tuna Strudel, 136
stuffings
  Baked Salmon with Mushroom
    Stuffing, 121
  Bread Stuffing, 182–83

stuffings (*continued*)

Marinated Roast Turkey with Cranberry Relish, 218–20

Minced Veal Stuffing, 183

Mostly Vegetable Stuffing, 499

Mushroom Stuffing, 122

Popcorn Stuffing Mounds, 261–62

Quick Matzo Meal Stuffing, 500

safety, 173

Stuffed Chicken Breasts, 499

Stuffed Shoulder Steak Rolls, 498

Stuffed Turkey Breast, 217

Stuffing Casserole, 262–63

Turkey Stuffing, 218

substitutions

in baking, 297, 345–47, 423

Passover substitutions, 492–94

*See also individual recipes*

sugar

Cinnamon-Sugar, 324

Fluffy Burnt Sugar Frosting, 362

how to process, 41

nutritional analysis, 47

Passover Icing Sugar, 493

Superfine/Fruit Sugar, 391

tips, 346, 349

Vanilla sugar, 493

summer squash. *See* zucchini

sun-dried tomatoes

Broiled Cheesy Fillets, 129

Sun-Dried Tomato Spread, 53

sweeteners

about sweeteners, 346

*See also* sugar

sweet potatoes

Baked Veggie Patties, 247

Carrot and Sweet Potato Soup, 95–96

Honey-Glazed Roasted Roots, 235

how to process, 31–32

Sweet Potato Bake, 507–8

Sweet Potato Kugel, 239

Sweet Potato No-Fries, 237

Sweet Potato Squash Soup, 99–100

Zucchini and Two Potato Soup, 96

swiss chard

how to process, 32–33

swiss cheese. *See* cheese—cheddar, swiss, mozzarella cheese

Tabbouleh Salad, 285

tahini

Hummus, 56

Tahini Dressing, 108

tapenade

Olive Tapenade, 54

tarts. *See* pies and tarts

teriyaki

Orange Teriyaki Grilled Salmon, 123–24

Teriyaki Chuck Roast, 180–81

Teriyaki Marinade, 108–9

Teriyaki Sauce, 109

Teriyaki Steak, 181

Teriyaki Turkey or Chicken Stir-Fry, 205–6

tips, tricks and techniques, 14–16

*See also* Smart Chart, 24–41

toffee/skor bits

Butterscotch Toffee Dreams, 439

Debbie's Decadent Delights, 433

High Skor Chocolate Cake, 365

how to process, 41

Toffee Coffee Cake, 373–74

Top Skor Torte, 404

tofu

as alternative to eggs, 391

Blended Tofu, 36

Chocolate Tofu Mousse, 410–11

Dairy-Free Cheesecake, 392

how to process, 36

Sticky Tofu, 249

tips, 391

Tofu Mayonnaise, 112

Tofu Smoothie, 410

to use in lasagnas, 140, 141

to use in stir-fries, 205

tomatoes

As-You-Like-It Vegetable Soup, 87

Broiled Cheesy Fillets, 129

Bruschetta, 68

Fresh Tomato Dressing, 289

Gazpacho, 85, 267

how to process, 33

Lasagna, 138–41, 512–13

Minestrone, 91–93

Moroccan Pepper Salad (Salade Cuite), 272

Penne with Roasted Tomatoes and Garlic au Gratin, 142–43

Penny's Tomato Bisque, 93

Quick Tomato Sauce, 105

Ratatouille, 233

Salad Niçoise, 276–77

Salmon Mediterranean, 512

Simply Salsa, 55–56

Sneaky Spaghetti Sauce, 200

storage, 266

Sun-Dried Tomato Spread, 53

Super Spaghetti Sauce, 199

Vegetable Cheese Chowder, 101–2

Vegetarian Cabbage Soup, 86

Vegetarian Spaghetti Sauce, 106

*See also individual recipes*

tortes, 389–92, 397–404

Basic Torte Layers, 397

Chocolate Fantasy Torte, 400–401

Chocolate Layer Torte, 399–400

Cinnamon Torte, 398

Fruit Variation, 399

Grasshopper Torte, 401

Hazelnut (Filbert) Torte, 402

Linzertorte, 402–3

Napoleon Torte, 399

Sour Cream Torte, 398

tips, 390–92

Top Skor Torte, 404

tortillas

Easy Nachos, 51

Mango Quesadillas, 67

Pitas, Wraps and Roll-ups, 51

Salmon Tortilla Pinwheels, 66

Tortilla Lasagna Florentine, 140–41

trifles, 404–8

Heavenly Chocolate Trifle, 407

Lemon Trifle, 407–8

Passover Trifle, 406

Terrific Trifle, 405–6

truffles
  Charoset Truffles, 495
  Chocolate Truffles, 425
  White Chocolate Truffles, 425
tsimmis
  Passover Carrot Tsimmis, 508–9
tuna
  Antipasto Spread, 61
  Asian Luncheon Salad, 278
  Crustless Passover Tuna Quiche, 511
  Favorite Tuna Casserole, 137–38
  Salad Niçoise, 276–77
  Salmon or Tuna Mousse, 63
  Sour Cream Tuna Quiche, 158
  Sweet and Sour Fish Patties, 133
  Swiss Tuna Bake, 137
  Tuna and Mushroom Lasagna, 138–39
  Tuna Patties, 135
  Tuna Patties in Spanish Sauce, 135–36
  Tuna Spread, 60–61
  Tuna Strudel, 136
turkey, 202, 205–6, 216–20
  food safety, 173
  grinding: Grind Your Own, 36
  Hamburgers à la Dutch, 196–97
  how to process, 35–36
  Marinated Roast Turkey with Cranberry Relish, 218–20
  Passover Chicken or Turkey Schnitzel, 213
  Roasted Turkey Breast Balsamico, 216–17
  Savory Turkey Breast, 178–79
  Stuffed Turkey Breast, 217
  Teriyaki Turkey or Chicken Stir-Fry, 205–6
  test for doneness, 219
  tips, 172–74, 217
  Turkey Cutlets with Peppers and Mushrooms, 217–18
  Turkey Gravy, 219–20
  Turkey Popcorn Shepherd's Pie, 202
  See also meatballs
turnips
  how to process, 33

using your food processor, 1
  basic processor parts, 1–6
  blades and how to use them, 9–12
  bowl capacity, 3, 13–14
  cleanups, quick, 7–8
  diagrams: processor parts, 2, 13
  dos and don'ts, 8–9
  how much food to process at a time, 13–14
  nested work bowls, 12–13
  optional blades and discs, 12
  safety tips, 6–7
  Smart Chart, 24–41
  tips, tricks and techniques, 14–16

vanilla, substitutions, 493
varenikas, 259
veal
  Baked Veal Chops, 185–86
  Chicken or Meat Filling, 257–58
  Chicken or Meat Turnovers, 75
  Chili, 197
  food safety, 173
  grinding: Grind Your Own, 36
  Hamburgers à la Dutch, 196–97
  how to process, 35–36
  Italian Roasted Veal, 183–84
  Minced Veal Stuffing, 183
  Moist and Spicy Meat Loaf, 201
  Oven Stew, 188
  Potato Kugel Meat Loaf, 201–2
  Rozie's Osso Bucco with Gremolata, 184–85
  Shipwreck, 203
  Sneaky Spaghetti Sauce, 200
  Stew Italiano, 189–90
  Super Spaghetti Sauce, 199
  Veal Brisket with Stuffing, 182
  See also meatballs
vegetables, 222–63
  As-You-Like-It Vegetable Soup, 87
  Baked Veggie Patties, 247
  Best Vegetable Dip, 52
  Chicken and Vegetable Bake, 211
  Confetti Bread, 313–14
  Easy Lentil Vegetable Soup, 90

Farfel, Chicken and Vegetable Kugel, 503–4
Grate and Bake, 506–7
Gratinéed Vegetables, 225
Hoisin Vegetable Stir-Fry, 248
Honey-Glazed Roasted Roots, 235
Horseradish, 110–11
how to process, 27–34, 224–25
how to purée, 32
Marinated Fresh Vegetable Salad, 270
microwaving, 225
Mom's Vegetable Soup with Matzo Balls, 87–88
Mostly Vegetable Stuffing, 499
Pareve Vegetable Quiche, 158–59
Pasta Vegetable Medley, 141–42
purées, 32
Quick Vegetable Broth, 84
Smart Chart, 27–34
tips, 14–16, 82–83, 224–25, 266–67
Vegetable Cheese Chowder, 101–2
Vegetable Kishka, 255
See also Passover vegetables and side dishes; salads; vegetarian dishes; individual vegetables
vegetarian dishes
  Baked Veggie Patties, 247
  Cheryl's Vegetable Casserole, 500–501
  Luscious Vegetarian Lasagna, 139–40
  Vegetarian Cabbage Soup, 86
  Vegetarian Chopped Liver, 57–58
  Vegetarian Egg Rolls, 76–77
  Vegetarian Minestrone, 91
  Vegetarian Spaghetti Sauce, 106
  See also dairy dishes; pareve dishes; salads; tofu; vegetables; individual recipes
vegetarian meat substitutes. See individual meat and poultry recipes
vinaigrette
  Balsamic Vinaigrette, 287
  Best Vinaigrette Dressing, 287

walnuts
    Applesauce Date and Nut Cake,
        354–55
    Charoset, 495
    Heavenly Squares, 460–61
    Morning Glorious Muffins, 338
    Passover Mud Cookies, 525
    Sour Cream Torte, 398
    Walnut Brandy Cookies, 437
    *See also* nuts
water chestnuts
    how to process, 31
watercress
    how to process, 30, 33
whipping cream
    Almost Whipping Cream, 391
    how to process, 41
    tips, 9, 391
    Whipped Cream, 387
white (béchamel) sauce, 103–4
wraps, pitas and roll-ups, 51
    *See also* pita

yams
    how to process, 31–32
    *See also* sweet potatoes
yeast doughs. *See* breads—yeast
    breads and doughs
yogurt
    Banana Yogurt Cake, 355–56
    nutritional analysis, 47
    Strawberry Swirl Popsicles,
        414–15
    Strawberry Yogurt Delight, 409
    as substitute for sour cream or
        buttermilk, 347
    Yogurt Cheese, 391
    Yummy Yogurt Salad Dressing,
        291–92

zucchini
    Baked Veggie Patties, 247
    Breaded Zucchini, 243
    Cheryl's Vegetable Casserole,
        500–501
    how to process, 33–34
    Mini Potato Zucchini Kugels,
        242
    Nana's Zucchini Bread, 334–35

No-Crust Zucchini Quiche,
    159–60
Ratatouille, 233
Sneaky Spaghetti Sauce, 200
Vegetarian Minestrone, 91
Zucchini and Two Potato Soup,
    96
Zucchini Latkes, 244
Zucchini Muffins, 335
Zucchini Noodle Soup, 97
Zucchini Puffs, 242–43
Zucchini Spice Cake, 378–79